The Evolution of
International Human Rights

Pennsylvania Studies in Human Rights

Bert Lockwood, Jr., Series Editor

A complete list of books in the series is available from the publisher.

The Evolution of International Human Rights

Visions Seen

Paul Gordon Lauren

WITHDRAWN
UTSA Libraries

PENN

University of Pennsylvania Press

Philadelphia

Copyright © 1998 University of Pennsylvania Press
All rights reserved
Printed in the United States of America on acid-free paper

10 9 8 7 6 5 4 3 2 1

Published by
University of Pennsylvania Press
Philadelphia, Pennsylvania 19104–4011

Library of Congress Cataloging-in-Publication Data
Lauren, Paul Gordon.
    The evolution of international human rights : visions seen / Paul
Gordon Lauren.
        p.   cm. — (Pennsylvania studies in human rights)
    Includes bibliographical references and index.
    ISBN 0-8122-3274-7 (hardcover : alk. paper). —
ISBN 0-8122-1521-4 (pbk. : alk. paper)
1. Human rights.   I. Title.   II. Series.
JC571.L285   1998
341.4′81′09—dc21   98-15215
                                                              CIP

Library
University of Texas
at San Antonio

To my teachers

What has been accomplished? This: we have kept a vision alive; we have held to a great ideal, we have established a continuity, and some day when unity and cooperation come, the importance of all these early steps will be recognized.

— W.E.B. Du Bois

Human rights were not a free gift. They were only won by long, hard struggle. This struggle, with all the efforts and sacrifices that it demanded, was inevitable: respect for individual rights, when it passes from theory to practice, entails conflict with certain interests and the abolition of certain privileges. Men and women everywhere should be familiar with the dramatic incidents — well-known and obscure — of a conquest which has been largely achieved through the heroism of the noblest of their fellows.

— UNESCO

Contents

Acknowledgments

One of the most enjoyable pleasures for any author is the opportunity that publication provides to acknowledge the generosity, assistance, and insights shared by others along the way. Many individuals and institutions in many places around the world contributed much to this book, and I am delighted to express my sincere appreciation to the following.

Herman Burgers, a rare individual of deep conviction and wide experience in the field of international human rights, for first challenging me to write this book and then graciously providing penetrating comments and helpful assistance along the way.

Bert Lockwood, Jr., the insightful and creative editor of *Human Rights Quarterly* and the Pennsylvania Studies on Human Rights, for inviting me to write this book and giving all the encouragement that any author could want.

The archivists and staff of the United Nations Archives in New York and Geneva, Archives de la Société des Nations et Collections Historiques in Geneva, U.S. National Archives and Manuscript Division of the Library of Congress in Washington, D.C., British Public Record Office in London, National Archives of New Zealand in Wellington, Hoover Institution Archives at Stanford University, Franklin D. Roosevelt Library at Hyde Park, Ministère des Affaires étrangères and Archives nationales in Paris, Politisches Archiv des Auswärtiges Amts in Bonn, and the Rare Book and Manuscript Library of Columbia University and Leo Baeck Institute in New York for granting access to rare materials and archival collections.

The librarians at the Maureen and Mike Mansfield Library and the Law Library of the University of Montana, Bibliothèque des Nations Unies at the Palais des Nations in Geneva, Green Library at Stanford University, Hoover Institution Library, Butler Library at Columbia University, Library of Congress, New York Public Library, Dag Hammarskjöld Library at the United Nations, Suzzalo Library at the University of Washington, Alexander Turnbull Library, British Library, Bibliothèque nationale, Massey University Library, Bibliothèque Publique et Universitaire de Genève, London School of Economics Library, University of Tokyo Library, Toyo University Library, Shanghai International Studies University Library, Columbus Memorial Library of the Organization of American States, and the Musée international de la Croix-Rouge et du Croissant-Rouge, for the use of resources and numerous courtesies.

The Rockefeller Foundation for an appointment as a Rockefeller Foundation Humanities Fellow, the Council for International Exchange of Scholars and U.S.-New Zealand Educational Foundation for an appointment as a Senior Fulbright Scholar, the Carter Rogers Montgomery Fund for the Study of International Relations, the Office of Research Administration and Department of History of the University of Montana, and the Tom and Ann Boone Endowment of the UM Foundation, for financial assistance.

Staff members of the Office of the High Commissioner for Human Rights/Centre for Human Rights in Geneva, especially senior advisors Tom McCarthy and Zdzislaw Kedzia, Jakob Moller, Alfred De Zayas, Fiona Blyth-Kubota, Laura Stryker-Cao, and Daniel Atchebro, for giving freely of their time to answer questions and provide invaluable insights about process and substance.

Those who graciously granted interviews, including Colin Aikman, Jimmy Carter, Frank Corner, Warren Hewitt, Clement John, Liu Binyan, J. M. Makatini, Jan Mårtenson, T. C. Ragachari, John Salzberg, Jerome Shestack, the late Clarence Streit, Brian Urquhart, Sandra Vogelgesang, and several who wish to remain anonymous, for sharing their vast experiences and perspectives on the political world of international human rights.

Maurizio Cortiello, Chief of Registry and Records at the United Nations Office in Geneva, and his assistant, Anna Rey-Mermier; and Marilla Guptil, Chief of the Archives Unit of the United Nations Archives in New York, for friendship and gracious assistance in finding documentary needles in haystacks; and Pierre Pelou, Director of the Bibliothèque des Nations Unies, and his staff, especially Nina Kriz Leneman, Carol Davies, Salvatore Leggio, Gary Meixner, Werner Simon, and Maggie Wachter, for assistance at every turn.

Professional colleagues and friends Edward Bennett, Timothy Bradstock, Dan Caldwell, Richard Pierre Claude, Richmond Clow, Gordon A. Craig, Richard Drake, John Eglin, Asbjørn Eide, David Emmons, William Farr, Linda Frey, Harry Fritz, Alexander George, Forest Grieves, Kerry Howe, Ayna Jabour, Darshan Kang, Mehrdad Kia, Peter Koehn, Marshall Lee, Ken Lockridge, Manny Machado, Barrie Macdonald, Michael Mayer, Leo Moser, Olatunde J. B. Ojo, Yunosuke Ohkura, Ralph Pettman, Henry Sekyi, Frederick Skinner, Anna-Lena Svensson-McCarthy, Van Symons, Howard Tolley, Warwick Tyler, Nobuchika Urata, and Pamela Volkel, for being willing to share knowledge from their own particular areas of expertise.

The Controller of Her Majesty's Stationery Office, the Director and Chief Archivist of the National Archives of New Zealand, and the Director of the Rare Book and Manuscript Library of Columbia University for granting permission to cite materials in their respective collections; and to Patricia Koo Tsien for authorizing the use of papers from her father, Wellington Koo;

Thomas Beal, Patricia Chapman, Mark Fritch, Kath McChesney-Lape, Kyu-Young Lee, Elsy Monsalve-Schmidt, Joyce Rosenblum, the late Tu Baixiong, and Linda Wheeler, for offering various forms of assistance and insight.

Eric Halpern and Noreen O'Connor of the University of Pennsylvania Press for seeing this project through to completion.

My wife, Susan, and our daughters, Sandy and Jeanne, for their constant and loving support.

Finally, I am grateful to all those who have taught me so much in so many different ways, to whom this book is dedicated.

Introduction: Visions and Visionaries

> Do not make the mistake of thinking that concerned people cannot change the world; it is the only thing that ever has.
>
> — Margaret Mead

There are times when the visions seen by people may provide a far better judge of their qualities and contributions than the immediate and measurable accomplishments of their lifetime. That is, those unique men and women who possess a capacity to go beyond the confines of what is or what has been, and to creatively dream or imagine what might be, sometimes have an impact on history that far transcends their own time and place. Indeed, visions of prophets, philosophers, religious and political leaders seen centuries ago in distant lands are still capable of capturing our imagination, inspiring our thoughts, and influencing our behavior today.

Among all these visions, perhaps none have had impact across the globe more profound than those of international human rights advocates. Thoughtful and insightful visionaries in many different times and diverse locations have seen in their mind's eye a world in which all people might enjoy certain basic and inherent rights simply by virtue of being human. They have viewed these rights or fundamental claims by persons to obtain just treatment as stemming from nature itself and thus inherited by all men, women, and children on earth as members born into the same human family entitled to be accorded worth and dignity. Moreover, with this premise they have envisioned a world without borders or other distinctions that divide people from one another in which all persons received equal treatment without any discrimination on the basis of gender, race, caste or class, religion, political belief, ethnicity, or nationality. Such visions of human rights have contributed to the long struggle for the worth and dignity of the human person throughout history. More recently, they have heavily shaped the entire discussion about the meaning of modern politics and society around the world, and in the process provided perhaps the most revolutionary concept of our own time.

The origins of these visions did not result from a single society, political system, culture, or region of the world. Some emerged out of religious belief and duty, compassion, or a sense of responsibility to care for brothers and sisters suffering in distress.

Others grew from philosophical discourse about the nature of government, natural law, and humankind itself, or out of theories concerning ethical limits on how individuals should treat one another or on what governments may be able to do to their own people. Still others emerged not from quiet contemplation or careful reflection, but rather from the heat of anger generated by a passionate sense of injustice being perpetrated or condoned in gross violation of the perceived fundamental human rights of the victims. Over the centuries these cases have spanned the globe and involved such circumstances as the exploitation of women or children, slavery, racial segregation and apartheid, caste or class discrimination, persecution of religious or ethnic minorities, violence against innocent civilians in times of war, torture of political prisoners, territorial conquest, and the mass exterminations of genocide or "ethnic cleansing." As one might expect, the responses to these wide-ranging abuses also have varied greatly depending on historical circumstances, with the result of not just one single, unified vision of human rights but rather many visions.

Despite their differences in origins and interpretations, however, all these visions of human rights confronted powerful opposition and forces of resistance every step of the way. The reason can be simply stated: they all raised profoundly disturbing issues about what it means to be human, thereby directly threatening traditional patterns of authority and privilege, vested interests and prerogatives, and the claims of national sovereignty. Visions of international human rights presented difficult philosophical questions about how individuals relate to society, whether people have responsibilities to others, and the role that ethical values should play in human behavior. They challenged the authority of the state over its own people, attempted to impose defined limitations on the arbitrary exercise of power, and sought to hold governments accountable to certain ethical norms of behavior. These visions similarly rejected the practice of hierarchy whereby certain people were treated as superior due to their gender or the color of their skin, refused to accept the argument that how a state treats its own people is its own business, and rejected the notion that the strong do what they can and the weak do what they must. It is precisely for this reason that the visionaries discussed throughout this book invariably found themselves ridiculed as naive idealists in a world of Realpolitik, criticized as speculative and impractical dreamers, reviled and persecuted as traitors to their own exclusive group or nation, and sometimes even tortured or killed as dangerous and seditious revolutionaries.

Despite all of the formidable odds and forces aligned against them, these visions could not be extinguished and those visionaries who saw them refused to be silenced. Upheavals in the eighteenth century and successes in the nineteenth century gave them hope. But the horrors and continued injustices of the twentieth century gave them determination. The plight of victims resulting from the World War I, the Bolshevik Revolution, and other upheavals of the time raised a new level of awareness about suffering. The fate of those abused by the regimes of Mussolini, Stalin, and Hitler made this discernment even more acute. Then the overwhelming brutality of World War II and the magnitude of genocide in the Final Solution created a consciousness about the extremes of cruelty inflicted by humans against each other so horrendous, in the words of contemporaries, as to "outrage the conscience of mankind."[1] These developments, when coupled with the demands of all those survivors who had been given promises about receiving their rights if they would only join in the crusade of war, created a force of global scale on behalf of international human rights that not only refused to be denied, but that continues to this day.

Carefully building on earlier efforts, and acutely aware of the sacrifices made by those who had gone before them, determined postwar visionaries set out to champion the cause of international human rights as never before in history. They believed that they had a duty to care for their brothers and sisters in need, that all human beings possessed certain inalienable rights, that respect for human rights contributed to global peace and security, and that war and victory provided unique opportunities for action. With strong and active support from individuals, minority groups, public opinion, nongovernmental organizations (NGOs), officials sympathetic to their cause, and governments that were themselves often victims of the Great Powers, they exerted pressure sufficient to create the Charter of the United Nations with specific provisions declaring that human rights henceforth would be a matter of international responsibility. Unwilling to rest on this accomplishment, they then labored diligently to proclaim a bold vision "for all peoples and all nations" known as the Universal Declaration of Human Rights. For the past fifty years, a new generation of visionaries has picked up the flaming torch and worked to extend freedom to literally millions of people, set standards, implement treaty obligations, promote and enhance human rights in innovative ways in order to help transform that vision into reality.

In this evolutionary process, these visions and those who saw them launched a revolution. All the visionaries imagined a world in which human rights would be respected more than they had ever been in the past, and they all believed that they could make a difference. Their efforts span the course of history, ranging from a time when they first communicated their visions by oral tradition or on parchment, pen-and-ink drawings, then pamphlets and books, then photographs, and presently by means of words and images from satellite transmissions, computers, and CD-ROMs. They knew before they ever began that throughout most of historical experience the international community remained largely silent on the issue of human rights, and regarded that how nations treated their own people was a matter of exclusive domestic jurisdiction and one of the political and legal prerogatives of national sovereignty. In this setting, individual victims of abuses could seek no redress or help beyond their own national governments, and were forced to remain as objects of international pity rather than as subjects of international law, suffering accordingly. Although abuses have not completely ceased, there are now universally accepted norms, binding treaties of human rights with implementation mechanisms, access by individual victims to global and regional machinery and opportunities to voice their concerns, and an international community much better informed through communication technology and less and less willing to accept the traditional claims of national sovereignty. Never before in history has there been what is now described with confidence as a "universal culture of human rights."[2] Today human rights play an exceedingly visible and important role in the conduct of international relations, and there is not a government on the face of the earth that is unaware of the Universal Declaration of Human Rights. The visions and the visionaries that made this dramatic revolution possible, and the powerful forces against which they fiercely contended and with which they determinedly worked, provide the subject of this book.

Chapter 1
My Brother's and Sister's Keeper
Visions and the Birth of Human Rights

Am I my brother's keeper?
— Genesis 4:9

The historical origins of powerful visions capable of shaping world events and attitudes like those of international human rights are rarely simple. Instead, they emerge in complicated and interrelated ways from the influence of many forces, personalities, and conditions in different times and diverse settings, each flowing in its own unique way like a tributary into an ever larger and mightier river. At times they flow gently through the calm meadows of religious meditation, prophetic inspiration, poetic expression, or philosophic contemplation. On other occasions, as we shall see, they smash through human events like torrents through precipitous canyons born of violence and pain from upheaval, enslavement, conquest, revolution, war, torture, and genocide.

Visions of human rights thus are not only complex, they are also often profound and disturbing. The reason for this is that they tend to strike at our very core and make us confront difficult and discomforting issues. They force us to examine critically the nature of men and women, consider what it means to be human, view both the best and the worst of human behavior, wrestle with how we ought to relate to one another, question the purposes of government and the exercise of power, and especially examine our own values and deeds in response to those who suffer.

One of the most agonizing issues presented by such visions, for example, is the matter of whether we have any responsibilities for the well-being of other people in need or pain. Thoughtful individuals in many different times and places have pondered whether they should possess a concern beyond themselves that extended to others who suffered or not. If so, they then had to ask further perplexing questions about the extent of concern that have continued for ages: Who is my "brother" or "sister," and what exactly does it mean to be a "keeper"? That is, just how wide should be the circle of responsibility and what form should concern for others take? A sense of obligation to immediate family members or friends and neighbors in close proximity might be readily apparent, but what about those beyond the community, the tribe, the clan, the class, the race, the faith, or, particularly in the modern world, the nation? Are these duties merely local or are they universal? Moreover, and equally troubling, is one obligated to express simply words of sympathy or sorrow over the fate of victims, or does responsibility entail the need to take concrete action to improve conditions and protect other human beings who suffer?

The historical evolution of visions of international human rights that continues to this day started centuries ago with efforts attempting to address precisely these difficult and universal questions. It began as soon as men and women abandoned nomadic existence and settled in organized societies, long before anyone had ever heard of the more recent expression, "human rights," or before nation-states negotiated specific international treaties. Moreover, this evolution began not with assertions of entitlement or demands for human rights but instead with discussions of duty.

Religious Visions: Brothers, Sisters, and Duties Beyond Borders

All of the major religions of the world seek in one way or another to speak to the issue of human responsibility to others. Despite their vast differences, complex contradictions, internal paradoxes, cultural variations, and susceptibility to conflicting interpretation and fierce argumentation, all of the great religious traditions share a universal interest in addressing the integrity, worth, and dignity of all persons and, consequently, the duty toward other people who suffer without distinction. Each seeks to provide ways that might direct personal thoughts and actions away from self-centeredness and toward the well-being of others in need. This concern is approached through various revelations, narratives, poetry, edicts and commandments, and stories or parables dealing with right and wrong, moral responsibility, ethical principles of justice and fairness, compassion, the essential dignity of each person, and the kinship and common humanity of all.

In Hinduism, the world's oldest religion, for example, the ancient texts of the Vedas, Āgamas, and Upanishads, among others partly written over three thousand years ago, continually stress that divine truth is universal and that religious belief must be a way of life. These scriptures address the existence of good and evil, wisdom, the necessity for moral behavior, and especially the importance of duty (*dharma*) and good conduct (*sadāchāra*) toward others suffering in need. They enjoin believers to fulfill faithfully their earthly responsibilities to all people beyond the self or family without distinction by practicing selfless concern for their pain, particularly charity and compassion for the hungry, the sick, the homeless, and the unfortunate, as discussed in the *Manava Dharma Sūtra* (Treatise on Human Duties). All human life, despite the vast differences among individuals, is considered sacred, to be loved and respected without distinction as to family member or stranger, friend or enemy. For this reason, the first and foremost ethical principle of Hinduism—and one as we shall see that became so important to Mahatma Gandhi who in the twentieth century regarded himself as a deeply traditional and orthodox Hindu—is noninjury to others. The edict is stated directly and universally: "Noninjury (*ahimsā*) is not causing pain to any living being at any time through the actions of one's mind, speech, or body."[1]

Genesis, the first book of Judaism's Torah written centuries ago, begins by telling of the shared fatherhood of God to all people and the fundamental importance of the creation of human beings as members of one family and as individuals endowed with worth. A discussion of the sovereignty of God, of the sacredness of the individual and the equal value of all God's children, of human relationships, and of explicitly defined responsibilities of individuals toward each other follows. The story of siblings Cain, a tiller of the soil, and Abel, a keeper of sheep, dramatizes the issue of obligation. When one of the two cannot be found, the other is asked about his brother's whereabouts and well-being. Attempting to escape blame and any responsibility for a murder, he denies knowing and then seeks refuge by posing a universal and enduring question: "Am I my brother's keeper?"[2] His answer is false and his question disingenuous, thereby setting the stage for subsequent books dealing with human nature and the meaning of history, ethical behavior toward others, social justice, injunctions that government decrees contrary to divine commands should be disregarded by men and women of conscience, the rights of foreign strangers in one's own land, the existence of one law that establishes a uniform standard of treatment and equality for all, and responsibilities toward those in need.[3] Among the writings of the prophets, for example, one of the most notable is commonly known as "the vision of Isaiah" instructing all believers "to loose the bonds of wickedness, to undo the tongs of the yoke, to let the oppressed go free . . . to share your bread with the hungry, and to bring the homeless poor into your house."[4] This injunction established a tradition that encouraged men and women to extend beyond themselves and take action on behalf of others in this world, observes Jewish theologian-philosopher Martin Buber in *I and Thou*. Such a process, he writes, "is a matter of leavening the human race in all places with genuine We-ness. Man will not persist in existence if he does not learn anew to persist in it as a genuine We."[5]

Buddhism, founded approximately 2,500 years ago in India by Siddhartha Gautama, also began by addressing the universal issues of human relationships, profound respect for the life of each person, and compassion in the face of pain suffered by fellow human beings. He explicitly attacked the rigid caste system of his day, democratically opening his order to all, stressing the worth of each individual regardless of their social or political position, and urging his followers to renounce differences "of caste and rank and become the members of one and the same society" practicing universal brotherhood and equality.[6] Scriptures like the Tripitaka and Anguttara-Nikaya pay considerable attention to the enduring problem of human suffering (*dukkha*), and stress that one's duty is to overcome selfish desires and private fulfillment by practicing charity and compassion (*karuna*) toward those in need. This ethic forms a part of Buddhism's Noble Eightfold Path that includes right thought, right speech, right action, and right effort toward "all beings." It also creates a religious tradition necessary to appreciate the Dalai Lama's more contemporary pronouncement that the world's problems will be solved only by showing kindness, love, and respect "for all humanity as brothers and sisters" and "if we understand each other's fundamental humanity, respect each other's rights, share each other's problems and sufferings."[7]

The founding of Confucianism by Kong Qiu in China at approximately the same time as the emergence of Buddhism brought still further reflections on human nature and responsible behavior. Indeed, Confucian thought articulated in the *Analects*, *Doc-*

trine of the Mean, and *Great Learning* focused much more on human relationships and an ethical life on earth than on the divine or spiritual matters in a realm beyond. Harmony and cooperation exist when all persons honor their duty and responsibility toward others, overcoming their own self-interest and egotism, treating all human beings as having equal worth, and recognizing that "within the four seas, all men are brothers."[8] Human nature is viewed as inherently good, and harsh warnings are given about oppressive governments that might exploit their people or fail to provide for their well-being. When the sage was asked whether there existed any single saying that one could act on all day and every day, he answered: "Do not impose on others what you yourself do not desire."[9] The basis of all the teachings can be found by following The Way (*Jen*), etymologically a combination of the character for "man" and for "two" that names the ideal and universal relationship between humans beings. It has been variously translated as goodness, benevolence, love, and human-heartedness. It represents the virtue of all virtues and the condition of being fully human in dealing with others, involving the display of human capacities at their very best and extending far beyond immediate personal or family relationships to include the world as a whole. As the well-known Confucian dictum explains: "If there be righteousness in the heart, there will be beauty in the character. If there is beauty in the character, there will be harmony in the home. If there is harmony in the home, there will be order in the nation. If there be order in the nation, there will be peace in the world."[10]

Christianity extended this theme of responsibility and compassion directly. During his ministry two thousand years ago, Jesus challenged the existing order of his day, taught about the value of all human beings in the sight of God, and spoke again and again about demonstrating love and compassion and of the need to give of one's self to others, of clothing the naked, of healing the sick, of feeding the hungry, of welcoming the stranger, of providing hope to the hopeless, and of caring for the oppressed of the world. He demonstrated a level of respect for women, children, outcasts, and outsiders that many of his contemporaries found inappropriate, using one of his most powerful and familiar teaching parables in the New Testament of the Bible to address the larger, universal, and provocative question: "Who is my neighbor?" Jesus responded by telling a story of a man traveling from Jerusalem to Jericho who fell among robbers. They stripped him and beat him, and left him nearly dead. By chance a priest journeying along the same road saw the victim, yet instead of stopping to help the poor man, the priest turned his eyes away and walked on the other side of the road. A passing Levite did the same thing, refusing to lend any assistance. But a Samaritan, regarded as an outcast in the community, came upon the man and had compassion. He stopped, bound up his wounds, set him on his own donkey, and carried him to an inn where he paid all the expenses until the victim recovered. The parable concludes with these words: "Which of these three, do you think, proved neighbor to the man who fell among the robbers?" The man who asked the initial question replied, "The one who showed mercy on him." And Jesus said to him, "Go and do likewise."[11] Lest there be any doubt on this matter, the apostle Paul further admonished all believers to recognize that "there is neither Greek nor Jew, nor slave nor free, nor man nor woman, but we are all one in Christ."[12]

The tenets of Islam, founded five hundred years after the lifetime of Jesus and revealed through the writings of Muhammed, also address aspects of being a brother's keeper. This begins with one of the pillars of belief: that of charity, or lifting the burdens of those less fortunate. The scripture of the Qur'an also speaks to matters regarding justice, the sanctity of life, personal safety, freedom, mercy, compassion, and respect for all human beings as rooted in the obligations owed by believers to God. Moreover, since Muhammed was not only a prophet and teacher, but also a government administrator and statesman, it is hardly surprising that Islam would recognize the inseparable connections between faith and politics, religion and society. In a society riven with class distinctions and the tyranny of vested interests, Muhammed preached an intense message of freedom from the various chains that bind, urging the reduction of injustices born of special privilege and insisting that in the sight of Allah, or God, all men are equal. Consequently, Islam teaches that there should exist absolute equality among races and that religious toleration should be guaranteed. Muhammed's announcement that "Jews [and later Christians] who attach themselves to our commonwealth shall be protected from all insults and vexations; they shall have an equal right with our own people . . . and shall practice their religion as freely as the Muslims," for example, has been described by at least one author as "the first charter of freedom of conscience in human history."[13]

These many and various religious visions—like all visions—expressed ideals rather than reality. They attempted to speak, with various levels of simplicity or sophistication, to the best of possible human relationships instead of the worst. Yet despite all of their efforts and at times vastly different approaches, none of these great religious traditions could escape secularization, perversion, or corruption in one form or another and in ways that provided a pretext for governments to engage in repression at home and aggression abroad or allowed the powerful to mask their greed. This is particularly evident among states that claimed to adopt one religion or another, and then proceeded to rule secularly in ways that had little to do with the original vision. Through time, values of simple and unadorned human charity often succumbed to cleverly devised theological arguments and justifications for elaborate rites, rituals, and the trappings of wealth and power concentrated in the hands of a few. The ideals of compassion for all those suffering in need or pain on many occasions gave way to notions of exclusivity or special "chosen people," military invasion against others in the name of the "Prince of Peace," persecution of "outcasts" or "untouchables," or "holy wars" of armed conquest against infidels. Historically, all these religions emerged from traditional, premodern, male-dominated societies characterized by considerable disparities, distinctions, discriminations, hereditary systems of inequality, and hierarchies headed by kings or emperors. Consequently, principles of respect and equal treatment for all frequently yielded to plush privilege for some and conquest, exploitation, and even enslavement for others based on notions of superiority in belief, gender, race, caste, class, tribe, clan, or some other criterion. In religious terms, humans often proved themselves to be precisely that—all too human.

As justified as much skepticism and cynicism over the use and abuse of religion in history may be, it is essential to remember that throughout the ages there also have always been those who have attempted by word or deed to follow faithfully the precepts of their teachers and prophets and to respond to their calling of being a keeper of brothers and sisters. Some became known as the saints of Christianity, the *murshids* and *pirs* of Sufi Islam, the *sadhus* or holy men of Hinduism, or the *bodhisattvas* of Buddhism, while others remained largely unrecognized and unknown to anyone except those to whom they extended selfless compassion and help. They lived in particular historical times and places that conditioned and at times determined what they could reasonably accomplish. Perseverance did not necessarily require success. Nor did these general religious concepts of responsibility developed in traditional, patriarchal, and hierarchical societies that far predated nation-states and modern concepts of individual rights necessitate the precise political, philosophical, or legal definitions of human rights of our own day. More often than not, they reflected simply an orientation of heart and spirit. If the tenets of helping those who suffered fell short in actual practice or precision, it did not diminish the ultimate value of the ideal as a goal toward which they or subsequent generations should strive.

In so doing, those largely unknown and unassuming men and women who rejected prevailing practices and attempted to follow precepts of religious faith through word or deed during their own lifetimes left a legacy that eventually made three significant contributions to the evolution of international human rights. In the first place, they established visions of values, normative standards, and ideals that proved to be enormously important sources of inspiration and strength for those who campaigned for human rights, especially during times of persecution and suffering. Second, by seeking to develop a moral imperative or universal sense of obligation toward humankind, these religious traditions helped establish an ingredient essential for any and all international human rights: a concept of responsibility to common humanity. Demands or assertions for human rights in one place would have remained forever unanswered, isolated, or localized unless there had been people elsewhere in the world who believed that they had larger responsibilities, or "duties beyond borders,"[14] to protect others regardless of station or place. Third, by developing concepts of duties, these religious traditions provided a inherent beginning for discussions about rights. Duties and rights are closely interrelated and correlative concepts because the responsibilities of some imply rights that can be claimed by others. As Gandhi insightfully observed, "The true source of rights is duty."[15] Thus, ideas about human duties led quite naturally to ideas about human rights.

Philosophical Visions: Human Nature, Natural Law, and Natural Rights

If religious traditions provided tributaries into the ever expanding and evolving river of thought about what would eventually be described as international human rights, moral and political philosophy contributed many others. Over the centuries, philosophers in many diverse times and places wrestled with difficult questions about reciprocal relationships between human beings both as individuals and as members of groups. They pondered the meaning of human nature, social justice, the universality of fundamental principles, responsibilities to brothers and sisters beyond borders, whether traditional rules-based societies could be transformed into rights-based societies, and whether governments possessed any responsibilities to protect certain rights of individuals and of groups. Despite their many differences of perspective and diverse approaches to these matters, they all sought understanding not through divine revelation or inspired scripture, but through secular inquiry and human reason.

Nearly twenty-four centuries ago in China, for example, the philosopher Mo Zi founded the Mohist school of moral philosophy. His writings emphasized the importance of duty, self-sacrifice, and an all-embracing respect toward all others, not confined merely to members of family or clan, but, in his words, "universally throughout the world."[16] Less than one hundred years later, and heavily influenced by Confucianism, the Chinese sage Mencius wrote extensively on the subject of human nature. He argued that humans by nature are fundamentally good, but that this goodness needs to be nourished. Toward this end, he stressed the need for benevolence in government and developed the older idea of the mandate of Heaven, according to which a dynasty ruled only as long as it ruled properly and addressed the well-being of the people. When a regime lost the mandate, rebellion was justified, and an evil ruler forfeited the right to rule. In language later recalled with considerable pride by Chinese human rights activists in the twentieth century, Mencius declared: "The individual is of infinite value, institutions and conventions come next, and the person of the ruler is of least significance."[17] At the same time, the philosopher Hsün-tzu asserted the same principle equally emphatically when he wrote: "In order to relieve anxiety and eradicate strife, nothing is as effective as the institution of corporate life based on a clear recognition of individual rights."[18]

Philosophers from other areas, cultures, and traditions made contributions as well, each in their own way. King Hammurabi of ancient Babylon, for example, proclaimed the necessity to honor broad principles of justice among people and thus created one of the earliest legal codes to govern behavior. "Let the oppressed man," he said, "come into the presence of my statue" to seek equal protection under the law.[19] Precepts from ancient Egypt sought to address explicitly issues of social justice and help for the weak by injunctions to "comfort the afflicted. . . . Refrain from unjust punishment. Kill not. . . . Make no distinction between the son of a man of importance and one of humble origin."[20] One pharaoh instructed his viziers to "make sure that all is done according to the law, that custom is observed and the right of each man respected."[21] Early Sanskrit writings from the Indian subcontinent specifically spoke of the responsibility of rulers for the welfare of people by declaring: "No one in his dominion should [be allowed to] suffer . . . either because of poverty or of any deliberate action on the part of others."[22] In the third century B.C., Aśoka of India issued edicts that guaranteed freedom of worship and other rights for his subjects. Others from the same area during the first century argued for impartial justice and social equality, maintaining, "Just as there is no distinction of classes among the fruits produced by one tree . . . in the form: 'this is a Brāhmana fruit,' 'this is a Ksatriya fruit,' etc., because they are all produced by one tree, even so there is no distinction [of castes] among men because they are all created by one Supreme Being."[23] The Hindu philosopher Chaitanya reinforced this same idea during the sixteenth century, as did others who argued against any distinction that would perpetuate an "untouchable" category of people, asserting simply: "There is only one caste — humanity."[24] Much later, the Sikh leader Guru Gobind Singh also proclaimed the need to create a global society by the universal emancipation of mankind from oppression and the elimination of caste distinctions, instructing his followers to "recognize all the human race as one."[25]

Similar philosophical positions expressing respect for the dignity of each person, protection of individuals, ethical behavior toward others, social justice, and law or rules above arbitrary power can be found in other areas ranging from the Middle East and Africa to pre-Columbian civilizations in the Americas. Cyrus the Great, for example, promulgated the famous "Charter of Cyrus" in the Persian empire more than two thousand years ago, recognizing certain rights of liberty and security, freedom of movement and religious belief, and even certain economic and social rights, thereby inspiring Sultan Farrukh Hablul Matin to write:

> For he, it was who, with supreme insight,
> Launched an Empire based not on physical might
> But on the vision of a family of nations
> Linked by bands of Humanity, truth, and right.[26]

Al-Farabi, an Islamic philosopher of the tenth century, wrote in his book *The Outlook of the People of the City of Virtue* of a vision of a moral society in which all individuals were endowed with rights and lived in love and charity with their neighbors.[27] Simple tribal communities relying on oral traditions rather than written language also produced concepts that contributed ultimately to discussions about human rights. A number of traditional African societies, for example, developed clear ideas about distributive justice designed to ensure the welfare of all and evolved a variety of thoughts about ways to offer protection from the abuse of political authority.[28] Others created sayings or proverbs to express their beliefs, such as that from the Akan tribe of Ghana warning, "One should not oppress with one's size or might."[29] A Burundi proverb expressing the importance of equality said simply, "Imana [God] creates men and draws no distinction between them."[30] Asserted an old Djerma-Songhai adage: "You should not [have to] solicit what is yours by right."[31]

Early ideas about general human rights thus did not originate exclusively in one location like the West or even with any particular form of government like liberal democracy, but were shared throughout the ages by visionaries from many cultures in many lands who expressed themselves in different ways. Although it is necessary to guard against the shallow and unhistorical view that all societies somehow have always subscribed to the same basic beliefs and values, it is also essential to recognize that the moral worth of each person is a belief that no single civilization, or people, or nation, or geographical area, or even century can claim as uniquely its own. The issue of human rights addresses age-old and universal questions about the relationship between individuals and their larger society, and thus is one that has been raised across time and across cultures. Indeed, as one insightful authority writes: "The struggle for human rights is as old as [world] history itself, because it concerns the need to protect the individual against the abuse of power by the monarch, the tyrant, or the state."[32] What the West did provide, however, was not a monopoly of ideas on the subject but rather much greater opportunities for visions such as these to receive fuller consideration, articulation, and eventual implementation.

At approximately the same time as Mencius in China, for example, a Western tradition began with a number of classical Greek philosophers who argued that a universal law of nature or God pervaded all creation. This law, they claimed, governed every element in the universe and provided the basis for an egalitarian framework of rights: equal respect for all citizens (*isotimia*), equality before the law (*isonomia*), equality in political power (*isokratia*) and suffrage (*isopsephia*), and equality of civil rights (*isopoliteia*). It was eternal and universal, and thus placed well above the narrow and self-serving dictates of a particular state, the rules of a specific society, or the will of a single lawmaker. Human conduct should thus be brought into harmony with this law of nature and judged according to it.[33] In his *Republic*, for example, Plato argued that a universal justice exists that transcends immediate circumstances and allows people in different political systems to recognize that some actions are clearly just and others unjust. Zeno of Citium spoke extensively of a universal law that binds all men together as brothers. Aristotle followed in *Politics* by claiming that the nature of a thing is what it is in the most perfect condition. Nature, in this case human nature, can best be perfected when people are good citizens in a good political order. He also declared that what is "just by nature" is not necessarily just by the laws of men. This theme is perhaps best represented by the example from Greek literature of Antigone, who, on being reproached by the king for denying his command not to bury her slain brother, asserts: "I did not think your orders were so strong that you, a mortal man, could over-run the gods' unwritten and unfailing laws. Not now, nor yesterday's, they always live, and no one knows their origin in time."[34]

The later Roman Stoic philosophers carried these ideas much further by broadening the scope of rights issues in practical affairs to include more beneficiaries than in the Greek tradition and by expanding views of nature to create the theories of classical natural law. In their thinking the law of nature provided the rational principle governing the entire universe that was entirely egalitarian and universal. Nature was conceived as a universal system of rules both physical, such as the law of gravity, and ethical, such as the obligation of all beings to respect one another as equals. It could be known through "right reason" inherent in the human mind, and if properly understood and obeyed, could guide all people toward perfection. The noted orator, statesman, and philosopher Marcus Tullius Cicero, argued that this natural law, supreme in nature and founded "ages before any written law existed or any state had been established," also provided the source of all real justice for the world. He wrote that this "universal justice and law" guided human nature to act justly and "be of service to others." As such, claimed Cicero, this natural law "binds all human society" together, applies to every member of "the whole human race" without distinction, marks the unique dignity of each person, imposes on all of us responsibilities to be keepers of our brothers and sisters, and provides norms of justice to guide states in creating laws by which they should be governed that "command right conduct and forbid wrongdoing."[35] He declared further that this "eternal and unchangeable law will be valid for all nations and all times."[36] Roman jurists subsequently elaborated on this theory by developing a remarkable body of law known as the *jus gentium*, or law of nations. They claimed that this law derived from nature and, hence, established certain universal duties and rights that extended far beyond those acquired by mere citizenship in specific states. This natural law thus imputed to all human beings a civic status of equality to all persons as members of the world community as a whole.

For centuries most of these early philosophical theories of natural law—just like those of religious doctrine—focused on universal responsibilities and duties rather than what are now described as rights. But the modifications of theories and then the transformations of theory into practice, as we shall see constantly, always have been tied to particular political, economic, social, and intellectual upheavals throughout history. For concepts of natural rights to come to the fore, major changes in the beliefs and practices of society needed to take place. In this regard, movements of monumental proportions spread over a period of five hundred years began to take place in Europe. The decline of feudalism and the expansion of commerce, for example, gave economic and then political power to an emerging middle class anxious for individual freedom. At the same time, the Renaissance and Reformation paved the way for the spiritual emancipation of the individual. In this context, resistance to political and economic bondage and to religious intolerance grew, criticisms that rulers had failed to meet their natural law obligations increased, and interest in freedom and individual expression expanded to unprecedented levels.[37] In the realm of politics, for example, the forcing of the Magna Carta, or Great Charter, from King John by the barons of England in 1215 early in this process helped to establish the principles that limits must exist on the powers of royal government, that kings must respect rights, and that liberties could be guaranteed by law. "To no one," read the text, ". . . will we deny or delay right and justice."[38] The Magnus Lagaboters Landslov issued by King Magnus of Norway in 1275 went further by promising equality before the law.[39]

In the realm of ideas, interest in rights followed in the wake of a growing religious consciousness of humanity. Christian philosophers during the same period like Saint Thomas Aquinas, for example, redefined the system of natural law as being divinely willed, and posited the duality of human existence wherein all people were subject both to the authority of humankind and to the authority of God. He believed that the living out of justice toward others was a living out of the love of the divine. Given his further belief in the universal brotherhood and sisterhood of all humankind, this made natural law theory support the important human rights principle that every person is an individual apart from his or her membership in a particular state. By the late fifteenth and early sixteenth centuries, these concepts received even further elaboration in the writings of Christian humanists and reformers who drew both on religious precepts of duty and compassion as well as principles of moral philosophy in championing political and social reform, ethical behavior, human dignity, and equality for individual men and women. "I would ask you to love one another," said the Czech professor Jan Hus just before he was burned at the stake, "not to let the good be suppressed by force and to give every person his rights."[40] "The doctrine of Christ," continued Erasmus of Rotterdam in the same spirit, "casts aside no age, no sex, no fortune, or position in life. It keeps no one at a distance."[41] All of this contributed to a considerable expansion of interest in justice, equality, and individual freedom, and thus to a corresponding shift from natural law as duties to natural law as rights.

A further transformation in the process of viewing natural law as entailing natural rights for all human beings occurred during the seventeenth century. The scientific revolution that expanded knowledge of physics, mathematics, astronomy, and medicine to previously unimagined levels also created a secular intellectual milieu that encouraged a belief that reason could not only discover laws of nature but also natural law in human affairs as well. In the world of ideas, the great Dutch jurist and diplomat who founded modern international law, Hugo Grotius, argued in *De jure belli et pacis* (On the Law of War and Peace, 1625) that natural law, both physical and moral, existed independently of political powers and authorities. It thus stood above all human-created governments and served as a measuring rod against with the laws and practices of any regime could be judged, he declared, and provided all humans with certain rights of protection and equal treatment without regard to any religious or civil status.

In the world of politics, events testified to the increasingly popular opinion that all human beings were endowed with natural rights that claims of "divine right" by kings simply could not diminish. Rebellions in France and Spain, for example, championed the right to resist absolutist governments who attempted to rule only as they wished. As the Dutch declared in renouncing their allegiance to the Spanish king: "God did not create the subjects for the benefit of the Prince, to do his bidding in all things, whether godly or ungodly, right or wrong, and to serve him as slaves, but the Prince for the benefit of the subjects . . . to govern them with justice and reason."[42] Further upheavals in England resulted in the Petition of Right of 1628 reasserting the right to be free from arbitrary arrest and imprisonment. The trying and dramatic experiences of more than forty years of English civil war, revolution, and turmoil, complete with the beheading of a king and the rise of a parliamentary dictator, produced a number of significant developments. One of these was the rise of a democratic movement known as the "Levellers" whose program of action entitled "Agreement of the People" explicitly called for guarantees of the natural rights of all to life, property, election of their representatives, freedom of religion, and freedom from conscription.[43] In 1679 Parliament passed the Habeas Corpus Act establishing the right to be protected against arbitrary detention or imprisonment and then the 1689 Bill of Rights, a monumental landmark in the history of civil and political human rights. Its specific provisions speak forcefully about limited monarchy, security of law and property, representative government and free elections, freedom of speech, religious toleration, trial by jury, and prohibitions against cruel and unusual punishment—all in the name of "ancient" and "undoubted" rights and all designed to protect people "from the violation of their rights, which they have here asserted, and from all other attempts upon their religion, rights, and liberties."[44]

These tumultuous developments also witnessed the emergence of John Locke, perhaps the most pivotal of all seventeenth-century philosophers. Writing initially from exile, he sought to innovatively weave universal natural law and universal natural rights together. His *Second Treatise of Government* (1690), still described as "one of the most influential political treatises of all time,"[45] argued that every individual person in the "state of nature" possessed certain "natural rights" prior to the existence of any organized societies. This concept applied, importantly, not just to those in Europe, but to "governments all through the world." People are born, Locke declared, in a "state of perfect equality, where naturally there is no superiority or jurisdiction of one over another." All humans, irrespective of the particular socioeconomic, cultural, or political conditions under which they live, thus possess, he wrote, "a title to perfect freedom and uncontrolled enjoyment of all the rights and privileges of the law of nature equally with any other man or number of men in the world and have by nature a power not only to preserve his property — that is his life, liberty, and estate — against the injuries and attempts of other men, but to judge and punish the breaches of that law in others."[46] From this premise it followed that people had formed societies and set up governments mainly to preserve those rights, not to surrender them. As a consequence, governments received their powers from the governed with whom they signed a contract. Any government that acted without limits imposed by the consent of the governed and thereby violated their natural rights, said Locke, thus dissolved the contract and gave people a right to resist. Such an argument for individual freedom rights, of course, was not only revolutionary in an age of entrenched privilege, but remains so in much of the world to this day.

Inspired by the provocative and suggestive theories of Locke and encouraged by the dynamic temper of the time, leading intellectuals of the eighteenth century known as the *philosophes* set about to develop modern conceptions of humanity by seeking to free human reason from dogma and the individual from absolute authority. "Man is born free," observed the French philosopher and visionary Jean-Jacques Rousseau in the stirring words of the *Contrat social, ou Principes du droit politique* (1762), "but everywhere he is in chains."[47] Rousseau and his intellectual colleagues like the Baron de Montesquieu, Voltaire, David Hume, and the Marquis de Condorcet called their movement the Enlightenment, the dawning of a new age of human reason and knowledge. Their interests focused not so much on "pure" scientific discovery and abstract system-building but instead on applied science and specific reforms relating to human nature and long-festering human problems of economic exploitation, social suppression, political despotism, torture, and ecclesiastical superstition and intolerance. Thus, they approached the age-old issue of being "a brother's keeper" from a secular and philosophical perspective rather than a religious one. For German philosopher Immanuel Kant this position resulted in the assertion of a "categorical imperative," a universal duty that protected the intrinsic worth of all individuals in order that human beings would be regarded not as means, but as ends in themselves.[48] Benevolence, a moral sense of obligation for the welfare of others, and the universal application of "a right to do, posses, or demand" those things that would enhance the general good of all, wrote the Scottish philosopher Francis Hutcheson in his *System of Moral Philosophy* (1755) represented the height of personal and civic virtue.[49] Collectively, these philosophers of the Enlightenment drew on the concept of natural law as discovered through human reason and brought it to the peak of its prestige. They believed that the fundamental rationality in the laws of nature could be applied to various aspects of the human condition, thus making humanity and society more rational and more perfectible through human effort. By extension, they said, such progress could result in greater happiness and liberty for all "without distinction of race or sect, towards perfection and happiness."[50]

Other philosophers of the Enlightenment sought to make this connection between natural law and rights even more explicit, perhaps being aided by the fact that in French the word *droit* covers both meanings. In the entry on "Natural Law" in his *Encyclopédie* (1755), for example, Denis Diderot wrote that the laws of nature are understood by virtually everyone. They provide the most basic foundation for human society by defining what is naturally and universally just for all human beings without any reference to kings, aristocracy, popes or bishops, class, country, or time period. Using the language of equal, individual human rights for all, Diderot challenged existing authority and asserted, "Tell yourself often: I am a man, and I have no other true, inalienable *natural rights* than those of humanity."[51] Shortly thereafter, Voltaire wrote his *Treatise on Toleration* (1763), arguing that natural law guaranteed the right of all people to freely practice their religion without fear of persecution. Starting from the same premises, Cesare Beccaria published his *On Crimes and on Punishments* (1764), advancing powerful arguments against the common practices of cruel treatment, torture, and the death penalty for prisoners. Abbé Guillaume Raynal, in his multivolume *Philosophical and Political History of Settlements and Trade of the Europeans* (1770), denounced slavery as a travesty against natural law and as a gross violation of the natural rights of its human victims.

Such philosophical ferment and expressions of natural law and natural rights, stressing as they did "inalienable" and "unalterable" individual freedom from control whether in politics, trade, societal conventions, intellectual endeavors, or religious belief, provided inspiration and justification for the revolutionary struggles against absolutist regimes that convulsed the West at the end of the eighteenth century. In fact, the abject failure of European monarchs to modify their privileged positions of power and thereby respect the most basic principles of freedom and equality inherent in natural law philosophy provoked the challenges in the first place. As one leading scholar writes, "absolutism prompted man to claim [natural, or human] rights precisely because it denied them."[52]

The first successful challenge to such absolutist authority came when the American colonists revolted against their British masters by firing those shots "heard around the world" due to their vast implications. The tenets of the Enlightenment increasingly separated many people in the colonies philosophically from absolutist monarchies. In addition, sheer distance by the vast Atlantic Ocean separated them geographically from threats of immediate government coercion. The combination of both elements thus afforded unique opportunities for considerations of greater independence and freedoms for the individual. Indeed, even prior to the revolution, the First Continental Congress enacted its own Bill of Rights in 1774, invoking entitlement to "life, liberty, and property" for all men. Lest such rights be restricted, and the expression "men" not refer to all people, Abigail Adams warned her husband to "Remember the ladies."[53]

Explosions of discontent into violence and then war produced further elaboration on human nature, natural law, and natural rights. Carefully schooled in the philosophy of the Enlightenment and extremely familiar with the political theory of Locke, Montesquieu, and Hutcheson, for example, Thomas Jefferson had no trouble in asserting that his countrymen were a free people "claiming their rights as derived from the laws of nature and not as the gift of their Chief Magistrate."[54] The Virginia Declaration of Rights, written by his modest and principled friend George Mason, argued that not just Virginians or even Americans, but "all men are by nature equally free and independent, and have certain inherent rights."[55] This language was followed shortly thereafter by one of the most eloquent statements of protest and visions of rights to ever emerge. Writing with his goose-quilled pen, Jefferson gave poetic expression to the philosophy of the time in the Declaration of Independence of 4 July 1776 by referring to "the laws of Nature and Nature's God." He stated the case for universal rights with these dramatic words:

We hold these truths to be self-evident, that all men are created equal, that they are endowed by their Creator with certain unalienable rights, that among these are life, liberty and the pursuit of happiness. That to secure these rights, governments are instituted among men, deriving their just powers from the consent of the governed. That whenever any form of government becomes destructive of those ends, it is the right of the people to alter or to abolish it, and to institute new government . . .[56]

This declaration was the most radical document Americans had yet produced — radical in its declaration of complete independence and radical in the rights it asserted for all.[57] It also was a call to revolution, of course, not only in the New World, but in the Old as well; for as Jefferson would go on to write: "a bill of rights is what the people are entitled to against every government on earth."[58]

Encouraged by this successful American experience, although pressed to the breaking point by its own internal problems and pressures, France also exploded into violent revolutionary upheaval in 1789. The resulting French Revolution not only destroyed a despotic monarch and the privileged elite of the old regime in France, but through its actions and its expressed ideology proved to be one of the most profound revolutions in history. Even before the fall of the Bastille prison on 14 July, revolutionary leaders sought to proclaim a declaration of rights not just for themselves, but for the world. Inspired by their own *philosophes* and by the American Declaration of Independence, for example, men like Abbé Sieyès and the Marquis de Lafayette, who had participated in the American Revolutionary War and who knew Jefferson well, spoke forcefully for the need to declare publicly the "natural rights" of all people. As their colleague, Duke Mathieu de Montmorency asserted in one speech that caused a sensation in the National Assembly, "The rights of man are invariable like justice, eternal like reason; they apply to all times and all countries. . . . Let us follow the example of the United States: they have set a great example in the new hemisphere; let us give one to the universe."[59]

The force and inspiration of their argument when combined with the upheaval of revolution quickly led the deputies in the National Assembly to proclaim loudly and vehemently their own Declaration of the Rights of Man and Citizen. Here they asserted that all men "are born and remain free and equal in rights," that these rights were universal and "natural and imprescriptible," and that they included "liberty, property, security, and resistance to oppression." The Declaration of 1789 delineated political rights to vote and participate in the process of politics and a number of very specific civil rights: the right to equality before the law, the right to be protected against arbitrary arrest or punishment, the right to be presumed innocent until proven guilty, the right to hold personal opinions and religious beliefs, the right of freedom of expression, and the right to possess property, among others.[60] By making the language of this declaration an integral part of their new constitution, the deputies transformed their vision of natural rights into positive national law. They established that the legitimacy of government no longer derived from the will of the monarch and a traditional order that granted privileges according to rank and status, but instead from the guarantee of individual rights under the law. The impact of this declaration on France and on other countries and peoples in the world struggling against oppression would be profound, and soon led the historian Lord Acton to describe it as "a single confused page . . . that outweighed libraries and was stronger than all of the armies of Napoleon."[61] Indeed, according to one authority, it "remains to this day the classic formulation of the inviolable rights of the individual vis-à-vis the state."[62]

The Declaration of the Rights of Man and Citizen immediately inspired additional efforts as well, for it demonstrated a level of success and attention that others sought to emulate.[63] In the one single, extraordinary year of 1791, for example, any number of developments shaping visions of human rights occurred. New articles of the French constitution specified protection by law of civil and political rights, including those of freedom of thought and worship, to Protestants and Jews who had been persecuted under the old regime. Additional provisions mandated public relief for the poor and free public education, items completely unknown in other constitutions of the time and ones that would come to inspire what eventually would come to be called social and economic rights. A self-educated butcher's daughter, Olympe de Gouges, issued her own Declaration of the Rights of Woman and Citizen, declaring in the very first article that "woman is born free and remains equal to man in her rights," and virtually shouting: "Women, wake up; the tocsin of reason sounds throughout the universe; recognize your rights."[64] In the National Assembly, the Marquis de Condorcet similarly attempted to make certain that the proclamation of these rights applied to women as well, pointedly observing that women played a vital role in the revolution itself and represented half the population. "Either no individual of the human race has genuine rights, or else all have the same," he argued, "and he who votes against the right of another, whatever the religion, color, or sex of that other, has henceforth abjured his own."[65] The slaves of Saint Dominique (now Haiti) also demanded equal rights and launched a massive and bloody revolt against their white, French owners in order to obtain them. In the United States during the same year, a majority of states ratified the first ten amendments to the Constitution, guaranteeing by law civil and political rights for citizens vis-à-vis the power of the federal government, and appropriately described as "The Bill of Rights."[66] At the same time in England, the impassioned writer Thomas Paine published his sensational and provocative best seller, *Rights of Man*. Drawing on the theory of natural law and

More Powerful Than Libraries and Armies: The Declaration of the Rights of Man and Citizen, 1789 (United Nations Photo).

natural rights, Paine introduced the specific expression, "human rights," perhaps for the first time.[67] He gave credit to religious traditions for observing the unity of all humankind and the equality of all individuals, and then argued that universal natural rights for individuals provided the original source of all subsequent rights for members of society. "Man did not enter into society to become *worse* than he was before, nor to have fewer rights than he had before," claimed Paine, "but to have those rights better secured."[68] Moreover, Paine returned to the earlier theme of responsibility for being a "brother's keeper" by explicitly responding to the French Declaration in these terms: "A Declaration of Rights is, by reciprocity, a Declaration of Duties also. Whatever is my right as a man is also the right of another; and it becomes my duty to guarantee as well as to possess."[69]

By the end of the eighteenth century, therefore, any number of highly diverse philosophical visions addressed issues of human rights in one form or another. At times both partial cause and effect of revolutions themselves, most stressed the existence of a relationship between human nature, natural law, and natural rights. Some of these visions became embodied in positive national law that emphasized secular and democratic values and sought to provide protection for individuals in the exercise of civil and political rights such as freedom of speech, press, religion, and assembly. Others waited for more than two centuries to be realized in practice, if even then. Moreover, at this stage these visions spoke in expansive philosophical terms, often raising more questions than providing answers about precise definitions of rights, the distinctions between "freedom to" and "freedom from," the rights of individuals and the rights of communities composed of individuals, and the mechanisms for the enforcement of rights and duties.

Most important, these early philosophical and secular visions of human rights also shared several fundamental features with the religious visions that preceded them. Like all visions, they spoke to an ideal rather than a reality. Abstract theories, as we shall see shortly, did not always match actual practice. By raising visions of the best rather than the worst in human nature, however, they, like their religious counterparts, contributed essential elements to the slow but steady evolution of international human rights. They helped to build an ideal that inspired the creation of normative standards and actions around the world in the centuries that followed. These visions greatly enhanced a universal sense about the essential unity of humankind and the larger responsibilities to be keepers of brothers and sisters elsewhere. Finally, they added the force of their considerable influence to the realization, articulated so well by Thomas Paine, that rights and duties are linked inextricably.

Traditions and Ideas of a Very Different Sort

These visions of human rights did not go unchallenged. Indeed, others not only did not share these visions, but vehemently contested both their claims and their dreams. If ideas can be weapons, then these provided the arsenal of the counterforces. Instead of seeing the possibilities for the best in human nature, they often saw the worst and had much history to support them. Rather than the universal, they stressed the particular. In place of rights, they demanded duties. Instead of justice, they wanted privilege. Rather than change, they pressed for tradition and continuity. In place of equality, they insisted on hierarchies and distinctions based on caste or class, race, gender, belief, ethnicity, or place of origin. Instead of being a keeper of brothers and sisters, they frequently looked no further than themselves or their own immediate family or exclusive group or gender. And, of particular significance to international human rights, rather than acknowledging the sovereignty of the individual or the existence of a human family, they emphasized the sovereignty and the authority of the nation-state alone.

On New Year's Day 1792, for example, a large and enraged mob dragged a pathetic effigy of Thomas Paine through the narrow streets of Coventry, England. A sign pinned to its chest revealed the real source of their contempt. It read: "Rights of Man." When reaching the public square the crowd quickly strung the effigy from a gibbet, a gallows device from which the bodies of criminals already hung were exposed in death for public scorn, and prepared a roaring fire. For effect, they let the likeness of Paine dangle for a while, twisting in the wind, and then watched as it erupted into flames. The spectators burst into cheers, and as the arms, legs, and face of the effigy were reduced to ashes and smoke, joined in a loud and energetic rendition of the song, "God Save the King."[70]

The publication of Thomas Paine's *Rights of Man* provoked not only this public spectacle, but many others as well. Government authorities encouraged further hangings of such effigies in public squares, burnings of his book, organizing anti-Paine meetings, publishing pamphlets against rights, and the issuance of a royal proclamation declaring Paine's writings to be seditious and calling for his arrest. It was all highly reminiscent of the earlier reaction toward the writings of Rousseau who, charged with inciting rebellion himself, had been forced into exile to save his life. The *Rights of Man* may have been an immediate best seller and spoken to the needs and the hopes of humankind at large, but its vision directly challenged powerful vested interests, privilege, and tradition. Moreover, it was a specific and direct assault on the thought of Edmund Burke, the distinguished founder of modern conservatism and author of the influential *Reflections on the Revolution in France* published in 1790. In this work, Burke attacked the French Revolution's destruction of established hierarchy and inheritance, antiquity and long tradition, and invaluable historical continuity. He criticized those responsible for this "great departure from the ancient course," argued that liberty could emerge only gradually out of the old order, and described the authors of the Declaration of the Rights of Man and Citizen as creating "a mine that will blow up, at one grand explosion, all examples of antiquity, all precedents, charters, and acts of parliament." Burke warned that those who composed this declaration had become carried away with dangerous theoretical extremes and "so taken up with their theories about the rights of man, that they have totally forgotten his nature." He considered humanity flawed, weak, and only intermittently rational. "History consists, for the greater part," wrote Burke, "of the miseries brought upon the world by pride, ambition, avarice, revenge, lust, sedition, hypocrisy, [and] ungoverned zeal," and warned that their nature was such that if people were given too many rights then they would "want everything."[71]

Critics also used this occasion to attack the theories of natural rights as they had evolved up to that point. For example, although he believed in natural law, conservative Edmund Burke nonetheless rejected the notion that so-called "rights of man" could be derived from it. Once again he denounced the Declaration of the Rights of Man and Citizen as so much "prattling about the rights of men" and its authors as "wantonly" creating "metaphysical declarations" that produced the "monstrous fiction" of human equality. Such notions, he argued, only served to inspire "false ideas and vain expectations in men destined to travel in the obscure walk of laborious life."[72] He feared, of course, that any public affirmation of natural rights would lead to social and political upheaval. Interestingly enough, from the other end of the philosophical spectrum liberal Jeremy Bentham, one of the founders of utilitarianism, was no less scornful. He worried that abstract declarations and proclamations of natural rights might easily replace positive law and specific legislation. "Rights," he wrote contemptuously, "is the child of law; from real law come real rights; but from imaginary laws, from 'law of nature,' come imaginary rights. . . . Natural rights is simple nonsense."[73]

Declarations of rights and the writings of authors like Paine were challenged not only by Burke, Bentham, and their many followers but, perhaps more significantly, by ideas about the nature of human beings and the nature of government that had developed over many centuries of time. Thomas Hobbes' powerful *Leviathan* written in seventeenth-century England and one of the fundamental works of Western political theory, for instance, also saw in humanity "a perpetual and restless desire of power after power." He wrote pessimistically that the nature of humans was such that without a strong government to protect them, they would turn on themselves and there would be "a war of every man against every man" and their individual lives would be "solitary, poor, nasty, brutish, and short."[74] To prevent such a state and to ensure the maintenance of order, Hobbes argued that the powers of a ruler had to be absolute and unquestioned while subjects were to obey. Even the illustration on the title page of his book conveyed this central theme, for it symbolically showed to both those who could read and the many more at the time who could not, that numerous tiny and insignificant individual humans needed to surrender themselves completely into the huge figure of the powerful monarch and the state. Under this arrangement, subjects were not entitled to change the form of government, protest or accuse the ruler of injustice, punish the monarch, or possess any individual rights. Whatever rights existed, insisted Hobbes, could be claimed only by the monarch, and these were "indivisible," "essential and inseparable." Such rights included the right to determine "false doctrines" and what truths could be taught, to make and enforce rules for law and order, to make war and peace "as he shall think most fit," to grant rewards, and to inflict punishments. Consequently, wrote Hobbes, "none of his subjects . . . can be freed from his subjection."[75] This kind of an argument, of course, was seized on immediately by those who believed in the divine right of kings and the need for absolute monarchs with strong and centralized political authority and who could sing "God Save the King" with genuine conviction. Other theorists followed with ideas of the "natural right of regal power,"[76] and one contemporary in France proclaimed: "The Prince need render an account of his acts to no one. . . . All the state is in him; the will of all the people is included in his. As all perfection and all strength are united in God, so all the power of individuals is united in the person of the prince."[77]

Even here, notions of divinely sanctioned, hereditary rulers born of royal families and governing unquestioning, obedient subjects extended back in time far beyond Hobbes and his contemporaries. The pharaohs of ancient Egypt, the caesars of Rome, the emperors of Byzantium, the caliphs of the Islamic world, the kings of Cambodia, the jarlar of Scandinavia, the khans of the Mongols, the emperors of China and Japan, the sultans and princes of the Indian subcontinent, the tsars of Russia, the kings of African tribes, the rajas of Java and Sumatra, and the emperors of the Aztecs and Incas in the New World, among many others and despite their considerable differences, all ruled traditional and highly stratified hierarchical societies. They drew sharp distinctions between the rulers and the ruled, and subjects were expected to respect and fear authority. The few governed the many, the rich and powerful dominated the poor and weak, and those with influence clearly sought to shape the prevailing culture in such a way as to reflect and reinforce their interests. Class and caste divisions and severe inequality predominated, and human bondage in slavery and serfdom existed in most places. Educational opportunities existed only for the most privileged or extraordinarily gifted, and the majority of people in the world could neither read nor write. Torture as a means of punishment, extracting confessions, or deterrence through grisly spectacle in public squares and places was not at all uncommon. Social stability and conformity prevailed over individual freedom or self-realization, and most certainly duties over rights. In fact, these political and cultural practices prevailed, and hierarchical and authoritarian governments dominated the world as it had evolved to that time.

Challenges to visions of human rights and of being keepers of brothers and sisters also came from those who believed in the fundamental importance of differences between people rather than similarities. For some, these distinctions should be made on the basis of age, education, or language, with preference given to the elderly over youth, the literate over those who could not read or write, or those who could speak in a particular tongue over those who could not. For others, they should be made on the basis of the possession of property, class, or caste. The Indian *varnashramadharma* system provided one of the most extreme examples with its strict divisions between castes and its essential assumption that there are fundamental and unchangeable differences in the nature of human beings that prevent any uniform or universal standard from being even considered, let alone applied. This view was strongly endorsed by Kautilya in his manual on how to seize, hold, and manipulate power known as the *Arthasastra* written over two thousand years ago. For some, depending on location, the critical distinctions should be based on associations with family, tribe, clan, village, walled city, province, country, empire, or continent. For others, the most critical factor distinguishing people from each other should be religious belief with sharp distinctions separating, for instance, Hindus of the orthodox Vedic tradition from Buddhists, Christians from Jews and "heathens," or those of the Islamic faith from "infidels"; or, for that matter, Catholics from Protestants or Sunnis from Shiites. The Spanish Inquisition, pogroms against Jews in Russia, the Tokugawa shogunate's persecution of Christians in Japan, Hindu repression of Buddhists, and the forced conversions of many religions, among other examples, all represented some aspect of extreme religious intolerance and discrimination.

Those powerful and influential religious leaders more committed to the existing secular order than some of the precepts of their faith also resisted any visions of human rights that might threaten the status quo. Kings and emperors around the world, of course, always had found it possible to secure support for their claims of divine right to rule over their subjects from popes, archbishops, patriarchs, clergy, rabbis, *ulema*, Brahmin priests, and others to whom believers looked for guidance. With the emergence of explicit assertions for human rights, this phenomenon became even more apparent. Clerical authorities in France, for example, readily banned Voltaire's writings arguing on behalf of the right to freely practice one's religion. Pope Pius VI strongly condemned notions of religious toleration or freedom of opinion contained in the French Declaration of the Rights of Man and Citizen, and urged Catholics not to be seduced by these new ideas. In the Islamic world, members of the conservative clergy denounced notions of civil and political rights as blasphemous and against the teachings of the Qur'an. Hindu religious leaders continued to urge their followers to resist visions of equal rights for all people that threatened what they claimed to be the divinely sanctioned natural order of caste divisions.

Two other elements of traditional difference also profoundly challenged larger visions of human rights and equality for all: gender and race. Prejudice by men against women and by men and women against those "of color" appeared to be nearly universal. Male-dominated societies represented the well-entrenched norm rather than the exception. Here notions of being a "brother's keeper" applied literally only to brothers, as daughters often received far less favorable treatment than sons from birth. Then, throughout their lives, many women could easily find themselves described as members of the "weaker" or "lesser" sex and subjected to various forms of discrimination, abuse, exploitation, and repression. Some males viewed females as simply inferior beings, incapable of performing so-called masculine tasks, and thus undeserving of equal treatment, whether under paternalistic Confucianism in China, Islamic culture, or the Christian West. Some considered them as no more than property to be bought and sold in what Westerners called the "white slave trade," and confined against their will to households, harems, or brothels. In a popular book entitled *Malleus Maleficarum* (Hammer of Witches), first written in 1486 and then widely circulated thereafter, for example, Jacob Sprenger declared that women were "feebler in mind and body" and "naturally more impressionable" than men, liars "by nature," "a defect" of creation, and represented nothing more than "an imperfect animal."[78] Others viewed them as dangerous threats, and the presence of misogyny, or hatred of women, manifested itself in a kind of patriarchal rage that considered females not as loving wives or caring mothers but rather as evil witches, lustful whores, and sources of deceit and subversive sexuality.

Through time such attitudes produced both customs and laws in many societies governing marriage and divorce, inheritance and primogeniture, employment, and exclusion from the political process, among other matters, resulting in what has been called the "gendering of power" and the systematic discrimination against women.[79] Most married women, for example, discovered their citizenship determined not by their parents or place of birth, but rather by that of their husband; and female nationals who married foreigners found themselves forced to be subjected to the laws and customs of their husband's country. The situation became even more critical for divorced, abandoned, or abused women, for being husbandless meant being stateless.[80] Even during the height of discussion about human rights during the French Revolution, leading deputies successfully called for advocates for the rights of women like Olympe de Gouges to be executed at the guillotine. Men like Jean Baptiste Amar asked, "Must women exercise political rights and meddle in the affairs of government?" He answered his own question with a resounding no, and argued:

Man is strong, robust, born with a great energy, audacity, and courage . . . [and] alone appears suited for the profound and serious thoughts [méditations] that require a great exertion of mind. . . . [While] in general, women are hardly capable of lofty conceptions and serious thoughts. And, if, among ancient peoples, their natural timidity and modesty did not permit them to appear outside of their family, do you want in the French Republic to see them coming up to the bar, to the speaker's box, to political assemblies like men, abandoning both the discretion that is the source of all the virtues of this sex and the care of their family?[81]

In terms of its impact on international relations, perhaps no issue confronted basic principles of human rights more directly than that of race. For centuries men and women ranging from Japan to the Islamic world and from the Indian subcontinent to Europe and then the Americas discriminated against those of "backward races" whom they regarded as racially inferior. Indeed, the traditions of a wide variety of societies around the world clearly demonstrate what has been called "the impulse to inequality" wherein skin color served to greater or lesser degrees as the badge of master and subject, of the free and enslaved, and of the dominators and dominated.[82] Among the many cases of racial prejudice, however, none came even close to eclipsing that of the white, Western world. From the ideas expressed by philosophers such as Aristotle, historians such as Herodotus and Tacitus, geographers such as Solinus, and chroniclers such as Gomes Eannes de Azurara, Europeans increasingly were led to believe in a natural inferiority of nonwhite human beings and, hence, in the legitimacy of treating them differently. In the sixteenth century, the noted geographer André Thevet claimed in his *Cosmographie universelle* that black Africans were "stupid, bestial, and blinded by folly," while the Jesuit missionary Alexandre Valignamo declared even more expansively that "all these dusky races" in the world beyond Europe "are very stupid and vicious, and of the basest spirits."[83] By the eighteenth century, respected scientists added their voices to these ideas of race, including the distinguished German physiologist and comparative anatomist who is often called the founder of anthropology, Johann Friedrich Blumenbach, who argued that from an international comparison of the races, "the white color holds the first place" while the others of black, yellow, brown, and red skin color are merely degenerates from the original.[84] All of these ideas, increasingly presented with the authority of science, easily could be seized on to justify or legitimate racial separation or segregation, imperial conquests, colonial exploitation, and especially the capture and sale of living human beings into life-long bondage via the international slave trade.

According to their defenders and beneficiaries, these various traditions and ideas and the regimes that flourished with them had produced societies of remarkable predictability and stability. Here, to use Burke's phrase, people knew "their proper place!" To maintain this long continuity and its benefits, he argued, "the body of the people must not find the principles of natural subordination . . . rooted out of their minds" by some misguided and inflammatory visions of human rights.[85] He and others believed that such dangerous ideas and revolutionary notions about liberty and equality for all people would raise unwarranted expectations, encourage challenges to traditional authority of all kinds, disrupt the rich continuity of history and custom, and thereby seriously threaten enviable conditions of law and order and private property that had proven themselves again and again over time and location throughout the world.

Burke's mention of property in this context is of great importance, for it revealed that visions and the language of rights could also present double-edged swords. That is, not all people shared the same vision, and the claimed rights of some could easily challenge the asserted rights of others or create difficult inconsistencies. This was particularly evident in the case of those who argued on behalf of property and private ownership.[86] Property rights had made a powerful appeal for many centuries to the minds of people by encouraging them to consider ownership as the rightful reward of those who had worked with the sweat of their brows or the intelligence of their minds. John Locke himself then helped to elevate these long-held notions of property rights to a higher philosophical plane by declaring that they were an integral part of "natural rights" and absolutely essential to the pursuit of happiness. Indeed, he argued that "the great and chief end" of forming governments in the first place was "the preservation of their property."[87] Rousseau joined in by describing the right of property as "the most sacred of all the rights of citizenship" and "even more important in some respects than liberty itself."[88] Hutcheson, Hume, Burke, Bentham, Jefferson, and Alexander Hamilton all added their voices to this chorus as well, as did others from non-Western countries.[89] It thus did not take much effort to use these arguments about property rights as a defense for the great holdings of the few rich against the poverty of the many unpropertied poor, and to do so when definitions of private property actually included living human beings: slaves, serfs, and women.

One other element directly and powerfully confronted any and all notions of international human rights: the doctrine of national sovereignty. As dynastic territorial states first emerged in Europe, they sought a variety of ways to strengthen and justify their use of growing and centralized power. The creation of large standing armies and of government bureaucracies provided invaluable and intimidating service in this regard, as did theories advocating the divine right of kings and the sovereign power of the state. This was precisely what Jean Bodin, the French political philosopher, wanted to achieve when he enunciated the principle of national sovereignty in his book, *Les Six Livres de la République,* during the second half of the sixteenth century. States, he asserted, possessed the unique feature of sovereignty, which he dramatically and defiantly defined as "power absolute and perpetual," "supreme," and "subject to no law." Indeed, claimed Bodin, such sovereign power provided "the distinguishing mark of a state." The state alone possessed the power to decide how it would behave in the world and how it would treat its own people within its own borders and those under its control in overseas possessions. Bodin described this power as "absolute authority over all the rest without exception" and "without the consent of any superior, equal, or inferior being necessary."[90] If a state desired to treat its subjects well and acknowledge that they might have rights, it could. If it wanted to abuse them, exploit them, persecute them, forcibly convert them, or enslave them, it could do that as well. The precise nature of the treatment, however, was considered to be a matter of exclusive domestic jurisdiction, and not at all subject to the opinions or values of other states or pressures from nonexistent international organizations. Individuals thus remained at the mercy of their own state.

This doctrine of national sovereignty, and its corollary of domestic jurisdiction, received reinforcement in a number of ways. The Treaty of Westphalia signed in 1648 provided recognition, in law as well as in fact, of the power and authority of sovereign, independent states to be the only legitimate actors in a decentralized international system. They recognized no universal authority like that of an emperor or a pope from above, and no claims from feudal barons or subjects from below.[91] The publication of *Leviathan* only three years later provided even further theoretical justification for the doctrine, particularly when Thomas Hobbes addressed what he described as "the essence of sovereignty."[92] Here he left no doubt about his belief that the sovereign powers of the state and the absolute monarch that acted in its name ruled without challenge. "In the span of a century," writes one noted authority of international politics, the doctrine of sovereignty "became unchallengeable either from within the territory or from without. In other words, it had become supreme."[93] Indeed, from the time that it was first enunciated to the present, no doctrine has served to thwart international human rights more severely than this one.

As traditional international law developed, for example, it became exclusively defined as that law governing relations between nation-states alone. This meant that only states could enjoy being subjects of international law and possess legal rights under it. To the extent that states had any international legal responsibilities relating to individuals, these were only deemed to be owed to other states. Such obligations arose either from rules concerning the treatment of foreign nationals or from special agreements concerning policies toward certain religious groups. In all other cases, states considered individuals as mere objects rather than subjects and as possessing absolutely no rights under international law. The manner in which a state treated its own people was regarded as strictly its own business. When these individuals suffered injury in any way, the rights of no other states were affected. Since international law did not regulate the rights of individuals vis-à-vis the state of their nationality, nations therefore deemed the entire subject to fall within their own exclusive domestic jurisdiction. This lack of regulation thus denied other states the right to intercede or intervene on behalf of the nationals of a state that abused them, thereby reinforcing the principle of national sovereignty even further.[94]

These many powerful forces thus stood firmly opposed to any visions of international human rights bound to challenge vested interests. The extension of rights to individuals irrespective of their caste or class, race, gender, belief, ethnicity, or place of origin

presented grave dangers to traditional forms of authority, hierarchy, privilege, property, and domestic and international law. No place on earth by the end of the eighteenth century, therefore, could claim that human rights for all were somehow broadly
based or solidly founded in their histories or cultures. In fact, it is for this reason that so
many contemporary defenders and beneficiaries of the status quo viewed those who
advocated rights—such as Thomas Paine—as dangerous revolutionaries and anar-
chists who threatened to overturn stability, destroy the public order, incite a state of
emergency, and jeopardize national sovereignty. They therefore vowed that they and
their successors would resist visions of human rights.

Visions and Reality

The interplay between these powerful visions that supported human rights, and those
ideas and traditions aligned in opposition, and the interests that both represented,
would move the course of much of history. Because they so often struck at the very core
of human nature and individual self-interest, religious doctrine, philosophical belief,
government power and authority, social and legal structures, and rights and responsibilities, they raised profoundly difficult issues about life, about the relationship between all individuals and families and societies in which they lived, and about history
and tradition. On occasion, at least some of these visions would complement each
other when human rights were seen as part of a seamless web in which the rights of one
affected the rights of another. At other times, however, they would compete, not just
with contemplative words or in the solemn decorum of legal proceedings, but in violence, revolution, and civil or foreign war. The results frequently indicated great contrasts between theory and practice, or between visions and reality.

Throughout history, for example, most individuals in the world found themselves
confronting hierarchical societies and imperial or authoritarian regimes of one kind or
another in which differences mattered. Whether their home was Western Europe, the
shores of the Mediterranean or the Baltic, the mountains or the plains of Asia, the
Indian subcontinent, the Near and Middle East, Africa, North America, Central and
South America, or islands of the Pacific, patterns of dominance and discrimination
prevailed. Sharp distinctions were made, depending on local and particular circumstances, on the basis of gender, age, education, religion, race, class or caste, ethnicity,
language, and tribe or clan, among other factors of difference used either individually
or in combination. Here, the theories such as those of the divine right of rulers or racial
superiority and customs of tradition, often ancient in origins, served to support these
practices. Even in democratic Athens, for example, less than half of the population ever
benefited from the theories of natural law. At times, some religious precepts actually
reinforced such behavior, as in the cases of religious zealots focusing on exclusivity
rather than universality and persecution rather than tolerance, Hinduism's texts about
the caste system and its "untouchables," or the opinion of Confucius that "women
indeed are human beings, but they are of a lower state than men and can never attain
full equality with them."[95]

More often than not, however, religious principles of care and compassion clashed with those secular desires of political power and privilege, thus making the distance between vision and reality all the more apparent. Some of those governments and peoples in the West who so vocally claimed to follow the precepts of Christianity and the "Prince of Peace," for example, came to be known internationally as among the most rapacious and the worst offenders against the well-being and rights of others. They practiced religious persecution of Jews and Muslims, discrimination against women and children, enslavement of Africans, and territorial conquest and exploitation of all those around the world whom they came to regard as racially inferior. Repulsed by the horrors of massacres and sufferings inflicted on these largely helpless victims, a few courageous individuals spoke out. The noted Dominican jurist of the sixteenth century, Francisco de Vitoria, for example, delivered a series of stinging lectures unequivocally condemning the Spanish government's brutal and un-Christian conquest of the Aztecs and Incas in the New World, and called for a new international law among nations with universal validity that would include rights and duties for all peoples. Shortly thereafter, the priest Bartholomé de Las Casas, motivated by his religious belief in being a brother's keeper, wrote a shocking account of these atrocities perpetrated by Spain, entitled *Brief Relation of the Destruction of the Indies*, in which he pleaded: "The Indians are our brothers and Christ has given his life for them. Why, then, do we persecute them with such inhuman savagery?"[96] Such words confronted one of the most powerful governments in the world with a public challenge to its professed ideals and the obvious gulf between vision and reality, but the practices continued. "To insist with Las Casas that Indians should be won over by persuasion only," writes one historian of these events, "was to abandon all future conquests and admit the injustice of past ones. The full implications of either theory were more than any self-respecting government of the time could stomach."[97]

The refusal of governments to halt or even restrict conquest was matched only by their unwillingness to end the profitable practice of slavery or the international slave trade. Slavery, of course, possessed an ancient tradition of vast scope that ranged from East Asia to Africa, from the Middle East to Europe, and from Southeast Asia to the Western Hemisphere. It was neither invented by Europeans nor confined exclusively to black Africans; and, in fact, whites themselves had known enslavement on the shores of the Mediterranean and Black seas, in Eastern Europe and what is now Russia, in European colonies, and in Africa and Asia.[98] But what emerged by the sixteenth, seventeenth, and eighteenth centuries dramatically transformed any and all slave patterns of the past. In terms of the total numbers of millions of human beings, focus on a particular race, creation of a justifying ideology of racial superiority, and magnitude of tragic brutality, it simply had no parallel in history. The extent of slavery and the slave trade at this time also made the practices extremely lucrative. Indeed, some of the largest and most successful business organizations of all time profited enormously from slaving and this traffic in human beings as products, including the Royal African Company, the Compagnie de Rouen of France, the Brandenburg Company of Prussia, the Maranhao Company of Portugal, and the Dutch West India Company, among others. The Board of Trade in London accurately reflected the opinion of investors in many other capitals when it concluded that it was "absolutely necessary that a trade so beneficial to the kingdom should be carried on to the greatest advantage."[99] Official state policy, often enhanced by investments from members of the royal families of Europe, guaranteed even further financial successes, the accumulation of capital, and the growth of commercial capitalism. As one leading authority on historical slave patterns observes, "black slavery was an intrinsic part of 'the rise of the West'" and for nation-states to refrain from participating in it "was almost as unthinkable as spurning nuclear technology is in the world of today."[100]

With the growth of the international slave trade and the practice of racial slavery, theories of the inferiority and superiority of one race over another gained even wider acceptance. Indeed, the concomitance of racial prejudice and the power to enslave blacks suggests a strong mutual relationship between the two. Both were, after all, twin aspects of the debasement of black men and women from people into property; and race relations obviously developed not only from theories but also from social and legal practices in which racial contact occurred.[101] In this regard, European slave traders and slave owners in the New World desperately sought to establish clear hierarchies and to keep the races segregated from each other. The Spanish Crown, for example, promulgated specific laws to "prohibit contact and communication between Indians and Mulattoes, Negroes, and similar races."[102] Portuguese settlers distanced themselves from what they called the *racas infectas* or "contaminated races" and created a caste system based on white supremacy and the institutionalized inferiority of colored slaves.[103] French slave laws, known as the *code noir*, also stressed the need for segregation and keeping the races apart, as did those of the Dutch. British colonists in North America acted in much the same way, constructing legal means to make black men and women slaves "for life," prohibiting miscegenation or interracial marriages, and granting any owner "absolute power and authority over his Negro slaves."[104]

When considering the contrasts between visions and reality at this time, it is also important to confront the attitudes and actions of a number of the Western *philosophes* themselves. Ironically enough, some of the greatest minds of the Enlightenment who espoused the democratic principles of liberation, equality, toleration, natural rights, and respect for the dignity of individuals and who challenged notions that a privileged few had a God-given right to rule over the vast majority of the population, at the same time revealed that they believed that these principles should be applied to their own gender and their own race alone. Rousseau, for example, could wax eloquently about freedom and justice, but at the same time refuse to acknowledge anything other than it was the order of nature for woman to obey men. "Women do wrong to complain of the inequality of man-made laws," he wrote, and claimed that "when she tries to usurp our rights, she is our inferior."[105] Montesquieu, the articulate exponent of individual worth, simultaneously claimed that black-skinned Africans were "savage and barbarian" and bereft of normal human traits.[106] Diderot, although he argued against the institution of slavery in theory, expressed similar opinions. Locke, the celebrated philosopher of human liberty, actually owned shares in the Royal African Company. Voltaire, too, held financial interests in the Compagnie des Indes, the fortunes of which came in part from the slave trade, and wrote that blacks possessed only "a few more ideas than animals" and that as "a result of a hierarchy of nations, Negroes are thus slaves of other men."[107]

Wrote the noted British philosopher David Hume, "I am apt to suspect the Negroes and in general all the other species . . . to be naturally inferior to the whites."[108]

Given this long and difficult historical context of theories and practices that had a bearing on human rights, many expected that the upheavals in America and France during the so-called Age of Democratic Revolutions at the end of the eighteenth century would mark a dramatic change of course and a marked reversal of the past. In many ways they did, particularly as they sought to give expression to natural rights theory, to restrict the prerogatives of monarchs and oligarchies, to extend the principles of democratic government, and to give definition to this first-generation of human rights that emphasized civil and political rights. Nevertheless, even revolutions, wars, and violence could not change everything at once, and the resistance to any broad-based extension of human rights for all remained determined and strong.

Despite the remarkable provisions of the new U.S. Constitution and its Bill of Rights, and the theories of natural law and inalienable rights that stood behind them, for example, actual practices denied equal rights to at least four categories of Americans: slaves, women, the unpropertied, and indigenous peoples. Slaves certainly found no protection from the Constitution when it prohibited Congress from taking action to eliminate the slave trade for twenty years, made no clear distinction between property rights and human rights, and by guaranteeing that fugitive slaves would be returned to their owners confirmed that slaves would be regarded not as citizens or as human beings endowed with rights but as articles of commerce, thereby providing official sanction for the practice of slavery. Both George Washington and Thomas Jefferson owned slaves themselves. Similarly, the Constitution did not mention women, and since the qualifications for suffrage were left to the decision of individual states, they would continue to deny the voting rights to American women for more than a century. In addition to gender, every state in the new nation restricted voting on the basis of age, race, and property or wealth, and thus denied the political right to vote and effective representation to the majority of the population.[109] Nor did these new documents or laws provide any protection for American Indians. Washington and Benjamin Franklin described them as "ignorant savages" and "beasts," while Jefferson himself argued that his country had no choice but to pursue them "to extinction."[110] For these disenfranchised and dispossessed groups, and despite the official rhetoric of rights, neither the Constitution nor its Bill of Rights provided any immediate protection whatsoever.

Revolutionary France experienced similar difficulties in the distance between vision and reality concerning human rights. Initially swept up in the excitement of radical change, leaders of the National Assembly decreed the abolition of what they called "the feudal regime," freed the few remaining serfs in the country, eliminated special privileges in matters of taxation and public office, issued the Declaration of the Rights of Man and Citizen, and then took the highly unusual step of extending citizenship to those of color and abolishing slavery in the colonies. These actions prompted immediate reactions, however, and some remained very short lived. Within only months, for example, the Assembly rescinded its decision about equal rights for blacks. Slavery in the colonies was reinstituted a short time thereafter, and few advocated any extension of human rights to the millions of indigenous peoples subjugated under the French

Empire. The political rights of voting and holding public office also possessed restrictions in practice. At first, only white men who passed a test of wealth, known as "active citizens," could exercise the franchise or hold office, as compared to those "passive citizens" of servants, the propertyless, and poor who could not. Women were theoretically citizens under the law, but practically could not vote, fully participate in the political process, or receive equal protection.[111] Revolutionary leaders here, as in America, understood that the extension of genuinely equal rights would entail vast social and political consequences that they were unwilling to accept.

In this regard, it is extremely important to recognize that the Declaration of Independence, the Constitution, and the Bill of Rights in the United States, as well as the Declaration of the Rights of Man and Citizen in France, reflected far more vision than reality. None of these documents were "deeply rooted" in either the practices of the West or even of these two countries, as others wishing to denigrate human rights within their own countries by distorting historical origins eventually would claim.[112] They emerged not out of long tradition or wide-spread experience or inclusive election, but rather out of war and revolution and had to be nurtured in the face of overwhelming opposition. In the context of the late eighteenth century when "democracy" and individual rights were regarded by many as synonymous with anarchy and subversion, they were statements of visions—ideals and aspirations toward which two nations pledged themselves to struggle in the future, but not to guarantee immediately at the moment.

The accuracy of this judgment can be seen in part by the number of outspoken critics who vowed that they would not rest as long as such blatant disparities between visions and realities in human rights existed in these countries. Some women, for example, viewed their exclusion from the extension of rights as a blatant betrayal of the promises of democracy. They wrote petitions, published tracts, and organized clubs to demand more participation. In the new American republic, Abigail Adams accused men of being "naturally tyrannical," and placed them on notice: "If particular care and attention is not paid to the ladies we are determined to foment a rebellion, and will not hold ourselves bound by any laws in which we have no voice or representation."[113] In revolutionary France, men like Condorcet and Pierre Guyomar and women like Olympe de Gouges and Etta Palm d'Aelders, argued courageously on behalf of the rights of women, sometimes sacrificing their very lives for the cause in which they believed. During 1792 Mary Wollstonecraft published her impassioned book in England entitled *A Vindication of the Rights of Woman.* Here she scathingly attacked the historical oppression of women by men, argued for gender equity, and demanded that the world establish "rights of humanity" for men and women alike.[114] Still others at the time worked to extend the boundaries of definition even further, such as Thomas Spence with his 1797 pamphlet entitled *The Rights of Infants.*[115]

Agitation and organized opposition against human bondage also grew appreciably during the same time. Indeed, absolutely nothing marked the vast distance between vision and reality more starkly than the institution and practice of slavery. As Patrick Henry, a revolutionary leader himself observed: "Is it not amazing that at a time when the rights of humanity are defined and understood with precision, in a country, above all others, fond of liberty, that in such a country we find men . . . adopting a principle as repugnant to humanity as it is inconsistent with the Bible, and destructive to liberty?"[116] Slaves themselves boldly petitioned for their freedom, arguing "for the sake of justice, humanity, and the rights of mankind."[117] Particularly from within the religious community of reformist churches came cries that the practice of slavery presented an absolutely intolerable obstacle to any concept of human rights and a violent offense against Christian principles to be keepers of all brothers and sisters. Fundamentally motivated during this period of religious revival known as the "Great Awakening" by their religious convictions and sense of responsibility, articulate and impassioned Protestant spokesmen like John Woolman, Granville Sharp, Benjamin Rush, Anthony Benezet, Samuel Hopkins, James Ramsay, and John Wesley all stressed in their arguments for abolition the relationship between spiritual and personal liberty, fusing the language of scripture with that of natural rights. For instance, in writing about all people equally being the subjects of "Christ's redeeming grace," Benezet declared: "At a time when the general rights and liberties of mankind . . . are become so much the subjects of universal consideration; can it be an inquiry indifferent to any, how many of those who distinguish themselves as the Advocates of Liberty, remain insensible and inattentive to the treatment of thousands and tens of thousands of our fellow-men who . . . are at this very time kept in the most deplorable state of slavery."[118]

Benezet and others from among nonconformist and anti-establishment congregations like the Baptists, Methodists, Congregationalists, Presbyterians, and especially the Quakers, who organized the first Society for the Relief of Free Negroes Unlawfully Held in Bondage and then the Society for the Abolition of the Slave Trade, presented their attacks against slavery as a vindication of the visions of Christianity, moral accountability, and the unity of all mankind. As one group wrote to another beyond their own borders:

We conjure you, as you love Liberty, to extend its influence, and investigate its import; examine your Declaration of Rights, and see if you can find in it a *term* which conveys the idea of *human* merchandise; examine your hearts, and see if you can find a spark of brotherhood for men who *deal* in men. To defend your own liberties is noble, but to befriend the friendless is Godlike; complete then your Revolution by demanding Commerce to be just, that Africa may bless you as well as Europe.[119]

They argued that the emancipation of slaves was fundamental to the message of love and compassion from the Gospels, the power of redemption, and Christ's injunction "to proclaim freedom to the captives." Collectively, they applauded Lord Mansfield's judicial decision in the *Somerset* case that holding slaves within Britain was against the law and worked to enact legislation for manumission and emancipation from slavery where they could, at least in the New England and mid-Atlantic states in North America.[120] They also quickly adopted as their symbol the image of a black slave on bended knee in chains, arms outstretched, and pleading: "Am I Not a Man and a Brother?" or "Am I Not a Woman and a Sister?" For them, the struggle against slavery presented an opportunity for their religious vision to become a progressive force in history and posed a decisive test for the strength of their convictions.[121] If human bondage in slavery be "excusable, or pardonable," wrote James Beattie bluntly in his 1793 treatise,

Brothers and Sisters: A Famous Emancipation Society Image (Library of Congress).

Elements of Moral Science, "it is vain to talk any longer of the external distinctions of right and wrong, truth and falsehood, good and evil."[122]

The application of theories of human rights to the world also suffered at this time in history from a very serious practical problem of accurate and timely information. That is, even those highly motivated to advance international human rights could take no action unless they could obtain news about the plight of others beyond their own borders, either by traveling themselves to different locations or by securing news of exploitation, conquest, massacre, or other abuses in sufficient time to relieve suffering. Given the power of authoritarian and autocratic rule, knowledge of these events often could be controlled or completely suppressed. Given the limitations of technology in an age before steamships, telegraphs, mass-circulation newspapers, popular novels, and photographs, such information simply could not be accurately or rapidly transmitted. As one observer who lived through this period insightfully and poignantly reflected: "In the old days, news travelled slowly; one scarcely heard what was happening at the other end of the world until the following year. If blood had been spilt, the earth had time to absorb it; if tears had been shed, the sun had time to dry them."[123]

If enormous chasms thus often existed between vision and reality concerning human rights, the same cannot be said with reference to the doctrine of national sovereignty. Here theory and practice mutually reinforced each other as independent nation-states often behaved exactly as they wished toward those under their control and human rights simply were not regarded as a matter of legitimate international concern. For several important reasons, states normally refused to become involved in disputes surrounding the treatment and well-being of people beyond their own borders. In philosophical terms, they found themselves consistently confronting the doctrine of national sovereignty and its uncompromising claims of domestic jurisdiction. In practical terms, they found themselves largely powerless to have much of an effect in the internal affairs of others. Their own lack of resources to project their will and the absence of any international organization or group that might assist in establishing some level of minimal standards let alone enforcement simply reinforced this conclusion. In political terms, they also found themselves afraid to intervene due to reciprocity. That is, criticism in the name of human rights within another country might well invite criticism of their own policies in return. States that made little or no effort to protect human rights of their own people at home could hardly claim justification for the protection of others abroad. These various philosophical, practical, and political factors, when combined with those many traditional ideas and practices that rejected human rights in the first place, all proved to be sufficient in erecting powerful obstacles in the path of anyone with visions of creating and protecting international human rights beyond the nation-state.

*   *   *

In the vast and complex history of the world, most people experienced not human rights, but to change meanings for a moment, human wrongs. During most times and places, from the beginning of recorded history to the end of the eighteenth century, those who lived and died found themselves confronting various forms of prejudice and discrimination based on gender, race, caste or class, belief, ethnicity, place of origin, or some other form of difference. They were never allowed to exercise whatever rights they might claim, or that others might assert on their behalf. Instead, traditional societies and imperial regimes from Asia to Africa and from Europe to Central America emphasized hierarchical relationships, distinct divisions between the few rulers and the many ruled, stratification between the powerful and the weak, and obedience rather than rights. Their cultures reflected and reinforced the interests of the powerful. Common patterns of dominance thus found expression in many varieties of privilege and poverty, intolerance and ignorance, despotism and violence, torture and conquest, arrogance and xenophobia, persecution and segregation, human bondage in serfdom and slavery, and even genocide. Moreover, in these practices virtually all governments regarded how they treated those under their control as a matter exclusively within their own domestic jurisdiction. Those who suffered as victims thus could not look beyond their state for any form of assistance or protection and were confined to their own locale, for their fate was not regarded as a legitimate subject of any possible international action.

Yet in the midst of this hostile historical environment and often in the face of entrenched traditional practices and fierce opposition, there were those creative and courageous enough to envision a different kind of world in which all people would be treated with dignity and equality. First with religious precepts, then with philosophical principles, and gradually with a few practical and concrete political results, slowly but nevertheless determinedly there began to emerge visions that all men and women had certain responsibilities to those in need and possessed certain natural or inalienable rights simply as the result of being human. Despite all of the realities and constraints aligned against them, these various visions gradually began to grow in power and influence. Their strength did not derive from their ability to immediately bring about human rights for all in practice, however, but rather to keep ideals alive for centuries, at times even during under brutal persecution, that might serve to inspire future generations to take more determined action when possible. By the end of the eighteenth century, these visions had helped to inspire wars, revolutions, declarations, constitutions, and nongovernmental organizations such as the Society for the Abolition of the Slave Trade, as well as individual acts of compassion. But this was only a foretaste of what lay just ahead. As one observer once noted, throughout most of history liberty remains more in shadow form than in substance, "yet the shadow is itself an earnest of greater things" to come.[124]

Chapter 2
To Protect Humanity and Defend Justice

Early International Efforts

> Now there are states of affairs in which human sympathy refuses to be confined by the [old] rules, necessarily limited and conventional, of international law. . . . Let us cast aside our narrow and ill-conceived construction of the ideas of a former period . . . in order to protect humanity and defend justice.
> — William Gladstone of Britain

Prior to the nineteenth century, the power of visions of human rights could be seen in inspiration, in the ability to create and then nurture an ideal of compassion and respect for others simply by the nature of being human brothers and sisters. Their capacity to influence actual behavior, however, was largely confined to specific individuals, locales, regions, or in a very small number of cases, nations. Traditional historical, philosophical, practical, political, and legal factors developed over the centuries all served to confine matters of human rights to the area of exclusive domestic jurisdiction, far from any global agenda, and thus removed from being considered as a legitimate issue for any kind of serious international action.

The seeds of vision sown in the past, often forced to lie dormant for generations, slowly began to germinate in the nineteenth century. Foreign and civil wars overthrew many power structures and vested interests, revolutions and the process of democratization challenged claims of state sovereignty and advanced more liberal political philosophies, industrialization and urbanization created new pressures for change, modernization unleashed forces opposed to pastoral tradition and more parochial ideas of former times, and appeals to the conscience on behalf of the welfare of others during this period increasingly began to fall on fertile soil. At the same time a technological revolution in transportation and communications in the West brought about by the railroad, steamship, telegraph, and especially the popular press and novels, meant that information about the fate of those who suffered in one form or another could no longer be controlled or delayed as in the past. Instead, they could be used to advance visions of international human rights, in the words of contemporaries, by giving expression to "the general sentiment of civilized mankind," "the principles of humanity," and "universal brotherhood," and thereby arousing "the fears and the hopes of thousands."[1] This simple fact would have profound implications, and the aspirations for rights would serve as both catalyst and outcome of intense upheaval. Those individual men and women devoted to advancing human rights thus found themselves as never before enabled to begin to pursue a direction of early international action in the name of humanity and justice by attempting to free the enslaved, to assist the exploited, to care for the wounded, and to protect the persecuted.

To Free the Enslaved

It is hardly surprising that the first efforts of the nineteenth century to protect human- ity and defend justice should focus on the tragic fate of those condemned to slavery. Nowhere were the violations of human rights—however defined—more blatant or brutal. The debasement of human beings from living people into mere property and their forceful capture, restraint with chains or neck irons, violent branding and torture, and life-long enslavement for themselves and their descendants dramatically revealed one of the most vicious and repulsive chapters in all of history.

Slavery, of course, possessed an ancient historical record of vast scope, extending over thousands of years and spread across Asia, Africa, Europe, the Middle East, islands of the Pacific, and the Americas. But what began to emerge during the sixteenth century with the first shipments of black Africans to the Western Hemisphere even- tually transformed any and all slave patterns of the past. In terms of numbers totaling in the millions, systematic focus on one particular race, creation of an ideology extolling racial superiority and a practice establishing racial segregation between masters and slaves, lucrative financial rewards, and impact on four continents, black slavery had no parallel in history. Few wanted to be left out of this enterprise and thus deny themselves either the power or the profits that flowed from it.[2] For this reason, and up to the beginning of the nineteenth century, the international slave trade flourished and hu- man bondage in slavery was legally practiced in most countries of the world.

Common practice and a widespread acceptance of slavery, however, did not mean unanimous approval. A small minority of thoughtful men and women refused to be swayed either by the prevailing arguments seeking to justify the owning of slaves or the powerful and well-financed vested interests of the time, and instead viewed the enslave- ment of human beings as completely contrary to the precepts of their religious faith and/or their political philosophy—and increasingly said so. They not only voiced their determined opposition to slavery, but began to organize early nongovernmental orga- nizations in the form of abolitionist societies to publish pamphlets and tracts, to preach sermons, to deliver public speeches, and to initiate active campaigns of agitation and protest in order to free the enslaved. Abolishing slavery, it is important to observe, was not a uniquely "Western" value. Indeed, plantation owners in the West devised and practiced one of most brutal and barbaric forms of slavery ever known in the world, and it was widely accepted by the majority. Others, including those of deep religious convic- tions among Muslims and Buddhists, also denounced the holding of human beings as slaves elsewhere in their own settings. What the West did possess, however, were the means to express opposition and influence opinion as well as the political institutions with the potential for responding to voting pressures and challenges to the status quo. In order to free the enslaved, abolitionists understood that they had to use these advantages to focus their efforts on achieving two difficult objectives: first, outlawing the international slave trade to stop the flow of human cargo from abroad; then, ending slavery at home.

The first serious efforts to render the slave trade illegal occurred simultaneously in the United States and Britain, where profits from slaving appeared most evident and where opposition in the name of human rights could be most forcefully mounted. Here all people, declared former slave trader and influential public speaker Thomas Branagan, had to confront the reality of the stark contrast between their stated theoretical principles and the practice of participating in the slave trade which made them "butchers of their brethren, destroyers of liberty and the rights of man, promoters and supporters of legal barbarity."[3] The intellectual and moral strength of this argument, when combined with a growing sense of guilt from the past, a crusading zeal of evangelical Christianity, a fear of the consequences of importing more slaves, and the emergence of new economic interest groups either unconnected with or even hostile to slavery, all played roles in leading the public to exert pressure against the trade. Fundamentally, they believed that it was wrong. Thus, President Thomas Jefferson, in his 1806 message to Congress, explicitly used the language of rights and urged the lawmakers "to withdraw the citizens of the United States from all further participation in those violations of human rights which have been so long continued on the unoffending inhabitants of Africa, and which the morality, the reputation, and the best interests of our country, have long been eager to proscribe."[4] At exactly the same time members of the Society for the Abolition of the Slave Trade in Britain escalated their public agitation and forced members of Parliament also to confront this issue in bitter debate about responsibilities for protecting human beings and defending justice in the name of "the common rights of humanity."[5] By 1807 the strength of those who wanted to end their own nation's involvement in the slave trade, particularly those within the nonconformist churches, had reached such proportions as to force votes in both Congress and Parliament. In the United States the result took the form of the Act to Prohibit the Importation of Slaves, declaring that those who brought persons seized from Africa for slavery would lose their ships and cargo, and face possible fines and imprisonment. In Britain the similar Act for the Abolition of the Slave Trade made it illegal to trade in, purchase, sell, barter, or transport any human cargo for the purpose of slavery.[6] Both of these laws provided a necessary beginning to eliminating the slave trade, but neither could solve all the difficulties at once. They lacked sufficient enforcement capabilities and applied only to their own areas of national territorial jurisdiction, and thus could not significantly influence the behavior of others beyond their own borders. In order to address this larger problem, therefore, those who wanted truly to end the slave trade turned their attention and energies toward an international solution.

All major breakthroughs in the long struggle for international human rights, as we shall see constantly, emerged in the wake of upheavals, wars, and revolutions. Although visions of human rights served as absolutely essential forces in these efforts, they rarely provided motives sufficiently powerful by themselves to move governments into effective action. Often ironically, they usually required significant shifts of power, the testing of existing institutions by disruption or chaos, or even violence and destruction to provide opportunities for serious reassessment and significant change. The abolitionists of the early nineteenth century appeared to understand this feature of human behavior better than most. For this reason they deliberately mounted a vigorous campaign to arouse public opinion in the aftermath of the American and French revolutions, the successful slave revolt in Saint-Dominique, upheavals in Latin America, the Irish rebellion, and the lengthy Napoleonic wars in such a way as to influence those diplomats attempting to restructure the international order at the Congress of Vienna in 1814–1815.

The leadership in this effort was taken by William Wilberforce and Thomas Clarkson, two charismatic and indefatigable British crusaders deeply inspired by their religious faith who viewed the slave trade as fundamentally a moral issue rather than a political matter. Wilberforce, for example, instigated a series of nearly eight hundred petitions to Parliament, initiated correspondence with leading political and literary figures, and even arranged for private meetings with Tsar Alexander I of Russia to discuss the importance of using the Congress of Vienna as the forum for the international abolition of the slave trade. Clarkson, described by the poet Samuel Taylor Coleridge as "the moral steam engine" of the crusade,[7] simultaneously prepared a special abridgment of his earlier report entitled *Evidence on the Subject of the Slave Trade* that could be easily read and quickly capture the imagination with illustrations of suffocatingly crowded conditions onboard slave ships and of shackles for restraining or punishing the helpless victims, thereby dramatically drawing attention to the horrors of the trade. In order to increase its influence internationally, friends then translated this pamphlet into French, German, Spanish, and Italian. A new preface encouraged all leaders and their representatives to seize the opportunity and abolish the abominable slave trade at Vienna.[8] Lord Castlereagh, the chief British delegate at the congress, found this public pressure and interference from private citizens to be particularly irritating and complained bitterly that it was wrong "to force it upon nations, at the expense of their honor and of the tranquility of the world."[9]

Delegates at the Congress of Vienna could not ignore this mounting public pressure, however, and consequently established a special committee on the international slave trade to deal with the issue. They quickly found themselves locked into a battle between power, principle, and prejudice. With both dispassionate reason and extreme emotion, they made and heard contesting arguments about human rights, religious imperatives, economic interests and profits, comparative strategic advantages, the unreliability of other nations, and the continued claims of national sovereignty. These representatives of governments knew that they had to avoid the dangers of the Scylla of achieving nothing and thereby provoking the wrath of the abolitionists and their public supporters or the Charybdis of accomplishing too much and thereby antagonizing serious vested interests. Through a complicated combination of threats and bribes ranging from money to territory, the delegates finally agreed to sign the Eight Power Declaration acknowledging that "the public voice in all civilized countries calls aloud for its prompt suppression," proclaiming that the international slave trade was "repugnant to

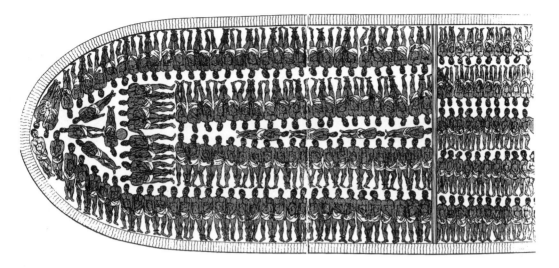

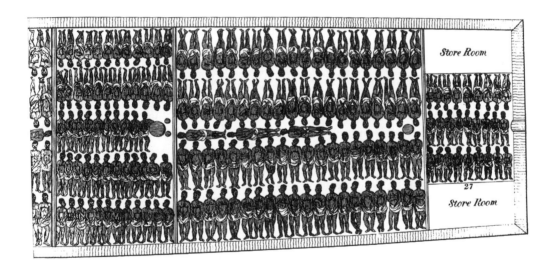

Human Beings as Property: The Horrors of Slavery (Thomas Clarkson, *Evidence on the Subject of the Slave Trade*).

the principles of humanity and universal morality," and recognizing that they possessed a responsibility to abolish the trade as soon as practicable.[10] This language, in turn, served to stimulate another treaty provision at the same time in which Britain, Russia, Austria, Prussia, and France pledged themselves to consider further measures "for the entire and definitive abolition of a Commerce so odious and so strongly condemned by the laws of religion and nature."[11] Britain and the United States similarly declared in the Treaty of Ghent during the same year that the traffic in slaves "is irreconcilable with the principles of humanity and justice" and agreed to work toward abolishing the slave trade.[12]

Many abolitionists hailed these new international declarations and pledges as tremendous accomplishments. Never before had powerful, sovereign nations been willing to discuss openly such a difficult and emotional subject as trading in human cargo. Never before had they been willing to acknowledge any sense of responsibility to end the slave trade in order to protect humanity and defend justice. At the Congress of Vienna they did. Yet, in so doing, these nations also began to reveal what other subsequent international human rights efforts all would realize in turn: agreement was easier to obtain on the general words of solemn declarations than on the specific provisions of enforceable commitments. The final texts of 1815, for example, did not make the slave trade illegal, sanction the arrest of slavers, provide machinery for enforcement, or authorize any activity that might challenge national sovereignty. Instead, in the words of one observer, they indicated that "while all were ready to concur in benevolent declarations, no one was prepared to take any action with teeth in it."[13]

Interestingly enough, however, even Wilberforce concluded that such declarations marked a significant beginning and, that given the long history of the slave trade and the powerful vested interests of the time, they represented all that could reasonably be expected in the world of practical politics and diplomacy. Rather than being discouraged and quitting in disgust or cynicism, he and his colleagues in the Society for the Abolition of the Slave Trade and the Aborigines Protection Society in Britain, along with like-minded individuals in the United States associated with the Society for the Suppression of the Slave Trade and the Association of Friends for Promoting the Abolition of Slavery and in France with the Société des Amis des Noirs and the Société de la Morale Chrétienne, determined to build on the words of these first declarations and to press onward for the "teeth" to abolish the trade. They unceasingly wrote letters, organized meetings, sponsored lectures by fugitive slaves, conducted investigations, supported boycotts of slave-produced goods, communicated with each other through the pages of the *Christian Observer*, and, convinced of the growing power of the printed word, launched press campaigns and published and distributed thousands of copies of Clarkson's *The Cries of Africa to the Inhabitants of Europe; Or, A Survey of That Bloody Commerce Called the Slave Trade*, which they translated into French, German, Spanish, Portuguese, Dutch, and Arabic. They rejoiced when the pope finally issued moral instructions to all Catholics to abstain from the slave trade. They appealed to national leaders, petitioned governments, and pressured diplomats to consider such actions as making the slave trade an act of piracy, granting navies the right to search ships suspected of transporting slaves, and creating an international agency on the coast of Africa with a maritime force and authority to halt the shipment of this human cargo at its source. In addition, they organized the British and Foreign Anti-Slavery Society (later becoming the Anti-Slavery International for the Protection of Human Rights and today noted as the oldest human rights NGO in the world) and by 1840 sponsored its first World Anti-Slavery Conference in order to arouse global opinion, provide convincing evidence that the problem was international in scope, and develop a sense of common purpose that extended beyond national borders.[14]

The British government proved to be the most responsive to this kind of public activity and pressure, and thus came to be the leading and unrivaled crusader to abolish the international slave trade. Indeed, for years it stood nearly alone among nations in efforts to suppress the trade. Inspired by moral principles and convinced of the righteousness of the cause, determined not to be excluded from financial profits or strategic influence accruing to competitors, armed with powerful naval squadrons, willing to shoulder heavy financial responsibilities, and supported by determined diplomats who created a special Slave Trade Department within the Foreign Office, the British led the way with mixed motives in enticing, bribing, and coercing others into signing agreements designed to gain international cooperation in suppressing the slave trade. As a result of their efforts, by 1862 a number of countries had signed formal treaties for a limited right to search suspected slave ships on the high seas, including Portugal, Spain, Denmark, the Netherlands, Sweden, Italy, Prussia, Russia, Austria, France, and the United States. Other components to this vast treaty network followed apace, and in less than twenty years later the total of bilateral treaties on the subject of the slave trade numbered more than fifty and included agreements with countries throughout Europe, North and South America, the Middle East, and rulers in Africa and Asia. These treaties proved to be of considerable importance in creating the beginnings of a maritime police force and a court system for the suppression of the slave trade and in drawing international attention to the violations of rights inherent in the practice of slavery. But they could only restrain certain activities of the traders and, even then, proved particularly difficult to enforce due to smuggling, maritime claims, colonial and commercial rivalry, and national sovereignty and pride.[15] Throughout this process it became increasingly evident that the necessary prerequisite for genuinely abolishing the slave trade abroad hinged on emancipation at home.

The great abolitionist campaign against slavery thus now began in earnest. New leaders in the struggle such as Thomas F. Buxton in Britain and Augustin Cochin in France and new organizations like the Confederação Abolicionista in Brazil emerged with determination. The intensity of the campaign became particularly strong in the United States where the issue of slavery increasingly tore the nation apart. Here William Lloyd Garrison, a journalist with an intense hatred of injustice, published in 1831 the first issue of *The Liberator* announcing: "I am in earnest. I will not equivocate — AND *I WILL BE HEARD*."[16] Through the pages of this enormously influential journal, he eloquently and passionately expressed his deeply held religious belief that slaveholding was a sin, and then quickly set about organizing the American Anti-Slavery Society. Others wrote articles and editorials in publications such as *The Rights of All* or *The Genius of Universal Emancipation*, drawing attention again and again to the chasm between the rights enunciated in the Declaration of Independence and the Bill of Rights and the practice of holding slaves. Still others sought to enter the political arena directly and created the Liberty Party in 1841, announcing their goal of achieving

Liberty — the liberty that is twin born with justice — the liberty that respects and protects the rights, not of the weak only, or of the strong only, but of the weak and the strong; and simply because they are human rights.[17]

Former slaves like the articulate Frederick Douglass and Sojourner Truth delivered hundreds of public speeches condemning the evils of slavery and encouraging their listeners to join in the cause for the "rights of man" and "human rights,"[18] and by mid-century nearly two thousand abolitionist societies existed, some of which launched acts of civil disobedience. Then, in 1852 a preacher's daughter named Harriet Beecher Stowe published her remarkable *Uncle Tom's Cabin*, described to this day as "probably the most influential novel ever published in the United States."[19] With a sense for drama, she created powerful images of slaves being ruthlessly beaten to death by heartless owners and fugitives fleeing across the ice on rivers, with babes in arms and bloodhounds baying at their heels, in order to reach their goal of freedom. Such scenes stirred emotion and captured the public imagination at home and abroad. Within the first year alone, Stowe's book sold over 300,000 copies in America, keeping eight new rotary steam presses operating around the clock. In Britain its circulation passed the million mark within eight months, and its eventual translation into twenty languages extended the impact even further in mobilizing international opinion against slavery.[20]

Such attitudes, whether inspired by compassion, a sense of responsibility, religious principle, and/or political conviction about human rights provided essential components in the process of freeing the enslaved. The most decisive elements, however, proved to be those transformations of power brought about by means of either revolution or war. Slavery in Spanish America ended only when the massive empire itself fell to what historian and diplomat Salvador de Madariaga called "the eagles of power."[21] Costa Rica, El Salvador, Guatemala, Honduras, and Nicaragua abolished slavery only after Spain had suffered armed invasion from the French army on land, humiliation from the British navy at sea, uprisings from revolutionaries at home, and military defeats during the wars for independence in Central America. Britain emancipated slaves in its colonies in 1833 only after a dramatic shift of political power at home, and France ended slavery in its colonial possessions only after the bloody chaos of the Revolution of 1848. Civil and foreign wars surrounded the abolition of slavery in Argentina, Colombia, Peru, and Venezuela during the 1850s. The United States began to free its slaves with President Abraham Lincoln's Emancipation Proclamation of 1863 and finally in 1865 with the Thirteenth Amendment to the Constitution, but only after the Civil War destroyed the power of slave-owning states and inflicted what remains to this day the most devastating conflict in the nation's history. Only Cuba and Brazil retained slavery in the Western Hemisphere longer than the United States, and they did not free their slaves until additional wars and struggles forced them to do so in the late 1880s. One observer saw these events as all portions of a whole, parts of "a great fight going on the world over . . . between free institutions and caste institutions, Freedom and Democracy against institutions of privilege and class."[22]

With these upheavals, the relationship between emancipation and the fate of the slave trade became apparent for the world to see. Once nations outlawed slavery within their own domains, the slave trade had no market; and once they withdrew their active support for, or passive acquiescence in, the trade, this commerce in human beings no longer could exist. Thus, after all the wars and revolutions of the nineteenth century most of those nations who had been so actively involved in trading realized that politically, diplomatically, economically, intellectually, and morally they simply could no longer sustain the slave trade. The realization of these facts, in addition to continued pressure from anti-slavery societies and the crusading efforts of religious leaders such as Cardinal Lavigerie of France and his L'Oeuvre antiesclavagiste, finally brought these nations together to search for international solutions. By 1885 they agreed under the Berlin Act that they shared a responsibility to free the enslaved and declared that "the trading in slaves is forbidden."[23]

Much more significantly, members of the international community quickly realized that the problem needed more than mere words of condemnation. Consequently, they sent delegates to Brussels to negotiate what became the 1890 General Act for the Repression of the African Slave Trade. Here, representatives ranging from the Great Powers of Europe, the United States, and the smaller Scandinavian countries to the Ottoman Empire, Persia, the Congo, and Zanzibar all professed their intention "of putting an end to the crimes and devastations engendered by the traffic in African slaves, of efficiently protecting the aboriginal population of Africa, and of securing for that vast continent the benefits of peace and civilization."[24] They thus signed a convention that bound them all to take practical action in repressing slave trading at places of origin as well as at sea and along inland caravan routes by capturing and searching slave ships, enforcing the punishment of offending slave captors and dealers, liberating captured slaves and granting them protection, sharing information and maintaining communication with each other, and creating for the first time an international machinery known as the "slave trade bureaux" located in Zanzibar and designed to facilitate the execution of the treaty. By so doing, they marked the triumphant culmination of the struggle to associate all of the major powers with a comprehensive international agreement to end the African slave trade. Despite its defects and potential dangers for interference into the domestic affairs and national sovereignty of others, the act embodied the principle that an international responsibility existed to deal with the trade and enslavement of human beings. It also marked an important step in establishing a moral standard for international behavior by which the powers might judge each other and the rest of the world might judge them. In addition, this convention, as we shall see, set a significant precedent for the League of Nations and the United Nations as they dealt with human rights in the twentieth century.[25]

To Assist the Exploited

Visions of protecting humanity and defending justice not only inspired these early international efforts to free the enslaved, but also to address the fate of others who were abused and exploited. The process of successfully breaking the chains of slavery and halting the ships of the slave trade increasingly helped to create an awareness of the international dimensions of need and to build momentum of reform that began to open up possibilities of other visions for human rights. In fact, at times they emphasized the interconnectedness of rights and mutually supported and reinforced each other. If the welfare of slaves heretofore without hope could be changed, reasoned many religious and humanitarian activists with a deep sense of responsibility, then why not the countless numbers of other brothers and sisters who also suffered from exploitation? Indeed, by the early nineteenth century the overwhelming majority of the world's population still found itself exploited in one way or the other and denied basic human rights due to their race, gender, and/or class.

The powerful impact of race on human affairs, for example, continued to plague and frustrate those who truly held a vision of equal rights for all, irrespective of the color of one's skin. They watched in both sorrow and outrage as the abolition of the institution of slavery often brought not an end to racial prejudice but rather an extension of racist ideology and exclusion in the form of racial segregation and discrimination. In one of the great paradoxes of the century, racism actually increased as democracy expanded.[26] The loss of slave status did not always bring with it a diminution of caste status, for freedom from slavery often exaggerated and even exacerbated existing prejudices of race. Emancipation from slavery in the West Indies, for instance, created a curious system of caste based on gradations of color. Freed blacks in the United States, despite new Constitutional amendments guaranteeing equality of protection under the law and the Civil Rights Act of 1866, faced intense prejudice and discrimination. "The Master he says we are all free," declared one former slave, "but it don't mean we is white. And it don't mean we is equal."[27] In frustration and anger many former slaves demanded: "Let's have our rights!"[28] Strenuous and often courageous attempts in the face of determined opposition were made to assist former slaves in receiving relief aid, finding employment, creating educational opportunities, fighting the "black codes" of racial segregation, obtaining protection from lynchings and other forms of violence, and securing basic civil and political rights through organizations such as the National Equal Rights League. Yet, given the politics and diplomacy of traditional vested interests and prerogatives of sovereignty and domestic jurisdiction at the time, these particular efforts rarely could move beyond the narrow confines of national borders.

Some early efforts did seek to address racial matters internationally, however, and these involved the fate of indigenous peoples subjugated and exploited by conquest. From a global perspective, one of the most striking and significant features of the nineteenth century was the tremendous outburst of imperialist activity by white Europeans and their cousins in North America, Australia, New Zealand, and South Africa against those whom they described as "inferior races" and "lesser breeds of color."[29] With an intensity that is still astonishing to recall, these Westerners rushed to conquer and carve out new imperial possessions in Africa, Asia, the Pacific, and North America by dispossessing, debasing, exploiting, and even exterminating the nonwhite native inhabitants. Not everyone, of course, supported these policies and several followed in the footsteps of the priest Las Casas by vocally criticizing their governments for destroying the unique historical and cultural traditions of other human beings, propagating myths of racial superiority, and violating the rights and the very lives of millions of indigenous peoples. Rather than trying to act only alone, however, they formed larger organizations in order to mobilize their efforts for more effective action. Some created Christian mission societies and launched the great missionary movement of the nineteenth century, taking seriously the Biblical injunction to "go ye into all the world."[30] Virtually hundreds of new organizations like the Friends Foreign Mission Association,

Société des Missions Évangeliques, Berliner Missionsgesellschaft, Russian Missionary Society of the Orthodox Church, Svenska Kyrkans Mission, American Board of Foreign Missions, Board of Foreign Missions of the United Presbyterian Church, Canadian Baptist Foreign Mission Board, Evangelical Union of South America, and World Missionary Conference emerged at this time and joined their Catholic Jesuit counterparts in sending out missionaries to all inhabited parts of the globe. By foot, horseback, cart, canoe, ship, or eventually train, they made efforts to reach people from the Eskimos in Alaska to the Zulus in Africa, from the Chinese and Koreans in Asia to the Amerindians in Latin America, and from the Blackfeet in the American West to the Maori in New Zealand.[31] Others created nongovernmental organizations like the Aborigines Protection Society founded by Quakers in Britain, the Société des Amis des Noirs in France, the Aborigines' Rights Protection Society in Africa, the Anti-Imperialist League, the Society for the Protection of Asiatic Sailors, and the Indian Rights Association, founded by a devout Episcopalian named Herbert Welsch who strongly believed in racial equality and wanted to create an organization dedicated "to secure to the Indians of the United States the political and civil rights already guaranteed to them by treaty and statutes."[32]

Although these organizations and their members always possessed the very real danger of being used and manipulated on the global stage by national governments eager to advance their own political, economic, and strategic interests, Christian missionaries and humanitarians made serious and earnest efforts, often at the cost of their own lives, to assist those of other races exploited far from their own shores. They sought to extend their medical, educational, technological, and agricultural knowledge to those who they believed could benefit from them, and bring the needs of these peoples to international attention through the pages of publications like the *Missionary Review of the World, Journal des Missions Évangéliques*, or *Allgemeine Missionszeitschrift*. In addition, they attempted to extend their legal protections of rights in the form of treaty law. Their efforts resulted in hospitals and schools, food and relief supplies, orphanages for children and stations for lepers, rescue homes for young girls and aged women, missions for former slaves, instruction for the blind and deaf, tools and trade, and treaties that explicitly addressed the rights of indigenous peoples. Those who worked for such purposes found themselves able to pressure the British Parliament into creating a select Aborigines' Committee "to consider what measures ought to be adopted with regard to the native inhabitants of countries when British settlements are made, and to the neighboring tribes in order to secure to them the due observance of justice and the protection of their rights."[33] In New Zealand they created the official governmental position of Protector of Aborigines and passed the Native Rights Act of 1865 to defend the rights of the Maori. In India they inspired the Caste Disabilities Removal Act, and in Canada the passage of the comprehensive Act Respecting Indians of 1880.

In the United States those who championed the rights of all not only helped to secure the position of the Commissioner of Indian Affairs, but were quick to draw attention to two famous court decisions and one celebrated speech of the time. The first decision came from the Supreme Court itself that stated explicitly, "By the protection of the law human rights are secured; withdraw that protection, and they are at the mercy of wicked rulers, or the clamor of an excited people."[34] A circuit court then went on to break new ground by ruling: "That an Indian is a 'person' within the meaning of the laws of the United States, and has, therefore, . . . the inalienable right to 'life, liberty, and the pursuit of happiness.' "[35] During the same year, Chief Joseph of the Nez Perce tribe declared in a moving speech:

Treat all men alike. Give them all the same law. Give them all an even chance to live and grow. All men were made by the same Great Spirit Chief. They all are brothers. The earth is the mother of all people, and people should have equal rights upon it.[36]

By 1885 the momentum of these many different national efforts was such as to draw international attention to the plight of indigenous peoples. At the conclusion of a major diplomatic conference, for example, fifteen nations pledged in the Berlin Act to provide international guarantees for the right of freedom of religion in imperial possessions and promising to "watch over the preservation of the native tribes and to care for the improvement of their moral and material well being, and to help in suppressing slavery."[37] The subsequent Brussels Act of 1890 reiterated this international humanitarian motivation and concern for "native welfare" further by committing seventeen signatory nations in a treaty to "efficiently protecting the aboriginal population of Africa" by not only suppressing slavery and the slave trade, but also by building transportation and communication systems and by restricting the importation of firearms, ammunition, and alcohol.[38]

These various international activities and treaty provisions, it must be acknowledged, did not always produce the intended result for the exploited of different races. The adoption of policies and their fulfillment can be two very different matters. Mixed motives, changing circumstances, unscrupulous white settlers unwilling to abide by the promises of treaty law, and other forces often beyond control continually revealed the familiar human rights problem of the gap between theory and practice, or between vision and reality. Through time some missionaries found themselves more interested in securing their own converts than in advancing the interests of indigenous peoples. Humanitarians came to realize that it often did not take much for ideals of self-sacrificing "trusteeship" to degenerate into arrogant paternalism by those more supportive of the assimilation of these populations into their own presumed superior culture and definitions of citizenship rather than in respecting self-determination or native rights considered on their own intrinsic merits. Diplomats discovered that invaders alone defined the meaning of rights declared in treaties with indigenous peoples and decided if, when, and to what extent they would be enforced in practice. Moreover, national governments bent on imperial aggression learned soon enough that humanitarian expressions contained in negotiated agreements also could be used as an excuse or justification for the partitioning of islands in the Pacific, carving up of spheres of influence in Asia or the Middle East, and seizing territory in North America or throughout the continent of Africa. In this process, those who devoted themselves to these early efforts thus began to realize an important lesson: namely, that religious or humanitarian motives and words of promise in declarations or treaties provided essential beginnings, but without the will to honor and enforce them they would be insufficient to realize visions of international human rights in practice.

Other visions of the time focused on those suffering exploitation on the basis of gender. Discrimination by males against females possessed a history extending over centuries and continents, and possessed an encrusted tradition more extensive than even that of slavery. Even the democratic revolutions of the eighteenth century and extension of liberal democracy in the early nineteenth century had failed to extend their full rights of citizenship to women, and many promises made often rang hollow for at least half of the population. Regardless of the form of government or location, however, the same pattern emerged around the globe. Women could not vote or hold elective office, participate in political organizations, own or inherit property, manage their earnings, sue in court, enter most professions or educational institutions, maintain custody of children after divorce, or have the right to personal autonomy and bodily integrity when legally regarded as the property of their husbands. This plight of women became particularly pronounced with the emancipation of black slaves, for the discussions about the rights of women emerged most explicitly at a time of debates about the meaning of rights for free blacks and linked both race and gender. Members of each group might be recognized as citizens, but still lacked the basic rights enjoyed by white males.[39] At a time of early efforts to promote human rights, therefore, it is hardly surprising that during and after the struggle for abolition attention would turn to women as well.

Most of those who became famous in the early crusade for women's rights began their reformist careers in the abolitionist movement. Here they first became conscious of the significance of the interrelationship of rights and the connection between race and gender. "In striving to strike his irons off," acknowledged Abby Kelley Foster referring to black slaves, "we found most surely, that we were manacled ourselves."[40] Here they discovered the vocal and active support of at least some men like George Thompson in Britain or William Lloyd Garrison and Frederick Douglass in the United States who through the pages of publications like the *Liberator*, *The Genius for Universal Emancipation*, and *The Rights of All* championed the exploited—whether they were slaves or women. Here they also learned practical techniques and developed leadership abilities for raising public consciousness through speeches and publicity, gathering petitions, organizing political protest and agitation, mobilizing resources and sympathetic churches, challenging traditional boundaries of what was considered to be appropriate feminine behavior, and the importance in a vision of rights of having conviction sufficient to overcome powerful opposition and intimidation. This could be seen in the efforts of the committed abolitionist and American Quaker Angelina Grimké, who forcefully argued that the struggle was one for human rights—not man's, not woman's, but equal rights for all human beings whatever their color, sex, or station.[41] Her influential sister, Sarah Grimké, wrote an early manifesto in 1838 entitled *Letters on the Equality of the Sexes and the Equality of Woman*, starkly comparing the exploitation of women with that of slaves, demanding equal rights in the name of religious and moral principle, and courageously arguing that rights could not be considered without responsibilities.[42] Elisha Hurlbut published similar ideas shortly thereafter in her suggestive book *Essays on Human Rights.*[43] After returning from the World Anti-Slavery Conference held in London, where they had experienced blatant gender discrimination again, Elizabeth Cady Stanton and Lucretia Mott determined to turn both their anger and their strong religious convictions into action by organizing a convention for the rights of women. Taking place in 1848, this convention was attended by nearly three hundred delegates and resulted in the famous Seneca Falls Declaration, asserting, "We hold these truths to be self-evident: that all men and women are created equal; that they are endowed by their Creator with certain inalienable rights." This declaration, which launched the women's rights movement and went on to inspire a vision for others far beyond the borders of United States, enumerates a long list of repeated injustices and injuries on the part of men toward women, calls for greater action and agitation to secure specific objectives, and especially demands "the equality of human rights."[44]

Philosophers and reformist writers contributed their thoughts and voices to this movement of liberation as well. The most influential proponent of liberalism during the nineteenth century, John Stuart Mill, articulated the interconnectedness of all rights by extolling the empirical value of human rights to society as a whole. Drawing his evidence from a wide array of historical examples ranging in location from Europe to Asia, he developed a broad theory of rights based not on belief in God or natural law but on man and utility, balanced between individual freedom and social necessity. In his 1859 treatise *On Liberty*, Mill argued that the protection of individual rights from unwarranted interference by others or from the arbitrary actions of governments was necessary both for the achievement of personal happiness and for the advancement of the welfare of society as a whole. In this regard, his outrage about the inequalities of gender prompted him ten years later to publish his classic *The Subjection of Women*. Based on collaborative studies with his wife, Harriet Taylor, he wrote about the traditional injustices in marriage, divorce, property, and law that denied freedom and rights to women. The translation of both of these important philosophical works into many languages rapidly spread Mill's ideas about human rights internationally, but writers from other countries made their own contributions as well. Iranian reformer Mirza Fath Ali Akhundzade, for example, shocked many of his contemporaries by challenging traditional Islamic practices and arguing strenuously for equality between men and women. In China, Tan Sitong focused his writings on the concept of *ren*, or benevolence, and addressed fundamental questions concerning humanity and the importance of securing gender equality. In Japan, Toshiko Kishida published her highly influential essay entitled "I Tell You, My Fellow Sisters," in which she forcefully argued that men and women alike should enjoy equal human rights.[45] Rosa Guerra similarly used her periodical *La Camelia* to champion equality for women throughout Latin America, and confidently asserted: "We are entering an era of liberty and there are no rights which exclude us!"[46]

These several manifestos, declarations, and treatises on philosophy, among others, provided an essential expression for grievances and an inspiration for action to those who fought for rights. But in order for their visions to be realized, they required significant transformations in the political, economic, and social forces of the past. The powerful mid-nineteenth-century explosions of the European revolutions of 1848, Crimean War, India Mutiny, American Civil War, upheavals and the abolition of slavery in the United States and Latin America, Taiping Rebellion in China, collapse of the Tokugawa shogunate and resulting civil war in Japan, and Franco-Prussian War with the revolutionary Paris Commune, among other crises, ignited just such a process and set into motion dramatic changes. These events disrupted, distorted, and in some cases actually destroyed traditional structures of both power and thought, thereby providing new opportunities to liberate many of those exploited in one way or another.

British women, for example, seized these openings and through time successfully pressured Parliament to reform laws governing marriage, the age of consent, and the use of their property and bodies. In France females secured the right to legalized divorce. German reformers — under the leadership of Helene Lange, Gertrud Bäumer, and their Allgemeiner deutscher Frauenverein, which fought for women's rights — gained improvements in educational opportunities and in labor conditions for working women. Swedish crusaders obtained equal property rights in marriage, and the right for women to work without their husband's permission. In India women secured the abolition of *suti*, or widow immolation, and the Hindu Widow's Remarriage Act which legalized intercaste marriages. Chinese females began to achieve reforms allowing them to hold supervisory offices in the bureaucracy and restricting the ancient and painful practice of mutilation by footbinding. In Argentina women gained recognition of certain civil rights in a new constitution. Women gradually secured gains in the United States as well, made all the more visible by the efforts of activists such as Elizabeth Cady Stanton and Susan B. Anthony who organized the American Equal Rights Association to advance their cause and created their own newspaper entitled *The Revolution*, published with the motto: "Men, their rights and nothing more; women, their rights and nothing less!"[47] They began slowly to break down the door that prevented female suffrage by obtaining the franchise in Wyoming, Colorado, Utah, and Idaho. Then, in 1893, after many years of unswerving effort by Kate Sheppard and her colleagues in the Women's Christian Temperance Union, New Zealand became the first country in the world to take the extraordinary step of extending to women the political right to vote.

Just like the other early efforts to promote and protect human rights, these activities on behalf of gender equality usually focused on particular nation-states. Crusaders for the rights of women understood all too well that the many domestic obstacles and resistance at home presented formidable enough challenges without having to confront the prerogatives of national sovereignty or worry about the world at large. Nevertheless, a number of individuals did consider that they had duties to sisters (and brothers) beyond their own borders, and ventured out to address the global issue of the exploitation of women. Using the century's new inventions in communication and transportation, activists like Flora Tristan of France, Margaret Bright Lucas of Britain, Stanton and Anthony of the United States, and Sheppard of New Zealand, among others, achieved international stature as speakers, writers, and advocates of women's rights. Although they sometimes had differences among themselves, together these women refused to let the gains they had made in their own countries remain isolated from the rest of the world; sharing their experiences with others, circulating translated copies of Mill's philosophy, of Stanton's *The Woman's Bible*, or of Henrik Ibsen's feminist drama *The Doll's House*, and encouraging the efforts to remove women from their "slave status" of the past. In addition, to give explicit expression to the global nature of their cause, crusaders for women's rights organized the first International Council of Women in 1888. Delegates arrived in Washington, D.C., from fifty-three American organizations and from eight countries, including India. They sought to commemorate the fortieth anniversary of the Seneca Falls Declaration, to take stock of progress already made, and to lay the foundation for unity and "universal sisterhood" of women's rights advocates.[48]

Still other visions of assisting the exploited during the nineteenth century focused on divisions of class. Indeed, when the century began, diplomats viewed their world more in terms of classes than nations, and sought to bolster the legitimacy of the existing order and the propertied rather than support any notions of the sovereignty of the people or of individual rights. Abuses derived from two sources: either traditional patterns of dominance tenaciously left over from feudalism, or from new ones created by modern capitalism and the Industrial Revolution. The promotion of rigid distinctions based on class by feudal or semi-feudal societies, for example, positioned serfs at the absolute bottom of a hierarchy where for generations they faced the hardships of forced labor and the deprivations of being regarded as the permanent legal property of their landholding owners. Masters could treat their serfs as they wished: exile them, buy and sell them, or severely punish them for attempting to escape. Indeed, little appreciable distinction existed between serfdom and slavery. Serfs could not own property themselves, move freely or marry by choice, obtain access to education or other employment, receive any protection from arbitrary oppression and exploitation, or secure even a semblance of any kind of human rights, as portrayed so clearly and passionately at the time by Nikolay Gogol's novel *Dead Souls*. As the nineteenth century progressed, however, these practices increasingly came to be questioned. Some challenged serfdom as being dangerous due to the possibilities of serf revolts, as an impediment to the creation of a trained army, or as economically antiquated at a time when industrial development and modernization required a free labor force. Others confronted the exploitation of serfs and the actual ownership of one human by other as not only being inhumane, but morally wrong, describing it as "the evil of evils."[49] For the first time many saw themselves and their own emerging social consciousness through the mirror of insight so often gained from an international or comparative perspective. As one Russian nobleman recounted in his memoirs: "One day we were sitting quietly on the terrace listening to the reading aloud of *Uncle Tom's Cabin*, a [recently translated] book which was then in fashion. My sisters could not get over the horrors of slavery and wept at the sad fate of poor Uncle Tom. 'I cannot conceive,' said one of them, 'how such atrocities can be tolerated. Slavery is horrible.' 'But,' said Bunny in her shrill little voice, 'we have slaves too.' "[50]

As in so many other cases, such a realization provided an essential element for considering and then directing change, but it ultimately took the wars, revolutions, and upheavals of modernization during the nineteenth century to break the practices of the past. Liberation came to the serfs in Prussia in 1807 after Napoleon's defeat of their country. Serfdom ended in the Austro-Hungarian Empire following the revolutions of

1848. Resistance to abolition in Russia ended with the catastrophic defeat in the Crimean War, and in 1861 the tsar launched the period of the "Great Reforms" by signing his dramatic edict that freed the serfs, sending out special envoys to carry the news to all of the remote villages of the vast empire. The abolition of serfdom in Russia, and then in Poland, by Alexander II—who came to be known as the "Tsar-Liberator"—marked a development of unprecedented scale. It directly liberated at least fifty million serfs. By comparison, emancipation of all the slaves in the United States just a few years later freed four million.[51] Declared Alexander's Decree of Emancipation: "In virtue of the new dispositions above-mentioned, the peasants attached to the soil will be invested within a term fixed by law with all the rights of free cultivators."[52] Shortly thereafter, the abolition of feudalism in Japan following the Tokugawa collapse also brought dramatic changes to the countryside under the new Meiji government and helped lead to peasants' support of the Jiyu-minken, or Popular Rights Movement.[53] At exactly the same time, the Iranian reformer Mirza Yusef Khan began writing about the importance of equality of all before the law, freedom of thought and expression, and *Huquq-i Insani*, or basic human rights.[54]

Not all class divisions during the nineteenth century, of course, centered on hereditary serfs or peasants toiling the land in agriculture. In fact, with the emergence and development of the Industrial Revolution, a rapid expansion in the numbers of exploited occurred among the working class of the urban proletariat in the new order of capitalism. In the factories, textile mills, and mines throughout the industrializing world millions of men and—at the very bottom—women and children, suffered in wretchedness in squalor, thick smoke and soot, disease-infested water, overcrowded slums, misery, and working conditions of oppression without any prospect of relief. Five-year-old boys chained around the waist hauled carts of coal in the mines, while girls of eight worked underground in complete darkness for twelve hours a day to open and close passage doors. Women stood on swollen feet for fifteen hours a day changing the thread on bobbins attached to power looms with no safety devices. Men labored under similar working conditions, received pitiful payment for their efforts, remained at the mercy of those who owned the means of production, and suffered back-breaking hardships of almost unimaginable duration. Estimates place the average workweek in Europe by mid-century at an appalling eighty-four hours.[55] The exploitation of this urban working class, often composed of the uprooted from rural environments or immigrants from other countries, with its attendant starvation, poverty, crime, prostitution, epidemics, and family dislocations became so tragic, in fact, that it simply could not be hidden. Personal observations, exposés in newspapers, reports from official commissions of inquiry, the provocative and brutal portrayal of poverty like *The Condition of the Working Class* written by Friedrich Engels, and the human struggles of characters dramatized by such widely-read and translated novelists such as Honoré de Balzac in *Les Paysans* or Charles Dickens in *Bleak House* and *Hard Times*, all contributed to a burgeoning public consciousness about the sufferings of those so exploited. Sermons from pulpits spoke with alarm about the growing chasms between the rich and the poor, and in one Easter message the archbishop of Paris publicly decried the subjugation of workers to "the new slavery of pauperism."[56]

Such obvious and severe misery endured by the working class ignited new and profoundly serious questions about the meaning of human rights. What good were civil rights such as the freedom of speech or political rights for voting, asked those who suffered, to people like themselves who had no food, no home, no clothing, no medical care, or no prospect of an education? What were the benefits of freedom from slavery or serfdom if the alternative was destitution? Did this mean that the expressions and declarations of human rights represented no more than the abstract ideas of philosophers, or parchment prose, or the empty platitudes of politicians? Or, when all was said and done, did human rights really remain no more than the exclusive possession of the ruling or rising classes marching under the banner of untrammeled laissez-faire and the "iron law" of wages?[57] With these questions in their minds, the have-not members of the working class and their leaders increasingly began to speak out not just about "negative" rights to be protected from unwarranted government interference but also about more "positive" rights to receive entitled state assistance. Labor spokesman William Cobbett charged during the 1830s, for example, that the poor had been cheated of their rights, and demanded before agitated crowds: "the right to have a living out of the land of our birth in exchange for our labour duly and honestly performed; the right, in case we fell into distress, to have our wants sufficiently relieved out the produce of the land, whether that distress arose from sickness, from decrepitude, from old age, or from inability to find employment."[58] He argued that society must assist the exploited, not necessarily out of a sense of charity, but because all individuals had a right to receive such succor. John Stuart Mill added his support to such claims for ameliorative action as well, declaring that among the exceptions to complete laissez-faire was the need to temper the worst consequences of the Industrial Revolution on the working poor of humanity by making relief "an absolute right."[59] It is out of this context of class exploitation that we thus discover the significant nineteenth-century emergence of a second-generation of human rights: namely, social and economic rights.

Faced with these problems and claims of the exploited poor caught in the forces of seemingly unrestrained capitalism, industrialization, and urbanization, many turned toward the path of reform. Indeed, the century was marked by an unprecedented reforming impulse accompanied by expressions of "service to humanity" and "the spirit of universal charity."[60] Particularly among upper- and middle-class women inspired by what they occasionally called the Social Gospel, or a strong religious sense of responsibility to assist those unable to care for themselves, a wide variety of religiously-oriented charitable organizations and movements emerged. In the West these included such notable efforts as the Salvation Army, Young Men's Christian Association, Young Women's Christian Association, Women's Christian Temperance Union, and the Paulist Fathers. These groups focused on social reform and addressed issues such as food for the poor, settlement and halfway houses for impoverished immigrant families, maternity care for mothers and infants, child welfare, temperance, prostitution, crime, prison and working conditions, and public education. In India similar efforts were made by the Ramakrishna Movement, which denounced the rigid caste system and spoke on behalf of the human rights of the poor, seeking to reduce social injustice and economic inequality by having Hindu precepts determine *sādhanā*, or social service, that addressed the universal needs of the exploited in practical ways.[61]

Some held other visions that connected rights and welfare but that were motivated more by political philosophy than by religious principles. Men like the Count Henri de Saint-Simon, Charles Fourier, and Robert Owen founded the ideas of early modern socialism. They and their followers envisioned socialist utopias in which workers would avoid exploitation by sharing harmonious, cooperative, and prosperous ways of life and set about creating ideal communities. Political liberals from very different perspectives sought to address other aspects of the claims for rights. At times they worked for extensions of the franchise by lowering the property qualifications for voting. They also launched the beginning of what has been called the "revolution in government" — activist state-supported welfare relief and regulation to assist in providing the greatest good to the greatest number.[62] Through their early efforts, the nineteenth century witnessed a series of new laws that for the first time improved the plight of the exploited poor by regulating some of the more egregious conditions of labor. National laws, influenced in part by pamphlets like *The Rights of Infants*, prohibited the employment of children under nine years old, limited working hours for teenagers, and banned women and children from having to labor underground in mines. Other legislative acts regulated domestic sanitation, minimum standards of food and drink, inspection to assure the observation of safety measures, and compulsory education. Building on the success of these national reform efforts, partly due to continuing pressure from organized labor, a number of nations began to consider the possibilities of extending protection to workers from exploitation at the international level. The results of their efforts would be seen in the first decade of the next century.

Others addressed these problems of the exploited poor and their rights by direct industrial action and even revolution. Impatient at the slow pace of moderate reform and unsatisfied by the perceived lack of genuine systemic change, more radical workers channeled their discontent into labor agitation, protest, trade unionism, pickets, strikes, and factory sabotage or destruction. The Chartist Movement, for example, under the influence of the fiery Irish journalist and speaker Feargus O'Conner, attracted thousands of workers, poor people, and middle-class radicals. They issued a "People's Charter," signed by more than a million people, demanding their rights, calling for universal suffrage and the elimination of property qualifications to hold office, and denouncing the rich as seeking to keep the rest of the people in social slavery and political degradation. Some workers turned toward the new theories of socialism expounded by Saint-Simon, Fourier, and Louis Blanc, attacking the competitive system of capitalism and asserting economic and social rights for all those exploited by the upper class. Still others grew weary of words and theories and turned instead to violence in the revolutions of 1848. These widespread upheavals throughout the continent of Europe fueled not only new kinds of demands for rights, but a clarion call for worldwide revolution.

At this point in history, Karl Marx, along with Friedrich Engels, emerged as the leading spokesmen. Their powerful *Communist Manifesto*, through many translations, inspired workers in Europe during the second half of the nineteenth century, and then, during much of the twentieth century, fired the imagination of Communist leaders throughout Asia, Latin America, Africa, and Europe. They viewed history as being determined by economic forces, and saw the end of feudal society as not bringing an end to class struggle, but rather new and global conditions of exploitation by the rich bourgeoisie of the impoverished proletariat, all in the name of the right to own private property. Marx and Engels therefore argued that liberal conceptions of civil and political rights, which sought to protect individuals by limiting the power of the state, represented only a "narrow bourgeois horizon of rights" that should "be left far behind."[63] They emphasized instead the idea that although the state would eventually wither away, in the interim phase of perfecting a communist society the state should expand its authority in order that each person, as a member of collective society, would be guaranteed his or her social and economic rights. Marx and Engels concluded that this vision — and thus the end of oppression and class warfare — could become a reality only by the forcible overthrow of existing institutions. "Let the ruling classes tremble at a Communist revolution," they shouted. "The proletarians have nothing to lose but their chains. They have a world to win. WORKING MEN OF ALL COUNTRIES, UNITE!"[64] In issuing this charge, Marx and Engels argued that only an international approach would enable exploited workers to claim their social and economic rights. Toward this end, they founded in 1864 the International Working Men's Organization, or First (Communist) International, exhorting their followers to form a "bond of brotherhood . . . between the workingmen of different countries" and, interestingly enough, "to master themselves the mysteries of international politics; to watch the diplomatic acts of their respective governments; to counteract them, if necessary, by all means in their power" in "the general struggle for the emancipation of the working classes."[65]

This relationship of human rights and the international exploitation by class as a result of the Industrial Revolution also attracted the attention of the Catholic Church. For years the deep and heartfelt concerns of both local clergy and laity about the severe problems caused by industrialization had met with only silence from a Vatican identified closely with monarchism and frequently with reaction. Finally, in the face of such overwhelming evidence of human deprivation and in light of his own personal observations of the sufferings of the exploited poor across national borders, Pope Leo XIII issued his 1891 encyclical known as *Rerum Novarum* (Of New Things), explicitly addressing what he called "the natural rights of mankind." Leo viewed society as a living whole whose members perform different functions and possess responsibilities, and where everyone has a right to procure for themselves and their families what is necessary to live. In this regard, he defended private property and rejected Marx's class hatred, but strongly opposed unrestrained capitalism and firmly warned that "the first concern of all is to save the poor workers from the cruelty of grasping speculators, who use human beings as mere instruments for making money. It is neither justice nor humanity so to grind men down with excessive labor as to stupefy their minds and wear out their bodies." For this reason, he declared, human rights

must be religiously respected wherever they are found; and it is the duty of the public authority to prevent and punish injury, and to protect each one in the possession of his own. Still, when there is question of protecting the rights of individuals, the poor and helpless have a claim to special consideration. The richer population have many ways of protecting themselves. . . . [But] wage-earners, who are, undoubtedly, among the weak and necessitous, should be specially cared for and protected by the commonwealth.[66]

Such pronouncements contributed still further to developing and legitimizing international claims for social and economic rights.

These many statements and efforts generated by the desire to assist the exploited during the nineteenth century reveal a number of significant issues in the history of human rights. Those men and women who worked to claim, to articulate, to extend, and to protect rights at this time all shared an intense desire to assist people suffering in one form or another from exploitation. They came to share an essential and wider sense of responsibility to make efforts beyond their own immediate borders and to call for international action despite their many assorted religious, philosophical, or political points of departure. In addition, they frequently confronted common opponents or forces resisting change and the same state claims of national sovereignty and domestic jurisdiction. Yet, there were differences as well, often profound and disturbing. Those who claimed that human rights belonged to all people without distinction and represented parts of a seamless web sometimes found themselves being challenged by those who insisted that some were more equal than others or more deserving on the basis of nation, race, gender, or class. Support for the rights of freed slaves or serfs, for example, did not necessarily guarantee an extension of effort to colonial or indigenous peoples, women, the working poor, or newly arrived immigrants. Those who believed that human rights came from God or were inherited from natural law frequently found themselves confronted by those who now argued that the source of rights could be found instead in rationalism, utilitarianism, secularism, or humanism. Moreover, reform liberalism claimed that the rights of men and women could be obtained best by working to protect personal life, liberty, equality, and ownership of property by individuals through the existing political process. Marx and his followers, on the other hand, emphasized the group rather than the individual. They argued that the most important human rights were not those of a civil or political nature, hopelessly individualistic and part of "bourgeois democracy," but rather those that focused on real human social and economic needs and that these rights could be secured only through revolution. Such different visions between those first-generation civil and political rights initially arising out of the eighteenth century and those second-generation social and economic rights emerging from the nineteenth century, and the often sharply different methods to achieve them, would play powerful roles in shaping the evolution of international human rights until our own day.

To Care for the Wounded

The history of the wounded in war spans the historical record of human existence. Ever since men began to fight each other they left the victims of armed combat scattered across countless blood-soaked battlefields, destined to be killed or captured by enemies, assisted by their comrades if possible, or simply left to fend for themselves as best they could. The vanquished, in particular, normally remained at the mercy of the victor, and mercy was not common.[67] Although the Chinese military theorist Sun Tzu wrote as early as the fourth century B.C. in *The Art of War* that an obligation existed to care for the wounded and prisoners of war, nations remained unable or unwilling to establish any mutually acceptable rules of behavior.[68] Those desperate and unfortunate soldiers wounded in battle had no international society, organization, or law to which they could turn for any protection or care, and hence remained largely forgotten — condemned to suffer and very likely die.

As warfare steadily escalated in destructiveness during the nineteenth century due to the technological capabilities of new weapons such as rifles and steam engines produced by the Industrial Revolution, as armies increasingly became composed of conscripts rather than professional soldiers, and as newspapers began to influence public opinion about the actual (as compared to only the imagined) conditions of war, the fate of the wounded came to be of much greater concern, and assertions of their rights as human beings increasingly came to the fore. Here, the efforts of three courageous and extraordinary women played an acutely significant role. During the Crimean War the Grand Duchess Elena Pavlovna of Russia, largely on her own, organized a group of nearly three hundred nurses known as the Sisters of Mercy to care for their wounded countrymen, thereby earning the gratitude of thousands of Russian soldiers and considerable public attention. Clara Barton, also on her own initiative, went to the aid of the wounded in the American Civil War, publicly urging others to join her and becoming widely known as "the Angel of the Battlefield." But the petite, dedicated, and strong-willed British nurse Florence Nightingale made the greatest impact. The granddaughter of a Member of Parliament who had served in the Commons for more than four decades championing the rights of factory workers, defending Jews and Dissenters, and supporting abolitionists, she believed deeply that God had called her into Christian service. When she traveled to the Crimea with other nurses to aid British soldiers, she confronted thousands of tormented men suffering from painful battle wounds, dysentery, starvation, cholera, exposure, and starvation in conditions of chaos and indescribable filth. Nightingale's experience changed her life and eventually that of a nation insofar as it cared for the sick and the wounded. She worked day and night to care for those in need herself, prolifically wrote letters to Queen Victoria and leading politicians asking for assistance, and insightfully campaigned for the press to bring the fate of the wounded and sick to broad public attention and literally into the homes of readers. Her remarkable successes in these endeavors, and the many reports of healed soldiers returning from the war, made Florence Nightingale extremely popular and highly influential, described by one group as a woman "whose heroic efforts on behalf of suffering humanity will be recognized and admired by all ages as long as the world shall last."[69] By mobilizing British public opinion she created a dramatic transformation in a sense of responsibility for rights of basic medical care, and by achieving innovative successes she served as a symbol of hope that inspired others to carry the cause of the wounded in war even further.

One of those directly inspired by the early efforts of Florence Nightingale was a man from Geneva by the name of J. Henry Dunant. He had helped to create the Young Men's Christian Union as the European counterpart to the newly formed Young Men's Christian Association (YMCA) and possessed an intense and abiding compassion in the plight of the wounded that extended far beyond caring for only those of one's own nationality. In 1859 he found himself a mere tourist in the tiny town of Castiglione della

Pieve in northern Italy when he suddenly encountered the horror of the monumental Battle of Solferino fought between the combined forces of the Italians and French against the Austrians with weapons produced by the Industrial Revolution. Three hundred thousand troops ferociously battled for their survival along a ten-mile front for fifteen hours under the suffocating heat of summer. When the fighting finally stopped, Dunant witnessed thousands of wounded soldiers mixed with the dead, sprawled across the destroyed landscape, and suffering in total exhaustion and excruciating pain without any medical assistance or supplies. He saw the immediate and tragic result of armies that had four veterinarians for every thousand horses but not even one physician for the same number of men. Dunant recorded his thoughts in an evocative and first-hand account written not to glorify war but rather to describe its butchery and the fate of those remaining just barely alive on "an immense field of slaughter." "One poor wounded man," he observed in appallingly detail, "has his jaw carried away; another his head shattered; a third, who could have been saved, has his chest beaten in. Oaths and shrieks of rage, groans of anguish and despair. . . . Brains spurt under the wheels, limbs are broken and torn. . . . [Men are] left behind, lying helpless on the naked ground in their own blood! . . . Heart-rending voices kept calling for help. Who could ever describe the agonies of that fearful night!"[70]

The care of these wounded men and their plight attracted Dunant's attention more than anything else. His intensely moving memoir, simply entitled *Un Souvenir de Solferino*, recounts their hideous wounds, painful sufferings, amputations conducted without anesthesia, infections, nauseating sounds and smells, vermin-covered bodies, and limbs rotting with gangrene. The numbers of wounded completely overwhelmed all efforts made by a pitifully small group of physicians, medical students, nurses, and volunteers such as Dunant to assemble rudimentary field hospitals or centers for care in farms, homes, churches, convents, and even outside in the open air. They exhausted themselves in trying to dress wounds, change bandages, give comfort, provide food and drink, promise to correspond with loving parents back home, and ease anguish. In this heroic endeavor, Dunant found himself struck with the fact that suffering makes no distinction between the wounded of the victors and those of the vanquished. He became convinced of the need for someone to speak on behalf of the common humanity of all and for the right to receive equal treatment in medical care. "Men of all nations lay *side by side* on the flagstone floors of the churches of Castiglione — Frenchmen and Arabs, Germans and Slavs," he recorded, reminding those who tried to care for them of the need to repeat the Italian phrase, *Tutti fratelli*, or "All are brothers," and acknowledging that "Our Lord Jesus Christ made no such distinctions between men in doing well."[71]

In addition to his graphic descriptions of human needs, Dunant's account became most notable for conveying his frustration of wanting to do more, his sense of duty, and his determination to make concrete proposals designed to care for the wounded in war. In these acute circumstances, he believed, all men and women must acknowledge the moral sense of the value of each human life and their worldwide responsibility to guarantee a right of medical treatment for all those who suffered wounds in war. Would it not be desirable, he wrote in what is in retrospect the single most important passage in his book, "to formulate some international principle, sanctioned by a Convention inviolate in character, which, once agreed on and ratified, might constitute the basis for societies for relief of the wounded in the different European countries?"[72] Toward this end, Dunant became a man with a vision: to create an international relief society of trained and dedicated volunteers with affiliates in all countries to care for the wounded as individual human beings without any distinction as to nationality, class, race, or any other form of difference.

Dunant's simple and poignantly realistic book aroused public opinion and became an instant topic of the day. It was read, reviewed, quoted, published in second and third editions, passed from hand to hand, and translated into several languages. The book made the fate of the wounded in war a tangible — and unacceptable — reality to those who read it, and attracted the attention of literary, political, and financial figures who offered to support Dunant in his crusade. His own optimism and tact, persuasiveness, simple dignity of presence, personal energy, genuineness of manner, and evangelical commitment to Christian service attracted others to his cause of creating a permanent system for international humanitarian assistance. An organizing committee, not without a little audacity, then decided to invite governments to send representatives to Geneva in order "to transpose Monsieur Dunant's ideas from the realm of theory to that of practice."[73] His resulting Geneva International Conference met in 1863 and attracted thirty delegates from fourteen different nations and four philanthropic societies. Although none of these participants possessed any authority to bind their countries to an agreement, they discussed thoroughly the means of carrying forward their vision and agreed to establish auxiliary medical societies in their own countries to assist in this important mission. They chose as their emblem the Swiss flag in reverse, placing a red cross on a white background, and created the private humanitarian organization based in Geneva called the International Committee of the Red Cross, described years later during a Nobel Peace Prize ceremony as "one of the great miracles in human history."[74] These delegates knew, however, that their vision could never be realized without the support of their respective governments and armies. For this reason, they pledged themselves to work for the participation of their own governments in a subsequent and more authoritative international conference.

Motivated by their Christian commitment to the unfortunate, desire to serve as Good Samaritans in the face of the horrors of war, and determination to assert the dignity and the worth of each individual human life,[75] Dunant and the other members of the International Committee energetically worked to organize such a second conference. In this regard, the skillful administration of the Geneva philanthropist Gustave Moynier proved to be particularly helpful, and within a year they had organized a conference attracting the representatives of sixteen governments. Here the assembled delegates negotiated the highly innovative Geneva Convention for the Amelioration of the Condition of the Wounded in Armies in the Field of 1864, the first multilateral treaty in history designed to protect the individual in times of war. The treaty required all signatories to acknowledge and respect the neutrality or immunity of military hospitals and their staffs of surgeons, nurses, orderlies, and others from attack or captivity in order that they might provide equal medical care for wounded soldiers regardless of their nationality.[76] In so doing, the signatories opened the way for the International Committee of the Red Cross and its affiliated national societies to become neutral intermediaries in the midst of war and authorized to conduct their work around the world in the name of common humanity. Ironically, the signing of this convention also demonstrated that it was war rather than peace—the care of soldiers rather than civilians—that stimulated and legitimized such active international interest in the rights of the individual.[77]

This Geneva, or Red Cross, Convention quickly established its utility as a means of caring for the basic needs of those wounded in battle. Immediately on ratification of the treaty, national Red Cross societies began to multiply, preparing for the time when their humanitarian services would be desperately needed. This came soon enough. Indeed, it came even before the details had been fully prepared, for the Red Cross emblem appeared for the first time on the battlefield during the 1864 Prussian-Danish War. Trained personnel, stocks of dressing material, surgical instruments, and horse-drawn ambulances quickly found themselves being mobilized to care for the wounded of the Austro-Prussian War of 1866. Further humanitarian efforts by Red Cross volunteers followed in the wake of the Franco-Prussian War of 1870-1871. In fact, their work during this bloody and protracted conflict so impressed eyewitness Clara Barton that she returned home to establish the American Association of the Red Cross and to urge her own government to sign the Geneva Convention. Other efforts followed apace. The Russo-Turkish War of 1877–1878 brought not only increased demands on the Red Cross, but also encouraged the creation of the Ottoman Red Crescent Society, the very formation of which reinforced acknowledgment of the universal nature of the need to care for the wounded, regardless of religious beliefs.[78] Not long thereafter the Nippon Sekijuji Sha, or Japanese Red Cross Society, was formed. Subsequent adherents to the convention soon included Siam and China in Asia, most of the Latin American countries, and the United States. Whenever a new war or armed conflict broke out, Red Cross units were there: the Serbo-Bulgarian War of 1885, Sino-Japanese War of 1894–1895, and the Spanish-American War of 1898. In each case, such early efforts sought to provide care for the wounded and respect the rights of all, "recognizing man as man, without any distinction whatever."[79]

The original Red Cross convention inspired additional efforts to create a series of treaties providing further international legal protection for the rights of victims of wars, and known variously as humanitarian law, Red Cross law, or human rights law in armed conflict.[80] In contrast with earlier "laws of war" that focused primarily on the use of objects such as weapons or ships, this new form of law focused on people. During the 1899 Hague Peace Conference, for example, delegates ranging in locations from Europe to Latin America and from Asia to the United States who could agree on practically nothing else and who jealously guarded their prerogatives of national sovereignty, publicly declared themselves to be jointly committed to "the laws of humanity and the requirements of the public conscience," and then adopted a Convention on the Laws and Customs of War on Land.[81] The text spoke explicitly of "rights"—the right of the wounded to receive medical treatment, the right of prisoners of war to be given food and clothing and protection under the law, the right of individuals to be considered inviolable if they carry a white flag and seek to communicate their intention to surrender, and the right of civilians to be protected from unlimited warfare. In addition, the treaty also established certain provisions recognizing the right of relief societies like the Red Cross to visit camps and provide medical assistance, inform home countries of individual whereabouts and physical condition, arrange correspondence with families and the sending of parcels, and facilitate the repatriation of the most seriously wounded. At exactly the same time, representatives also signed the Convention for the Adaptation to Maritime Warfare of Principles of the Geneva Convention, guaranteeing the neutrality of hospital ships and their medical staff and extending protection to those individuals wounded at sea.[82]

These conventions, like other features of the Hague Peace Conference, were necessarily gradual and tentative. Given the context of the time and the uneasy combination of broad international humanitarianism and parochial national interests, they could hardly be expected to be otherwise. All nations continued to insist that there would be no compromise with their own interpretations of sovereignty, and thus could choose to either ratify or reject the treaties. Each also refused to include any specific enforcement provisions within the texts of the treaties or impose penalties for those who violated the provisions. Most seemed to be motivated by elemental dynamics of mutual self-interest rather than broad principles of humanity. Moreover, and particularly troublesome to the International Committee of the Red Cross, was the tendency of these same national governments to subvert the original and universal mission to care for all wounded by intoxicating their respective national Red Cross societies with the heady brew of nationalism and leading them toward an exclusive patriotism that sought to provide attention only for their own.[83]

Despite these difficulties, however, the creation of the International Red Cross, the Hague Conventions, and the subsequent emergence of humanitarian law in armed conflict marked dramatic advances for visions of human rights. For the first time, positive law in the form of international treaties established certain rights for the protection of individual victims of war. These early efforts began by acknowledging the "dictates of the public conscience," by focusing on the rights of those combatants wounded in battle and suffering in pain on land and sea, and by articulating the principles of the "laws of humanity." They continued by establishing rights for individuals captured as prisoners of war. They then expanded the scope of rights still further by including the protection of civilians to be free from torture, mutilation, pillage, attack on undefended dwellings, and destruction of places of worship. Together, they all helped to lay the critical foundations for humanitarian law recognizing that individuals in time of war possessed certain basic human rights and that their protection was a legitimate issue that demanded international action.[84]

To Protect the Persecuted

Most of these efforts to advance some dimension of international human rights during the nineteenth century required the voluntary cooperation and compliance of sovereign nation-states. That is, attempts to free the enslaved, to assist the exploited, and to care for the wounded in the world could not succeed unless these governments who controlled these victims agreed to cooperate. Given the political realities of the time, the definitions of internal affairs and the legitimacy of state behavior, and the principles of the doctrine of sovereignty, independent nations had to be willing on their own accord to sign and abide by the terms of international treaties, or to allow international relief organizations into their countries, in order for human rights to be promoted and protected. Otherwise, nothing would change. The one important exception to this took the form of humanitarian intervention.

A number of the early founders of international law addressed themselves to the complicated question of whether any nation or group of nations ever could intervene in the internal affairs of others when the mistreatment of subjects became so brutal that it exceeded the limits of acceptable behavior. Alberico Gentiti, for example, expressed the opinion at the end of the sixteenth century that resort to arms could be justified in defending the "common law of humanity," for "in the violation of that law we are all injured, and individuals in turn can find their personal rights violated."[85] Hugo Grotius, writing in the next century at a time of absolute monarchies, asked whether a just war could be launched for the purpose of defending subjects "from injuries by their ruler," and concluded that "if a tyrant . . . practices atrocities towards his subjects, which no just man can approve, the right of human social connection is not cut off in such case."[86] Emerich de Vattel wrote in a similar vein, arguing that "if a prince, by violating the fundamental laws, gives his subjects a lawful cause for resisting him; if, by his insupportable tyranny, he brings on a national revolt against him, any foreign power may rightfully give assistance to an oppressed people who asked for its aid."[87] Through time, their writings and those of others contributed to the theory that if any state rendered itself guilty of cruelties and persecution against its own people to such an extent that it attracted international attention and generated international outrage, then intervention by others might be considered legitimate.

This theory of humanitarianism, of course, immediately clashed with other theories of diplomacy and international relations, especially those of sovereignty and its uncompromising corollaries of independence, domestic jurisdiction, and nonintervention, and, of growing importance in the nineteenth century, intense nationalism. It went far beyond the practice of merely protecting alien nationals,[88] and proposed to deal directly with the protection of the citizens or subjects of other countries. Humanitarian intervention also confronted the practical and political realities of power and the prospects of reciprocity. Any nation considering launching an unwelcomed and uninvited intervention into another state understood perfectly well that it possessed limitations on its ability to actually project its own power onto another and thereby to coerce particular forms of behavior.[89] In addition, intervening in the internal affairs of another nation in the name of human rights might well invite criticism of abuses at home and dangerously risk prompting others to reciprocate with their own interventions in return. The costs of implementing the theory of humanitarian intervention into practice, in short, were considerable. Nevertheless, by the nineteenth century, a growing concern about human rights on a global scale increasingly encouraged governments to be willing to reevaluate at least some of the traditional reluctance to consider domestic affairs as matters of legitimate international concern and to consider a new level of direct action on behalf of the persecuted.

Not surprisingly, victims who suffered from religious or ethnic persecution attracted early attention among those who considered the possibilities of international protection and humanitarian intervention. Indeed, the fate of minorities persecuted for their religious convictions or ethnic affiliations certainly could be counted on to draw the interest of those of the same group elsewhere, even beyond their own borders. They would be the ones, for example, most likely to hold a vision of exercising a right of religious freedom and most determined to protect that right if threatened by persecution. In the past, these concerns received only slight international attention from states unwilling to challenge any prerogatives of national sovereignty.[90] The experience of upheavals early in the nineteenth century began to change this timid approach, however, and accelerated the evolution of international human rights. In this case, those diplomats who gathered at the Congress of Vienna during 1814 and 1815 were prepared to slowly, but nevertheless explicitly, recognize the beginnings of an international right of religious freedom and to acknowledge that intolerance on the basis of religion might jeopardize other aspects of international peace and security. In several specific instances they pledged themselves to maintain "religious equality" and "assure equal protection and favor to every sect" in Belgium,[91] and to guarantee "without any distinction of Religion . . . the same political and civil rights which are enjoyed by [other] inhabitants" in Switzerland.[92] At the same time, they agreed to a significant new departure in the history of diplomacy by pledging themselves to stand behind the consideration of means of effecting "an amelioration in the civil state of those who profess the Jewish religion in Germany," paying "particular attention to the measures by which the enjoyment of civil rights shall be secured and guaranteed to them."[93] The fact that these unique provisions occurred as integral parts of multilateral, negotiated treaties provided an important early step in establishing the principle and the practice of international guarantees to protect such rights, for they entailed the clear implication that any failure by the responsible governments to abide by these conditions due to religious or ethnic persecution could result in international enforcement by means of humanitarian intervention.

The most significant case of protecting the persecuted in the nineteenth century and subsequent development of the practices of humanitarian intervention emerged particularly with reference to the fate of Christians living in the Ottoman Empire. Given the volatile religious history of its vast territorial expanse ranging from Algeria across north Africa through the Middle East and to Asia Minor and the Balkans, the Ottomans could maintain internal peace only by recognizing various *millets*, or religious communities, which acknowledged at least minimal interests and customs of Greek Orthodox Christians, Muslims, Jews, and Armenian Christians. Yet, even under this system, the *dhimmîs*, or non-Muslim subjects of the sultan, suffered various forms of discrimination.[94] Of these victims, however, only the Christians had powerful friends with a long-standing interest in their fate and able to exert pressure beyond their own borders.[95] The Great Powers of Europe alone possessed the capabilities of exerting influence and practicing coercive diplomacy, if they so chose, by employing a variety of means ranging from diplomatic pressure to military intervention.

Reformist Europeans, who already had taken some measures to ensure greater religious toleration within their own borders by such efforts as the Catholic Emancipation Acts of 1829 and 1832 and the Religious Disabilities Act of 1846 in Britain and the relaxation of many legal restrictions against Jews in several countries, now brought some of their influence to bear by using diplomatic persuasion. Expressions of interest, grave remonstrances, and formal protests about the treatment of Christian subjects within the Ottoman Empire emerged early. Many Ottomans responded with resentment and outrage, regarding this behavior as blatant coercion and overt interference in their own internal affairs. A number of other reform-minded government officials, interestingly enough, actually welcomed this international pressure and used it as a means of bringing about change within the Ottoman Empire. Regardless of the initial response, however, the result took the form of the *Hatti-i Sherif* promulgated by Sultan Abdulmejid and his foreign minister in 1839. This famous decree, uniquely and deliberately read for the first time before an assemblage of foreign diplomats, guaranteed certain legal, social, and political rights to "all our subjects, of whatever religion or sect they may be; they shall enjoy them without exception."[96] Further pressure forced the sultan to issue a more extensive decree in 1856 known as the *Islahat Fermani*. "Every distinction or designation," it reads, "pending to make any class whatever of the subjects of my empire inferior to another class, on account of their religion, language, or race, shall be forever effaced from administrative protocol."[97] In the subsequent Treaty of Paris negotiated during the same year following the Crimean War, Sultan Abdul-Aziz similarly pledged before the world his acceptance of an international obligation to honor "the welfare of his subjects . . . without distinction of religion or race" and "his generous intentions towards the Christian population of his Empire."[98]

When diplomatic protests proved to be insufficient in the minds of European states to protect the persecuted, they were prepared to escalate their means and use direct military intervention if necessary. After several years of passively watching extensive human suffering and the slaughter of many Greek Orthodox Christians at the hands of the sultan's forces, for example, the Great Powers resolved in 1827 to actively intervene. Britain, France, and Russia, acting in concert and in the name of the international community in order to stop the bloodshed, ignored the claim by the sultan that the conflict in Greece was an "internal affair" of the empire and agreed to send naval vessels and troops to the region. Their motives of such intervention, they announced in a most unusual formal treaty, could be found in their desire of finally "putting a stop to the effusion of blood" and "of re-establishing peace between the Contending Parties, by means of an arrangement called for, no less by sentiments of humanity, than by interests for the tranquility of Europe."[99]

The Great Powers added more precedent to this new pattern of humanitarian intervention in the wake of the suppression and massacre of many Christians in Syria. Reports of the horrible persecution and then murder of perhaps as many as eleven thousand Christian Maronites by Muslim Druze from this area of the Ottoman Empire began to circulate during the summer of 1860. "It is to be hoped," wrote one official, "that there may be some exaggeration in them. Still, if but a tenth part be true, enough has occurred to excite universal reprobation."[100] Indeed, observed another diplomat, these "calamities" caused such a "profound emotion" of outrage that governments found themselves forced to confront the question of whether they had certain interna-tional responsibilities or "duties" to protect the persecuted.[101] Austria, France, Britain, Prussia, and Russia, with the agreement of the Ottoman Turks themselves who wanted to avoid anything worse, consequently authorized an expeditionary military force of six thousand men to be sent in the name of them all to restore order in the region and to protect the Christian subjects of the sultan. Interestingly enough, these six powers also created a ground-breaking International Commission to investigate the causes and the extent of the persecution, to consider means of punishing the guilty and of assisting the victims, to draft a new constitution for the Lebanon region that guaranteed re-ligious protection, and to prevent the outbreak of such developments in the future.[102] Said the British secretary of state for external affairs in explaining the reason for this intervention: "It is to be hoped that the measures now taken may vindicate the rights of humanity."[103]

Religious persecution in the Balkans produced an even greater escalation of human-itarian intervention, for here the flames of crisis fanned international passions as never before. Years of notorious misrule and unrelenting persecution of Christians in Bosnia, Herzegovina, and Bulgaria finally produced revolts against the Ottoman Empire by the late 1870s. When the sultan sent in troops to crush the rebellion, they behaved in such a way against non-Muslims as to provoke international horror and outrage. Reports of unrestrained killing, looting, raping, burning, pillaging, and torturing increasingly appeared to have all too much basis in reality. The slaughter of no fewer than twelve thousand Christians during a single month prompted even some of the restrained and mild-mannered commentators to describe this behavior "as the most heinous crimes that had stained the history of the present century."[104] Pen-and-ink drawings in news-papers provided visual images of rapacious Turkish troops burning homes, riding over dead bodies, and massacring innocent children and women who were clearly wearing medallions of the Christian cross.[105] More impassioned commentators created further images of persecution with their words. William Gladstone, the fiery orator who even-tually would serve as the British prime minister on four separate occasions, published a book entitled *The Bulgarian Horrors* that sold forty thousand copies in just three days, and many more thereafter. He described "the horror and infamy" of scenes of villages "burned down by the scores" and "men, women, and children murdered, or worse than murdered, by thousands" in "Satanic orgies" conducted by a "great anti-human specimen of humanity."[106]

Gladstone saved his greatest eloquence and passion not to merely describe, but to arouse government leaders and public opinion into taking action. He urged his readers and listeners to go beyond their own selfish, luxurious, and indifferent lives, the naked-ness of their minds, and the feebleness of their wills to consider the fate of those who are persecuted. Again and again he spoke of "rights and duties" and the need to take action, not for narrow national interests, but out of a sense of global responsibility "for the deep interests of humanity."[107] Gladstone argued that under these extreme circum-stances, the international community possessed a moral obligation to challenge the traditional restrictions of past practices and now actively intervene in order to protect humanity and defend justice. Solemnly he declared:

Victims of Persecution (*Illustrated London Times*, 1876).

A little faith in the ineradicable difference between right and wrong is worth a great deal of European diplomacy, bewildered by views it dare neither dismiss nor avow. . . . What civilization longs for, what policy no less than humanity requires, is that united Europe, scouted, as we have seen, in its highest, its united diplomacy, shall pass sentence in its might, upon a Government which unites the vices of the conqueror and the slave, and which is lost alike to truth, to mercy, and to shame.[108]

Consequently, Gladstone concluded, "for the purposes of humanity alone" the fleet should be "so distributed as to enable its force to be most promptly and efficiently applied, in case of need, on Turkish soil, in concert with the other Powers, for the defense of innocent lives, and to prevent the repetition of those recent scenes at which Hell itself might almost blush."[109] Such action, he believed, collectively and effectively would convey one simple message: "You shall *not* do it again!"[110]

All the outrage and indignation thus generated by the atrocities in the Balkans prompted national leaders to call first for an international conference designed to take appropriate action to protect persecuted Christians. The Ottoman Turks refused to bow to any such pressure, arguing that how they treated their own subjects was a matter of exclusive domestic jurisdiction. In response to this rejection, Russia declared war on Turkey and the intervention began. Given the asymmetry of power in this case, the result was not difficult to determine, and the Great Powers met collectively several months later in order to forge the 1878 Treaty of Berlin. In the midst of the expected terms covering a variety of territorial changes and strategic considerations in the Balkans, the signatories also made certain that this treaty would address much more explicitly than in the past an important provision on human rights. They wanted to make certain that the principles of religious freedom and nondiscrimination received international approval. For this reason, they wrote into the text of the treaty that henceforth in the Ottoman Empire "differences in religious creeds and confessions shall not be alleged against any person as a ground for exclusion or incapacity in matters relating to the enjoyment of civil and political rights, admission to public employments, functions, and honors, or the exercise of the various professions and industries in any locality whatsoever." In addition, they negotiated other terms concerning the rights of ethnic as well as religious minorities that acknowledged the need to protect the Armenians from persecution at the hands of the Circassians and Kurds, providing such articles as those declaring that "in the districts where Bulgarians are intermixed with Turkish, Roumanian, Greek, and other populations, the rights and interests of these populations shall be taken into consideration."[111] A short time thereafter, the same powers signed the International Convention of Constantinople, containing specific articles guaranteeing the right of Muslims to freely practice their religion with complete equality in territories restored to Greece.[112] At the time, such provisions as an integral part of international treaties represented a striking departure from traditional practice.

Their efforts did not stop here, however. Within just two years, the six signatory powers of the Treaty of Berlin issued a highly publicized collective note to Sultan Abdul Hamid, strongly criticizing his mistreatment and suppression of Armenians within his empire. He quite naturally resented such interference and threats of further intervention from what he described as "over-zealous people" and argued that his government was being unfairly singled out for criticism of practices "which naturally occur in every country in the world."[113] Yet he found himself under considerable international pressure that he could not ignore, and thus began to temporarily curtail the extent of persecution. These nations responded again during 1895 and 1896 when renewed massacres of Armenians occurred not only in distant rural areas but within full view of the diplomatic community in Istanbul itself. Britain, France, and Russia publicly demanded a commission of enquiry and an immediate halt to all such bloodshed and violations of basic rights.

Persecution of minorities within the Ottoman Empire provided a highly visible focal point for international attention, condemnation, and action, much in the same way that the atrocities of the Third Reich in Germany and apartheid in South Africa would do in the next century. But, significantly, these efforts were not confined to violations of human rights by the Turks alone. The government of tsarist Russia, for example, found itself widely criticized for its brutal suppression of the Poles. The Hungarians similarly discovered themselves to be the subject of international outrage over their policy of forced assimilation known as Magyarization, whereby they deliberately persecuted minority ethnic or religious groups within their territories by means of educational and cultural policies, administrative and electoral laws, political trials, and the use of armed force. The Evangelical Alliance, composed of churches from throughout Europe and the United States, also drew widespread attention to new variants of "Russification" which deliberately persecuted non-Orthodox believers. Jewish organizations also consistently urged governments to take action that might protect their coreligionists from anti-Semitic pogroms, and at times achieved successes. A number of serious representations were made by Austria, France, Great Britain, Greece, and the United States to the Romanian government on behalf of Jews suffering from discrimination, persecution, and murder.[114] Similarly, the United States formally protested on several occasions against Russian treatment of Jewish citizens, arguing that while it had no desire to challenge municipal laws and regulations, it could not remain silent in the face such abuses of rights and the "claims of our common humanity."[115]

These early efforts for the purpose of protecting the rights of the persecuted contributed heavily to the growing theory and practice of humanitarian intervention and its slow but steady acceptance as an increasingly important component of customary international law. They helped to develop the emerging legal principle that certain basic and fundamental *lois de l'humanité*, or laws of humanity, must be applied to behavior in the world, and that there were certain limits to the freedom that states could enjoy under international law when it came to dealing with how they treated their own nationals. Legal scholars described these limitations in terms of natural law, antecedent and superior to any national legislation, and explicitly used the expression, "human rights," so essential that their egregious violation simply could not be ignored by other states and the global community. These human rights included life, liberty, and equal protection under the law. It followed from this vision that various forms of pressure and force could thus be justifiably used by a group of powers acting collectively or "in concert" in the name of humanity for the purpose of protecting the rights of inhabitants in another state unable to defend themselves from inhumane treatment by their own government, but only if it became so abusive and oppressive as to shock the conscience of humankind and clearly exceeded the limits of reason and justice. In addition, those statesmen of the nineteenth and early twentieth centuries began to at least consider the possibility that the violation of human rights in one country might well endanger the tranquility and peace of all countries.[116]

Humanitarian intervention both in theory and practice also helped to identify serious and troubling problems created when trying to transform visions of international human rights into reality. Even at this early stage, for example, it became evident that international intervention in the name of "humanity" might well be genuinely beneficent and justified, but at the same time always carried the dangerous potential of providing a convenient pretext for coercion or a guise for masking more suspicious motives of national self-interest and aggrandizement.[117] Similarly, difficulties arose as to precisely what nations or group of nations could legitimately or precisely define the "laws of humanity," "the conscience of mankind," and the meaning of "human rights" for the world as a whole while at the same time avoiding accusations of having arbitrary standards that applied to some but not to all.[118] The Great Powers who demonstrated such eagerness to protect the rights of the persecuted in the Ottoman Empire, for example, also happened to be the same ones known to persecute and discriminate against indigenous peoples within their own overseas empires. In addition, whereas carefully negotiated and solemn treaty provisions concerning human rights indicated a strength of desire, the lack of enforcement provisions revealed a lack of will. "Whether use will be made of this — probably the last — opportunity which has been thus obtained . . . by the interposition of the Powers of Europe," conceded one diplomat at the conclusion of a particularly arduous discussion, "or whether it is to be thrown away, will depend [ultimately] upon the sincerity with which the Turkish statesmen now address themselves to the duties of good government and the task of reform."[119] Finally, and not surprisingly, those engaged in this activity worried about what they described at the time as "the inconveniences and dangers which an intervention of this kind might produce."[120] Humanitarian intervention always carried the risk that it could provoke even worse reactions against the very people that it wanted to protect. Even more serious in terms of international relations, such intervention could create the risk of a dangerous precedent that might be turned against those who employed it and thus threaten their own independence, domestic jurisdiction, territorial integrity, and national sovereignty. Each of these difficult problems would continue to confront those who struggled to advance international human rights for many years to come.

$$*\quad*\quad*$$

Despite obvious limitations and the persistence of particular problems, these early international efforts on behalf of human rights represented remarkable achievements. At the beginning of the nineteenth century, slavery was common in many countries and the slave trade flourished, often with government sanction and support. Hereditary systems of inequality and traditional exploitation due to race, gender, or class continued unabated. The wounded in war were left to suffer and die where they fell on battlefields. Moreover, states could engage in persecution against religious or ethnic minorities with impunity and without the slightest fear of criticism from abroad. In the face of all this members of the global community responded to the pleas of the enslaved, the exploited, the wounded, and the persecuted with pronounced passivity and stark silence. By sharp contrast, when the century ended, most of the living victims of slavery, the slave trade, and serfdom were emancipated and those who suffered from exploitation, warfare, and persecution possessed at least a prospect of being helped in some small, or possibly even significant, way from others beyond their own borders.

What had happened, of course, is that a number of major upheavals during the century had opened dramatic new opportunities for change, and growing awareness of the plight of those who suffered stirred the collective conscience of thoughtful men and women who vowed that they would no longer remain passive or silent and would organize themselves to bring about change. Wars and revolutions played vital roles in this process, as did thought-provoking books with their now-revealed power to mobilize public opinion into action at critical times over egregious wrongs. International concern for human rights, ironically, thus became the most intense when abuses were the most obvious and blatant: in slavery, in exploitation, in war, and in persecution. Those who struggled to free, to assist, to heal, or to protect their brothers and sisters elsewhere did so not only confronting forces and doctrines from the past, but without guidelines and in the face of prevailing contrary pressures arising from intense nationalism, imperial conquest and manifest destiny, racism, immigration restrictions, and laissez-faire.[121] These visionaries and activists experienced both frustrations and successes, and through their cooperation and clashes often raised more questions about human rights than they answered. But they believed that their efforts would make a difference — and they did. Never before had the members of the international community been so willing to examine such dark places and practices in the world and to confront evils long taken for granted. Never before had they been so willing to begin establishing some kind of a moral framework for action in the name of protecting humanity and defending justice. Together they experimented, and demonstrated that they actually could begin exploring expanded definitions of human rights, developing a larger sense of moral awareness and obligation toward humanity as a whole, creating political precedents and practical mechanisms for taking international action, and cautiously challenging the traditional boundaries of domestic jurisdiction and national sovereignty. In all of this their greatest contribution thus was not in reaching a definitive destination, but rather in successfully establishing a direction — a direction that would give encouragement to visions of human rights carried forward into a new century.

Chapter 3
Entering the Twentieth Century

World Visions, War, and Revolutions

> We must do away with boundaries of nations and unify the world, do away with boundaries of class and make all people equal, do away with boundaries of race and render all races the same, do away with boundaries of sex and protect individual independence, . . . [and] do away with boundaries of suffering to reach universal harmony.
>
> — Kang Youwei of China

The experience of entering a new century invariably provides rather special opportunities to reflect on the process and the meaning of historical change and continuity. For those whose lifespans cross the threshold from one century into another, the event is often emotionally moving, filled with elements of concern and hope about how the future might differ from the past. In this regard, those with visions of human rights at the beginning of the twentieth century had reasons for both trepidation and genuine excitement. They knew that the old forces of resistance, prejudices, vested interests, and the doctrine of national sovereignty with domestic jurisdiction would not simply disappear and would continue to confront them. Yet, they also hoped that the momentum gained from their successes during the nineteenth century could not only be maintained, but perhaps even accelerated. What they did not and could not know, of course, was that within just a few years their world would explode into its first "total" war of global proportions and precipitate revolutions. This in turn would cause unprecedented human suffering and death, destroy four empires, create new states from the ashes of old monarchies, shift the world balance of power, loosen the bonds of imperialism, bring about a wide-ranging peace conference, create a new global organization — and help to advance the evolution of international human rights.

Ferment and the Anticipation of Rights

The turn into the twentieth century brought ferment and anticipation to the world. Indeed, the years between 1900 and 1914 unleashed a dynamic period bursting with discovery, change, development, creativity, energy, and visions. "Thought had more than once been upset, but never caught and whirled about in the vortex of infinite forces," wrote intellectual Henry Adams on the threshold of the dawn of the new century. "Power leaped from every atom, and enough of it to supply the stellar universe. . . . Man could no longer hold it off. Forces grasped at his wrists and flung him about as though he had hold of a live wire or runaway automobile." His essay "A Law of Acceleration" virtually vibrated with expressions of energy and motion: "dynamic theory," "unlimited power," "new forces," and, more importantly, "the inadequacy of old implements of thought."[1] Those who visited the remarkable 1900 International Exposition held in Paris expressed similar thoughts, as they inspected the latest demonstrations of people's growing ability to harness the world's resources to their own purposes. The very categories of the exhibition halls testified to the scope of this bursting inventiveness: machinery, textiles, civil engineering and transportation, mining and metallurgy, chemical industries, and electrical inventions which heralded the transformation from the nineteenth "Century of Steam" to the twentieth "Century of Electricity." One ominous portent of the future, however, lay in the number of visitors standing spellbound before the exhibits of Schneider-Creusot's long-range cannon and Vicker-Maxim's rapid-firing machine guns.[2]

Change was in the air, and these many innovations in technology soon found themselves matched by those in other realms by thinkers and artists sensitive to the new century's mood. In theoretical physics the quantum theory of energy and Albert Einstein's dissertation on relativity soundly shook established Newtonian concepts of the universe and opened new perspectives on mass, time, and space. Sigmund Freud's early ideas of psychoanalysis began to revolutionize explanations of human behavior. The popularity of William James's *Pragmatism* and Henri Bergson's *L'Evolution créatrice* indicated dramatic shifts in philosophy toward empiricism and the immediate and practical needs of people. Exuberant productions by Serge Diaghilev began to transform choreography and stage production in ballet, while in music the works of Igor Stravinsky, Claude Debussy, and Arnold Schoenberg all repudiated romanticism and opened up creative new possibilities for composers who called themselves "modernists." Artists experimented with color and technique to further develop expressionism, Pablo Picasso used highly unusual geometric forms to create cubism, and others developed a style known as *art nouveau*. The pioneering work of Frank Lloyd Wright and Walter Gropius increasingly led architecture and design to emphasize function rather than ornamentation. And, throughout the entire period leading up to the war, vocal advocates of the ideas of "modernization" appeared from Brazil to China, from Japan to Iran, and from Russia to Egypt, urging their own countries and the world to abandon traditional restraints and enter the dynamics of the twentieth century by embracing change.

An important and growing interest in the world as a whole also emerged at this time. Technological innovations in communication with wireless telegraph and in transportation, made particularly dramatic with Louis Bleriot's sensational first crossing of the English Channel by airplane in 1909, captured the popular imagination. These inventions appeared to nullify many previous notions about distance, time, geographical barriers, and national boundaries, and thereby "shrank" the globe. The mental construct of "the world" thus began to change, and people and places once seemingly far removed became closer than ever before. For this reason, observers increasingly spoke of "world politics," "global affairs," and the truly "international" aspects of diplomacy.[3] In the words of one diplomat of the time, all this suddenly forced geography to become "a grand new subject."[4] Foreign ministries familiar with the old Eurocentric features of the past now needed to respond to this change by developing more sophisticated maps. Within just a few years, to cite but one example, those rudimentary and simplistic representations in the French *Annuaire diplomatique* which placed all of Asia on a single page showing Japan in possession of only five cities were quickly transformed into detailed maps of China, Japan, and Korea covered with place names, cities and towns, and special insets. This same pattern emerged with the transformation of maps representing the United States, Latin America, Africa, and the islands of the Pacific.[5] None of the countries or their cities were new, of course, but in the past they had simply been diplomatically ignored. It became increasingly clear that in the twentieth century this would no longer be possible. As one political leader observed, the impact of scientific discovery and application, the "logic of history," and "world-wide repercussions" of events all produced a new situation in which "the affairs of the world now interest all the world."[6]

Global perspectives also suggested global solutions to common problems, hence the emergence at this time of an intense interest in internationalization. Advances in technology and the growing economic interdependence of nations called for coordinated action across borders to provide solutions for a wide variety of problems. These included the practical application of telegraph and wireless communications, rail transportation, sanitation, postal services, shipping regulations, navigational charts and signals, assistance and salvage at sea, protection of patents and copyrights, law enforcement, scientific discovery, trade statistics, tariffs, business transactions, trade union activity, suppression of opium and other drugs, and sporting events, among many other functional matters requiring some form of international cooperation. Remarkably, in the few years between the turn of the century and the outbreak of World War I, officials and private citizens alike established thirteen intergovernmental bodies and three hundred and four NGOs to deal with these kinds of international issues.[7] Among these were the International Association of Chambers of Commerce, the International Institute of Agriculture, the World Missionary Conference, and the International Federation of Permanent Committees for Expositions. The formation of the Union of International Associations itself provided a visible capstone of this globalization activity as it began to coordinate the scheduling of programs, conferences, and other endeavors of these many organizations, as well as publishing its own journal, appropriately named *La Vie Internationale*.

This larger context, climate of opinion, and movement toward globalization all played vital roles in thinking about visions of international human rights as well. Change in general encouraged those who worked for the expansion and protection of rights denied for so long in the past, for it challenged the status quo. The shrinking of the world by technology and economic interdependence made it easier to view events in distant places as being related to each other and to more fully consider people beyond national borders as being brothers and sisters. More specifically, the proponents of global "modernization" focused attention on the many benefits that might be derived from political systems based on law and justice, constitutional limits of authority, representative institutions and extensions of the franchise, individual liberty, economic and social freedoms, availability of medical care and educational opportunities, and equal protection of the rights of all. In this setting, and in anticipation of an active future, it thus came as no surprise when the NGO known as the Ligue des Droits de l'Homme emerged with its first publication in 1901, announcing that its vision to promote liberty, equality, fraternity, and justice applied not just to those in France — but "to all humanity."[8] Toward this end, the members of the Ligue passed resolutions, sponsored studies, published exposés, pressured governments, and organized conferences on subjects ranging from religious and ethnic persecution, the rights of indigenous peoples, victims of unjust and brutal regimes, class inequalities, and the oppressed everywhere. Their attention went wherever violations of human rights occurred, whether in France, Algeria, China, the Ottoman Empire, Ivory Coast, Senegal, the Balkans, Indochina, Madagascar, or the Congo, pledging their constant support for the rights "of all human beings, without exception."[9]

At exactly the same time, other advocates of human rights engaged in similar discourse in different parts of the globe. In Iran, for example, Talibov-i Tabrizi published his *Izāhāt dar Khusus-i Azādi* (Explanations Concerning Freedom), provoking considerable discussion about the relationship between the rights of individuals vis-à-vis the state, the teachings of Islam, and the comparative practices of other countries.[10] In North America, the Lake Mohonk Conference of Friends of the Indian expanded its concern about rights to the international level and in 1904 added a new expression to its official name: "and Other Dependent Peoples."[11] Simultaneously, according to one authority, "Early twentieth-century China was imbued with an enthusiasm for human rights, ranging from a concern with the nature of the family and its components of individual persons, and the status of women in society, to the balancing of the rights of individuals with the community as a whole."[12] The visionary Chinese author Kang Youwei, for instance, began publishing the first parts of his *Datong shu* (The Book of Great Harmony) which promotes individual liberty, freedom, equality, and the natural rights of all humanity. In this pathbreaking work from Asia, he argued that the achievement of these universal rights and the alleviation of human suffering required eliminating the barriers of gender and liberating women, abolishing all divisions based on race and class, and erasing national boundaries and viewing the world as a single entity.[13]

Visions of international human rights also received attention during this time of ferment and anticipation from some governments under pressure to continue their efforts of progressive reform by using the power of states to protect the human condition and to provide assistance, especially on behalf of the exploited, wounded, or persecuted.[14] They founded the International Association for the Protection of Labor, with the International Labor Office as its executive organ, to articulate rights for workers and to protect them from some of the life-threatening dangers of industrialization. Toward this end, after meeting in Berne, Switzerland, they successfully negotiated and opened for signature the two innovative conventions of 1906 focusing on economic and social rights and creating obligations under international law on governments vis-à-vis each other concerning the treatment of their own citizens. These treaties included the International Convention Respecting the Prohibition of Night Work for Women in Industrial Employment, and the International Convention Respecting the Prohibition of the Use of White (Yellow) Phosphorus in the Manufacture of Matches. That same year witnessed the international reconsideration of the original Red Cross Convention on behalf of the rights of combatants suffering on battlefields and the new and expanded Convention for the Amelioration of the Condition of the Wounded and Sick in Armies in the Field. In 1907 delegates to the second Hague Peace Conference extended this coverage of humanitarian law even further by securing the signatures of forty-four nations from Asia to the United States and from Latin America to Europe on the Convention Respecting the Laws and Customs of War on Land and the Convention for the Adaption to Maritime Warfare of the Principles of the Geneva Convention. The International Office of Public Health also was created during this year to advocate a global right to health and to protect people around the world from the threat of diseases such as cholera which had the potential for causing epidemics.[15]

These years marked an increase as well in the interest in international humanitarian intervention as a means of protecting the rights of the persecuted. In several cases of egregious abuses sufficient to attract outside attention, nations refused to remain silent in the face of persecution, and thereby further challenged the doctrines of national sovereignty and domestic jurisdiction. Sometimes their concern took the form of diplomatic representations or protests. Austria, France, Britain, and the United States, for instance, officially complained to the Romanian and the Russian governments over the discrimination and persecution of their respective Jewish populations. The European powers issued protests to the sultan of Morocco in 1909 demanding that he abolish the use of bodily punishments leading to mutilation or slow death against political prisoners and "observe henceforth the laws of humanity."[16] Formal complaints were issued to the Peruvian government on behalf of aborigines who had been subject to cruel and inhumane treatment, as well as to Belgium protesting behavior against the native peoples of the Congo. Renewed atrocities against Christians in the Ottoman Empire prompted more than words, and several nations joined together to actually force the Turks to institute reforms for protecting rights, to disband irregular forces, to remit taxes to those victimized, and to accept the presence of foreign military officers as a guarantee of compliance.[17] In addition, a new outbreak of persecutions against Armenians by the Turkish government prompted a strong American protest accompanied by a presidential message about "the interest of humanity at large" and the "fundamental rights" of all people with the following fascinating observation:

Ordinarily it is very much wiser and more useful for us to concern ourselves with striving for our own moral and material betterment here at home than to concern ourselves with trying to better the condition of things in other nations. We have plenty of sins of our own to war against, and under ordinary circumstances we can do more . . . here at home than by passing resolutions about wrongdoing elsewhere. Nevertheless there are occasional crimes committed on so vast a scale and of such peculiar horror as to make us doubt whether it is not our manifest duty to endeavor at least to show our disapproval of the deed and our sympathy with those who have suffered by it. The cases must be extreme in which such a course is justifiable. There must be no effort made to remove the mote from our brother's eye if we refuse to remove the beam from our own. But in extreme cases action may be justifiable and proper.[18]

Such thoughts and endeavors concerning international obligations to protect human rights across borders attempted to address a number of serious problems prior to World War I, but certainly not all. To those who still suffered in one form or another, and to those excluded from the coverage of treaties or the attention of humanitarian interventions, these efforts represented only partial and much too narrowly selective attempts for the protection of the rights of all people. Instead, they viewed these actions as steps in the proper direction but as insufficient in addressing the denial of their particular rights. More specifically, declared the critics, governments around the world still continued to exclude those victimized due to their race, gender, or class. To change this situation, activists determined to expand the boundaries of existing visions and increase their efforts even further.

Not surprisingly, racial discrimination drew the immediate attention of those interested in human rights. In fact, after the turn of the century, long-standing prejudice actually seemed to escalate as never before with serious discussions about "the rising tide of color," "lesser breeds," "inferior blacks," "savage reds," "ignorant browns," the "yellow peril," "superior whites," "racial destiny," "racial purity," and possible "race wars" extending throughout the globe.[19] Consequently, during the very first Pan-African Congress meeting in London during 1900, the determined and talented black intellectual and activist, W.E.B. Du Bois, made his much-celebrated statement repeated many times around the world: "The problem of the twentieth century is the problem of the color line — the relation of the darker to the lighter races of men in Asia and Africa, in America and the islands of the sea."[20] Three years later he published *The Souls of Black Folk* and then, due to his dissatisfaction with the accommodationist approach of Booker T. Washington for securing rights from whites, went on to organize the Niagara Movement for more aggressive action to combat all distinctions based on race. This quickly led in turn to the formation of the National Association for the Advancement of Colored People (NAACP) within the United States, designed to overturn the color bar of discrimination, to stop the horrifying practice of lynching, and to obtain all manner of equal rights as guaranteed by the Constitution. "We will not be satisfied," thundered Du Bois,

to take one jot or title less than our full manhood rights. We claim for ourselves every single right that belongs to a freeborn American, political, civil, and social; and until we get these rights we will never cease to protest and assail the ears of America. . . . It is a fight for ideals, lest this, our common fatherland, false to its founding, become in truth the land of the thief and the home of the slave — a byword and a hissing among the nations for its sounding pretensions and pitiful accomplishment.[21]

Many miles away but at the same time, Mohandas Gandhi began his public protest against the racial discrimination toward Indian immigrants in South Africa, attracting international attention by resisting the 1907 Asiatic Registration Act and by articulating his vision of justice and the worth of each and every human being that eventually would lead others to describe him as the man who "made humility and truth more powerful than empires."[22] All of this helped to reveal the global scope of the racial problem and resulted in the first meeting of the Universal Races Congress in 1911 with its participating delegates committing themselves toward securing basic human rights for all regardless of the color of their skin.

Race also pervaded imperialism with its language of "the white man's burden" and the necessity to overpower the "backward colored races," and for this reason a number of those who struggled to advance international human rights turned their attention toward halting Western imperial conquest and promoting the self-determination of indigenous peoples. A number of critics came from the West itself, often actively participating in organizations like the Anti-Imperialist League and writing vehement attacks against the conquest and exploitation of natives caught under the nets of colonial empires. J. A. Hobson's pioneering 1902 book *Imperialism* condemned with angry passion wealthy men and financial monopolies, politicians who served as their willing accomplices, national and racial chauvinists, and all others who turned their backs on religious and humanitarian principles and instead gloated "in the perils, pains, and slaughter of fellow-men."[23] Radicals, Socialists, and Marxists added their voices to this opposition to imperial conquest and exploitation, as did liberal reformers such as E. D. Morel, with scathing indictments of French and Belgian practices in the Congo and Henry Nevinson with his castigations against the violations of human rights in Portuguese Angola and São Tomé.[24]

In any number of cases during the years between the turn of the century and the outbreak of World War I, the victims of imperialism began to rise up themselves, demanding their own independence, and putting words into action by launching attacks against those who would deny them their rights. The Ashantis launched an uprising against the British in the Gold Coast (now Ghana), the Hottentots and Hereros arose against the Germans in South-West Africa (now Namibia), the Congolese and Indochinese began armed rebellion against the French, Ethiopians and Somalis initiated attacks against the Italians, Filipinos began fighting against the Americans, and the members of the Boxer Rebellion in China violently struck against all Westerners. Japan's stunning defeat of Russia in their 1904–1905 war provided a particularly dramatic psychological turning point for those who struggled for self-determination, for as described by one contemporary, it represented "the most important historical event which has happened, or is likely to happen, in our lifetime: the victory of a non-white people over a white people."[25] The charismatic French socialist leader Jean Jaurès took all of these developments as signs of what was to come and declared: "There are all these people of all races who have seemed inert . . . and sunk deep in an eternal sleep, who are now awakening, demanding their rights, and flexing their muscles."[26]

Advocates for women's rights also contributed their voices and efforts with renewed vigor during this time of anticipation and ferment, confirming Lady Frances Balfour's opinion of "new winds blowing hard through society."[27] Some of this activity focused on the general emancipation of women from discrimination in the past, and included efforts to obtain equality in marriage, access to education, the opportunity to own property, improvement for women's working conditions in sweat shops, and birth control, often under the slogan of "Let us be our sister's keepers."[28] Many efforts in the West focused primarily on enabling women to benefit from the gains of liberalism and parliamentary representation by securing the right to vote, not necessarily as an end in itself but as a means of securing a broad range of other rights. Finnish females over the age of twenty-four and Australian women obtained the right to vote on an equal basis with men in 1906. Women in Norway secured the franchise in 1913. But that was all. In fact, prior to World War I, these countries joined New Zealand as the only ones in the entire world that granted women the right to vote. Under the general influence of the Progressive movement that attacked the inequalities in American life, and the efforts of the newly formed National Woman's Party, the franchise had been extended to females in eleven of the western United States by 1914, but this did not apply to the nation as a whole. But when other governments refused to enact similar legislation, they provoked at least some suffragists to escalate their pressure through bold public activism and even violence. In Britain, for example, Emmeline Pankhurst and her daughters formed the Women's Freedom League and began a campaign of militancy by organizing protest parades, disrupting meetings, smashing windows, slashing works of art, chaining themselves to the gates of Parliament, setting fires, and holding hunger strikes that, when arrested, led to brutal and highly publicized force-feedings by the authorities. Others believed that the best way to secure rights for women was to organize not just nationally but globally and, with the help of tireless crusaders like Susan B. Anthony and Carrie Chapman Catt, created the International Woman Suffrage Alliance for the world with affiliates in many nations.[29]

For women who lived in countries without established parliamentary forms of government, of course, the right to vote represented a vision far removed from any immediate reality. They worked instead to liberate themselves during these years from 1900 to 1914 from centuries of traditional gender oppression and to secure greater equality. For them, the issue of women's rights was linked intrinsically with larger movements of modernization and political change and often with struggles of self-determination against Western imperialism. The revolutionary feminist Qiu Jin organized the first women's association in China, for example, spoke out against the oppression of women within the traditional patriarchal system, launched the journal *Zhongguo Nübao* (Chinese Women) to advocate "equal rights for women," and openly declared: "We want our emancipation! Men and women are born equal, why should we let men hold sway?"[30] In Japan, Hideko Fukuda began publishing her *Sekai Fujin* (Women of the World) and reporting on the activities of the recently created Society for the Reinstatement of Women's Rights and suffragist movements overseas, Raicho Hiratsuka organized a group called Seitosha (Bluestockings) to promote equality for women, and revolutionary Suga Kanno revealed her anger by shouting: "Rise up, women! Wake up!"[31] Concepción Felix formed the Asociación Feminista Filipino in the Philippines and the publication of *Filipinas* declared itself to be devoted entirely to matters affecting "the rights of women."[32] In Turkey, Ahmet Agaoglu forcefully argued that the rights of women were completely in accordance with the tenets of pure Islam cleansed of its misinterpretations, while Nuriye Ulviye Mevlan organized the Ottoman Association for

Women Struggling for Equal Rights: Emmeline Pankhurst under Arrest (Culver Pictures).

the Defense of Women's Rights. Similar organizations and efforts appeared in Egypt, Iran, India, Sri Lanka, Indonesia, Vietnam, and Korea, all working on behalf of extending basic human rights to women.[33]

Still others sought to address the rights of females by focusing on the fate of those caught up in the international white slave trade and forced into prostitution against their will. Several new nongovernmental organizations formed for the purpose of protecting the rights of women and girls treated like private property and forced into "involuntary sexual slavery." Toward this end, they worked at closing down bordellos wherever they existed in the world and combating what they regarded as the injustice of state-supported prostitution that placed restrictions on women but not their male customers. These reformers assisted in hiring social workers to meet incoming ships and offer assistance to females traveling alone or under suspicious circumstances, and sometimes provided flyers in different languages proclaiming that no one could be forced to become a prostitute. Indeed, they gained publicity sufficient enough to successfully pressure thirteen governments to negotiate, then ratify, two groundbreaking international agreements that actually created agencies to monitor and prosecute those who traded in women and girls across national borders.[34]

The fate of those denied their rights as a result of class distinctions attracted considerable attention as well. Activists strongly resisted any notion that rights somehow belonged only to people of wealth or property. Toward this end, many worked as reformers within the existing system to extend the franchise, elect representatives sympathetic to those victimized by industrialization or other forms of exploitation, provide social security benefits, and organize labor unions. In Britain they supported the Fabian Society, formed the new Labour Party, and successfully secured the National Insurance Act of 1911 protecting workers against the worst ravages of accident, sickness, and unemployment. By 1912 German reformers committed to the needs of the working class had made the Social Democratic Party the largest parliamentary group in the Reichstag. Belgian activists obtained old-age pensions, compensation for accidents, and improvements in housing and public services for members of the working class. Their counterparts in Sweden acquired universal men's suffrage for elections to the lower house and the property qualification for election to the upper house was reduced. Members of the Ramakrishna Movement in India continued to provide practical humanitarian service and to work to reduce social and economic inequalities. At the same time, Progressives within the United States worked to arouse the public's conscience toward social responsibility and to create legislation to help the poor in a variety of ways. These efforts resulted in a whole new array of laws pertaining to food, housing, education, children, public health, labor conditions, and elections, including the Seventeenth Amendment to the Constitution in 1913 providing for the right of people to elect U.S. senators directly. Not content with these national gains, many reformers sought to cooperate and coordinate beyond their own borders, and did so through the creation of international NGOs and international federations of trade unions such as the International Ladies' Garment Workers' Union.

Not all of those dedicated to advancing the rights of workers and others economically or socially disadvantaged due to their class were persuaded by these efforts or by their reformist sponsors who sat cheek by jowl with the upper classes in parliaments. They found extensions of voting, social legislation, and trade union activity to be certainly helpful, but often too seductive and fundamentally inadequate for the needs at hand. For them, visions of true emancipation for workers and a full realization of their rights could be accomplished not in voting majorities or in the moderation of unions collecting insurance funds, but only through the "direct action" of more militancy, strikes, sabotage, syndicalism, and industrial combat that would one day paralyze capitalism and inaugurate revolution. In France they formed the Confédération Générale du Travail (CGT); in Germany they followed the radical Marxist Karl Kautsky; and in the United States they created the radical Industrial Workers of the World (IWW) in 1905. At a more global level, a number of radical socialists felt disaffected by the reformist trend of the the Second International with its headquarters in Brussels, and advocated more extreme upheaval around the world. This group quickly found its most effective spokesman in the exiled Russian revolutionary V. I. Lenin, whose 1902 pamphlet *What Is To Be Done?* castigated the reformers who would bourgeoisify the class struggle, and called for a disciplined elite of professional revolutionaries as a means of securing the rights of the oppressed and exploited around the world.

Revolutionary upheaval, however ideologically inspired, also clearly marked these years of anticipation and ferment, contributing much to the discourse on human rights. The explosion of the 1905 Russian Revolution began this process when a protest march to the tsar's Winter Palace erupted after troops opened fire and killed or wounded hundreds of people. This bloodshed immediately prompted general strikes, peasant revolts, and military mutinies, forcing a reluctant Alexander II to issue the so-called October Manifesto, granting a national legislative assembly, a constitution limiting autocratic power, decrees abolishing most of the restrictions on the personal liberties of peasants, and guarantees protecting the rights of freedom of the press, of speech, and of assembly. Then, the Young Turk Revolt occurred in 1908, first with a revolutionary party committed to modernization and then with widespread popular support, compelling the despotic Sultan Abdul Hamid to agree to elections for a parliament, constitutional changes that promised to transform Turkey into a more liberal state, and the extension of certain political rights. The Mexican Revolution followed in 1910, setting off a series of subsequent uprisings, the emergence of Emiliano Zapata and his landless peasant followers demanding justice and their rights, several years of strife and civil war, and what was to become the first major social revolution of the twentieth century. All of these upheavals, in turn, helped to inspire others elsewhere, particularly as discontent within their own countries mounted. This certainly proved to be the case in China. Here leaders such as Sun Yat-sen who had written the "Three Principles of the People" dealing with the ideals of universal harmony and individual freedom, the members of a women's brigade, and others associated with the Revolutionary Alliance launched the 1911 Chinese Revolution and helped to dramatically end more than two millennia of imperial history. They deposed the last emperor of the Qing dynasty, declared the creation of the new Chinese Republic, established a constitution guaranteeing equal protection under the law and providing for freedom of worship and assembly, committed themselves to moving toward more democratic principles like political and social equality, and announced that they henceforth would promote "the equalization of human rights."[35]

World War, Revolutions, and Rights

The outbreak of the World War I in 1914 provided the prospect of an even greater acceleration in the evolution of both visions and practices of international human rights. A rare few understood that this armed conflict would produce dramatic upheavals, as in the case of the unusually prescient German Chief of Staff Helmuth von Moltke who wrote on the very first day of battle that the world was entering "the struggle that will decide the course of history for the next one hundred years."[36] Most observers, however, possessed little idea of what was in store and blithely entered the war with blind enthusiasm. They believed that the war would be short and mobile, eliminate domestic conflict by generating patriotic unity, be confined strictly to military combatants in uniform, and result in a relatively small loss of lives. They were wrong. Years of building modern armaments, forming rival and rigid alliance systems, designing detailed war plans against enemies, and engaging in imperial rivalries all created conditions that now quickly turned a few shots from a political assassination in Sarajevo into a global conflict that produced not only a "total" war but revolutions with unimagined consequences as well.

In terms of death and devastation, people around the world staggered in disbelief as this conflict extended not for a several months but for years and, in the words of one military authority, "provided a preview of the Pandora's box of evils that the linkage of science with industry in the service of war was to mean [for the twentieth century]."[37] The combination of scientific patterns of machine-gun fire and barbed-wire entanglements, artillery capable of firing exploding shells to targets several miles away, poison gas, land mines, torpedoes, submarines and battleships deployed on a massive scale, aircraft for combat on the ground and in the sky, and armored tanks all unleashed unparalleled slaughter of human life and destruction of property and entire provinces, often leaving little difference between the "victor" and the "vanquished." It let loose the most destructive war in history up to this point, inflicting an average of five and a half thousand casualties per day for more than four years. In the end, the military dead alone included two million Germans, almost as many Russians, a million and a half Frenchmen, more than a million Austrians, almost as many Englishmen, half a million Italians and nearly as many Turks, and more than one hundred thousand Americans. Those wounded, maimed, disfigured, or incapacitated for the rest of their lives numbered least thirty million.[38]

The sheer magnitude of this kind of bloodshed and carnage obviously forced people as never before to consider the value of humanitarian law and the rights of the sick and wounded, and often dying, during armed conflict. Indeed, in its first circular after the outbreak of the war, the International Committee of the Red Cross accurately predicted: "From now on, the Red Cross movement will have to commit itself to a degree of activity unprecedented in its intensity."[39] Lacking any paid staff, its members largely put aside both their personal and professional lives to devote themselves for the duration of hostilities to their humanitarian mission. Beyond the details of operating the agency itself, personnel of the International Committee amassed an index file containing seven million cards, sent nearly two million parcels, assisted with the repatriation of captured medical personnel and of the severely wounded, condemned the use of chemical warfare and deliberate attacks on appropriately marked hospital ships, and constantly and forcefully worked to remind all belligerent countries of their obligations under the Geneva Convention concerning individual rights. In addition, they created the International Prisoner of War Agency to care for those captured during combat whose fate had yet to be regulated effectively by the Geneva Convention, collecting and forwarding correspondence and gifts at the rate of nearly thirty thousand per day and serving as a neutral and reassuring intermediary for the exchange of information between prisoners and their anxious families. Wartime exigencies also greatly increased membership in the national Red Cross societies and forged new linkages among several of them that demonstrated again the practical importance of international cooperation beyond national borders when dealing with the rights of sick and wounded combatants.[40]

Not just the numbers but the composition of the armed forces greatly influenced the discussion of human rights during the World War I. The consumption of young men at such a phenomenal rate over such a long period of time forced belligerent governments to conscript larger quantities of soldiers and sailors from minority races and working or peasant classes to fill the rapidly depleting ranks of combatants. Therefore, it is not surprising that while providing military service and thus risking their very lives in warfare such individuals would begin to ask not whether but rather when the rights of citizenship given to some of their countrymen would now be extended to them. In both Europe and the United States, for example, labor unions increasingly began to insist on greater social and economic rights in return for their sacrifices. In France, no other segment of society was so hard hit by mobilization as the peasantry, of whom contemporaries noted "went into the war docile and resigned, [and] came out resentful and ready to complain."[41] The sprawling multiethnic empires of Russia and Austria-Hungary experienced serious protests for rights among their minorities called to sacrifice on the battlefront. This phenomenon became even more pronounced when the United States entered the war with black troops, which eventually constituted nearly one-third of the entire armed forces. In some cases draft boards actually exempted single white men but conscripted black fathers. Many of those who served believed that their military sacrifices would pay dividends and that in the end the "war to make the world safe for democracy" would extend visions of the full rights of citizenship to them as well. Even Du Bois subscribed to this vision and encouraged his readers in a famous essay to "close ranks shoulder to shoulder with our white citizens and the allied nations that are fighting for democracy" as a means of achieving their rights.[42] If this hope were not enough to stimulate such thinking, then enemy propaganda provided a constant reminder of the failure of America to fulfill its promise of equal rights. "Do you enjoy the same rights as the white people in America, the land of Freedom and Democracy," asked a German circular scattered over black troops, "or are you rather not treated over there as second-class citizens? Can you go into a restaurant where white people sit? . . . Is lynching and the most horrible crimes connected therewith a lawful proceeding in a democratic country?"[43] All of this could not help but foster a growing consciousness of racial inequality and a resolve to do something about it. Kelly Miller provided ample expression of just such determination when he wrote of the experiences and emotions of these black soldiers in one book called *An Appeal to Conscience: America's Code of Caste a Disgrace to Democracy*. He followed this with an even stronger treatise, tellingly entitled *The World War for Human Rights.*[44]

The issue of international human rights was also powerfully raised by the composition and origin of still other troops who fought in the war. Although it clearly began in Europe, the armed struggle rapidly expanded to assume global dimensions as well and imperial competitors launched attacks in accordance with wartime imperatives and alignments. Portugal, Japan, and the Ottoman Empire quickly joined the original belligerents, and then the overseas colonies of the British, Germans, French, Belgians, and Portuguese all entered the war. At the same time, Australian and New Zealand forces attacked German possessions in New Guinea, Samoa, and the Solomon, Caroline, and Marshall Islands, among others in the Pacific. British troops fought throughout the

Middle East and sailors plied the Atlantic and Indian Oceans, while their Japanese allies attacked Germans in Kiaochow and then moved along the Shantung Peninsula in China. Not content with taking the war to Africa and Asia, Europeans took Africans and Asians to the war. Desperate for manpower, they determined that they could use their vast reservoir of imperial subjects as soldiers in Europe. It is estimated that nearly two and a half million colonials fought for Britain, and thousands more served as noncombatants. They came from India, British East and West Africa, Egypt, the West Indies, South Africa, Mauritius, Fiji, and China. France similarly pressed into service hundreds of thousands from Algeria, Morocco, Senegal, and Dahomey in Africa and still others from French Indochina, while the Russians drafted Muslims from Central Asia. It did not take much imagination for these troops to realize immediately that they all were regarded as equal when it came time to fight and die, but not for protection under the law, voting, immigration, or other forms of basic human rights.

This extensive participation of nonwhites and non-Westerners in the combat of World War I proved to be of extraordinary importance in the subsequent development of African and Asian nationalism and visions of human rights, including that of self-determination. It helped to destroy the myth of "superior" and "invincible" whites, accelerated discussion about the meaning of rights beyond national borders, struck blows that shook the existing imperial system, and greatly politicized many of those who survived by heightening their collective sense of confidence and entitlement. Soldiers from diverse parts of the world established contacts for the first time with like-minded, politically conscious individuals also drawn unwittingly and unwillingly into this war who thus began to expand their heretofore restricted horizons and to consider what this conflict might ultimately mean for their rights. In fact, several of those who would become major leaders in the movement of decolonization including Ho Chi Minh, Zhou Enlai, and Lamine Senghor first became politically active as a result of their experiences during World War I. In 1916 the Congress Party began openly to demand home rule for India in exchange for all its sacrifices in wartime, and during the 1917 and 1918 Imperial War Conferences the Indian delegates explicitly raised the issue of human rights and racial equality within the Dominions. Mohamed Duse, the articulate editor of the first Afro-Asian journal, *African Times and Orient Review*, similarly began to argue that the combat experience of the black, brown, and yellow races of the world proved that they were every bit the equal of whites. As he wrote in one essay designed to encourage his readers to see the relationship between war and human rights: "We are forced to observe that the once despised black man is coming to the front in the battle for freedom, and the freedom which he helps to win for the white man must also be meted out to him when the day of reckoning arrives. . . . In helping the British Empire and the French Republic in the hour of need you are helping yourselves to a freedom which cannot be denied to you and to a glory which shall be engraved upon the brazen tablets of fame which the rains of the ages shall not wash away."[45]

Among these many features that so characterized World War I from other previous armed conflicts, perhaps none provided more significance than the impact of the war on civilians. Indeed, by obliterating the traditional distinction between combatants and civilians during warfare, this struggle introduced modern, "total" war to the twentieth century. In earlier wars, even in the protracted and destructive campaigns against Napoleon, it was only occasionally that the average citizen at home felt the war's effects, and often entirely possible for them to forget that the fighting even existed. During World War I, this kind of detachment proved to be virtually impossible. Citizens of all the belligerent countries discovered that the exigencies of war subjected their lives and their rights to ever-increasing levels of control, determining their freedom of action, their employment, their diet, and even what they could say or think. Moreover, those people of Belgium, northeast France, and Poland, who saw their countries overrun, their homes commandeered as billets, their farms and factories destroyed, and their families and friends held hostage by occupying forces, knew the war, in the words of historian Gordon A. Craig, "as intimately as the troops who passed through their streets."[46] But they were by no means alone. It is estimated that in Russia, Serbia, and Bulgaria the civilian loss of life actually exceeded those of the military.[47] Added to these staggering deaths were the countless numbers of refugees forced to flee from their homelands and others literally crying and begging for some form of relief.

Such unanticipated and incalculable human suffering by civilians immediately and completely overwhelmed the capacity of every existing relief organization. The International Committee of the Red Cross had been organized to address wounded combatants, not civilians, and therefore possessed no authorization or mechanism to meet this sudden challenge. All the private, religiously oriented, charity groups had never before in history been confronted with this magnitude of need, and try as they might, could not possibly deal with the unexpectedly long queues of the homeless, sick, starving, and destitute that lengthened with each day of the war. In addition, with the existence of armed combat, naval blockades, and obvious danger in taking any action across national borders, no government was prepared to assume any responsibility for the fate of these victims during time of war on its own. It thus appeared as though they would be condemned to suffer and starve, perhaps even to die, entirely without outside assistance.

Desperate times often call for desperate measures, and into this breach stepped dedicated humanitarians who believed that these victimized civilians possessed the right to food and care simply by the nature of being human. Under the direction of an American businessman of Quaker background named Herbert Hoover, they created an innovative nongovernmental organization called the Commission for Relief in Belgium. With its head office in London and main branches in New York, Rotterdam, and Brussels, the commission operated with unofficial endorsement from American, Spanish, and Dutch governments, engaging in what Hoover would describe as "a perfectly gigantic struggle."[48] It coordinated the work of an extraordinary five thousand separate volunteer committees in raising funds, cajoling national governments, fighting bureaucracies, collecting food and supplies throughout North and South America to India, transferring these necessities through war zones and over belligerent frontiers, and finally distributing them to those in need in what was described as a "work of mercy" and a "great humanitarian task." When the war finally ended, the Commission had distributed five million tons of food and had spent $1 billion in loans and private donations. Nearly four million signatures appeared on letters and scrolls sent directly to Hoover, in addition to expressions of appreciation embroidered on used flour sacks, from grateful recipients of this relief.[49] In the end, the whole experience not only saved the lives of these individuals, but contributed heavily to developing a sense of responsibility to those who suffer beyond national borders, a successful mechanism for administering international relief, and to what Hoover later described as "a sensitive adjustment of conflicting rights and interest through a spirit of decency and cooperation in human relationships."[50]

Innocent civilians suffered in other ways during the war as well, for at times armed conflict provided either an excuse for violence or a mask to conceal government brutality against presumed enemies of the state. Ethnic and religious minorities caught between the Austro-Hungarian and Ottoman Empires in the Balkans, for example, suffered considerable loss of life throughout the fighting. The most egregious case, however, occurred when the Turkish government launched a program of genocide against the Armenians on the charge that they were aiding the Russian enemy. Early in 1915, Armenian political, religious, educational, and intellectual leaders in Istanbul were arrested, deported to Anatolia, and systematically murdered. Those serving in the Ottoman armies and already segregated into unarmed battalions were then taken out in groups and killed. Following this, the government rounded up masses of Armenian civilians from throughout the empire, forcing them out of their ancestral homeland, marching them across deserts and mountains, and deliberately exposing them to starvation and disease in order to cause death. Many eyewitnesses recorded this calamity, including one Italian diplomat who painfully wrote:

The passing of the gangs of Armenian exiles beneath the windows and before the door of the consulate; their prayers for help, when neither I nor any other could do anything to answer them; the city in a state of siege, guarded at every point by 15,000 troops in complete war equipment, by thousands of police agents, by bands of volunteers and by the members of the "Committee of Union and Progress"; the lamentations, the tears, the abandonments, the imprecations, the many suicides, the instantaneous deaths from sheer terror, the sudden unhinging of men's reason, the conflagrations, the shooting of victims in the city, the ruthless searches through the houses and in the countryside; the hundreds of corpses found every day along the exile road . . . ; the children torn away from their families . . .—these are my last ineffaceable memories of Trebizond, memories which still . . . torment my soul.[51]

Reliable estimates place the Armenian dead at numbers of at least one million.[52] Such deliberate genocide on such a massive and shocking scale could not possibly escape wider international attention, and consequently drew considerable protests from governments around the world announcing their intent to hold the Turks individually and collectively accountable for these gross violations of the most basic of all human rights —namely, the right to exist—and "crimes against humanity."[53]

While some visions of human rights for civilians thus came to the fore during World War I due to persecution, others arose due to liberation. That is, by stretching existing institutions and practices often to the breaking point, wartime demands also released certain groups and individuals from traditional restraints or prior restrictions. Among the most significant of these were women. The introduction of the "home front" in this war to match the efforts on the battlefront resulted from the realization that modern, protracted, total war with naval blockades that imposed siege conditions on domestic populations simply could not be waged without using all available resources. As young men were sent off to combat and their jobs became vacant, it became quickly apparent that no nation could continue this war without somehow replacing their vital contributions in factories, on farms, and in public service. Consequently, women discovered that dramatic changes affecting men now affected them, that definitions of "manpower" began to shift, and that positions never before open to them now became available. At first with a trickle, and then with a flood, women found themselves actually being recruited to work in family businesses, turn out shells in munitions industries, provide medical care, conduct railroads, buck rivets in shipyards, drive public trolleys and ambulances, deliver the mail, and police local areas. Some even provided military service, resulting in innovative creations like the British Women's Army Auxiliary Corps, composed of those who worked as secretaries, recruiters, nurses, mechanics, and physicians, at times with such distinction that they received military decorations. Together, these experiences opened up opportunities for liberation, silenced a number of critics with gender prejudices, exposed past discrimination against women through what Millicent Garrett Fawcett called "the great searchlight of war," and all the while created new levels of self-confidence that encouraged the assertion of rights.[54]

Many of these wartime demands for rights focused on suffrage, and the extension of the right to vote for women in Denmark and Iceland during 1915 stimulated this pressure even further. The following year, Jeannette Rankin was elected from the state of Montana to be the first women ever to serve in the U.S. Congress, but the lack of a national franchise led to the formation of the more militant National Women's Party and its rallying cry: "HOW LONG MUST WOMEN WAIT FOR LIBERTY?"[55] Russia extended voting rights to women in 1917. At the same time, Sarojini Naidu actively campaigned for women's franchise rights in India. Pressure mounted for equal treatment in Britain and the Dominions from organizations like the Women's Freedom League, Dominions' Women's Suffrage Union, and United Suffragists, all of whom asked whether the assumption of the duties of men in war would result in the assumption of their rights as well. "Votes for heroines as well as heroes," they demanded.[56] Similar expressions even were heard the in Parliament where one male member declared: "Women of every station . . . have proved themselves able to undertake work that before the war was regarded as solely the province of men. Where is the man now who would deny to women the civil rights which she has earned by her hard work?"[57] By the war's end, such arguments proved to be irrefutable, and females successfully secured at least partial voting rights in Britain and Ireland through the Qualification of Women Act of 1918. Women in Australia secured the right to vote on a national basis during the same year. This considerable activity surrounding the war helped to inspire others to consider the rights of women in different settings, including the Turkish writer and sociologist, Ziya Gokalp, who at the same time expressed in poetry:

All must be equal, marriage, divorce, wealth.
No nation can ever bloom if its daughters
Are not given the weight they deserve.
We have fought for and won all our other rights.

Only the family is still in its dark age.
Why do we still turn our backs on women?
Tell me, have they not a part in our struggles?[58]

World War I also accelerated the evolution of visions about human rights by denying them. Men and women alike discovered that with the emergence of the "home front," governments increasingly engaged in political centralization, economic regimentation, and thought control. Authorities sought to ensure that full civilian resources would be mobilized for the war effort and that the fighting spirit would be properly maintained. To do this, they subjected their people to extraordinary levels of control — regulating their lives, conditions of employment, diet, freedom of action, and even what they could think or say — all in the name of national security emergency. This regulation occurred not just in belligerent countries of absolute monarchies where the tradition of parliamentary government was weak and resulted in the imposition of military dictatorships, but in presumably democratic nations as well. In Britain, the Defense of the Realm Act authorized the government to do virtually anything it pleased with citizens suspected of sins against the war effort. The act made it legally possible for houses to be searched without a warrant, persons to be held liable for possessing literature considered subversive by some overzealous magistrate, deportation and internment to take place without trial, public meetings to be prohibited by police without the right of appeal, newspapers to be subjected to vigorous censorship, and the exercise of the right of freedom of speech to be considered unpatriotic and result in prison sentences. In France, the government exerted enormous pressure against the Ligue des Droits de l'Homme to desist from its advocacy of the rights of individuals and groups during a time of warfare control, court martial, censorship, and conscription. In the United States, the 1917 Espionage Act and the notorious 1918 Sedition Act, effectively suspended any number of provisions in the Bill of Rights, as predicted by dissenting members of Congress, particularly among pacifists, wartime critics, socialists, and left-wing workers who suffered the worst repression. These laws imposed severe penalties of fines and prison terms for any person who would "willfully utter, print, write, or publish any disloyal, profane, scurrilous, or abusive language" about the American form of government, the Constitution, the flag, or even service uniforms; or would in any way "incite, provoke, or encourage resistance" to the government; or "advocate any curtailment of production . . . of anything necessary or essential to the prosecution of the war."[59] Such provisions launched a wartime orgy of hysteria, witch-hunting, persecution, and mob violence that violated the rights of anyone suspected of being unpatriotic. Self-appointed vigilante groups attacked individuals on city streets and on farms without fear of legal reprisals, while official agents of the Department of Justice and army troops advanced on radicals in mining or lumber camps. Some were killed, like Joe Hill of the Industrial Workers of the World, and well over one thousand citizens were imprisoned, including the Socialist Party's presidential candidate, Eugene V. Debs, for merely being suspected of some kind of disloyalty. In this setting of wartime violations of rights, it is thus not surprising that membership would increase dramatically in organizations such as the French Ligue des Droits de l'Homme, or the newly created predecessor to the American Civil Liberties Union, the National Civil Liberties Bureau.[60]

Some of these governmental efforts to maintain fighting resolve by exerting ever greater control through the denial of rights failed, and failed completely. In fact, as death, destruction, starvation, and other hardships of the prolonged conflict continued, the war created conditions that produced not only cracks in the "home front" but chasms that resulted in actual revolution itself. This began in 1916 when a group of Irish nationalists attacked government buildings in Dublin and launched the Easter Rebellion in an effort to wrest independence from Britain. The same year riots and strikes broke out in Germany, Russia, Austria, and Italy, often pitting civilians against one another, divided along class lines. Throughout the sprawling Austro-Hungarian Empire nationalist groups increasingly resisted centralized authority, envisioning equal treatment and their right of self-determination. The Czechs, for example, began a vigorous anti-Hapsburg campaign and created the Czechoslovak National Council to escalate pressure on the government. The Poles, Croatians, Slovenes, and Serbs all took similar action to assert their rights. In addition, mutinies began to occur in the armies, as soldiers refused to follow the orders of their officers. By early 1917, one observer warned clearly: "We are living on a volcano."[61]

The eruption took place in Russia. Long frustrated by the autocratic government of Nicholas II, the shortage of food, the lack of rights, and the absence of peace, people took to the streets in March 1917. Masses of workers, women, peasants, soldiers, and moderate and radical politicians participated in widespread protests and rioting. This action resulted in the abdication of the tsar and the emergence of elected soviets, or councils of workers and soldiers, and a provisional government that promised a constitution guaranteeing civil and political rights. In the hopes of destabilizing Russia even further, the German High Command provided safe rail transportation for V. I. Lenin, the exiled leader of the Russian Bolsheviks, to return to his homeland in order to launch a revolution. Upon arriving in Petrograd, Lenin issued his April Theses, a document that called for Russia to withdraw from the war, for the soviets to seize power on behalf of workers and peasants, and for all private land to be nationalized. Within months, he and his followers launched the Bolshevik Revolution, seizing control by force, and urging Communists everywhere to use the chaos of the war as a springboard to rise up against their oppressors, to assert their rights, and to overthrow the capitalistic order around the world.

Massive disruption and confusion resulting from the combination now of both war and revolution in turn quickly produced renewed and extremely serious questions about war aims and human rights. Why was the war still being fought after all, and what could people expect in victory or in defeat? Would their many sacrifices and sufferings in wartime provide an extension of their rights as promised, or would they be ignored once the emergency passed? Who would make a stand on principle, and what kind of rights could be legitimately addressed by the international community? The Ligue des Droits de l'Homme in France, the Women's Freedom League and United Suffragists in Britain and the Dominions, the National Association for the Advancement of Colored People and the National Civil Liberties Bureau in the United States, the Society for the Advancement of Women in the Philippines, the Patriotic Women's League in Korea, the Indies Social Democratic Party in Indonesia, and the Congress Party in India, among many other NGOs around the world, all added their different voices and suggested answers to these questions about human rights, as did writers such as Du Bois in the pages of *Crisis* and Duse in *African Times and Orient Review*. In a very important and widely-discussed speech, Japanese Premier Shigenobu Okuma declared that for peace and for "the harmonization of different civilizations of the east and the west" practices of "inferiority must end," announcing that his country was determined to champion the basic human right of racial equality.[62] In 1917 the Mexican government announced a new constitution with radical provisions for the rights of labor that had never been seen before in the Western Hemisphere. A Chilean jurist and diplomat named Alejandro Alvarez drafted a document during the same year entitled "International Rights of the Individual," arguing for the need to establish international human rights for all and asserting that individuals possess rights not based on their citizenship in a given state but on their membership in the human family.[63]

Perhaps the most ultimately influential statements about the meaning of rights in this world of war and revolution emerged from the political leaders of those two countries destined to greatly shape global affairs during the rest of the twentieth century: the United States and Russia. President Woodrow Wilson had announced with stirring eloquence as early as the first year of the war that he looked forward to the time when the world would know that his country "puts human rights above all other rights" and that "her flag is the flag not only of America, but of humanity."[64] He subsequently went on to give enthusiastic encouragement to those with a vision about such rights by pledging that the United States was fighting this war "to make the world safe for democracy" and create a "new diplomacy," and by promising in his Fourteen Points to support liberty, the right of people to determine their own form of government, and equality of rights across national borders. Not stopping there, Wilson went on to forcefully declare: "Self-determination is not a mere phrase. It is an imperative principle of action, which statesmen will henceforth ignore at their peril."[65] Lenin also spoke about human rights, but with extremely significant differences. He placed emphasis on social and economic rights rather than those of a civil or political nature, and focused on class and group rights rather than those of the individual, fiercely declaring that these rights could best be obtained through revolutionary Communism rather than evolutionary and capitalistic democracy, and that the right of self-determination should apply not simply to Europeans but to the entire world. As he wrote in *Imperialism, the Highest Stage of Capitalism*, and elsewhere during the war, this right should apply to all, including "the Orient, Asia, Africa, the colonies, where [it] is not a thing of the past but of the present and the future."[66] In so doing, Lenin made two important arguments that would greatly influence many subsequent discussions of international human rights: first, that there existed an inextricable connection between the national liberation movements of decolonization and the class struggle; and secondly, that the right of self-determination was a universal right.[67] Lenin's initial actions in this regard appeared to give a certain credibility to his words, for almost immediately on seizing power his new government issued the Declaration of the Rights of the Peoples of Russia, abolishing all privileges and disabilities based on nationality or religion and granting all the right of self-determination.

All these visions, words, and policies involving human rights became even more pronounced during the final and chaotic events of war and revolution in 1918 and 1919. The All-Russian Congress of Soviets, for example, adopted what it called the Declaration of Rights of the Toiling and Exploited Peoples, boldly pledging "to suppress all exploitation of man by man, to abolish forever the division of society into classes, ruthlessly to suppress all exploitation, and to bring about the socialist organization of society in all countries."[68] Facing punishing new offensives, German soldiers fled from the front, sailors mutinied onboard ship, and workers demonstrated in the streets with sufficient force to launch the German Revolution, depose Kaiser William II from the throne, end their participation in the war, and begin a halting experiment with rights in a democracy. The Austro-Hungarian Empire collapsed in defeat and revolution, its ruler abdicated, and its new leaders declared a republic. Crowds of Czechs and Slovaks and Croatians announced their independence in the name of the right of self-determination. Nationalists declared their independence throughout Eastern Europe. Revolutionaries proclaimed soviet republics in Bavaria and Hungary. Uprisings occurred in colonial empires scattered from Asia to Africa. In each and every one of these events, discussions and claims of human rights proceeded with unparalleled intensity and vigor. Given the circumstances of the time, however, the actual realization of any of these visions would be determined initially not so much by the people in the streets or behind the barricades but rather by those who assembled to negotiate an international peace settlement.

Peacemaking and Human Rights

The great and the small, the famous and the unrecognized who gathered together at the Paris Peace Conference beginning in January 1919 were, for a short moment in time, the arbiters of the world. Indeed, their decisions influenced people scattered throughout the far reaches of the globe, thus allowing observers to accurately describe their deliberations as "the clearing house of the Fates."[69] Here the silent influences of the more than ten million dead joined with the tumultuous demands of the living who had sacrificed and suffered so much and now wanted a peace settlement that would prevent such carnage in the future. Nations, empires, races, men and women, political parties, pressure groups, NGOs, and individuals all met to vie with each other over both selfish spoils and lofty principles. Although some of the more callous among them believed that they were only cleaning up the folly of a civilization gone mad and needed to grab whatever they could, others genuinely saw themselves as creating an entirely different world in which some form of human rights would be honored. "We were journeying to Paris," wrote one diplomat in recording the mood, "not merely to liquidate the war, but to found a new order. . . . We were preparing not Peace only, but Eternal Peace."[70]

For those with such dreams of peace and justice, this conference represented a special opportunity to negotiate a series of treaties that would institute a "new" diplomacy different from the past and that would include some dimensions of international human rights. Some, of course, optimistically and somewhat naively believed as a matter of faith that this would occur simply because of the sheer righteousness of their cause, and thus saw no reason to develop a plan of action, create prior agreement on an agenda, or define precisely what they meant by rights. But even those with a more pragmatic sense of politics and diplomacy had identifiable reasons for hope as well. The experience of World War I, after all, had demonstrated the international aspects of shared life and death, and thus reinforced the importance of responsibilities beyond one's own national borders. Millions of people had sacrificed and suffered during the course of the war and many solemn promises about rights had been made that were now due to be fulfilled. In addition, they thought that the presence of new participants with different kinds of voices heretofore excluded from the "inner sanctum" of previous Great Power diplomacy would guarantee the realization of these visions of human rights. One of the most striking differences, for example, was the arrival of non-European states, a sign that the age had passed when it could be claimed that Europe represented "the lever that moved the world."[71] Among the newcomers were Australia, New Zealand, Canada, South Africa, Japan, and the United States. Others came as well. With irrepressible enthusiasm, Du Bois described the gathering as "THIRTY-TWO NATIONS, PEOPLES, AND RACES. . . . Not simply England, Italy, and the Great Powers are there, but all the little nations. . . . Not only groups, but races have come — Jews, Indians, Arabs, and All-Asia."[72] Another observer similarly noted, "Chinamen, Japanese, Koreans, Hindus, Kirghizes, Lesghiens, Circassians, Mingrelians, Buryats, Malays, and Negroes and Negroids from Africa and America were among the tribes and tongues forgathered in Paris to watch the rebuilding of the political world system and to see where they 'came in.' "[73] All of this was unique in the annals of global diplomacy, and thus the time appeared particularly ripe to work for advances in the evolution of international human rights.

The collective right of self-determination, or of the freedom to choose one's own form of government, surfaced immediately and powerfully at the peace conference. Indeed, U.S. Secretary of State Robert Lansing described this principle and its application as "simply loaded with dynamite."[74] Not only had so much been promised during the war about precisely this matter, especially by Wilson and Lenin, but groups of Poles, Czechs, Serbs, Armenians, Jews, Arabs, Indians, Senegalese, and Vietnamese, among many others, descended on the assembled in Paris to exert pressure for their own national independence and make certain that these promises were honored.[75] To make matters more acute, all parties knew that the complicated intermixture of populations defied any clear means of demarcating one national or ethnic group from another, and that any granting of self-determination would involve redrawing critical borders and freeing people heretofore under the control of someone else. Nothing at an international conference, even in the best of times, produces greater intensity and emotion than the taking of power and territory from one country and giving them to another. But in this case, war and revolution had destroyed the German, Austro-Hungarian, Russian, and Ottoman empires, and now many waited to claim their rights from vast spoils that seemed to be at their disposal on three continents.

Negotiations designed to realize this right of self-determination at the Paris Peace Conference proceeded along tortuous routes due to a volatile mixture of issues and forces pulling in different directions. Like so many other cases in the long evolution of international human rights, those making decisions here both carried and confronted a variety of mixed motives. In addition to the genuine desire to maintain fidelity to the promises of the past and to satisfy the legitimate claims from nationalist groups were those motivations of a more calculating and brutal nature that addressed matters of Realpolitik. For example, carving up old empires into new states in the name of self-determination would create at the same time the benefits of allies who owed their very existence to these peacemakers, thus forming a more favorable balance of global power for the victors. Taking away land and power from defeated enemies would exact revenge and levy punishment for losses sustained in the war. And, if such changes took place in Eastern Europe, they could contribute toward erecting a *cordon sanitaire,* or sanitary barrier, to quarantine what many leaders in West perceived as the infectious disease of Communism emerging from Lenin's Russia. One British general, for example, strongly argued that the Soviets presented "a danger to the world" that had to be resisted in part by creating a series of new nations—not because of the right of self-determination, but instead "to create a ring of States all round Bolshevik Russia, the object being to prevent Bolshevism from spreading; to deprive it of supplies and power of expansion, and to reduce it to absolute exhaustion."[76]

Arriving at a fair and just settlement in the midst of these mixed motives, complicated issues, and competing claims not only between nations but between individual and group rights in the wake of war and revolutions, would have profoundly challenged the most brilliant, well-meaning, and experienced of statesmen. At the Paris Peace Conference, the task nearly overwhelmed those making decisions and lent credence to the observations made at the time that it is relatively easy to formulate abstract principles when compared with engineering their practical application and that "peace is very much more complicated than war."[77] In the end, this caused great inconsistencies and eventual problems. Nevertheless, the resulting international treaties dramatically liquidated multinational empires and redrew existing borders all the way from the Baltic in the north to the Adriatic and Aegean Seas in the south.[78] The Finns, Estonians, Latvians, Lithuanians, and Poles all gained their independence. The treaties authorized the Czechs and Slovaks to create Czechoslovakia, the Hungarians to separate themselves completely from the Austrian Hapburgs, the Romanians to expand their territory and influence, and the Albanians to have their own state. Then, in a complicated arrangement fraught with potential danger, the leaders at Paris joined the Serbs, Slovenians, Bosnians, Croatians, Herzegovinians, and Montenegrins into a single state called Yugoslavia. Never before in history had so many new nation-states been created at one time in the name of the right of self-determination.

The human rights of minorities also attracted considerable attention and care at the Paris Peace Conference. Humanitarian intervention as a means of protecting religious or ethnic minorities from persecution, of course, had arisen well before the war; but concern had been greatly intensified by the recent experience with genocide against the Armenians and other wartime loss of human life. To make this issue even more acute, the very act of establishing new states created sizable numbers of new minorities within their frontiers, thereby raising serious questions about their rights. If any of these governments persecuted those populations under one guise or another who had just been joined to their states, genuine threats could be posed to both domestic and international stability. "Nothing," acknowledged Wilson at a plenary meeting of the peace conference, "is more likely to disturb the peace of the world than the treatment which might in certain circumstances be meted out to minorities."[79] The realization thus very slowly began to emerge (although it would take the experience of another world war to be appreciated more fully) that violations of human rights at home ran perilous risks of jeopardizing world peace abroad. This could be seen in the large number and wide-ranging scope of proposals submitted to the conference by private citizens, nongovernmental organizations, and official representatives in the name of protecting the rights of minorities. They argued for the right of minorities for the preservation of their culture and ethnic character, the right to use one's own language, the right of equality for all before the law, and the right of freedom of worship and religion.[80] "All citizens," urged one proposal, "without distinction as to race, nationality, or religion, shall enjoy equal civil, religious, political, and national rights."[81] The most critical factor in all of these proposals, of course, was not their assertion of rights but rather their call for responsibilities. That is, all the proposals strongly urged members of the international community to cross that important intellectual and political threshold imposed by strict definitions of national sovereignty and now establish that they possessed a collective responsibility beyond their own borders to guarantee protection for the rights of minorities.

After lengthy and often difficult negotiations, the decisionmakers at Paris created an international legal foundation for such protection through a series of highly innovative agreements known collectively as the Minorities Treaties. This protective regime began with five separate but related treaties that required the beneficiaries of the peace settlement such as Poland, Czechoslovakia, Yugoslavia, Romania, and Greece, as a condition of their creation or expansion, to assume obligations toward citizens within their borders. Similar obligations were then imposed by provisions in the peace treaties on four of the vanquished states from the war, including Austria, Bulgaria, Hungary, and Turkey. Together, these treaty provisions (with others that would soon follow) required the signatory states "to assure full and complete protection of life and liberty" to all of their inhabitants "without distinction of birth, nationality, language, race, or religion." In addition, they provided that all nationals would be equal before the law and able to fully enjoy the same civil and political rights. Finally, they specified a number of guarantees for minorities, including the right to freely use their own language, and the right to establish charitable, religious, social, and economic institutions of their own choosing. Precise terminology, for example, provided specific protection for Jewish and Muslim minorities. Of particular importance in this regard, the signatories explicitly recognized in these treaties "that the stipulations in the foregoing articles, as far as they affect persons belonging to racial, religious, or linguistic minorities, *constitute obligations of international concern* and shall be placed under the guarantee of the League of Nations."[82]

Those who gathered at the peace conference devoted significant time discussing the human right to life as well. The memory of those millions recently killed and the never-ceasing reminders of those refugees and other victims of war and revolution who died

daily from starvation constantly brought the issue of death and life to the fore. Especially after the successful efforts of the Commission for Relief in Belgium to provide
basic food and care during the war, it appeared unconscionable for the world now to
simply turn its back on these suffering individuals and their families huddled together
in countless cities and villages on an unprecedented human scale. In addition, some
political leaders feared that continued death and starvation would only breed turmoil
and chaos. "It is impossible to discuss the peace of the world," warned Herbert Hoover
in discussing the fate of an estimated one hundred and twenty-five million people,
"until adequate measures have been taken to alleviate the fear of hunger."[83] The
arguments of the right of all people to have enought food to live, particularly when
combined with considerations of instability, proved to be sufficient to cause the victors
to announce that they would create a new administrative structure known as the inter-
allied Supreme Council of Supply and Relief, with Hoover serving as its director general, to distribute tons of food, clothing, and other supplies to those in need.[84] The U.S.
Congress subsequently passed the 1919 Relief Bill, creating the American Relief Administration and authorizing $100 million to be contributed on behalf of those who
suffered. This new international endeavor, declared those who envisioned and then
created these mechanisms for relief, resulted primarily out of a "high sense of human
duty and sympathy" and for the "humanitarian purpose of saving lives."[85]

The rights of labor also received significant attention during the Paris Peace Conference. Laborers had sacrificed much during World War I and, in order to maintain
war production strength and unity on the "home front," governments had made many
promises for the extension of social and economic rights once hostilities ceased. Between 1914 and 1919 all of the major British, French, Belgian, and American trade
unions, among others, had announced detailed plans designed to improve the international condition of workers and to allow them to share in the benefits of democracy for
which the war was presumably being waged. During the same time, no less than twelve
international conferences of workers were convened by trade unions, socialist organizations, or other reformist groups in places like Leeds, Stockholm, and Berne. Together,
they came to agree on several basic demands: advance social welfare through international action, establish conventions governing working conditions, include representatives of labor in the peace negotiations, and, interestingly enough, create a basic "charter" of fundamental rights.[86] The fires of revolution in Russia and Germany at precisely
this time added yet another dimension to the discussion, causing a number of the
leaders at Paris to fear what might happen if labor or class unrest spread into their own
countries due to an absence of construction action. As delegates from the American
Federation of Labor told U.S. President Wilson in no uncertain terms, "*something must
be done*" to secure workers' rights in the peace treaties and "*organized labor must have this
recognition*" or serious consequences would follow.[87] Once again, a variety of pressures
thus impinged on the peacemakers, and in response to mixed motives they created a
Commission on International Labor Legislation to draft appropriate proposals and
give them advice about how to proceed.

Comprised of labor representatives from nine different countries, this commission
met on thirty-five separate occasions and in its own words, attempted to address "the

sentiments of justice and humanity."[88] Toward this end, the delegates listened atten-
tively to a variety of appeals, including those ranging from moderate to radical worker's
organizations and the International Women's Council and the Conference of Allied
Women Suffragists. Despite the many differences expressed, however, all agreed on one
fundamental proposition: that peace and economic and social justice in the twentieth
century were indissolubly linked. They believed that without this kind of justice there
could never be lasting peace and that uniform justice could be secured only through
international action. Consequently, the commission boldly produced two important
documents. The first took the form of a highly unusual draft convention containing
provisions for the establishment of a permanent organization for international labor
legislation. Its purpose would be to promote "lasting peace through social justice" by
improving the conditions of working men — and women. Its members still would be
sovereign nation-states but they would be very uniquely represented by a tripartite
delegation composed of representatives of government, management, and labor sitting
side by side and enjoying equal status. The second document took the form of a
statement on general principles, often described as the Labor Charter, and began with
the declaration that "labor should not be regarded merely as a commodity or article of
commerce" but as human beings entitled to "a reasonable standard of life." Other
principles called for the adoption of an eight-hour day, abolition of child labor, inspection of factories, and a variety of rights, including the right of association for the
employed as well as for the employers and the right of women to receive equal pay for
equal work. Such provisions and proposals were regarded as truly radical measures and
marked significant legal and political departures from the past. Thus, it came as a
surprise to many when the peacemakers at Paris not only actually adopted the recommendations, but made them integral parts of the binding peace treaties themselves.[89]
In so doing, they agreed to establish for the first time a permanent body called the
International Labor Organization (ILO) with machinery devoted to labor issues well
beyond mere national borders and set the stage for much subsequent effort and action
on behalf of human rights.

As a result of these remarkable treaty provisions, many people, with justifiable reason,
eagerly anticipated a great extension of their rights — but not all. Others carefully
examined the terms and wondered just where they and their rights "came in." As they
saw it, all the innovative provisions up to this point appeared to have one major, un-
spoken qualification: they were confined almost entirely to the interests of the white,
male victors of World War I. Why, they asked poignantly, did the protection of equal
rights for minorities not extend to minority races and indigenous peoples in Asia,
Africa, the Middle East, Latin America, the United States and Canada, or islands of the
Pacific? Where were the tons of food, clothing, and other relief supplies for the refugees
and needy outside of Europe? Why was there so little mention in the treaties about the
rights of women? What were the advantages of international labor legislation to pre-
industrial societies of peasants barely surviving on the land? And, especially, where was
the solemn principle of the right to self-determination when it involved colonial possessions? Some, with biting criticism like Du Bois, attempted to attract attention to these
questions by organizing a Pan-African Congress to meet in Paris at exactly the same

time, demanding strict adherence to principles of human rights, and bringing "all pressure possible on the delegates at the Peace Table in the interest of the colored peoples of the United States and the world."[90] Others, such as Jane Addams and Jeannette Rankin from the United States and Gertrude Baer from Germany, held a simultaneous conference of their own, attracting delegates from sixteen countries. They were fearful that the terms of peace would be largely determined by "diplomats who are necessarily bound by the traditional conventions which have so long dominated all intercourse between nations." "Such men," they declared, "are seldom representative of modern social thought and the least responsive to changing ideas" who must be convinced of "the importance of certain interests which have hitherto been inarticulate in international affairs."[91] To accomplish this task, they formed the Women's International League for Peace and Freedom and vowed to exert continual pressure on governments. Still others critics continued to hold their tongues for just a little while longer, waiting with restraint to see whether their remaining aspirations might be realized by the negotiations involving the much-anticipated Covenant of the League of Nations.

The Covenant: Rights Proclaimed and Rights Rejected

Great hope and drama surrounded the creation of the League of Nations. For generations, some people had dreamed of a kind of international organization that might be able to prevent the anarchy caused by the extremes of sovereignty practiced by nation-states and to bring about a world of peace. The traumatic experiences of recent war and revolution provided even greater impetus to this vision, particularly when it was adopted and then actually advocated by Woodrow Wilson in one of his Fourteen Points. When the war ended, he promised, his efforts would be devoted toward ushering in a period of "new diplomacy" with lasting global peace and justice through the creation of "a general association of nations . . . formed under specific covenants for the purpose of affording mutual guarantees of political independence and territorial integrity to great and small states alike."[92] This vision inspired millions of people who greeted Wilson when he first arrived in Europe, hung portraits of him in their homes, held spontaneous parades in his honor, and hailed him as "the spokesman for world humanity."[93]

Wilson's insistence on the creation of this new international organization and his chairmanship of the Commission on the League of Nations, as well as the widespread public support that it engendered, made discussions on this subject an integral part of the entire peacemaking process. In fact, the delegates determined to make the governing Covenant of this body an actual legal component of the peace treaties themselves. They decided that this organization would be composed of the Assembly in which all member states would be represented, the Council in which the Great Powers would have permanent seats with four others assigned to different states for shorter periods, and a secretariat composed of civil servants whose loyalty would not be placed with their own nation-states but with the international organization itself. There was genuine hope that once established, the League and its sister bodies, such as the International Court of Justice, would make possible the achievement of peace and justice and the promotion of human rights through collective action. Thus, the negotiators in Paris quickly assigned the League responsibilities for guaranteeing the borders drawn in the name of the right of self-determination, enforcing the provisions of the Minority Treaties, assisting in the distribution of relief supplies, and providing financial support for the International Labor Organization, all of which marked significant new departures.

In attempting to address the relationship between justice and peace even further, the delegates created several other specific provisions within the Covenant relating to the evolving visions of human rights. All members of the League of Nations, for example, pledged themselves "to secure and maintain fair and humane conditions of labor for men, women, and children, both in their own countries and in all countries to which their commercial and industrial relations extend." They also agreed to support the enforcement of agreements relating to the traffic in women and children and in opium and other drugs, and to take steps for the international prevention and control of disease. They promised to secure and maintain the right of freedom of communication and transit. In addition, they committed themselves to expanding the original scope of humanitarian law by encouraging and promoting national Red Cross organizations in their efforts for the improvement of health, the prevention of disease, and in very broad terms, "the mitigation of suffering throughout the world." Finally, and in interesting language that perhaps raised more questions than it answered, they pledged themselves "to secure just treatment of the native inhabitants of territories under their control."[94]

Once these many determinations had been made and innovations created, the real question at this stage revolved around just how far the delegates would go in extending benefits and human rights to those thus far excluded. If the Covenant was truly designed to govern the operations of the new international organization responsible for world peace and justice for the great and the small alike, asked those who still waited in line for their turn, then should it not be as inclusive as possible? Should there not be more provisions, they queried, dealing with the right of women to be guaranteed equal rights or with the right of all to have freedom of religion? One draft proposal, for example, suggested that members of the League of Nations recognize "religious persecution and intolerance as fertile sources of war" and therefore agree to promise "that they will make no law prohibiting or interfering with the free exercise of religion, and that they will in no way discriminate, either in law or in fact, against those who practice any particular creed, religion, or belief."[95] Any number of delegates, including Wilson himself, strongly and personally supported this or other draft articles on the right to practice religion freely and the right to be protected against religious discrimination. Indeed, some even wanted to include provisions authorizing the League of Nations to use humanitarian intervention if necessary as a means of protecting these rights. But in the end, these proposals failed primarily because of the great fear that they might create a dangerous opportunity for opening an even more controversial issue of international human rights: racial equality.[96]

Perhaps no single issue at the Paris Peace Conference attracted more genuinely global attention than that of race. For the hundreds of millions of people around the world subjected to colonial exploitation and control, excluded by immigration restrictions, persecuted by prejudice, and victimized by the long-term effects of the legacy of slavery, racial discrimination was of fundamental importance.[97] Indeed, according to Du Bois, it presented "*the* problem of the twentieth century."[98] Even less passionate observers objectively described racial equality as "the burning question" and one "filled with explosives."[99] In the past, generations of people from around the world seeking to combat racial discrimination could be completely ignored due to the fact that they possessed little power or influence and thus could be excluded from having any voice at all during serious diplomatic deliberations. At the Paris Peace Conference this could no longer be tolerated, for too many global participants had been involved in World War I. Among the official victors was none other than Japan, the first nonwhite country ever to be invited to such a momentous gathering, and one fully determined to speak out as a victim of prejudice and to insist now on international recognition for the right of racial equality. "As to the terms of peace, Japan should insist on the equal international treatment of all races," wrote the newspaper *Asahi* in unsolicited advice to the delegation. "No other question is so inseparably and materially interwoven with the permanency of the world's peace as that of unfair and unjust treatment of a large majority of the world's population." "If the discrimination wall is to remain standing," it concluded, "then President Wilson will have spoken of peace, justice, and humanity in vain, and he would have proved after all only a hypocrite."[100]

The Japanese delegation of Kimmochi Saiongi and Nobuaki Makino, and their many supporters in other countries, ran into precisely this formidable wall of racial discrimination, for the powerful in Paris were largely prejudiced whites. They sought a single clause in the Covenant of the League of Nations supporting the principle of the right of all to racial equality, but met with immediate and intransigent opposition. Woodrow Wilson, who had a record of supporting immigration exclusion against the "Yellow Peril" abroad and racial segregation within the United States, did all that he could to thwart their efforts.[101] The British foreign secretary expressed the opinion that he simply did not believe that all men were created equal and most certainly "not that a man in Central Africa was created equal to a European."[102] The Australian prime minister represented a country that continued to persecute Aborigines and had personally campaigned on a platform that included the statement: "Our chief plank is, of course, White Australia. There's no compromise about *that*." Moreover, he announced that he "would not deviate an inch" from his position, and declared that if the Covenant contained a provision on racial equality his country would refuse to join the League of Nations itself.[103] New Zealand's prime minister expressed similar attitudes, receiving support from newspapers such as the *Otago Witness* printing the opinion that "though the American Declaration of Independence begins by asserting all men are born equal in the sight of God, it makes no mention of niggers and Japanese."[104]

Statements such as these prompted immediate and angry reactions, especially among those who had been hailed as "close allies" or "invaluable soldiers" during the recent war. Thirty-seven different Japanese NGOs devoted to rights mobilized a mass meeting in Tokyo and collectively organized the Association for the Equality of Races, declaring that any perpetuation of racial discrimination would not only strike against the great principles of liberty and equality but would endanger all future international relations. "If it is allowed to remain," asserted their joint statement, "all the alliances and treaties will only be castles of sand, and the general peace of the world will not be secured."[105] The Chinese delegate, Wellington Koo, announced that he and the people of China were "profoundly interested" in this question of human rights and "in full sympathy" with the movement to secure racial equality.[106] Similar expressions came from throughout the colonial world elsewhere in Asia, Africa, and Latin America who viewed prejudice of race as being at the core of their plight, and who listened in horror as they heard many of the decisionmakers at the Paris Peace Conference refer to them as "primitive" and "racially inferior" peoples, "savage tribes," and too "backward" for self-government. Within the United States, the National Association for the Advancement of Colored People publicly and pointedly asked Wilson, with reference to his famous statement about saving the world: "Mr. President, why not make America safe for democracy?"[107]

Great global attention thus was focused on the meeting of the Commission on the League of Nations, chaired by Wilson himself, designed to resolve this issue of human rights. Wilson had desperately hoped to avoid taking any vote at all on this issue, even if the Japanese were willing to water down their original proposal. On this matter he knew his own heart and believed that the U.S. Senate would never ratify a treaty if it contained any article about racial equality. But the Japanese and their supporters insisted, arguing that the larger principle was too important to remain unsettled or left out of the Covenant. He therefore reluctantly and nervously called for a vote. The final tabulation indicated eleven out of seventeen in favor of a provision in the Covenant on racial equality — a clear majority. Confronted with this result, Wilson suddenly declared from the chair that the proposal had failed. It could not be adopted, he announced without warning, because it had been unable to secure the unanimous approval of the entire commission. This decision shocked the majority of delegates, for they knew perfectly well that no such thing as a unanimity "rule" existed at all. The French legal expert quickly brought this to the attention of the assembled, now in an uproar, and stated that a majority had just voted in support of the principle of racial equality. Wilson was forced to admit this fact, but said that in this particular case there simply were "too serious objections on the part of some of us" to have it inserted into the Covenant.[108] He therefore refused to acknowledge any additional challenges and adamantly declared the debate to be over.

This unilateral and shocking decision by such a presumed champion of human rights immediately produced storms of international reaction and protest. Newspapers blared headlines announcing: "Peace Delegates Beat Japan's Proposal for Racial Equality."[109] In the United States, Du Bois angrily denounced Wilson as blatantly violating the principles for which the war had been fought and turning his back on promises made to black soldiers. Riots broke out in a number of cities throughout the country, including the nation's own capital of Washington, D.C., accompanied by lynchings, burnings, and destruction marking what some described as nothing short of a "race war."[110] Other critics elsewhere lashed out at what the *Asahi* and the *Nichinichi* in Japan called "the paralyzed conscience" and hypocrisy of the "so-called civilized world" of the Anglo-Saxons, and decided to create their own League for the Abolition of Race Discrimination.[111] "The root of [the problem] lies in the perverted feeling of racial superiority entertained by the whites," reflected one highly experienced diplomat from Asia. "If things are allowed to proceed in the present way, there is every likelihood that the peace of the world will be endangered. It, therefore, behooves all well-wishers of mankind to exert their utmost to remove their gross injustice immediately."[112]

Once this decision about racial equality was made, it sealed the fate of those who thought that the right of self-determination solemnly delineated elsewhere in the peace treaties also might be applied to them. If this right could be authorized for those in Eastern Europe, they had assumed, then surely it would be granted for those who suffered even worse from oppression and exploitation in the colonies. Moreover, they too had sacrificed in the war and been given the promise by Wilson himself that "a free, open-minded, and absolutely impartial adjustment of all colonial claims" would take place in which "the interests of the populations concerned must have equal weight" with those of the imperial powers.[113] These hopes now were crushed. The decision makers at Paris determined that the right of self-determination might be applied to those living in Europe, but most certainly not to people elsewhere. When Wellington Koo asked at an early stage about the Western powers using this opportune time to end their practice of extraterritoriality or special privileges in China, he received the brusque reply that it "was out of the question."[114] Now the British, French, Italians, Americans, Belgians, and Japanese all revealed that they were not at all eager to release their grip on their imperial possessions. In fact, the treaties disclosed that they used their victory in the war, despite their many promises, to actually extend their power at the expense of others. The British and the French carved up Arab land in the Middle East formerly belonging to the Ottoman Empire, partitioning Palestine, Lebanon, Syria, Transjordan, Iraq, and Persian Gulf territories between them and then took former German possessions in Tanganyika (now Tanzania), the Cameroons, and Togo. Not to be outdone, the Belgians extended their control into Ruanda-Urundi (now Rwanda and Burundi) and the Italians seized a sphere of influence in western Turkey. The South Africans took control of former German colonial possessions in South-West Africa. The Japanese extended their influence on the Shandong peninsula in China and in Manchuria, and took over Pacific islands north of the equator formerly controlled by Germany. The Australians and New Zealanders grabbed what they could in the South Pacific. In the event that all this taking and trading appeared too crass, the powers called their new acquisitions "mandates" rather than possessions, promising to care for "the well-being and development" of the inhabitants, but declaring that they would govern until such time as these "backward" peoples not yet ready for self-government were "able to stand on their own feet in the strenuous conditions of the modern world."[115] Confided one diplomat in Paris: "However fervid might be our indignation regarding Italian claims to Dalmatia and the Dodecanese, it could be cooled by reference, not to Cyprus only, but to Ireland, Egypt, and India. We had accepted a system for others which, when it came to practice, we should refuse to apply to ourselves."[116]

Once these details of the peace treaties and Covenant of the League of Nations became known, widespread demonstrations broke out throughout the world among those who saw their wartime service unreciprocated and promises dishonored. Oppressed peoples perceived nothing but continued racial prejudice and new schemes for continued control, and described the mandate system as "the crudity of conquest draped in the veil of morality," "moral wrapping paper," and mere "fig leaves" designed to conceal the nakedness of imperialism.[117] The Destour Party formed immediately in Tunisia to organize for action that might lead to independence from France. Riots broke out in Egypt and Palestine against the British, and demonstrations erupted in Korea against the Japanese in the name of human rights. Ho Chi Minh realized that for his people in Indochina these decisions in Paris indicated the beginning of what would be called "the bright shining lie": that the right of self-determination applied only to whites—"not to the brown and the yellow peoples of Asia or to the blacks of Africa."[118] In India, where more than one million troops and noncombatants served in the allied war effort, those who wanted their freedom launched massive protests against new repressive measures imposed by the colonial government, igniting the April 1919 massacre at Amritsar when British troops opened fire and killed four hundred unarmed and unprotected civilians. Within three weeks, mass riots against these treaties and the loss of territory they conferred to the Japanese erupted in China as well, beginning first with students in Tiananmen Square and then spreading throughout the country, igniting what came to be called the May Fourth Movement. Among the most significant demands of those who protested, in the words of one of the movement's intellectual founders, Chen Duxiu, were two: "equality and human rights."[119]

*   *   *

When the peace conference finally ended and the delegates returned home to their respective nations still trying to recover from world war and revolutions, those who had championed the cause of international human rights found cause for both deep disappointment and genuine celebration. The many exaggerated expectations, often encouraged by political leaders themselves, that somehow all the sacrifices made in wartime would be rewarded and thereby suddenly transform the nature of rights around the globe did not materialize. And those who believed that the sheer righteousness of their cause would be sufficient to bring about justice came to realize something of the power of vested interests, resistance, revenge, greed, prejudice, and national sovereignty. According to the terms of the peace treaties and the Covenant of the League of Nations, the standards and obligations to protect human rights did not fall on all equally, the benefits did not extend universally to everyone, the enforcement provisions remained uncertain, and the final power of action continued to reside in the hands of sovereign nation-states who could chose to join the new organization or not. As the Ligue des Droits de l'Homme noted with concern, the final settlement resulted from the decisions made by governments rather than peoples.[120] On the other hand, these same legal instruments also marked unparalleled achievements. Never before in history had a peace conference produced so many treaties or programs with so many provisions about the right of self-determination, the right of minorities to be protected, the right to enjoy life by receiving relief assistance, and the rights of laboring classes, or produced an international organization formally charged with guaranteeing these particular rights. Never before had the global community made such a direct connection between peace and justice, or been willing to acknowledge such extensive responsibilities. For the beneficiaries, these provisions thus held out an extraordinary promise that the future would be far different from the past. For the excluded, they provoked a realization of the necessity to exert continual pressure and a determination never to give up until they realized their vision. In both cases, however, there appeared to be a realization that as the world was about to embark on a new era of presumed peace, finding a solution to these problems of international human rights now marked, in the words of one diplomat, opportunities and challenges and ultimately "the responsibility of twentieth century diplomacy."[121]

Chapter 4
Opportunities and Challenges

Visions and Rights Between the Wars

> Considering that at the present moment these rights might be so formulated as to ensure that every inhabitant of a State should have the right to the full and entire protection of his life and liberty, and that all the citizens of a State should be equal before the law and should enjoy the same civil and political rights, without distinction of race, language, or religion; Expresses the hope that a world convention may be drawn up under the auspices of the League of Nations, ensuring the protection and respect of such rights.
> — Delegation to the League of Nations from Haiti

Those who survived in the aftermath of a world war, revolutions, and an international conference designed to create lasting peace had good reasons for both deep anxiety and hopeful optimism. The all too recent experience of devastation, massive deaths and wounds, monumental human suffering, and sense of betrayal provided an unmistakably clear warning about what the future might hold. If the forces of extreme nationalism, state power over its citizens, ideological intolerance and prejudice, and modern technology in the service of war or persecution as recently revealed were ever unleashed again, then the prospects for peace, justice, and the extension of human rights appeared limited indeed. As a returning soldier in Erich Maria Remarque's *All Quiet on the Western Front* comments:

I am young, I am twenty years old; yet I know nothing of life but despair, death, fear, and fatuous superficiality cast over an abyss of sorrow. I see how peoples are set against one another, and in silence, unknowingly, foolishly, obediently, innocently slay one another. I see that the keenest brains in the world invent weapons and words to make it yet more refined and enduring. And all men of my age, here and over there, throughout the whole world, see these things.

"What will happen afterwards?" he asks, "And what shall come out of us?"[1] Not everyone, of course, approached the future with such overwhelming depression, and instead considered their recent experiences as a prod for humanity to redeem itself and as a chance for hope. For them, the war, revolutions, and peace conference revealed the capacity to dream dreams and see visions in desperate times, ultimately create treaties with provisions about human rights, and even establish an innovative international organization to guide the world into a better future. These sharply contrasting perspectives now came to influence the course of events, for as people around the globe moved into the period between the wars they would witness both opportunities and challenges in the evolution of international human rights.

A Flourishing of Visions

One of the most striking features of the period that began with this new era of peace was a dramatic increase in the number and scope of open and often very frank discussions focused on international human rights. Motivated both by the fear of accomplishing nothing and thus failing in the face of opposing forces and by the hope of positively advancing the cause of rights, and encouraged by such developments as the establishment of the new League of Nations with its promise of a better future, visions of rights at this time began to flourish. A wide variety of publicists and activists around the world suddenly began to make particularly significant contributions as individuals and as NGOs to these visions. Indeed, in the words of one perceptive observer, "the idea of human rights arose as a wave."[2]

Visions of international human rights always have required the capacity to consider responsibilities extending beyond national borders and to visualize the world as a whole. In this regard, the time between the wars marked a significant development. The global dimensions of World War I and the experiences of its participants who had traveled far from their own shores to assist others side by side as allies, for example, made an indelible impression that lasted long after the fighting ceased. Advances in communication and transportation technology further contributed to this perspective by inexorably bringing the people and places of the globe, heretofore far removed from each other, much closer together. The flow of goods, services, and capital from one continent to another with increased levels of international trade did much the same. Moreover, the creation of the League of Nations with responsibilities for the world as a whole enhanced this view even more, prompting numerous expressions about the "international idea," a "new world order" and "internationalism."[3] As one commentator noted, all this "implies a new international attitude: the attitude of sacrifice as the earnest of its reality, the attitude of universalism as the pledge of its continuity."[4]

For many thoughtful women and men, a vital part of this enhanced international perspective centered on human rights. They viewed the rights of one person as related to the rights of others, irrespective of place, and attempted to use this period as an opportunity to expand their visions of human rights to encompass the world. Rather than being deterred by the actions (or inactions) of their own governments, they created new NGOs to promote the cause of rights. The formation immediately after the war of the Women's International League for Peace and Freedom (WILPF) provides but one example. In the words of Jane Addams, one of its founders, the league sought "to inaugurate a new type of international life in the world" and thereby advance "the hopes of mankind."[5] To accomplish this goal, its members created an organization with an international headquarters in Geneva and national sections around the globe ranging from Mexico and Peru, from Japan to New Zealand, and from Sweden to the United States. Together they worked diligently to advance peace and social justice, reduce armaments, provide food and relief assistance, advocate gender equality, encourage educational opportunities, decrease racial and class discrimination, promote internationalism over nationalism, and champion basic human rights. "They all alike had come to realize," said Addams, "that every crusade, every beginning of social change, must start from small numbers of people convinced of the righteousness of a cause."[6]

Such convictions certainly motivated those who worked on behalf of women's rights, as did the achievements gained during these years. In the two years of 1919 and 1920, for example, women secured the right to vote in Germany, Austria, the Netherlands, Luxembourg, Czechoslovakia, Poland, and Canada. The passage of the Nineteenth Amendment to the Constitution in 1920 finally enfranchised twenty-six million women of voting age within the United States. Three years later, women introduced for the first time the proposed Equal Rights Amendment which states that "Equality of rights under the law shall not be denied or abridged by the United States or any State on account of sex."[7] These accomplishments inspired others in turn, especially those without suffrage like Fusae Ichikawa in Japan, who organized the Fusen Kakutoku Domei (Women's Suffrage League) that issued a manifesto demanding "the right to take part in politics, and cooperate with one another regardless of any political, religious, and other differences we may have."[8] Similar women's organizations and movements emerged in Turkey, Iran, India, Ceylon (now Sri Lanka), Indonesia, the Philippines, China, Korea, and Vietnam, many of whom were encouraged when Kemal Atatürk publicly asserted from a Muslim country:

Let us be frank: society is made of women as well as men. If one grants all the rights to progress to the one and no rights at all to the other, what happens? Is it possible that one half of the population is in chains for the other half to reach the skies? Progress is possible only through common effort.[9]

New organizations such as the Women's International League for Peace and Freedom, the International Woman Suffrage Alliance, the International Council of Women, and the International Alliance of Women all simultaneously emphasized the necessity that equal rights of gender be extended around the world and witnessed the successful extension of the right to vote in one form or another for women in Burma, Ecuador, Greece, Hungary, Mexico, Mongolia, and Sweden.[10] During the Fifth Conference of the American Republics in Santiago, Chile, in 1923 the delegates agreed to sponsor studies of how constitutional and legal limitations imposed on women could be abolished and of how they might achieve full civil and political rights, and in 1928 at their next conference in Havana, Cuba, established the Inter-American Commission on Women for just this purpose.[11] Moreover, these were the years when Margaret Sanger of the United States, Ellen Key of Sweden, and Shizue Ishimoto of Japan, among others, launched their campaign for women's rights by speaking openly and often in the face of great opposition, providing contraceptive information to a mass audience for the first time in human history, and asserting the rights of reproduction for women wherever they might be.[12]

At exactly the same time as these efforts, other visionaries pushed forward to create additional NGOs specifically devoted toward advancing the cause of international human rights. The prestigious Institut de Droit International, to illustrate, as early as 1921 began to study the possibility of issuing a declaration on behalf of the rights of all people.[13] In addition, under the leadership of the courageous Victor Basch, the French Ligue pour la Défense des Droits de l'Homme quickly established contact with former German enemies immediately after the war to seek reconciliation. Among those was Carl von Ossietsky, who served as the chair of the recently formed Deutsche Liga für Menschenrechte and who would be awarded a Nobel Peace Prize, only to later die at the hands of the Nazis. They took the initiative to bring fourteen other national human rights leagues and leaders into contact, including Miguel de Unamuno who founded and chaired the Spanish organization, the Italian human rights leader Giacomo Mateotti who within several years would be assassinated for his resistance against Benito Mussolini and the Fascists, and a representative from China. Together they established in 1922 the Fédération Internationale des Droits de l'Homme (FIDH), specifically designed to advance human rights across borders around the world. Its program of action entailed creating new national leagues in those countries where they did not exist, developing a central bureau of information and assistance, promoting social justice, defending all varieties of human rights, including those of indigenous peoples under colonial domination, and engaging in a campaign to pressure the League of Nations into enlarging its activities in the area of international human rights. In addition, the organization actively began to advocate for the first time the idea of a world declaration of human rights for all people.[14]

Advocates for human rights who viewed themselves as parts of this larger and dynamic international movement emerged in a myriad of diverse places during these years. In Asia, for example, a number of Chinese intellectuals and activists found themselves increasingly influenced by journals appearing with titles such as *New China*, *New Youth*, and *New Dawn*, and joining organizations devoted to political and social change. Some enthusiastically joined the liberal and democratically oriented China League for Civil Rights founded by Cai Yuanpei and Lu Xun. Others decided to follow the much more revolutionary Chinese Communist Party, finding inspiration in the early prediction of its leader Mao Zedong declaring: "In a very short time . . . several hundred million peasants will rise like a mighty storm, like a hurricane, a force so swift and violent that no power, however great, will be able to hold it back. . . . They will sweep all the imperialists, warlords, corrupt officials, local tyrants, and evil gentry into their graves."[15] At the same time the Japanese experienced a blossoming of parliamentary government and free expression such as had never been known before. The dramatic 1925 electoral law created universal adult male suffrage, thereby increasingly the electorate from three million to more than twelve million with a single stroke and initiating even more discussion about the nature and extent of rights.[16] From Latin America, the Chilean jurist Alejandro Alvarez continued to work and write on behalf of international human rights through his extensive publications, participation in the League of Nations, and work with such organizations as the Institute of International Law, the American Institute of International Law, and the Carnegie Endowment for International Peace.[17]

Elsewhere in the world the movement for rights became part and parcel of efforts to gain independence from colonial rule. Gandhi increased his activities of civil disobedience in India to secure the right of self-determination by organizing successful strikes and protests, calling on his oppressors to be faithful to their own professed religious principles, and developing his belief in the redemptive power of love to convert even brutal opponents by its *satyagraha*, or "soul force." He explicitly warned the British in *Hind Swarāj* (Indian Home Rule) that he would use passive resistance as a deliberate method "of securing rights."[18] In Indonesia, Sukarno (who would eventually become the first president of his country) led a loose federation of various groups united behind the common theme of securing independence from the Dutch. A similar relationship developed in Vietnam where Ho Chi Minh (who would become the leader of his nation) and his Communist Party quickly realized the power to be gained by mobilizing revolutionaries and others who worked for the rights of peasants and workers and women's rights with those seeking freedom from the French.[19] The leaders of the Soviet Union also saw vast opportunities in such potent combinations of the discontent and exploited, and through the Third (Communist) International, or Comintern, actively encouraged those trying to unite revolution with national liberation. At the same time, representatives from Nigeria, Sierra Leone, Gambia, and the Gold Coast (now Ghana), met in Accra during the 1920s and founded the National Congress of British West Africa to assist each other in promoting the vision of self-determination. Activists in the French colonies formed an international union for exactly the same purpose. In addition, this vibrant period marked the beginning of the political education of a number of those who would eventually lead their countries into independence throughout Africa, including Nnamdi Azikiwe in Nigeria, Kwame Nkrumah in the Gold Coast, Jomo Kenyatta in Kenya, Kenneth Kaunda of Zambia, and Habib Bourguiba in Tunisia. Declared the latter in making a connection between self-determination and other human rights: "The Tunisia we mean to liberate will not be a Tunisia for Muslim, for Jew, or for Christian. It will be a Tunisia for all, without distinction of religion or race, who wish to have it as their country and to live in it under the protection of just laws."[20]

Assertions of the right to political independence often were accompanied by those relating to the right to be free from discrimination. No issue raised more complications, for not only was race closely tied to class, but all too intimately related to imperial domination and exploitation in the colonies and policies of immigration exclusion (with their insistence on the prerogatives of national sovereignty) based on racial prejudice. It is thus not surprising at all that any discussions of human rights during the years between the wars would entail many visions of racial equality, actively pressed by the emergence of additional NGOs. In Asia, for example, the Japanese formed the League for the Abolition of Race Discrimination and the newly created Pan-Asian Society in China focused on the issue of race and through its publication entitled *Ta Ya* which explicitly addressed itself to the "1,000 million souls of Asia" who suffered "from the oppression of the white races of Europe and America."[21] The organization of larger Pan-Asian conferences beyond national borders emphasized this theme of racial discrimination even further and demanded that those basic human rights so discussed in the West be extended to Asians. Representatives from Japan, China, India, the Philippines, East Indies, the Malay states, Egypt, and Turkey gathered in 1925 to establish what they called the "Colored International" to support "the abolition of racial discrimination in the immigration policies of certain white nations, and to combat the assumption of social and ethnological superiority by the white races."[22] At the same time, delegates from around the Pacific basin created the Institute of Pacific Relations to address common problems, especially those of race. Walter Nash, who led the New Zealand delegation to the Institute (and who eventually came to be such an outspoken advocate for human rights in the International Labor Organization and in the formative years of the United Nations), returned from the 1927 meeting so convinced of the critical nature of racial prejudice that he took a highly unpopular stand by publicly urging his countrymen to "look behind the mask of race and color and nation" and extend equal rights to all.[23]

Demands for racial equality and the right of nondiscrimination came from other sources as well. Those who created the Ligue Universelle pour la Défense de la Race Noire, as they stated in the name of the organization itself, dedicated themselves to protect the rights of those discriminated against because of the color of their skin wherever they might be. Intellectuals such as Jean Price-Mars and Aimé Césaire of Haiti and Léopold Senghor of Senegal adopted the same cause under an even larger banner of what they called "Négritude," developing journals such as *L'Etudiant Noir* and *La Revue du Monde Noir* to give expression to their visions. W.E.B. Du Bois and his supporters instituted the Pan-African Association, organized Pan-African conferences, and issued what they called their "Declaration to the World" demanding "the absolute equality of races" as the ultimate fulfillment of human liberty around the globe — "in Asia, in Africa, America, and the isles of the sea."[24] More radical elements followed Marcus Garvey, a native of Jamaica who had worked for the *African Times and Orient Review* in London, moved to Harlem in New York City, and founded the Universal Negro Improvement Association as a vehicle for public agitation. His International Conventions of the Negro Peoples of the World brought delegates from around the globe, and his newspaper *The Negro World* appeared in English, French, and Spanish and was distributed over several continents until banned by many colonial governments. "Up, you mighty Race!" Garvey exhorted his followers. "Now we have started to speak and I am only the forerunner of an awakened Africa that shall never go back to sleep."[25]

Visionaries and champions of human rights emerged in many other different places and with other organizations as well. In fact, a remarkable array of individuals with considerable international experience became publicists and activists for human rights during these years. These included Alejandro Alvarez, who from Chile already had written about the need for future international law to provide for rights of the individual; André Mandelstam, the diplomat once appointed head of the legal office of the Russian Ministry of Foreign Affairs prior to the Bolsheviks; Antoine Frangulis, the Greek jurist and diplomat who at an early stage had represented his country at the League of Nations; Eduard Beneš, the Czech leader who would become president of his country; and Colonel Edward House, the diplomatic advisor to Woodrow Wilson in the United States. Together, and along with others, they formed in 1926 the Académie

Diplomatique Internationale (ADI) with its headquarters in Paris, and almost immediately set up a commission to study the question of international protection of human rights. With active participation by Frangulis and Mandelstam, this commission diligently began its work by carefully analyzing the rights covered by the obligations delineated in the Minorities Treaties. After thorough study, the members concluded that some of these provisions should now serve as a more broadly based, generalized, and extended model for others. They thus recommended that all inhabitants of all states should have the right to receive full and complete protection of life and liberty, and that all nationals of a state obtain equality before the law and the enjoyment of the same civil and political rights without distinction as to race, language, or religion. The academy as a whole accepted this recommendation in 1928 and in a formal resolution called for a worldwide convention brought about under the auspices of the League of Nations that would ensure the protection and the respect for these basic human rights.[26]

Simultaneous with these efforts, the Institut de Droit International invested significant time and energy in considering a draft text of an statement envisioning the role that human rights should play in the global community of the future. Mandelstam, who had been named as the rapporteur of the organization's Commission for the International Protection of the Rights of Man and Citizen and of Minorities, took the initiative for this effort. With determination and conviction he pushed for extensive measures and argued strongly among his colleagues for a three-step strategy of a declaration, a convention, and then sanctions. After much lively discussion over the course of nearly eight years, and consistent with its position that international law encompassed more than just the relationships between states, its illustrious members formally adopted during their 1929 plenary session what they boldly called the Declaration of the International Rights of Man. The preamble began by asserting that "the juridical conscience of the civilized world demands the recognition for the individual of rights preserved from all infringement on the part of the state," declaring that "it is essential to extend international recognition of the rights of man to the entire world." Articles within the text that followed defined the duties of each state, as members of the international community, and called on them to protect a number of rights, including the equal rights of every individual to life, liberty, and property "without distinction of nationality, sex, race, language, or religion." By formally adopting such language and taking this public stand for the rights of individuals in international law, the Institute saw itself as speaking out on behalf of humanity as a whole, courageously challenging the absolute sanctity of the doctrine of national sovereignty, and thereby marking a significant point of departure for a new era of international human rights.[27]

This Declaration of the International Rights of Man inspired and emboldened other individuals to speak out and write in the name of human rights, especially those who themselves had suffered at the hands of governments or been forced into exile due to political upheaval. Boris Mirkine-Guetzévitch, a former Russian professor of international law and a victim of the Bolsheviks, for example, edited a collection of the human rights provisions in the constitutions of all countries, and then published a work on the new trends in creating declarations of human rights.[28] Antoine Frangulis, who had fled from the Greek military dictatorship, often thrust himself into highly public debates over the contest between human rights and national sovereignty. André Mandelstam in particular, with his intense and scholarly eyes looking out through wire-rimmed glasses, wrote, taught, and worked unceasingly in exile from his native Russia. His prolific publication of substantial articles in both French and German in leading journals of international and comparative law, and a 1931 book entitled *Les Droits internationaux de l'Homme*, all sought to analyze recent developments, consider new opportunities, stir the conscience, and share an expansive vision of international human rights.[29] He then introduced a course on human rights at the Institut Universitaire des Hautes Études Internationales in Geneva and taught a special seminar on the international protection of human rights at the Académie de Droit International at The Hague. In addition, he indefatigably labored to involve NGOs such as the Institut de Droit International, the Académie Diplomatique Internationale, the Fédération International des Droits de l'Homme, and the International Institute of Public Law in matters relating to the protection of human rights around the world.[30]

The outbreak and then extension of the Great Depression that came to encompass much of the world also generated a new increase and intensity in visions of rights. As misery and suffering spread first across the industrialized West and then gradually to seemingly far-removed locations around the globe, so too did calls for human rights relating to class, particularly social and economic rights. Many moderates and reformers looked for answers in visions that entailed more effective welfare services provided to the needy by religious or charitable groups, NGOs, states, or the League of Nations itself. Others sought to secure rights to food, housing, jobs, and medical care through labor and socialist political parties or through the International Labor Organization and International Federation of Trade Unions to advance the cause of rights for workers. Some turned to more aggressive labor unions, organizing discontented workers into more militant action, calling for general strikes, and demanding an extension of rights to alleviate human suffering. And, with ominous signs of storm clouds rising in the future, still others began to turn toward extremes like the Third (Communist) International, militarism, or even emerging fascist parties, announcing that rights (at least for certain select groups) could be secured only through violence and revolution. Regardless of the wide variety of proposed solutions and different interpretations of human rights, however, the harsh experience of the Depression dramatically increased international discussion of social and economic rights as never before.

All these developments contributed tributaries into a ever-growing river of interest in and concern over human rights around the world, and together encouraged activists not to remain passive and try to push even further. Members of the International Union of Associations for the League of Nations, for example, mobilized their non-governmental organization in assisting and coordinating the activities of various national associations of citizen groups to provide support for and to exert pressure on the League of Nations to do more. Toward this end, André Mandelstam urged the International Union to draw the attention of the League of Nations to the desirability of convening a conference of all states for the elaboration of a general convention for the international protection of human rights. This proposal generated highly animated discussions between those who argued on behalf of human rights irrespective of the dangers and those who worried that if every infringement of rights could constitute a problem under international law, then any violation inside a state might implicate the League of Nations itself. In the end, a revised text of a resolution abandoned the idea of such a conference for the moment, but charged a special committee in 1933 to examine on what basis a draft convention on international guarantees for human rights might be established. This committee included, among others, Mandelstam, Jacques Dumas of France, and Henri Rolin of Belgium (who later as a delegate to the 1945 San Francisco Conference insisted on opening the United Nations Charter with the words, "We the peoples," and became in 1968 the president of the European Court of Human Rights). The same resolution of the International Union also declared that the principle of legal equality between people as well as between states required a global acceptance of responsibility for protecting human rights, including the use of humanitarian intervention if necessary.[31]

Other groups also sought to add their collective voices and perspectives to this flourishing of visions for international human rights generated by both hope and fear. The Fédération Internationale des Droits de l'Homme with the support of its affiliates around the world, for example, formally passed a resolution endorsing the principles set forth in the Institut de Droit International's Declaration of the International Rights of Man.[32] This, in turn, inspired the French Ligue pour la Défense des Droits de l'Homme, which viewed itself as an organization designed to hold a visionary ideal aloft and to pressure governments on behalf of human rights, to take more determined action. Consequently, the Ligue and its members (one of whom was René Cassin who later would participate in drafting the 1948 Universal Declaration of Human Rights) held a special conference at Dijon and produced its own Complement to the Declaration of the Rights of Man and of the Citizen, consisting of a preamble and fourteen specific articles relating to human rights. Perhaps not surprising given the harsh realities and human suffering in poverty and unemployment during the Depression, this document addressed a number of more radical social and economic rights than did previous statements. Nevertheless, its very first article secured widespread support from all of those who had visions of global human rights at this time by reading: "The international protection of human rights must be universally organized and guaranteed in such a manner that no state can deny the exercise of these rights to any human being living on its territory."[33]

Almost all of these visions of international human rights came from individuals acting on their own or from NGOs. But on some occasions, governments sought to make their own contributions to as well. Those from Latin America, for example, demonstrated a particular interest in formulating and articulating visions of rights. Meeting in a series of Inter-American Conferences during the interwar years, they sought to explore definitions of individual rights beyond national settings and ways in which those rights might be protected regionally and internationally. In this regard, they created the Inter-American Commission on Women to focus on women's rights, and to begin addressing the rights of indigenous peoples, workers, and immigrants. Representatives adopted the "Lima Declaration in Favor of Women's Rights" calling for political treatment, the enjoyment of civil status, and full protection in and opportunities of employment on the basis of equality with men. They then went on to approve a more broadly based statement entitled "Defense of Human Rights" expressing the hope that the rights of men and women alike would be respected throughout the world whenever conflict arose.[34] During these years the Latin Americans, among others, also found themselves turning to the opportunities provided by the new League of Nations.

Opportunities for New Departures

Much of this flourishing of visions, of course, can be attributed to the emergence of the League of Nations, described as "the great innovation of the peace."[35] Created in the wake of devastating war and revolutions, this new international organization generated extraordinary expectations among millions of people around the world. It held out the promise of a "new diplomacy," a fresh beginning in international politics, a chance to correct whatever flaws might exist in the Versailles settlement, an opportunity for global approaches to common problems, a prospect to advance the cause of peace and justice, and a strong possibility of promoting human rights. A sense of all these hopes in the future could be seen and heard when the delegates first assembled with excitement at Geneva in 1920. They described the event as being of "unprecedented greatness," as presenting a "unique opportunity," as one that "will have a permanent influence on the evolution of the nations," and as presenting "the divine seed of future harvests, the witness of the world to be."[36] "Let us dedicate ourselves to humanity," declared another with earnestness. "Working together, let us seek to prepare and step by step to achieve the reign, so long awaited, of international morality and human rights."[37]

In attempting to realize these visions, the League of Nations immediately found itself possessing a remarkable array of opportunities for new departures. Specific provisions within the Covenant and the peace settlements assigned to this newly created international organization a wide variety of highly unusual responsibilities in several different areas of human rights. Suddenly the League was expected to guarantee the provisions of a whole series of new Minorities Treaties regarding nondiscrimination and equal protection in civil and political rights. It became charged with protecting the right of self-determination and political independence of all of its members and for fulfilling its "sacred trust of civilization" to administer a new mandate system of non-self-governing territories who wanted to become independent. The Covenant required this body to create a Permanent Court of International Justice, and to encourage and promote the establishment and cooperation of Red Cross organizations for "the improvement of health, the prevention of disease, and the mitigation of suffering throughout the world." Moreover, it assigned to members of the organization responsibilities for securing "fair and humane" working conditions, obtaining "just treatment" for the native inhabitants under their control, dealing with international traffic in women and children and dangerous drugs, and maintaining freedom of communication and transit.[38] What all of this would mean in actual practice, of course, was completely unknown as the League set about in the absence of experience and with few real guidelines or road maps to meet these broadly generalized responsibilities, begin its work, and explore both the possibilities and the limits of politics and diplomacy that lay ahead.

   Among the very first efforts made in this regard were those involved in first creating, and then activating, the International Labor Organization. Designed to provide global attention to the rights of workers in the name "of justice and humanity" and supported by funds from the League of Nations, this body began its work with energy and determination. Under the direction of Albert Thomas, the dynamic and highly respected French Socialist,[39] the organization set out with an ambitious and active program of creating an International Labor Office staffed by civil servants, conducting investigations of working conditions, assembling statistical information, issuing publications such as the *International Labour Review*, considering complaints, organizing international conferences, coordinating contact between national labor unions, promoting social justice, and especially drafting international treaties on labor matters. Within just the first two years of the organization, for example, more than thirty different international agreements of one kind or another were prepared. By 1933, the International Labor Organization had drafted and submitted for ratification to governments an extraordinary forty separate and often lengthy conventions. These addressed an extremely wide array of issues, including limits on the hours of work, maternity leave, unemployment, conditions of labor at night for women and children, equality of treatment in workers' compensation, minimum age at sea, weekly rest, forced or compulsory labor, prohibition of dangerous chemicals, sickness insurance in industry and agriculture, medical examinations, and the right of association. For those involved in creating such international treaties for the very first time, it appeared entirely appropriate to conclude that the International Labor Organization clearly represented an integral part of "the great evolutionary movement" toward human rights that would endure.[40]
   Other opportunities for new departures emerged under the auspices of the League of Nations as a result of the Minorities Treaties. Their provisions sought to grant legal equality to individuals belonging to a minority on the same basis as other nationals and to make possible the preservation of a minority group's traditions and characteristics. When first signed, these treaties applied only to the recently created or enlarged countries of Poland, Czechoslovakia, Yugoslavia, Romania, and Greece, and to the vanquished states from the war of Austria, Bulgaria, Hungary, and Turkey, along with the acknowledgment that such protections "*constitute obligations of international concern* and shall be placed under the guarantee of the League of Nations."[41] These provisions obviously marked a beginning, but once the League began its operations, pressure for further extensions arose immediately. Those countries subjected to the treaties, for example, complained that they were being unfairly singled out and held to standards not applied to all. At the same time, others began to have a growing sense of responsibility that the rights of racial, religious, or linguistic minorities should be recognized as a universal human right and, based on the precedents of humanitarian intervention, therefore protected much more broadly around the world.[42] Consequently, members of the League decided to initiate several new efforts. One of these was to make admission into the League for certain states with significant minority populations actually contingent on a pledge to protect minority rights. Finland, Albania, Lithuania, Latvia, Estonia, and Iraq all faced this requirement before they could become members, and thus had to promise to guarantee equal protection of civil and political rights for

minorities within their borders, freedom of religion, and the right of minority groups to use their own language. In addition, the League actively encouraged states to sign bilateral agreements protecting minority rights between them, as in the case of the 1922 German-Polish Convention on Upper Silesia, which soon would assume tremendous importance. The organization also expressed its collective hope

that the States which are not bound by any legal obligations to the League with respect to Minorities will nevertheless observe in the treatment of their own racial, religious, or linguistic minorities at least as high a standard of justice and toleration as is required by any of the Treaties and by the regular action of the Council.[43]

Moreover, members of the League created special mechanisms to help monitor and implement this regime of treaty obligations including Minorities Committees, commissions and tribunals, the office of Director of the Minorities Section, and procedures for bringing violations of human rights before the Permanent Court of International Justice.

Due to these innovations, minority groups now possessed some means whereby they could bring complaints against states who violated their rights before the international community assembled as the League of Nations and petition for protection. Indeed, it is estimated that nearly nine hundred petitions were submitted on behalf of minorities.[44] If the secretary-general of the League considered that a charge possessed merit, he could recommend to the Council that it appoint an ad hoc Minorities Committee to investigate the matter and try to reach a mutually acceptable settlement. If this failed, the complaint could be sent to the Council as a whole or to the Permanent Court of International Justice. Precisely such a development occurred with the *Minority Schools in Albania* case, in which the court insisted on the necessity of maintaining equality in fact as well as in law and held that the closing of minority schools would help destroy the means of preserving uniqueness and thus was incompatible with equal protection.[45] The German-Polish Convention on Upper Silesia, to use another important example, not only guaranteed equal protection for the rights of minorities, but also set up a Minorities Office on each side of the common frontier and established a Mixed Commission and an Arbitral Tribunal each with an independent president appointed by the League Council. The Mixed Commission focused on conciliation and handled more than two thousand cases during the fifteen years of its existence. The Arbitral Tribunal was a judicial body with competence to hear claims by individuals and render judgments binding on the courts and administrative authorities of the two countries. Serious differences of opinion, of course, always could be submitted to the Permanent Court of International Justice, as occurred with the 1928 *Rights of Minorities in Upper Silesia* case. Here the court ruled that the application of any racial, linguistic, or religious criteria for school admission was unacceptable and "subject to no verification, dispute, pressure or hindrance whatever on the part of the authorities," thereby reiterating the essential dimension of nondiscrimination in equal protection.[46]

In addition to these activities, the Council, the Assembly, and the various committees of the League regularly and consistently devoted considerable time seriously debating the issue of minorities. Time and time again the delegates confronted the increasingly familiar tension between their interest in avoiding criticism of the internal affairs of other member states on the one hand, and their desire to address their growing sense of responsibility for protecting the rights of minority populations on the other. As one official described it: "No debate in Committee is more animated or is followed with closer interest than the yearly discussion on Minority questions. . . . I am yet able to state, and my statement is based on personal observation, that this debate . . . shows that the League is by no means dead or even dying."[47] Together, these intense discussions when combined with the many new treaty obligations, rulings, opinions, resolutions, mechanisms, and various activities by the League on behalf of minorities all created significant precedents for increased international protection of human rights. Each sought to address the fact that millions of people lived without normal legal protection and desperately needed outside guarantees from a permanent international body willing to challenge some of the traditional claims of national sovereignty.[48]

The members of the League of Nations also turned their attention to the rights of indigenous peoples in colonial areas in Africa, the Near East, and the Pacific brought under the Mandates System after the war, which in some ways paralleled its efforts for the protection of minorities, trying to determine precisely the meaning of such vague expressions in the Covenant as "the well-being and development" of these peoples and the "sacred trust of civilization" at a time of imperial control. To begin this task, they created the Mandates Commission and decided to make it composed strictly of experts nominated by the Council rather than those beholden to their own governments, and included an assessor from the International Labor Office concerned with the rights of workers in the mandated territories. Importantly, they deliberately designed it in such a way as to make the majority of its members come from those states not holding mandates. The commission first began its meetings in 1921 with Wellington Koo of China as chair. It held two long sessions every year, exhaustively collected materials, received petitions, independently examined many reports between meetings, possessed the power to call often-reluctant and resistant governors and other high officials of the various mandates before it, made commendations that encouraged humanitarian administration in the field, issued reprimands against those who violated the letter of the law or the spirit of conditions of responsibility to do such things as guaranteeing freedom of conscience and religion, and gave wide publicity to abuses through published annual reports. As early as 1922, for example, and with the support of the Haitian and Indian delegates in the Assembly, South Africa found itself publicly criticized for harshness and injustice when dealing with the rights of native tribes in South-West Africa. In terms of the right of self-determination, the Mandates Commission also attempted to secure independence for the "Class A" mandates of the Arab countries of Iraq, Syria, Lebanon, and Transjordan. In these efforts, the Mandates Commission and members of the Assembly worked to place colonial administration under the continuous watch and open criticism of an international body and thus, in the words of Lord Balfour, "to make it quite impossible that any transaction of general interest should take place except in the full glare of the noonday sun of public opinion."[49] In this way the majority of members of the League sought to distance themselves from the old practice of direct, no-questions-asked, colonial annexation and abuse of native peoples by the powerful, working instead to develop a greater sense of moral responsibility for the rights of indigenous and dependent peoples wherever they might be around the world.[50]

This concern for human rights focused attention on the matter of slavery as well. The Covenant specifically required nations with mandates, for example, to prohibit any remnants of the slave trade in territories under their control. To meet this responsibility, members of the League initiated the drafting and negotiation of a whole series of Mandate Treaties addressing slavery. Treaties establishing the British mandate for the Cameroons, Togoland, and East Africa, those for the French mandate for the Cameroons and Togoland, and the Belgian mandate for East Africa all contained explicit provisions for suppressing all forms of the slave trade, the eventual emancipation of all slaves, and the prohibition of forced labor except for essential public services, and even then only in return for adequate remuneration. Similar terms appeared in those treaties creating the British, Australian, New Zealand, and Japanese mandates in former German territories in the Pacific.[51] The League then created a Temporary Slavery Commission consisting of eight experts in colonial questions, instructing them to make all necessary inquiries concerning practices of slavery, to communicate their conclusions to the Council of the League, and to make proposals for eradicating the last vestiges of slavery and the slave trade wherever they still existed. Their discovery of the persistent remnants of royal slaves, domestic servitude, and compulsory labor in places like Ethiopia, the Belgian Congo (now Zaire), India, Sierra Leone, Rio de Oro on the western Sahara, Borneo (now part of Indonesia, Malaysia, and Brunei), New Guinea, Burma, Afghanistan, and the Hedjaz (now part of Saudi Arabia) convinced members of this commission that the international community needed to take further action.[52] They consequently worked to draft a new comprehensive and far-reaching treaty known as the International Convention on the Abolition of Slavery and the Slave Trade of 1926. Here, the text provided for the first time a precise and legal definition of slavery and the slave trade, committed the signatories to bringing about the complete abolition of slavery and forced labor in all of its forms in all territories under their control or tutelage — not just in Africa but everywhere — and to make adequate provisions in their own laws for the imposition of severe penalties for any infractions.[53] The purpose of all of this activity, noted one observer, was to protect basic human rights and to affirm internationally that personal freedom "is the rightful possession of every human being."[54]

The League of Nations also launched new departures in global politics and diplomacy by giving international consideration to the rights of women and children. The Covenant spoke explicitly of both only in the context of working conditions and illicit traffic for the purposes of prostitution, but this provided an opening that was quickly seized. NGOs such as the Women's International League for Peace and Freedom, the Association Féminine Internationale, the Union Internationale des Ligues Féminines Catholiques, and the International Woman Suffrage Alliance played extremely important roles both in giving support for the extension of the franchise and in keeping the issue of equal rights constantly before the members of the League, as they said, on behalf "of the whole world."[55] They took enormous pride, for example, in watching the rights of women be extended in one form or another during the 1930s in Brazil, Ceylon, Chile, Cuba, India, Nicaragua, Peru, the Philippines, Romania, South Africa, Siam (now Thailand), Turkey, and Uruguay.[56] They also were pleased that members of the League made participation on the Council, Assembly, various commissions, and secretariat open to women as well men, watching as a number of women served with distinction, such as Henni Forchhammer of Denmark, an active member of the Women's International League for Peace and Freedom appointed to the Permanent Mandates Commission. The League further established the Advisory Committee on the Suppression of Traffic in Women and Children, initially for dealing with problems of prostitution and the protection of young women and then with larger matters of consent in marriage, the exploitation of women, and the welfare of families. This body was composed of twelve official delegates together with a considerable number of assessors from some of the primary private organizations already attempting to cope with these problems, the Health Organization of the League, as well the International Labor Office. Among other accomplishments sponsored by this committee, the League successfully produced the International Convention for the Suppression of the Traffic in Women and Children in 1921 and then the International Convention for the Suppression of the Traffic in Women of Full Age in 1933.[57] Following this action, the League agreed to sponsor an extensive study on the status and rights of women at the joint request of the delegations of Argentina, Bolivia, Cuba, Dominican Republic, Haiti, Honduras, Mexico, Panama, Peru, and Uruguay. Members quickly realized, after assembling and studying reports from Africa, the Americas, Asia, Europe, and the Pacific, the international extent of abuses and anomalies that existed in extending full and genuinely equal rights unrestricted by age, property, or marital status. The League Assembly therefore resolved to create a special committee of experts charged with preparing and then publishing comprehensive reports on the legal status and rights of women around the world.[58]

Those attentive to women's rights during this period invariably found themselves concerned about the rights of children as well, and many spoke of the intimate relationship between being a woman and being a nurturing mother. Here, nongovernmental organizations devoted to women joined with others like the Jewish Association for the Protection of Girls and Women, the Save the Children Fund, the Union Internationale de Secours aux Enfants, or the Association Catholique Internationale des Oeuvres des Protections de la Jeune Fille, among others, to create pressure for action on behalf of those least able to defend or care for themselves: children. "All rivalries, all racial or religious antagonisms," declared one appeal to the League, "have vanished in the face of the agony of the children—who are the sacred heritage of the human race."[59] In response to this pressure and their own growing sense of responsibility to help those unable to help themselves, members of the League created the Advisory Committee for Child Welfare. This committee was composed almost exactly like its counterpart focused on women and charged it with devoting itself to addressing the needs of children. As it began working on matters of life and health in early infancy, starvation and homelessness, blindness and sickness, and orphans and illegitimacy,[60] the committee also found itself asked to consider what the International Council of Women described as the responsibility of the community to care for all children and to recognize what they described as the universal and "inalienable rights" of every child.[61] Interestingly enough, and after much consideration of this matter, members of the League of Nations decided to make another new departure by drafting the very first declaration ever officially adopted by an international organization of sovereign nation-states on an issue of human rights: the 1924 Declaration of the Rights of the Child. This declaration, signed by fifty nations, announced that "mankind owes to the child the best that it has to give" and charged all countries to "accept as their duty" the universal protection of the rights of all children irrespective of race, nationality, or creed. Toward this end, the declaration coupled the rights of children with the responsibilities of nations, asserting that the hungry child must be fed, the sick child helped, the delinquent child re-claimed, and the orphaned child sheltered and succored, and that children must be the first to receive relief in times of distress.[62] For the delegate from Japan, such a declara-tion, along with other actions by the League, accurately reflected the truly universal concern for the rights of children across all other barriers and demonstrated how "so many nations in the different continents — nations of most varied customs, traditions, systems of morality, and civilizations — have joined forces, with that sense of respon-sibility of the human conscience which is the spiritual treasure of all mankind."[63]

Delegates used similar expressions as they began to address what they described as the right of all people around the world to a minimum level of decent health. Confront-ing not only the historical problem of caring for the sick but also a near explosion of serious postwar epidemics of influenza, typhus, cholera, and typhoid that claimed more lives than those taken during all of World War I, they created the Health Organi-zation of the League of Nations, composed of highly skilled medical personnel from Europe, the Americas, and Asia. This body drew on leading scientific institutes and individual experts who often gave freely of their knowledge and their time to its service, and eventually became one of the most successful operations of the League itself and one whose output of work on behalf of those who suffered far exceeded its financial resources. Indeed, it was the Health Organization that often made the League of Nations a reality in distant places where it otherwise would have remained no more than an abstract name. With energy and zeal its members launched an international campaign against epidemics, addressed the care of those inflicted with leprosy, orga-nized conferences on world health, sent missions to the Middle East and Asia at the specific request of host countries, prepared extensive studies of tropical diseases in Africa, wrote studies on water quality and sewage disposal, drafted conventions for sanitation control, made suggestions on providing adequate housing, and standardized a number of critical vaccines. In light of new discoveries with vitamins and minerals, it also called on experts to develop schedules of the dietary needs of the human body and initiated pioneering studies on nutrition and health. These startling reports publicized the fact that even in the richest countries, large numbers of the population suffered from serious undernourishment, and that, taking the world as a whole, an enormous proportion of human beings were being denied, through poverty or ignorance or government policy, their right to get the food necessary for the maintenance of health and life.[64] Concurrent with these many activities were those of the Advisory Committee on Traffic in Opium and Other Dangerous Drugs, also created by members of the League in the name of the right of all humans to health. In addition to conducting investigations and leading public criticisms of governments who often colluded with drug traffickers, this committee produced the original drafts for the International Opium Convention of 1925 and the Convention for Limiting the Manufacture and Regulating the Distribution of Narcotic Drugs of 1931, which, for the first time, gave authority to an international body to regulate the importation of drugs into more than sixty countries.[65]

Members of the League also viewed issues of the right to health as applying not just to civilian populations, but to military combatants as well. It is for this reason that they sought to extend the coverage of humanitarian law to those capable of being wounded or killed by horrifying new inventions of the twentieth century and to those captured as prisoners during times of war. More specifically, they sought to establish that no one would ever become a victim of the use of chemical and biological weapons in warfare. As a result of several years of effort and negotiation, and in the name of human rights, the League of Nations therefore created and submitted for signature the famous Geneva Protocol of 1925. This treaty prohibited the use in war of asphyxiating, poisonous, or other gases and of bacteriological agents. Although criticized at the time for being overly idealistic, it established a regime of provisions and prohibitions that were successfully respected later during World War II.[66] Shortly thereafter, nations negotiated the 1929 Geneva Convention Relative to the Treatment of Prisoners of War, stipulating that prisoners and those wounded on the battlefield "shall at all times be humanely treated and protected" and guaranteeing the right to receive medical attention, food, and clothing.[67]

In addition to all of these other efforts on behalf of various aspects of human rights, the League of Nations launched a dramatic new departure in the area of assisting refugees. World War I had produced a flood of human victims across the borders of Europe, but the revolutions, civil wars, military coup d'états, famines, and other upheavals that followed unleashed even more. To illustrate, from Russia alone, at least two million men, women, and children were forced to flee from the new Bolshevik regime, warfare, and then famine in their country to Europe or Asia. They were usually destitute or with few resources, without work, and suddenly thrown on the charity of countries who themselves struggled with difficulties of all sorts. Others quickly followed when war and violence spread throughout Turkey, forcing more than one million Turks, Greeks, Armenians, and Assyrians across borders. Wherever these refugees appeared, neither the national governments nor the private relief organizations that tried to help could begin to provide sufficient assistance. As one eyewitness reported:

we found ourselves confronted with 140,000 Russians who had arrived . . . on some 75 ships in a starving condition. It was a sight I shall never forget. . . . Then some 75,000 Turkish refugees arrived. Hearing of the misery amongst them I went to visit some of the camps myself. A more pitiable sight I never saw. We then tried to help these unfortunate people. . . . Our task seemed hopeless. The calls for charity could not continue. The Americans were feeding some 17,500 Russians a day. The British Relief were feeding some 10,000 Russians and 10,000 Turks a day. The future became black indeed. Funds were exhausted. The French could go on feeding the Russians no longer. Similarly the Americans. . . . The situation became very serious. . . . There appeared to be no machinery capable of dealing with this avalanche. . . . The death rate was appalling, reaching some 1,500 a week.[68]

In the face of this tragic human suffering and in the absence of sufficient relief from any other sources, desperate appeals turned to the League of Nations. Here, the members knew that nothing existed specifically in the Covenant as foreseen by its founders that obligated the organization to accept any such magnitude of responsibilities. Nevertheless, they knew that they now would have to decide whether this problem fell within the terms of reference of the new international organization. After considerable debate (and one that would be repeated many times again in later years under the United Nations), the majority of members became convinced that they simply could not turn their back on these most unfortunate people crying out for assistance. They concluded that refugees had "become a question of international importance," and thus decided to expand their vision of responsibility for human rights by establishing the Refugee Organization.[69]

This organization set out as best it could to meet these desperate needs. In this regard, its overworked and underfunded staff received much energy from its first high commissioner, the dynamic and resolute Norwegian explorer Fridtjof Nansen, who adamantly refused to be swayed from his vision of protecting the basic human rights of refugees. Since they possessed no experience in these matters and no clear guidelines for this new departure, the staff experimented as they went along and did what they could, often taking great risks in their faith that somehow funds would come in. Nansen continually received personal appeals like that from one relief worker who wrote: "All the governments seem quite willing to let these people convicted of no crime die of starvation. . . . Those of us . . . who see this suffering and injustice at first hand, feel it keenly and the shame it casts on a so-called civilized age, beg you most earnestly to use your influence to end this impossible situation, something which no one else seems to have the power to do."[70] Without even knowing the precise amount of funding necessary, he responded by saying, "It must be possible to find some definite solution of the problem. . . . and you can draw on me and I will have the money sent you as soon as I know what sum is required. . . . Whatever happens, we cannot allow this people to starve, that is obvious."[71] Nansen and his staff at the Refugee Organization worked with representatives of the International Labor Organization and hundreds of dedicated volunteers from Red Cross and Red Crescent societies, among others, to send money, distribute food and clothes, provide medical attention, secure housing, seek employment opportunities, prepare legal documents on naturalizations and certificates of indigency, assist in evacuations, search for parents and children, and intervene with governments for the repatriation or resettlement of individual refugees. Their activities extended from Asia to the Middle East and from Europe to Latin America. In addition, they invented something called the "Nansen Passport," a certificate delivered by national authorities on the recommendation of the high commissioner or his authorized representatives, eventually accepted as the equivalent of a passport by more than fifty countries, that enabled stranded refugees stuck at border crossings to find an escape to freedom. Even at an early stage, members of the international community began to recognize the importance of this activity and described Nansen as a "creative genius" and a "saint" who "deserves the gratitude of all mankind" for saving "from misery and often from death hundreds of thousands of human beings."[72]

All of these many and varied activities by the League of Nations marked significant new departures in the evolution of international human rights. They were followed by others, such as the creation of the International Relief Union designed to coordinate the efforts of governments, organizations such as the International Committee of the Red Cross to administer relief efforts for victims of disasters, the Convention Relating to the International Status of Refugees marking the beginning of international refugee law and speaking explicitly of rights, and the International Penal and Penitentiary Commission laboring on behalf of the basic rights of prisoners.[73] In addition, although it did not attempt to define human rights with any degree of precision, the organization began to wrestle with the difficult philosophical and political issue of the relationship between rights and responsibilities. As it poignantly noted on one occasion,

> While the Assembly recognizes the primary right of the Minorities to be protected by the League from oppression, it also emphasizes the duty incumbent upon persons belonging to racial, religious, or linguistic minorities to cooperate as loyal fellow-citizens with the nations to which they now belong.[74]

In this way and in many others, the League launched out, seized unique opportunities, and clearly attempted to address the rights of labor, the rights of ethnic and religious minorities, the rights of indigenous peoples in mandates and those condemned to slavery, the rights of women and children, the rights of all to a minimal standard of health, and the rights of refugees, among others. Successes occurred frequently, and literally thousands on thousands of people directly benefited from these efforts. Yet, at exactly the same time, problems continually emerged, again and again confronting those who worked on behalf of human rights with serious challenges.

Challenges of Old Problems

Not all people between the wars embraced these visions or the cause of international human rights. In fact, many individuals and nations actively opposed any efforts at all to continue this historical process of freeing the enslaved, assisting the exploited, caring for the wounded, or protecting the persecuted. Instead, they squirmed and temporized, condemned the League as representing no more than unrealistic sentiment, and sought to prevent change and presented resistance in order to maintain their privileged positions. In this regard, they found themselves enormously assisted by their old allies of vested interests, fear of the unknown, selfishness, skepticism, greed, prejudice, money and power, and especially the doctrine of national sovereignty.

In order to understand and appreciate both the successes and the failures of the League of Nations, it is essential to understand that the organization, as a product of politics and diplomacy, reflected a whole series of uneasy compromises from the very beginning. The organization itself, for example, was a product of the Versailles Treaty, tied to the end of a specific war and authored by the victors. For this reason, the membership revealed significant differences between the universalists and those who would restrict the numbers of participants according to the victors and the vanquished of World War I. The level of its power resulted from the interplay between those who desired to create a unified world government emphasizing internationalism on the one extreme and those who would not budge beyond the nation-state or nationalism on the other. The structure and decisionmaking authority of its Council and Assembly represented the tension between the Great Powers and all other states. The terms of the Minorities Treaties marked the differences between the idealists who wanted to promote a principle and the politicians desiring leverage over the vanquished and weaker states. The composition and scope of its Mandates Commission indicated the conflicts between the interests of the mighty imperial powers who wanted to retain a free hand in their colonial possessions and those who wanted to eliminate colonies altogether and grant the right of self-determination to all peoples. Moreover, the highly generalized provisions in its Covenant concerning human rights demonstrated the sharp differences between those with expansive visions who wanted to use the new international organization as a vast opportunity to extend universal rights to all people on the one hand, and those on the other who felt absolutely no responsibility toward others whatsoever and who intensely wanted to protect their existing privileges and prerogatives under the banner of national sovereignty and domestic jurisdiction.

As a consequence, the League was plagued by a number of fundamental structural problems from the outset. It never secured universal membership, for example. The United States not only never joined the League at all, but especially during the early years did much to deliberately obstruct its activities and diminish its effectiveness. Germany did not gain membership for a number of years, and the Soviet Union joined only after several years. Britain and France largely agreed to exclude their colonies from participation, but beyond that held fundamental differences about the extent of authority that the League should possess. Since it was composed of nation-states claiming sovereignty, the League of Nations never possessed any more power to take action or impose sanctions than its members were prepared to give it. The Council, composed primarily of the Great Powers, retained considerable power over the larger and more representative Assembly, but in both cases no action could be taken without unanimity among all of the members. The governing document of the League made provision for important exemptions by noting that certain subjects remained "solely within the domestic jurisdiction" of member states and by explicitly stating: "Nothing in this Covenant shall be deemed to affect the validity of international engagements, such as treaties of arbitration or regional understandings like the Monroe doctrine [asserting a special sphere of influence and privilege for the United States in Latin America], for securing the maintenance of peace."[75] In addition, the constitution of the International Labor Organization specifically declared that in cases of federal states, "it shall be in the discretion of that Government to treat a draft convention . . . as a recommendation only."[76] Such factors hardly boded well for those interested in the future effectiveness of international efforts on behalf of human rights.

Beyond the immediate and structural limitations of the League of Nations itself, however, were challenges presented by some old, larger, and perhaps more serious problems of history, aspects of human nature, and global politics. This is precisely what Woodrow Wilson's own Secretary of State Robert Lansing worried about from practical experience when he considered the inherent lack of "altruistic cooperation" in the world and the "national selfishness and the mutual suspicions which control international relations."[77] These proved to be formidable obstacles that came to confront every single one of the efforts made by the League of Nations, including those promoting human rights, between the wars. In so doing, they also revealed the nature, strength, and persistence of the problems that would continue to reappear and, as we shall see, later plague the United Nations in its own struggles to advance international human rights.

The very creation of the League of Nations and its internationalist approach, for example, directly threatened the sovereignty of nation-states and their prerogatives as the major actors in international affairs. If an organization, however structurally flawed or compromised, could be created with certain claims to speak on behalf of the people of the world as a whole, then the exclusive privileges held by nations in the past thereby would be placed in jeopardy. What if the League somehow found a way to restrict the power of a state to unilaterally advance its own national interests or control its own people? What would happen, to be more specific, if it suddenly decided to take action on behalf of the rights of racial or religious minorities, colonial peoples, women, children, workers, the enslaved, refugees, immigrants, or anyone else heretofore regarded as subjects of domestic jurisdiction? When faced with these kinds of questions, nations began to dig in their heels. As the League considered one possible international convention, for example, a participant ventured:

if I may express a personal opinion, I would say that it is much to be hoped that attempts, of which this is an example, to regulate matters which are national in character, will be brought to an end, and that the League will in future more and more concern itself only with those tasks provided for in the Covenant.[78]

Others, like Australian leader William Hughes, were even more direct, observing that matters "solely within the domestic jurisdiction of a nation" could not be "the proper subjects for inquiry" by the League, and declaring: "We must choose between doing our way . . . [or] having the matter taken out of our hands."[79] Still others, like the United States, simply refused to even be a part of the enterprise and rejected joining the League of Nations altogether. Raising all kinds of fears of internationalism, Senator James Reed of Missouri posed a problem in language that speaks for itself: "Think of submitting questions involving the very life of the United States to a tribunal on which a nigger from Liberia, a nigger from Honduras, a nigger from India . . . each have votes equal to that of the great United States."[80] His colleague Henry Cabot Lodge, who led the fight in the Senate on behalf of isolationism, declared bluntly in debate, "We do not want a narrow alley of escape from jurisdiction of the League. We want to prevent any jurisdiction whatever."[81]

Some states continually displayed resistance to efforts made on behalf of human rights in other ways as well. Despite the creation of the International Labor Organization and a whole series of treaties designed to protect the rights of workers, for example, governments presented one challenge after another. Albert Thomas, his staff, and their supporters were constantly accused of pushing far beyond the original intent of the organization, of wasteful administration and excessive expenditures, of utilizing international labor legislation as camouflage to interfere into the domestic affairs of member states, and of using the ILO as a vehicle to spread worldwide revolutionary propaganda of class warfare. Some even accused them of seeking to deal with matters outside of their authority, like the government representative who in response to a proposal relating to the rights of workers and the distribution of resources declared:

I say . . . this conference has no more jurisdiction over the question of the distribution of raw materials, which the delegate from Italy referred to, than it has over the question of discovering a way of navigating from the earth to the moon. It might just as well be clearly understood that the nations which have raw materials will deal with them as they believe fair and in the national interest, but they will deal with them by their own parliaments, their own legislatures, and they will not accept international regulations with reference to the control of their private property.[82]

Others criticized them for seeking to impose uniformity on a diverse world, noting that the abolition of night work for women may make sense in the temperate climates of industrialized countries, but may be inappropriate in tropical regions where the only cool period of the day is after sunset. Still others complained of excessive expectations and expenditures, maintaining: "You cannot ask the Governments when they have the greatest difficulty in meeting their financial obligations to commence drafting ideal legislation for their citizens. . . . Every class is suffering. The working class is not alone in that respect."[83] Bitter criticism also arose when the organization granted small states the same vote as large states, despite their vastly different economic resources. Many large business interests and employers strongly resisted the imposition of the eight-hour day, changes in working conditions, international investigations or interference into their activities relating to unemployment or production, or any other "dangerous innovations," and frequently placed considerable pressure on their governments to not ratify the labor treaties. At times the more rabid critics engaged in what labor representatives described as reactionary "sinister attacks," publicly denouncing those involved with the International Labor Organization as being nothing short of Communist revolutionaries, bent on destroying industry, free enterprise and capitalism, national sovereignty, and the nation-state itself.[84]

Serious problems confronted those administering the Minorities Treaties as well. Through time those countries subjected to the treaty provisions concerning the rights of racial, religious, and linguistic minorities within their populations increasingly complained that they were being unfairly held to standards not applied to the majority of countries. They were joined by the representative from India who declared that "there are minority questions outside Europe," pointing to the fate of those suffering discrimination in South Africa, and asserting: "We believe in one truth and one justice, universal for all men."[85] The Chinese delegate spoke in similar language, reminding members of the Assembly that this matter "raised not only the question of nationalities but that of races, and consequently directly concerned China."[86] In the name of making the protection of such rights truly universal, a number of members therefore approached the Assembly in 1925 with a proposed resolution to create a general convention obligating all members of the League to guarantee the rights of minorities. It met with immediate rejection. Two other attempts, one in 1930 and another in 1932, resulted in the same fate, as other states refused to impose such obligations on themselves. Each time the powerful argued that the rights of minorities raised "very delicate matters" and "touched sensitive spots in many countries," declaring with determination that they had no intention of surrendering control over their own citizens or subjects to an international organization, thereby restricting their national sovereignty. "Prudence," said one representative opposed to change, "requires that innovations should be avoided and that the prerogatives of the Council should be left in tact."[87] In addition, although the Minorities Committees greatly stretched the original terms of the treaties by receiving petitions, the influential members of the League insisted that such communications be regarded as simply reports rather than appeals, thus possessing no legal status, and that delegations of minority populations never be allowed to appear before the Council where only the accused state governments could be represented, and thus were not likely to call for punishment against themselves.[88]

One of the reasons why states demonstrated such resistance to any international attention of minority protection, as the Chinese among other non-Europeans quickly pointed out, was the persistent problem of race. Any number of nations, especially those of white settlement, possessed significant numbers of racial minorities (or even majorities) descended from indigenous peoples, slaves, or more recently, immigrants. Most of these people suffered as victims of prejudice, experiencing severe forms of racial discrimination through variations of segregation or apartheid, denial of full civil and political rights, unequal protection under the law, and exclusion. Those very states who just a short time earlier at the Paris Peace Conference had prevented the inclusion of a racial equality clause in the Covenant of the League did not change their minds or their hearts, and now demonstrated even further intransigence. They steadfastly refused to modify discriminatory policies at home, and actually tightened immigration restrictions during these years between the wars with bold public statements about "race wars," "racial alliances," "racial purity," and the "Yellow Peril," insisting throughout the entire process that all such matters remained exclusively within the domestic jurisdiction of their own national sovereignty.[89] "The 'racial equality' question in its present state," stated one confidential and blunt memorandum written by the British Foreign Office with reference to one aspect of this problem,

primarily concerns the following countries: Japan, China, British India, United States of America (especially California and the Pacific States), Canada, Australia, New Zealand, South Africa. The first three countries demand the right of free immigration and freedom from discrimination disabilities for their nationals in the territories of the last five countries. The question can be regarded from an economic or from a political point of view, but in its essence it is a racial one. . . . The white and the colored races cannot and will not amalgamate. One or the other must be the ruling caste.

The report thus concluded that the international racial issue would remain "highly combustible," presenting the world with a problem for which there was "no solution" and "no cure."[90]

Attitudes such as these more than manifested themselves when racially discriminated groups approached the League of Nations for assistance. If they came from countries subjected to the provisions of the Minorities Treaties, they likely would meet a reception allowing them to submit a petition of complaint. If they came from any other nation, however, and operated under the mistaken assumption that the provisions about nondiscrimination and equal protection in these treaties somehow would apply to them as well, they faced rejection. At a very early stage, for example, a group from the National Colored World Democracy Congress petitioned the League to go back and correct an earlier mistake by inserting a racial equality clause in the Covenant and to assert "the ultimate ascendancy of the Right over Might."[91] Others appealed to the "equality of race treatment by all nations in the League."[92] W.E.B. Du Bois and the Pan-African congresses called on the League to "turn its attention to the great racial problem as it today affects persons of Negro descent," to "promote Peace and Justice," and to "take a firm stand on the absolute equality of races."[93] Even stronger petitions came from Marcus Garvey and his Universal Negro Improvement Association and African Communities League, which claimed to represent "six million members scattered in Africa, the West Indies, South and Central America, North America, Europe, and Asia," asserting in their "Petition of the Negro Race": "Your Petitioners desire to impress upon you the fact that the four hundred million Negroes of the world are no longer disposed to hold themselves as serfs, peons, and slaves, but that it is their intention to look forward to the higher benefits of human liberty, human rights, and true democracy."[94] Still more petitions and letters poured in from South Africa, Australia, New Zealand, India, France, Cuba, Canada, and the United States, among other countries. Regardless of whether they were typed and eloquent in their use of language, or arrived handwritten on notepaper with misspellings and improper grammar, they all requested the same thing: racial equality.

These many petitions and pleas clearly placed the League of Nations in a most awkward and difficult position. As one internal staff note observed, "They have a real case which we cannot totally ignore and should not greatly encourage." If the League tried to respond adequately to the petitioners, it would exceed the authority given to it by its members, alienate powerful states, and threaten vested interests in the world. To deal with these letters from the United States, for example, warned one official from the secretariat confidentially, "might antagonize many of our friends in America, who might think that the League was meddling in the Negro question in the States, where this question is a very burning one."[95] Yet, if it did not respond, the League would violate its own stated principles of higher purpose and the expectations of millions of people around the world, thereby subjecting itself to charges of double standards and hypocrisy. When faced with this dilemma, the majority of members would not let the League assist the many petitioners. Consequently, when Du Bois, Garvey, the Maori leader from New Zealand T. W. Ratana, or others traveled to Geneva to personally deliver their pleas, they received only statements that "the rules of procedure" did not allow for consideration of their requests. Time and time again petitioners were told simply that "it is not possible for the Secretariat to take up this question."[96] When Deskaheh, a leader of the Six Nations Iroquois Confederacy, journeyed to Geneva to present an elaborate petition that he called *The Redman's Appeal for Justice*, he received a sympathetic hearing from the delegates from Persia, Ireland, Estonia, and Panama (who themselves had known the taste of oppression), but provoked the anger of Canada who described the petition as "absurd," and of Britain who blocked any formal consideration by the League by warning other members that it constituted "impertinent interference in internal affairs."[97] In fact, the flood of petitions about racial discrimination proved so embarrassing to a majority of the League's member states that by 1928 they found it necessary to reaffirm publicly their commitment to the principles of national sovereignty and domestic jurisdiction by declaring their determination "to insure that states with a minority within their borders should be protected from the danger of interference by other powers in their internal affairs."[98]

Similar challenges to those working on behalf of human rights in the League of Nations emerged with the matter of mandates or colonial empires where racial prejudice also played a critical role. Despite the often heroic efforts of the Mandates Commission, the imperial powers resisted any international attempts to seriously interfere in their control over colonial peoples or to actually grant the right of self-determination. Some of them referred openly in the Assembly itself to the inhabitants under their jurisdiction with black, yellow, brown, and red skin color as "the savage races," "the uncivilized races," and "the savage hordes"—rather than as people.[99] One delegate even went so far as to include in the official records a copy of a suggestion made to impose a system of segregation on natives in the mandates and "to prevent equality between white and black, to uphold the status of the white men."[100] Other representatives resented the commission as "an unfriendly intruder" and "an unwelcomed critic," and argued that the League could only advise on the mandates, but most certainly not exercise control.[101] Some also could not restrain their hostility toward those who struggled for independence from empire or sought the League's assistance in gaining the right of self-determination. Winston Churchill in Britain vehemently reacted to what he described as "the nauseating and humiliating spectacle of this one-time Inner Temple lawyer, now seditious fakir, striking half-naked up the steps of the Viceroy's palace, there to negotiate and parley on equal terms with the representative of the King-Emperor," declaring that "Gandhism and all it stands for must ultimately be grappled with and finally crushed."[102] With attitudes like these, decolonization would have to wait until yet another world war shattered the strength of imperial powers beyond recognition or repair. But until this occurred, the number of new states would remain very limited and the majority of membership in the League would stay largely in the hands of white Europeans.

Resistance to various aspects of human rights occurred in other ways as well. When negotiating the International Convention on the Abolition of Slavery and the Slave Trade, for example, a number of states expressed skepticism, worked to limit the mechanisms of enforcement, or challenged the very competence of the League to even deal with this matter. "The question of slavery is of a very special kind," declared the Belgian government with skeletons in its own closet, arguing: "It is not merely a technical question; it is mainly administrative and political and . . . therefore . . . in all questions of this nature, the League of Nations and its organizations cannot engage in any investigation except through the intermediary of the States directly concerned."[103] When dealing with issues of women or watching the evolution of the Declaration of the Rights of the Child, some delegates expressed dismay over the involvement of women in the first place, protested that children either had no rights at all or that if they did they had no place in the important discussions of an international organization, or that all matters of family relationships remained exclusively within the domestic jurisdiction of member nation-states. Even in seemingly neutral matters of the right of health for all, opposition occurred. India, the Dutch East Indies, the Malay states, and other British, French, and Portuguese possessions that drew a proportion of their revenue from the opium trade all resisted overly strict international controls over opium and other narcotic drugs; and countries with powerful chemical industries like Switzerland opposed limitations on drug manufactures. The efforts of the Refugee Organization often generated resentment and opposition from some governments, who argued that they should not be asked to contribute funds or assistance to foreigners when their own people were starving and out of work. Similarly, activists promoting human rights for NGOs such as the Fédération Internationale des Droits de l'Homme, the Académie Diplomatique Internationale, and the Women's International League for Peace and Freedom frequently found themselves unwanted, unappreciated, and criticized by governments who resented their "interference" and "pushful energy."[104]

The challenges of such continued resistance by so many governments insisting on their national sovereignty, in addition to the structural limitations of the League of Nations itself, made the struggle for human rights exactly that—a struggle. The various committees, commissions, affiliated bodies, nongovernmental organizations, declarations, and treaties that addressed matters of human rights all sought to realize some aspect of visions to care for the basic and fundamental needs of people. But in the near absence of enforcement capabilities, these efforts essentially depended on conciliation and moral suasion. At times these worked. Yet, on other occasions, as one report sadly noted, "these were often not enough."[105] To the great frustration of those who held visions of human rights, for example, seemingly nothing could be done to actually assist those victimized by the Communist regime in the Soviet Union, Catholics oppressed by the anticlerical Mexican government, or Armenians still persecuted by the Turks.[106] This could be seen with striking and foreboding clarity as even more severe storm clouds began to gather on the horizon for the League and the world.

The Gathering Storm

With the emergence of Benito Mussolini and the Fascist Party in Italy, the rise of militarism in Japan, and especially the advent of Nazism in Germany marked by Adolf Hitler's seizure of power, those who labored on behalf of international human rights had reason for profound concern. Not one of these regimes believed in internationalism, "universal laws of humanity," the League of Nations, gender equity, or racial equality; and certainly none cared about protecting the rights of individuals. Instead, each sought to glorify the nation-state, increase its power over people, secure discipline through submission and blind obedience, obtain strength and unity by eliminating

perceived weaknesses or differences, gain territory by imperialist expansion, and literally destroy those at home or abroad who stood in their way. Mussolini resented any
foreign criticism of his actions, and proclaimed it all to be unwarranted interference of
Italian national sovereignty and domestic jurisdiction. When the League condemned
Japanese aggression against Manchuria in 1931, Japan simply walked out and severed
all connections with the organization and its values. Even before coming to power,
Hitler had expressed his opinions unequivocally in his autobiographical *Mein Kampf*
(My Struggle), advocating the transcending power of a nation-state and a superior
"master race," condemning Communists and liberals, cursing Jews, and describing the
League of Nations as no more than a worthless organization of idealists with "pious
hopes" foolishly and dangerously "chasing after the phantom." Visions of international
human rights, the worth of the individual, compassion for others, international care for
the persecuted or exploited, universal responsibilities beyond borders toward the suffering, and racial or gender equality, he asserted, were "drivel" and reflected only the
inventions of cowards, weaklings, religious bleeding hearts, and fools—"for Nature
does not know them." Armed struggle alone is the father of all things, wrote Hitler,
declaring: "When the nations on this planet fight for existence . . . then all considerations of humanitarianism . . . crumble into nothingness."[107]

It did not take long for such attitudes to dramatically impact practical policy. Indeed,
immediately on assuming power in January 1933, Hitler set about to put his ideas into
action and, with the enthusiasm and assistance of the members of his Nazi Party, to
build the edifice of the Third Reich. He vowed to "exterminate Marxism root and
branch," and began by restricting freedom of press, by unleashing the police and his
own storm troopers to terrorize political opponents and Jews, and by seizing the occasion of a fire in the Reichstag to abrogate constitutional provisions protecting individual rights and to arrest alleged enemies of the state at will. Through raw intimidation,
Hitler secured by March an "Enabling Act" giving him personal power to rule by
decree, suppress all remaining rights, and thereby make himself a dictator. A series of
new orders commanded a public boycott of Jewish businesses, discharged Jewish civil
servants, excluded Jewish lawyers from legal practice, removed Jewish physicians from
practice for health-insurance funds, and placed limits on the admission of Jewish pupils
into schools. Hitler and the Nazis naturally declared that all such actions clearly fell
within the prerogatives of German national sovereignty and that they therefore could
do exactly as they wished. To their surprise and shock, this position was challenged by a
single man named Franz Bernheim who decided to transform this domestic matter into
an international issue by unexpectedly taking his case directly to the League of Nations.

Franz Bernheim, a thirty-two-year-old German national of Jewish descent, maintained that he had been unfairly and illegally discharged from his job in Upper Silesia
solely as a result of Hitler's new decrees against Jews. This action, he claimed, represented a clear and unequivocal violation of the minority clauses of the German-Polish
Convention regarding Upper Silesia that specifically guaranteed equality of all Germans before the law in respect to civil and political rights, equal treatment regarding
employment, and protection of the life and liberty of all inhabitants without distinction
or discrimination as to race, language, or religion. Bernheim also argued that any

reading of the convention would reveal that it assigned the Council of the League of Nations authority to pronounce judgments on either individual or collective petitions directly addressed to it by members of a minority. Consequently, he publicly submitted a petition requesting the Council itself declare these Nazi measures against Jews to be null and void for Upper Silesia, and then to issue instructions that the conditions guaranteed by the convention be restored and that the victims be reinstated in their rights.[108]

By throwing down the gauntlet so suddenly and directly, Bernheim's petition caught everyone off guard, but guaranteed that it could not be pushed aside or ignored. Indeed, one correspondent predicted immediately that it "may turn out to be the most important matter to come before the seventy-second session of the Council of the League of Nations."[109] With the submission of this petition, the League found itself forced by "an unknown Jew" to address the issue of international protection for the rights of minorities immediately and in the light of much public attention.[110] The German Foreign Office did not want this to occur at all, of course, and told its delegate in Geneva: "Debate on the Jewish question in the League Council is absolutely undesirable, and is to be avoided at all costs."[111] Given the circumstances, however, such a debate could not be avoided and the Council, composed mainly of ministers of foreign affairs or their deputies, devoted an unprecedented series of discussions during May and June 1933 to what the representative of Mexico described as "the great difficulties" raised by this case.[112] Here their debate ranged from very specific questions over whether Bernheim had legal standing and could legitimately submit a petition in the first place and if he genuinely did "belong to a minority," to much larger issues such as whether the League possessed the competence or the "moral right" to deal with this matter, the difficulty posed by protecting minorities in some select countries but not all, the relationships between international and municipal law, the conflicting claims of international organizations and national sovereignty, and the likely reaction of world public opinion if the League obfuscated or refused to take any meaningful action. At the end of the extended debate, and after careful consultation with the Committee of Jurists, the Council decided that discrimination as described represented a breach of treaty obligations and that Bernheim should receive compensation. But on the larger principle, the Council importantly ruled that the interests of a minority *could* be represented by one individual, and that any offense against an individual was therefore ipso facto against the entire minority to which he or she belonged.[113] This decision opened the floodgates and determined that more serious and intense debate would soon follow.

When the larger Assembly of the League of Nations took up this matter of the international protection of minorities during its sessions of September and October 1933, the lines were more sharply drawn. By this time the delegates had become much more aware not just of Bernheim, but of the much larger problem of the persecution throughout Nazi Germany; and some, especially those from Denmark, Sweden, and Norway, were fully determined in advance to bring this matter to international attention. If they did not evince sufficient concern about the fate of these victims themselves, or privately admitted as some did that they were "very much averse from raising this question at Geneva in any form,"[114] then individual citizens and NGOs such as the gutmachung geleistet werde.

VI./   Der unterzeichnete Franz Bernheim bittet
ferner, das Generalsekretariat des Völkerbundes,
dieser Petition Dringlichkeit zuzuerkennen.

Er begründet diese Bitte damit, dass, wie die
oben zitierten Gesetze und Verordnungen beweisen,
die Durchführung des Grundsatzes der Ungleichheit
gegenüber den Reichsangehörigen nichtarischer,
also jüdischer Abstammung, systematisch auf allen
Gebieten des privaten und öffentlichen Lebens fort-
gesetzt und durchgeführt werden, dass bereits eine
Unzahl von jüdischen Existenzen vernichtet wurde,
und dass bei fortgesetzter Anwendung dieser heute
im Deutschen Reiche geltenden Tendenzen in kür-
zester Zeit sämtliche Juden in ihrer Existenz dau-
ernden Schaden gelitten haben werden, sodass irgend-
eine Wiedereinsetzung und Wiedergutmachung dann
unmöglich sein wird, und viele Tausende und Zehn-
tausende in ihrer Existenz vollkommen zugrunde ge-
richtet sein werden.

8 Beilagen
Prag, am 12. Mai 1933

Franz Bernheim

Osvědčuji /

A Single Individual Appeals to the International Community: The Bernheim Petition (Archives de la Société des Nations).

Federation of League of Nations Unions would apply pressure on their foreign ministries and diplomats to take action.[115] Committee reports revealed increased physical violence and coercion, deprivations of rights, new laws forcing Jews from their jobs and homes, and growing numbers of refugees tragically forced to flee their country. The sudden and rather sensational appearance of Joseph Goebbels, the Nazi propaganda minister who often served as Hitler's mouthpiece, in Geneva raised even more concerns and thereby brought additional and larger questions of principle to the fore. What, for example, should the League do to meet its international responsibilities to protect the human rights of minorities, and how could Germany reconcile its discriminatory legislation and action with its earlier obligation to treat all nationals with tolerance and justice? Acting under instructions from his government who argued that this was "a purely internal affair,"[116] the German representative, August von Keller, refused to comment at all on the Bernheim case in plenary session. In committee, however, he announced the new German philosophy based on *Volkstum*, an organic and ethnic nationality defined in terms of race. Over the sharp criticism of other delegates, and in a complete reversal of how he had previously argued over the fate of German-speaking minorities living in other countries, von Keller bristled and insisted that the "Jewish problem" fell exclusively within the domestic jurisdiction of Germany and thus remained completely outside the scope of the obligations of the minority clauses and of the authority of the League of Nations.[117]

This kind of argument and these developments profoundly troubled those concerned about international human rights. They watched in frustration and alarming anxiety as the League found itself confronted with the Bernheim petition, the seeming inability to increase protection of minorities, and reports of brutal violations of human rights by totalitarian regimes, especially the overt anti-Jewish policies of Nazi Germany. Unwilling to simply sit by and watch this gathering storm rise and their visions of human rights collapse in the process, they decided to make an attempt to do something more. Consequently, and simultaneously with the discussion over the Bernheim case, they submitted proposals calling for more extensive international guarantees of human rights, not just in those few countries with Minorities Treaties but around the world.

The delegation from Haiti took the first step in proposing a more generalized regime of protection for human rights. Speaking as its representative, Antoine Frangulis, who soon would be described as "the delegate of the rights of man,"[118] opened the discussion by criticizing the selective system for the protection of minorities as being far too limited. He painfully contended that recent experience revealed the "equality of rights so ardently desired for the nations has not yet been given any real international guarantee in the domestic sphere of the different countries" and, therefore, that "the fundamental principles governing human societies have been shaken and the most sacred rights of men and of citizens are no longer respected."[119] Giving testimony to the influence of NGOs in this area of human rights, Frangulis referred specifically to the thoughtful proposals drafted earlier by the Académie Diplomatique Internationale, the Declaration of the International Rights of Man passed by the Institut de Droit International and subsequently endorsed by the Fédération Internationale des Droits de l'Homme, and most recently by the Federation of League of Nations Unions in June

1933, concerning various forms of universal guarantees. He believed that these should serve as the basis for new efforts, arguing that

there is not only one category of citizens of a State, described as a minority, which deserves attention, but . . . all the citizens of which human communities are made up are entitled to the same freedom and the same protection, [and] the League of Nations must consider the problem as a whole from the aspect of the rights of man — that is to say, of the rights which men possess as such, whether they belong to a minority or a majority — and it must seek the solutions which are necessary.

Toward this end, he maintained that the "League of Nations cannot remain indifferent" to the fate of those who suffered, and therefore proposed that it draft a comprehensive world convention for the protection of human rights everywhere.[120] The delegates from Greece and Ireland also offered public support for a universal agreement safeguarding human rights.

But once again, these proposed plans on behalf of human rights confronted their old adversaries of national sovereignty and vested interests. Despite whatever diplomatic niceties governments might say in public sessions of the League, or harsh denunciations that they might level against Nazi behavior against Jews in Germany, once these proposals were sent into committee behind closed doors, opposition reared its head. The majority of members of the League of Nations, including the military dictatorships and civilian oligarchies in Latin America and even those representing democratic governments, had no interest in a general convention that might be turned around to apply to them. They began by trying to denigrate the activists in NGOs who pushed for such things as rights for "people of no great importance."[121] More seriously, they feared that if they extended protection to minorities not yet covered by the treaties, the obligations incurred might stimulate separatist tendencies, force them to eliminate immigration restrictions, risk outside intervention into their own domestic affairs, and encourage racial minorities within their own countries or indigenous peoples within their colonial territories to be more aggressive in demanding rights.[122] As one British official said, he "did not wish to be quoted," but declared that "the acceptance of such a proposal by His Majesty's Government would be entirely impossible in view of our colonial empire."[123] Such determined opposition again revealed the fact that the League itself possessed no power other than that given to it by member states — and they were willing to surrender very little. In the end, the Assembly could muster enough votes only to reaffirm "the hope" that all nations would treat their minorities with justice and toleration. The proposals that the League adopt more universal protection for human rights thus, in the words of one delegate, "fell to the ground."[124] Even more ominously for the future, within three days of the close of the Assembly session, Germany announced abruptly that it was withdrawing from the League of Nations itself.

This represented only part of the picture, for the storm clouds continued to build on several fronts, bringing in their wake unparalleled assaults against human rights. In the Soviet Union, despite the language of rights in the constitution, Joseph Stalin continued to ruthlessly rule his totalitarian state. He expelled thousands of opponents to the Siberian Gulag, instituted state terrorism to persecute and a series of trials to punish those with any opinions except those reflecting a devotion to the regime, and used secret police and other agents to execute officials and officers for disloyalty. To compound this tragedy, Stalin forced the masses of peasants at gunpoint into collective farms under the control of the Communist Party, and then into deliberate famine. The sheer magnitude of this assault (described by writer Boris Pasternak as so horrendous as to "not fit within the bounds of consciousness")[125] is revealed by the fact that the state published the deaths of livestock but not people, and by estimates that place the total number of those who died at the staggering figure of more than fourteen million human beings.[126] In 1935 Mussolini launched a war against Ethiopia, itself a member of the League of Nations, deliberately bombing hospitals marked with the Red Cross insignia, shamelessly employing outlawed mustard gas, and attacking defenseless women and children, all while describing black Ethiopians as an inferior barbaric race unworthy to stand side by side with superior whites. A short time thereafter, he issued his infamous Manifesto of Fascist Racism, openly declaring: "It is time that the Italians proclaimed themselves frankly racist" and recognize that the Fascist regime "has been based upon racism."[127] In 1936 General Francisco Franco staged a coup d'état, thus beginning a civil war in Spain that would destroy liberty in that country and bring the international conflict between democracy and dictatorship to a new intensity. In complete violation of the obligations of the Versailles Treaty, Hitler announced rearmament for the German army, the creation of an air force, and the occupation of the demilitarized Rhineland. While these events occurred in Europe and Africa, Japan forced its way further into Manchuria and initiated armed invasions against China, provoking worldwide revulsion over its deliberate 1937 bombardment against innocent civilians in Shanghai and the brutal rape of Nanjing. "The women," confessed one Japanese soldier, "suffered the most. All the women were raped, from the youngest to the oldest. . . . There wasn't a soldier who missed this chance. . . . Usually we killed the girl after we had finished."[128]

To make the situation even worse, additional human suffering occurred along with these acts of violence to rights at home and aggression abroad. Serious unemployment, poverty, starvation, homelessness, economic and social collapse, and other consequences still left in the wake of the Great Depression all placed severe stress on democratic institutions and on international efforts by the League to alleviate misery. Many governments under pressure from their budget constraints and labor unions, for example, began to question why they should expend money and effort on foreigners beyond their borders when they could not even feed or house or employ their own nationals who were suffering at home. In addition, some argued that assisting refugees fleeing from their homeland not only strained resources, but simply compounded problems by increasing the number of some other nation's minorities as well. These complaints reached such a crescendo, in fact, that members of the League refused to contribute any further funds to the important Refugee Organization, and instructed that it cease operations. Those charged with implementing this decision painfully did what they were told, but observed that this would violate the rights of all those desperate for help, often members of minorities seeking refuge from persecution, and noted that "there remains a truly appalling number of refugees who require substantial assistance and will continue to require it even after 1938, unless they are to die of hunger or be driven to desperate courses." Moreover, they sadly warned: "the liquidation [of this office] will naturally not do away with the *refugee problem*."[129]

Those with visions of international human rights watched these developments and events with horror. Much of the world and many of their accomplishments seemed to be falling apart before their very eyes as dictatorships displaced democracies, depression crushed prosperity, hatred overrode compassion, violence (especially armed force against innocents) overpowered reason, and isolationism and passionate nationalism overwhelmed international cooperation. Their frustration only increased when they saw the failure of some political discussions to even address the concept of human rights.[130] In this process, however, they slowly began to see an emerging relationship between domestic and foreign affairs: namely, that how a nation respects the rights of its own people at home may have significant implications for peace and security abroad. But this vital connection and realization would not be appreciated until the world had gone through yet another war. At the moment, the majority of members of the League of Nations would not bring themselves to grant sufficient authority to the organization to keep commitments, believe that international law could cover the relation of the citizen to the state as well as the relations between states, impose sanctions, or take meaningful collective action. Instead, they sought refuge in narrow definitions of interests, reduced support for projects that might cause political problems, hoped that they might strike individual deals and thereby divert the pending disaster, worried that if they interfered with the national sovereignty of other states they would become victims themselves, and feared that they might provoke the aggressors toward even more dangerous and destructive violence. "We had hoped," sighed an exhausted Nansen, "for a disarmament of souls: but the spirit of hostility and national hatred is growing worse than ever between former enemies and even between former allies. Everything that happens seems to hasten the catastrophe. We have decided for a policy of words."[131] Consequently, they allowed the League only to express "concern," "note" aggression, and "deplore" the violation of human rights.

This lesson was not lost on the dictators and those bent on aggression. Seeing no visible international restraints to keep them in check either at home or abroad, they believed that they could proceed exactly as they wished without fear of serious consequences. Hitler, in particular, threw caution to the wind and directed the mechanisms of the state to escalate the process of "Aryanization" in order to secure "racial purity." This quickly resulted in the Law for the Protection of German Blood and Honor. Next, the Nazi publication *Neues Volk* poured out increasingly venomous articles praising Mussolini's racist policies in Ethiopia, segregation and lynching in the United States as well as the "efficiency" of earlier genocide against American Indians, British and French imperialism over indigenous colored peoples, the exclusion of Asians through immigration restrictions, and intense hatred against Jews.[132] State-sponsored anti-Semitism ignited the ferocity and brutality of *Kristallnacht* (Night of Broken Glass) in November 1938 when Nazis and their supporters openly burned synagogues, looted Jewish businesses, and, rampaging through in the streets in an orgy of violence. As an ominous sign of even more tragic things yet to come, several thousand Jews were shipped off to concentration camps bearing the names of Dachau, Sachsenhausen, and Buchenwald. The same year Hitler annexed Austria and, with the open assistance of those who would appease him in Britain and France, dismembered Czechoslovakia. These successes and conquests simply convinced Hitler of his own infallibility and of the potency of his ideas, and whetted his appetite for more. He moved into Prague in March 1939, and then instructed his generals to ready themselves and their troops for the coming war. "Close your hearts to pity," he ordered, and be prepared to "act brutally."[133]

*   *   *

Given these incredibly hostile times, severe limitations, and the active resistance of so many governments between the wars, the surprise should not be that in the end the League of Nations collapsed (for so did the whole international system) — but that it accomplished anything at all. That the League did so is remarkable testimony to those men and women with visions who seized the opportunities, confronted the challenges, and labored so hard to make the whole enterprise work. The achievements of the International Labor Organization, the administration of the Minorities Treaties, the opinions and judgments of the Permanent Court of International Justice, the investigations of the Mandates Commission, the work of the Slavery Commission and its International Convention on the Abolition of Slavery and the Slave Trade, the promotion of the rights of women and the Declaration of the Rights of the Child, the studies of the Health Organization and its international conventions on dangerous drugs, the Geneva Protocol and Conventions on humanitarian law in times of war, and the assistance the Refugee Organization provided to hundreds of thousands of suffering human beings all bear witness to remarkable efforts in the face of extraordinary difficulties. Never before in history had members of the global community ventured so far into what heretofore had been regarded as domestic affairs or attempted so much in the arena of international human rights. These efforts eventually would provide invaluable practical experiences, teach many indispensable lessons, and serve as an inspiration for those who followed with the United Nations holding visions of their own. Before any of this could happen, however, the human inhabitants of the earth would have to go through yet other unimagined horrors and the Holocaust of World War II.

Chapter 5
A "People's War"

The Crusade of World War II

> This is in very truth a people's war. It is a war which cannot be won until the fundamental rights of the peoples of the earth are secured. In no other manner can a true peace be achieved. . . . We must pursue this with courage and with vision.
>
> — Sumner Welles of the United States

The trauma of World War II shook the world to its very foundations. Never before in human history had any armed conflict resulted in so many million deaths, so much massive devastation, or so much global upheaval. For six brutal years, this total war extended in one way or another to most parts of the world, consumed the financial and material resources developed over generations, launched what some at the time called an international "race war," fanned hatreds and produced massive genocide, mobilized the instruments of modern science and the mysteries of the atom into service as instruments of destruction, and exposed entire populations of men, women, and children to horrifying death. In fact, for the first time in modern history, more civilians lost their lives than did combatants. For this reason, participants often described World War II as a "people's war"[1] that consumed not only military commanders and those in uniform, but everyone caught in its inferno, demanding service, sacrifice, exposure, and sometimes life itself.

It is difficult to imagine that a war of this magnitude, lasting for so long, spreading across the globe, and causing the deaths of more than fifty million human beings could create, at the same time, new and unanticipated opportunities for the advancement of international human rights. But it did. World War II was a testing time for values and ideas as well as for weapons and warriors. It exposed, as nothing else had ever been able to do, the ultimate consequences of allowing nations to hide behind the shield of national sovereignty and claims of exclusive domestic jurisdiction. It forced people as never before to examine themselves, their past, and their values in a mirror, and to begin the process of redefining the full meaning of "peace" and "security." By requiring the total mobilization of all resources of nations and empires for survival, the war brought about the emergence of minority groups, smaller nations, and colonial populations heretofore excluded now demanding to be heard. Moreover, by becoming a "people's war," this armed struggle compelled governments fighting against aggression to enunci-ate the principles for which they stood and the war and peace aims for which they were fighting. This elaborate process, with its many interconnecting variables all forged in the intense crucible of war, became a crusade that in turn set into motion what would become a veritable revolution on behalf of international human rights.

War, Genocide, and Self-Reflections

When World War II began, only the most idealistic few could possibly hold out any hope for the future of human rights. Facing woefully unprepared victims, those aggressors who deliberately launched the war operated nearly at will. The mechanized German forces of the Third Reich crushed Poland with a *Blitzkrieg* lasting only a few weeks in September 1939. With this success behind him, Hitler ordered them to turn west in the spring of 1940, invading Denmark and Norway in April and then the Netherlands, Belgium, and Luxembourg in May. Seemingly invincible, they then smashed into French soil and raced toward the English Channel, and by June marched unopposed under the Arc de Triomphe in Paris itself as France capitulated. Once these continental positions and air bases were secured, Hitler ordered that the Battle of Britain would begin with the deliberate use of aerial bombardment in order to pound the civilian population in cities like London and Coventry into submission. During spring 1941, German forces moved to assist Mussolini and his Italian troops in territorial conquest, and successfully attacked Yugoslavia, Greece, Crete, and North Africa. In June, Hitler made one of his most fateful decisions and invaded Russia, giving explicit warnings to his commanders that this would be no ordinary military conflict but a war of extermina-tion that would require unmerciful, unrelenting ruthlessness. Toward this end, he entrusted "special tasks" to the *Einsatzgruppen* with orders to round up innocent civil-ians near battles in occupied territories, march them naked toward open ditches, and then kill them by the hundreds of thousands. International jurists eventually estimated that perhaps two million defenseless human beings in Russia alone were murdered, describing it as "a crime of such unprecedented brutality and such inconceivable savagery that the mind rebels against its own thought image and the imagination staggers in the contemplation of a human degradation beyond the power of language to adequately portray."[2]

Not content with this kind of murder on the mere edges of battlefields, Hitler deter-mined to make a more determined commitment of resources in order to obsessively pursue his program of "cleansing" presumed racial inferiors from the face of the earth. The world faced an "ideological and biological" struggle of race, he insisted, that required determination and a strength of will undeterred by any legal or moral limita-tions on behavior. To emerge victorious in this ruthless genocide, Hitler appointed Heinrich Himmler as the Reichsführer SS and gave him the power to engage in what-ever "special treatment" might be necessary. This took the form of segregation, expro-priation, internment, forced labor, and eventual deportation and extermination of all Jews, "degenerate-looking Orientals," "the Asian-Mongol virus" of Slavs, and others deemed to be racial *Untermenschen*, or subhumans.[3] When the Nazi leadership decided after several months that the mass shootings, mobile gas vans, and carbon monoxide asphyxiations in abandoned farmhouses would no longer be sufficient for the extent of the task that lay ahead, they then designed special annihilation centers out of sight where large numbers of innocent men, women, and children could be killed as quickly and as efficiently as possible. Thus, relatively early in the war they began construction of these camps at Auschwitz, Chelmno, Belzec, Sobibor, Majdanek, and Treblinka for one simple and terrifying purpose: mass extermination.

The military triumphs of the Germans in Europe and North Africa demonstrated the glaring weaknesses of the democracies, and thereby served to whet the appetites of Japanese expansionists who wanted more than just their recent conquests in China. The fall of the Netherlands, the collapse of France, and the absorption of Britain in her own survival meant that these countries could not defend their Asian and Pacific colonial possessions that now suddenly appeared ripe for the taking. Thus, as early as June 1940, the government of Japan began demanding special rights and bases in Southeast Asia. After signing a pact with Germany and Italy, it continued to press for more. In July 1941 Japanese troops moved into Indochina and Thailand, again taking action against innocent civilians, and began making menacing threats in the direction of the Philippines, Burma, Singapore and other areas on the Malayan peninsula, and Indonesia. The only power temporarily standing in the way of the direct conquest of these peoples by the Japanese was a very uncertain United States.

The United States, of course, had not played a significant role in international affairs since World War I and the Paris Peace Conference twenty years before. It deliberately had chosen not to participate in the League of Nations at all, actually tried to obstruct a number of international efforts in the area of human rights, and largely removed itself from any global responsibilities by means of a policy of isolationism. The outbreak of war and the successes of the aggressors, however, suddenly confronted the illusion that the nation somehow could remain completely aloof from global affairs, forcing President Franklin Roosevelt to begin a serious self-reflection and to formulate some kind of response. Toward this end, he sent Under Secretary of State Sumner Welles on a critical fact-finding mission in March 1940. Welles, who would soon work so hard to promote the evolution of international human rights during the course of the war, pessimistically reported back that he saw only increasing drift, war, and an absence of any real security. "What is imperatively required," he wrote pointedly to Roosevelt, "is statesmanship of the highest character, marked by vision, courage, and daring."[4] The president responded to this challenge in his next annual message to Congress and the nation with a dramatic departure from the recent past. He spoke forcefully not just about the narrow interests of the United States, but about the world at large, discussing the relationship between domestic liberties and international peace and proclaiming that he sought to secure "four essential human freedoms" for all. These included freedom of speech and expression, freedom of worship, freedom from want, and freedom from fear — "everywhere in the world." "Freedom," he declared, "means the supremacy of human rights everywhere. Our support goes to those who struggle to gain those rights or keep them." This, he concluded, "is no vision of a distant millennium. It is a definite basis for a kind of world attainable in our own time and generation."[5] To achieve this objective, Roosevelt protested the aggression of Germany and Italy, gradually extended aid to the Chinese government of Chiang Kai-shek (Jiang Jie-shī), applied restrictions against certain materials to Japan, and explored ways in which the United States might give greater assistance to the British. With reference to the latter, it became increasingly clear to Roosevelt, although his country was technically still a nonbelligerent, that he needed to meet secretly with Prime Minister Winston Churchill. It was necessary for them to formulate a common strategy and to respond to growing pressure from within their own countries to declare a common purpose.[6] Toward this end, they mutually agreed to meet in August 1941 "somewhere in the Atlantic."[7]

Roosevelt and Churchill, traveling along with their respective staffs (including Sumner Welles representing the Department of State) aboard warships and heavily protected by other naval forces, rendezvoused at sea off the Newfoundland coast at Placentia Bay.[8] They had corresponded with each other at length and admired each other from afar, but now met each other for the very first time. They joined together for a Sunday morning religious service on the quarterdeck, with several hundred sailors and marines from both countries standing under the imposing barrels of fourteen-inch guns, singing "Onward, Christian Soldiers" and "Our God, Our Help in Ages Past." As Churchill later described the event with obvious emotion, "Every word seemed to stir the heart. It was a great hour to live. [Yet] nearly half those who sang were soon to die."[9] They subsequently began to discuss the details of the United States serving as "the arsenal of democracy," of lend-lease assistance to Britain and Russia, strategies to combat aggression by Germany and Italy in Europe and North Africa and by Japan in Asia, and, following the suggestion initiated by Roosevelt that would come to assume great importance, a joint statement laying down certain broad purposes and principles of common policy. A somewhat reluctant Churchill wrote the first draft on stationery from 10 Downing Street, then Roosevelt and his staff suggested a few amendments. In the end, they produced and jointly issued an eight-point declaration known as the Atlantic Charter, the most famous result of their meeting. In this document, they publicly announced that in the name of "their hopes for a better future for the world," they wanted no territorial aggrandizement themselves, supported freedom of trade and of the seas, and respected "the right of all peoples to choose the form of government under which they will live." In addition, they boldly declared that they sought the right to have "improved labor standards, economic advancement, and social security" in all nations, wanted people everywhere to be able to have the right to "live out their lives in freedom from want and fear," and desired "a wider and permanent system of general security" for the world.[10]

By issuing the Atlantic Charter, both Roosevelt and Churchill sought to delineate a sharp contrast between themselves and their adversaries, declare a purpose for their endeavors, and to provide principles around which their people could rally for a crusade. Both men knew from their own personal experiences in leading their nations through difficult times about the power of visions, ideas, and words, and thus sought to bring them to bear as they confronted World War II. The Voice of America quickly seized the Charter as a banner to rally forces around the globe, and Welles described it

The Crusade Begins: Roosevelt, Churchill, and the Atlantic Charter (Franklin D. Roosevelt Library).

as "the agreement that was to bind together the United Nations."[11] U.S. Senator Alben Barkley predicted that it would "find an enthusiastic response in the hearts of all peoples everywhere who believe in freedom and democracy."[12] During the first meeting of the Inter-Allied Council in September, all of the European allies, including the Soviet Union, unanimously declared their support for the principles of the Atlantic Charter. One month later at the International Labor Organization conference in New York, the delegates from more than thirty countries enthusiastically welcomed the declaration and pledged to give their cooperation in trying to make the vision of the charter a universal reality. It also greatly impressed two New Zealand leaders with strong religious and labor backgrounds who soon would make very significant contributions to international human rights far out of proportion to the size of their country. One of these was Peter Fraser, who actually had been imprisoned for his beliefs opposing conscription during World War I, but now as prime minister of his country participated in the War Cabinet discussions in London and helped to contribute the language about labor standards and social security in the Atlantic Charter, viewed it as a most welcomed contribution to the war effort and to broader discussions about human rights. His close colleague and Deputy Prime Minister Walter Nash, similarly described the statement as "a modern charter of human liberties" and without hesitation boldly predicted that it constituted nothing short of "a declaration more potent for good than any other in the records of human history."[13] In addition, the principles enunciated here also greatly impressed a young black lawyer in South Africa named Nelson Mandela, who writes in his autobiography:

The Atlantic Charter of 1941, signed by Roosevelt and Churchill, reaffirmed faith in the dignity of each human being and propagated a host of democratic principles. Some in the West saw the Charter as empty promises, but not those of us in Africa. Inspired by the Atlantic Charter and the fight of the Allies against tyranny and oppression, the ANC [African National Congress] created its own Charter, called African Claims, which called for full citizenship for all Africans, the right to buy land, and the repeal of all discriminatory legislation. We hoped that the government and ordinary South Africans would see that the principles they were fighting for in Europe were the same ones we were advocating at home.[14]

Not all reactions to the Atlantic Charter, however, were so enthusiastic. The Germans, Italians, and Japanese, as might be expected, viewed the statements as nothing more than a wartime "maneuver" or "propaganda bluff" that lacked substance and smacked of hypocrisy.[15] Others, including those within the United States and Britain, expressed deeper concerns and asked tough questions. How, asked isolationists and those belonging to organizations like the America First Committee, could the president commit to such a declaration without drawing their nonbelligerent country closer to war and then into perhaps long-term international entanglements and responsibilities? How, asked those with vested interests, could pledges for more liberalized trading practices be given without jeopardizing protective tariffs, or for improved labor standards, economic advancement, and social security without risking the spread of dangerous socialism? Would this announced commitment to human rights, asked others, apply to the domestic laws of racial segregation or immigration restrictions based on race in the United States, Canada, Australia, New Zealand, or South Africa? Or, would the pronouncements about the right of self-determination in the Atlantic Charter actually apply to the indigenous people in the colonial possessions of Britain, France, the Netherlands, Portugal, Spain, or the United States extending over the four hemispheres of the globe?

These deeper questions of what the principles of the Atlantic Charter would mean for the United States and others in the world immediately assumed greater significance when the Japanese attacked Pearl Harbor on 7 December 1941 without warning. The specially designed torpedoes launched from planes not only sunk the unprepared American battleships moored at the naval base in Hawaii but, ultimately more momentous, the strength of American isolationism. In stunned and angry response to this surprise attack, Congress dramatically reversed its policies and declared war against Japan, and then against the other Axis powers of Germany and Italy. Thus within only a few days the United States suddenly found itself wrenched completely away from nonentanglement of the past and engaged in a global war. For the moment, however, the military advantage still remained with the Japanese, who used the next several months to extend their conquests over other peoples in Asia and the Pacific. Two days after Pearl Harbor, forces from Japan invaded the Philippines and began a program of staggering brutality against captured survivors, including the notorious Bataan Death March in which thousands died of starvation, beatings, and exposure. They simultaneously conquered those living on the Malayan peninsula, taking Singapore and then Burma, thereby cutting off all land communications with the free world. Other conquests quickly followed in Sumatra, Java, Borneo, New Guinea, Wake, and Guam, and the Japanese seemed poised to invade India, Australia, New Zealand, or Alaska if they chose. For those attempting to defend themselves against this aggression and for those possessing any visions of human rights at all, the future appeared bleak indeed.

In order to hold out hope, however, and to mobilize all the resources necessary to mount a people's war against the Axis, twenty-six nations agreed to sign the Declaration of the United Nations on 1 January 1942. Here, countries such as the United States, the Soviet Union, Britain and China, joined with Canada, Haiti, Cuba, India, New Zealand, and South Africa, among others, in making a highly public pledge before themselves and their peoples. They promised to devote their full resources to the crusade of World War II, to refrain from signing any separate armistice or peace agreement with their enemies, and to adhere to the principles enunciated in the Atlantic Charter on behalf of individuals as well as states. By the end, a total of forty-six nations signed this declaration, adding their names and reputations to all others pledging to engage in the "common struggle against savage and brutal forces seeking to subjugate the world." They announced their commitment to secure "decent life, liberty, independence, and religious freedom" for the world. In addition, and in a particularly important breakthrough in the evolution of international human rights, all the states at war against Germany, Italy, and/or Japan pledged in the Declaration of the United Nations to join themselves in a crusade "*to preserve human rights and justice in their own lands as well as in other lands.*"[16] Lest there be any misunderstanding of the mission at hand, Roosevelt announced that this was nothing short of a global struggle against "tyranny and cruelty and serfdom" in which there could never be a compromise "between good and evil" and where "only total victory" could bring about the realization of human rights.[17] Within just a few weeks, the Ministers of Foreign Affairs of the American Republics meeting in Rio de Janeiro reaffirmed the same goals and committed themselves to supporting the principles of the Atlantic Charter.[18] Many of those who now entered the war strongly believed in the objectives of this crusade, and when the war finally ended after staggering losses and sacrifices they fully intended to insist that their governments honor these promises.

In the evolution of international human rights, World War II thus provided the opportunity and the motivation to not only enunciate basic principles, but to make certain public pledges to people around the globe as well. But it did far more than this. The experience of war and genocide also greatly heightened awareness of human rights by the sheer magnitude and brutality of their violation. Indeed, it was World War II that demonstrated as never before in history the extreme consequences of the doctrine of national sovereignty and ideologies of superiority. This, in turn, forced those engaged in the war to look in a mirror and see their own reflections, and consider whether they had any responsibility to change their ways.

No case during the war so dramatized the horrors of pain and suffering inflicted on other human beings as a deliberate part of state policy more than the Nazis of the Third Reich. Hitler began his persecution of Jews and other opponents immediately on seizing power, and escalated his program of securing "racial purity" once German armies invaded other countries. But soon even these mass murders were deemed to be insufficient for the "historic mission" of purging the world of presumed racial inferiors and other undesirables. Thus, in January 1942, the very month of the Declaration of the United Nations, Nazi officials described at the infamous Wannsee Conference their intention to begin a program of mass extermination of entire populations of people, based solely on distinctions of race. They even provided a name for their policy: the "Final Solution of the Jewish Question." Within several weeks, the first group of Slovakian Jews arrived at Auschwitz, followed by others from the ghetto of Lublin who were sent to Belzec. Although even the minister for propaganda, Joseph Goebbels, described the program as "barbaric,"[19] it continued and gathered frightful momentum. The Nazis and their many non-German, anti-Semitic collaborators rounded up those whom they regarded as racial inferiors undeserving of any human rights in France, Belgium, the Netherlands, Luxembourg, and Norway. They gathered others from Germany, Austria, Italy, Poland, Russia, Latvia, Estonia, Lithuania, Czechoslovakia, Hungary, Romania, Bulgaria, and Greece. These helpless victims were crowded together in suffocating cattle cars and then sent on their way to the specially prepared camps that awaited them.

Once they arrived, these terrified men, women, and children ripped apart from their larger families, homes, and countries, met a fate described by eyewitnesses in the following words:

The first train arrived . . . 45 freight cars with 6,700 people, of whom 1,450 were already dead on arrival. . . . A large loudspeaker blares instructions: undress completely, take off artificial limbs, glasses, etc. Hand in all valuables. . . . Women and girls to the barber, who cuts off their hair in two or three strokes and stuffs it into potato sacks.

Then the line starts moving. . . . At the corner a strapping SS-man announces in a pastoral voice: Nothing will happen to you! Just breathe deeply inside the chambers, that stretches the lungs; this inhalation is necessary against the illnesses and epidemics. . . . For a few of these unfortunates a small glimmer of hope which suffices to have them take the few steps to the chambers without resistance — the majority knows what is ahead, the stench tells their fate. . . .

The wooden doors are opened. . . . Inside the chambers, the dead are closely pressed together, like pillars of stone. . . . They still hold hands, so they have to be torn apart to get the chambers ready for the next occupants.[20]

It is estimated that a total of as many as eleven million human beings were killed, including six million Jews and a nearly equal number of others ranging from children and the aged, homosexuals, Slavic slave laborers, prisoners of war, Communists, members of the German resistance, gypsies, and Jehovah's Witnesses.[21] Such a policy and such staggering numbers seem so grotesque, so perverse, so inhuman, and so self-defeating that they defy credulity. But tragically, the horrors of this Holocaust and its assault on humanity were all too real.

The language of superiority, exclusivity, and racial hatreds, however, was most certainly not confined during World War II to the German Nazis. In their attacks against

Toward the "Final Solution" (International Military Tribunal).

other peoples in Asia and the Pacific, for example, the Japanese also used blatant pronouncements that defied human rights. Like their counterparts in the West, and despite their earlier efforts at the Paris Peace Conference in the name of equality, the leaders of Japan declared their own superiority as *shido minzoku*, or the leading race. At home, they spoke of "racial solidarity," "racial purity," and "racial destiny," as well as the need to engage in a "race war" to secure land for the benefit of the superior "Yamato race." During the war the civilian bureaucracy in Tokyo produced a multi-volume study entitled *An Investigation of Global Policy with the Yamato Race as Nucleus*, which articulated the goal of assuming their "proper place" over all others. This ideol-ogy of racial superiority extended to non-Japanese Asians subjected to conquest as well as to Caucasians characterized as decadent demons, selfish devils, bestial monsters, and "hairy, twisted-nosed savages" of subhumans.[22] These attitudes, in the judgments of most Asian historians, produced horrendous violations of basic human rights and bru-tality by Japanese troops against captured soldiers and civilians alike in the form of punishment, forced labor, sex slave "comfort women," mutilations, and murder.[23]

In addition, the leaders and ideologues of Japan deliberately manipulated the divi-sive and highly emotional issue of race to mobilize support in Asia against what they called the "White Peril." That is, during the intensity of war, they spoke not of universal principles for all peoples, but instead portrayed the struggle as a battle of the East versus the West and of colored versus white. They declared their desire to pursue a "holy war" to "liberate East Asia from white invasion and oppression."[24] Toward this end, they claimed that their conquests should not be viewed as victories against their neighboring brothers and sisters, but rather as humiliations against the Americans, British, French, and Dutch. To those who had long suffered from racial discrimination, exploitation, imperialism, and immigration restrictions for many years, these claims struck a responsive cord. Indeed, they often provided exhilarating hope, a sense of racial solidarity, and pride in ties of blood and color that for some temporarily outweighed the fact that the Japanese discriminated against them and that old conquerors simply were being replaced by new ones. "Although my reason utterly rebelled against it," admitted one Asian, "my sympathies instinctively ranged themselves with the Japanese in their fight against the Anglo-Saxons."[25] Others in the region similarly reported their satisfaction in seeing early Japanese military victories attack the myth of white omnipotence, create "great disgrace on the white race," and heighten the differences between races rather than promote the similarities of humankind.[26]

The Western allies also contributed heavily to this division, international hatred, and racial antagonism. Indeed, once the war began in all of its global dimensions, their actions — and inactions — often spoke far louder than their many words about human rights. Despite their vigorous condemnations of the Third Reich's policy of genocide, for example, none of the Allies would take specific measures to provide relief to those of the Jewish faith trapped in Hitler's inferno. They rejected efforts to revise immigration restrictions, to grant asylum to those who might successfully escape, to consider possible rescue attempts, or to provide emergency aid through neutral countries, and prosecuted anyone engaged in the purchase of exit visas to ransom Jews as guilty of trading with the enemy. In one early case that attracted considerable public attention, for example, nearly one thousand Jewish refugees onboard a ship were forced out of port by immigration officials first in Cuba, then the United States, who refused to let them enter, prompting the *New York Times* to editorialize that such crass behavior "cries to high heaven of man's inhumanity to man."[27] Protestant churches, except for those in Scandinavia, remained noticeably silent in the face of the Holocaust, and Pope Pius XII steadfastly refused to issue any public protest against the Nazi atrocities, let alone take any action. Stalin himself was a long-standing and virulent anti-Semite, and many high ranking British and American officials harbored a poorly concealed abhorrence toward Jewish refugees, describing them as "these useless people" and as part of a serious "racial problem."[28] Moreover, once the battles of the Pacific began, they brought into sharp focus other dimensions of the tensions of race that had existed for several centuries and encouraged those who saw the world not in terms of human unity, but rather as a place of combat of "the Yellow Race against the White Race."[29] Governments and the popular press in the West quickly created an image of the Japanese as a "racial menace" of scheming, "murderous little ape men" or "vermin," as "yellow bastards," and as savage, slant-eyed "subhumans."[30] The Hearst newspaper chain in the United States boldly declared: "The war in the Pacific is the World War, the War of Oriental

Races against Occidental Races for the Domination of the World."[31] Churchill spoke publicly and contemptuously of the inferior "little yellow men."[32] Others generated a vehemence certainly not matched against German or Italian enemies, describing the war against Japan as "a holy war, a racial war of greater significance than any the world has heretofore seen." In fact, writers supporting the cause of China and a free Asia, such as Pearl S. Buck and Lin Yutang, were so appalled by the way Westerners saw the war in the Pacific in such sweeping racial terms that they warned of World War III within a generation between whites and nonwhites.[33]

Lest these expressions be somehow dismissed as simply wartime rhetoric against opponents, it is important to recognize that similar attitudes by the West were revealed with reference to friends and allied partners fighting the Axis as well. Similarly, despite the publicly praised status of China and India as members of the Grand Alliance, their white allies in the United States, Canada, Australia, New Zealand, and South Africa still blocked immigration by their nationals during most of the war because of the color of their skin. "Why be apologetic about Anglo-Saxon superiority [to other races]?" said a brazen Churchill more generally, "We are superior."[34] When he was asked whether the principles enunciated in the Atlantic Charter concerning the right of self-determination would apply to those in the colonies sacrificing on behalf of the war effort, he declared in a widely quoted response: "We mean to hold our own. I have not become the King's First Minister to preside over the liquidation of the British Empire."[35] Even when passing through Allied Africa, U.S. military commanders continued to reveal their contempt by referring to people there as "fuzzy wuzzies" and "niggers."[36] Moreover, when Ruth Benedict published her famous wartime pamphlet *The Races of Mankind* warning about the dangers of international racism, especially as practiced by whites, it was banned by the U.S. Army and denounced in Congress.

Tragically enough, this revelation of such prejudices and hatreds by so many in the West toward enemies, friends, and allies, even applied to some citizens and soldiers. Throughout the Western hemisphere, for example, governments viewed men, women, and even children of Japanese descent as potential enemies solely because of their race. In Mexico and Peru, immigrants from Japan were rounded up and confined in special camps. In Canada, more than twenty thousand were evicted from their homes in the coastal regions of British Columbia and interned. In the United States, the situation was even worse when in February 1942 Roosevelt signed Executive Order 9066 authorizing the secretary of war to exclude, remove, and then detain U.S. citizens of Japanese origin and their parents. With no legal charges being made, more than one hundred thousand Japanese-Americans accused of belonging to "an enemy race," suddenly found themselves forced out of their jobs and homes, then herded into "relocation centers," or what government documents at the time described as "concentration camps" surrounded by barbed wire, dogs, and armed guards.[37] Even those fighting against the Axis in the name of freedom faced discrimination. Colored colonial troops certainly were not treated equally during war. Blacks drafted for military service in the United States quickly realized that their government wanted them as soldiers, but not as complete citizens or human beings deserving full equality, as evidenced by segregated units and discriminatory medical treatment. As Representative John Rankin of Mississippi explained the official policy, any mixing of blood plasma in field hospitals would "mongrelize America" and he would never allow anyone to "pump Negro or Japanese blood into the veins of our wounded white boys."[38] Similar experiences confronted blacks in South Africa who, although their country was fighting the Axis, confronted white Afrikaners in the Ossewa Brandwag organization committed to a separation of the races through apartheid.

This flagrant disparity between the language of the Atlantic Charter and the promises of the Declaration of the United Nations on the one hand, and the reality of such blatant actions on the part of the Allies both at home and abroad on the other, simply became impossible to dismiss or ignore. In part this resulted from highly successful efforts by the Axis to draw widespread attention to Allied hypocrisy.[39] More important, it occurred because of the painful truthfulness of the arguments advanced by those who actually suffered. The claim by the Allies that they were engaged in a crusade for human rights, while at the same time fully practicing their own forms of violating some of those very rights, often rang hollow and revealed a wide and glaring chasm between words and deeds. There were people within the Allied countries, and even more within their vast colonial empires, still victimized by fear and by want. All citizens in this "total" war experienced severe wartime restrictions on their freedom and liberties. Women confronted barriers of various kinds, and even those working in defense industries did not receive equal pay. Differences of religion, nationality, ethnicity, and age still perpetuated injustices. Class distinctions continued, with many arguing that the poor were more likely to be drafted into military service than the rich. And, of course, nothing could hide the highly visible discrimination based on racial prejudice. When those called on to fight in this war of peoples increasingly began to ask how some of these attitudes and practices compared with those of their opponents, they not only posed troubling questions difficult to answer but held up a mirror to themselves and saw their own reflection. As such, the war proved to be a battleground for ideas and values as well as for warriors and weapons.

When these self-reflective criticisms came from such a widespread base generated during the crusade of a "people's war," Allied governments thus found themselves forced — as never before — to acknowledge their hypocrisy. In Britain, for example, the Foreign Office had to admit that with reference to issues of human rights, there existed very legitimate grounds for complaint.[40] The secretary of state for the colonies even went so far as to declare: "If we are fighting for liberty, we cannot set the bounds to the advance of other races. . . . We must avoid any reproach that, when we blame Hitler for his poisonous doctrine of the Herrenvolk, we had a similar doctrine lurking in our own hearts."[41] The same pattern emerged with government leaders in Australia and New Zealand who asked remarkably, "Are we afraid to do justice?"[42] In South Africa, General Jan Smuts reluctantly admitted: "I have heard natives saying, 'Why fight against Japan? We are oppressed by the whites and we shall not fare worse under the Japanese.' "[43] Even the reactionary prime minister of the Netherlands, P. S. Gerbrandy, publicly acknowledged for the first time the role that violations of human rights played in perpetuating empire and fostering international and interracial tensions.[44] This theme of global problems was developed even further by Walter White of the NAACP when he wrote directly to Roosevelt that "the colored peoples of the world, who constitute four-fifths of the world's population" need to be assured "that no longer will black, brown, and yellow peoples be treated as inferior or exploited by white peoples."[45]

The self-reflection from this wartime mirror became virtually impossible to avoid in the United States, especially as it increasingly sought to lead the crusade itself. Eleanor Roosevelt, wife of the president and strong in her own convictions, publicly spoke out as a determined advocate for human rights, particularly the rights of women, children, and racial minorities. "The nation," she declared on one occasion, "cannot expect colored people to feel that the United States is worth defending if the Negro continues to be treated as he is now."[46] How, asked Gunnar Myrdal again and again as he prepared his monumental wartime study entitled *An American Dilemma: The Negro Problem and Modern Democracy*, could the United States oppose the racial policies of the Nazis and Fascists with such vehemence abroad, yet support them so vociferously at home?[47] Penetrating and unrelenting questions such as these forced themselves on the country, and thus thrust on many the conclusion that they had reached a critical turning point. "Today it is becoming increasingly apparent to thoughtful Americans that we cannot fight the forces and ideas of imperialism abroad and maintain a form of imperialism at home," acknowledged Wendell Willkie, former presidential candidate of the Republican Party. "The war," he conceded in a remarkably revealing message,

had done this to our thinking. . . . So we are finding under the pressures of this conflict that long-standing barriers and prejudices are breaking down. The defense of democracy against the forces that threaten it from without has made some of its failures to function at home glaringly apparent. Our very proclamations of what we are fighting for have rendered our own inequities self-evident. When we talk of freedom and opportunity for all nations the mocking paradoxes in our own society become so clear they can no longer be ignored.[48]

Because these striking and paradoxical contrasts could not be ignored, individuals, NGOs, and sometimes even governments themselves fighting in this crusade of a "people's war" turned to the task of developing visions and drafting proposals on the subject of international human rights.

Crusaders, Visions, and Proposals

The first elaborations of visions for human rights during World War II, not surprisingly, came from individual crusaders rather than governments. Building on so much of the inspiration and effort during the years of the League of Nations, they saw the outbreak of violence as necessitating a crusade against totalitarian regimes characterized by their complete disregard for human life and liberty through aggression abroad and complete dictatorship at home. As early as the second month of the war, for example, the prominent British utopian writer (and, hence, no stranger to imagining visions of different worlds), H. G. Wells launched a vigorous and large-scale campaign to bring human rights to the attention of the public. At the age of seventy-three and from his perspective as president of PEN International, a nongovernmental organization deeply committed to freedom of expression, he began by writing a letter to the *Times* declaring:

At various crises in the history of our communities, beginning with the Magna Carta, and going through various Bills of Rights, Declarations of the Rights of Man and so forth, it has been our custom to produce a specific declaration of the broad principles on which our public and social life is based. . . . The present time seems particularly suitable for such a restatement of the spirit in which we face life in general and the present combat in particular.[49]

To begin this process, Wells drafted a "Declaration of Rights," opening with a preamble, then proposing clauses for the right to equal protection without discrimination, nourishment, housing, medical care, education, and the right to work. He then formed a committee of well-known citizens like Lord Sankey (former president of the House of Lords and a member of the Académie Diplomatique Internationale) to help attract notice and draw up the final text of a declaration and secured the willingness of the *Daily Herald* to devote space to a series of articles under the title of "The Rights of Man."[50] At the same time, he frequently spoke in public, wrote articles in the *Manchester Guardian* and other periodicals, and worked to gain the support of NGOs such as the National Peace Council. Using this momentum to full advantage, Wells went on to publish a book in early 1940 containing his original draft and an extensive commentary on the nature of human rights. To emphasize the crusading spirit of the war at hand, he significantly entitled this book *The Rights of Man or What Are We Fighting For?* In this work he called on all people to spread the idea of the rights of man around the world, declaring emphatically: "There is no time to waste. Do not wait for 'leaders.' Act yourself."[51]

Wells did not stop his campaign on behalf of human rights at the edge of his own borders. Indeed, he sought to make his vision an international one and extend it as widely as possible around the globe. He made sure that *The Rights of Man* received widespread distribution throughout forty-eight countries and that his declaration was published in many different translations ranging from all of the European languages to Chinese, Japanese, Arabic, Urdu, Hindi, Bengali, Gujerati, Hausa, Swahili, Yoruba, Zulu, and Esperanto. His ideas received considerable attention by the Western press and were even attacked by Mussolini's *Popolo d'Italia* and on Goebbels's radio. Not content with this coverage, Wells sent a copy of his draft declaration to Dorothy Thomson, America's best-known female journalist at the time, who in turn wrote a column on the subject of human rights. He spoke or corresponded with many leading figures of the time, including Franklin and Eleanor Roosevelt, Jan Masaryk and Eduard Beneš of Czechoslovakia, Chaim Weizmann of the Jewish Agency, Jan Smuts of South Africa (who at the end of the war would draft the preamble of the United Nations Charter), Gandhi and Jawaharlal Nehru of India, and a number of philosophers in China, and learned much about the relationship between rights and duties and about the importance of incorporating different philosophical traditions into any statement of universal principle. In addition, during the autumn of 1940 he conducted a highly publicized lecture tour throughout the United States, often bluntly criticizing what he regarded as the hypocrisies of the West and always raising the vision of international human rights for the world.

Other individuals and nongovernmental organizations added their own contributions to these crusading visions as well. Immediately after the outbreak of war, the American League of Nations Association created a special Commission to Study the

Organization of Peace. Under the leadership of James T. Shotwell, the eminent historian at the Carnegie Endowment for International Peace who had served as a member of the United States delegation at the Paris Peace Conference, this group began to devote considerable time to the subject of the international safeguarding of human rights, publishing studies and exerting substantial influence on public opinion. A group of citizens in London organized themselves as the Atlantic Charter Society and worked to bring about the realization of its stated aims on rights. The international journalist Clarence Streit published his book, *Union Now: A Proposal*, urging all democratic nations of the world to unite on behalf of individual freedoms and what he called "the rights of man."[52] In 1940 the Movement for Federal Union published a pamphlet entitled *How Shall We Win?* which proposed an international charter of freedoms for all peoples. Several other proposals followed the next year. The Catholic Association for International Peace advocated that "the rights of man and of peoples must be defined and recognized, and an institutional way established to ensure human rights" while at the same time proposing the creation of an international bill of rights.[53] Private citizens created the new International League for the Rights of Man (subsequently the International League for Human Rights) with headquarters in New York City, and the World Citizens Association assembled a conference of experts on international relations that produced a report entitled *The World's Destiny* calling for recognition of the "new rights of man" in any postwar international organization.[54] The British Labour Party went on record as supporting a statement of the Rights of Man, and J. L. Brierly of Oxford University submitted a proposal for "an international bill of rights" guaranteeing certain civil and political rights to all people to the Royal Institute of International Affairs for consideration.[55] Lecturing in exile, Beneš spoke on the same theme and declared: "After the present war a charter of Human Rights throughout the whole world should be constitutionally established and put into practice."[56] The growing popularity of this vision of setting forth basic rights could certainly be seen in a number of different ways by early 1942 when a widely circulated public statement by the National Conference of Christians and Jews concerning "inalienable rights" and the publication of a book by Jacques Maritain entitled *Les Droits de l'Homme et la Loi Naturelle* (The Rights of Man and Natural Law) stimulated still further discussion about the prospects for some kind of bill of rights that might protect all people.[57] These many men and women who labored in adopting visions and creating proposals on behalf of human rights became even more convinced of their crusading mission when Roosevelt decided to commemorate the first anniversary of the signing of the Atlantic Charter. On this occasion he responded to their concerns and inspired them by declaring:

A year ago today the nations resisting a common barbaric foe were units or small groups, fighting for their existence. Now, these nations and groups of nations in all the continents of the earth have united. They have formed a great union of humanity, dedicated to the realization of that common program of purposes and principles set forth in the Atlantic Charter. . . . Their faith in life, liberty, independence and religious freedom, and in the preservation of human rights and justice in their own lands as well as in other lands, has been given form and substance and power through a great gathering of peoples now known as the United Nations. . . . When victory comes, we shall stand shoulder to shoulder in seeking to nourish the great ideals for which we fight. . . . We reaffirm our principles.[58]

Such broad declarations of principle and proposals for bills or charters of guarantees provided essential elements for the evolution of international human rights, but for many activists they did not offer sufficient specificity. For them, it was necessary to take the generalities of these visions and proposals to the next step and focus them on very concrete problems. Toward this end, they consciously drew on the theme of a "people's war" and directed their energies to the specific needs and rights of a variety of people around the world.

Enormous attention, for example, focused on the fate of those millions of indigenous peoples still suffering as conquered subjects under colonial empires. The promise of the right of self-determination first enunciated in the Atlantic Charter stirred hopes of freedom. It stimulated great excitement among individuals like Du Bois and George Padmore of the Pan-African movement, Nkrumah of Ghana, Azikiew of Nigeria, and Amy Jacques Garvey, and among NGOs such as the Universal African National Movement and Council on African Affairs, for realizing their dreams of independence for Africans. Harold Moody and his League of Colored Peoples, for example, proposed a "Charter for Colored Peoples" claiming their right to be free from the colonial powers and to secure self-determination.[59] At the same time, the raw power of successful Japanese military victories against the Americans, British, French, and Dutch stripped away the facade of presumed Western superiority in Asia and provided inspiration for independence heretofore considered virtually impossible. For the first time, colonial peoples saw the prospect of a different future. Everything, recalled S. Sjahrir of Indonesia in *Out of Exile*, "was shaken loose from its moorings. . . . All layers of society came to see the past in another light. If these [Japanese] barbarians had been able to replace the old colonial authority, why had that authority been necessary at all? Why, instead, hadn't they handled the affairs of government themselves? . . . [Now] national self-consciousness . . . developed a new and powerful drive beyond anything known before."[60] For their own part, the Japanese actively encouraged these visions by deliberately cultivating nationalist leaders like Subhas Chandra Bose of India, Ba Maw of Burma, José Laurel of the Philippines, and Sukarno of Indonesia during the war. Pearl S. Buck, the widely read author and interpreter of Asian affairs to the West, watched all these developments carefully and warned: "The deep patience of colored peoples is at an end. Everywhere among them there is the same resolve for freedom and equality that white Americans and British have, but it is a grimmer resolve, for it includes the determination to be rid of white rule and exploitation and white race prejudice, and nothing will weaken this will."[61]

Raising the issue of race abroad, of course, elevated it at home. Aborigines in Australia, Indians and Inuits in Canada, blacks in South Africa, and Maori in New Zealand, among others, wanted to know how the principles of the Atlantic Charter would apply to them.[62] In this light the Institute of Pacific Relations called on the Allies to establish "conditions of racial, political, and economic justice and welfare" for all.[63] The same question arose with even greater force in the United States where the right of non-discrimination had been contested ever since the nation's founding with particular reference to rights of indigenous peoples and slaves, and now escalated with the active participation of several million blacks as servicemen in the armed forces and as workers in defense industries. During 1942 the Congress of Racial Equality organized its first campaigns for political action, proposing that all peoples should be treated equally without distinction as to the color of their skin. At the same time, many members of the National Association for the Advancement of Colored People actively participated in what they called the "Double V Campaign": victory over the Axis abroad and victory over racial discrimination at home. Race riots and continued segregation even within the armed forces and on military bases made the disparity between the principles of the Atlantic Charter and actual practice all the more stark. "Just carve on my tombstone," declared one draftee with pointed bitterness, "Here lies a black man, killed fighting a yellow man, for the protection of the white man."[64] Statements such as these were given widespread public attention, and thus helped to generate a growing number of specific proposals, including those for the right to vote without poll taxes or other obstacles, equal protection through a federal anti-lynching law and Justice Department intervention in cases of civil rights violations, the elimination of Jim Crow laws of segregation, an end to imperialism and colonial possessions, and desegregation in the military.[65] The activities of the Indian Rights Association and the formation of the more militant National Congress of American Indians on behalf of both individual and "tribal rights" during the war added still further momentum to this movement.[66]

Other proposals emerging from the experience of the war focused specifically on the rights of women. Not only did women suffer as much if not more than men when civilian population centers were attacked in this total war, but they contributed heavily to volunteer activities, the work force, and actual military service or resistance against occupation forces. In these circumstances, it is not surprising that women and those men who supported them among the Allies in the crusade of this "people's war" would make proposals for complete equality in rights. The extension of the right of women to vote thus granted during the war in the Mongolian People's Republic, the Dominican Republic, and by the French Provisional Government in Algiers, served in turn to inspire others.[67] Struggles during the war also stimulated visions of the liberation of women in China, particularly among the members of the Chinese Communist Party such as the well-known writer Ding Ling with her influential essay "Thoughts on 8 March [International Women's Day]" and the proposal by one regional government for "raising women's political, economic, and cultural position in society on the basis of the fundamental principle of equality between the sexes."[68] In the United States, the government and media suddenly changed their criticisms of women who worked, and instead embarked on a campaign to get them to enter the work force in the name of a crusading patriotic duty. Over six million women subsequently took jobs outside the home, and in the process watched their wages leap upward, their unionization increase, their efforts praised publicly with popular images of "Rosie the Riveter," and their economic independence and self-confidence grow as never before. Indeed, the Women's Bureau declared this role during the war to be "one of the most fundamental social and economic changes" in the nation's history, and indicated that women had every intention of insisting on the full extension of their rights when the war finally ended.[69]

Women also played a particularly significant role during the war as advocates for the rights of children. As in virtually all other cases in the evolution of international human rights, a consciousness of victimization provided the essential impetus. It became increasingly clear during the tragic course of this conflict that innocent children remained starkly incapable of defending themselves against the ravages of war and horrors of genocide. As victims, their plight could hardly be ignored by Allies crusading in the name of the value of human life and rights. At first, efforts such as those of the National War Orphans Shelter Association in China sought to provide immediate assistance of food, clothing, and refuge for children suddenly deprived of their parents and without any other form of protection. NGOs in the West devoted to the welfare of children, including many based on religious belief, took similar action in the face of such obvious need. As the war progressed and as the number of infant and young victims mounted, other efforts began to focus on establishing an international recognition of rights for children. The Inter-Allied Conference of Educational Experts, for example, proposed a "Children's Charter" to draw attention to this issue. The Pan-American Child Congress offered a similar proposal, as did the U.S. Children's Bureau with its "Children's Charter in Wartime," addressing the rights of the child.[70]

Still other proposals for human rights emerged with an emphasis on class and caste. Since this "people's war" and its ensuing crusade required sacrifices from all citizens, they in turn might reasonably expect that their efforts would be rewarded and their rights recognized. In fact, to secure support, Allied governments made such promises to their people. Workers and those impoverished in the United States with vivid memories of the recent Depression still on their minds certainly interpreted Roosevelt's pledge about freedom from want, especially in the context of his New Deal social legislation, in just such a light. They welcomed his call for a new "Economic Bill of Rights" that would complement the Constitution's traditional Bill of Rights.[71] The expectations of those who voted for the Labour Party in Australia and New Zealand were much the same as they listened to their governments declare: "We are fighting for a moral issue, . . . to institute the rule of law . . . and to increase the welfare of the people."[72] They listened intently as Peter Fraser and Walter Nash spoke continually in Wellington and abroad about how the war, although a calamity, also presented an unparalleled opportunity to extend justice, the principles of the Atlantic Charter, and the rights "of all mankind" to improved labor standards, full employment, economic advancement, and social security as "the rightful heritage of all human beings."[73] The formation of the Mahila Atmaraksha Samiti in India at the same time similarly stressed the need to eliminate the great disparities between castes of the rich and the poor in society.[74] Perhaps the most dramatic and influential of all these wartime proposals dealing with such class differences and rights was the Beveridge Report of 1942 in Britain. "Now, when the war is abolishing landmarks of every kind," it declared, "is the opportunity for using experience in a clear field. A revolutionary moment in the world's history is a time for revolutions, not for patching."[75] Toward this end, the report maintained that the state should offer security for service and contribution made by people during the war, and therefore proposed that Churchill's conservative government acknowledge the right of all citizens to have a decent level of subsistence and a minimum level of social security through family allowances, disability benefits, national health insurance, old-age pensions, and a national minimum income. The report thus came to serve as the conceptual foundation of the modern welfare state in Britain and its authors found themselves being praised for their "pioneering vision."[76]

These proposals about the rights of all people to have a certain minimum level of protection and to have the freedom from fear and from want also pervaded the whole area of wartime relief. The experience of World War II all too often provided tragic evidence of the old adage that "war is the great equalizer" when it came to human suffering. Distinctions of the past quickly seemed to pale when it came to masses of people victimized by wartime destruction, disruption, and dislocation, made all the more extensive and spread across continents by the weapons of modern science. Graphic accounts and photographs of displaced, huddled human beings in pain from starvation, exposure, destitution, and illness from around the world moved humanitarians to again consider their universal responsibilities and render critical assistance. Many private organizations and religious charities rushed to provide relief of distress, as did the Red Cross, and did so until they simply were overwhelmed with the magnitude of the problem. In an attempt to address this unmistakable need and critical emergency, forty-four nations agreed to create the United Nations Relief and Rehabilitation Administration (UNRRA), described by one authority as "the first and in some ways the most fruitful of broadly based international organizations" to emerge from the war.[77] By contributing their collective resources, they sought to provide humanitarian aid and assistance in ways that none of them could accomplish alone to those who suffered so terribly in Asia and Europe, ranging from small villages in China to seaports along the Baltic and Adriatic. The organization eventually dispensed tons of food, built hundreds of hospitals, prevented epidemics of diphtheria and cholera, revived transportation systems, and cared for an estimated one million displaced persons. Moreover, the members and workers of UNRRA pledged that at no time would relief and rehabilitation supplies be used as a political weapon and that no discrimination should be made in the distribution of relief supplies because of race, gender, creed, class, political belief. Such nondiscrimination, they declared, in addition to receiving a minimum level of food and supplies necessary to sustain life, constituted basic human rights that belonged to all humankind.[78]

As all these incalculable human needs became more apparent during the course of the war, and as the crusading dimensions of this global conflict grew, individuals and nongovernmental organizations devoted even more effort to promoting visions of international human rights. The Commission to Study the Organization of Peace, composed of prominent scholars and foreign policy experts, released a highly suggestive report in 1943 entitled "Human Rights and the World Order." Written by the noted international legal authority Quincy Wright, it argued that the members of the global community now needed to pay particular attention as to how they might protect human rights across national borders.[79] Shortly thereafter the International Bill of Rights Committee of the Twentieth Century Association sponsored the publication of *The International Bill of Rights and Permanent Peace Concordance*, and representatives from forty-seven different colleges and universities throughout the United States submitted a proposal for an international bill of rights.[80] During the same year, Hersch Lauterpacht, perhaps the most famous expert on international law of the time in the world, began his advocacy of an international bill of human rights with a public lecture at Cambridge University and subsequently published his proposals in *An International Bill of the Rights of Man*.[81] Then, following two years' worth of work by a committee of advisers representing the major cultures of the world, the American Law Institute, composed of members from throughout the Western Hemisphere, released its *Statement of Essential Human Rights*. This report (which would later serve as one of the principal sources for drawing up the first draft of the Universal Declaration of Human Rights) was heavily influenced by Latin American jurists. It delineated a variety of civil and political rights and social and economic rights, and called on the leaders of the world to recognize that "at this crucial moment in human history . . . new concepts [of human rights] affecting the future development of man and society are being crystallized."[82]

Greatly encouraged by all these many proposals, the International Labor Organization sought to add its influence and voice to this groundswell of support for human rights as well. Thus, during its first regular session since the outbreak of war, under the leadership of Walter Nash, its members from forty-one different countries enthusiastically endorsed what they called The Declaration of Philadelphia. Here, in early 1944 they spoke with a great sense of urgency of the need to see themselves as "the conscience of mankind" and to create "a people's peace." Toward this end, they reaffirmed the universal applicability of the principles of the Atlantic Charter and their original constitution, reiterating their belief that all men and women, regardless of race, creed, or any other factor of difference, have the right to pursue their material well-being and spiritual development in conditions of freedom and dignity, economic and social security, and equal opportunity. Following the adoption of the declaration, Nash spoke eloquently of "a vision of a different post-war world unfolding truly amazing possibilities of a better life for all of us." He acknowledged the sacrifices made by people across the continents during the war and argued that there could be no genuine peace without a recognition of the rights of all people to life, some level of prosperity, and equality. Then, in perhaps the most moving part of his speech he declared that the world must recognize that "there are no superior people" and that "there can be no justification for discrimination." "Men and women of all races, of all creeds, of all nationalities, and of all classes" around the world, he concluded, henceforth must be treated equally and accorded their basic human rights.[83]

All of these proclaimed visions increasingly constituted what René Brunet, a former delegate to the League of Nations, described as a "vast movement of public opinion" that "grew incessantly in force and in scope as the war rolled on." "Hundreds of political, scholarly, and religious organizations," he observed personally with great interest, collectively contributed to the crusade for human rights. These crusaders fervently believed in their mission, and sought to build momentum and bring as much influence to bear on governments as they possibly could. Through their many publications, manifestos, and appeals for action, he concluded, they created visions and proposals that "have spread and impressed the idea that the protection of human rights should be part of the war aims of the Allied Powers, and that the future peace would not be complete if it would not consecrate the principle of international protection of human rights in all States and if it would not guarantee this protection in an effective manner."[84]

Such effectiveness, of course, constituted the critical problem. How to actually guarantee protection for human rights constantly plagued all of the visions emerging from World War II, as acknowledged by the influential Commission to Study the Organization of Peace in its most pathbreaking 1944 report entitled *International Safeguard of Human Rights*. Hardhitting and highly critical of both the horrifying abuses of rights by the Axis and of the double standards practiced by the liberal democratic Allies, the report argued that the world stood on the verge of a new future. It emphasized that the dramatic change could begin to take place only if people and governments first acknowledged the intimate connection between human rights in domestic politics and world peace, then took deliberate international action to safeguard those rights. Toward this end, the commission specifically proposed to convene a United Nations Conference on Human Rights without delay, establish a permanent Commission on Human Rights to develop standards and methods of protection, recognize the right of individuals and groups to petition this body, and to develop effective means of enforcement. The members of the commission fully recognized that such a task would not be easy, for traditions inhibit innovation, prejudices run deep, and diplomatic agreement is always hard to achieve. But among all of the obstacles to be faced, the report singled out one for special attention: "the bogey of national sovereignty," which allowed states to claim a special privilege of domestic jurisdiction and to dismiss any interest by other states into the abuse of rights of their own people as unjustifiable interference into their internal affairs. In the past, observed the report, the guarantee of human rights remained the separate, exclusive, and independent responsibility of each nation. The individual person thus had to rely on his or her own government — the most likely source of abuse in the first place — for protection, but could not look beyond their borders for help. The commission vowed that in the name of international human rights, after the experience of war and genocide, this simply could no longer be tolerated, and declared with as much intensity as it could command:

We are determined that hereafter no nation may be insulated and wholly a law unto itself in the treatment of its people.[85]

The acceptance or rejection of this vision would be determined not so much by those many individuals or NGOs who proposed it, however, but by the very claimants of national sovereignty, namely the governments of nation states themselves.

Human Rights and National Sovereignty in Postwar Planning

The many proposals and visions of international human rights generated during the course of World War II presented Allied governments with an unanticipated and serious dilemma. On the one hand, all these thoughtful discussions about rights provided enormous advantages. They helped to make a dramatic and positive distinction between themselves and their wartime adversaries, establish encouraging purposes for which they were fighting the war, and provide principles capable of genuinely inspiring their people to participate and make sacrifices on behalf of a universal crusade. Yet, at the same time, such discussions also presented difficult problems by creating a troublesome mirror that reflected their own abuses of rights, raising dangerous expectations that might not be met, and potentially threatening their own power and claims of national sovereignty. It did not take long for governments, particularly as they began to make plans for the postwar world, to confront this dilemma and the contest between international human rights and national sovereignty directly, and to recognize the profound difficulty of trying to have it both ways.

There were times during the war when some Allied governments actually appeared to be enthusiastic in leading the crusade for human rights. The visionary language of the Atlantic Charter and then the forceful and wide-ranging Declaration of the United Nations, eventually signed by forty-six nations, marked a dramatic departure in the evolution of international human rights. Innumerable public addresses subsequently made by Winston Churchill and his Secretary of State for Foreign Affairs Anthony Eden in Britain, Charles de Gaulle and René Cassin of the Free French National Committee, Prime Minister William Mackenzie King of Canada, Madame Chiang and Minister of Foreign Affairs T. V. Soong of China, Prime Minister Robert Menzies and his Minister for External Affairs Herbert Evatt of Australia, Peter Fraser and Walter Nash of New Zealand, Jan Smuts of South Africa, President Manuel Camacho of Mexico, and especially Franklin and Eleanor Roosevelt, Sumner Welles, and Secretary of State Cordell Hull in the United States, among many others, all reconfirmed the commitment to principles of human rights in official and highly visible ways.[86] At times they even dropped copies of H. G. Wells's *The Rights of Man* behind enemy lines.[87] Additional encouragement came from Latin American governments when their Inter-American Juridical Committee issued its preliminary Recommendation on Postwar Problems surprisingly addressing the need for nation-states to modify their traditional interpretations of national sovereignty by taking into account moral law, peace, and social justice for all in the larger international community.[88] More evidence appeared when a number of Allied governments signed the 1942 United Nations Declaration on Jewish Massacres, publicly condemning Hitler's violation of "the most elementary human rights" and solemnly promising the world to punish those responsible for the atrocities of mass extermination.[89] Their signing of the Moscow Declaration pledging a commitment to a new United Nations organization on the conclusion of the war and their financial support of UNRRA and its efforts at alleviating human suffering gave even further credence to their statements about international human rights.[90]

Other statements and actions, however, revealed a very different direction. When pressed, most of those leaders who spoke so eloquently about human rights quickly noted that statements like the Atlantic Charter and Declaration of the United Nations represented only goals rather than legal agreements that might jeopardize national interests or threaten national sovereignty. It is in this context that Churchill made his celebrated statements about not allowing stated principles such as that of the right of self-determination to precipitate the liquidation of the British Empire, and describing the Atlantic Charter as "no more than a simple, rough and ready, war-time statement of a goal" toward which the supporting governments "mean to make their war" instead of a binding treaty with firm commitments.[91] When H. G. Wells lectured in the United States to promote a vision of international human rights, officials in the Foreign Office contemptuously referred to him as "a somewhat senile, half-extinct prophet . . . much better kept at home."[92] Governments reacted with similar hostility when in a hard-hitting essay on human rights entitled "Your Sovereignty — or Your Nation's?" Clarence Streit challenged them by reminding all of those fighting this "people's war" that states were made for the benefit of men and women rather than the reverse.[93] Moreover, and as we have seen, the Allied governments displayed great reluctance to take any serious action that might actually dissolve their colonial empires, assist those Jews caught in Hitler's Holocaust, modify their exclusive immigration restrictions, release those interned for the war solely because of their race, or change their domestic policies of segregation. In following these policies, it must be acknowledged that government officials understood perfectly well that they did not act in political isolation, but enjoyed the support of large numbers of their own citizens who clearly did not want other countries telling them what they could or could not do. As one study attempting to promote human rights during the war reluctantly noted: "There are many voters to whom national sovereignty is a very dear thing. They will surrender it [if at all] . . . only after long argument, and even then with reluctance."[94]

This tension between those who advocated human rights and those unwilling to surrender national sovereignty revealed itself in any number of ways, not the least of which could be found in efforts of postwar planning. Many of the Allied governments, to one extent or the other, created special, official, interdepartmental committees charged with analyzing the profoundly changing nature of relations among states and the forces at work within and between them, anticipating future peace and security, and preparing for the vast and complicated problems that eventually would confront them and the world on the conclusion of the war. The most elaborate of these occurred in the United States, which appeared to have resolved that it had no intention of reverting back into isolationism once the conflict ended and now to play an active role in global affairs. Toward this end, Roosevelt authorized the creation of the Advisory Committee on Postwar Foreign Policy. Its membership came first from the Department of State, including Hull, Welles, special assistant Leo Pasvolsky, legal advisor Green Hackworth, and Harley Notter, who became advisor to the assistant secretary for United Nations affairs. Other members came from the Senate and House of Representatives, the White House, a member each from the War and Navy Departments and the Joint Chiefs of Staff, and, as if to confirm the theme of a "people's war," several nonofficial individuals, including Hamilton Fish Armstrong, the editor of *Foreign Affairs*; Anne O'Hare McCormick, the foreign affairs analyst of the *New York Times*; Norman Davis of the American Red Cross and the Council on Foreign Relations; James Shotwell, who concurrently chaired the nongovernmental Commission to Study the Organization of Peace; and representatives of the American Federation of Labor, among others. The committee set out to accomplish its wide-ranging assignments in early 1942 by establishing a division of labor and creating subcommittees for political issues, territorial matters, reconstruction, economic policy, security questions, and general coordination. The most important of these, and the one whose judgment heavily influenced all the rest, was the Subcommittee on Political Problems chaired by Welles.[95]

Sumner Welles brought a wealth of experience and valuable assets with him to this assignment of postwar planning. He had traveled widely, served in diplomatic posts and on special assignments from Asia to Latin America and Europe, held the position of under secretary of state, and enjoyed a long personal friendship and confidence with President Roosevelt. Welles had played important roles onboard ship at the historic negotiation of the principles of the Atlantic Charter, at Washington during the signing of the Declaration of the United Nations, at the meeting in Rio de Janeiro when the Ministers of Foreign Affairs of the American Republics endorsed the Atlantic Charter, and as Cordell Hull suffered from increasingly serious illness, effectively became the secretary of state. In addition, Welles fervently believed in international human rights. Both in private conversations and in highly publicized speeches, he spoke frequently and fervently about a vision of humanity, the needs of those who suffered, equality, responsibilities beyond national borders, the importance of ending colonial possessions and supporting indigenous peoples, the relationship between the respect for rights and world peace, and the necessity of using this "people's war" to advance the inherent rights of every human being, "guaranteed to the world as a whole — in all oceans and in all continents."[96] Under his direction, therefore, it is hardly surprising that the Subcommittee on Political Problems and its various ad hoc working groups would turn their attention to such matters as peace, international law, the pacific settlement of disputes, the creation of an effective international organization (described at this planning stage as the "United Nations Authority") to replace the League of Nations, and the possibilities of an international bill of human rights.

Consequently, the first ad hoc drafting group within the State Department to be created under this committee structure for postwar planning received the charge of considering the issues that might surround an international bill of human rights. Known as the Special Subcommittee on Legal Problems,[97] it became perhaps the very first governmental group of a nation-state ever to address this subject officially in such detail. It met at least once a week for months in confidential deliberations. Indeed, most of its documents were marked "Secret. Not to be removed from the State Department building." Encouraged by Welles, the members assumed that the international recognition and, within each state the guarantee, of basic human rights would be conducive to the development of conditions favorable to the maintenance of peace. They therefore aimed to formulate a set of the rights of individuals that they thought would be universally respected, even if not formally subscribed to by all states, in a forceful statement of general principles. Toward this end, and appreciating the value of understanding the experiences of history, they consulted the texts of the English Bill of Rights, the U.S. Bill of Rights, the French Declaration of the Rights of Man and of the Citizen, the Declaration of the International Rights of Man adopted by the Institut de Droit International, proposals of the Fédération Internationale des Droits de l'Homme, and various suggestions from the American Institute of International Law and the Commission to Study the Organization of Peace, among others. Based on both the letter and the spirit of these documents and proposals, and their own visions of the future of the world, the members of this State Department group produced a number of drafts that included both traditional civil and political rights such as equal protection under the law, freedom of expression and religious belief, and the right to assemble, as well as social and economic rights such as a minimum standard of well-being and access to educational opportunities that were becoming increasingly accepted as basic by those people engaged in the war. At the end, they recommended that this international bill of rights conclude with these words:

These human rights shall be guaranteed by and constitute a part of the supreme law of each state and shall be observed and enforced by its administrative and judicial authorities, without discrimination on the basis of nationality, language, race, political opinion, or religious belief, any law or constitutional provision to the contrary notwithstanding.[98]

The critical difficulty with this draft, of course, came from the language "shall be observed and enforced . . . any law or constitutional provision to the contrary notwithstanding." "It becomes immediately apparent," observed Durward Sandifer, a specialist in legal matters providing advice, that "the principal problem is that of implementing the guarantees contained in any bill of rights."[99] Words and phrases were one thing, he pointed out to the other members of the special subcommittee not eager to hear him, but that implementation and enforcement presented something quite different. Any international guarantees of human rights by their very nature would impinge on the claimed prerogatives of national sovereignty and domestic jurisdiction. Confronted with this conflict, Sandifer continued to advise against any proposal that might involve international sanctions and cited the earlier opinion of André Mandelstam in *Les Droits Internationaux de l'Homme*, who even as a strong advocate of human rights also reluctantly acknowledged the power of national sovereignty when he wrote:

The signature, by all states, of a general convention of the rights of man would be at present unattainable, if such a convention should include any sanctions. . . . In fact, it would be falling victim to strange illusions to imagine that at the present time, when the Powers have not yet reached an understanding on the subject of the establishment of collective sanctions against the state which breaks its solemn obligations to maintain the *external peace*, that the same Powers would consent to the institution of a juridical system permitting the international community to render judgements followed by sanctions in the demand of *internal peace*.[100]

As a result of this argument, Sandifer recommended that an international bill of rights to promulgated—but without establishing any provisions for enforcement. "This would represent the simplest and least complicated method of putting an international bill of rights into effect," he wrote in a document classified as secret. "It is a device used many times in the past. States agree on the adoption of new rules of law or a formulation of existing rules and proclaim them to the world in a formal international agreement. Reliance is placed primarily upon the good faith of the contracting parties. . . . Such a procedure has the advantage of provoking the minimum of opposition, which is important in a step as radical in character as giving universal legal recognition to individual human rights."[101]

These same kinds of warnings confronted those concerned about human rights in those postwar planning subcommittees dealing with territorial questions and with proposals for an international organization. The Territorial Subcommittee, for example, assumed that virtually every region of the globe would be affected by the war. Its members knew that when hostilities ended complicated and difficult questions would arise over border readjustments, the desire of the victors to hold strategic possessions, the fate of the League of Nations mandates, and the applicability of the principle of the right of self-determination, among others, to indigenous peoples in colonial empires, as declared in the Atlantic Charter. Yet, they also encountered the fact that most of those imperial powers were military allies necessary for defeating common enemies and not at all inclined to surrender their possessions or their prerogatives of sovereignty. This problem confronted the Special Subcommittee on International Organization as well. When the members began their work under the chairmanship of Welles, they believed strongly in the need to make human rights provisions an integral part of their planning for the postwar world, and thus to regard the individual as well as the nation-state as both the object and subject of the international organization that would follow. To do this, however, they realized that they could not avoid what they called "the underlying question": "*How* do we limit sovereignty?"[102]

Members of this postwar planning committee found it extremely difficult to find satisfactory answers to this question. They spent several months carefully drafting a proposed charter for a postwar international organization, for example, including very specific provisions dealing with human rights. These included the enumeration of civil and political rights regarding freedom of conscience, speech, press, petition, association, and assembly, and certain safeguards of persons accused of a crime. The draft also contained provisions for economic and social rights, including the right to participate in public education, property rights, and the right to enjoy minimum standards of well-being. One of the most important articles provided for the right of equal protection and nondiscrimination on the basis of race, nationality, language, political opinion, or religious belief. Such a ban on discrimination, believed members of the committee, would be "fundamental because without it no person's rights are assured and those of all may be undermined."[103] Yet, when one internal evaluator provided an assessment of this issue of human rights, she soberly noted that given the politics of the time, this provision of nondiscrimination suffered from several problems. One of these was the absence of any mention of discrimination on the basis of gender "because agreement on this point could not yet be attained." In addition, she feared, the language of race would never be allowed to "interfere with the laws of some of our states for the segregation of the races." For these reasons, among others, the draft revealed what she called "the most notable omission": namely, "the absence of guarantees or measures of enforcement." Any such provisions would raise "constitutional or political difficulties in various states," be "politically unacceptable," and interfere with domestic jurisdiction and national sovereignty. As such, she predicted, any provisions regarding enforceable protection of human rights would be "out of the question at the present time."[104]

The avoidance of any challenges to national sovereignty by means of international human rights certainly resonated with the cautious and sometimes cynical Secretary of State. Cordell Hull, along with his supporters, continually praised the value of their own "realism" when dealing with power politics while portraying Welles as no more than a Don Quixote tilting at windmills, criticizing him for his unrealistic visions spawned by "idealism," zealotry, and "crusading liberalism."[105] Neither Hull nor Welles hid their considerable differences of personality or policy, and their smoldering conflicts that sometimes flared out in the open provided a vivid reminder of the fact that govern-ments and their officials rarely speak with the same voice. This became particularly evident over the issue of human rights. Although they both could deliver magnificent public speeches about the importance of rights, for example, it was Hull who did so to mobilize wartime support rather than out of genuine conviction. Within the Depart-ment of State he used the authority of his office to reiterate that no nation should interfere in the domestic affairs of another, that the colonial powers should not be forced to dismantle their empires too precipitously, that the proposed United Nations organization should not be given too much power, and that the doctrine of national sovereignty should not be sacrificed on any altar of human rights. When presiding over one of the State Department postwar planning meetings, for instance, he specifically attacked the proposed international bill of human rights and reminded all of those present (including most pointedly Welles) that no self-respecting nation would ever allow other countries to determine its relations with its own people, accept a concept of rights that applied vertically from the world down to the local level, permit enforce-ment procedures to be imposed by outsiders, or surrender any feature of its basic sovereignty. "Any proposal requiring a derogation of national sovereignty," he an-nounced with determination, would "meet the opposition" of the United States.[106]

Opposition from the Great Powers

The bitter struggle and wrenching hardship of World War II forced most nations into a dramatic realization of the necessity to find some kind of solutions on an international scale to their acute problems. Even the strongest realized that traditional national borders, geographical barriers, and local or regional scale of the past simply could no longer completely protect them. Global market forces were generated in far away financial capitals and the migration of peoples dramatically shaped their own econo-mies in ways they often did not fully understand. Distant military conflicts among participants equipped with modern technology could quickly envelop them with little warning and could create destruction of such overwhelming magnitude that their own resources were rendered completely insufficient. In order to defend themselves, they came to understand that they needed the combined military strength of all of the members of the Grand Alliance and thus hold international conferences and establish procedures to coordinate their prosecution of the war. In order to help those who suffered as a result of the conflict, they came to realize that they needed to collectively pool their resources and institute mechanisms like the United Nations Relief and Rehabilitation Administration to provide humanitarian food, medicine, clothing, and other emergency necessities. Moreover, in order to prepare for the transition from war to peace that would follow, they concluded that long-term peace and stability required that they develop coordinated monetary and financial policies and thus decided at the Bretton Woods Conference to create the International Bank for Reconstruction and Development (or World Bank) and the International Monetary Fund. With Allied successes in the Pacific, huge Soviet advances westward, and the Anglo-American D-Day invasion of Normandy in 1944, the course of the war began to change profoundly and brought the belligerents nearer to the battlegrounds where the final struggles would be fought to decision. This forced the coalition partners to give even more serious and urgent attention to the postwar world that their victory would likely bring. Toward this end, the Great Powers among the Allies decided that it was imperative for them to meet immediately and together draft a charter for a new international organization that would become known as the United Nations.

For seven weeks from August to October 1944, representatives of the United States, Britain, the Soviet Union, and China met in the elegant colonial residence at Dumbarton Oaks on the secluded outskirts of Washington, D.C. Prophetically, the inscription carved on the mansion wall read: *Quod severis metes*— "you shall reap what you sow."[107] Here they sought to negotiate agreement on the design and authority of a postwar international organization that would replace the League of Nations and maintain world peace and security. They held their conversations in secrecy, during two different phases, addressing such matters as the structure and scope of the proposed organization, security arrangements and the enforcement of decisions concerning any aggression or breaches of the peace, and the pacific settlement of disputes.[108] Among themselves they reached ready agreement over Roosevelt's basic concept of the "Four Policemen," which stated that those nations with the most preponderant strength would act as guardians over the rest of the world. As described by Hull, the "major responsibility" for maintaining peace and security after the war "must inevitably" be borne by these powers, and that no possibility existed for a successful international organization unless these four powers supported it.[109] Toward this end, they hammered out a preliminary charter of the United Nations that provided in the first instance for a powerful Security Council, that they, as the Great Powers, would dominate through their permanent membership and power of the veto. They agreed that a considerably weaker General Assembly would be composed of representatives of all nations, that an Economic and Social Council be created, and that an International Court of Justice be established to facilitate the peaceful resolution of disputes. They also agreed that the national sovereignty of each member state of the new organization would be respected.[110]

Despite the significant differences between them on other matters, the Great Powers also agreed on their opposition to any meaningful provisions concerning international human rights. Despite all of the solemn declarations, moving speeches, crusading rhetoric during the "people's war," and even Roosevelt's own reported feeling that some provision about human rights was "extremely vital,"[111] the movers and shakers at Dumbarton Oaks resisted the inclusion of articles in the charter that might involve giving the United Nations any authority to enforce rights that might interfere with their sovereignty. The only exception to this (and particularly ironic given the nature of the claims of subsequent regimes about the "imposition" of rights by the West on the rest of the world) was China. Even before the conference began, for example, the Chinese announced that in order for the international organization to be enabled to enforce justice for the world, their country would be willing "to cede as much of its sovereign power as may be required."[112] In addition, they determined to raise the issue of the right of all people to equality and nondiscrimination. Chinese leaders were well aware of the ignoble fate of the Japanese proposal for racial equality at the earlier Paris Peace

Conference, and thought that perhaps the experience of another war now might result in more positive changes. "I am particularly grateful to you and Secretary Hull," wrote Chiang to Roosevelt in advance, "for the insistence on the necessity of China's being represented at the conference. Without the participation of Asiatic peoples, the conference will have no meaning for half of humanity."[113] The Chinese then followed this correspondence with an official proposal that the new organization "shall be universal in character," strive to secure social welfare, support the self-determination of peoples, and that "the principle of equality of all states and all races shall be upheld."[114] Lest there be any question about China's interest in this matter, Wellington Koo went on to speak out about the influence of Confucius, Mo Zi, and Sun Yat-sen, explaining that "the thought of universal brotherhood has been deeply rooted in the minds of the Chinese for more than two thousand years."[115] His colleague, H. H. Kung, went on to declare in a speech given considerable publicity that China wanted "to strive toward the realization of a world commonwealth, in which all nations, great and small, will live in peace and equality, and all peoples are protected in their inalienable rights and assured the enjoyment of the fruits of their labor. The United Nations have now a unique opportunity to work together toward that ideal."[116]

This Chinese proposal drew fire at once from the other Great Powers during the first phase of the Dumbarton Oaks conversations, who shared a deep concern over "the equality of race question" specifically and the larger issue of human rights in general. The United States delegation no longer included Sumner Welles at the helm of postwar planning, for he had been forced to resign by Hull. They now received instructions instead from Hull and his new, handpicked Under Secretary of State Edward Stettinius directing them to shift away from previous and detailed State Department proposals about human rights completely and certainly from any stark or explicit article about equality as proposed by China.[117] The Soviets opposed the Chinese proposal immediately. Sir Alexander Cadogan, leading the British delegation, and well aware of Churchill's attitude toward race and vehement opposition to any right of self-determination in the empire, worried about creating the possibility that the organization would engage in criticism of the internal policies of member states and thereby threaten national sovereignty and domestic jurisdiction.[118] He acknowledged that China alone had raised this question and telegraphed the Foreign Office:

Discussion has taken place here of the attitude which should be adopted if the Chinese delegation press for inclusion in the agreed proposals of a provision on racial equality. Argument strongly advanced is that it would be against our interest and tradition as a liberal power to oppose the expression of a principle denial of which figures so prominently in Nazi philosophy and is repugnant to the mass of British and foreign opinion. Such action would moreover prejudice British and American relations in a sphere of greatest delicacy by supplying ammunition to critics who accuse us of reactionary policy in the Far East.

Cadogan then went on to propose a way out of the dilemma by suggesting a difference between words and deeds:

Recognition of the principle commits us to nothing more than we have always stood for. But there might be a revival of the quite unfounded fears of 1919 that immigration problems are involved.

These are, of course, . . . matters of domestic jurisdiction and would be covered if a satisfactory solution of this question is reached. We may be sure that if it were thought that such questions were involved by the recognition of the principle, the United States Delegation would oppose it.[119]

This was a safe bet. The United States tentatively considered the possibility of authorizing the United Nations to conduct studies and make recommendations concerning human rights, but certainly not to take action.[120] Stettinius indicated a willingness to support a general statement of principle about human rights, but not one that would threaten national sovereignty or speak explicitly about racial equality. If the new United Nations formally recognized such a principle of equality, he and others feared, it could seriously challenge domestic jurisdiction and control of their own internal affairs. The denial of rights to American citizens due to segregation and restrictive immigration legislation on the basis of race could then be brought into question by the international community. The Senate already had passed a resolution expressing that United States membership in any international organization should be conditional on a strong domestic jurisdiction clause. Members of the House of Representatives and the Republican presidential candidate Thomas Dewey and his foreign affairs advisor John Foster Dulles conveyed similar warnings about granting too much "coercive power" to the United Nations that would provoke negative reactions in domestic politics. They and other elected officials knew that the American nativism that had served as the wellspring for isolationism and super-patriotism always lay just below the surface for many voters who could be counted on to oppose any "foreigners" telling them what they could or could not do. In addition, recent naval victories in the South Pacific were beginning to change the attitude of the Joint Chiefs of Staff regarding the right of self-determination. They began to strongly resist any suggestions about surrendering islands of strategic importance captured from the Japanese after much loss of life and thus sought to tone down previous statements about the evils of colonial possessions. All of these factors represented component parts of what Welles described as "the powerful influences" opposed to granting too much authority to the United Nations.[121] Consequently, the United States proposed a statement that tried to have it both ways by reading: "The International Organization should refrain from intervention in the internal affairs of any state, it being the responsibility of each state to see that conditions prevailing within its jurisdiction do not endanger international peace and security and, to this end, to respect the human rights and fundamental freedoms of all its people and to govern in accordance with the principles of humanity and justice."[122]

The British and the Soviet delegations would not even support this statement that took away with one hand what it gave with the other. They feared that a general statement about human rights and fundamental freedoms in the section on general principles for the United Nations would open a Pandora's box and release dangerous forces that would seriously threaten their sovereignty and power. British officials in London and those stationed in overseas possessions, for example, worried that such language would greatly endanger their control over a vast empire with its sprawling holdings throughout the world. They also expressed the conviction that rights were not necessarily "absolute" at all times or in all places, and voiced concern about the possibility of having to create "an international detective service" to monitor compliance should there be any stated principles of human rights. The British thus dug in their heels.[123] Moreover, the maintenance of Stalin's dictatorial regime of forced collectivization, ruthless purges, state terrorism, and the Gulag could never possibly survive any serious efforts on behalf of human rights within the Soviet Union. In addition, despite innumerable wartime pledges, Stalin had no intention of discussing the right of self-determination for the Baltic states, eastern Poland, Bessarabia, and part of Finland that he was about to annex outright with the armed might of the Red Army. Andrei Gromyko, the dour Soviet representative, bluntly declared that any reference to individual rights and basic freedoms "is not germane to the main tasks of an international security organization."[124] Consequently, the British and Soviets reluctantly agreed to an innocuous phrase that the organization should promote respect for human rights and fundamental freedoms, but only if it related to the single area of international cooperation in social and economic matters.[125]

By the time the Chinese began their direct participation in the second phase of the Dumbarton Oaks conversations, therefore, the Big Three (Great Britain, the Soviet Union, and the United States) had already agreed among themselves to bury any mention of human rights deep within the text and confine it to social and economic cooperation, and to completely eliminate all mention of racial equality as originally proposed by China. Wellington Koo, as the chair of the delegation at Dumbarton Oaks, complained at the very first opportunity in a private conversation with Cadogan that "nothing was said about justice" in the draft text of the charter.[126] In frustration, he spoke about "law and justice," "equality," and "humanity at large," and then went on to explain his argument at greater length in a memorandum combining both principle and pragmatism:

The new organization aims at the maintenance of peace and security throughout the world. It hopes to lay the foundation for a durable peace in order that the genius and resources of mankind may be devoted entirely to constructive purposes. For the successful attainment of this object, the faith, understanding, and cooperation of all peoples will be needed. As a means of promoting this . . . it will be highly desirable to consecrate the principle of equality of races as of states in the fundamental instrument of the new institution. Reference to this principle . . . in the preamble of the new charter will not only give moral satisfaction to the greater part of humanity, but will also go far to pave the way for the realization of the ideal of universal brotherhood inseparable from the ideal of permanent world peace.[127]

The other Great Powers opposed this position, telling Koo and other members of his delegation in no uncertain terms that it simply would not be approved by them. In doing so, they presented a serious dilemma for the Chinese. If they simply accepted the draft text as a fait accompli, they risked losing the principles at stake. If they pushed the issues of race or of colonies too strongly, however, they risked attracting criticism of their own regime of Chiang Kai-shek and alienating the very allies on whom they depended. The cost was especially high when considering the United States, who seemed at times to possess a near infatuation with China, serving as their absolutely essential benefactor of military supplies and financial assistance in wartime and sponsor of diplomatic status in postwar planning. Churchill, for example, had opposed even inviting them to attend the Dumbarton Oaks negotiations, dismissing them contemptuously as not being a world power at all but only a "faggot vote on the side of the United States."[128] In the end, the Chinese had to choose between relative priorities. They decided that although this issue might be important, it was not vital when compared to the risk of jeopardizing their immediate strategic and political needs by offending the other Great Powers, particularly since they knew they already had been outvoted. They did not remain silent, however. In providing an assessment of developments, Koo avoided the sensitive word, *race*, but spoke about all of the sacrifices made during the war, the great body of public opinion around the world, and the need to adopt basic principles of justice and humanity for international conduct. These represented matters, he said, to which China "attached a great deal of importance." "It would be highly desirable to do everything possible," Koo continued, "to remove any suspicion on the part of the peace-loving peoples of the world that this new organization, though originally set up for the maintenance of peace and security, might eventually degenerate into an organization of power politics. If we could do something to give a moral tone to the character of the new organization, we would go a long way toward fostering confidence and removing misgivings, possibly based upon cynicism, doubts, or suspicions."[129]

For the moment, these particular words and warning of the Chinese largely fell on deaf ears at Dumbarton Oaks. The draft charter that emerged from the conversations among the Great Powers, in the words of one observer, lacked any "humanity" and emphasized "the actual facts" of Realpolitik in the international situation.[130] First and foremost among these facts was the intention of the Great Powers of creating an international organization that they could control. As described by one leading authority on this subject, "the Big Three saw the defense of their own security, the protection of their own interests, and the enjoyment of the fruits of their victory in the world war as more important than the creation of an international organization to maintain world peace."[131] Their design for the new body sought to guarantee that they would dominate the powerful Security Council with their permanent membership and vetoes capable of thwarting any action against themselves. This would ensure that the organization would never be able to oppose any aggression that they launched. They also designed a much weaker General Assembly in which all states would sit, but one that largely would confine itself to discussions and debates about international questions falling within the scope of the charter. In the confidential words of Roosevelt (and thus not designed for public consumption), this assembly "should meet about once a year" and enable "all the small nations . . . to blow off steam at it."[132] In addition, their language for the charter wanted to ensure that an emphasis would be placed on the rights of states rather than individuals, that no reference would be made about colonial possessions at all, and that no mention would be made about human rights either in the principles of the organization as a whole or in the functions of the Security Council and General Assembly. Instead, they would permit the only reference to human rights and fundamental freedoms to appear within the confines of general economic and social cooperation. When one member of the Chinese delegation dared to ask for an explanation of what the other Great Powers meant by this single mention, Leo Pasvolsky of the Department of State replied that the details of both principles and mechanics would be left to the assembly of the organization. After making appropriate studies, he observed, it might propose international agreements with regard to the observance of human rights, but that any such accords would become effective only when accepted by the respective sovereign states. "This," he bluntly predicted, "would not be likely to happen for some time."[133]

*   *   *

Most of those particular representatives of the Great Powers who drafted a charter for the United Nations at Dumbarton Oaks thus seemed to have little appreciation for the power of the visions of human rights generated during World War II. They came to realize much sooner than they ever anticipated, however, that crusades once unleashed are not easily reined in or halted. Expectations had been raised, promises made, and proposals issued during this "people's war" that were not about to be denied. Countless men and women, including those among minority groups, smaller nations, and colonial peoples, had been led to believe that their personal sacrifices in war and their witness to genocide would bring certain results to the world. Advocates for international human rights thus reacted with immediate shock, resentment, and anger when they read the proposals emanating from the Great Powers that contained all the old provisos about national sovereignty but almost nothing about rights. Welles, perhaps with a broader perspective gained from much experience, responded by suggesting to them that not everyone had yet been heard on this subject. There would not be any "signing on the dotted line," he said, "by nations that have not yet been given a chance to take part in conferences and who may not be willing to accept the general lines in the proposals of Dumbarton Oaks."[134] This is exactly what happened, for those who had been excluded up to this point now determined that they would not remain passive in the face of Great Power opposition or silent on the subject of human rights as the time approached for a more broadly based international conference designed to create a new peace.

Chapter 6
A "People's Peace"

Peace and a Charter with Human Rights

As we have had a people's war, so shall we now have a people's peace.
— Walter Nash of New Zealand

After enduring so much suffering, surviving so much devastation, and hearing so many promises from their leaders about human rights, it is hardly surprising that many of those who sacrificed so much during World War II would demand better conditions for the peace that would follow. They had fought in this crusade for a purpose, and with the end in sight were not about to let the pledges be broken or their visions be denied. After years of brutal struggle, their adversaries finally bordered on the verge of collapse and peace was just a few months away. The diplomacy of the Great Powers at Dumbarton Oaks concerning an international organization and the strategic positioning of vast armies and navies around the face of the globe revealed that powerful forces already were seeking to mold the postwar world in particular ways, and that the language of a broadly based peace for all people employed during the war was giving way to the terms of narrow national security. Indeed, their deliberations gave every appearance of having everything to do with geopolitics and almost nothing to do with human rights. Consequently, voices arose in many quarters to protest what they regarded as a betrayal by the Great Powers and to reassert their own visions and proposals tempered so recently by sacrifices in the crucible of battle. To do this, they sought to reshape the direction of the discussion about the actual terms of the United Nations Charter by insisting that sacrifices made in the "people's war" now be rewarded by a "people's peace" that fully entailed dimensions of human rights.

Insisting on a Peace with Rights

The expectations for the Dumbarton Oaks conversations had been exceedingly high. After all, victory over fierce adversaries seemed assured within a few months and those Great Powers around the table already had pledged themselves before their own people and before the world to honor the principles of the Atlantic Charter and the Declaration of the United Nations. The very fact that the meetings were held in the United States, the "arsenal of democracy" and the home of Franklin Roosevelt who had done more than any other person to bring human rights to the attention of the globe during the crusade of war, provided additional hope. Public statements by the participants themselves about creating a new international organization to establish lasting peace for all nations generated even further excitement and enthusiasm about the prospects for the postwar world. As Cordell Hull said on behalf of the president at the opening session: "We meet at a time when the war is moving toward an overwhelming triumph for the forces of freedom. It is our task here to help lay the foundations upon which, after victory, peace, freedom, and a growing prosperity can be built. . . . This war moves us to search for an enduring peace — a peace founded upon justice and fair dealing for individuals and for nations."[1]

Perhaps the very height of these expectations made the fall so precipitous when they failed to materialize. Instead of all the idealistic features of peace and an international organization promised during the wartime crusade and suggested anew by the grandiose statements of Hull and others, the Dumbarton Oaks proposals revealed something quite different. Once these plans became known through open publication and word of mouth, they opened up a vociferous public debate and launched a storm of protest that extended around the world. In the minds of those who advocated a new kind of universal peace with human rights, the meetings exposed the crass self-interests and the old politics of the Great Powers alone. The prominence of the Security Council, the diminution of the General Assembly, the emphasis on states rather than individuals, the absence of any provision at all concerning colonial empires, and the sole mention of human rights practically buried in the text and confined to social and economic cooperation thus provoked shock, resentment, and anger. As one diplomat who watched these proceedings very carefully described it, the proposals emerging from Dumbarton Oaks amounted to "very little more than an undertaking by the . . . Great Powers to meet from time to time to discuss the situation as it appeared, and to decide what they thought might best be done, and in taking this course they expected the assistance and collaboration of the smaller powers." If they were allowed to stand, he warned, the result would be the very "negation in the international field of those principles of democracy for which this war is being fought" on behalf of all nations, colonies, minorities, and others denied their basic rights. The United Nations, he predicted, thus would become "merely another alliance with the obvious fate of all alliances" and would fail to protect human rights and thus fail to keep the peace.[2]

Many members of the alliance, NGOs, and private citizens alike thus felt an enormous sense of betrayal at the hands of the Great Powers. For this reason, they expressed their feelings in language that often spoke of pledges dishonored, debts unpaid, and promises unkept, and returned again and again to text of the Atlantic Charter. When addressing the Canadian House of Parliament in anticipation of this issue, for example, Peter Fraser referred to the catastrophes, cynicism, and despair that occurred when governments ignored promises made during World War I and warned that it must never be allowed to happen again. "The principles of the Atlantic Charter are not platitudes," he declared. "They are principles that must be honored, because thousands have died for them."[3] He reminded his listeners that countless numbers of people had sacrificed during this war on land and sea, in the air, in workshops, on farms, in mines, and in factories because they believed in what their leaders told them. If these hope-filled promises about rights now turned into lies and visions of rights transformed into dust, he cautioned, a precarious future awaited the world. Others expressed similar ideas, particularly among colonial peoples and minority groups, who vehemently complained that the Dumbarton Oaks proposals flagrantly violated both the letter and the spirit of the promises made by the Atlantic Charter, the Declaration of the United Nations, and the leaders in the crusade of the Grand Alliance such as Roosevelt, who had pledged a commitment to human rights in the peace that would follow victory.

New Zealand proved to be one of the most vigorous and vocal opponents of the Dumbarton Oaks arrangements made by the Great Powers. Exercising an influence far out of proportion to the physical strength or geographical size of their country, staunch advocates for human rights like Fraser and Nash reacted with indignation and immediate criticism. They had believed in the principles of the Atlantic Charter from the very beginning, viewed themselves as men of the people and champions of the underdog, and used their considerable energy and passion to fight for them wherever they traveled and spoke on behalf of the war effort. They envisioned an international organization that could keep the peace by treating nations equally, protecting the political independence and territorial integrity of all member states from external aggression, and developing a system of trusteeship for colonial possessions that advanced "the well-being and development of native peoples" and led toward self-determination. They also believed in the importance of advancing social and economic justice on a global level as they had done through their labor policies at home, promoting the "moral principles" of human rights, and mobilizing the loyalty of men and women around the world for this "people's peace" that would thereby be created.[4] Mincing few words, Carl Berendsen, the ambassador of New Zealand to the United States, expressed his criticisms of the Dumbarton Oaks package of proposals directly:

Too much emphasis on Great Powers and not much real machinery for joint action even among them. Too much vagueness. No guarantees, no pledges, no undertaking except in general terms. . . . With the emphasis on the Great Powers no adequate opportunity for small countries like New Zealand to exercise influence or express views. . . . Too much emphasis on Council, too little on Assembly. . . . No adequate machinery for securing peaceful change and economic justice — only words.

Consequently, he tersely concluded: "It aims too low."[5]

Other allies among the British Commonwealth also voiced objections to what they regarded as the elitism and high-handedness demonstrated by the Dumbarton Oaks proposals and the fact that the leaders of their great allies were not seriously concerned about their opinions at all. Often disregarding human rights problems and abuses within their own countries, they complained that the plans simply smacked of Realpolitik and imperialism from the past, reeked with arrogance and the presumption of permanent predominance, and completely ignored promises made by the

Atlantic Charter. India protested that no provisions appeared regarding the right of self-determination or racial equality, and Gandhi and his many followers escalated their calls for independence. Australia, Canada, and South Africa—all of whom believed that they had contributed significantly to the war effort—wanted to know why they and their views had been so completely ignored in the plans by the Great Powers for the new international organization. In an attempt to counteract their exclusion from the deliberations and to influence the course of future discussions about the postwar world, therefore, representatives from Australia and New Zealand decided to formulate a joint position. Meeting in Wellington during November 1944, they quickly agreed to press for more influence by the smaller powers, a greater role for the General Assembly, the creation of an international trusteeship system on behalf of native peoples, and explicit provisions relating to human rights, particularly those having to do with social and economic welfare. "The Charter of the Organization," they collectively declared, "should make clear to the peoples of the world the principles on which the action of the Organization is to be based," and toward this end should draw on "the essential principles" regarding human rights delineated in the Atlantic Charter and the Declaration of Philadelphia from the International Labor Organization.[6] Now the shoe was on the other foot, and the British did not like it at all. They especially objected to the statement about international trusteeship of colonial possessions, which they regarded as a threat to their empire. "In our view," they announced in an unusually sharp comment, "in a matter of this kind all members of the British Commonwealth ought to take every care to coordinate as far as possible their respective views before entering public declarations of policy. We can only express our regret that this public announcement has been made on behalf of the Australian and New Zealand governments without prior consultation with, or warning to us."[7] The replies of leaders from both Australia and New Zealand to this protest from London, in the words of even the polite official history, "were, to say the least, unrepentant."[8]

When they read the provisions contained in the Dumbarton Oaks proposals, the countries of Latin America also raised their voices in loud complaint. A long history of outside exploitation ranging from the conquistadors of the sixteenth century and colonialism by Europeans to heavy pressure and intervention from the United States in more recent years already had made them sensitive to abuse at the hands of the Great Powers. Moreover, they felt betrayed by the United States, who had not invited them to Dumbarton Oaks despite promises that as allies in the Western Hemisphere they would be fully consulted on any plans on a postwar organization. Thus, when the proposals were first released, it did not take much to provoke their reaction against what appeared as continued arrogance, power politics, and imperialism. Uruguay declared that it would support a "new League of Nations" organization, but wanted one that clearly supported genuine equality among its members, promoted liberty and justice, advanced respect for the dignity of the human person, and rejected any doctrine of racial preeminence.[9] Mexico insisted on changes as well, and in a lengthy proposal actually spent several pages arguing for the essential importance of including statements about the rights and duties of nations and individuals in the principles of the organization. In this regard, the Mexican government cited the influence of those visions seen in historical documents such as the French Declaration of the Rights of Man and the Citizen, the writings of internationalists like André Mandelstam and Alejandro Alvarez, the efforts of the League of Nations, the promises made by officials during the crusade of World War II, and the reports of nongovernmental organizations such as the Commission to Study the Organization of the Peace and its *International Safeguard of Human Rights*.[10] Venezuela complained that by emphasizing the Great Powers and their interests alone, the Dumbarton Oaks proposals created a "fundamental defect" that ignored the aspirations of the medium and small powers. To correct this problem, it called on all nations to return to "the great and humanitarian principles" of the Atlantic Charter, promote respect for the rights of people and fundamental freedoms, and make provision for the disposition of the colonies and protection of the rights of their inhabitants.[11] Pressure for changes came from other countries as well, including Brazil, Guatemala, and Panama, who joined with their colleagues and argued for the rights of the "common man," pointedly noting that the Dumbarton Oaks proposals "had not touched on the question" at all.[12] These complaints mounted to such a degree that the governments throughout Latin America decided to call for an extraordinary meeting in order to formulate a collective policy and exert as much pressure as possible by means of a united front.

The representatives of twenty nations thus assembled together at the famous and imposing Chapultepec Castle in Mexico City in February 1945 for the Inter-American Conference on Problems of War and Peace were determined to make a difference. Here they proceeded to go through the Dumbarton Oaks proposals, in the words of one observer, "paragraph by paragraph."[13] Although the United States sent a large and active delegation, this hardly deterred the other nineteen from expressing their criticisms.[14] Serious concerns surfaced about the dominance of the Great Powers, the relationship of regional arrangements for security and cooperation vis-à-vis the larger international organization, economic and social problems, and the role that human rights should play in the postwar peace. The delegates submitted more than one hundred and fifty draft resolutions, and certainly used the occasion to voice their opinions in deliberations followed closely by the world press and by China.[15] Sometimes forgetting their own less-than-exemplary records, they contended that if the crusade of World War II was in the name of democratic principles, then surely the new international organization should be based on democracy. Bolivia argued for the need to precisely define the rights and responsibilities of both nations and individuals, and to make specific guarantees an integral part of the plan of the organization. Venezuela proclaimed the necessity of creating a global system of law, justice, and equity that supported human rights and fundamental freedoms. Licenciado Alfonso García Robles of the Mexican Ministry for Foreign Affairs vigorously advanced what he called the program for the "Protección de los derechos internacionales del Hombre," or Protection of the International Rights of Man. He fully acknowledged the visions of human rights seen by H. G. Wells, the Institut de Droit International, and the American Law Institute, among others who had gone before, and insisted that now was the time to make them an integral part of the peace.[16] One of the female members of the Mexican delegation, along with Minerva Bernardino of the Dominican Republic, who served as president of

Speaking Out for a "People's Peace" with Human Rights: The Latin Americans at the Chapultepec Conference (Organization of American States).

the Inter-American Commission of Women, spoke strongly on behalf of women's rights. Cuba even went so far as to submit two elaborate proposals, one entitled "Draft Declaration of the International Duties and Rights of the Individual," and the other designated as the "Draft Declaration of the Duties and Rights of Nations." "The juridi-cal conscience of the civilized world demands that the rights of the individual be recognized rights free from infringement by the State," declared the Cuban proposal elaborating a whole series of civil and political rights and social and economic rights in some detail. "It is important," concluded the Cubans, "to extend to the whole world the international recognition of these rights of man."[17]

In the end, all of the delegates agreed to a number of resolutions and the text of the Final Act of the Inter-American Conference on Problems of War and Peace. These related to a wide variety of issues, ranging from continued military cooperation and common defense, the punishment of war crimes, and reciprocal assistance for American solidarity to economic cooperation, to the incorporation of international law into municipal legislation and proposals for the new international organization and human rights. Taking a deliberate jab at the Great Powers, they again reminded everyone for the record that "the Republics here represented . . . did not take part in the Dumbarton Oaks Conversations." They agreed that the Dumbarton Oaks plan provided a valuable contribution in setting up an international organization and could serve as a basis for further discussion, but declared that the proposals "are capable of certain improvements with a view to perfecting them and to realizing with greater assurance the objectives which they enunciate," especially regarding an organization that "must reflect the ideas and hopes of all peace-loving nations participating in its creation."[18] Toward this end, the delegates subscribed to the principles of the Atlantic Charter, a charter on the rights of women and children, the right of freedom of access to information, declarations of economic and social rights, and a resolution recommending "every effort to prevent racial or religious discrimination." In addition, those assembled at Chapultepec endorsed a list of fundamental principles that they desired to have applied to the future peace. These included the sovereign equality of all states, international law as a standard of conduct, repudiation of territorial conquest, support for the principles of democracy, justice, and "the rights of man" encompassing a variety of civil, political, economic, and social rights for all people. Instead of just stopping there, however, a resolution went on to declare support for "a system of international protection of these rights" and called on the Inter-American Juridical Committee to prepare a draft "Declaration of the International Rights and Duties of Man."[19]

At the conclusion of the Chapultepec Conference, most of the Latin American countries hailed this declaration as a significant contribution toward promoting the vision that human rights possess a universal moral validity across all national boundaries. Indeed, some of the attendees even spoke of the "spiritual experience" of their gathering and of the majority of delegates approaching their task with "missionary zeal and devotion." They expressed the hope that it would help in the creation of a "people's peace" that addressed the needs of "the common man" and all the "peons, coolies, and other social outcasts throughout the world" and advance the process of transforming the individual from being merely the subject to the actual object of international law.[20] The Great Powers reacted differently. Stalin's Soviet Union, for example, certainly had no intention of endorsing principles of democracy or any broad ranging application of civil and political rights. The British noted disparagingly that "although considered of great importance by the Mexican Delegation, it is not clear what practical application it will have."[21] Edward Stettinius, now as U.S. secretary of state, hailed the declared "principles of humanity" before the press with a flourish in public, but in private the delegation tended to discount the declaration as perhaps no more than a means of embarrassing the United States or certainly to dismiss it as sop designed to satisfy Mexican prestige.[22] Moreover, the Department of State chose not to publish the declaration at a time or in a place along with other resolutions and results of the conference as a whole.[23] Serious questions thus persisted about the true intentions of the Great Powers with reference to the role that human rights should play in the new international organization and in the peace.

Governments from Australia and New Zealand and the Latin American countries were not the only ones asking these questions. In fact, many NGOs and private citizens alike joined in as well. The invitation of representatives from labor movements, social organizations, and educational associations normally excluded from diplomatic affairs to the Chapultepec Conference, for example, certainly facilitated this process. Within the United States, some of the most serious questioning actually occurred inadvertently. That is, President Roosevelt, Stettinius, and their advisors remained acutely aware of the failure of Woodrow Wilson to secure American participation in the League of Nations at the end of World War I. They desperately sought to avoid any repetition with the new United Nations. The Department of State consequently launched a vigorous program that marked a significant departure in its relations with the public. Under the direction of the Office of Public Affairs, it sent officials across the country to deliver addresses and held a series of seminars and panel discussions with many groups in Washington, D.C., itself, all in a campaign to build popular support for the Dumbarton Oaks proposals and the new international organization that would emerge from them. In slightly more than a month, for example, departmental personnel participated in more than one hundred separate sessions in a number of widely scattered cities. They met with representatives from business and labor, education, farm groups, service clubs, women's associations, churches, and those specializing in the study of international relations. The audiences in these sessions listened — but they also asked questions, and many wanted to know how the secretary of state himself could use the expression, "a people's peace," and yet at the same time be so blind as to exclude international human rights.[24]

In these public discussions, representatives of NGOs such as the American Bar Association, the American Federation of Labor, the American Law Institute, the Congress of Industrial Organizations, the Brookings Institution, the Farm Bureau Federation, the National Association for the Advancement of Colored People, and the Carnegie Endowment for International Peace, among many others, for example, frequently voiced to officials from the Department of State their concerns about human rights. Members of the newly formed Americans United for World Organization issued and distributed what they called a *Statement of Essential Human Rights*.[25] The influential Commission to Study the Organization of Peace invariably used these occasions to advance the ideas recently presented in their *International Safeguard of Human Rights*. Pulling no punches, they forcefully argued that the new international organization had to include more than suggested by the Dumbarton Oaks proposals. They specifically and prophetically called for more provisions about human rights in the Charter, the convocation of a United Nations Conference on Human Rights without delay, the promulgation of an international bill of rights, the establishment of a permanent Commission on Human Rights to develop standards and methods of protection, and the promotion of effective means of enforcement.[26] At the same time, the Joint Committee on Religious Liberty created by the Federal Council of Churches responded similarly to what it regarded as the weakness of the Dumbarton Oaks proposals, and issued a memorandum advocating the establishment of a specialized agency under the authority of the proposed Economic and Social Council with specific responsibility for human rights and endorsed the creation of an international bill of rights. The American Jewish Congress and the Synagogue Council of America quickly endorsed these ideas as well.[27]

Religious values also played a significant role in the response of the Commission on a Just and Durable Peace regarding international human rights. Representing forty-five denominations and affiliated agencies, this organization issued a report in early 1945 entitled *Christian Standards and Current International Developments* analyzing the "omissions and shortcomings" of the proposals by the Great Powers and suggesting measures "to bring the Dumbarton Oaks plan into closer harmony with Christian ideals." It recommended that the new international organization "reaffirm those present and long-range purposes of justice and human welfare which are set forth in the Atlantic Charter and which reflect the aspirations of peoples everywhere," develop international law, limit armaments, and protect the weak from the arbitrary exercise of power by the strong. In addition, the Commission on a Just and Durable Peace advocated the creation of a special Commission on Human Rights and Fundamental Freedoms that actively protected, among other rights, those of religious and intellectual liberty and "equal and unsegregated opportunity for all races." Moreover, they directly called on all colonial powers to renounce their empires and proclaim their support for the right of self-determination and freedom for indigenous peoples around the world. "We cannot in good conscience," declared the committed members of the Commission, "be a party to the dismantling of Japanese colonial possessions without at the same time insisting that the imperialism of the white man shall be brought to the speediest possible end. We cannot have a sound or stable community so long as their is enforced submission of one people to the will of another in Korea, in India, in the Congo, in Puerto Rico or anywhere else."[28]

Individuals also joined in this rising chorus of criticism about the absence of meaningful provisions about human rights in the Dumbarton Oaks proposals. Through letters to editors, speeches, press conferences, sermons, and other forms of protest, they expressed their disappointment and resentment over what they regarded as the unfair process and the meager results of Dumbarton Oaks. Congresswoman Clare Boothe Luce, for example, complained that part of the cause could be found in the absence of any women delegates from the United States, Britain, the Soviet Union, or China during the conversations.[29] Some individuals wrote that they did "not want to recommend that the churches give their support to the Dumbarton Oaks Proposals as these stand at present," offering the opinion that in terms of human rights "the Atlantic Charter and the Four Freedoms promised America and the world a much more courageous plan than Dumbarton Oaks turned out to be."[30] One writer attributed the lack of vision in the resulting plan to one major factor: "In the preliminary peace talks at Dumbarton Oaks only one colored group participated, the Chinese, and [thus] the equality and basic problems of Negroes and colonial colored people were not on the agenda."[31] Professor Rayford Logan of Howard University openly criticized the proposals for completely ignoring the rights of colonial peoples.[32] W.E.B. Du Bois weighed in as well, castigating the proposals for giving the Great Powers too much control over the new organization and neglecting human rights, particularly those of minorities and of indigenous peoples living under subjugation in the colonies. He warned that unless these problems were addressed, the United Nations would never be able to create or maintain a lasting peace.[33]

These many criticisms of the Dumbarton Oaks proposals, whether originating with governments, NGOs, or private individuals, contributed to the evolution of international human rights in two significant ways. The first of these was to raise the issue of human rights much higher on the global agenda as the war neared its end. They did this by reminding especially the Great Powers of their promises made to people during the crusade of World War II and by serving notice that these could not—and would not—be ignored in any further planning for the new international organization. The documents creating the United Nations, they declared, would not be allowed to exclude important provisions on human rights. Secondly, they placed visions of human rights directly in the center of concepts of peace. For them, peace defined exclusively and narrowly in terms of deterrence among the Great Powers in a geopolitical balance of power would no longer suffice. Instead, they proposed a much broader "people's peace" that did not ignore collective security, but that would entail by definition the international protection of certain basic human rights.

This idea of a peace with rights owed a great deal to the recent experiences of the Depression, Hitler and the Third Reich, and World War II. Many of those who survived these individual and collective traumas believed that they could learn lessons from history, and thus sought to create a peace that would avoid perceived mistakes of the past. In looking back over their own personal experiences, for example, they came to regard the economic and social hardship suffered during the course of the Depression as contributing greatly to the rise of fascist regimes, the emergence of severe global competition, and ultimately to the outbreak of war itself. For this reason, those concerned about the longstanding and pernicious divisions of class or caste in society like Fraser, Nash, Du Bois, the American Federation of Labor, and various socialist and communist parties, despite their many differences, all insisted that the maintenance of a genuine "people's peace" required a guarantee to protect certain economic and social rights for all people. They believed that poverty, misery, unemployment, and depressed standards of living anywhere in an age of a global economy and a technological shrinking of the world bred instability elsewhere and thereby threatened peace. This is why Roosevelt's language about freedom from want and the inclusion of economic and social rights within the Atlantic Charter resonated so strongly with them. Those delegates of the International Labor Organization that endorsed the Declaration of Philadelphia thus could declare with conviction that "experience has fully demonstrated the truth of the statement . . . that lasting peace can be established only if it is based upon social justice." Peace, in their mind, thus required that "all human beings, irrespective of race, creed, or sex, have the right to pursue both their material well-being and their spiritual development in conditions of freedom and dignity, of economic security, and equal opportunity."[34]

Many also began to define peace as more clearly entailing the protection of civil and political rights for all people. After their own recent history, they were no longer willing to accept the old proposition that how a government treated its own people remained an exclusive and simple matter of "domestic jurisdiction." The crushing of all opposition, the denial of freedom of speech and assembly, the elimination of due process, and the expansion of the power of the state over the lives of individuals and groups by Hitler, Mussolini, and the militarists in Japan — all behind the protective shield of national sovereignty — convinced them that the abuse of rights at home could all too quickly spill over national borders and lead to war and even genocide. "As basic human rights are protected in each country, the prevention of war is made easier," declared the Commission to Study the Organization of Peace. The reason for this, they believed, could be stated directly and in light of recent experience:

Now, as a result of the Second World War, it has become clear that a regime of violence and oppression within any nation of the civilized world is a matter of concern for all the rest. It is a disease in the body politic which is contagious because the government that rests upon violence will, by its very nature, be even more ready to do violence to foreigners than to its own fellow citizens, especially if it can thus escape the consequences of its acts at home. The foreign policy of despots is inherently one which carries with it a constant risk to the peace and security of others. In short, if aggression is the key-note of domestic policy, it will also be the clue to foreign relations.[35]

The ordeal of World War II similarly contributed to the concept that any lasting peace would require an implementation of the right of self-determination. Part of this, of course, resulted from the many promises made by the Allies to distance themselves from their adversaries and to solicit support for the larger crusade. They promoted the idea at every opportunity that the right of all people to choose the form of government under which they would live remained one of the most essential ingredients of any peace settlement. Thus, the Atlantic Charter, the Declaration of the United Nations, the many speeches by Allied leaders, and even the Declaration on Liberated Europe emerging as late as February 1945 from the Yalta Conference between the United States, Britain, and the Soviet Union, all fostered this concept.[36] But there was something more as well. The war produced millions of new European victims of aggression at the hands of the Axis powers. As a result, their own first-hand experience made them much more sympathetic than ever before to the sufferings of others forced to live under conquest and subjugation, including those indigenous peoples within their colonial empires, who vowed that there could never be lasting peace as long as they were denied their freedom. Thus, many victims in the West began to join with many others like Gandhi in India, Ho Chi Minh of Indochina, Nkrumah and Kenyatta of Africa, Carlos Romulo of the Philippines, and Fonoti of Western Samoa in regarding the right of self-determination as absolutely necessary for international peace.[37]

New visions of peace also entailed the closely related matter of the right to receive equal treatment and protection under the law without discrimination or persecution. Coverage by the international press and attention by the League of Nations and many nongovernmental organizations concerned about violations of human rights over Hit-

ler's tyranny against Jews and others who he detested had raised international awareness of this issue to new heights even before the war began. Yet, as more and more
details about the shocking extent of the Holocaust began to seep their way out from
under the earth of unmarked mass graves in occupied territories and from under the
barbed-wire enclosures of the extermination camps into the world, it became nearly
impossible to ignore the connection between racial and religious discrimination, especially as revealed by the recent extremes of Nazi philosophy, on the one hand and
genocidal war on the other. This appeared all the more evident when their own actions
and statements during the war forced the Allies to look into a mirror and see their own
reflections of blatant and violent prejudice.[38] Based on this experience, global opinion
thus increasingly began to consider much more fully that the persecution of any individual or group anywhere potentially threatened the peace everywhere. It is for this
reason that nearly all serious proposals for peace emerging from governments, NGOs,
and individuals alike — with the notable exception of the Dumbarton Oaks proposals
from the Great Powers — contained some explicit provision providing for the fundamental right of all people to equality and nondiscrimination, often in the context of a
larger declaration of international human rights.[39] The proposal from the American
Jewish Committee, for example, contained just such a proposition in its *World Charter for
Human Rights*.[40] As those assembled for the Inter-American Conference on Problems of
War and Peace formally declared: "World peace cannot be consolidated until men are
able to exercise their basic rights without distinction as to race or religion."[41]

Finally, and not surprising given the crusading nature of the war, those proposals
emerging at this time continually argued that peace could be neither created nor
sustained unless it contained elements of "justice." Definitions of international justice
appeared in many different forms. For some, it meant freedom from aggression and
that small states would be treated if not equally, then certainly fairly, by the Great
Powers in the postwar world. For others, it entailed the rule of law, principles of democracy, an international court of justice, free trade, or the reduction of armaments. Yet,
for most, concepts of a "people's peace" with universal justice required the protection
of some form of basic human rights, however defined or asserted. "The relation between human rights and a just peace," proclaimed the Commission to Study the Organization of Peace as a maxim, "is close and interlocking."[42] The Commission on a Just
and Durable Peace set up by the Federal Council of Churches argued in exactly the
same way. Here, economic and social rights, civil and political rights, the right of self-
determination, and the right to nondiscrimination based on race or religion, as discussed, all played prominent roles. But other dimensions, also enhanced by recent
experiences, appeared as well. These included proposals for the protection of rights for
women and children, the right to be protected by humanitarian law in times of war, the
right of all people including refugees and displaced persons to have access to relief
during periods of distress, and the rights of indigenous peoples and ethnic minorities,
among others. Those who asserted such rights, either singularly or collectively, invariably did so in the name of the relationship between peace and justice.[43]

These various visions of peace with rights could never be applied in practice, of
course, unless and until the peoples and the nations of the world agreed to implement

them as their collective international responsibility. Although World War II contributed profoundly and as never before to the concept of responsibilities to other people far beyond one's own national borders, any discussion about such continued responsibilities in peace remained confined to speculation until the fighting actually ceased. But by spring 1945 the end of the war seemed to be a distinct possibility, and it thus appeared absolutely vital for those engaged in this monumental struggle to finally gather together and somehow negotiate a plan for an international organization to keep the peace that would be acceptable to them all. "This time we shall not make the mistake of waiting . . . to set up the machinery of peace," said Roosevelt in drawing a lesson from recent history. "This time, as we fight together to get the war over quickly, we work together to keep it from happening again. . . . We shall have to take the responsibility for world collaboration, or we shall have to bear the responsibility for another world conflict."[44] Toward this end, fifty nations decided to send their representatives and their respective plans for peace to a conference held in San Francisco.

Politics and Diplomacy at the San Francisco Conference

The opening speeches of the United Nations Conference on International Organization delivered in the elegant setting of the San Francisco Opera House during April 1945 conveyed a spirit of extraordinary euphoria and sense of responsibility. Flushed with continued military victories against their adversaries and excited about participating in what they knew would be one of the century's most historic events on the road to peace, several hundred representatives and their staffs could hardly contain their enthusiasm. Never before in the history of the world had so many nations of such various sizes been so widely represented at such a high-level international conference. Never before had Asia and the Pacific Rim been given so much recognition. At the same time, they understood that the occasion also came with a heavy responsibility. They perceived that they had been given a second chance after the failure of the Paris Peace Conference at the end of World War I, and knew that war-weary people around the globe expected them to create a viable international organization to keep the peace. The sudden death of Franklin Roosevelt less than two weeks before the conference itself produced a great sense of loss at a time of enormous need and thus gave this burden of responsibility even more weight. For this reason, the delegates spoke of the seriousness of the tasks before them and the necessity to make their gathering a "landmark" and a "milestone" on the long march toward a better future. "For there can be no doubt anymore," said the seasoned Prime Minister Jan Smuts of South Africa, "that for us, for the human race, the hour has struck. Mankind has arrived at the crisis of its fate, the fate of its future as a civilized world."[45] "If we should pay mere lip service to the inspiring ideals and then later do violence to simple justice," declared the brand-new and untested U.S. President Harry Truman in exactly the same tone, "we would draw down upon us the bitter wrath of generations and yet unborn. . . . We must build a new world — a far better world — one in which the eternal dignity of man is respected."[46]

Other delegates spoke in similar language about the opportunities and the responsibilities for now creating a "people's peace." They urged each other to put past practices behind them, to rise above their own narrowly parochial national self-interests, to promote the larger international good of all, to honor the promises made during the war, and to create an organization founded not on power politics but on principle. Toward this end, speeches encouraged the participants to be guided by "the vision of the ideal" and to commit themselves "to vindicate the fundamental rights of man, and on that basis to found a better, freer world for the future."[47] Interestingly enough, some of the delegates also warned each other about the dangers in settings such as this of excessive oratorical flourishes that might create a false sense of euphoria, conceal serious problems, or ignore the reality of global politics and diplomacy. Ramaswami Mudaliar of the Indian delegation responded by arguing that given the promises made and the pressures unleashed during the war, those who would define "reality" solely in geopolitical terms would be making an error of equal seriousness. "We are all asked to be realists," he said, "we are asked to recognize various factors in the world set up as it is today." "There is one great reality," he continued,

one fundamental factor, one eternal verity which all religions teach, which must be remembered by all of us, the dignity of the common man, the fundamental human rights of all beings all over the world. Those rights are incapable of segregation or of isolation. There is neither border nor breed nor color nor creed on which those rights can be separated as between beings and beings. And, speaking as an Asiatic, may I say that this is an aspect of the question which can never be forgotten, and if we are laying the foundations for peace we can only lay them truly and justly. . . . Those fundamental human rights of all beings all over the world should be recognized and men and women treated as equals in every sphere, so far as opportunities are concerned.[48]

Following all the opening ceremony and initial speeches in the light of full publicity, the conference delegates set about to address the tasks at hand. Nearly three hundred official delegates labored with the help of two and a half thousand advisors, while over two thousand journalists and radio announcers conveyed the deliberations to the world. The organization of the conference into several working commissions and committees created a unique and democratic process that provided many more opportunities for vigorous debate and discussion than any other diplomatic conference ever held before. In this setting, the different agendas of the participants thus became quickly apparent. The Great Powers, of course, still desired to adhere as closely as possible to their original Dumbarton Oaks proposals that would enable them to protect their own interests and enjoy the fruits of their military victory. These provisions would allow them to dominate the Security Council, possess the power to veto any action that might be taken against them, create a weak General Assembly, place an emphasis on the rights of state rather than individuals, and exclude any reference to colonial possessions at all. In addition, this particular plan would allow only one reference to human rights, and that would be confined to general economic and social cooperation alone. In fact, the lengthy, elaborate, and carefully indexed briefing book prepared for members of the U.S. delegation did not contain a single agenda item for human rights.[49] The meeting at the Yalta Conference confirmed that the United States, Britain, and the Soviet Union intended to stick with these proposals and to let the Dumbarton Oaks plan serve as the basis of all further discussion.[50] Indeed, when the United States suggested at Yalta that they might want to reconsider their collective position on colonial territories and perhaps create some kind of machinery for international trusteeship, Churchill exploded with wrath and declared that he would never "consent under any circumstances to the United Nations thrusting interfering fingers into the very life of the British Empire."[51] Seeking to avoid any further alterations or surprises of this nature and to maintain as much solidarity as possible, the Great Powers agreed that they needed to maintain close and constant communication with each other, and did so through their private evening consultations in Secretary of State Stettinius's penthouse apartment high atop the Fairmont Hotel while participating in the San Francisco Conference. They also often cooperated closely within committee meetings, as revealed somewhat perversely by Sir Alexander Cadogan of the British delegation who privately but proudly described the process in these words: "I generally sit next to the American . . . and we conspire together to try to whack obstructionists on the head. . . . I tell him he's our heavy artillery and I am the sniper. It works quite well and we wiped the floor with a Mexican last night: I think we must have shut him up for a week or so."[52]

Despite such callous bombast, however, these delegates of the Great Powers knew perfectly well that they had serious differences between themselves and understood that if push came to shove they might not always be able to speak with the same voice. The Americans, Chinese, and Soviets might find common ground in their opposition to the British Empire, for example, but discover many other areas of disagreement such as the role that France should play in the new organization, regional defense, the nature of truly democratic regimes, or the meaning of human rights in the world. Particularly troublesome was the growing level of serious tension between the United States and the Soviet Union. On the very first day of the San Francisco Conference, their respective troops from west and east met each other on the banks of the Elbe River in Europe and enjoyed a brief moment of joyous celebration that symbolized their cooperation as allies in a successful coalition. Before the conference concluded, however, Nazi Germany surrendered; and with the defeat of the common enemy that had forced them together, both powerful nations began to perceive that they no longer needed each other in the same way. This change appeared as early as Molotov's opening speech during the first plenary session. Here he spoke of the hardships of the war and the need for security, but noticeably said nothing about the principles of the Atlantic Charter or even the social and economic human rights of workers. Instead, he accused some of those very nations listening to him of having turned the League of Nations "into a tool of various reactionary forces and privileged powers" and warned about the need of creating a new international organization to be alert to the "many irreconcilable enemies in the camp of the most aggressive imperialists."[53] Truman conveyed this hostility as well and told his advisors in his own blunt way that "if the Russians did not wish to join us they could go to hell."[54]

Disagreements also existed even within the delegations of the Great Powers. In order to avoid the bitter partisanship suffered by Woodrow Wilson at the end of previous war, for example, the U.S. delegation consisted of rival Democrats and Republicans, including individuals as different as former isolationist Senator Arthur Vandenberg from Michigan, Senator Tom Connally from Texas, who earlier had belligerently participated in filibusters against anti-lynching and fair employment practices legislation, and John Foster Dulles. Virginia Gildersleeve, the dean of Barnard College, served as the only woman on an otherwise all-white, male delegation and who saw herself as representing no particular political party but rather the interests of women and the public at large. Early in the conference she was personally petitioned to help secure gender equality and rights for "the world's most long-suffering minority—women."[55] Moreover, to make matter even more complicated, the Great Powers were very much aware of many criticisms already leveled at their Dumbarton Oaks proposals and of the amendments that would be officially submitted by others insisting on changes. Leo Pasvolsky of the Department of State informed members of his own delegation that references about promoting human rights and fundamental freedoms already "had caused a great deal of difficulty" during the drafting stage and would likely continue to do so.[56] The Foreign Office in London similarly received advise about the flaws in the Dumbarton Oaks proposals. "Great as is the advance represented by these various provisions," wrote one advisor, "there are other respects in which the tentative proposals either represent a retrogression as compared with the Covenant [of the League of Nations] or fail to deal with practical problems having a legal aspect which proved during the interwar period to be of substantial importance." To solve these difficulties, he suggested, "we cannot afford to forget that the tentative proposals can be made a reality only by the release of moral and political forces." He therefore offered the not particularly welcomed advice that all parties would need to avoid the emotional exaltation of the moment and recognize "long-term political realities," but at the same time dedicate the international organization to a "high purpose" beyond power politics that "will ring through ages to come as a challenge . . . to establish right and justice as the basis of the world community."[57]

The medium and small nations of the world also came to the San Francisco Conference with their own agendas. Australia and New Zealand certainly had not been timid in announcing their objectives in advance. News releases from India and the Philippines revealed their interests and intentions. The large Latin American contingent even had widely circulated some of its recommendations resulting from the Chapultepec Conference just two months before. In contrast to the Great Powers, despite their many differences of geography, politics, culture, language, race, religion, and ethnicity, all of these countries shared a desire to shape the new United Nations into an organization that reflected both their particular interests and their visions of peace. Toward this end, they sought to reduce the influence of the proposed Security Council, increase the authority of the more widely representative General Assembly, provide more explicit statements about purposes and principles, and make sure that the organization committed itself in a variety of different ways to clearly supporting international human rights. They wanted definite changes in the Dumbarton Oaks proposals, and said so.

As a first step toward this objective, delegates from these countries submitted official amendments to the conference regarding human rights provisions in the United Nations Charter, starting with the very first chapter. Such formal proposals could not be easily ignored or quickly dismissed. They expressed great dissatisfaction with the vague statements of purpose and stark omissions of the Dumbarton Oaks proposals from the Great Powers. The declared purposes of the new organization, they argued, should go beyond old concepts of peace and security defined only in narrow geopolitical terms, and include those principles promised to people throughout the world during the crusade of World War II. Consequently, at an early stage, the governments of Egypt, Mexico, France, Guatemala, Paraguay, and South Africa all submitted suggestions and amendments to include provisions declaring that support for human rights constituted one of the essential purposes of the United Nations.[58] These were quickly followed by proposals of exactly the same nature by India, New Zealand, Norway, Lebanon, and Cuba.[59] In each and every case, these proposed amendments, and others that would follow, sought to insert explicit provisions supporting international human rights for all people at the very beginning of the Charter itself. "We must recognize that the realization of these ideals involves a long-sustained effort that may be considered as overstepping the limits set forth by the Dumbarton Oaks proposals," maintained the Egyptian government. "It is however indubitable that the principles of the Atlantic Charter have fostered so much hope throughout the world, that they ought to be put forward as the aims of the new World Organization."[60]

In this effort to explicitly address matters of human rights in the United Nations Charter, the delegates from these medium and small powers received enormous support and encouragement from many nongovernmental organizations. Indeed, one of the major characteristics of the San Francisco Conference and its efforts to create a "people's peace" was the extraordinary and unprecedented influence exerted on the deliberations by groups and individuals not a part of any government at all who came to advance the interests of people rather than those of states. Some of these operated from a considerable distance, such as World Trade Union Congress, Provisional World Council of Dominated Nations, West Indies National Council, Sino-Korean People's League, and the Council of Christians and Jews headquartered in London. This latter NGO (composed, in the words of one Foreign Office staff member, of "some heavy backers" such as the archbishop of Canterbury, the archbishop of Westminster, the Chief Rabbi, and the moderator of the Church of Scotland, among other religious leaders) issued a petition entitled "Memorandum for Submission to His Majesty's Government for Their Consideration in View of the San Francisco Conference" urging that human rights be considered as an essential matter and be given prominence by the British delegation.[61] The Non-European United Committee from Cape Town, South Africa, printed "A Declaration to the Nations of the World" on behalf of several million black Africans, Indians, and those of mixed color, proclaiming that unless action were taken by the United Nations to address racial equality, all individuals other than whites in South Africa would "live and suffer under a tyranny very little different from Nazism."[62] The Six Nations Iroquois Confederacy similarly pressed the Canadian government to support the rights of indigenous peoples and racial justice in the Charter.

No nation experienced the pressure of more nongovernmental organizations represented at the San Francisco Conference than the United States. A largely democratic society, the guarantee of certain civil and political rights, an open and active press, and simple geographical proximity all contributed to this development. Moreover, in an effort largely to generate public support, the Department of State took the usual move of overcoming its reservations about "open diplomacy" by actually inviting forty-two NGOs to send delegations of representatives to serve in the capacity of "consultants."[63] These individuals included Clark Eichelberger of the American Association for the United Nations, Helen Reid of the American Association of University Women, David Simmons of the American Bar Association, Robert Watt of the American Federation of Labor, Joseph Proskauer of the American Jewish Committee, James Shotwell of the Carnegie Endowment for International Peace and the Commission to Study the Organization of Peace, Thomas Finletter of the Council on Foreign Relations, Walter Van Kirk and Frederick Nolde of the Federal Council of Churches, Richard Pattee of the National Catholic Welfare Conference, and Jane Evans of the National Peace Conference. This group also included Walter White, W.E.B. Du Bois, and Mary McLeod Bethune of the National Association for the Advancement of Colored People, who publicly announced that they wanted to advance an international bill of human rights, the dismantling of colonial empires, and a racial equality clause similar to that proposed by the Chinese at Dumbarton Oaks, and in the case of Bethune, the rights of women of all races. Representatives from many other nongovernmental organizations not invited to enjoy formal consultant status such as the Fraternal Council of Negro Churches, Council on African Affairs, and the Universal Negro Improvement Association, simply decided to appear in San Francisco in order to make their influence felt as aggressively as they could and to prevent only white, middle- and upper-class males from dominating the discussions.[64]

Much to its surprise, and sometimes to its annoyance, the Department of State came to realize that when people are given the opportunity to express their opinions, they just might do so. These "consultants" believed passionately in their visions of human rights and most had spent years of their lives as political, social, and religious activists. They most certainly were not the type to meekly sit by, take an oath of silence, or be content, in the words of one of them, to serve as mere "window dressing" for the benefit of their government's public image at San Francisco.[65] They thus energetically held news conferences, issued press releases, spoke in local churches, sought allies where they could find them, lobbied with representatives of foreign delegations, attended sessions as observers, and applied pressure to their own delegation. On one particularly dramatic occasion, they insisted on meeting as a group with Stettinius himself. The Department of State official who was present recorded the event as follows:

Mr. Stettinius was in the chair. Human rights was the topic of discussion. I see it all as if it had happened yesterday. I can see Judge Proskauer rise to his feet and address an impassioned plea to Secretary Stettinius. "It isn't enough," he said, "for the charter to speak of universal respect for and observance of human rights. If there is to be freedom in this world, and peace, human rights must be safeguarded and there must be machinery within the United Nations to promote such freedom, to make fundamental human rights a reality. It is for you, Mr. Secretary," he continued —he pointed at him— "it is for the American delegation to take the lead in this matter, to live up to what is best in our traditions, to write into the charter a provision which would give meaning to the articles which pledge the nations of the world to promote human rights and fundamental freedoms." Judge Proskauer's appeal was taken by other people at the meeting—people representing different races, creeds, and political opinions. I accompanied Mr. Stettinius at the end of that meeting to a meeting of the American delegation. We went straight there. And all the way up in the elevator, then way down the long corridor on the fifth floor, down the corner room, where the American delegation was meeting, he didn't say a word. He was obviously moved.[66]

While some governments waited to see how Stettinius and the United States would respond to these pressures, others sought to push ahead and propose amendments for an explicit provision in the United Nations Charter concerning equal protection and nondiscrimination. The new organization, in the words of the formal amendment submitted by India—and advanced with particular vigor in public by the dynamic female excluded from the official delegation, Vijaya Lakshmi Pandit—should promote "fundamental human rights for all men and women, irrespective of race, color, or creed, in all nations and in international relations and associations of nations one with another."[67] The government of the Philippines returned to the issue raised by the sole voice of China at Dumbarton Oaks and proposed that the United Nations commit itself "to develop friendly relations and the spirit of brotherhood and racial equality among nations" and to act in accordance with the principles of the Atlantic Charter, while Iraq argued that racial discrimination constituted a "Nazi philosophy" that had to be "discarded forever" in international relations.[68] Others, including Brazil, the Dominican Republic, and Mexico submitted an amendment calling for the organization to ensure respect for human rights and fundamental freedoms without discrimination against race, sex, condition, or creed.[69] The American and Chinese women delegates felt very strongly about the right of equal treatment and stressed during a number of sessions that "women should be regarded as human beings."[70] Uruguay proposed that the new organization endorse "the essential rights of mankind, internationally established and guaranteed," while Panama suggested inserting a declaration of "essential human rights" and a clause guaranteeing equal protection against discrimination because of race, religion, sex, "or any other reason."[71] And, unique among the Europeans at an early stage, France similarly advanced an amendment calling on the United Nations to see to it that the essential liberties of all are respected, without distinction of race, language, or creed.[72] In each and every one of these proposals, nondiscrimination was seen as absolutely essential to any provision about international human rights—a point emphasized with devastating poignancy at precisely this time by shocking photographs of piles of emaciated corpses found by Allied forces as they liberated Nazi extermination camps. Then, in a move that surprised many delegates when it became public, the Soviet Union announced that it would support such a clause in the Charter prohibiting discrimination. Given the previous and unequivocal Soviet opposition to human rights at Dumbarton Oaks, and given the increasing tension between their two countries now that the common military adversary was almost defeated, the U.S. representatives interpreted this action as being motivated by politics and diplomacy, and dismissed it as no more than "playing up to the small nations."[73]

Yet it was precisely these "small nations," many of whom were nonwhite, that had suffered so much in the past from discrimination, exploitation, and exclusion from participation in international deliberations. Their people, who consistently found their rights abused or denied, long had been the victims, the subjects, and the pawns in the great chess game of diplomacy. Now at the San Francisco Conference, and after all the promises of the crusading war, they and their supporters demanded change and did so with particular vehemence over the issues of the right to self-determination and the welfare of indigenous peoples in colonial territories. The principles of the Atlantic Charter must be applied universally, said the representative of Australia, and human rights acknowledged as a matter of international concern rather than being confined to just territories formerly belonging to adversaries of the world war. "Otherwise," he noted pointedly, "native peoples would be in a better position merely because they had once been under enemy sovereignty."[74] China re-entered the public debate on this issue that it alone had formally raised months before at Dumbarton Oaks, and argued again for the necessity of supporting the principle of the equality of all races and their right to self-determination.[75] This time the Chinese found themselves surrounded by many others in support. General Carlos Romulo of the Philippines, for example, reminded all of the delegates that many different races and peoples had fought in World War II together, and yet not all of them enjoyed the same protection of their basic rights. "This is a victory for the whole world," he stated, "not for one race, one nation, or one leader, but for all men. Before this war broke out, I toured the Asiatic territories and I learned from the leaders and from the people of the flame of hope that swept the Far East when the Atlantic Charter was made known to the world. Everywhere these people asked the questions: Is the Atlantic Charter for the Pacific? Is it for one side of the world, and not for the other? For one race and not for them too?"[76]

So strong was the pressure at San Francisco on this point completely excluded by the Big Three at Dumbarton Oaks that the delegates decided to design an entirely new committee to deal with the issue of the human rights of people in the colonies and dependent territories.[77] They created the Trusteeship Committee and elected Peter Fraser of New Zealand to serve as its chair. Like many other things that he did, Fraser threw himself into this assignment with conviction, principle, and a deep sense of responsibility, and used it as an opportunity to address what he called the vision of "the fundamental rights of men and women" around the world.[78] Long before the San Francisco Conference even began, he and Herbert Evatt of Australia had announced their support for a system of trusteeship that would go far beyond the mandates program of the League of Nations in placing an international emphasis on the welfare and the economic, social, and political development of indigenous peoples. Many delegations endorsed the idea of creating a strong Trusteeship Council as an integral part of the United Nations that would have the authority to compel the colonial powers to begin the process of decolonization, eventually dismantling their empires. Others opposed this plan as being too slow, too patronizing, and for not going far enough, and instead demanded immediate self-determination for all peoples under colonial domination. Those holding colonies, of course, resisted any plans that might interfere with their interests whatsoever and argued that the international organization could not be engaged in the theft of their possessions. Others, like Harold Stassen of the U.S. delegation urged extreme caution and warned that independence was "a dangerous word."[79] Such sharply conflicting positions revealed a level of politics and diplomacy rarely matched elsewhere at the conference, particularly when displayed by those who vigorously represented Australia, Belgium, Britain, China, Egypt, France, Iraq, the Netherlands, the Philippines, South Africa, the Soviet Union, and the United States. All this produced, as might be expected, contentious debate, intense maneuvering, and what Fraser himself described as "protracted negotiations" so difficult that they often had to take place in private "outside the Committee."[80]

Simultaneous with these efforts, many delegates also worked diligently to increase both the number and the scope of human rights provisions in other sections of the United Nations Charter. They lobbied hard, for example, to increase the relative influence of the General Assembly where all nations would have an equal vote by giving it the authority to consider any matter within the sphere of international relations. Among these, they wanted to give it the explicit power to initiate studies and make specific recommendations concerning human rights for the world.[81] In addition, those delegates who believed strongly in a connection between peace and social and economic justice sought to elevate the status of the proposed Economic and Social Council within the organization. Rather than making this council simply a body responsible to the General Assembly as proposed by the Dumbarton Oaks plan, they wanted it to stand alone, to be a "principal organ" of the United Nations itself, and to possess clear responsibilities in the area of international human rights. These included such matters as economic justice, social and cultural affairs, the right of self-determination, equal treatment and nondiscrimination, as well as humanitarian and relief activities. But here a great controversy arose between those who represented labor governments such as Australia and New Zealand, who wanted to include statements about the right to "full employment," and those such as the United States, who regarded such a provision as too specific and too communistic.[82]

In the midst of all this discussion and debate, the Great Powers decided that they simply could not ignore these extraordinary pressures to place provisions for international human rights squarely within the United Nations Charter. All the public statements, private conversations, official speeches, formal proposals, and actual votes generated by other governments and NGOs concerning human rights—and the intensity with which they were presented—sent the "Big Four" into further deliberations. Spurred on by pressure from its own consultants who argued that human rights represented "a matter of tremendous importance" that absolutely required "much greater emphasis" in the Charter, and by members of its own delegation like Virginia Gildersleeve, the United States suggested to the other Great Powers that certain changes be made in the Dumbarton Oaks proposals.[83] As a result of intense discussions among themselves, they agreed to submit a collective and formal package of amendments themselves. It incorporated many suggestions advanced up to this point in the conference by others, including specific provisions on human rights and nondiscrimination as they related to the purposes of the organization, the terms of reference for the General Assembly, arrangements for international economic and social cooperation, and the functions and powers of the Economic and Social Council. Their amendments still refused, however, to even mention the fate of colonies or to address the issue of trusteeship. In addition, they wanted to insert in the Charter an explicit provision reaffirming the principle of national sovereignty and domestic jurisdiction to protect all states from outside interference from the United Nations itself.[84]

All these various amendments from delegations and proposals from nongovernmental organizations regarding human rights, along with the personalities and the nations who presented them, added powerful forces to the volatile mixture of politics and diplomacy at the San Francisco Conference. There were other important and strategic factors as well. Neither vigor of protest nor urgency of argument, for example, could alter the plain fact of Great Power dominance. The delegates understood perfectly well that, for better or worse, the United Nations could never be created or sustained unless the most powerful nations agreed to give their support, and that this would come only at a cost of certain conditions.[85] Similarly, they realized that no organization seeking to claim universal principles would ever emerge unless endorsed by the medium and small powers who had their own agendas and could claim to speak for the overwhelming majority of people in the world. The Latin American countries alone, for example, held twenty out of fifty votes at the conference.[86] In addition, all delegations (including those from nondemocratic countries) knew all too well of the many domestic critics and pressures of one form or another that would scrutinize their decisions once they left the exciting mood of an international meeting and the quaint Victorian homes and cable cars of San Francisco. This was particularly true in the case of the United States, where opposition party members even served as members of the delegation, constantly reminding the others that Senate approval would be necessary for ratification of any treaty and declaring again and again that the principles of national sovereignty and domestic jurisdiction must never be surrendered.[87] Moreover, of particular importance to the subject of human rights, since governments are usually the most egregious violators of such rights, their representatives eventually came to the realization that they were being asked to consider provisions that would actually restrict the ability of their own governments to treat their own people as they wished. The complicated interplay of these many forces and factors finally came to seen in the text of the Charter of the United Nations.

The Charter of the United Nations

Exactly two months after opening their historic conference, the delegates of the nations of the world reached agreement on the terms of the Charter that would create the United Nations. President Truman boarded an airplane and returned to San Francisco in order that he could be present at the final signing ceremony. On the next day, 26 June 1945, all the delegates assembled in the Veterans Building auditorium before a witnessing throng of excited correspondents and photographers from across the globe. Under an imposing backdrop of the assembled flags of all participating countries, the heads of each delegation gathered behind a massive desk placed on a bright blue circular carpet. When the hands of the clock stood together at noon, Wellington Koo solemnly stepped forward to represent the country that had suffered the longest as a victim of the war. Then, with a traditional Chinese ink brush in his hand, he carefully inscribed the characters of his name as the first signature on the leather-bound copy of the text before him.[88] The rest followed in turn. When all the signatures had been secured, they enthusiastically yet solemnly presented to the world a blueprint for the most ambitious experiment in international organization ever attempted in history: the Charter of the United Nations.

In many ways the Charter closely resembled the Dumbarton Oaks proposals. It established a powerful Security Council assisted by a Military Staff Committee with primary responsibility for the maintenance of international peace and security, dominated by the Great Powers through their permanent membership and veto. It created a General Assembly where all nations could have equal votes and address matters of common concern to them all. The Charter instituted an Economic and Social Council to encourage cooperation among nations in a variety of areas and an International Court of Justice. In addition, it established a Secretariat for the organization as a whole administered by a secretary-general and a staff. In other ways, the Charter of the United Nations marked a notable departure from the Dumbarton Oaks proposals submitted by the Great Powers. This was particularly evident in the area of international human rights.

The very first sentence of the Charter, for example, announced the departure immediately. Rather than the traditional language about the plenipotentiaries of nation-states, yet entirely consistent with their recent historical experience and their visions of the component elements of a "people's peace," the signatories declared in inspiring tones:

WE THE PEOPLES OF THE UNITED NATIONS
DETERMINED
to save succeeding generations from the scourge of war, which twice in our lifetime has brought untold sorrow to mankind, and

to reaffirm faith in fundamental human rights, in the dignity and worth of the human person, in the equal rights of men and women of nations large and small, and

to establish conditions under which justice and respect for the obligations arising from treaties and other sources of international law can be maintained, and

to promote social progress and better standards of life in larger freedom . . .

HAVE RESOLVED TO COMBINE OUR EFFORTS
TO ACCOMPLISH THESE AIMS.

The text then carried this resolve directly into Article 1 where the signatories boldly pledged themselves and their organization to very new international responsibilities:

To develop friendly relations among nations based on respect for the principle of equal rights and self-determination of peoples, and to take other appropriate measures for international peace;

To achieve international cooperation in solving international problems of an economic, social, cultural, or humanitarian character, and in promoting and encouraging respect for human rights and fundamental freedoms for all without distinction as to race, sex, language, or religion. . .[89]

Such explicit provisions regarding human rights provided only the beginning, however, for the Charter went on to say much more on this subject. It gave the General

Assembly considerably more authority than ever originally proposed by the Great Powers, providing authorization to discuss virtually any questions or matters within the broad scope of the United Nations Charter, including those of human rights. In addition, it explicitly charged the Assembly with responsibility for initiating studies and making recommendations for the purpose of assisting in the realization of international human rights without racial, sexual, linguistic, or religious discrimination. This meant that although a recommendation from the General Assembly would not possess the binding force of law, any resolution dealing with human rights that passed unanimously or by consensus most certainly had the potential of significantly impacting on the behavior of the United Nations as a whole. The Charter also instructed the Security Council to act in accordance with the larger purposes and principles of the organization, to investigate any dispute that might lead to international friction, and to act to maintain or restore peace and security. In this regard, it possessed the authority to determine whether any serious human rights violation constituted a "threat to the peace," and thus to decide on possible action, including humanitarian intervention, on the part of the United Nations.[90]

The majority of delegates at San Francisco also made certain that the Charter addressed a broad spectrum of rights in the economic and social arena in considerable detail. Indeed, in the words of Peter Fraser, "No section of the Dumbarton Oaks proposals underwent more extensive changes for the better than that which dealt with international cooperation in economic and social matters."[91] The Charter explicitly drew a connection between human well-being and international peace, announced support again for the principle of equal rights and self-determination, and committed the organization to promote universal respect for, and observance of, human rights and fundamental freedoms without discrimination — "for all." To achieve this, it elevated the Economic and Social Council to be one of the principal organs of the United Nations and authorized it to initiate studies, make recommendations to the General Assembly and to those specialized agencies such as the International Labor Organization focused on addressing humanitarian tasks, prepare draft conventions, and call international conferences on matters related to human rights. In addition, more importantly, the Charter mandated that this Economic and Social Council create commissions in economic and social fields and for the promotion of human rights, and such other commissions as may be required for the performance of its functions.[92]

Then, in a radical departure from the original proposals from the Great Powers, the Charter explicitly addressed one of the most contentious and bitterly debated issues of the entire conference: the rights of indigenous peoples around the world. The text began with a broad-based provision entitled the Declaration Regarding Non-Self-Governing Territories in which the members of the United Nations that have or assume responsibilities for the administration of territories whose peoples have not yet attained a full measure of self-government recognize the principle "that the interests of the inhabitants of these territories are paramount, and accept as a sacred trust the obligation to promote to the utmost, within the system of international peace and security established by the present Charter, the well-being of the inhabitants of these territories." Toward this end, the signatories pledged themselves to ensure, with due respect for the culture of the peoples concerned, their political, economic, social, and educational advancement, their just treatment, and their protection against abuses. In addition, they promised to aid in developing their self-government, to take due account of the political aspirations of these peoples, and to assist them in the progressive development of their free political institutions.[93] At the same time, the Charter also provided for the creation of an International Trusteeship System that went far beyond the restricted confines of the earlier mandate system of the League of Nations and one openly dedicated to securing peace and security and to ensuring equal treatment and the administration of justice without prejudice. In addition, and very importantly, it committed the United Nations to several basic objectives for this trusteeship system, including

the political, economic, social, and educational advancement of the inhabitants of the trust territories, and their progressive development towards self-government or independence as may be appropriate to the particular circumstances of each territory and its peoples and the freely expressed wishes of the peoples concerned

and

respect for human rights and for fundamental freedoms for all without distinction as to race, sex, language, or religion, and . . . recognition of the interdependence of the peoples of the world.

To administer and supervise this system, the Charter then went on to establish a Trusteeship Council with the power to consider reports, accept petitions, provide for periodic visits, and to take action in conformity with the terms of specific trusteeship agreements.[94]

The delegates at San Francisco who negotiated and signed the Charter also sought to make provision for the International Court of Justice to potentially deal with cases involving human rights. They made this body the judicial organ of the United Nations, for example, and thus responsible for achieving and maintaining the purposes and principles of the organization as a whole, including those of human rights. In addition, each signatory pledged to comply with the decision of the court in any case in which it was a party. Moreover, and particularly important for matters involving human rights wherein governments might want to censor certain details or facts, the Statute of the International Court of Justice annexed to the Charter itself gave it the authority to request information from intergovernmental organizations relevant to cases before it and even to receive information presented by such organizations on their own initiative.[95] This established the mechanism whereby the court could render decisions, either in an adjudicatory or an advisory capacity, on questions regarding international human rights.

Never before in history had any treaty ever given human rights such a prominent place as did the Charter of the United Nations. Those delegates and their allies among NGOs, individuals, and colonial peoples who had worked so hard to insert these specific provisions thus possessed many reasons for genuine pride and a sense of remarkable accomplishment. They had refused to renege on the promises made during the course of the war. They had not been deterred by Great Power pressure or by arguments that their visions represented only idealistic and naive dreams in a world dominated by power politics. And, they had resisted the attempts made by critics to "eliminate as much repetition as possible" in the "controversial" articles about human rights and defended phrases associated with such rights that opponents found "offensive."[96] But it was not over. In order to secure these provisions, they needed to concede others. Thus, a more detailed reading of *all* the provisions in the Charter revealed that the politics and diplomacy of the San Francisco Conference also had produced important qualifications, omissions, and other problems that would confront the evolution of international human rights for many years to come.

The much-heralded and innovative International Trusteeship System with its goal of ultimately extending independence for everyone, for example, did not apply to all colonial territories. Indeed, those states possessing empires insisted that it apply only to former mandates, territories detached from enemy states as a result of World War II, and those territories voluntarily placed under the system with conditions to be determined by nations responsible for their administration. Such a qualification, of course, allowed countries such as Britain, France, Portugal, Spain, the Netherlands, Belgium, and the United States to retain and exploit whatever colonial possessions they wished. In addition, they made sure that the Charter allowed any area in a territory under trust to be designated a "strategic area" if so desired and placed under the auspices of the Security Council where the Great Powers could use their veto to maintain exclusive control over a trusted area (a method quickly employed by the United States to seize former Japanese possessions in the Pacific, including the Caroline, Mariana, and Marshall Islands). Moreover, they sought to restrict the powers of the Trusteeship Council and successfully resisted the efforts of those who wanted to give it independent authority to investigate, to compel reports from the administrating nations, or to otherwise push colonial powers further than they wanted to go in respecting the rights of indigenous peoples.[97]

The Charter also spoke in new and eloquent ways about responsibilities for the United Nations in the area of international human rights. It provided unparalleled specificity for a treaty of this wide-ranging nature in language against discrimination on the basis of race, gender, language, and religion. But it did not define precisely what was meant by the expression, "human rights." Due to the politics and diplomacy at San Francisco, not the least of which involved the growing tension between the democratic and capitalist states of the West with those who advocated Communism, the Charter did not discuss the details or conditions of civil and political rights or economic and social rights. Similarly, it did not explain what the nations of the world actually intended by "fundamental freedoms" or "just treatment." Nor did it elaborate the meaning of "political, economic, social, and educational advancement" or those aspects of international relations possessing a "humanitarian character." The language of the Charter remained generous but vague on each of these points.

A much greater problem emerged in the matter of enforcement. Several representatives at San Francisco, especially those of the Great Powers, indicated a willingness to include words and statements of principle about human rights, but not provisions for practical or effective means of enforcement. Any proposals from other governments that the United Nations be required to actually and actively "safeguard," "protect," "preserve," "guarantee," "implement," "assure," or "enforce" human rights died an unceremonious death in committee.[98] Instead, the active verbs that could gain an acceptance by the majority were generally relatively innocuous ones such as "should facilitate," "may discuss," "initiate studies," "consider," "make recommendations," "reaffirm," "assist," "encourage," and "promote."[99] Even then, delegates carefully explained that they did not want these words to assume any greater meaning or authority than they already possessed. As the Costa Rican representative announced bluntly during the course of negotiations, with specific reference to provisions on human rights: "The propagation of ideas and principles whose objectives are these is of immense value to mankind; but surely if the word 'promote' is understood as implying the ability to coerce states . . . not one of the states concerned will recognize this principle."[100]

International human rights, once again, thus smashed against the rock of national sovereignty. This obviously came as no surprise. In fact, many observers had accurately predicted in advance that the principle of national sovereignty which had plagued so many efforts on behalf of human rights in the past certainly would resurface with a vengeance once negotiations for the United Nations began in earnest. "We have taught the layman to worship the arch-fiction of the sovereign state," forewarned legal scholar Philip C. Jessup, "and thereby have built a Maginot line against the invasion of new ideas in the international world, and behind that rampart the demagogue and the reactionary are enthroned."[101] James Shotwell similarly cautioned in the *International Safeguard of Human Rights*, issued by the Commission to Study the Organization of the Peace, that "each state, jealous of its sovereignty, had regarded any expression of foreign interest in the welfare of its citizens at home, as an interference in its own affairs," and would like to continue to do so. But, he wrote, "Now as a result of the Second World War, it has become clear that a regime of violence and oppression within any nation of the civilized world is a matter of concern to all the rest," and thus urged all delegates to overcome their traditional defense of national sovereignty for the sake of international peace and human rights.[102] This would not be easy, for as Arthur Vandenberg of the U.S. delegation candidly announced in the very beginning (and thereby foreshadowing an issue that would grow in intensity in the future), national sovereignty and the prevention of outside interference into domestic affairs were matters "dear to our hearts."[103]

The fundamental difficulty and ultimate paradox, of course, stemmed from the fact that those very governments most guilty of violating the human rights of their own people were being asked to provide active and determined protection against themselves. For this reason, the overwhelming majority of states remained unwilling to sacrifice elements of their sovereignty for the sake of human rights by authorizing the international community to intervene in their own internal affairs. The United States could speak eloquently about civil rights around the world, for example, but not if they exacerbated what Dulles called "the Negro problem in the South."[104] The British had no trouble supporting the principle of extending political rights for others, but not if it applied to their empire. The Soviets could support economic and social rights, but not if they threatened to impose civil and political rights on Stalin's dictatorship. The Chinese could strongly advocate the right of self-determination in colonial possessions or racial equality, but not if they entailed drastic reforms at home. But this could not simply be laid at the doorstep of the Great Powers alone. The Australians and New Zealanders could endorse a broad extension of human rights for the globe, but not if this jeopardized control over their own immigration policies against Asians or their respective populations of Aborigines or Maori. Jan Smuts of South Africa could enthusiastically draft the language about rights for the preamble to the Charter, but not if it committed his country to giving equal treatment for blacks. The Indians could argue passionately for the rights of all people, but not if required them to eliminate their caste system. The Iranians could declare their agreement with principles of equality and justice, but not if it forced them to modify their policies toward women at home. The Cubans had no trouble supporting an international declaration of the rights and duties of all individuals, but not if this in turn threatened the strong-armed rule of Fulgencio Batista.[105] As Herbert Evatt remarked during an extremely candid moment, "Every country represented in this conference has its own internal problems, its own vital spheres of domestic policy in which it cannot, without forfeiting its very existence as a state, permit external intervention."[106] The international protection of human rights seemed perfectly acceptable if extended over the domestic jurisdiction of other nations — but not to their own.

For precisely these reasons, and despite all of the other language of the Charter as described, a number of representatives insisted on features that would guarantee the interests and prerogatives of their states. Although the language of the preamble spoke of "We the Peoples," for example, the text of the Charter was agreed to by governments and not by peoples. Moreover, and of particular importance, they inserted one of the most critical provisions of entire Charter. In very large part due to the specific fear that international human rights would present too great a threat to national sovereignty and control over internal affairs, Article 2 (7) reads as follows:

Nothing contained in the present Charter shall authorize the United Nations to intervene in matters which are essentially within the domestic jurisdiction of any state or shall require Members to submit such matters to settlement.[107]

With such language, some delegates hoped that they could thus defend the sovereignty of their own nations and prevent the new international organization from interfering with their own particular domestic problems. In the words of one delegate from the United States, this provision "was sufficient to overpower all other considerations."[108]

When one reads this article on domestic jurisdiction it is easy to conclude that the delegates who drafted and signed the Charter of the United Nations engaged in nothing less than deliberate duplicity. That is, they cynically and capriciously took away with one hand what they had given with the other. They could return home claiming to their people and the world that they had supported human rights, while at the same time knowing full well that the organization now could not interfere with the way that they treated their own people. There is some truth to this argument. But it is insufficient as a full explanation and does not do justice to the complexities of the issues or the range of motivations among the participants, a number of whom believed that without Article 2 (7) the Charter would have never been approved in the first place. The evidence suggests that many delegates, trying to be conscientious in representing competing interests—and thus balance pressures on them—either did not completely understand the full implications of their decisions or somewhat naively believed that they just might be able to have their cake and eat it too. They wanted to ensure that individual people would be protected from severe abuses and the violations of their rights at the hands of governments, while at exactly the same time to make sure that the new international organization did not have the authority to intervene in their own domestic affairs.[109] Those with little experience in politics and diplomacy did not appreciate that *international* human rights and *national* sovereignty could be diametrically opposed to each other. Some fell victim to their own wishful thinking and convinced themselves that all of the provisions and principles in the Charter were internally consistent and contained no inherent contradictions. Still others believed that, if nations cooperated with each other in good faith, the problems created by the necessity of compromise at the San Francisco Conference somehow would work themselves out through time and that many opportunities still existed to resolve remaining difficulties. They noted, for example, that although it was true that the Charter provided no definition of "human rights," it similarly did not define the highly imprecise expression, "essentially within the domestic jurisdiction" of member states.

Differing Reactions and Assessments

The final provisions of the Charter of the United Nations, including those specifically dealing with human rights, produced a wide variety of differing reactions and assessments. For many, they marked an unprecedented accomplishment and level of achievement. Never before in history or the annals of diplomacy had issues of international human rights been so openly discussed, strongly advocated, or made such an integral part of a negotiated agreement with formal obligations and enlarged responsibilities by so many nations around the world. Those with visions about the importance of extending rights to all people had refused to be intimidated by pressure, to be dismissed by the skeptics as mere idealists, or to be silenced for the sake of expediency. They had done their best to keep promises made during the war and to create a "people's peace" in which rights would be respected. The actual inclusion of explicit provisions in the Charter for human rights and fundamental freedoms, equality and nondiscrimination, justice, economic and social advancement, humanitarian assistance, self-determination and independence, the welfare of indigenous peoples, and the opportunity for public international organizations to provide information to the International Court of Justice on their own initiative seemed simply unbelievable.

For these reasons, the concluding speeches of many of the delegates at San Francisco and the private assessments that followed spoke profusely of "one of the great moments in history," an "epoch-making document," and a "milestone in the evolution of human freedom." They discussed the historic and unique role of the San Francisco Conference and its profoundly significant contribution. They praised the Charter as one of the most important agreements ever negotiated in the entire history of the world and hailed it as representing the embodiment of highest aspirations of all men and women. They enthusiastically embraced its wider definitions of global peace that included justice, the welfare of "untold millions" of people, and human rights. "The words upon its parchment," declared one delegate, "chart the course by which a world in agony can be restored and peace maintained and human rights and freedoms can be advanced."[110]

Others reacted much differently and accused the delegates at San Francisco of not doing enough and producing a Charter of little or no value. *Time* magazine compared the idealistic promises made during the war with the end result and concluded that the final agreement represented no more than "a charter for a world of power."[111] Seasoned activist Rayford Logan characterized the results as a "tragic joke."[112] He noted that the organization just created, although heavily armed with principle, lacked clear practical procedures to implement the human rights provisions or the power to actually enforce them. Even the signatories to the Charter themselves already had violated some of the terms by denying full rights to their own citizens and subjects. The domestic jurisdiction clause, of course, drew immediate criticism for having slashed with a single stroke the very life out of all the articles dealing with human rights. In addition, those indigenous peoples who believed that they had been promised the right of self-determination were angry and sorely disappointed to learn that the colonial powers would still be able to retain their empires. Du Bois, who had just finished writing *Color and Democracy*, declared in testimony before the Senate Foreign Relations Committee that all of this reflected nothing more than "the national interests, the economic rivalries, and the selfish demands" of those governments represented at San Francisco. The new United Nations, he argued, should be created to serve "not only white peoples of English descent, but Latins and Slavs, and the yellow, brown, and black peoples of America, Asia, and Africa." "The proposed Charter," concluded Du Bois, "should, therefore, make clear and unequivocal the straightforward stand of the civilized world for race equality, and the universal application of the democratic way of life, not simply as philosophy and justice, but to save human civilization from suicide. What was true of the United States in the past is true of world civilization today—we cannot exist half slave and half free."[113]

Instead of complaining that the Charter accomplished too little, some critics angrily charged that it did too much. They feared that the delegates at San Francisco had created some kind of world government or super-state that would seriously jeopardize the prerogatives of their own nation. Particularly when reading the explicit provisions about human rights in the founding document of the new organization, they feared that even the domestic jurisdiction clause would not be "water tight" and might not be able to sufficiently protect complete national sovereignty from interference by the world community. Given the growing sense among many during the war of the often close relationship between foreign and domestic affairs, they wondered, who would actually determine the precise definition of "domestic jurisdiction"? Or, even more difficult, who would decide the meaning of "essentially" within the domestic jurisdiction of member states? Would this authority rest with each government, with the Security Council, with a majority of the General Assembly, the Commission on Human

Rights, or with the International Court of Justice? Thus, depending on their particular interests and problems, government officials worried aloud how the provisions of the Charter would affect their treatment of indigenous peoples in colonial areas, of those seeking immigration, or of their own citizens suffering from discrimination due to their race, gender, language, or religious beliefs.[114]

Still other participants and observers viewed the Charter, including its human rights provisions, neither as a simply magnificent achievement that suddenly would create heaven on earth nor as a horrendous tragedy that would destroy the cherished nation-state. Instead, they saw it in the context of the time and considered it to be a remarkable accomplishment in the evolution of international human rights. They regarded the practice of politics and diplomacy as the art of the possible, balanced somewhere between the cynics and the perfectionists, and knew that no nation or group could obtain everything they wanted over the course of two months of negotiation. They believed that those who assembled at San Francisco had accomplished about as much, if not more, as could realistically be expected given the heavy legacies of the past, the circumstances of the war, the magnitude of the tasks, the differences between the Great Powers and the medium and small nations, the divergent opinions among states and nongovernmental organizations, the prejudices of the time, and the often exaggerated hopes for the future. No one, they concluded, reasonably could expect the delegates, even if they had nothing else to do, to agree on a precise definition or enumeration of human rights — let alone draft an actual bill or charter of rights as proposed by some — in such a politically complex and philosophically diverse world within just a few weeks. "We cannot indeed claim that our work is perfect or that we have created an unbreakable guarantee of peace," said Lord Halifax in a moment of remarkable candor. "For ours is no enchanted palace to 'spring into sight at once' by magic touch or hidden power."[115] He told the other delegates that they had forged an instrument that would enhance peace only if nations were ready to make sacrifices for the common good and that only time would tell whether their efforts rested on shifting sand or solid rock. Jan Smuts reached the same assessment, describing the Charter as an imperfect document, full of compromises over difficult and tangled problems, but nevertheless a substantial advance over any previous plan ever created.[116] Peter Fraser returned home with a comparable opinion, saying that the Charter certainly was not perfect and contained many defects. It nevertheless marked, he said, the best possible hope of realizing a vision of peace with human rights for millions of men, women, and children of all nations around the world.[117]

In his concluding speech to the San Francisco Conference, President Harry Truman offered a similar assessment. Before all of the delegates assembled for the final session, he explained that in his judgment the Charter represented somewhat of a wonder to have been even negotiated at all. Many pressures had been exerted on the participants to keep them from making concessions or reaching compromises. The result was not perfect, he acknowledged, but certainly marked an essential first step in moving toward the future. "This Charter, like our Constitution," he said, "will be expanded and improved as time goes on. No one claims that it is now a final or a perfect instrument. It has not been poured into a fixed mold. Changing world conditions will require read-

International Recognition of Human Rights: The San Francisco Conference and the United Nations Charter (United Nations Photo).

justments — but they will be readjustments of peace and not of war." Then, significantly, Truman publicly declared what many others believed that they had learned over the course of their experience with recent history in the twentieth century: namely, that peace and human rights were inseparably connected. "The Charter is dedicated to the achievement and observance of human rights and fundamental freedoms," he concluded. "Unless we can attain those objectives for all men and women everywhere — without regard to race, language, or religion — we cannot have permanent peace and security in the world.[118]

*   *   *

Visions of creating a "people's peace" that contained provisions for human rights would not be denied as World War II came to an end. People around the world had endured too much suffering, made too many sacrifices, heard too many promises, and witnessed too much of the staggering capacity of modern states to oppress, torture, and kill millions of their own fellow human beings on a global scale to ever simply return to an unchanged past. The United Nations Charter thus sought to address a number of their concerns, and by providing explicit provisions focused on human rights in a formal treaty as never before in history, dramatically challenged and changed some of the most essential parameters of international discourse and behavior. In so doing, those who negotiated the Charter discovered themselves caught in the vortex of a dramatic and powerful struggle between a long tradition of national sovereignty and a dynamic new direction pushing for the internationalization of human rights. As they struggled with this in the aftermath of war, they found themselves unable and unwilling either to completely abandon a conservative past or to wholeheartedly embrace a potentially revolutionary future. For this reason, they simultaneously wrote provisions into the Charter containing language about both domestic jurisdiction and human rights, and about both governments and individuals. Assuming responsibilities to respect "the principle of equal rights and self-determination" and to promote "universal respect for, and observance of, human rights and fundamental freedoms for all without distinction as to race, sex, language, or religion," while at the same time avoiding all intervention "in matters which are essentially within the domestic jurisdiction of any state," appeared confusing at best and completely contradictory at worst. The existence of these difficulties thus set into motion a global debate about the philosophical and political meanings of these expressions and the precise nature of duties beyond national borders, and in the process launched what would become a revolution in international human rights.

Chapter 7
Proclaiming a Vision

The Universal Declaration of Human Rights

> Are human rights essentially within the domestic jurisdiction of the State? My answer is no, and a hundred times no. I submit that by the San Francisco Charter human rights have been taken out of the province of domestic jurisdiction and have been placed within the realm of international law.
>
> — Ricardo Alfaro of Panama

Those who negotiated and signed the Charter of the United Nations opened a veritable floodgate to new possibilities of expanding international human rights as never before in the history of the world. Explicit provisions suddenly placed the signatory states and the organization itself on public record and in international law as supporting universal respect for and observance of human rights and fundamental freedoms for all. The members of the United Nations formally pledged themselves to promote these rights, including those of self-determination and economic and social advancement, without any distinction as to race, sex, language, or religion. Just how these objectives would be met in practice with the machinery recently created, of course, remained to be seen. There were those with visions who now possessed expansive hopes to actively use the new organization as a means of advancing international human rights beyond all previous limitations and restraints. Yet, there also were others committed to vested interests and national sovereignty, and armed with the domestic jurisdiction clause of the Charter, vowed to resist change, at least insofar as it might involve their own country. Both sides believed that any resolution of their sharply conflicting positions would take time and would depend on changing historical circumstances, but few anticipated just how soon the contest would be joined. It began immediately, for those who demanded change refused to wait. The ensuing contest would determine much of the future, and that future would reveal revolutionary developments for those seeking to proclaim a vision of international human rights to the world.

The Revolution Begins

The activists who saw in the language of the Charter and the momentum that created it unprecedented opportunities to advance international human rights wasted no time at all. They were unwilling to sit by patiently and absolutely determined not to accept the proposition that the domestic jurisdiction clause precluded any and all challenges to the prerogatives of national sovereignty. Instead, they claimed that the "spirit and purpose" of the Charter imposed important moral *obligations* on members of the global community. Signatory states had made solemn promises to themselves and to the world to uphold certain principles of public morality in international behavior, and that these now needed to be honored. They also argued that the Charter recognized fundamental rights of the individual and, as a legally binding treaty, thereby for the first time in history transformed individuals from mere objects of international compassion into actual subjects of international law.[1] Thus, even before the United Nations formally met for the first time, they seized a number of initiatives and launched a variety of new efforts. These produced frustration and fear among those governments and individuals who opposed them, but brought hope and encouragement to those who shared their visions.

Within only days of the signing of the United Nations Charter in June of 1945, for example, the Pan-African Federation, the Federation of Indian Associations in Britain, the West African Students' Union, the Ceylon Students' Association, and the Burma Association all combined their resources, energies, and aspirations to organize the All-Colonial People's Conference. Here, and explicitly using the language and the promises of the Charter, they demanded their rights of self-determination and racial equality. This served to inspire the larger and more influential Fifth Pan-African Congress held during October in Manchester. Representatives came from Antigua, Barbados, Bermuda, British Guiana (now Guyana), Gambia, the Gold Coast (now Ghana), Jamaica, Kenya, Liberia, Nigeria, Nyasaland (now Malawi), St. Kitts, St. Lucia, Sierra Leone, South Africa, Tanganyika, Tobago, Trinidad, and Uganda, among others, including Du Bois from the United States. Reflecting both the radicalizing effect of World War II and the expectations raised by the Charter, they indicated that they were no longer inclined to ask modestly for some slight favor from on high to alleviate discrimination and exploitation, but now determined to demand independence, an end to racial discrimination, and respect for human rights. From their ranks emerged leaders such as Nkrumah and Kenyatta, who became powerful figures in the international movement for decolonization with a resolve to take their destiny into their own hands. They agreed to adopt a strategy for organizing their peoples through political parties and trade unions and for engaging in struggle if necessary. In a resolution entitled "The Challenge to the Colonial Powers," they asserted: "The delegates to the Fifth Pan-African Congress believe in peace. . . . Yet if the Western world is still determined to rule mankind by force, then Africans, as a last resort, may have to appeal to force in the effort to achieve Freedom, even if force destroys the world." The text of another resolution, "The Declaration to the Colonial Peoples of the World," conveyed this new determination as well by ending with a ringing slogan reminiscent of the concluding words of the *Communist Manifesto:* "Colonial and Subject Peoples of the World — Unite!"[2]

This, of course, marked only the beginning. Not all peoples possessed the patience to wait for the results of resolutions from international meetings of nongovernmental organizations or for the as yet untested deliberations of the United Nations. Instead, they sought to take matters into their own hands and to exploit the unique conditions that came in the wake of the immediate aftermath of war. These included the weaknesses of the exhausted European colonial powers, the new promises of the Charter of the United Nations, and the defeat of Japan after the dropping of the atomic bombs that created a temporary vacuum of power in Asia. They were fully prepared to use armed force if necessary to gain their independence and the right of self-determination, and thus launched campaigns and insurrections against the British in Burma, Egypt, India, Iraq, Malaya, and Palestine; the French in Algeria, Indochina, Lebanon, and Syria; and the Dutch in Indonesia.[3] Violence occurred within the United States as well with the outbreak of several major race riots caused by a revival of the Ku Klux Klan, lynchings, and black ex-service men and women returning from a war to defend democracy in no mood to live again in a racially segregated society that denied their human rights. In the opinion of Walter White, all of these struggles against exploitation, imperialism, and racism were global in nature and closely interrelated, whether they occurred in Asia, Africa, the Middle East, the islands of the Pacific, North or South America. As he wrote in warning at the time: "A wind *is* rising — a wind of determination by the have-nots of the world to share the benefits of freedom and prosperity which the haves of the earth have tried to keep exclusively for themselves. That wind blows all over the world. Whether that wind develops into a hurricane is a decision which we must make now."[4]

Inspired by the provisions in the Charter, nations, non-governmental organizations, and individuals also suddenly became much more active in criticizing the abuses of human rights both at home and abroad. The African National Congress publicly condemned the practice of apartheid in South Africa. The World Jewish Congress and the Conseil Représentatif des Juifs de France pushed strongly for provisions in the peace treaties signed with former adversaries that would protect human rights. A radio station in Texas broadcast a series of programs about the unequal treatment of Hispanics, claiming that such discrimination clearly violated the new Charter of the United Nations. India joined with the National Association for the Advancement of Colored People and the Indian Rights Association in castigating racial segregation in the United States with newspaper headlines like "A Shameful Act" and "Treatment of Negroes a Blot on U.S." The United States reciprocated by drawing attention to the discrimination of the caste system in India. Czechoslovakia vehemently criticized the Soviet Union for suppressing the rights of those people living in Eastern Europe by means of the power of the Red Army. China condemned the immigration policies of Australia, Canada, and New Zealand. The Soviet Union loudly proclaimed that capitalists in the West abused the economic and social rights of poor classes. Iraq, Egypt, and most of the Latin American countries, among many others, condemned the British, French, and Dutch for trying to perpetuate their colonial empires and deny indigenous peoples their right to self-determination.[5] And, in the autumn of 1945, Uruguay launched a campaign to protest the violation of civil and political rights of the people of Argentina by their own government. As the Uruguayan Minister for Foreign Affairs Eduardo Rodríguez Larreta declared in taking such action, the principle of nonintervention into the domestic affairs of another state could no longer "shield without limitation the notorious and repeated violation by any republic of the elementary rights of man and of the citizen, nor the nonfulfillment of obligations freely contracted by a state with respect to its external and internal duties and which entitle it to be an active member of the international community."[6]

Those states subject to such criticism, of course, reacted swiftly and vehemently. They claimed that how they treated their own people was strictly their own business, regardless of whatever new pledges had been made. The long-standing doctrine of national sovereignty, the principle of nonintervention, and the Charter's own Article 2 (7) about domestic jurisdiction, they said, precluded any outside interference whatsoever into their own internal affairs. The government of Argentina, to use just one example, declared that any accusation against its human rights record was "unexpected as it is dangerous" and raised "a matter of extraordinary transcendency." This kind of interference, it asserted, could result only in threatening traditional practices, spreading defamation, sowing confusion, and raising the specter that members of the international community could intervene in the domestic affairs of any state whenever they wished. Argentina thus announced that it would never accept the proposition that its own policies at home might somehow be "subject to the will or the judgement of foreign powers."[7] Such expressions of resistance threw fuel on the fire of the escalating global debate and mobilized those with visions of international human rights to vow that they would challenge the traditional claims of national sovereignty even further and in any forum possible.

During exactly this same time, to illustrate, a variety of international conferences organized for different purposes all tended to eventually turn to matters of human rights. The International Labor Conference met in the autumn of 1945 to create a new constitution for the International Labor Organization that would determine its critical future direction in the postwar world. Acutely aware of their own role in promoting the concept of "a people's peace" and in adopting the Philadelphia Declaration's strong statement about rights, the delegates who assembled in Paris sought to address their traditional concerns about class within a larger context of international human rights extended around the world. To do this, in the words of one scholar, they sought to go "beyond the nation-state" and to strengthen their organization by expanding its representation and extending its scope to address the general welfare needs of all people. The delegations from Australia, Egypt, India, and most of Latin America thus inveighed against the near monopoly of industrial Western states in major organs of the International Labor Organization and demanded representation on a more global scale. They argued on behalf of the universal rights of all people, particularly those of an economic and social nature. They stressed labor inspection, freedom of association, equal remuneration for men and women, the right to be free from forced labor, nondiscrimination, and minimum standards of living. Toward this end, a number of delegates emphasized the need to provide aid and technical assistance to those who suffered in developing countries. The Committee on Social Policy in Dependent Territories worked further to secure the inclusion of obligations on colonial powers to apply legal conventions to their possessions and to submit special reports on the actual progress of implementation.[8] Similarly, when diplomats assembled shortly thereafter for the purpose of creating the United

Nations Educational, Scientific, and Cultural Organization (UNESCO), they quickly felt compelled to comment on the causes of the catastrophe of armed conflict they all had just experienced. They easily could have blamed any of the traditional explanations such as territorial ambition, economic greed, human aggressiveness, the accumulation of armaments, the absence of collective security and appeasement, or the lack of prudent statecraft, among others, but did not. Instead, they focused on only one factor, and poignantly concluded in a most remarkable statement: "The great and terrible war which has now ended was a war made possible by the denial of democratic principles of the dignity, equality, and mutual respect for men, and by the propagation in their place, through ignorance and prejudice, of the doctrine of the inequality of men and races."[9] For this reason, they committed themselves to move as far as possible from these ideas by devoting their educational, scientific, and cultural resources toward the promotion of international human rights.

The opening of the International Military Tribunal at Nuremberg attracted even greater—and at times, riveting—attention. Information concerning Nazi atrocities increasingly had become available throughout World War II. But prior to the actual occupation of Germany and Poland, these horrific acts always could be conveniently dismissed or discounted as no more than wartime propaganda simply too exaggerated to be believed. Once Allied forces entered the extermination camps and witnessed the evidence that made even the strong turn away, however, the unbelievable became all too tragically real. Policymakers, including many of those who attended the San Francisco Conference, had received some sense of the horror before, but had no idea of the staggering extent of torture and genocide. By November, when the trials began, there were few illusions on the part of the prosecutors, who declared that they possessed far more than sufficient evidence to charge the remaining Nazi leaders with crimes to commit conspiracy, crimes against the peace, war crimes, and, an important new category: "crimes against humanity," or those involving persecution, mass deportations, and extermination on political, racial, or religious grounds.[10] Never before in history had a legal proceeding attempted to make government leaders internationally responsible as individuals for crimes against humanity covering so much time, so many nations, or so many people, including their own citizens. "The wrongs which we seek to condemn and punish," declared Justice Robert Jackson in his opening statement, "have been so calculated, so malignant, and so devastating, that civilization cannot tolerate their being ignored, because it cannot survive their being repeated." History, he argued, does not record any crime perpetuated against so many victims with such cruelty or such violations against the "inalienable rights" of all human beings. "Our proof," he predicted without exaggeration, "will be disgusting."[11]

It was. Massive registers of meticulous documents revealed the names and the numbers of those helpless human beings exterminated like insects. Shocking personal testimony described the massive deportations, forced labor, torture, and unspeakable medical experiments. Grotesque photographs of the "Final Solution" displayed mounds of human bones, piles of eyeglasses or gold fillings stolen from helpless victims, and scratches in solid concrete made by the clawing fingers of those about to be gassed to death. Gruesome newsreels showed bulldozers shoving heaps of naked and limp bodies

"We Were a Sovereign State and That Was Strictly Our Business": The Holocaust
(International Military Tribunal).

of men, women, and children being dumped unceremoniously into earthen pits and
mass graves. To make it worse, the defendants claimed that they were not responsible,
and Hitler's deputy Hermann Goering declared: "But that was our right! We were a
sovereign State and that was strictly our business."[12] The proceedings at Nuremberg
forced the world to peer into the abyss of overwhelming horror and to hear incompre-
hensible crimes that claimed the lives of several million human beings justified in the
name of national sovereignty. Many who saw this evidence and heard this testimony
became convinced in their shock, agony, and moral outrage that such actions against

humanity and excuses about sovereignty must *never* be allowed to happen again. For them, the ideology of Nazism, the experience of the war, and the horrors of the Holocaust provided a defining and irrevocable turning point.[13] They thus determined that they would no longer remain silent or inactive, but vowed instead that they would eagerly participate in the revolution to promote respect for human rights.

The cumulative effect of these many international efforts could hardly be ignored, and before the year was out, they began to produce important changes within the domestic politics of a number of states as well. Explicitly and specifically citing the human rights provisions of the Charter of the United Nations, for example, aggrieved persons and parties sought to challenge discriminatory policies within their own nations. Aborigines in Australia, Maori in New Zealand, blacks and Asians in South Africa, and various indigenous peoples in both North and South America all increased pressure on their governments to comply with the new international commitments. They scored a major victory in Canada when the High Court of Ontario in the *Re Drummond Wren* case dismissed racially restrictive real estate covenants and specifically cited the human rights provisions within the Charter as the reason for doing so. Similar developments emerged in New Zealand with the signing of the Maori Social and Economic Advancement Act and in the United States where negotiations began for what would become the Indian Claims Commission to consider some form of redress for Native Americans.[14] Bolivia, Guatemala, Hungary, Italy, Liberia, and Portugal granted women the right to vote.[15] Elections in Britain brought a new Labour Government into power promising drastic changes from the past, including the commitment to reduce class divisions at home by means of launching a welfare state and to consider the rights of indigenous peoples abroad by implementing "a revolution in Imperial attitude."[16]

These revolutionary developments marked only the beginning, however, for 1946 brought even more changes. This single year, for example, witnessed dramatic constitutional changes that specifically addressed equality in rights in a number of geographically diverse countries. These included Albania, Brazil, Ceylon, China, Ecuador, France, Japan, Panama, and Yugoslavia, and immediately affected the rights of millions of people, especially women.[17] The new Japanese Constitution, to illustrate, turned its back on centuries of tradition by prohibiting discrimination in political, economic, or social relations because of race, creed, social status, family origin, or sex, and went on to proscribe:

> Marriage shall be based only on the mutual consent of both sexes and it shall be maintained through mutual cooperation with the equal rights of husband and wife as a basis.
> With regard to choice of spouse, property rights, inheritance, choice of domicile, divorce, and other matters pertaining to marriage and the family, laws shall be enacted from the standpoint of individual dignity and the essential equality of the sexes.[18]

During the same year, the leading victors of World War II acting through the Council of Foreign Ministers, deliberately used the language of the United Nations Charter to include broad guarantees for human rights within the peace treaties with Bulgaria, Hungary, Italy, and Romania. When concerns arose that such provisions might interfere with the internal affairs of these states, they were dismissed with the argument that how nations treat their own people at home now must be regarded as an international responsibility.[19]

The majority of efforts to advance international human rights during 1946 focused on the United Nations itself. Most of those determined to promote their visions for rights pinned their hopes on this new organization and its charge under the provisions of the Charter. They thus wasted no time at all in turning their attention to its first meetings, which they knew would be both historical and critical. Indeed, not at all content to wait on the evolution of the precise committee structure or the deliberate procedures negotiated to facilitate the long-term work of the United Nations, they immediately launched full-scale debate within the General Assembly dealing with a number of highly explosive and controversial issues of human rights. During the very first session, for example, delegates began discussing specific charges of state violations against individuals in Bulgaria, Greece, Hungary, Spain, and the Soviet Union, among others.

One of the most important of these early efforts to draw global attention to human rights by means of widespread publicity within the General Assembly occurred on the initiative of Egypt. Inspired by the principles enunciated in the Charter, and strongly encouraged by the strong political support from most of the Latin American states and all of the existing Afro-Asian countries then members of the United Nations, the Egyptian delegation swiftly introduced a resolution. It condemned racial and religious persecution and called on all governments to take prompt and energetic action to end discrimination. Other delegates quickly rose to lend their support, describing this matter of discrimination as a "burning question," a "vital" issue of "immense importance," and as "one of the most important questions which the conscience of this august Assembly must face." Emilio Saint-Lot of Haiti passionately spoke in favor of the resolution, asserting the need for the whole world to proclaim the value and the dignity of each individual human being. The delegate from India echoed the same theme and argued that global peace and security must be based "on freedom for all people, on the recognition of human dignity, on the fact that the human soul has the same value whether it is encased in a white, brown, or black body."[20] The force of this principle in light of the provisions in the Charter could hardly be denied, and the Assembly unanimously passed the resolution condemning persecution and discrimination.

Enormously encouraged by this strong international support on the issue of racial equality, and long the victim of discrimination through various forms such as imperialism and immigration restrictions, India decided to raise the stakes. It decided to go far beyond seeking support for a general statement of principle without enforcement, and instead attempted to single out a specific country for violating the principles of the Charter and to call for remedial action. To throw down the gauntlet and thereby launch the attack, the Indian government sent the intense and articulate Vijaya Lakshmi Pandit, the first woman leader of any delegation to the General Assembly, to the very first session of the United Nations to condemn South Africa for its policies of racial discrimination. Standing erect at the podium, she accused the government of South Africa of grossly violating the basic human rights of Indians and others with darker skin colors, in total contradiction of the principles and purposes of the Charter. She declared that this case was not simply one between two countries, but one with potential consequences for the entire world and for the integrity of the United Nations itself, and called on her fellow delegates to listen to their collective conscience and rise to meet their new international responsibilities. Her speech produced an immediate and violent reaction from Jan Smuts of South Africa who had personally and directly clashed with Gandhi over this issue before, and was outraged to have his own reputation and that of his country now put on trial for all the world to see. He rose and shouted that his country was protected by Article 2 (7) of the Charter. The treatment of Indians, coloreds, and mixed races, he said, was purely and simply a matter of "domestic jurisdiction." Smuts warned ominously that if the delegates authorized the United Nations to intervene in South Africa, then an extremely dangerous precedent would be set for doing the same in any other country, thus destroying national sovereignty. Pandit arose again and dismissed this legal argument about domestic jurisdiction as being "late in the day and far-fetched" and as making a mockery out of the principles enunciated in the Charter. "Millions of voiceless people," she asserted, "who because of their creed or color, have been relegated to positions of inferiority, are looking to us for justice, and it is only on the foundation of justice that we can create a new world order. . . . We must remember that, in the present case, the minds of millions of people in India and in other parts of Asia and Africa have been moved to intense indignation at all forms of racial discrimination which stand focused upon the problem of South Africa. This is a test case."[21]

All sides of the debate agreed that it was indeed a test case that would establish a most critical precedent. A number of other states rallied behind India's position. Wellington Koo of China argued that all Asians took a great interest in this case of South Africa, for they wanted to see racial discrimination eliminated from the face of the earth. The Mexican delegate rose in strong support to describe the issue as "one of the most important questions of our time," and Carlos Romulo of the Philippines called it "a moral question of the first magnitude" that could be ignored only at great risk. "Can this Assembly," asked the representative from Poland, "remain indifferent when so fundamental a problem is involved?" Ricardo Alfaro of Panama argued passionately that he would never consider human rights as the exclusive prerogative of individual states hiding behind the cloak of domestic jurisdiction, claiming that the Charter gave birth to the new principle that individuals as well as states now were subjects of international law. In sharp contrast, South Africa angrily lashed out against those who dared to interfere in its internal affairs, and in heated debate dismissed the General Assembly as a "mere political forum" of activist troublemakers. Australia, Britain, Canada, and the United States, among others, fearful that their own problems at home might attract international attention, supported the South African position, arguing that the United Nations possessed no legal jurisdiction in this matter involving national sovereignty. In the end, the resolution recognizing that the treatment of Indians in South Africa failed to be in conformity with international obligations under the Charter and calling on the two governments to discuss their problem and report back to the General Assembly passed with the necessary two-thirds majority.[22] As such, it marked a revolutionary departure and signaled to all governments in the world that the members of the United Nations would no longer be silent on this question or be swayed by the traditional arguments that how a nation treated its own people was somehow exclusively its own business.

Within only days of passing this resolution, for example, the General Assembly energetically turned its attention to the issue of genocide as well. Once again, the initiative came not from white nations or the Great Powers, but from others who had been victimized in the past. Cuba, India, and Panama led the charge, but were quickly joined by others. They and their allies observed that extermination had existed for many centuries, including the tragic cases of the Hereros and others in Africa, Aborigines in Australia and Tasmania, Armenians in Turkey, and native Indian tribes in North and South America. But they argued that the extreme nature of genocide during World War II and the recent horrifying revelations of the "Final Solution" and other crimes against humanity at the Nuremberg trials demonstrated an enormous danger to global peace that simply could not be ignored or tolerated. They consequently determined to place genocide squarely on the international agenda for human rights by speaking out collectively against such monstrous atrocities and to reaffirm the right of all to a human existence. Toward this end, they passed a resolution condemning mass extermination as completely contrary to moral law and to the spirit and aims of the United Nations. The resolution, in significant language, declared that genocide "is a crime under international law which the civilized world condemns, and for the commission of which principals and accomplices — whether private individuals, public officials, or statesmen, and whether the crime is committed on religious, racial, political, or any other grounds — are punishable."[23] This decision, like the final judgment of the Nuremberg Tribunal condemning Nazi war criminals just a few weeks before and the ongoing deliberations of the Tokyo War Crimes Trials helped to establish the principle that individuals, and not just nations, would now be subjects of international law.[24]

Simultaneous with these intense debates on the new human rights agenda about discrimination and genocide were those that raged over the right of self-determination. World War II had released powerful psychological and political forces in Africa, Asia, the Caribbean, Middle East, and the Pacific demanding rights for indigenous peoples and an end to colonial empires. These clashed directly and often violently with the resistance of the imperial powers to give up control over their possessions. Considerable pressure had been brought to bear by the majority of states represented at the San Francisco Conference to write provisions into the Charter concerning the Declaration Regarding Non-Self-Governing Territories, recognizing the principle that the interests of the inhabitants of these lands were paramount and pledging to work toward self-government and to authorize the creation of an International Trusteeship System within the United Nations. But this represented only a tenuous compromise. The majority within the General Assembly, who themselves had once been victims of imperialism, still were not satisfied, and decided to use their very first session to push further. They agreed to create the Trusteeship Council, but in addition to having administering powers serve on this body, they elected such countries as China, Iraq, Mexico, and the Soviet Union, who were all well known for their public statements about anticolonialism. They battled over the text of each and every trusteeship agreement, trying to drive the specific conditions toward a greater emphasis on the rights of the peoples of these territories. In this regard, they strongly criticized a number of the early draft proposals from the large colonial powers, but praised the commitment from New Zealand that its agreement with Western Samoa would be "in effect a self-contained Bill of Rights for the inhabitants."[25] They adamantly rejected the plan by South Africa to annex South-West Africa. And, over the strong objections of the colonial powers who complained about unwarranted interference into the domestic affairs of sovereign states, the General Assembly passed two important resolutions. One of these sought to take the information and reports about the conditions within the trust territories and the well-being of their people out of the exclusive control of the Trusteeship Council, and place it in the hands of the General Assembly as a whole through the secretary-general and through a special ad hoc committee composed of such vocal advocates of decolonization as China, Cuba, Egypt, India, the Philippines, Soviet Union, and Uruguay. In addition, another resolution called on those members who administered trust territories to convene special conferences of representatives of the peoples living in these lands in order that they might articulate their wishes and aspirations for self-government. Such action, they declared, would help to give practical effect to both the letter and the spirit of the human rights provisions within the Charter itself.[26]

Not content with all of these efforts, delegates to this first session also turned their attention to the issue of gender. Inspired by the language in the Charter concerning the prohibition of discrimination on the basis of sex that stood in such marked contrast with centuries of historical practice, a number of members sought to push the United Nations and the world even further toward securing genuine equality. They began this effort by creating a formal and permanent Commission on the Status of Women, declaring:

The position which women hold today has not been won without hard and often bitter struggle and a great deal of work is still required. But today for the first time in history the women of the world have in the Commission an international body solely devoted to achieving complete equality for them.[27]

Bodil Begtrup of Denmark then forcefully reminded her fellow delegates, a number of whom were well-known activists in their own countries, that women around the world still suffered solely due to their gender. An explicit statement sponsored by the General Assembly, she argued, would provide moral support and encouragement to all those around the world, including those in Islamic nations, who struggled to improve the status of women. Tireless in her efforts, she gained the active support of others like Minerva Bernardino of the Dominican Republic, Fryderyka Kalinowska of Poland, and Madame W. S. New of China, all of whom argued that international human rights could not proceed unless the global community paid due attention to the rights of half of the population of the human race. Agnes McIntosh of New Zealand stressed the importance of developing a larger sense of responsibilities as citizens of the world beyond national borders, and maintained that unless the United Nations took a stand on this matter, women in country after country would be forced to fight long and bitter battles by themselves to secure equal rights. After months of work, these women and their male supporters gathered enough votes to secure a resolution recommending that all member states adopt measures necessary to fulfill the purposes and aims of the Charter by granting political rights to women.[28] As Secretary-General Trygve Lie said during the course of the debates: "We will not rest until women everywhere enjoy equal rights and equal opportunities with men."[29]

The General Assembly threw itself into a discussion of the relationship between human rights and freedom of information as well. According to General Carlos Romulo, the representative of the Philippines who first raised the issue, the rights of citizens were most likely to be respected in those countries who had an unfettered press capable of ensuring the free flow of truthful and unbiased information. He and others pointed out that recent experience with totalitarian governments demonstrated all too well the dangers of censorship and the manipulation of propaganda that destroyed rights, threatened the peace, and, as described by Aase Lionaes of Norway, "poisoned the minds of millions."[30] They thus sponsored a resolution calling for an international conference on freedom of information, recognizing that the technological inventions of radio and film must be included in any discussion about the press, and acknowledging the existence of a "moral obligation" to seek facts without prejudice. The motive behind this effort, as stated in language passed unanimously by the General Assembly, could be found in the conviction that "freedom of information is a fundamental human right and is the touchstone of all the freedoms to which the United Nations is consecrated."[31]

In addition to political and civil rights, the General Assembly spent considerable time discussing social and economic rights and what the delegates regarded as their collective responsibility to guarantee the basic right of all people to a minimum standard of life and living conditions guaranteed by international humanitarian assistance. A number of the discussions began in the Third Committee (Social, Humanitarian, and Cultural Affairs), chaired by Peter Fraser, who had spoken so forcefully about these kinds of rights during the San Francisco Conference. With constant references to human rights, both as ends in themselves as well as means toward peace, they created a whole series of mechanisms designed to address the needs of those who suffered from various forms of urgent social and economic problems. To provide help to the hundreds of thousands of refugees and displaced persons still left in the aftermath of war, for example, the General Assembly established the International Refugee Organization (IRO) and charged it with tasks of repatriation and resettlement. In this context, as a representative of the Netherlands described it, all delegations had "the first opportunity and the duty to demonstrate in a practical way the true significance of the Rights of Man, so often extolled during the years of war, and also often referred to after victory."[32] To render assistance to children and adolescents, they created the United Nations International Children's Emergency Fund (UNICEF). To secure and maintain fair and humane conditions of labor, they brought the International Labor Organization (ILO) into a relationship with the United Nations as a specialized agency. To raise levels of nutrition and standards of living, they established the same relationship with the new Food and Agricultural Organization (FAO). To advance the general level of education and knowledge, they repeated the process with the United Nations Educational, Scientific, and Cultural Organization. To collect and distribute relief and to provide social welfare, they decided to redistribute some of the functions of the wartime United

Nations Relief and Rehabilitation Administration (UNRRA) among the office of the secretary-general, the Economic and Social Council, and the specialized agencies, and encouraged member governments to work closely with the Red Cross and Red Crescent societies in their humanitarian mission. And, to give medical attention to those suffering from physical or mental ailments, disease, or infirmity, they urged member governments to accept the constitution of the World Health Organization (WHO), one of whose essential provisions read significantly: "The enjoyment of the highest attainable standard of health is one of the fundamental rights of every human being without distinction as to race, religion, political belief, economic or social condition."[33]

Finally, and significantly, members of the first General Assembly sought to speak to the question of an international bill of human rights. Visions of such a bill had emerged during deliberations by the League of Nations, during the course of World War II, and during preparations for a "people's peace."[34] Even President Truman in his closing address to the San Francisco Conference had urged that such a bill be created and be given priority in such a way that it would "be as much a part of international life as our own bill of rights is a part of our Constitution."[35] But up to this stage there had never seemed to be enough time to draft such a document or to secure sufficient acceptance by most governments. The many decisions made and the resolutions passed by the United Nations during this first year, however, seemed to indicate that the mood had changed dramatically and that the time was now ripe to take more determined efforts. Consequently, the untiring Ricardo Alfaro of Panama seized the initiative and submitted a statement on the rights and duties of states and a draft Declaration on Fundamental Human Rights and Freedoms. He received strong support from Chile, Cuba, Ecuador, Egypt, France, and Liberia, among others. After listening to the arguments, the General Assembly then voted to renew its support for the creation of an international bill of rights, but given the complex nature of such an instrument, voted to send the draft declaration on human rights to the Economic and Social Council with instructions to forward it for further study and action to the new Commission on Human Rights.[36]

Members of the United Nations invested considerable time and care in creating the Commission on Human Rights. They understood that the Charter mandated them to do so. Perhaps more importantly, they knew that many people throughout the world deeply concerned about human rights would be watching them carefully and that expectations ran high. The United States Secretary of State, in fact, actually concluded prophetically that the creation of the commission "may well prove one of the most important and significant achievements of the San Francisco Conference. . . . It is a promise from this generation to generations yet unborn that this war, fought in the cause of freedom, will not have been fought in vain."[37] In addition, many believed, as expressed by one diplomat in the British Foreign Office, that "the work of this commission may be of considerable importance, and that many subjects of particular concern to this country, in particular subjects such as the rights of colonial peoples, may be raised."[38] Consequently, the United Nations member states took the advice of the Preparatory Commission, particularly the strongly worded recommendations about protecting international human rights, very seriously and began preparations to establish a commission on a permanent basis.[39] In order to provide it with sufficient and professional staff support and to prepare an annual *Yearbook on Human Rights* to inform all peoples of the status of rights around the world, the secretary-general created the Human Rights Division within the Secretariat. His assistant Henri Laugier, who once served as the president of the Fédération Internationale des Droits de l'Homme, then named Canadian professor John Humphrey as the division's first director with the promise that the assignment would prove to be "a great adventure."[40] Then, in order to draft recommendations concerning the precise terms of reference and composition of the Commission on Human Rights, the Economic and Social Council named nine individuals to a special "nuclear," or preparatory, commission. This group immediately by acclamation elected as its chairperson none other than Eleanor Roosevelt, the former First Lady of the United States and a remarkable woman already well known for her outspoken and often courageous positions on human rights.

With intelligence, compassion, graciousness, commitment, and determination, Eleanor Roosevelt set about to guide this commission in accomplishing its task before the eyes of the world. Her enormous popularity and prestige attracted attention, but it was her vision that generated inspiration and offered hope. She believed in an international community that respected the value and variety of all human life where no nation or individual person could be truly free as long as others were not. Consequently, as she expressed herself in thought and action, it became clear that her commitment to human rights embraced presidents and ambassadors as well as the "everyday people" of the world, and extended from the large citadels of government power to tiny hamlets and villages. People sensed her gift of profound sincerity and her capacity to care for and understand the human condition, and thus wrote and told her that they shared her hope in the United Nations and its potential for creating a more decent future.[41] She thus quickly became aware of the fact that "this Commission means a great deal to a great many people," telling her colleagues that "they look upon us, regardless of the governments that we spring from, as *their* representatives, the representatives of people of the world."[42] But in this process, she knew that neither she nor the commission could please everyone and that not all people and governments would like the results. As she declared publicly and with the voice of experience: "Sometimes issues arise where one has to advocate something that may be difficult for one's own government to carry through, and yet, if one believes it is right, I think one should advocate it, hoping that if it would be good for the world, it would, therefore, in the end, be good for one's own government and one's own people too."[43] With precisely this in mind, Roosevelt and her committee recommended an ambitious program for the Commission on Human Rights and suggested that three subcommissions be created, one for Freedom of Information and of the Press, one for Protection of Minorities, and another for Prevention of Discrimination. In addition, and most daring, they recommended that the Commission on Human Rights be composed of individual experts rather than representatives of governments in order that it might acquire greater independence and integrity, and that it be empowered to actively aid the Security Council by pointing out cases where violations of human rights constituted threats to world peace.[44]

Some of these recommendations received ready acceptance, but as Roosevelt had predicted, others produced immediate hostility. For some governments, parts of the proposals were too ambitious and too threatening to their own national sovereignty and domestic jurisdiction. Thus, the delegate from Britain received ciphered instructions to be very careful about this "extremely delicate" subject with enormous implications while at the same time being warned "not to give the impression that we are being obstructive. We suggest our right course is to play for time, leaving it as far as possible to other delegations to bring out the difficulties."[45] The British need not have worried, for others quickly did jump into the fray, including the Soviets who insisted adamantly that they would never accept individual experts acting in their own capacity instead of state-appointed government representatives. In the end, and after the dust had settled, the Economic and Social Council decided to establish the Commission on Human Rights as a permanent body, composed of eighteen members. The council remained unwilling to grant it too much freedom, however, and thus determined that those members would serve as official representatives of their respective governments. The commission was charged with responsibilities for submitting proposals, recommendations, and reports regarding international declarations or conventions on civil liberties, the status of women, freedom of information, and similar matters; the protection of minorities; and the prevention of discrimination on grounds of race, sex, language, or religion. The council gave one task first priority, however, and assigned the commission to begin its work by drafting an international bill of human rights.[46] This, in turn, immediately raised extremely difficult issues of philosophy and politics, and thereby confirmed the judgment of one veteran observer that "no part of the Economic and Social Council contains more explosive material than the Commission on Human Rights."[47]

Challenging Questions of Philosophy

It is likely that no issue of public policy in the world raises more difficult philosophical questions than that of human rights. Nevertheless, up to this stage in the historical evolution of international human rights, diplomats had only been on the margins of serious philosophical discourse. In their more private moments they may have pondered issues of philosophy and ethics, but as representatives of nation-states in formal negotiations they rarely ventured far beyond the realm of immediate political interests. They never before had been required to provide any precise definition or clear articulation of the meaning of "human rights" or "fundamental freedoms," to wrestle with moral diversity on a global scale, nor to create any thoughtful assessment of what the extension of rights might mean for the world as a whole. Instead, visions of human rights based on some normative theory of natural law, justice, or the intrinsic value of each individual person largely had come from scattered religious leaders, philosophers, individual men and women with a sense of responsibility toward victims of abuse, or NGOs determined to act on principles very different from that of national sovereignty. This changed dramatically once the United Nations decided that its Commission on Human Rights, composed of government representatives, should draft an international bill of rights capable of securing universal acceptance. Such a formidable task suddenly confronted the members of the commission with a whole series of inescapable and difficult philosophical questions.

Those who understood something about the nature of international human rights clearly anticipated that these issues of philosophy would arise with force and drama. Thus, when the Commission on Human Rights held its first session at the end of January 1947, observers packed the visitors' seats to capacity in the council chamber in order that they might witness what they knew would be a fascinating discussion. Even more telling, governments appointed as their representatives on this commission not political flunkies but a remarkable collection of individuals of unusual quality and stature who they believed would be thoughtful, articulate, and intellectually capable of understanding the complicated issues that would confront them. Several, in fact, held Ph.D. degrees. China named Dr. Peng-chun Chang, a career diplomat with a strong background in Confucianism and a deep commitment to the values inherent in Asian culture and philosophy, who earlier had served as a professor at Nankai University. Lebanon appointed Dr. Charles Malik, a former professor of philosophy and a brilliant scholar heavily influenced by the writings of Saint Thomas Aquinas who ardently believed in natural law, liberalism, and democracy. France designated Dr. René Cassin, a brilliant and widely published professor of international law, who had represented his country at the League of Nations, been a long-standing and active member of the Ligue des Droits de l'Homme, and who would later serve as the president of the European Court of Human Rights. The Philippines selected the dynamic Carlos Romulo, an experienced public official, a devote Catholic, a brigadier general during the war, and recipient of a Pulitzer Prize for journalism. Charles Dukes, a trade unionist and an articulate and active member of the Labour Party, represented Britain. Hansa Mehta, a determined advocate for human rights who pushed for measures of implementation, came from India. Chile appointed Don Felix Nieto del Rio, a career diplomat who also served as editor of *El Mercurio* and was acknowledged as perhaps his country's most distinguished writer on foreign affairs. Panama named Dr. Ricardo Alfaro, its own foreign minister, former professor of history and law, and judge on the Permanent Court of Arbitration at The Hague. Iran appointed Dr. Ghasseme Ghani, a distinguished author, member of parliament, advisor to the crown prince, former minister of culture, member of the first Academy of Iran, and also fluent in Persian, Arabic, and French. Dr. Don José A. Mora served as the representative for his country of Uruguay. The Soviet Union appointed Alexander Bogomolov, an urbane career diplomat with considerable experience and the recipient of the Order of Lenin. Vladislav Ribnikar, a son of the wealthy owners of the newspaper *Politica* who had joined the partisans during the war and had become a Communist, represented Yugoslavia. The United States named Eleanor Roosevelt as its representative, and her prestige was such that even this distinguished group quickly and unanimously elected her as chair of the commission itself.[48]

Profound differences of philosophy about the individual, the state, and ethical values surfaced immediately. In opening the very first session on behalf of the secretary-general, for example, Laugier announced that with the General Assembly's recent and highly visible vote on India's complaint about discrimination in South Africa, the international community had determined that long-established principles of human rights for each person would now take precedence over the principle of national sovereignty and that individuals and groups within nations could seek protection from their own governments. Ribnikar rose to challenge this position, arguing in orthodox Marxist language that it stemmed from the errors of bourgeois, individualistic philosophy generated during the eighteenth and nineteenth centuries rather than some eternal verity. In the modern world, he declared, the right of the state superseded the so-called rights of the individual, and that real liberty could be reached only by achieving a complete harmony between individual people and the collectivity of the state. Malik responded that totalitarian states had seriously threatened, and in some cases destroyed, individual human rights, and that their excesses now needed to be curbed by an international proclamation that the individual human person was infinitely more valuable than any group or state to which he or she belonged. Dukes retorted that unrestricted individual liberty was virtually impossible in any modern community and organized society, and stressed the value of associations such as trade unions, which could play a critical role in moderating between the state and each person. They strenuously debated whether human rights derived from God, from natural law, or from the authority of the state. Some claimed that human rights fundamentally centered on political rights like voting or holding office and civil rights like freedom of religion and the right to own property, while others heatedly countered that these rights were of secondary importance when compared to the basic economic and social rights to have employment, shelter, social security, and health for all men, women, and children. In addition, they argued whether rights were universal in nature or context-dependent on particular times, places, cultures, and circumstances.[49] All this represented, in the words of one observer, "an astonishing spectacle." "Here was a body preoccupied mainly with ideas, trying to deepen moral concepts, philosophical doctrines, and legal and sociological theses in a common effort to build a new soul for the international body."[50]

Thus, from the very first meeting of its first session, the Commission on Human Rights confronted a number of fundamental and not easily answered philosophical questions that would continue to shape many subsequent deliberations. What exactly are "human rights" and what is the meaning of "fundamental freedoms"? Do human rights originate from a deity, from eternal religious precepts, or from enduring philosophical principles, or are they granted by the authority of temporal states under exclusive "domestic jurisdiction"? Can they be universally claimed by all people without distinctions as members of the larger human family, or in a fragmented world with many different forms of government and value systems are they restricted to membership within a given state, culture, or stages of development? Should the basic right to life be applied at the time of conception, or must it wait until birth? Do rights apply only to people, or can states claim certain rights such as that of national sovereignty? What is the relationship, if any, between human rights for individuals and lasting "peace" and "security" for the world? Should the purpose of the state be to largely stay out of the lives of people and give them as much freedom as possible, or should it be to actively intervene and take positive steps to assure the realization of certain rights? What is the relationship between human rights and distributive justice? Do the rights of individuals possess greater value than the rights of collective groups, or are they truly indivisible and interdependent? Are some human rights more "fundamental," antecedent and necessary to other rights? Are political and civil rights, for example, more important than economic and social rights, or must they all be respected in equal measure? If all human rights have the same value and are ultimately indivisible, then what happens if the claims of one right conflict with those of another?

These questions only began the discussion, for they raised others that quickly followed. Does the simple assertion of a right make it so, or must it be tested against some established norm? Are human rights absolute, or must they be conditioned and modified by particular circumstances? What if the right of free speech is used to actually inflame racial hatred, goad class antagonisms, arouse religious intolerance, or incite war? What is the precise relationship between individual rights and corporate or social responsibilities? Is any society entitled to expect that every human right will be exercised with responsibility and due regard for the rights of others? Is it possible to establish international normative standards of behavior for the world while at the same time respecting different philosophical and cultural values? And, is there any value in proclaiming a vision of international human rights if means are not simultaneously provided for their implementation?

The answers to these vexing questions, as accurately described by those who wrestled with them, "were far from clear," particularly since they consciously sought to discover universal principles by creating a discourse "wherein no regional philosophy or [single] way of life was permitted to prevail."[51] Indeed, their extraordinary and pioneering efforts to consider a wide range of opinions and values certainly belies later charges that they somehow conspired to "circumvent fundamental differences" or engaged in "cultural imperialism."[52] To help them resolve some of the issues as they prepared a draft international bill of rights, for example, members of the Commission on Human Rights deliberately decided to draw on a number of different sources above and beyond whatever instructions they received from their governments. Some of their own group — Cassin, Malik, and Chang — already possessed sufficiently credible intellectual credentials to offer suggestions, to command respect when they spoke, and to understand the pluralistic philosophical and cultural traditions of Europe, the Middle East, and Asia. Staff from the Secretariat, such as Laugier and especially Humphrey, provided a wide range of significant knowledge, experience, and documentation on the laws and constitutional provisions of the member states of the United Nations. Experts from specialized agencies such as the International Labor Organization, UNESCO, World Health Organization, and the preparatory International Refugee Organization gave valuable assistance and insights.[53] International lawyers working on the Nuremberg and Tokyo war crimes trials offered assistance in explaining how emerging definitions of crimes against humanity might contribute to the evolving meaning of human rights.[54] Governments, nongovernmental organizations, and private individuals contributed ideas, ideological formulations of theory, suggestions for specific language, and even complete proposals detailing what they believed should be included in any international bill of rights. They came from Britain, Chile, Cuba, Ecuador, India, Panama, and the United States; the Inter-American Juridical Committee of the Pan American Union, the World Government Association, the Institut de Droit International and the Fédération Internationale des Droits de l'Homme; the editors of *Free World*; the American Law Institute, the American Association for the United Nations, the American Jewish Congress, and the American Federation of Labor; and from individuals like international legal expert Hersch Lauterpacht and those who forwarded copies of the writings of Alejandro Alvarez and H. G. Wells, among many others.[55] In addition, and in recognition of the complexity of the issues that faced them, the members of the Commission on Human Rights also could draw on assistance from a group of philosophers assembled by the United Nations Educational, Scientific, and Cultural Organization.

In what surely amounted to one of the most unique developments in the entire history of diplomacy, UNESCO called together a group of experts on philosophy to provide solicited advice on a critical matter of international policy. The organization had considered convening a large and lengthy "Conference of Philosophers," but the press of time on the Commission on Human Rights and the immediacy of drafting a bill pushed them in the direction of acting quickly. They consequently planned to gather together as soon as possible, but only after they had obtained the considered opinions of many individuals. Given the nature of the subject of international human rights, they knew that they could not rely simply on Western philosophy, but needed to obtain wide-ranging perspectives from around the world. Toward this end, they consequently invited written comments from one hundred and fifty very different people, directly asking them for their thoughts on some of the specific philosophical questions raised by international human rights. Their invitation began with a dramatic challenge that in itself revealed the complexities at hand:

The world of man is at a critical stage in its political, social, and economic evolution. If it is to proceed further on the path towards unity, it must develop a common set of ideas and principles. One of those is a common formulation of the rights of man. This common formulation must by some means reconcile the various divergent or opposing formulations now in existence. It must further be sufficiently definite to have real significance both as an inspiration and as a guide to practice, but also sufficiently general and feasible to apply to all men, and to be capable to modification to suit peoples at different stages of social and political development while yet retaining significance for them and their aspirations.[56]

Responses came from many individuals invited to offer their opinions. Although many, often deep, philosophical differences existed between them, they each attempted in their own way to address the nature of humankind and of governments, the efficacy of natural law, the relationship of the individual and the larger society and world in which they live, the necessity to curb abuses of power, cultural differences, the importance of shaping policy according to values and moral conscience, and whether it was even possible to create an international bill of human rights in the first place. Some, like the Italian philosopher and historian Benedetto Croce, doubted the entire enterprise, while the author of *The Condition of Man* and *Values for Survival* Lewis Mumford of the United States strongly supported the effort and urged the creation of a truly universal vision of rights. F. S. C. Northrop, a professor of philosophy at Yale University and the author of *The Meeting of East and West*, provided similar endorsement, but warned that the pluralistic nature of the world absolutely required the avoidance of ethnocentrism by incorporating the accepted ideologies and values of many different cultures, schools of thought, and nations into any final document. In his response, Jacques Maritain, a former professor of philosophy at the Institut Catholique de Paris heavily influenced by the writings of Thomas Aquinas and author of *Les Droits de l'Homme et la Loi Naturelle*, cautioned that no bill of rights could ever be exhaustive and final, and by necessity must always be expressed in terms of the state of the moral conscience and of civilization at any given time in history. Others responded from a variety of religious and cultural perspectives, including poet and philosopher Humayun Kabir on "Human Rights: The Islamic Tradition and the Problems of the World Today" and political scientist S. V. Puntambekar of India on "The Hindu Concept of Human Rights." Le Zhongshu from Nanjing University in China wrote with conviction about "Human Rights in the Chinese Tradition," and a short time thereafter sent a personal letter to U.S. Secretary of State George Marshall declaring: "I believe that the Declaration of the Rights of Man for the entire world is required."[57] Anthropologist A. P. Elkin of Australia, author of *Wanted: A Charter for the Native Peoples,* stressed the importance of the rights of all indigenous peoples, particularly the right of self-determination. Concerned about the implications of new technologies of mass destruction emerging from the war, physical and biological scientists like R. W. Gerard and W. A. Noyes of the United States and J. M. Burgers of the Netherlands, argued for the importance of the right to freedom of conscience and expression. In their responses, many of these commentators also focused on the importance of recognizing the relationship between rights and responsibilities in any international bill.[58] Among these, Gandhi wrote most pointedly: "I learned from my illiterate but wise mother that all rights to be deserved and preserved came from duty well done. Thus the very right to live accrues to us only when we do the duty of citizenship of the world. From this one fundamental statement, perhaps it is easy enough to define the duties of Man and Woman and correlate every right to some corresponding duty to be first performed."[59]

Following the receipt of these various opinions and suggestions from leading thinkers from around the world, UNESCO convened the special Committee on the Philosophic Principles of the Rights of Man in Paris during the early summer of 1947. Here they gathered as much information as they could about the differing philosophical, political, scientific, and social values spread across the vastness of the globe and carefully analyzed several centuries of the historical evolution of theoretical concepts of rights in different times and places. They determined that their purpose was not to achieve doctrinal consensus among all ideologies, but rather to develop a formulation of what common grounds for agreement might be found in order to draft an international bill of human rights. Toward this end, they concluded that despite whatever differences might exist between them, all people shared certain basic and fundamental principles that applied to human rights. Consequently, they asserted, a solemn obligation existed for the United Nations "to declare, not only to all governments, but also to their peoples, the rights which have now become the vital ends of human effort everywhere." These rights, they argued, "must no longer be confined to the few," but as they historically have been extended within states, must now be extended beyond them to be legitimately claimed by men and women in all places. "Human rights," they concluded after much deliberation, "have become, and must remain, universal. All the rights which we have come slowly and laboriously to recognize belong to all men everywhere without discrimination of race, sex, language, or religion. They are universal."[60]

The Committee on the Philosophic Principles of the Rights of Man then went on to explain those human rights that it regarded as universal in nature. "Varied in cultures and built upon different institutions," it reported, "the members of the United Nations have, nevertheless, certain great principles in common. They believe that men and women, all over the world, have the right to a life that is free from the haunting fear of poverty and insecurity" and to have rights "without discrimination of any kind." Among such rights, the committee delineated several, including first and foremost the right to live. Following this, they listed certain economic and social rights such as the protection of health and the right to work, to own property, to education, and to share in progress. The committee also identified specific political and civil rights, including the right to information, to free inquiry, to self-expression, to justice, and to political action. They enumerated the right of all people to freedom of speech, assembly, association, worship, and the press. Finally, they listed the right of citizenship and the right to rebellion and revolution if regimes become too oppressive. As the committee recognized in a moment of pragmatism at the very end, however, the members of the Commission on Human Rights would have to resolve how they would take these general principles of philosophy and implement them in practice through an international bill of human rights in a world immersed in politics.[61]

Difficult Problems of Politics

Those men and women who served on the Commission on Human Rights, of course, hardly needed to be reminded of the political environment in which they operated. Despite all of the philosophical discourse and the many expressions of goodwill for the international community as a whole, they faced politics at every turn. Each of the rights identified by the Committee on the Philosophic Principles of the Rights of Man raised a political problem of some kind somewhere in the world. If the United Nations attempted to implement any of these rights in practice it would immediately provoke fears of world government and prompt claims by states about the protection of their sovereignty under Article 2 (7) of the Charter against outside intervention in their own domestic affairs. In addition, the members of the commission came to realize all too well that they served not as individuals free to make their own decisions, but rather as official representatives of their governments who provided them with "position papers" and "letters of instruction" on behalf of political agendas.[62] Their meetings consequently became the focus not only of what the participants themselves called "fireworks," but major "battles."[63]

Problems of politics surfaced immediately. Indeed, even before it formally began its meetings to draft an international bill, the Commission on Human Rights found itself as the unexpected recipient of a veritable flood of petitions. Literally thousands of people from all over the world sent written appeals to the commission begging for help against the abuses of their own governments and pleading for the United Nations to apply the principles delineated in the Charter to them.[64] Due to her stature and integrity, her emerging reputation as the "First Lady of the World," the vision she represented, the hope she inspired, and her genuine compassion for those in need, Eleanor

Roosevelt discovered that many of these petitions were addressed to her personally. It is difficult to read these without feeling the pain, sensing both the desperation and the hope, and being reminded of the human face of human rights among those writing to her. They pleaded with her to help those who suffered from racial prejudice or religious persecution, women who confronted discrimination, victims of concentration camps, conscientious objectors being forced against their will to perform military service, and children still lacking food, shelter, or medical attention. They thanked her for her compassionate spirit and her concern "for the welfare of all mankind."[65] A telegram sent in the name of five thousand displaced Ukrainians far from their own homes, for example, spoke about the need for justice in the world, and while struggling with grammar but not with conviction, expressed their belief "that you venerable lady and the committee you preside over will protect us from any acts of ill treatment and violation of the rights of man just now a time of hard trial arrived and your assistance most necessary."[66]

Under these kinds of circumstances, virtually all governments quickly realized that none of them could remain immune from criticism. If petitions could be received and heard by the United Nations, then this would only fuel further dissent at home or in the colonies, embarrass them in front of the entire international community, and increase the risk of outside intervention into what they regarded as their own internal affairs. Over the objections of certain members of the commission—Romulo, Mehta, Cassin, and Roosevelt, for example, who personally responded with sympathy toward these urgent and often desperate appeals—they suddenly put a stop to this practice by issuing explicit instructions for their representatives to publicly declare that the commission had no power to take any action in regard to complaints by individuals about alleged violations of human rights by governments.[67] This precluded the possibility of governments taking reprisals against the authors of such petitions, but also prevented the commission from making serious charges public. Politics from the very beginning thus forced the commission, in the words of one authority on its activities, to make "a critical declaration of impotence" with reference to petitions.[68]

Yet, even stark statements about the lack of jurisdiction and public declarations trying to discourage petitions did not halt the wave of complaints. In fact, in some cases, they seemed to make the challenge all the more necessary. One of the most striking examples of this occurred when the indefatigable and nearly eighty-year-old W.E.B. Du Bois determined to petition the United Nations. On behalf of the National Association for the Advancement of Colored People, he supervised the writing of a lengthy and bitter complaint describing the long history of racial discrimination in the United States, the denial of basic rights to blacks solely because of the color of their skin, and the solemn obligations regarding human rights incumbent on all members of the United Nations under the Charter. News of this explosive document began to leak out, prompting Walter White to write privately to Eleanor Roosevelt that the press "from all over the world" wanted advance copies of the petition and observing that "the matter cannot be kept secret, so great is the interest."[69] Du Bois, of course, did not want secrecy or quiet diplomacy, and in the full publicity of as much media coverage as he could attract, formally presented the complaint to the United Nations in October 1947. He gave the petition the provocative title: "An Appeal to the World: A Statement on the Denial of Human Rights to Minorities in the Case of Citizens of Negro Descent in the United States of America and An Appeal to the United Nations for Redress."[70] With fire in his voice, Du Bois shouted in a statement prepared for the Commission on Human Rights that justice could no longer be denied and appealed to the nations of the world to stand by their promises on behalf of the rights of all people.[71] In taking this action, the NAACP clearly understood the implications. They agreed that the original cause of the petition represented "primarily an internal and national question," but argued with considerable insight that it "becomes inevitably an international question, and will in the future become more and more international." They believed that this petition would go far beyond the problem of racial discrimination in the United States and give encouragement to the oppressed everywhere, including those in colonial empires. "The eyes and ears of the chancelleries of the world," they predicted,

will be focused and attuned to this petition. For depending upon what stand the United Nations takes in this appeal will determine in part, the policy to be followed and the measures to be adopted by the colonial powers in their future relations with their wards, and the procedures to be put into practice by countries who practice some form of discrimination. While on the part of submerged and underprivileged groups, it is likely to inspire and stimulate them to carry their cases directly to the world body in the hope of redress.[72]

This is exactly what governments feared, and they understood the possible consequences immediately. This petition confirmed what would become some of the most difficult and sensitive political problems of the remaining twentieth century. If the United Nations became a gigantic "complaint bureau" for human rights, then there would be no end of challenges to national sovereignty. With or without justification, individuals or groups could go over the heads of their own governments and seek redress from the international community, thereby vastly restricting the traditional meaning of domestic jurisdiction and greatly increasing the power and authority of the United Nations. The widespread publicity given to this petition of Du Bois by journalists from around the world who believed that they were witnessing an extremely important event demonstrated just how embarrassing such issues might be for other governments as well if given attention. The intensity with which the few delegates from Asia and Africa viewed this petition as their own in the name of the right to racial equality and the right of self-determination provided sufficient evidence that the continued existence of all colonial empires could be in serious jeopardy. Moreover, and of particular significance for politics, the eagerness with which the Soviet Union seized on this NAACP petition and brought it to the Commission on Human Rights in order to exploit flaws of the United States offered dramatic proof that human rights also could be used as ammunition to fight in the monumental struggle rapidly becoming known as the Cold War.[73]

The founders of the United Nations knew that success for the new international organization would be heavily dependent on whether the Great Powers could maintain their collaboration exhibited during World War II in times of peace.[74] Yet, it did not take long after the defeat of the common enemy for the pledges of mutual cooperation to give way to confusion, suspicion, and then vehement hostility. Disputes about the suppression of freedom in Eastern Europe by the Soviet Union, exclusive possession of the atomic bomb and occupation of Japan by the United States, the "Iron Curtain" speech of Winston Churchill accusing Communists of brutal aggression, and new crises in Greece and Turkey all seemed to propel the great wartime allies into becoming implacable enemies. When the United States enunciated the Truman Doctrine in March 1947 after the first meeting of the Commission on Human Rights and declared that everyone in the world now faced a choice between freedom or totalitarianism, the Soviets responded by describing the action as "aggressive," "hostile and bellicose," and one specifically designed "to interfere in the affairs of other countries on the side of reaction and counter-revolution."[75] This increasingly venomous animosity quickly carried over into the United Nations and virtually all discussions about human rights. The United States accused the Soviets of punishing dissidents without trial, persecuting religion, imposing censorship, forcing refugees to return to the Soviet Union against their will, and opposing citizen committees designed to monitor human rights violations, among many other abuses. The Soviets responded by charging the United States with making "false and slanderous allegations," suppressing basic economic and social rights by means of "a clique of magnates" from "capitalist monopolies," and resorted to personal attacks against Eleanor Roosevelt on the Commission on Human Rights, accusing her of being a "meddling old woman" and "hypocritical servant of capitalism."[76] Then, in what proved to be its most powerful and effective argument, the Soviet Union accused the United States of being a hypocrite of the worst sort by talking boldly about human rights, yet at the same time violating the fundamental civil and political rights of its black citizens guaranteed by its own constitution, a result of the festering sore of racial discrimination. Suddenly caught completely off guard, the United States found an issue heretofore regarded as exclusively a domestic matter, exposed and then exploited as its vulnerable Achilles' heel for all the world to see.[77] Under this new international attention (made all the more acute by its own desire to be the leader of the "free world" in the Cold War and the fact that so many nonwhite delegates and staff of the United Nations witnessed this discrimination with their own eyes), the United States could no longer hide from its failure to extend voting rights to blacks, prohibit blatant segregation, or prevent such insidious practices as lynching. Indeed, even when President Truman's own Committee on Civil Rights in their report entitled *To Secure These Rights*, described by one authority as "one of the most outspoken and impressive documents of all time bearing upon human rights,"[78] they reached the same conclusion. "Throughout the Pacific, Latin America, Africa, the Near, Middle, and Far East," they warned, "the treatment which our Negroes receive is taken as a reflection of our attitude toward all darked-skinned peoples" and "plays into the hands of Communist propagandists. The United States is not so strong, the final triumph of the democratic ideal is not so inevitable that we can ignore what the world thinks of our record."[79]

Political problems were hardly confined to the Cold War, however. In fact, virtually all of the activities of the United Nations in the area of human rights—by their very nature—threatened existing policies and practices, and thus suddenly confronted governments with a whole range of new and unexpected difficulties with severe political implications. When the General Assembly debated South Africa's policies of apartheid and the Sixth Committee (Legal Affairs), the Ad Hoc Committee on Genocide, and the Committee on the Codification of International Law started to draft a convention on genocide, for example, each government with minority populations within its borders or under its control began to realize that it would be subject to greater international scrutiny than ever before. When the Secretariat appointed the black American and determined advocate of equality for all races, Ralph Bunche, as the first director of the Trusteeship Division, it served notice that colonial empires with their racial discrimination and exploitation would be severely challenged. When the Commission on the Status of Women initiated its survey of gender practices around the world, all governments began to understand that their particular policies toward women would receive unprecedented global attention. When the Sub-Commission on Prevention of Discrimination and Protection of Minorities began asking questions about the status of Aborigines in Australia, Maori in New Zealand, Inuits and Metis in Canada, and Amerindian tribes in Latin America, it indicated that every country with populations of indigenous peoples would sooner or later come under examination. Even something as "simple" as preparing an annual and seemingly innocuous *Yearbook on Human Rights* produced immediate difficulties. Never before in history had governments ever been asked to provide wide-ranging information about the protections of rights in their constitutions and laws, their treatment of minorities, or their policies toward women for all of the rest of the world to see and examine. The request from the Secretariat to supply such details suddenly forced all governments to agonize over how much they would reveal and how much they would conceal about the protection or the abuse of human rights within their own countries. They therefore began to realize that an aggressive pursuit of international human rights would likely attract global attention to their own problems, seriously jeopardize their own national sovereignty, and perhaps threaten other aspects of their perceived national interests.

Not surprisingly, these many political difficulties produced immediate criticisms and hostilities. Government officials began to speak of using human rights violations as "weapons" against their adversaries, condemn the role of "irresponsible if not actually hostile groups" who wanted to embarrass them, and criticize the "careless idealism of certain members" of the Commission on Human Rights "willing to agree to anything, possible or impossible, in order to advance the cause of human rights."[80] National parliamentarians accused the United Nations of being in a "violent hurry" that would result in disaster.[81] General Smuts of South Africa complained that much of this resulted from the fact that the organization was becoming dominated by the "colored peoples" of the world.[82] Department of State representatives expressed the fear that some of the members of the Commission on Human Rights, such as Cassin, were "manifesting fellow-traveller tendencies" and might actually be "crypto-Communist."[83] Soon-to-be U.S. Secretary of State Dean Acheson distrusted the internationalists who he contemptuously called "True Believers," criticized the Charter as "impracticable," regarded the location of the United Nations Secretariat as no more than "a crowded center of conflicting races and nationalities," and revealed his attitudes toward broader gender roles by asking V. L. Pandit, who became the first female president of the United

Nations General Assembly, "Why do pretty women want to be like men?"[84] The many concerns of these critics were only exacerbated when John Humphrey, the Director of the Division of Human Rights, in an important speech that would subsequently haunt him for the rest of his career in the Secretariat declared:

Human rights are largely a matter of relationships between the state and individuals, and therefore a matter which has been traditionally regarded as being within the domestic jurisdiction of states. What is now being proposed is, in effect, the creation of some kind of supranational supervision of the relationship between the state and its citizens. . . . What the United Nations is trying to do is revolutionary in character."[85]

Still other political problems surfaced with the activities of NGOs, who had been emboldened by their influence during the San Francisco Conference. These groups often could mobilize considerable domestic pressure at home and, as the United Nations emerged as a forum for international discourse, most certainly could generate significant embarrassment abroad, as demonstrated beyond doubt by the National Association for the Advancement of Colored People. But this represented only one of many nongovernmental organizations seeking to influence the outcome of human rights activities by the international community. Most wanted to push governments much further than they wanted to go. Some of these stressed very broad issues of human rights, such as the International League for the Rights of Man, the Fédération Internationale des Droits de l'Homme, the Commission to Study the Organization of Peace, the Inter-American Bar Association, the Union pour la Défense de la Personne Humaine, the International Law Association, and the Women's International League for Peace and Freedom. Others focused on the rights of all people to receive humanitarian protection and relief, for example, the International Committee of the Red Cross, the International Missionary Council, the Union Internationale des Ligues Féminines Catholiques, the Commission of the Churches on International Affairs of the World Council of Churches, and many different religious groups. NGOs such as the International African Institute, the Centre Against Imperialism, and the Pan-African Congress emphasized the right of self-determination. Gender provided the center of attention for the International Alliance for Women for Equal Rights and Equal Responsibilities, the International Council of Women, the Liaison Committee of Women's International Organizations, the Pan-American Women's Association, and the World Woman's Party for Equal Rights. The right of equal protection served as the focal point for the World Jewish Congress, while the rights of children occupied the energies of the International Union for Child Welfare. The American Federation of Labor, the Worker's Defense League, the World Federation of Trade Unions, and the International Federation of Christian Trade Unions all concentrated on securing economic and social rights.[86] At the same time, however, other nongovernmental organizations, described by one experienced official as the "enemies . . . of the United Nations human rights program," applied pressure in the opposite direction.[87] In the United States, for example, the Republican Party and Southern Democrats waged an active campaign against a serious international bill of human rights, as did the American Bar Association which according to one of its more distinguished members, "almost went wild" over the drafts, arguing that they would invariably threaten national sovereignty and the domestic jurisdiction of states.[88]

All these pressures came to bear on the Commission on Human Rights at every stage as it attempted to meet its charge of producing an international bill of human rights. Indeed, even many procedural issues generated controversy. After considerable debate and after discounting Australian Colonel W. R. Hodgson's opinion that "no concrete results could be achieved by a drafting committee composed of government representatives expressing different points of view,"[89] the commission decided to start by creating a drafting committee composed of Eleanor Roosevelt, P. C. Chang, and Charles Malik, with K. C. Neogy of India serving as rapporteur. This arrangement proved to be short-lived, however, for considerable criticisms and protests emerged from those determined not to be excluded.[90] This resulted in the addition of representatives from Australia, Chile, France, Britain, and the Soviet Union — an arrangement described as "strictly political,"[91] but one that nevertheless brought together West and East, Communist and non-Communist, industrialized and developing countries. They began their work by exhaustively pouring over a mammoth, four-hundred-page compilation of all the rights and freedoms mentioned in the various proposals that had been submitted or currently a part of national laws and a draft text initially prepared by John Humphrey.[92] They frequently met into the early hours of the morning, arguing over both philosophy and politics, and trying to decide exactly what might be meant by an "international bill of rights." Should such a bill be in the form of a convention or covenant, which on ratification would be binding on governments and become an integral part of the basic law of nations? Or, should it be a declaration of principles, enumerating and explaining the still-undefined meaning of "human rights" that would take the form of a recommendation from the General Assembly to all member states? This was no simple dilemma, and feelings ran strong in the committee. The Soviet representative warned sternly, for example, of the danger of "embarking on a voyage which would lead it in a direction where is might cross the border which divides international from internal law — the border which divides the inter-relationships of governments from the field where the sovereign rights of nations must prevail."[93] In sharp contrast, with passion that far exceeded any authorization from her government, Hansa Mehta decried any timidity regarding enforcement, and let the committee know in no uncertain terms that, "Unless it is binding on the states Members of the United Nations it will have no meaning."[94] Observed one official watching all this very closely:

The setting up of international machinery to protect individual human rights would be one of the greatest international achievements in history. It would assert that just as the real purpose of a State's government is to ensure the welfare of the individual human being, so the real concern of international law is with the welfare of individuals. It would at the same time be a more drastic limitation of sovereignty than any State has yet been prepared to accept.[95]

Others reached the same conclusion. Right in the midst of these deliberations, Eleanor Roosevelt received most unwelcomed instructions telling her to focus her efforts on a declaration of principles on human rights, where the United States government felt "on safer ground," and that any discussion about legal commitments and enforcement "should be kept on a tentative level and should not involve any commitments by this Government."[96] Months of work, study, and argument led to other detailed reports, then to the important second session of the Commission on Human Rights meeting in Geneva at the end of 1947.[97] Here the commission determined that an international bill of rights should be composed of three parts: a declaration, a binding convention, and specific measures for implementation. Toward this end, they produced a Draft International Declaration on Human Rights and a Draft International Covenant on Human Rights, and offered suggestions on ways in which these documents might be implemented.[98] They hoped that together these might become "the basis of one of the most significant documents in history: a charter of the fundamental rights and freedoms of men and women the world over."[99]

Before any parts of this vision could be realized in practice, of course, these drafts needed to be circulated to all sovereign member governments directly and to their representatives on a number of different bodies within the United Nations for their comments, suggestions, and ultimate approval. This process revealed and escalated the difficult problems of politics even further, for the drafts had captured the headlines of the world, developed a momentum with high public expectations, and demanded a response that could not be hidden, thereby forcing governments into a true test of conviction about what they would or would not be willing and able to do on behalf of international human rights. This required that they devote considerable time and energy to studying the language of the draft texts, considering the philosophical premises on which they were based, and analyzing what they described as "practical politics" at home and "the international political situation" abroad should the drafts be adopted.[100] Toward this end, governments often exchanged views with each other, asked for advice, received unsolicited opinions from individuals and NGOs, and at times even created elaborate interdepartmental committees to help them work through the challenges. The British Foreign Office created a special Working Party on Human Rights, for example, while the United States Department of State established an Interdepartmental Committee on International Social Policy (ISP) with a Subcommittee on Human Rights, and the New Zealand Ministry of External Affairs formed its own Human Rights Committee.[101] Some governments sought to work collectively with others in order to formulate common or regional responses if they could, such as the Latin Americans who adopted an "American Declaration of the Rights and Duties of Man" during their Ninth International Conference of American States meeting in Bogota.[102] Throughout this entire process, governments found themselves to greater or lesser degrees constantly caught between public pressure for some achievement in this area along with activists who wanted to initiate a revolutionary program for the international protection of human rights, and those who insisted on maintaining all of the traditional prerogatives of national sovereignty and resisted any restrictions on their domestic jurisdiction or vested interests.

These arguments continued within the United Nations itself as representatives made their points and lobbied for their positions in a number of different ways and settings, as they found themselves caught between wanting to achieve something on behalf of human rights while at the same time protecting domestic jurisdiction and what one diplomat described as "their own sacred cows."[103] Many governments sent their comments and suggestions directly to the secretary-general or the Secretariat, freely expressing their opinions.[104] South Africa, for example, wrote that the proposed draft "trespasses upon matters which should be left where they belong, in the domestic sphere of the member states" and thus declared it to be "completely unacceptable."[105] Some governments conducted frequent and lengthy communication with the staff of the Division of Human Rights.[106] Others approached the Sub-Commission on Prevention of Discrimination and Protection of Minorities, the Sub-Commission on Freedom of Information and the Press, the Commission on the Status of Women, and especially the Commission on Human Rights,[107] seeking to influence both the drafting committee and the commission as a whole, where it was reported that governments sometimes presented "violent objection" and "determined opposition" to certain proposals or strong support of others.[108]

The Commission on Human Rights considered all of these many reactions, comments, and suggestions during its third session in May–June 1948. In addition, its own members sought to influence the course of discussion by making recommendations themselves. China, for example, stressed the utmost importance of having provisions on the right of equality without discrimination, freedom of conscience, and freedom of speech and expression.[109] Others did the same, arguing at length for their particular point of view. The commission finally agreed on a draft declaration consisting of an elaborate preamble and twenty-eight articles, which they submitted to their parent body, the Economic and Social Council, for further deliberation during July and August. Here, often contentious meetings also revealed sharp differences. Some members wanted to defer consideration of the declaration until agreement had been reached on a covenant and system of implementation as well. Others argued that an attempt to reach consensus on such a complicated and elaborate package on the constantly evolving totality of human rights would only lead to a loss of momentum and a long delay in the proclamation of the declaration, and perhaps even a weakening of its contents. They believed that if they insisted on getting both a declaration and a covenant at the same time, and tried to enforce undefined norms against unwilling states, they likely would secure nothing at all. In the end, ECOSOC decided to transmit the draft declaration as it stood to the United Nations General Assembly for consideration and decision.[110]

The Universal Declaration of Human Rights

When the General Assembly met during its September–December 1948 session in Paris, it did so in a mood that juxtaposed both fear and hope. On the one hand, the ominous fall of Czechoslovakia to a Communist coup and the frightful risk of war resulting from the Soviet blockade of Berlin created a plummeting and terrifying frigidness to the Cold War. On the other hand, two years of extraordinary effort and extensive preparation involving countless individuals, many NGOs, the staff of the secretariat, and all governments members of the United Nations had produced a draft declaration on human rights for all people in the world. The majority of members decided that, despite all of the other difficulties and problems that confronted them, so much had been invested and too much was at stake to allow this opportunity to pass. They thus agreed to turn their attention to what participants and observers alike described as the "miracle" of the "great debate" by the General Assembly on what would become the Universal Declaration of Human Rights.[111]

The greater part of this most serious and impassioned debate occurred within the General Assembly's Third Committee responsible for social, humanitarian, and cultural affairs, sometimes described as "perhaps the most turbulent body in the United Nations."[112] Here, well over fifty delegations, including some of the same individuals who represented their governments on the Commission on Human Rights,[113] participated in nearly ninety meetings that considered one hundred and sixty-eight resolutions containing amendments for the draft declaration. Even normally bland official accounts described the setting as one in which delegates "thrashed out" their differences and poured over the draft text "line by line" and "word by word."[114] Due to the philosophical issues raised by human rights, the participants engaged in a vigorous and fascinating debate most unusual for diplomacy about spiritual values and religious belief, cultural relativism, whether there should be a reference to the divine origin of the human being, the ideal relationship between an individual and larger society, the connection between rights and responsibilities, whether concepts of "natural law" could have universal validity, the nature of men and women, the purpose of the state, when life began and whether children have rights, justice and morality, definitions of "freedom" and "democracy," and the meaning of "the public good" and "the dignity and the worth of the human person." And, owing to the highly political nature of human rights, they exchanged accusations over whether human rights were abused more in colonial empires or behind the Iron Curtain, argued about the limitations on national sovereignty, debated whether issues any longer could be considered to be exclusively "within the domestic jurisdiction of member states," and discussed the possibility of what one Soviet delegate described as "the destruction of governments" should the United Nations push too far.[115]

Most of the arguments had been made before, but time and previous debate had not diminished the intensity and passion of those who believed in the necessity of proclaiming a vision of international human rights. They would not be dissuaded by whatever philosophical questions still remained, by old and new political problems, or by not obtaining everything that they wanted. Thus, despite the fact that they came from a wide variety of backgrounds and had a wealth of differences between them, the overwhelming majority of delegates at the United Nations were determined to do something that had never been done before: create a declaration of universally accepted norms or standards of human rights, developed after full consideration of the philosophies, cultures, and political systems of the world, and designed to establish what Eleanor Roosevelt described as a common standard valid "for all peoples and all nations."[116] They succeeded in reaching consensus or near-consensus on almost all of the articles. When disputes emerged, solutions often were prepared by small drafting groups that met after the official meetings and sometimes labored until well after midnight. Less than one week before the closing date of the General Assembly session, the Third Committee finally reached agreement that the proposed text should be submitted to the plenary as a whole.[117]

The text of this declaration on international human rights was designed to create and then proclaim a vision. They did not intend for it to become, in the words of one observer, a narrow set of legally binding provisions confined to "a document for lawyers," but rather a declaration of universal principles concerning human rights that could be widely understood and serve as an inspiration for subsequent action.[118] Toward this end, the text began with a broadly based preamble. It spoke first of philosophy, expressing the belief in the "inherent dignity" of each person and the "inalienable rights of all members of the human family" as the foundation of freedom, justice, and peace in the world. The preamble then went on to address history and politics, noting that "disregard and contempt for human rights have resulted in barbarous acts which have outraged the conscience of mankind," observing that the peoples of the United Nations have reaffirmed their faith in the worth of the person and in equal rights for men and women, and drawing attention to the fact that member states have pledged themselves to promote universal respect for and observance of human rights and fundamental freedoms. At this time in history, it asserted, a "common understanding of these rights and freedoms is of the greatest importance for the full realization of this pledge."[119]

In order to articulate this understanding for all governments and peoples alike, the text then presented a total of thirty separate but related articles for consideration, declaring its purpose to be the creation of "a common standard of achievement." Of particular importance, and in language that merits considerable attention and reflection, it insisted on beginning with two fundamental points. The first of these declared that "*all* human beings are born free and equal in dignity and rights." Second, the text presented a general application clause, significantly expanding on the principle of nondiscrimination established by the Charter and declaring that all the rights and freedoms set forth in the rest of the document be made applicable to *everyone* "without distinction of any kind, such as race, color, sex, language, religion, political or other opinion, national or social origin, property, birth, or other status." Then, lest any question at all still remain about the universal intent or the particularities of East or West, North or South, the language boldly proclaimed that no distinction would be made on the basis of the political, jurisdictional, or international status of any country or any territory to which a person belongs.[120]

The vision under consideration then addressed a number of different kinds of human rights. Many of the articles, for example, spoke to civil rights. These included the right to life, liberty, and the security of each person; the right to be free from slavery or servitude; and the right to be free from torture and cruel or inhumane punishment. They encompassed the right to recognition as a person before the law, the right to equality and equal protection under the law, the right to a fair trial, the right to freedom from arbitrary arrest or exile, and the right to be presumed innocent until proven guilty. All people, according to the text, possessed the right to freedom of movement, opinion, expression, conscience, and religion, as well as the right to peaceful assembly and association. Other provisions entailed the right to marry and form a family, and equal rights in marriage for men and women. In addition the proposed declaration provided for the right of everyone to own property alone as well as in association with others and for the right to be free from any arbitrary deprivation of that property.[121]

This proposal on behalf of international human rights also explicitly included important political rights. One provision, for example, addressed the right of all people to have a nationality. Then, in what has been described as "a revolution within a revolution," one of the most critical articles declared the right of all people to take part in the government of one's own country, either directly or indirectly through freely chosen representatives.[122] Other items encompassed the right to equal access to employment in the public service of one's nation. Moreover, in language that subsequently would cause considerable difficulty for a number of governments, the text stated that the "will of the people shall be the basis of the authority of government" and that all people possessed the right to vote in periodic and genuine elections with universal and equal suffrage.[123]

Significantly, the text contained a number of articles addressing economic, social, and cultural rights, thus placing them on the same level as civil and political rights. These included the right to social security, the right to work and free choice of employment, the right to just and favorable conditions of work, and the right to equal pay for equal work. They also contained the right to an adequate standard of living, including food, clothing, housing, medical care, and necessary social services. and the right to assistance for motherhood and childhood. Everyone, according to the text, had the right to social security in the event of unemployment, sickness, disability, widowhood, old age, or other lack of livelihood as a result of circumstances beyond their control. Additional articles spoke to the right to education, including at least free elementary education, and equal access for all, on the basis of merit, to higher education. A separate provision declared the right of each person to participate freely in the cultural life of their community.[124]

Then, this vision of international human rights sought to directly address the philosophical and the political issue of the relationship between individual rights and collective responsibilities, or what has been called "the other side of the coin."[125] The many, many authors who contributed to the final text wanted to acknowledge the advice of Gandhi and others that the enjoyment of rights entails responsibilities to others and to a larger society.[126] For some, the primary motivation for including such a provision derived from religious conviction and a sense of responsibility to those in need beyond one's self. For others in the General Assembly, the motivating factor came from a belief that the requirements of society represented a greater concern over those of the individual. "Everyone," the text declared, despite different points of departure, "has duties to the community." The language then went on to explain that in the exercise of their own rights and freedoms, each individual has the responsibility to respect the same rights of others and to meeting the just requirements of morality, public order, and the general welfare.[127]

Great care, countless numbers of meetings and discussions, compromises seeking to accommodate differing ideologies and diverging viewpoints from all over the world, and considerable effort all had been given to bring this vision of international human rights to this particular point. Now, in the plenary debates of the General Assembly, some delegates argued that the text contained too many rights, while others claimed that it embraced too few. They argued about its likely benefits, and considered its possible curses. The Soviets proposed to delay consideration for another year and tried to introduce a number of last-minute amendments, but could gain only the support of their Communist allies.[128] Finally, in the evening of 10 December 1948, Herbert Evatt of Australia, who was serving as the president of the General Assembly, announced that the time had come for a vote to be taken. Acutely sensing with anticipation that they were about to make history, conveyed by excited murmurings throughout the normally solemn chamber of the Palais Chaillot, each delegate listened to the votes of others and prepared to cast their own. In the end, the president announced the final vote: forty-eight in favor, none opposed, and eight abstentions.[129] In the midst of spontaneous rejoicing, the delegates arose and gave Eleanor Roosevelt a standing ovation. Then they and members of the news media alike left the large assembly hall to announce that the United Nations had just proclaimed a vision on behalf of all peoples in the world to be known as the Universal Declaration of Human Rights.[130]

This remarkable proclamation unleashed an enormous sense of achievement and a veritable flood of praise. To René Cassin, the Universal Declaration represented "a milestone in the long struggle for human rights" that by setting normative standards established "the first international document of ethical value" and one absolutely certain to provide a "beacon of hope for humanity."[131] Hernan Santa Cruz of Chile hailed it as being of "exceptional importance" as a safeguard for the rights of all human beings, and Charles Malik praised it as "destined to mark an important stage in the history of mankind."[132] P. C. Chang declared that China greatly welcomed the document as establishing normative standards that finally could be acknowledged as being truly universal in nature and that applied to all countries. Evatt lauded the proclamation for marking the first time in the entire course of history that the community of nations had ever made a declaration of universal human rights on behalf of millions of people all over the world who could now turn to it for help, guidance, and inspiration.[133] Other delegates joined their voices to this chorus of acclaim, such as Belarmino de Athayde of Brazil, who described the Universal Declaration as a "remarkable achievement" in the historical evolution of international human rights that possessed "great moral authority," and Mohammed Khan of Pakistan, who hailed it as "an epoch-making event."[134] The representative of Norway praised it as finally putting to rest the claim that human rights somehow fell within the exclusive jurisdiction of states.[135] Eleanor Roosevelt, who had done so much to guide the proclamation through two full years of drafts, committees, and meetings, acknowledged in the end that it was not a perfect document but one that nevertheless marked a point of departure and "may well become the international Magna Carta of all men everywhere." She spoke of "the moment of achievement," and concluded: "We stand here today at the threshold of a great event both in the life of the United Nations and in the life of mankind. . . . At a time when there are so many issues on which we find it difficult to reach a common basis of agreement, it is a significant fact that . . . [so many] states have found such a large measure of agreement in the complex field of human rights."[136] Many nongovernmental organizations and private individuals also rejoiced at the approval of the Universal Declaration, describing it as an unprecedented accomplishment in the historical evolution of international human rights and praising it for achieving "the very near impossible."[137]

Nevertheless, not all people reacted so positively to the Universal Declaration of

The "Magna Carta" of Mankind: Eleanor Roosevelt and the Universal Declaration of Human Rights (United Nations Photo).

Human Rights. Indeed, the critics who represented those continuous forces of vested interests and tradition, the power of states over the lives of individual people, or domestic jurisdiction and national sovereignty, all reacted sharply to this revolutionary proclamation. Communist governments, for example, consistently complained that the document tried to challenge their authority and restrict their power. They criticized the Universal Declaration for being too "vague" on certain points and possessing "many gaps" and serious "deficiencies."[138] The representative of Poland even went so far as to accuse the proclamation of being "a step backward" in the movement for genuine human rights.[139] Andrei Vyshinsky of the Soviet Union, who often clashed publicly with Eleanor Roosevelt, reluctantly admitted that the proclamation would probably assist in the lives of "little people," but soundly condemned it for having "serious defects" and, most importantly, for not addressing "the sovereign right of States."[140] South Africa similarly and vehemently complained that the Universal Declaration went "far beyond" the rights contemplated by the United Nations Charter and thereby seriously interfered with the national sovereignty and domestic jurisdiction of member states. Its delegate feared — correctly, as it turned out — that this proclamation would be interpreted as an authoritative definition of fundamental rights and freedoms that had been left largely undefined by the Charter, and that, if this happened, those states who voted for the Universal Declaration would feel bound in the same manner as if they had signed a convention embodying those principles.[141] The president of the American Bar Association also reacted negatively, declaring that the document represented a revolutionary and totally new concept in the field of law and government that would drastically threaten the principle of national sovereignty.[142]

As the advocates hoped, and as the critics feared, the Universal Declaration enormously accelerated the evolution of international human rights. Despite many efforts to present and portray the document as a "mere" statement of principle with no legally binding authority at all,[143] the vision proclaimed struck a cord among the peoples of the world and rapidly began to take on a life of its own. It quickly came to assume, as we shall see, growing moral, political, and even legal force through customary law. This, in turn, inspired a veritable revolution in international, regional, and national actions on behalf of human rights. Indeed, it is precisely for this reason that the vision of the Universal Declaration of Human Rights is still described as "the greatest achievement of the United Nations" and as "one of the greatest steps forward in the process of global civilization."[144]

*   *   *

In creating the Universal Declaration of Human Rights, an international body representing the community of nations for the first time in all of history agreed on a universal vision of human rights on behalf of all men, women, and children everywhere in the world. The participants remarkably joined together to both reflect and transcend their many different political and economic systems, social and judicial structures, religious and cultural backgrounds, philosophical and ideological beliefs, stages of development and cultural settings, and histories of exclusive national sovereignty in such a way as to create the Universal Declaration of Human Rights that spoke of the "human family" as a whole and to establish a set of normative standards for all peoples and all nations. The fact that there was no single author, but rather hundreds — or, arguably, even thousands — who contributed to drafting the text, gave the proclamation and its vision even greater authority and prestige. Its vision proclaimed that all people everywhere possessed certain basic and identifiable rights, that universal standards existed for the world as a whole, and that human rights were matters of legitimate international concern and no longer within the exclusive domestic jurisdiction of nation-states as in the past. Yet, as those familiar with the long struggle for human rights knew from experience, tremendous distances often existed between abstract theory and actual practice. In fact, at the time of the adoption of the Universal Declaration of Human Rights no state — not one — regardless of location, level of development, or culture, could meet its standards of achievement.[145] Champions and opponents of human rights alike thus wondered what would happen and what it all would mean. The answer, of course, lay in the future and ultimately would depend on if, when, and how the world decided to transform this internationally proclaimed vision into reality.

Chapter 8
Transforming Visions into Reality

Fifty Years of the Universal Declaration

> The Universal Declaration of Human Rights [has] . . . inspired, guided, and directed national and international energies toward the achievement of a worldwide awareness of the human person . . . as well as standards and machinery to protect human rights; and these have far outstripped the vision of many at the time of the proclamation. The universality and continuing relevance of the Universal Declaration of Human Rights in a vastly changed world is not due to its legal style or precision, nor to the expertise of its authors [but] . . . because it reflects profound truths about human nature and the requirements of human dignity.
>
> —Jan Mårtenson of Sweden

The many women and men who worked so hard to draft and then secure international approval for the Universal Declaration of Human Rights wanted to make certain that the vision proclaimed in the text would be realized in practice. They knew that visions without action remained only wishful thinking at best or verbiage at worst, and wanted the rights declared to be enjoyed in the daily lives of all people around the world. Both the United Nations and its member states had proclaimed a new commitment to promote respect for these rights and freedoms by teaching and education and to secure their universal and effective recognition and observance by progressive national and international measures.[1] This call for action profoundly influenced the evolution of international human rights for the next fifty years. During this time, the Universal Declaration assumed ever-greater importance by establishing a standard by which to judge behavior and the human condition, acquiring significant moral and political force, influencing legal instruments and measures of implementation, contributing to customary international law, and serving as a major source of inspiration and direction for determined efforts to advance its proclaimed vision. It became one of the best known and most frequently cited documents in history. Often in the face of determined opposition from countervailing forces of resistance, the world responded to both the promise and challenge of the Universal Declaration in a variety of ways that sought to transform visions into the reality of practical politics and legal obligations by extending, protecting, promoting, and enhancing international human rights.

Extending Rights and Setting Standards

The champions of the Universal Declaration of Human Rights understood perfectly well that if it were to have any chance of producing an impact on the world as a whole, they would have to proclaim its vision widely. People and nations, in short, would have to know of its message before they could act. With precisely this fact in mind, the delegates in the General Assembly immediately resolved that "the text of the Declaration should be disseminated among all peoples throughout the world" and recommended that the organization and the governments of all member states use every means at their disposal to cause it to be displayed, read, and expounded. They also invited all of the specialized agencies and NGOs to do their utmost to bring the text to the attention of as large an audience of individuals and groups as they possibly could. As one member of the Secretariat observed to another: "What we are called upon to do is to change attitudes and re-orient . . . values in nearly all parts of the world."[2] Toward this end, one of the first necessary steps entailed a translation of the declaration into as many languages as possible in order that the vision might be proclaimed around the globe. Reports quickly indicated that copies were sold out as soon as they became available.[3]

It did not take long for the Universal Declaration to begin having an impact. Several new national laws and constitutions, including those of Costa Rica, El Salvador, Haiti, Indonesia, Jordan, Libya, Puerto Rico, and Syria, incorporated either specific language or principles of the declaration into their text. Judicial opinions and court cases, both from national courts as well as from the International Court of Justice referred to the vision as well. Indigenous peoples in the colonial possessions of the imperial powers eagerly seized on its proclaimed rights. The new Japanese Peace Treaty specifically announced that one of its purposes was to enable Japan to "strive to realize the objectives of the Universal Declaration of Human Rights."[4] Other bilateral treaties and formal and informal complaints by one government to another about the treatment of individual citizens made explicit mention of the declaration. Some countries, such as Canada, created a Special Senate Committee on Human Rights and Fundamental Freedoms to draft its own national bill of rights. Schools and universities planned special instruction and seminars to provide information about the rights proclaimed in the Universal Declaration, and public events including exhibitions and concerts of well-known artists sought to attract even greater publicity. Newspapers printed articles and radios broadcasted programs on the meaning of the declaration, as did the new technological medium of television. The Division of Human Rights actively engaged in collecting information from all member countries for what would become its annual publication of the *Yearbook on Human Rights*, and suddenly found itself as the unprepared recipient of all kinds of requests dealing with a wide variety of different aspects of human rights. UNESCO and other specialized agencies launched similar programs that constantly referred to the vision of the Universal Declaration. Indeed, without exaggeration, one observer watching all this dynamic activity concluded within only a very short period that "there is an impressive amount of evidence to show just how much influence this Declaration has exerted throughout the world . . . since it was adopted and proclaimed."[5]

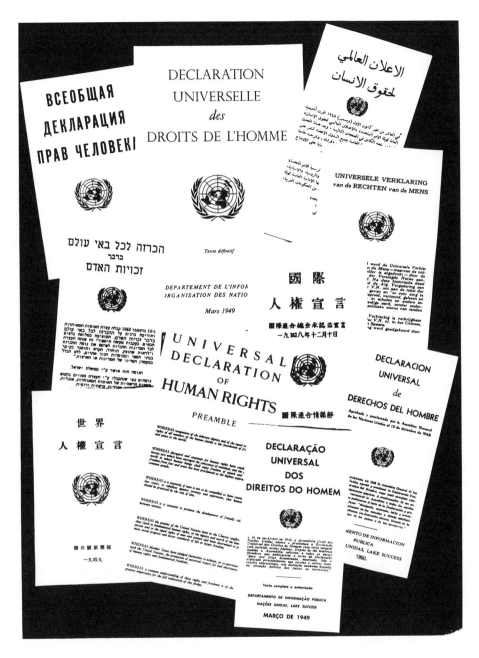

For Everyone: The Universal Declaration in Many Languages.

It soon did much, much more. In fact, the Universal Declaration greatly assisted in the important process of setting standards, or establishing norms, through declarations and legally binding conventions covering a wide variety of specific aspects of international human rights. Its vision, for example, encouraged states to begin ratifying the Convention on the Prevention and Punishment of the Crime of Genocide, which established genocide as a crime under international law and held those who committed or incited such extermination responsible for their actions.[6] Its broad context and especially its provision on the right to life for all people then helped to influence the creation of the 1949 Geneva conventions and their elaboration of humanitarian law dealing with the amelioration of the condition of the sick and wounded on land and at sea, the treatment of prisoners of war, and, most innovatively, the protection of civilian populations in time of war.[7] By the next year members of the Council of Europe specifically referred to the Universal Declaration by name and its aim of "securing the universal and effective recognition and observance of the Rights contained therein" in signing the extremely important European Convention on Human Rights creating binding obligations and providing for a far-reaching system of supervision of the observance of these rights.[8] The momentum thus created also enabled the International Labor Organization to draft the Right to Organize and Collective Bargaining Convention, the Convention Concerning Equal Remuneration for Men and Women Workers, which finally secured the provision long sought by advocates for women's rights of equal pay for equal work, and the Discrimination (Employment and Occupation) Convention. Simultaneous with these standard-setting instruments were those of the 1951 Convention Relating to the Status of Refugees falling under the supervision of the recently created United Nations High Commissioner for Refugees; the 1952 Convention on the Political Rights of Women; the 1954 Convention Relating to the Status of Stateless Persons; the 1956 Supplementary Convention on the Abolition of Slavery, the Slave Trade, and Practices Similar to Slavery; and the 1957 Convention on the Nationality of Married Women, each specifically citing the vision of the Universal Declaration of Human Rights within their texts.[9]

All of these innovative treaties broke significant new ground, providing extremely important contributions and precedents for much of what would still come. But many of the champions of international human rights desired more. They appreciated the value of these specific conventions on focused subjects, but wanted a much broader-based covenant directly tied to the wide-ranging provisions of the Universal Declaration. They knew that the delegates who had adopted the declaration itself had understood the importance of putting words into action in order to transform visions into reality, and for this reason had simultaneously passed a resolution entitled "Preparation of a Draft Covenant on Human Rights and Draft Measures of Implementation." This drew attention to the fact that the original plan called for the creation of an international bill of rights with three parts: a declaration, a covenant to set more precise and elaborate standards, and then finally implementing measures. The resolution therefore urged the Commission on Human Rights to proceed immediately toward the next stage of a covenant, assigning it their highest priority. The delegates and their many supporters among individuals and nongovernmental organizations knew that the commission already had produced a draft "International Covenant on Human Rights," and thus assumed that such a treaty could be negotiated quickly.[10] Even intimate insiders believed that results lay just around the corner.[11] They were wrong.

The adoption of the Universal Declaration and the early groundbreaking covenants that followed all created a wave of euphoria among those interested in advancing international human rights that temporarily masked several underlying problems and countervailing forces of resistance. States willing to adopt declarations of principle, for example, did not always share a similar enthusiasm for accepting binding obligations that might restrict their freedom of action, challenge their vested interests, or threaten their national sovereignty. After adopting the Universal Declaration of Human Rights, to illustrate, they argued intensely over the highly controversial and emotionally charged question of whether this proclamation imposed international legal commitments or not.[12] In addition, of particular seriousness were the complicating problems of international politics on the United Nations itself. The United States and its allies in the Cold War increasingly came to fear that the organization was falling under the radical influence of Communists and those interested in threatening the status quo by destroying colonial empires. The Soviet Union and those allied with it, on the other hand, came to believe that the United Nations was leaning in the direction of anti-Communist, imperialistic, and capitalist forces, particularly after the refusal to seat the representative of the People's Republic of China following the 1949 revolution and the use of the organization in support of South Korea during the Korean War. This East-West confrontation soon became global in geographical scope and affected nearly everything that the United Nations attempted, ranging from such matters as the election of the secretary-general and voting procedures to substantive issues concerning collective security in the face of threats to the peace, arms control, and interpretations of international human rights.[13]

Of particular importance, and despite their extremely serious differences, however, both of the superpowers of the Cold War ironically shared one critical characteristic in common: both greatly feared measures by the United Nations in the area of human rights that might threaten their national sovereignty. The Soviets, for example, strongly opposed any decision or mechanism that would allow an international authority to investigate or interfere in their own internal affairs. They opposed the creation of local human rights citizen groups and the granting of free access to international correspondents, which they felt would introduce "spies" into their country, arguing that any such action would be contrary to Article 2 (7) of the Charter regarding domestic jurisdiction. They adamantly refused to respond to the thousands of letters received by the Commission on Human Rights from women regarding their sons and husbands still imprisoned against their will as prisoners of war and against the principles of the Universal Declaration of Human Rights.[14] They denied that political and civil rights represented anything other than "bourgeois" values, and thus of little or no value for most of the world. They resisted any investigations of their one-party state, secret police, suppression of freedom of speech, persecution of religion, and political prisoners or victims of conscience confined to the Gulag's brutal prisons. For all these reasons, they and their Eastern European allies continually opposed any proposal that might estab-

lish a system of "international pressure" that could become "an instrument of interference" in the internal affairs of states, which might undermine their independence
and national sovereignty.[15]

Similar fears, for different reasons, emerged in the United States as well. Here,
the rise of McCarthyism with its jingoistic nationalism, isolationism, and rabid anti-
Communism portrayed the specter of a United Nations infested with foreign enemies
attempting to destroy the nation's values. The American Bar Association issued ominous warnings about the implications of international agreements usurping the authority of federal and state law, and openly opposed the Genocide Convention and the draft
covenant on human rights. The Daughters of the American Revolution did the same,
while at the same time issuing personal attacks on Eleanor Roosevelt. Many business
and political leaders argued that any discussions of social and economic rights represented a distinct "scarlet hue" with an insidious wedge of Communist ideology designed to destroy the system of free enterprise. In addition, racial segregationists continued to fear anything that the United Nations and its "alien elements" might do to
bring about changes in immigration laws or equality for black men and women.[16] With
these several factors in mind, Republican Senator John Bricker decided to introduce
legislation demanding that the United States withdraw from all covenants, conventions,
and treaties emerging from the United Nations having anything to do with human
rights. "My purpose in offering this resolution," he declared to his colleagues, "is to
bury the so-called covenant on human rights so deep that no one holding office will
ever dare to attempt its resurrection."[17] He went on to describe the proposed covenant
as "completely foreign to American law and tradition" and described it as nothing less
than a "U.N. Blueprint for Tyranny."[18] Then, on the floor of the Senate itself Bricker
stridently announced to his colleagues: "I do not want any of the international groups,
and especially the group headed by Mrs. Eleanor Roosevelt, which has drafted the
covenant of Human Rights, to betray the fundamental, inalienable, and God-given
rights of American citizens enjoyed under the Constitution. That is really what I am
driving at."[19]

Powerful political forces of resistance such as these joined with others and confronted the Commission on Human Rights every step of the way. In fact, for precisely
this reason, it took several years for the commission to reach agreement on setting
standards in the covenant portion of an international bill of rights. But then, as one
participant in the process noted, this attempt to create global protection of human
rights "represents a radical departure from traditional thinking and practice." "We are
in effect asking States to submit to international supervision their relationship with
their own citizens, something which has been traditionally regarded as an absolute
prerogative of national sovereignty."[20] Representatives thus disagreed on whether national means would suffice or whether international agencies would be required to
implement whatever provisions appeared in a covenant. Some sought to insert articles
about rights not covered in the Universal Declaration of Human Rights, while others
attempted to weaken principles already formulated through such means as arguing
about gender or suggesting that they did not apply to indigenous populations in the
colonies. In addition, they argued strenuously about the relationship, enforceability,

and priority of different kinds of rights. Stated somewhat differently, various nations saw not one, single, unified vision of rights, but rather different and sometimes conflicting visions. The preliminary text, for example, embraced the view of Britain and the United States that only civil and political rights could be included in a legally binding treaty. The Soviets protested this arrangement as being hopelessly bourgeois and typically capitalist, arguing instead that any covenant ought to contain provisions emphasizing economic and social rights. The General Assembly, watching all this bickering, decided to direct the commission to study ways of including the right of nations and peoples to self-determination and to prepare a single comprehensive document that recognized that "the enjoyment of civil and political freedoms and of economic, social, and cultural rights are interconnected and interdependent" and that contained "an explicit recognition of equality of men and women."[21] Nevertheless, the disputes between the superpowers and their respective allies of the Cold War continued to rage and resulted in an uneasy compromise whereby the commission would proceed with its standard-setting activities by creating drafts of two separate covenants, each focused on different kinds of rights.

Negotiations thus began to shape a draft of the International Covenant on Civil and Political Rights and the International Covenant on Economic, Social, and Cultural Rights. But once again, differences, pressures, and resistance emerged immediately, turning the Commission on Human Rights into what has been described as "a focus for political controversy" and "a forum of political conflict."[22] Representatives debated over such basic issues as whether governments themselves should be considered as oppressors or benefactors, whether special escape clauses should be included covering "public emergencies," and whether international enforcement machinery was even necessary in the first place. The Soviet Union, for example, insisted that national institutions alone had the exclusive authority to enforce any provisions, warning that any supranational mechanisms would impinge on a state's sovereignty and control over its own people. On the opposite extreme, Australia advocated an International Court of Human Rights with authority to protect individuals against their own governments. Colonial powers heatedly debated with those committed to decolonization about the right of self-determination. With reference to specific rights such as that of freedom of speech, the United States with the support of NGOs such as the American Civil Liberties Union argued that no limits should exist on expression, whereas delegates from the nonwhite world and Europeans victimized by Hitler's propaganda strongly believed that the language of the proposed covenant should prohibit any deliberate advocacy of racism or war. Some members of the Sub-Commission on Prevention of Discrimination and Protection of Minorities lobbied heavily for provisions guaranteeing equal treatment, but others with serious racial problems, such as the United States and South Africa, expressed deep concern about interference in domestic affairs and threats to national sovereignty. Indeed, it was precisely this concern that ultimately prompted the administration of President Dwight Eisenhower and his Secretary of State John Foster Dulles to dramatically reverse the policies of their predecessors. In 1953 they refused to reappoint Eleanor Roosevelt to the Commission on Human Rights, even thought she still had two years remaining before the end of her term. Then, they suddenly announced to a shocked world that the United States would not become a party to *any* human rights treaty approved by the United Nations.[23] With this, the issue was no longer one of personal hurt, but rather one of policy, and Eleanor Roosevelt lost no time in responding. She declared publicly and bluntly: "We have sold out to the Brickers and McCarthys. It is a sorry day for the honor and good faith of the present Administration in relation to our interest in the human rights and freedoms of people throughout the world."[24]

To those who genuinely sought to transform the vision of the Universal Declaration of Human Rights into reality, these developments produced disappointment, frustration, and anger. In their minds, several valuable years had been needlessly squandered in political posturing and debate with no appreciable result or further achievement in standard setting. It seemed to them that the majority within the United Nations appeared more interested in protecting their own vested interests and national sovereignty and in fighting the Cold War rather than in advancing the cause of international human rights. Now, their champion and spokeswoman Eleanor Roosevelt had been sacked and the United States announced that it was turning its back on the entire enterprise of covenants. They would have felt even worse if they had known that this decision by Eisenhower and Dulles would set a tone and a direction that would be followed by subsequent Republican and Democratic successors alike, and thereby largely removing their country from the effective and constructive role in the evolution of international human rights that it could have played for the next two decades. The Soviets enthusiastically seized on this change of policy as an incredible gift given to them as ammunition for the propaganda war, and now argued before the world that since the United States would not even become a party to the covenants and conventions, it had no right to lecture others on the subject of human rights. "The hopes," wrote one disheartened observer, "have been so far sadly frustrated" and concluded that this deadlock would likely continue for many years to come.[25]

What he and many others could not fully anticipate was the impact on international human rights of one of the most powerful developments of the entire twentieth century: the collapse of colonial empires and the emergence of newly independent nations and peoples. In this regard, the vision proclaimed in the Universal Declaration of Human Rights would be both profound and revolutionary as it began to extend to literally millions of men, women, and children around the world. It could hardly be otherwise if one honored the words of the text about "the equal and inalienable rights of all members of the human family." More pointedly, Article 2 recognized no exceptions whatsoever. Inserted primarily as a result of the unceasing pressure exerted by the Asian, African, and Latin American countries who themselves had suffered so severely from racial discrimination, marginalization, colonial conquest, exploitation, and sometimes genocide, it states that all of the rights and freedoms set forth in the Universal Declaration applied to "*everyone* . . . without distinction of any kind," and proclaims: "Furthermore, no distinction shall be made on the basis of the political, jurisdictional or international status of the country or territory to which a person belongs, whether it be independent, trust, non-self-governing territory or under any other limitation of sovereignty."[26]

Given this unequivocal language, it is hardly surprising that those responsible for following the instructions of the General Assembly would reach the conclusion that a new and firm responsibility now existed to extend the proclaimed principles. "Whatever its legal character," in the judgment of those within the Secretariat after consultations with member states, "the Universal Declaration should be considered an effective instrument in any institution or organ directly under the United Nations."[27] This applied with particular reference to the Trusteeship System, already established under the Charter to encourage respect for human rights and already containing specific agreements of honoring these rights.[28] They, and those states supporting decolonization and the right to self-determination, thus saw the task at hand as making these visions a reality. "Now that the Universal Declaration of Human Rights has been adopted," they concluded, "it is both logical and feasible that the United Nations should make that Declaration a common standard of achievement for all territories and peoples under the Trusteeship System."[29] In this context the International Committee of the Congress of Peoples Against Imperialism thus held its first meeting to decide how best to bring about the collapse of colonial empires.[30]

Those indigenous peoples in the colonies seeking independence, and their supporters elsewhere, did not require the Universal Declaration of Human Rights to launch the process of decolonization. They had already been promised the right of self-determination with the Atlantic Charter, the war had already weakened the strength of Western colonial powers and destroyed the myth of white invincibility while increasing their own sense of self-confidence, and the United Nations Charter itself had included the Declaration Regarding Non-Self-Governing Territories. But the Universal Declaration contributed two new elements that would prove to be of great importance. One of these was a confirmation of hope and an affirmation of principle, for its vision offered an authoritative and universal expression of their deepest aspirations for the extension of human rights and freedom around the world. Secondly, it provided an international and widely acknowledged legitimacy to their efforts. Almost all nations in the world — including the major colonial powers themselves — had not voted no or abstained, but instead had openly given their positive vote and highly visible support to the principles contained therein. As the representative of Uruguay said during the debates, the Universal Declaration provided a natural elaboration of the United Nations Charter itself, and thus the enforcement and respect for its provisions would become one of the obligations of all member states.[31] These two factors could not be lightly dismissed. In fact, the colonial powers understood the implications perfectly well. Most of them wanted to retain their imperial holdings as long as possible and thus deliberately and actively sought to delay any publicity about, or application of, the Universal Declaration within their overseas possessions. In a secret despatch to governors of the British colonies, to illustrate, the Colonial Office warned that the declaration would be "a source of great embarrassment" that would produce only "difficulties" and "undesirable implications."[32] Others similarly complained of the "widespread anti-colonial bias in the United Nations."[33]

In this setting, there is no question that the human rights program of the United Nations played a critical role. The Trusteeship Division under Ralph Bunche could not have been more committed to decolonization, both for those under the Trusteeship System and the many more outside that particular arrangement desiring the right of self-determination. The same could be said about many of those on the Trusteeship Council who quickly adopted a lengthy questionnaire for all trust territories regarding the observance of specific human rights and, significantly, adopted rules of procedure allowing for periodic visits and special missions to these lands and for the right of petitions to be submitted verbally or in writing. With the strong support of those who served on the Fourth Committee (Trusteeship Affairs), and especially in the Third Committee where the issue of the right of self-determination, not surprisingly, was raised most directly, they also created the Special Committee on Information from Non-Self-Governing Territories.[34] Then, and of great importance, the membership in the General Assembly became increasingly committed to extending human rights to colonial peoples. Under a joint initiative taken by Afghanistan, Burma, Egypt, India, Indonesia, Iran, Iraq, Lebanon, Pakistan, the Philippines, Saudi Arabia, Syria, and Yemen, and with constant reference to the Universal Declaration of Human Rights in discussions, the majority decided to include an article on the right of self-determination in whatever covenants for implementing human rights might emerge. They also specifically asked the Commission on Human Rights to make recommendations to them concerning the international respect for the right self-determination of peoples.[35] Here, intense struggles raged between the colonial powers and most others, and between the United States and the Soviet Union competing for the affections of emerging nations. The whole subject, in the words of one staff member, was full of "political complexities."[36] Those who watched all these powerful forces at work concluded that sooner or later "something is going to happen."[37]

It did. The process that began when the United States gave independence to the Philippines and when Britain relinquished control over India, Pakistan, Burma, Sri Lanka, and Palestine, now proceeded like a flood in Asia. Those who did not receive their freedom as a gift from their colonial masters determined to take it—by force if necessary. For this reason, insurgent guerrilla movements and wars of national liberation erupted in French Indochina, the Dutch East Indies, and British Malaya. With the strong support of most members of the United Nations, as well as that of the new Communist regime of Mao Zedong in China, willing to pass resolutions in the General Assembly and the Security Council, apply political and diplomatic pressure, engage in economic boycotts, and provide assistance, the empires began to collapse. In 1949, for example, the Dutch found themselves forced to grant self-determination to Indonesia, thus ending a colonial regime begun three and a half centuries before. Laos secured its independence from the French in 1953, and Cambodia and South Vietnam soon followed. After several years of bloody and costly fighting, Malaya gained its freedom from British colonial rule in 1957. In the midst of all this activity, many of those who had just been freed and those wishing to be so convened at Bandung and held what host Indonesian President Sukarno described as a "new departure" and "the first international conference of colored peoples in the history of mankind."[38] Here, such notables as Romulo of the Philippines, Jawaharlal Nehru of India, and Zhou Enlai of China referred specifically to the vision proclaimed in the Universal Declaration of Human

Rights. They announced their determination to act as agents of history by advancing the cause of international human rights, especially those of self-determination and racial equality, and to make sure that those rights obtained in Asia were extended to Africa as well.[39]

As late as 1955, still only four countries in the entire continent other than South Africa could claim to be independent: Egypt, Ethiopia, Liberia, and Libya. All the rest remained under some form of colonial control. Yet, they too realized that powerful forces for change were sweeping the world, ranging from the vision of the Universal Declaration of Human Rights to diplomatic pressure from the United Nations and the use of armed force, and that in this setting the colonial powers of the past would not be able to "cling on to their imperial ermine" forever.[40] Europeans, reminded of their own words and promises and frightened by forces that they could no longer control, came to the same realization. Thus, in a dramatic shift of policy, France reluctantly relinquished control in Tunisia and Morocco and Britain conceded independence to Sudan. Kwame Nkrumah announced with tears in his eyes that in 1957 the colony formerly exploited for its gold and black slaves would gain self-determination under the new name of Ghana, vowing that he would do whatever he could to serve as a catalyst for extending this right to others. Toward this end, he organized the highly successful All-African Peoples' Conference in Accra the next year, inviting representatives from anglophone West and East Africa, francophone black Africa, the Belgian Congo, and Arab lands to the north. Not about to miss a historic opportunity like this, the ninety-year-old Du Bois demonstrated that age had not diminished his passion for human rights at all, and exhorted the assembled delegates to unite in a common effort: "You have nothing to lose but your chains! You have a continent to regain! You have freedom and human dignity to attain!"[41]

A virtual revolution occurred within just a few short years, and cracks in the edifice of empire became chasms. Guinea became free in 1958, but the dam burst in 1960, frequently described as "The Year of Africa."[42] Suddenly, the people of almost half of the entire continent secured the right of self-determination as seventeen separate states gained political independence. These included Cameroon, Central African Republic, Chad, Congo (Brazzaville), Côte d'Ivoire, Dahomey (now Benin), Gabon, Madagascar, Mauritania, Mali, Niger, Nigeria, Senegal, Somalia, Togo, Upper Volta (now Burkina Faso), and Zaire (now Democratic Republic of Congo). Sierra Leone and Tanganyika gained their freedom the next year, while Frantz Fanon published his powerful and angry book entitled *The Wretched of the Earth* that provided even further articulation of self-determination as a basic human right.[43] Algeria, Burundi, Kenya, Malawi, Rwanda, Uganda, Zambia, and Zanzibar (which united with Tanganyika to form Tanzania) soon followed. During this same period elsewhere in the world, the people of Cyprus, Jamaica, Kuwait, Malaysia, Mongolia, Tobago, and Trinidad also gained their independence. This development marked one of the greatest political changes in human history, for never before had so many people gained emancipation in such an incredibly short period of time. In just a few years, decolonization destroyed empires often built up over several centuries, liberated vast territories on the globe from colonial rule, transferred power from whites to nonwhites, and secured the right of self-determination for more than one billion people. Indeed, one participant in this process describes it as "the greatest extension and achievement of human rights in the history of the world."[44]

This revolutionary destruction of colonial empires and emergence of many newly independent nations and peoples in Africa and Asia also dramatically transformed the composition, character, tone, language, and much of the agenda of the United Nations itself. In sheer numbers alone, they now captured the majority and hence voting strength within the organization as a whole, and therefore were able to elect U Thant from Burma as the first non-Western and nonwhite secretary-general. But perhaps more important, they brought a new and shared commitment to certain aspects of international human rights. In order to appreciate this factor, it is essential to understand that this Afro-Asian group represented the most heterogeneous bloc within the United Nations. Geographically, its members ranged from Japan on the Pacific to Morocco on the Atlantic and from Tunisia on the Mediterranean to Madagascar on the Indian Ocean. Religiously, they varied from Hinduism to Islam and from Christianity to Buddhism. Politically, they spanned the distance from pro-Western Thailand and Lebanon, to vociferously nonaligned Egypt and Indonesia, to pro-Communist Mongolia, and even those leaning toward communism found themselves sharply divided in the Sino-Soviet split. But what they shared, and what was certain to bring them together, related to human rights. They believed that they had directly benefited from the efforts of the United Nations and from the vision proclaimed by the Universal Declaration of Human Rights—and said so. At the time of independence, for example, virtually all of the new states praised the Universal Declaration which had given them hope and legitimacy, and either referred to it by name or incorporated some of its provisions into their own national constitutions.[45] In addition, and more specifically, they all held a particular passion for two intimately intertwined issues: the right of self-determination for those people not yet free from colonial domination, and the right to equality for those still suffering from racial discrimination. To address these problems directly, they set out to mobilize the resources of the United Nations and to finally break the deadlock that had immobilized the entire process of standard setting for international human rights.

With the knowledge that they increasingly controlled a majority within the United Nations, and with the conviction that they had a responsibility to do whatever they possibly could to facilitate the historical process of emancipation, eighty-nine states from Africa, Asia, Latin America, and all the Communist countries along with others in Europe, joined together in 1960 to adopt a General Assembly resolution called the Declaration on the Granting of Independence to Colonial Countries and People.[46] Its language boldly proclaimed that the subjugation of peoples to alien domination, discrimination, and exploitation constituted a flagrant violation of the vision and the provisions of the Universal Declaration of Human Rights, an infraction against the United Nations Charter, and an impediment to the promotion of world peace. Supporters announced their determination to assist their brothers and sisters still under foreign domination in gaining their right of self-determination. Toward this end, they then voted to establish a new and special committee to explore ways in which this declaration might be implemented. Its members set about their task with vigor and determination. Over the objections of its Australian, British, and U.S. members, but with the full support of Secretary-General U Thant who criticized the antiquated policies of "the ruler and the ruled, the master race and the subhuman,"[47] the committee took the dramatic decision to invite petitioners from colonial territories to come and bear witness about the violations of their human rights before representatives of the United Nations. They organized meetings outside of United Nations headquarters in places such as Addis Ababa, Dar-el-Salaam, Lusaka, and Tangier, boldly requesting specific information from the colonial powers about the political conditions in their dependencies and making explicit recommendations regarding how the Universal Declaration of Human Rights should be implemented in practice.[48]

Throughout all of these efforts, Asian and African delegates within the United Nations never lost sight of the related issue certain to bring them together: the right to racial equality.[49] A long and heavy history of subjugation, exploitation, enslavement, segregation, exclusion, and sometimes genocide all had long since convinced them of a clear pattern of the violation of basic human rights by white Western powers on the basis of race. They returned to this theme without ceasing and consistently cited the Universal Declaration of Human Rights in doing so when they met at the Asian-African Conference in Bandung, the All-African Peoples' Conference in Accra, the Summit Conference of Independent African States creating the Organization of African Unity in Addis Ababa, the Afro-Asian Peoples' Solidarity Organization in Cairo, and in meetings of the United Nations in New York and Geneva. The intensity of their feeling grew even more as they watched the determined refusal of whites to give up power in territories controlled by Portugal, Southern Rhodesia, and South Africa; the continual marginalization of indigenous peoples and immigration policies of "White Australia," "White New Zealand," and "White Canada"; and the persistence of racial discrimination and the emergence of the civil rights movement and Martin Luther King, Jr., within the United States. Of particular importance in this regard was the unrelenting practice of racial persecution and segregation known as apartheid against a overwhelming majority of blacks by a small, white minority regime in South Africa. When police attacked an unarmed crowd gathered at Sharpeville in 1960 and massacred black civilians, it proved to be more than the Asian and African countries would tolerate. They called for a special emergency session of the Security Council to consider the dangers that violations of human rights under apartheid presented for world peace and to condemn racial discrimination. This prompted the white South African Prime Minister to lash out at what he called the "international forces" intervening within his country's domestic jurisdiction and threatening its national sovereignty.[50] In sharp contrast, the charismatic black leader Nelson Mandela embraced such external pressure, declaring before being imprisoned for twenty-seven years: "The Universal Declaration of Human Rights provides that all men are equal before the law."[51]

With all these violations of racial equality, the new majority of Asian and African countries decided that it was time for them to do whatever they possibly could to help transform this particular feature of the vision of the Universal Declaration of Human Rights into reality. They began by creating the Special Committee on the Policies of Apartheid and called on all member countries to pressure South Africa by severing diplomatic relations, boycotting its products, embargoing goods (including weapons), and enacting legislation prohibiting its ships or aircraft from using any port facilities.[52] Casting a broad net, they then went on to adopt an important document known as the Declaration on the Elimination of All Forms of Racial Discrimination, condemning any ideology or policy that resulted in racial segregation or apartheid and called for the international community to take concrete action against them. "We are not forgetting for a single instant," said one delegate, "that even the best resolutions are of value only in so far as they are effectively applied. . . . The hour for decisive action has struck. Let us not allow it to pass by."[53] Toward this end, again citing the Universal Declaration of Human Rights by name, they worked to create and adopt the remarkable International Convention on the Elimination of All Forms of Racial Discrimination in 1965. For the first time in history, states negotiated a standard-setting and binding treaty that defined racial discrimination, pledged themselves to adopt all necessary measures to prevent and eradicate racial discrimination as it applied to a wide variety of human rights, agreed that they could be subject to criticism from other states party to the convention and individual petitioners, and, significantly, authorized the creation of the first international machinery for any United Nations-sponsored human rights instrument to implement compliance with the treaty itself.[54]

These remarkable actions finally broke the political deadlock that had existed for well more than a decade within the General Assembly, thereby stalemating completion of work on the covenants. They proved that if the political will existed among the majority, the United Nations could move forward in the process of extending rights and setting standards. As the spokeswoman from Colombia observed:

the change is not purely numerical. . . . There has been a change of ideas, modes of expression, attitudes, objectives, and even ideals. There has been an awakening of the world conscience to a duty that cannot be denied, an awakening of peoples to a clear right — that of strengthening the foundations of justice, society based on equality, the obligations of States to promote conditions that will permit every person the full enjoyment of his rights.[55]

Consequently, and with the full and active support of an ever-growing number of NGOs, work now started in earnest to complete the languishing international bill of human rights that would make respect for the rights proclaimed in the Universal Declaration a legal responsibility of states. An indication of the intensity of this new determination can be seen in the fact that it took only the single, pivotal year of 1966 for both the historic International Covenant on Civil and Political Rights and the International Covenant on Economic, Social, and Cultural Rights (approved before in draft form by the Commission on Human Rights and ECOSOC) to move through the General Assembly and finally to be adopted and opened for signature.[56] Both treaties begin by referring to the Universal Declaration of Human Rights and firmly and unequivocally established that human rights are essential matters of international concern, hence no longer residing within the exclusive confines of the domestic jurisdiction of those states parties to the covenants. They also prohibit discrimination based on race, color, gender, language, religion, political or other opinion, national or social origin, property, birth, or other status. In addition, both covenants provide not just for the human rights of individuals, but also of "peoples" or "collective" rights relating to the right of self-determination and the right to control their own natural resources and means of subsistence. Moreover, each establishes a distinct and compulsory international enforcement system designed to ensure that the states parties to the treaties comply with their explicit obligations. Participants at the time thus described them as marking a "historic event," "a new era, a new epoch, in the development of positive international concern for human rights," and a "major advance" toward realizing the vision proclaimed by the Universal Declaration of Human Rights.[57]

Provisions in the International Covenant on Civil and Political Rights, originally supported by Western powers but opposed by Communist governments, build on the text of the Universal Declaration but provide much greater juridical specificity and expand on the number of rights enumerated. A total of fifty-three articles address such rights as the right to life, liberty and security; a fair trial; privacy; freedom of thought and religion; freedom of conscience and expression, assembly, association, movement, voting and political participation; equal protection; and the right of all to be regarded as a person before the law, among others. Provisions also create undertakings by states to provide for the right of detained persons to be treated with humanity and not to deny members of ethnic, religious, or linguistic minorities the right to enjoy their own culture, to profess and practice their own religion, or to use their own language. In addition, the text provides for certain rights on behalf of all children to have a name, acquire a nationality, and be protected against discrimination on the basis of such criteria as race or gender. Members of the General Assembly also agreed at the same time to couple with this covenant a separate treaty known as the Optional Protocol, making provision for private parties claiming to be victims of a violation of civil or political rights to file individual complaints against states parties to its terms. Later they opened a Second Optional Protocol to the covenant for signature, committing those states that ratify its terms to take whatever measures might be necessary to abolish the death penalty within their countries.[58]

The International Covenant on Economic, Social, and Cultural Rights also broke significant new ground in standard setting. Its articles, originally pushed by the Soviet Union and its allies and some states sympathetic to social welfare, gradually gained the support of others. The International Labor Organization, for example, stressed the importance of including provisions regarding the right to work, UNESCO for the right to education and to participate in cultural life, WHO for the right of all people to health, and the Food and Agricultural Organization for the right to be free from hunger. The political factor that tipped the scales for final adoption by the General Assembly, however, and confirmed the connection between the extension of rights and the setting of standards, was once again the emergence of the new and developing countries just released from the bonds of colonialism who possessed great interest in achieving economic, social, and cultural rights. The thirty-one articles of the covenant reflect this collective and widespread support by not merely listing these rights, but describing and defining them in considerable detail. At times they even set out the steps that should be taken to achieve their progressive realization. Among such rights so addressed are those of the right to work, the right to the enjoyment of just and favorable conditions of work including equal pay for equal work, the right to form and join trade unions, the right to social security, the right to protection of the family including special assistance to mothers and children, the right to an adequate standard of living including food, the right to the highest attainable standard of physical and mental health, the right to education, and the right to take part in cultural life.

The new majority, along with their supportive colleagues among other delegations within the United Nations, took much justifiable pride in watching the adoption of these two standard-setting covenants. They knew that although the treaty language had been negotiated in draft form earlier, it was their collective effort that had been responsible for finally breaking the long and debilitating political deadlock. This success encouraged them to embark on even more activity, including expanding the composition of the Commission on Human Rights itself. In 1967 they were able to enlarge the membership of the commission to thirty-two, and thereby secure significant influence in determining priorities. Perhaps more important in terms of emphasizing the universal nature of the enterprise, a new formula allocated seats in strict accordance with a regional formula, with Africa securing eight, Asia six, Eastern Europe four, Latin America six, and Western Europe and all others eight.[59] At the same time they found themselves agreeing with the opinion of Seán MacBride, who had recently helped found the nongovernmental organization of Amnesty International, that the vision of the Universal Declaration of Human Rights needed to be made "the Charter of liberty of the oppressed and the downtrodden" everywhere.[60]

This momentum and the commitment to advance international human rights by an expanding number of states could be seen almost immediately. As early as 1968, for example, the General Assembly adopted and opened for signature the Convention on the Non-Applicability of Statutory Limitations to War Crimes and Crimes Against Humanity.[61] By 1973 its members agreed on the International Convention on the Suppression and the Punishment of the Crime of Apartheid dealing with the highly emotional issue of race, declaring that apartheid "is a crime against humanity" and establishing particular measures to implement its provisions and punish those deemed guilty.[62] Six years later, believing that gender discrimination can be found in almost every country in the world, they followed this action with the landmark Convention on the Elimination of All Forms of Discrimination Against Women, which defines discrimination as "any distinction, exclusion, or restriction made on the basis of sex" that impairs the enjoyment by women of "human rights and fundamental freedoms in the political, economic, social, cultural, civil, or any other field." States parties to this treaty also pledged themselves

to modify the social and cultural patterns of conduct of men and women, with a view to achieving the elimination of prejudices and customary and all other practices which are based on the idea of the inferiority or the superiority of either of the sexes or on stereotyped roles for men and women.[63]

In 1984, after an increase of yet another eleven members on the Commission on Human Rights, and with the unceasing assistance and prodding from individuals in NGOs like Niall MacDermot of the International Commission of Jurists and Jean-

Jacques Gautier of the Comité Suisse Contre la Torture, the majority in the General Assembly approved the International Convention Against Torture and Other Cruel, Inhuman, or Degrading Treatment or Punishment.[64] Then, in rapid succession, delegates to the United Nations went on to adopt and open for signature the groundbreaking treaties recognizing a responsibility for those particularly vulnerable individuals least able to defend themselves with the 1989 Convention on the Rights of the Child and the 1990 International Convention on the Protection of the Rights of All Migrant Workers and Members of Their Families.[65]

Never before in history had so many treaties been created in such a short amount of time on behalf of international human rights, and every single one of these specifically cited the Universal Declaration of Human Rights by name. Of particular importance is the fact that all of these standard-setting instruments resulted from the approval of representatives from one hundred to more than one hundred and fifty states (as compared to the approximately fifty that had created the United Nations), and thus became all the more remarkable for reflecting the normative values not of a particular group or narrow region of states but of the modern international community as a whole. Once they achieved this, the next task—and the ultimate test in the face of continued abuses—became one of avoiding mere lip service by actually protecting these enumerated rights through implementation.

Protecting Rights Through Implementation

Those familiar with the struggle for international human rights knew from long experience of the constant problem posed by the distance between theory and practice. For this reason, they took great pride in the accomplishments of actually being able to extend rights and set standards following the proclamation of the Universal Declaration. But, for the same reason, they also knew that difficulties and serious questions still lay ahead. What would be the practical effect of all these efforts in the lives of individual people, how long would it take for them to be implemented, and what if states simply refused to ratify these covenants and conventions, thereby preventing them from ever entering into force? As one delegate noted, the challenge would be to acknowledge the achievements while at the same time avoiding "pompous statements" and "tempting promises" and seeing to it "that these new covenants are strictly observed everywhere."[66] To achieve this, those who wanted the established standards to be implemented in practice knew that they now would have to work to secure ratification of the treaties.

International covenants and conventions become binding, contractual treaties with the authority of law only when the necessary and predetermined number of states agree by their own free will to accept the obligations contained therein. Such will is usually first manifested by the signature of authorized representatives of states parties to the agreement in a public ceremony with much fanfare, and then by subsequent ratification or accession in accordance with the basic law of each country, with some involving the approval of only a small number of individuals and others, like the United States, requiring a two-thirds majority in the Senate. This second phase generally presents the most difficult and serious problems, for here the influences of domestic politics often play determining roles, and struggles rage between various personalities and competing interest groups who demand to be heard. In addition, some states will not ratify treaties unless or until their own national laws are already in conformity with the conditions of the international agreements. These several factors explain why there often is such a lengthy lag in time between standard setting and actual treaty implementation in the form of precise methods and machinery of enforcement. Fundamentally, the determining factor in whether treaties are ratified rapidly, after a long delay, or not at all is political will.

The International Convention on the Elimination of All Forms of Racial Discrimination, for example, possessed such strong support from Asian, African, Arab, and Latin American countries that it entered into force in 1969 only four years after adoption by the General Assembly. Once it became legally binding on those states who ratified its terms and thereby accepted its obligations, appropriate enforcement machinery could be created. The resulting Committee on the Elimination of Racial Discrimination (CERD) established the first international mechanism built within the framework of measures for implementation in a United Nations-sponsored treaty in the field of human rights. It is composed of eighteen members elected by the states party to the convention but, importantly, who serve in their individual capacities rather than as government representatives. They possess the power to review the periodic reports required of all states acceding to the convention, to request additional information if they so desire, and to make whatever recommendations they consider appropriate in their annual report to the United Nations General Assembly. The convention also gives them the authority to receive any interstate complaints and provides an optional provision for individual petitions concerning alleged violations of human rights on the basis of racial discrimination. In fulfilling their implementation task, the members of CERD have adopted the practice of inviting states submitting reports to send a representative to participate in the proceedings, answer questions, provide explanations, and listen to criticisms if necessary. Moreover, they have energetically indicated to states party to the convention the form and character that their reports must take, refused to accept very brief reports simply stating that no racial discrimination existed in the country under review, required the production of demographic information about the existence of minorities, and made it very clear in its view that racial discrimination is not practiced only by whites against blacks.[67]

The important Covenant on Civil and Political Rights, by contrast, took a full decade to enter into force in 1976; for many of those states eager to sign the text (including a number of the originally enthusiastic countries of Asia and Africa) demonstrated reluctance when it came to assuming binding obligations. According to it provisions, states party to the treaty are subject to the jurisdiction of the implementation mechanism of the Human Rights Committee (HRC). The essential task of its eighteen members serving in their individual capacities is to ensure that states party to the covenant comply with their incurred obligations. They examine reports required by states on measures adopted for the enjoyment of those specified rights, administer an interstate complaint mechanism, receive individual petitions as provided under the Optional

Protocol, and are free to draw on their own knowledge as experts in the area of human rights and on information provided by nongovernmental human rights organizations. One evaluation of this whole procedure has noted, "Even the most skeptical observers have been impressed by the apparent seriousness that many states from different parts of the world, with diverse political systems, have taken toward their reporting obligations, as reflected by the quality of the reports and the calibre of the representatives, as well as their willingness to answer the Committee's questions."[68] In recent years the members of HRC also have adopted a number of advisory opinions that interpret the meaning of some of their responsibilities and developed a valuable body of case law stemming from charges brought against such geographically diverse countries as Canada, Colombia, Finland, Madagascar, Mauritius, and Uruguay, among others.[69]

Once the International Covenant on Economic, Social, and Cultural Rights entered into force in 1976, states party to the treaty also committed themselves to submitting obligatory reports on the measures taken and the progress made in achieving observance of those rights recognized in the covenant. At first the Economic and Social Council provided the monitoring mechanism, but its sheer size and that fact that its members were official representatives of governments subjected to constant political pressures inhibited its ability to perform the required tasks objectively. Consequently, with remarkable political courage, the majority of members agreed in 1985 to create the permanent Committee on Economic, Social, and Cultural Rights (CESCR), composed of eighteen individuals acting in their own personal capacities to implement the treaty. Members of this committee have devised an elaborate and obligatory reporting system in order that they might determine whether states party to the covenant are honoring their commitments, and annually submit recommendations to ECOSOC for its consideration and action.[70]

This means of implementing human rights treaty obligations through monitoring mechanisms of experts elected by ratifying states but acting in their own capacities to determine compliance established a successful pattern followed with other international conventions. When the Convention on the Elimination of All Forms of Discrimination Against Women entered into force in 1981, for instance, those states incurring the appropriate obligations agreed to establish the Committee on the Elimination of Discrimination Against Women (CEDAW). Its twenty-three members possess the authority to evaluate obligatory country reports, but not the jurisdiction to receive interstate or individual complaints. When the International Convention Against Torture and Other Cruel, Inhuman, or Degrading Treatment or Punishment came to have the force of law in 1987, the parties established the Committee Against Torture (CAT) to supervise its implementation. This ten-member committee is mandated to administer a required reporting system as well as an optional interstate and individual complaint mechanism. Of particular importance, and a potential source of considerable enforcement power, it possesses the authority in certain cases to undertake actual investigations of suspected abuses, as it has done in an recent inquiry involving torture in Turkey. In addition, when the Convention on the Rights of the Child entered into force in 1990, it provided for the creation of the Committee on the Rights of the Child (CRC) to monitor compliance with this unique treaty that singles out the rights of children for international protection, particularly against sexual and economic exploitation, emergency situations like armed conflict, abandonment, and ill treatment. In this capacity, it may invite the specialized agencies, UNICEF, and other United Nations organs to submit reports on the implementation of the convention in areas within the scope of their respective activities. Today, one hundred and ninety states are parties to the Convention on the Rights of the Child, making it the most widely ratified treaty in the history of the world.[71]

All of these standard-setting treaties and their respective implementing mechanisms inspired by the vision of the Universal Declaration of Human Rights have increasingly transformed the law of nations. Under traditional and heavily entrenched international law, only states possessed legal standing and enjoyed recognized rights. This horizontal system between sovereign states ruled supreme, and individuals remained outside. But with the advent of this whole body of legal instruments in the form of binding covenants and conventions with monitoring bodies, this system has increasingly changed into a more vertical arrangement, whereby individual men, women, and children find themselves being increasingly transformed into legitimate subjects of international law to be legally respected, and entitled to the protection of their rights against violations by their own governments, as well as by other states. In fact, noted one lawyer recently, "A hundred years from now, jurists may well be saying that the most important, most radical indeed, development in international law in the twentieth century was the growth of an international law of human rights."[72]

As impressive as these legal instruments might be, however, they most certainly could not solve all problems dealing with international human rights. Authoritarian governments engaging in serious violations of rights of their own citizens, for example, still could continue to refuse to ratify the new treaty texts or the optional protocols and thus remain outside of the established commitments. Or, certain covenants and conventions might not contain provisions for receiving interstate or individual complaints about human rights abuses. Or, states could become parties to the treaties, but do so only with certain attached conditions or reservations. Or, when pressures became too great, could try to claim special privileges, refuse to acknowledge the competence of the particular monitoring body, or take refuge under a "derogation clause" exempting them from obligations in times of public emergencies.[73] For all of these reasons, the advocates of international human rights, whether serving as state officials, members of NGOs, or individuals understood that they could not rely exclusively on their achievements in creating these various legal instruments or rest on their accomplishments in creating convention-based mechanisms. The realization of the vision of the Universal Declaration required more, and toward this end they set about to simultaneously establish a number of extremely significant non-treaty procedures and mechanisms as well.

From the very beginning of efforts to advance international human rights, one of the most critical features has always been whether the possibility existed for individuals to bring complaints about violations to the attention of appropriate bodies for possible action. Throughout most of history, those persons wanting to complain about abuses of rights had no organization to which they could turn, or confronted an institution with no power, or found themselves denied recognition or standing and thus ignored, or were silenced by their own governments seeking to avoid any criticism by hiding behind claims of national sovereignty and domestic jurisdiction. Only in very unique circumstances, as in the Bernheim petition before the League of Nations, did this ever change. In fact, for many years the United Nations itself followed the well-established pattern. When confronted with a veritable flood of tragic and politically dangerous petitions from victims suffering from one kind of abuse or another, governments instructed their representatives on the Commission on Human Rights to formally and publicly declare that their body "has no power to take any action in regard to any complaints concerning human rights."[74]

Remarkably, despite this widely publicized decision and its appearance of complete futility as a means of seeking remedy, hundreds of thousands of individuals and NGOs writing on their behalf still chose to send letters to the unprepared Commission on Human Rights. Those who wrote believed that they had no one else to whom they could realistically turn, and thus continued to correspond in both desperation over the lack of alternatives and hope in what the United Nations might become in transforming the vision of human rights into a reality for their lives. Some pleaded for help in dealing with the fate of individuals, particular families, or certain groups. Still others requested assistance in dealing with broader subjects such as the protection of minorities, the right of people to self-determination, freedom of religion, the right of asylum, forced labor, prevention of discrimination, conscientious objection, or prisoners and victims of war. Regardless of the issue, however, people would write every day of every year without ceasing. Indeed, during one year alone, the commission received more than twenty-five thousand communications concerning alleged violations of human rights.[75]

The members of the Economic and Social Council had to confront this problem directly. For political reasons, they could not take action on these petitions, but by the same token they could not completely ignore them either. After all, many of the communications contained references to the Universal Declaration of Human Rights by name, the principles of which these same governments had endorsed themselves. One close observer put his finger precisely on the problem by writing that this issue of petitions raised "the whole question of state sovereignty" and provided

a constant invitation to the United Nations to intervene in what may properly be regarded as the internal affairs of a sovereign state. Nevertheless, it is this very encroachment of the international community into the affairs of states which lies at the root of all progress in the field of human rights.[76]

As a beginning step of working their way through this delicate dilemma, they decided to create a system whereby the staff of the Human Rights Division would compile a confidential list of the communications, then convey them to the Commission on Human Rights and the Commission on the Status of Women. Member states not represented on the commissions would be informed of the substance of the communications that concerned them directly, but the identity of the authors would be kept secret unless they chose to reveal themselves. Yet, access to this list was severely restricted, information contained therein could never be used to initiate any action in specific cases, and the entire nature of the process provoked resentment from governments. The possibility of petitioning against alleged violations of human rights thus remained dead-locked for years under the early "no power" decision with only the slightest of modifications.[77] Like so many other efforts in the long evolution of international human rights, action could proceed only when a problem of such proportions arose that it simply could no longer be ignored. This occurred, once again, over the issue of racial discrimination.

When confronted not only with the continued injustice of apartheid and colonialism, but also the fixed determination of the white governments to persist in their policies despite constant resolutions, declarations, and embargoes to the contrary, the new and determined majority within the United Nations decided to take even further action. They strongly supported, for example, the creation by the Commission on Human Rights in 1967 of an Ad Hoc Working Group of Experts to investigate the treatment of prisoners in South Africa, Namibia, Southern Rhodesia, and Portuguese territories in Africa, and to invite individuals to bear witness to abuses of human rights in these countries. Then, in order to focus global attention on what they regarded as an unmitigated evil of racism and to go far beyond the polite diplomatic parlance of criticizing "certain countries," these states from Africa and Asia with the strong support from Latin America and Arab countries wanted to expose apartheid and specifically cite South Africa by name. Toward this end, they gathered not only the necessary number of votes, but more important the sufficient political will, to pass an important resolution authorizing the Commission on Human Rights "to examine information relevant to gross violations of human rights and fundamental freedoms, as exemplified by the policy of apartheid as practiced in the Republic of South Africa" and to report its findings with recommendations to the Economic and Social Council.[78] This action opened a critical door that had been slammed shut from the beginning, and thereby made possible many other efforts that went far beyond apartheid. Broader discussions soon followed, for example, about racial discrimination, segregation, the remaining vestiges of colonialism, Israeli policies in occupied territories, the seizing of power by a military junta in Greece, and the brutality of the Duvalier regime in Haiti. This, in turn, encouraged the members of ECOSOC in 1970 to pass Resolution 1503. Over the strong objections of a minority who argued that it would threaten the principle of national sovereignty, they authorized the creation of machinery for implementing a procedure for dealing with petitions concerning abuses, with a view "to determining whether to refer to the Commission on Human Rights particular situations which appear to reveal a consistent pattern of gross and reliably attested violations of human rights requiring consideration."[79] Then, in an extremely important decision the next year, and referring specifically to the Universal Declaration of Human Rights, the subcommission decided to open the door still wider by determining that communications would be admissible if

there are reasonable grounds to believe that they reveal a consistent pattern of gross and reliably attested violations of human rights and fundamental freedoms, *including* policies of racial discrimination and segregation and of apartheid *in any country, including* colonial and other dependent countries and peoples.[80]

A Voice Finally Gained: A Former Prisoner Bearing Witness to Abuses Before the World, 1968 (United Nations Photo).

The widespread possibilities—and challenges—of giving voices to those heretofore confined to silence created by this new procedure and its machinery of implementation to deal with large-scale or systematic violations of human rights were seen immediately. When the chief of the Communications Unit of the International Instruments and Procedures Section in the Human Rights Division brought the first collection before the Commission on Human Rights in 1974, he carted more than two thousand pages of material into the room. Here, it was dumped in the laps of those hitherto involved in the somewhat more philosophical and abstract issues of standard setting rather than practical application and specific identification of offending regimes. The shocking and politically sensitive content of this material struck like a bombshell, and commission members suddenly realized why they had been instructed to close this kind of meeting to the public for the first time in their history.[81]

With this auspicious beginning, the Commission on Human Rights started to work its way through a process of receiving, considering, and acting on what is described as "thousands, thousands, and thousands" of communications.[82] Some governments, like that of the Shah of Iran, Fidel Castro of Cuba, or Ferdinand Marcos of the Philippines, dug in their heels and launched a counteroffensive to divert the commission from focusing on concrete and individual human rights abuses by swamping it with other issues, claiming that only collective abuses such as apartheid or colonialism should be considered, or misrepresenting the confidentiality requirement of the 1503 procedure to exclude particularly vocal nongovernmental organizations. But the number of complaints submitted to the commission increased dramatically, for added to the petitions from single individuals in the past were those generated by massive letter-writing campaigns and carefully gathered information provided by NGOs such as Amnesty International, the Fédération Internationale des Droits de l'Homme, International Commission of Jurists, International League for Human Rights, Women's International League for Peace and Freedom, and the World Council of Churches. In addition, a number of highly visible and politically charged situations attracted considerable global attention and generated demands for action, including persistent apartheid by the white minority regime of South Africa, the treatment of Palestinians in occupied territories by Israel, the torture of political opponents by the brutal dictatorship of Augusto Pinochet in Chile, and the launching of the "dirty war" against human rights by the military junta in Argentina.[83] Within this context, the procedures and machinery of 1503 began to provide an extremely important dimension to the means available to the members of the international community to deal with violations of human rights wherever they might occur. Indeed, since the creation of this mechanism and its subsequent modifications,[84] the Commission on Human Rights has considered complaints against more than seventy different countries, behind closed doors and with a rule of confidentiality. These range all the way from Afghanistan, Argentina, Armenia, and Azerbaijan to Gabon, Germany, Indonesia, and Israel; and from Japan, Kenya, Korea, and Kuwait to Uganda, the United States, Vietnam, and Zaire.[85]

Those who have observed and participated in these developments bear intense testimony to the striking contrast between past practices and the implementation of this 1503 procedure. Prior to this mechanism, responses of states to communications sent by the secretary-general charging them with human rights violations usually contained no more than a few, terse lines often contained in a single sentence. "The Government of ——," they frequently read, "views such charges as slanderous propaganda, libelous allegations, a threat to our national sovereignty, and unwarranted interference into our internal affairs as protected by Article 2 (7) of the Charter."[86] Today, such replies are no longer acceptable, for few governments believe that they can get away with claiming that they are somehow unaccountable or immune from scrutiny under the international standards of the Universal Declaration of Human Rights and subsequent instruments. None is anxious to be forced to go through an elaborate and highly embarrassing process before the representatives of other governments that determines whether their specific situation requires a thorough "study" and "report" or an "investigation" into serious violations of human rights. For this reason, considerable effort is expended by governments in preparing official responses to charges brought against them, often sending presidents, prime ministers, or ministers of foreign affairs or justice in person to address the Commission on Human Rights. On some occasions, governments have even foregone their prerogatives of confidentiality and voluntarily opened their own files to the public in order to clear the name of their country.[87]

Not content with even these remarkable developments, the majority of members on the Commission on Human Rights decided to invoke the vision of the Universal Declaration and push to further develop still other non-treaty procedures and machinery that might provide some form of protection for victims against serious abuses of human rights. They sometimes found the elaborate 1503 mechanism, for example, to be overly cumbersome and confidential, thus preventing sufficient public disclosure and discussion. With the constant encouragement from activist-minded Theo von Boven from the Netherlands, who became Director of the Division of Human Rights in 1977, they successfully determined to implement their broader authority under resolutions to place charges of gross violations on their agenda by creating new means.[88] Over time, these have taken the form of various working groups composed of experts acting in their individual capacities as well as independent women or men designated as rapporteurs, representatives, or experts. The mandates given to such procedures and mechanisms, collectively known as special procedures, are to examine and publicly report on major phenomena of human rights violations worldwide or on human rights situations in specific countries or territories. Their precise directives are determined by the specificities of particular situations and needs, but in all cases designed to bring particularly egregious cases to greater public attention.[89]

Among these various special procedures created by the Commission on Human Rights, to illustrate, one finds a number of working groups dealing with such topics as enforced or involuntary disappearances, arbitrary detention, situations of gross violation of human rights, structural adjustment programs for economic, social, and cultural rights, and the right to development. Other working groups are given the task of drafting new standard-setting instruments such as a declaration on human rights defenders, optional protocols for the International Convention Against Torture and the International Convention on the Rights of the Child. Special rapporteurs for worldwide thematic issues are appointed to study, analyze, and report on such subjects as summary or arbitrary executions, torture, religious intolerance, the use of mercenaries, child prostitution and child pornography, and freedom of opinion and expression. Still others are charged with focusing their attention on violence against women, racism and xenophobia, internally displaced persons, independence of the judiciary, and the illicit movement and dumping of toxic and dangerous products. Special rapporteurs of the Sub-Commission on Prevention of Discrimination and Protection of Minorities include those concentrating on such diverse topics as the health of women and children, cultural property of indigenous peoples, discrimination against people with HIV or AIDS, and conscientious objection. Each of these subjects, of course, continue to raise difficult practical as well as political questions.

Particularly sensitive issues are presented when the Commission on Human Rights creates a mandate for special rapporteurs or representatives to focus on charges of violations within specific countries. In these cases, issues of domestic jurisdiction and national sovereignty rise immediately and passionately to the fore, and nations perhaps willing to have such means applied to others vehemently resist any effort to focus attention on themselves. Nevertheless, when sufficient political will can be found among the majority of members convinced of their broader responsibilities, the commission in recent years has established special rapporteurs or representatives for Afghanistan, Burundi, Cambodia, Cuba, Equatorial Guinea, Guatemala, Haiti, and Iran. Others have been appointed for Iraq, Myanmar (Burma), the Israeli-occupied territory of Palestine, Rwanda, Somalia, Sudan, the former Yugoslavia, and Zaire.

These many procedures and mechanisms designed to protect human rights by implementing either specific legally binding treaty obligations or more general non-treaty resolutions have created remarkable change on the road of transforming the vision of the Universal Declaration of Human Rights into reality, particularly insofar as gross violations are concerned. Together, along with evolving interpretations of both standard-setting documents and instruments as well as the creation of a United Nations High Commissioner for Human Rights, they have enabled the world to address publicly particularly egregious situations more forcefully than ever before in history. The international community has determined that it will no longer accept the argument by governments engaging in massive and systematic violations that they are somehow sheltered by the Charter's Article 2 (7) on domestic jurisdiction. Quite to the contrary, it now maintains that any serious disregard for the vision of human rights proclaimed by the Universal Declaration and elaborated in other standard-setting documents and treaties constitutes instead a serious breach of obligations of all members of the United Nations, hence requiring appropriate measures. This stance marks a dramatic departure from centuries of traditional international law and behavior.

Promoting Rights

Those who strongly advocated international human rights firmly believed that the vision proclaimed in the Universal Declaration of Human Rights could not be realized in practice without information and widespread popular support. Leaders such as Carlos Romulo and others strongly believed that the abuses of human rights could only be overcome by information made possible through freedom of expression. As one member of the United Nations Secretariat observed, "Governments move slowly, except under the pressure of opinion or events," and that without an informed public, the effort on behalf of human rights will lose "the most important factor." "This latent potential demand," he concluded, "must be organized, if we are to succeed."[90] With precisely this in mind, a number of members of the United Nations, the Secretariat, nongovernmental organizations, and individuals actively worked to promote human rights around the world.

They began by energetically promoting the vision proclaimed by the Universal Declaration of Human Rights in nearly every part of the globe. Toward this end, the Secretariat expanded its initial translation of the Universal Declaration of Human Rights into thirty-six different languages and reproduced several million of copies of the document for widespread distribution. Moreover, its staff quickly realized the promotional value of regular publications such as the *Yearbook on Human Rights*, in which reports about the status of human rights in each country were given wide publicity. UNESCO produced study guides, books, films, posters, radio programs, exhibits, and books like *Human Rights: Comments and Interpretations* to carry the vision into the lives of men, women, and children throughout the world.[91] At the same time, the member states of the United Nations declared that 10 December of each year should officially be designated as "Human Rights Day" and designed to commemorate and rededicate the collective commitment to the vision of the Universal Declaration of Human Rights. Working with the Secretariat, NGOs, and private individuals, they then went on to expand public observance of this anniversary by means of a wide array of ceremonies, conferences, seminars, concerts, dances, specific programs in schools, and special features in the press, on the radio, and with the new invention of television transmission. Other efforts followed in rapid succession. In fact, for a considerable period of time, while politics prohibited other efforts, promotional activities became the primary focus of the Commission on Human Rights itself.[92]

Publications became one of the most effective means of promoting human rights. Staff members of the Secretariat regularly began to write and publish articles about human rights in journals such as the *United Nations Bulletin*; then the *United Nations Chronicle*; *Refugees*, published under the auspices of the United Nations High Commissioner for Refugees; and the *Human Rights Newsletter*, produced by the Centre for Human Rights. Similar coverage occurred in the ILO's *International Labour Review* and UNESCO's *Courier* and *Chronicle*. The Sub-Commission on Prevention of Discrimination and Protection of Minorities sponsored a whole series of special publications such as the *Study of Discrimination in Education*, *Study of Discrimination in the Matter of Political Rights*, *Study on Racial Discrimination*, and *The Realization of Economic, Social, and Cultural Rights: Problems, Policies, and Progress*, and made them widely available to libraries.[93] The reception of these reports encouraged others, such as the Secretariat's broad-based and comprehensive report entitled *United Nations Action in the Field of Human Rights*.[94] On the occasion of major anniversaries of the adoption of the Universal Declaration on Human Rights, the secretariat began to publish *Human Rights: A Compilation of International Instruments* consisting of the texts of conventions, declarations, and certain recommendations adopted by the United Nations and its specialized agencies. These came to be supplemented with annual publications of *Human Rights: Status of International Instruments* describing in considerable detail the signatures, ratifications, and accessions to human rights treaties. In addition, the annual reports and documentation published by regional, intergovernmental organizations like the European Commission on Human Rights, the Inter-American Commission on Human Rights, and the African Commission on Human and People's Rights also contributed to this growing body of readily available material to promote international human rights.[95]

Many others contributed to this increased publicity as well, particularly the growing number of nongovernmental organizations deeply committed to human rights and anxious to utilize their own essays, reports, studies, and journals as means of promotion activities. Indeed, the initial premise of Peter Benenson, who first envisioned Amnesty International, was precisely that publicity campaigns based on accurate evidence would serve as the most effective means of embarrassing governments guilty of abuses and thereby protect the rights of prisoners of conscience. The widespread success of his original "Appeal for Amnesty, 1961" prompted many subsequent activities, such as the hard-hitting *Amnesty International Report* that regularly brings violations of human rights to the attention of the world. Similar publications include *The Review* of the International Commission of Jurists, various handbooks and reports from the Asian Forum for Human Rights and Development, the *Human Rights Africa Bulletin*, *Human Rights Watch World Report*, the *Revue annuelle* of the Fédération Internationale des Droits de l'Homme, *Human Rights Bulletin* of the International League for Human Rights, and the *Human Rights Monitor* of the Human Rights Service, among many others. In addition, new journals like *Human Rights Quarterly* and *Human Rights Law Journal*, in addition to the *Revue des Droits de l'Homme*, also provide opportunities to promote independent and scholarly attention to the subject of human rights. One of the most important features of these nongovernmental and scholarly publications is that since they do not represent official positions, they often prove to be much more blunt and critical than some United Nations-sponsored studies, which must reach political accommodation, and are thus particularly effective in speaking truth to power and promoting rights.

This momentum continued to accelerate, and those who championed visions of human rights became enormously heartened by the convergence of several different developments from sometimes unexpected sources that greatly assisted promotion activities. Some of these occurred when the governments of Australia, Canada, and New Zealand began to enact new legislation for their immigration laws and policies toward indigenous peoples, publicly acknowledging "that the winds of change are blowing" and declaring their desire to conform more closely with the principles proclaimed in the Universal Declaration of Human Rights.[96] At the same time, Pope John XXIII issued his powerful encyclical *Pacem in Terris*, where he spoke of justice, charity, liberty, the common good, responsibilities, and international human rights, which he described as a part of the natural law applying to every human being. The authority of the world community, he asserted, must have "as its special aim the recognition, respect, safeguarding, and promotion of the rights of the human person." He went on to make specific reference to the vision of the Universal Declaration and concluded:

It is therefore Our earnest wish that the United Nations Organization may be able progressively to adapt its structure and methods of operation to the magnitude and nobility of its tasks. May the day not be long delayed when every human being can find in this organization an effective safeguard of his personal rights; those rights, that is, which derive directly from his dignity as a human person, and which are therefore universal, inviolable, and inalienable.[97]

Nearly simultaneous with this remarkable pronouncement, over two hundred thousand people gathered at the Lincoln Memorial in Washington, D.C., to hear Martin Luther King, Jr., deliver his "I Have a Dream" speech, in which he eloquently described his vision for a world in which all people would be judged by the content of their character rather than the color of their skin, then watched in astonishment as the 1964 and 1965 Civil Rights Acts entered into law. At the same time, of course, the process of decolonization and the extension of the right of self-determination continued with the force of a tidal wave.

All of these changes occurred at such a rapid pace that serious assessment was frequently difficult. The many achievements and benefits were not always fully appreciated or understood, nor were the problems. Among the latter, for example, the signing of treaties for international human rights did not necessarily ensure ratification, and implementation mechanisms frequently required adjustments. In addition, many governments among the Asian, African, and Arab countries came to realize, often with considerable difficulty, that independence alone did not automatically bring civil or political rights in its wake or afford economic development or social well-being. Consequently, in order to address these issues and to draw as much attention as possible to the Universal Declaration of Human Rights on the occasion of its twentieth anniversary, the General Assembly, with strong support from many NGOs, declared 1968 as the International Year for Human Rights. In doing so, its members specifically cited the vision of the Universal Declaration as being "of the highest importance," stressed the importance of protecting rights through implementation procedures and mechanisms, and expressed their belief that intensified promotion and development of respect for human rights would contribute to strengthening peace throughout the world. They called on all member states to intensify their efforts and undertakings in the field of human rights, urged them to ratify the human rights treaties and accept the incumbent obligations, and encouraged them to make the International Year for Human Rights "truly universal." Toward this end, they created a committee composed of representatives from different geographical areas, ideological orientations, religious faiths, cultures, and stages of development from around the globe and charged them with organizing a major international conference to promote human rights as far as possible.[98]

The resulting International Conference on Human Rights was held in Teheran during 1968 and was attended by delegations from eighty-four countries, representatives from United Nations bodies and specialized agencies, officials from regional organizations such as the League of Arab States and the Organization of African Unity, and members of nongovernmental organizations ranging from the International Alliance of Women and the League of Red Cross Societies to the World Council of Churches and the World Muslim Congress. With vast and worldwide media attention, the participants evaluated the effects of the Universal Declaration of Human Rights and publicly called on all states to help transform this vision into reality by ratifying the standards and obligations of the emerging covenants and conventions. They devoted considerable effort to analyzing issues of rights surrounding the specific problems of racial and religious discrimination, apartheid, self-determination for those still under colonial domination, armament races and humanitarian law in armed conflicts, illiteracy, continued discrimination against women, and protection for families and children. Significantly, and reflecting the ideas and interests in development of the new majority within the United Nations, the delegates went on to declare that "since human rights and fundamental freedoms are indivisible, the full realization of civil and political rights without the enjoyment of economic, social, and cultural rights is impossible." As they looked toward the future, the conference participants urged "all peoples and governments to dedicate themselves to the principles enshrined in the Universal Declaration of Human Rights and to redouble their efforts to provide for all human beings a life consonant with freedom and dignity and conducive to physical, mental, social, and spiritual welfare." Moreover, and of particular interest given later attempts by certain governments to characterize international human rights as a "Western invention," all of the majority of non-western states solemnly proclaimed:

The Universal Declaration of Human Rights states a common understanding of the peoples of the world concerning the inalienable and inviolable rights of all members of the human family and constitutes an obligation for the members of the international community.[99]

Toward this end, the members of the United Nations then decided to begin a series of promotional activities in which particular issues of human rights would be the focus of international attention for an entire decade. Not surprising, given the intensity of emotion on the subject, the General Assembly began by declaring that 1973 marked the initiation of the Decade to Combat Racism and Racial Discrimination, and announced its determination to speak out for dignity and equality. "The ultimate goals of the Decade," declared the enabling resolution, "are to promote human rights and fundamental freedom for all, without distinction of any kind on grounds of race, color, descent, or national or ethnic origin," with the aim of eliminating the persistence of racist beliefs, policies, and practices wherever they might exist.[100] To accomplish these goals and objectives, the overwhelming majority of member states of the United Nations agreed on a specific and ambitious Plan of Action that included such concrete measures as providing assistance to victims of racial discrimination, denying political and diplomatic support to governments that practiced racial discrimination, seeking ratification and implementation of relevant standard-setting instruments, conducting further studies on race, and sponsoring the World Conference to Combat Racism and Racial Discrimination. Both the successes of this program, which eventually saw the creation of CERD as a treaty-monitoring body and the end of apartheid in South Africa, as well as the emergence of new problems, such as "ethnic cleansing" in the former Yugoslavia and genocide in Rwanda, caused the members of the United Nations to twice renew the decade's theme and to rededicate themselves to its goals.[101]

The achievements of this program in promoting aspects of human rights encouraged the international community to establish others in turn. Consequently, in 1976, members of the United Nations launched the Decade for Women following the World Conference of the International Women's Year held in Mexico City. Working closely with the Commission on the Status of Women and with many NGOs, the participants engaged in a wide variety of efforts to draw attention to the rights of women around the globe as well as developing a plan of action. They focused on problems related to socioeconomic development, employment, education, social benefits, health and family planning, peace, and violence. In the process they conducted special studies about gender discrimination, revealing that "while women represent 50 percent of the world's population, they perform nearly two-thirds of all working hours, receive only one-tenth of the world income, and own less than 1 percent of world property."[102] In addition, they successfully worked during the course of the decade to gain adoption by the General Assembly of the Convention on the Elimination of All Forms of Discrimination Against Women, to secure the necessary number of ratifications for it to enter into force, and then to create the treaty-monitoring body of the Committee on the Elimination of Discrimination Against Women. The concluding World Conference to Review and Appraise the Achievements of the United Nations Decade for Women held in Nairobi during 1985, attracted close to fourteen thousand participants to a NGO forum and more than one thousand five hundred official conference attendees from one hundred and fifty-nine nations. In the end, and in an effort to continue the momentum for the future, they adopted a program of action entitled Forward-Looking Strategies for the Advancement of Women that in the words of the secretary-general "constitute the principal instrument of overall policy of the United Nations in the promotion of the rights of women."[103]

These two decades of promotion not only received the encouragement and support of the overwhelming majority of members of the United Nations, but also benefited from several other simultaneous developments. In Eastern Europe, a group of Czechoslovakian citizens, including the future president Václav Havel, created an association called Charter 77 to draw worldwide, public attention to violations of rights, announcing that their inspiration came from the vision of the Universal Declaration of Human Rights, which made possible "a new era in history, an era of immense significance, because it means a decisive turn in people's consciousness, in their relationship towards themselves and society."[104] In the Soviet Union, noted dissidents such as Andrei Sakharov and Elena Bonner increasingly spoke out at great personal risk about flagrant abuses of human rights by their government, often with specific references to the Universal Declaration. In Latin America, Archbishop Oscar Romero delivered public sermons about the necessity to respect human rights, which would soon cost him his life. In the United States, the efforts of Congressman Donald Fraser to hold hearings about the violations of rights in light of internationally established standards, and especially the election of Jimmy Carter as president, brought the kind of attention to the subject of human rights that the nation had not seen since the days of Eleanor Roosevelt. "As President," Carter later wrote, "I hoped and believed that the expansion of human rights might be the wave of the future throughout the world, and I wanted the United States to be on the crest of this movement."[105] To achieve this objective, he announced that human rights would serve as a central core and "soul" of his foreign policy, and to help make this happen appointed black civil rights leader Andrew Young, and subsequently Don McHenry, as ambassadors to the United Nations, and Jerome Shestack of the International League for Human Rights as a representative on the Commission on Human Rights. Carter then pressed both adversaries as well as friendly but authoritarian allies in the Cold War alike to improve their human rights practices, personally went before the United Nations to draw attention to the Universal Declaration of Human Rights and to reiterate that no nation — including his own — could hide any longer behind the excuse of national sovereignty and domestic jurisdiction in the treatment of its citizens.[106] At the same time, the World Council of Churches appointed a Human Rights Advisory Group and launched an active program on behalf of international human rights. Then, Amnesty International's receipt of the Nobel Peace Prize, directly in the midst of attacks from some Latin American, Arab, and Communist governments on those groups that pried too closely into their affairs, suddenly gave marked visibility and legitimacy to human rights nongovernmental organizations. Shortly thereafter, the Organization of African Unity — strongly encouraged by developments throughout their continent such as the collapse of the last remnants of the Portuguese empire and the coming into power of a black majority government in Zimbabwe — made specific reference to the Universal Declaration and adopted the African Charter of Human and People's Rights.[107]

All of these activities and developments encouraged others and greatly strengthened the belief that promotion was essential to the progressive evolution of international human rights. Indeed, when he became Under Secretary-General of Human Rights and assumed direction of the Centre for Human Rights in Geneva, Jan Mårtenson described promotion efforts as one of the three "pillars" of United Nations human rights program, the other two being standard setting and implementation. As he declared publicly: "A key element in the realization of human rights is the knowledge by each person of his or her inalienable rights and the means that exist to protect them."[108] With the launching of the United Nations World Public Information Campaign for Human Rights in 1988 on the occasion of the fortieth anniversary of the Universal Declaration, and with the release of Amnesty International's annual *Global Report on Human Rights* charging that gross violations had increased in proportion to the amount of lip service governments paid to human rights, these activities expanded even further. The new Centre for Human Rights (designed to replace the former Division of Human Rights just a few years before) began publication of a series of fact sheets and the *Human Rights Newsletter*, expanded its contacts with nongovernmental organizations, cosponsored a large NGO World Congress on Human Rights in New Delhi, and worked closely with the Commission on Human Rights and a special preparatory committee to plan for a major, worldwide conference designed to assess the entire status of international human rights and to see whether visions had indeed been translated into reality.

Not all governments welcomed this plan for a new international conference on human rights. In fact, some vehemently opposed the effort and attempted in any way that they could to thwart the efforts of Ibrahima Fall of Senegal and scores of others trying to organize the conference and to prevent the gathering from even taking place at all. Failing at that, they then not only tried to keep it from addressing politically sensitive issues but also to prevent certain individuals or representatives of particular groups or NGOs from being allowed to speak. They believed that this kind of additional attention to, and promotion of, international human rights would result in embarrassing criticism of their own abuses before the eyes of the world. Even documents usually noted for their use of polite diplomatic language described the confrontations and disputes between these states and those who supported the objectives of the conference as nothing short of "difficult," "divisive," and "intense."[109] The Chinese government, for example, still furious at the global attention and unrelenting criticism resulting from the 1989 Tiananmen Square massacre, its occupation policies in Tibet, and general abuses of civil and political rights, increasingly staked out a hard-line position much different from its earlier support of international standards and did what it could to thwart the process. It worked with similar-minded governments to create a "gag rule" that forbade any finger-pointing or discussion of specific violations by individual member states, sought to exclude NGOs like Amnesty International that had been extremely critical of its violations of human rights, and fought to keep the Dalai Lama from having any opportunity at all to address the conference participants.[110] In addition, it led the movement joined by Indonesia, Malaysia, and Singapore to endorse the "Bangkok Declaration," which challenged the very notion of international norms as proclaimed by the Universal Declaration of Human Rights and asserted instead the importance of relative norms that recognized the "particularities" or differences of nation, region, history, culture, and religion.[111]

These maneuvers provoked strong reactions among advocates for human rights within other governments and most certainly among NGOs. Among the latter, those in Asia were particularly incensed. They accused these states of being cynically interested in nothing more than creating a shield under the expression of "cultural relativism" to protect themselves against criticism and accountability. Said one spokesman, they came up with this argument because they "have something to hide on the protection of human rights in their own countries."[112] More than one hundred Asian-Pacific NGOs, in fact, went so far as to publicly issue their own parallel declaration, strongly supporting the norms of human rights proclaimed in the Universal Declaration as belonging to all members of the human family. They warned others to be aware of the legitimate claims of differences and cultural pluralism, but not to be seduced into thinking that these somehow allow repressive regimes to set their own norms as it suits them and absolve themselves from internationally established standards.[113] The Burmese activist and Nobel Peace Prize-winner Aung San Suu Kyi subsequently responded in a similar manner, forcefully declaring that claims of "cultural relativism" by her government and others were only cynical manipulations "intended to justify the policies and actions of those in power" and designed to serve as an excuse for denying human rights. The serious differences, she said bluntly, were not between cultures, but rather between universal norms of human rights and the unrestricted exercise of power.[114]

Despite all of the difficulties, obstacles, and arguments thrown in their way, and last-minute fears that the entire enterprise might completely collapse, the will of the majority of members of the United Nations prevailed to the point that they could hold the World Conference on Human Rights in Vienna during 1993. Acutely aware of its highly visible, promotional mission, Secretary-General Boutros Boutros-Ghali of Egypt announced in his opening comments that the conference "marks one of those rare, defining moments when the entire community of States finds itself under the gaze of the world. It is the gaze of the billions of men and women who yearn to recognize themselves in the discussions that we shall be conducting and the decisions that we shall be taking in their name." He went on to challenge all the participates to rise above their differences, avoid "verbal battles" and "sterile polemics," and recommit themselves to realizing visions of international human rights based on the quintessential value of the worth of each and every human being.[115] But with the presence of over two thousand delegates from one hundred and seventy-one nations, speakers that included heads of state and other government officials, representatives from specialized agencies and intergovernmental bodies, and nearly four thousand representatives of over eight hundred NGOs, as well as all those who demonstrated in the streets outside the conference, it is not surprising that many serious and contentious problems arose. In the end, and after considerable compromises, the participants finally agreed on the Vienna Declaration and Program of Action. In this document, they invoked what they described as "the spirit of our age and the realities of our time" that supported international human rights. They recognized that they all came from different cultures and backgrounds, but nevertheless turned their backs on the argument of relativism and reaffirmed their commitment to the vision of the Universal Declaration of Human Rights as a common standard for all peoples and all nations by unequivocally declaring: "The universal nature of these rights and freedoms is beyond question." Moreover, they boldly rejected the old claims of domestic jurisdiction by asserting that *all* human rights represented a legitimate concern of the international community. In addition, they acknowledged the indivisible and interrelated nature of human rights, stressing the importance of taking specific action on behalf of all women, children, indigenous peoples, refugees, the racially or religiously oppressed, the economically exploited, and others abused in one way or another. Finally, they urged states to support democracy and development, secure additional ratifications of the human rights instruments, encourage NGOs to become more active, authorize increased funding for the Centre for Human Rights, and consider creating a new position of High Commissioner for Human Rights to coordinate as many of these activities as possible, thereby enhancing international human rights even further.[116]

Enhancing Rights and Expanding Activities

From the very beginning, those committed to realizing the vision proclaimed by the Universal Declaration of Human Rights understood that the transformation of theoretical principles into practice would require the development and utilization of a variety of innovative means. They knew that in this process they would confront many obstacles and face determined opposition. They thus began to travel their way through largely uncharted waters, inspired by this vision but finding it tempered by political realities that constantly reminded them of diplomacy being the art of the possible. The extension of rights coupled with standard setting, the implementation of treaties and enabling resolutions, and the many promotional campaigns of individuals, NGOs, national governments, intergovernmental regional bodies, and the United Nations with its own organs and specialized agencies all made overwhelmingly significant contributions in this endeavor. When operating at their best, they all mutually reinforced each other. In addition, they collectively helped in developing a remarkably wide array of other procedures, programs, and mechanisms all designed in one way or another to enhance the realization of international human rights.

Beyond the promotion of rights through publicity but less than the enforcement of rights through treaty implementation, for example, staff within the Division of Human Rights, then the Centre for Human Rights, along with the specialized agencies and the support of the majority of members of the United Nations, gradually developed a number of means to offer practical help and instruction in concrete measures to be taken on behalf of those in need. These included the sharing of technical knowledge and advice by experts, special seminars, fellowships and scholarships for those persons having direct responsibilities in implementing human rights in their respective countries, and regional training courses all known as "advisory services in the field of human rights."[117] Early expert advice provided to governments, to illustrate, involved specific suggestions on such matters as how to administer fair elections and how to prepare women for participation in political affairs. Seminars and training programs sought to offer practical help to those concerned with realizing the principles stated in the Universal Declaration through concrete measures dealing with such issues as social welfare and development, enhancing the public administration of justice, drafting the language of national legislation, improving the status of minorities and aboriginal populations, helping to secure equal pay for women workers, suggesting ways to provide all people with education and health care, assisting refugees, and providing relief to victims of disaster. Of particular importance, United Nations personnel took these programs wherever they received an invitation, and traveled from Japan, India, Mongolia, the Philippines, and Thailand in Asia to Cameroon, Ethiopia, Ghana, and Zambia in Africa, and from Argentina, Chile, Colombia, and Mexico in Latin America to Austria, Britain, Italy, and Poland in Europe.[118]

Any number of governments, especially those of newly independent and developing countries, eagerly desired such assistance and directly asked for technical and advisory services in the field of human rights. They had endorsed the Universal Declaration of Human Rights and made its principles part of their own constitutions, but needed to develop machinery and trained personnel in public administration and the judicial system to encourage the adoption of appropriate policies and procedures. Toward this end, they specifically requested conferences, seminars, and training sessions to prepare politicians, civil servants, and educators in their own country. Others, however, viewed these advisory services as embarrassing, and thought that by making a request they might simply draw attention to a particular human rights problem at home. For many years, to illustrate, the Secretariat could not find an Arab state willing to host a conference or seminar on the rights of women. Some governments argued that such activities represented matters "beyond the competence" of the Secretariat or, worse, interference into their own internal affairs. Those who attempted to provide technical assistance thus constantly found themselves confronting what they called "these intricate and complicated problems" and especially "the political atmosphere" of domestic and international behavior.[119]

Yet despite this kind of political resistance and various obstacles thrown in its way, a majority of states increasingly viewed the program of advisory services and technical assistance as a valuable means of enhancing rights. This became particularly true as they sought to take full advantage of the "window of opportunity" made possible by the fall of the Berlin Wall and the collapse of Communist regimes in the Soviet Union and Eastern Europe — events inspired themselves in large part by visions of human rights — and the end of the Cold War. In fact, for this reason they made sure that provisions in the Vienna Declaration and Program of Action emerging from the World Conference on Human Rights called on the Centre for Human Rights to actually increase and strengthen its activities in this area of providing practical assistance to states in elaborating and attaining plans of action. Thus, when the members of the General Assembly with strong support from nongovernmental organizations created the position of the United Nations High Commissioner for Human Rights, naming José Ayala Lasso from Ecuador as its first occupant in 1994, they specifically mentioned advisory services as one of the tools essential for the enhancement of other international activities and machinery in the field of human rights and for the realization of the vision of the Universal Declaration of Human Rights.[120] Whether funded from the regular budget of the United Nations or the new UN Fund for Technical Cooperation in the Field of Human Rights, these efforts today entail specific projects such as building national and regional human rights infrastructures, strengthening democratic institutions, drafting new constitutions, explaining treaty reporting and international obligations, creating confidence-building measures in often fragile societies, reforming penal and correctional institutions, training officials and security forces, conducting seminars for judges and lawyers, developing educational strategies and materials, assisting the media in covering human rights, and at times serving as active agents of prevention. Current programs conducted by the staff of the Centre for Human Rights, among many examples, involve direct assistance to the African Commission on Human and Peoples' Rights, the African Centre for Democracy and Human Rights Studies, and the Arab Institute for Human Rights, as well as regional and national field offices located in Abkhazia of Georgia, Burundi, Cambodia, Colombia, Gaza (at the request of the Palestinian Authority), Malawi, and Mongolia, with plans to set up others elsewhere.[121]

Similar activities also include the creation of special field operations assigned as needed to address particularly gross violations of human rights. In response to the Haitian crisis of military dictatorship, for example, the General Assembly authorized the participation of the United Nations along with the Organization of American States in the International Civilian Mission to Haiti; then, in monitoring an agreement regarding negotiations for a peace settlement ending nearly thirty years of internal conflict in Guatemala, authorized the creation of the United Nations Mission for the Verification of Human Rights in Guatemala mutually acceptable to both the government and the opposition Unidad Revolucionaria Nacional Guatemalteca.[122] Responding to the shocking brutality and "ethnic cleansing" in Bosnia and Herzegovina, the United Nations created the Human Rights Field Operation in the Former Yugoslavia. It is charged with enhancing freedom of movement, helping internally displaced persons return to their homes, assisting NGOs, providing expertise for reforming law-enforcement institutions, and providing public information and education on behalf of democratization initiatives and human rights. Similarly, in response to the slaughter and extensive carnage inflicted by Hutus against Tutsis in Rwanda, the Commission on Human Rights and the High Commissioner for Human Rights, acting with the cooperation of the host government, instituted the Human Rights Field Operation in Rwanda. It is staffed with specialists mandated to investigate the genocide and other breaches of international human rights and humanitarian law, to monitor the ongoing situation, to deter further human rights violations, to assist refugees and internally displaced persons, and to assist the government in the rehabilitation of their justice system.

Much of this expanding activity, of course, could be traced directly to the increasingly energetic efforts and ever-expanding roles of those who serve the Commission on Human Rights itself. This body that originally numbered only eighteen now meets with fifty-three members. In addition to membership, the length of time allocated for its annual sessions has expanded, as has the commission's ever-enlarging agenda. In one way or another, along with the Centre for Human Rights and the High Commissioner for Human Rights and its own Sub-Commission on Prevention of Discrimination and Protection of Minorities, it is involved in drafting new standard-setting instruments and declarations, seeking further ratifications of existing treaties, dealing with complaints about human rights violations, developing extra-conventional mechanisms or special procedures, dispatching fact-finding missions, supporting advisory services and technical assistance, working with NGOs and regional intergovernmental bodies, making recommendations for further action to improve respect for international human rights, and assisting in promotional activities. With reference to just the latter, for example, it currently promotes the Third Decade to Combat Racism and Racial Discrimination (1993–2002), the United Nations Decade for Human Rights Education (1995–2004), and the International Decade of the World's Indigenous People (1995–2004).[123] In addition, when the commission conducts these activities in public sessions, it draws hundreds of people together into the large, circular, and wood-paneled Salle XVII of the Palais des Nations in Geneva. Participants include delegations from the states that are members of the commission, representatives from most other countries in the world (often including high-ranking government officials), staff from the Secretariat and specialized agencies of the United Nations, and sometimes even the secretary-general himself. Also included are those representatives of many NGOs trying to find a seat or a place to stand in the packed room.

Such an assemblage of delegates and representatives, sometimes numbering over eight hundred, surrounding the open meetings of the Commission on Human Rights provides its own kind of enhancement of human rights. That is, it possesses an influential deterrent value, for few nations relish the prospect of standing before this huge and potentially hostile group, occasionally covered by television cameras beaming transmission signals to overhead satellites for instantaneous broadcast, and being called on to publicly defend their record on human rights in light of internationally established norms before the opinion of the world. In fact, it normally is sufficient to compel most governments to expend considerable energy to comply with the universal standards in advance. If this fails, governments then find themselves working very hard to keep the commission from taking any further action against them. In a particularly heated debate during the 1997 session, to illustrate, China lobbied intensely for a motion of "no action" that would prevent the commission from investigating reports of violations of human rights obligations in treaties to which it is a party, restraints on the rights of its citizens regarding freedom of assembly and expression, abuses of the right to a fair trial, and restrictions on the religious and cultural rights of Tibetans.[124] The Chinese ambassador found himself surrounded by news media that nearly smothered him and in the unenviable position of accusing most human rights advocates of "outrageous distortion" and "sanctimonious posturing," of arguing for national sovereignty over universal standards, of implying threats of economic retaliation against those who would vote against his country, and of ominously warning: "What happens to China today will happen to you tomorrow."[125] Most states make considerable effort to avoid being placed in this kind of situation in the first place.

Concurrent with all of these developments are those of the United Nations Department of Humanitarian Affairs, the specialized agencies, and other international bodies with concern for and responsibilities in the area of enhancing human rights. Many of UNESCO's efforts, for example, are focused on the right to an education, cultural rights, and human rights education. The Food and Agricultural Organization addresses matters relating to the right to sustain life by providing sufficient food supplies. Consistent with its original mandate, UNICEF concentrates on realizing the rights of the child. The extensive operations of the United Nations High Commissioner for Refugees devote their efforts to the rights of refugees and displaced persons, wherever they might be, and since its creation has provided direct assistance to more than thirty million refugees. Most of the work of the World Health Organization centers on the right of all to health. The United Nations Development Program directs its efforts toward the right to development. The ILO focuses its activity on the rights of labor, the right to receive equal pay for equal work, and protection of the rights of the children in the workplace. The International Committee of the Red Cross and the International Federation of the Red Cross and Red Crescent Societies continue their often courageous efforts to provide humanitarian relief and to protect the rights of both civilians and combatants in times of armed conflict, as well as launching new campaigns for the abolition of land mines. Moreover, today the World Bank and the International Monetary Fund are responsible for conducting human rights impact assessments prior to making investments and loans.[126]

Among the more unexpected of these many new and expanding activities are those initiated by members of the Security Council itself. When the United Nations was first created, most of the founders believed that issues of human rights would remain narrowly defined and exclusively confined to the Economic and Social Council. Only with the greatest reluctance and only when confronted with particularly egregious violations, as in the case of the oppression against blacks by the white minority regime in Rhodesia in 1966 and 1968, and apartheid in South Africa illustrated by the Soweto massacre in 1976 and the murder of black activist Steven Biko the following year that attracted the attention of the world, would the Security Council ever authorize the use of sanctions. In recent years, however, members have increasingly become convinced that violations of human rights ultimately and seriously jeopardize international peace, as they explicitly stated in their 1991 resolution dealing with Iraq's persecution of its Kurdish population, and therefore have given much more serious thought to the possibilities of humanitarian intervention.[127] Indeed, according to some close observers, the Security Council has exhibited "a dramatic new vision of human rights" that includes a willingness to impose sanctions when necessary and the launching of a number of innovative and precedent-setting initiatives at both the operational and jurisdictional levels.[128] Its mandates establishing and deploying United Nations peace keeping forces, for example, have steadily incorporated important human rights components as a part of their mission, including those sent to Namibia, El Salvador, Cambodia, Mozambique, Bosnia, Herzegovina, and Croatia. It went on to create in 1993 the International Criminal Tribunal for the Former Yugoslavia to prosecute those responsible for "ethnic cleansing," torture, the rape of women, detention camps, and other violations of human rights and obligations under the genocide convention and international humanitarian law in Bosnia and Herzegovina, and then followed the same pattern by establishing the International Tribunal for Rwanda in 1994. Even more recently, the Security Council has taken action to deal with human rights in Afghanistan, the creation of a Human Rights Protection Office in Georgia, and the endorsement of a Human Rights Ombudsman in Bosnia and Herzegovina.[129]

The extraordinary range, geographical extent, and complexity of these many expanding activities has been so vast as to prompt considerable efforts just to explain them. The Office of the High Commissioner for Human Rights and the Centre for Human Rights, to illustrate, published a comprehensive study entitled *The United Nations and Human Rights* and launched a new series of publications called *Notes of the United Nations High Commissioner for Human Rights*, the first of which focused on the theme "Making Human Rights a Reality."[130] Working in close cooperation with the United Nations Library at Geneva, and seeking to utilize the latest means for the efficient storage and retrieval of data, they produced their first CD-ROM in 1997 under the title of *Human Rights: Bibliographical Data and International Instruments* containing seventeen thousand references to United Nations documents and publications.[131] Moreover, seeking to use the most recent technology as a means of promotion, they also recently created a website for the Office of the High Commissioner for Human Rights with a homepage prominently and fittingly displaying the first article of the Universal Declaration of Human Rights reading: "All human beings are born free and equal in dignity and rights."[132]

Finally, all these international developments seeking to implement the Universal Declaration have inspired, encouraged, and assisted in innumerable other activities in what is frequently described as a worldwide "human rights movement."[133] Many of these involve countless numbers of relatively unknown men and women who eagerly seize on the instruments, mechanisms, tools, and even a Human Rights Hot Line now available to them twenty-four hours a day in their struggles to realize visions where they live, at the grassroots level.[134] They are the people on the front line who dodge bullets, who speak out against brutality and tyranny, who search for the "disappeared," who write on behalf of the imprisoned and tortured, who try to defend the exploited and repressed, who seek to stop carnage and impoverishment, and who work in common ways to bring human rights to life. They also are the ones participating in a vast new field of action in which ordinary but dedicated people are constructing human rights projects, organizing practical training sessions in local communities, and sharing their knowledge with others through education now in virtually every quadrant of the globe.[135]

*   *   *

In the fifty years that have transpired since the adoption of the Universal Declaration of Human Rights the world has witnessed a veritable revolution in transforming visions of international human rights into reality. Never before have there been so many achievements in extending rights to former colonial peoples, setting standards through declarations and binding covenants, protecting rights through mechanisms of treaty implementation and non-treaty procedures, promoting rights through education and the media, and enhancing rights through such means as advisory services and technical assistance in the field where people actually suffer. Together they have helped millions of people gain their independence and assisted unknown numbers of others by preventing abuses, securing freedom from torture or prison, acquiring access to monitoring bodies and humanitarian aid, and obtaining national and international legal protections for their rights. In addition, they have inspired regional intergovernmental organizations and states acting on their own or in conjunction with others to use the observance or violation of human rights as a criteria for their foreign policies. Never before in history has there been what is now described as such a "universal culture of human rights" in which the rights of so many men, women, and children are given so much attention in so many diverse places under the watchful eyes of the world and in which the international community refers to human rights as "the common language of humanity."[136] But the revolution remains unfinished, for gaps between theory and practice still exist, abuses continue, sources of resistance remain, and problems persist. Given these facts, the ability to move the vision of the Universal Declaration of Human Rights any closer to reality in the next fifty years may well depend on how well we understand what can be learned about visions and the evolution of international human rights in the past.

Conclusion
Visions and the Evolution of International Human Rights

> To all the heroes and heroines in this country and the rest of the world who sacrificed in many ways and surrendered their lives so that we could be free. Their visions have become reality.
>
> — Nelson Mandela of South Africa

The history of the evolution of international human rights, as we have seen throughout this book, is a history of the long and determined struggle for freedom and dignity. It is one inspired by visions of what it means to be truly human and a sense of responsibility to other members of the same human family. It is a history brought about by visionaries and by those men and women of determination willing to make sacrifices and sometimes take considerable risks in confronting vested interests, privilege, prejudice, and the claims of national sovereignty. Moreover, it is one in which revolutions, wars, and upheavals have played prominent and often critical roles in accelerating a process, accentuating the influence of politics, and helping visions become reality.

The Nature and Power of Visions

Visions, by their very nature, challenge our imaginations, cause us to reexamine our assumptions, and often raise profound and disturbing questions about our values. They tend to address some of the larger and more abstract issues of life that do not always lend themselves to simple solutions. They are sometimes imprecise, and what may be seen by one visionary in his or her own mind may not be at all clear to others or may be subject to different interpretations. Visions present hypothetical conditions and situations that require both a willingness and an ability to go beyond existing experience by means of imagination. In addition, visions focused on human rights pose their own particular difficulties. At precisely the time that they seek to address the best in people, for example, they are generally forced to confront the worst. Ironically, visions of human rights have always gained the greatest support during times of greatest human abuses, including slavery, torture, segregation and apartheid, conquest, or genocide. In these circumstances, how is one to determine the genuine nature of human beings and what is possible? Such visions during challenging times also pose difficult and vexing questions that do not lend themselves to quick or conclusive or even satisfactory answers. Do we possess certain basic rights simply because we are all human beings? If so, what exactly are these rights and do they have universal applicability? Are some rights more important than others, or are they really indivisible and interdependent? What is the relationship between the individual and the larger society in which we live, and does the respect for rights entail corresponding responsibilities to other brothers and sisters?

It is exactly these kinds of difficult, thought- and conscience-provoking questions that endow visions of human rights with a power that encourages, enables, or actually forces people to test existing values, reexamine their assumptions, and sometimes change their minds. For this reason, those who witnessed the evolution of international human rights at one stage or another constantly commented on the remarkable power of visions to transform society by "stirring the conscience of humanity" and "changing patterns of thought," even those entrenched with centuries of encumbered tradition behind them.[1] They have the capacity to cause men and women to consider the possibilities that kings and emperors may not be divine, that aristocratic class or caste divisions may not be part of the "natural order," or that slavery may be morally wrong. They pointedly suggest the prospect that women deserve the same rights as men, that empires are not inevitable, that indigenous peoples are human beings, or that torture and genocide are ethically reprehensive and need not be tolerated. Similarly, they ask people to imagine that international norms can be established and that nation-states need not be allowed to claim that however they wish to behave and treat people is strictly their own business.

In addition, these visions possess a remarkable power to inspire, for they serve as carriers of hope. It is not at all difficult to understand how dreams of a world at peace and harmony as a result of the mutual respect of basic rights generate inspiration. They see the best in us rather than the worst. They look toward the possibilities of what might be rather than what is or what has been in an imperfect world, and call us to rise above the limitations and experiences of the past. These visions consider what we share as members of the same human family and what brings us together rather than what drives us apart. They see a world of common humanity without borders where the worth and dignity of each man, woman, and child is honored. They imagine the elimination of suffering based on distinctions of gender, race, caste or class, belief, ethnicity, or nationality. Moreover, they point the way toward behavior based on ethical norms and values rather than the exercise of raw power and brutal force. All this helps to explain why visions provide such enduring inspiration to those seeking human rights.

Indeed, these are the reasons why certain visions have touched people in powerful ways at their core, uplifted the human spirit, and enabled them to dream of what might be even at times of great cost and peril. They inspired countless numbers to follow those religious leaders who preached the brotherhood and sisterhood of all human beings. They encouraged others to embrace the visions of philosophers who spoke of ethical values and justice that respected the dignity of each person everywhere. These visions gave hope to those who dreamed of freeing the enslaved, assisting the exploited, caring for the wounded, and protecting the persecuted, wherever they might be. They provided strength to millions seeking a time when women would enjoy the same rights as men, when racial discrimination and apartheid would end, and when colonial empires would crumble. In addition, these visions inspired those who hoped that the international community would someday be able to create an organization that placed a value on people rather than just states and that could develop standards of human rights that would be universally accepted and applied around the world. Today they do the same for those like José Ramos-Horta and his struggle for rights in East Timor, the successors to Mother Teresa as they care for the suffering, and Rigoberta Menchú Tum from Guatemala and her dreams of a world that respects the rights of women and indigenous peoples.

These same visions that inspire, however, also enrage, produce fear, and provoke resistance. To imagine a world in which each and every individual is treated with respect and dignity, receives equal protection, enjoys freedom, and is accorded social justice is to threaten virtually any tradition or practice based on privilege and hierarchy, birth or wealth, exclusivity, and prejudice. The reason is not difficult to explain, for as one experienced observer notes succinctly: "The struggle for human rights has always been and always will be a struggle against authority."[2] Visions of human rights, by their nature, defy the legitimacy and threaten the existence of all forms of political, economic, social, or cultural despotism, tyranny, dictatorship, oligarchy, or authoritarian control. Moreover, if they seek to apply these principles to the world as a whole, they challenge the jealously guarded claims of national sovereignty or cultural uniqueness. They are thus capable of presenting a potent focus and a resounding rallying cry for those who want change. This is why these visions of human rights are so frequently and strongly resisted and why some governments have resisted even publicizing, let alone implementing, the Universal Declaration of Human Rights in territory under their control.

Given these factors, the power of visions should never be underestimated. Ideas know no boundaries and have the capacity to change the world. Men and women who draw inspiration from visions of human rights understand this — as do those who fear them. In fact, it is for precisely this reason that visionaries and those who follow them so frequently face enormous pressure to keep their visions to themselves and to remain silent. At times they may be ridiculed as naive idealists or criticized as impractical dreamers, as discovered by the Buddhist *bodhisattvas*, Mo Zi when he wrote about moral philosophy, Al-Farabi when he described his vision of virtue from the perspective of Islam, Thomas Clarkson when he imagined ending the slave trade, Alejandro Alvarez and André Mandelstam when they dreamed of formulating international standards of rights, and Peter Benenson when he considered forming Amnesty International. Sometimes, they may be reviled and coerced, as experienced by Jean-Jacques Rousseau when forced into exile, Thomas Paine when burned in effigy, Emmeline Pankhurst when imprisoned and force-fed in jail, or Nelson Mandela when sent into confinement for twenty-seven years. On other occasions, the price to be paid for their visions of human rights is death, as experienced by Jan Hus when burned at the stake, Olympe de Gouges when guillotined, Mohandas Gandhi and Martin Luther King, Jr., when assassinated, or Steven Biko when killed in a South African jail. The same fear of the power of visions of human rights exists today, as evidenced by all those largely unknown victims censored, punished for their beliefs, arbitrarily arrested, imprisoned without trial, tortured, starved, denied medical treatment, and otherwise coerced into being silent about human rights, as well as the more noted cases involving the attempts on the life of Bishop Carlos Felipe Ximenes Belo by the political leaders of Indonesia, and the house arrest of Aung San Suu Kyi and her followers by the military commanders of Burma (Myanmar), and the bounty offered by the government of Iran for the assassination of writer Salman Rushdie.[3]

Despite all of the historical evidence of the capacity of visions of human rights to transform attitudes, to create inspiration, and to provoke resistance, it is interesting that not all observers understand or appreciate this power. Instead, they dismiss these visions as "just dreams," "only words," "merely statements," or "impractical specula-tions" unlikely to create anything more than a ripple on the course of human events. There were those who believed that an empire could never be seriously threatened by the ideas in a Declaration on the Granting of Independence to Colonial Countries and Peoples or a Declaration of the Asian-African Conference, that monarchy and aristoc-racy could never be dangerously contested by the concepts in some Declaration of the Rights of Man and Citizen, or that gender discrimination could never be significantly changed by statements in a Seneca Falls Declaration or a Declaration of Mexico on the Equality of Women. There were those who simply could not imagine that racism might be profoundly challenged by the words in a speech entitled "I Have a Dream" and a Declaration on the Elimination of All Forms of Racial Discrimination, or that national sovereignty and domestic jurisdiction might be critically jeopardized by the principles enunciated by some Atlantic Charter, or that norms of behavior might actually be created by ideas expressed in international declarations. Upon the adoption of the Universal Declaration of Human Rights, for example, any number of commentators tended to belittle the achievement. They described the text as "a mere declaration" and "a statement of principles devoid of any obligatory character."[4] John Foster Dulles noted somewhat contemptuously that the Universal Declaration "merely sets up a standard."[5] Others of the same mind dismissed it as "innocuous," "ineffectual," "purely declaratory," "of no more value than a recommendation," "a mere statement of political and moral principle," and "a grandiloquent incantation" destined for only "futility."[6] In the light of the subsequent impact of the Universal Declaration of Human Rights, it is unlikely that they would hold these same opinions today.

People of Vision and Action

Although visions possess this unusual degree of power and influence, they do not have the capacity to spring to life on their own or bring themselves to fruition. For this task they need people, or what Nelson Mandela calls the heroes and heroines. Such men and women may be quiet religious leaders teaching through prophecy or parables, they may be contemplative philosophers or poets providing influence through the written word, they may be eager activists engaging in civil disobedience, they may be unlikely citizens reluctantly propelled by the course of events to become involved, or they may be government leaders.

The evolution of international human rights, as we have seen, has required in the first instance people serving as visionaries. There must be thoughtful men and women not only capable of imagining possibilities beyond existing experience themselves, but also of conveying these visions to others. They may do this through their teachings, as in the messages of the prophets Isaiah and Muhammed, the parables of Jesus, the instructions of Kong Qiu, or the lessons of Siddhartha Gautama and Chaitanya. They may achieve this through other forms of communication that infuse dreams such as the speeches of Cicero or Franklin Roosevelt, the poetry of Sultan Farrukh Hablul Matin or Ziya Gokalp, the letters of Abigail Adams, the manifestos of Karl Marx, the journals of Hideko Fukuda, the pamphlets of H. G. Wells, the decisions of the judges presiding over the International Military Tribunal at Nuremberg, the encyclicals of Pope John XXIII, or the songs of the civil rights movement such as "We Shall Overcome." These visionaries may transmit their ideas to others by means of lengthy treatises such as the published writings of Bartholomé de Las Casas, John Locke, Mary Wollstonecraft, or Kang Youwei. Or, they may convey visions through resolutions or proclamations such as the Universal Declaration of Human Rights.

For many, however, actions speak louder than words. It is clear from the experiences of history that one of the most effective ways of conveying visions of human rights to others has been by means of personal example. The actual behavior of dedicated and courageous women and men believing that they could make a difference and willing to make great sacrifices — sometimes including their lives — on behalf of principles of human rights provides credibility and inspiration that cannot be matched in any other way. Such people are a Francisco de Vitoria willing to risk imprisonment by criticizing his government's extermination of indigenous peoples, a Florence Nightingale willing to risk her own health by tending to the needs of wounded soldiers, a Qiu Jin willing to risk punishment by organizing the first woman's movement in China, or a Fridtjof Nansen willing to put himself in danger by helping refugees. They include a Franz Bernheim willing to risk persecution by drawing international attention to the plight of Jews under the Nazi regime, a W.E.B. Du Bois willing to risk lynching by publicly criticizing racism in the United States before the world, a Kwame Nkrumah willing to risk his life by standing up to the mighty British Empire, an Andrei Sakharov and Elena Bonner willing to risk internal exile by speaking out on the abuses of rights by the Soviet Union, or a Václav Havel willing to risk imprisonment and possible torture by drawing international attention to the violations of human rights by his government. They also include cases of a worker for the International Red Cross worker delivering relief in the crossfire of a civil war or a staff member of the United Nations Centre for Human Rights providing technical assistance in a country known for its extrajudicial executions and arbitrary arrests.

In addition, time and time again in the long struggle for international human rights we have seen so many of these efforts made by the nonelite and relatively unknown. These include those historically willing to participate in peoples' protests, struggles, revolutions, and even wars, in addition to daily and often common activities on behalf of human rights. They are the ones described by Eleanor Roosevelt as "everyday people" who take human rights seriously and work for, organize on behalf of, and sometimes sacrifice and suffer for a vision in which they truly believe. As she observed:

Where, after all, do universal human rights begin? In small places, close to home — so close and so small that they cannot be seen on any maps of the world. Yet they ARE the world of the individual persons; the neighborhood . . . , the school or college . . . , the factory, farm, or office. . . . Such are the places where every man, woman, and child seeks equal justice, equal opportunity, equal dignity without discrimination. Unless these rights have meaning there, they have little meaning anywhere. Without concerned citizen action to uphold them close to home, we shall look in vain for progress in the larger world.[7]

These are the men and women who discuss human rights where they live and work and who construct projects at the grassroots level to bring rights to life. They are the people who gather in streets and public squares, sign petitions, teach others, speak out, participate in letter-writing campaigns, passively resist, and march or chain themselves to fences as a means of drawing attention to abuses. They also are the individuals sometimes suddenly confronted with the unexpected, like the unknown man willing to risk death in the name of human rights by standing completely alone, planting his feet in the path of a moving column of armored tanks in Beijing.

There are times, of course, when individual people do not need to stand entirely by themselves. Instead, they can draw strength and support from other visionaries and activists by forming and participating in nongovernmental organizations. Within larger groups they can combine their energies and resources to draw widespread attention to particular abuses and create pressure sufficient to challenge authority and bring about change. As we have seen, the contributions made by people through NGOs often have been extremely important in the evolution of international human rights. The Society for the Abolition of the Slave Trade and the Société Française pour l'Abolition de l'Esclavage, for example, played critical roles in bringing an end to the shipment and sale of human beings as cargo and property. The International Woman Suffrage Alliance and the Fusen Kakutoku Domei made significant contributions in raising awareness about equal rights for women and in securing agreements on suppressing the traffic in women and children. The Commission to Study the Organization of Peace and the Institut de Droit International provided invaluable assistance and mobilized powerful pressure to create human rights provisions within the United Nations Charter. The Fédération International des Droits de l'Homme and the International League for the Rights of Man, among many others, all played vital roles in helping to shape and secure the Universal Declaration of Human Rights. The Pan-Asian Society and the Pan-African Congress contributed heavily to discussions and then actions concerning the right of self-determination and the rights of indigenous peoples. The National Association for the Advancement of Colored People and the League for the Abolition of Race Discrimination did the same for the eventual International Convention on the Elimination of All Forms of Racial Discrimination. Amnesty International and the International Commission of Jurists provided similarly vital contributions to the International Convention Against Torture.

Actions Speaking Louder Than Words: Beijing, 1989 (AP/Wide World Photos).

Today, people continue this tradition by playing invaluable roles through NGOs. Some support and participate in those NGOs that approach international human rights with a religious orientation such as the Baha'i International Community, the Commission of the Churches on International Affairs of the World Council of Churches, the Friends (Quakers) World Committee for Consultation, the International World Conference on Religion and Peace, the World Fellowship of Buddhists, the World Jewish Congress, and the World Muslim Congress. Other men and women are actively engaged with those having a more secular perspective including the Human Rights Internet, Human Rights Watch, the International League of the Rights and Liberation of Peoples, the Asian Coalition of Human Rights Organizations, and the International Service for Human Rights, among many others. Together they draw attention to abuses, provide support for the promotion of human rights, lobby for continued standard setting, apply pressure for serious implementation of existing treaties, conduct independent reports of their own, file human rights complaints, and submit information in international judicial and quasi-judicial proceedings containing material normally not included in state reports. Given the fact that they do not represent the interests or official positions of governments, they are less restricted by diplomatic protocol and the responsibility to balance other policy considerations, and therefore possess the freedom to focus directly on human rights issues for their own sake and be much more vocal, outspoken, and fiercely critical of violations that occur. As Edith Ballantyne of the Women's International League for Peace and Freedom said recently when informed that NGOs might not be invited to high-level meetings concerning the Office of the High Commissioner for Human Rights: "If we are not invited, then too bad. We will simply attend anyway."[8] Indeed, at times people in nongovernmental organizations are so successful that governments fear them, attempting to restrict their activities and to control their access to the meetings of the Commission on Human Rights. Secretary-General Kofi Annan of Ghana recently acknowledged their great contributions, while one official at the Centre for Human Rights observed, "Without the people of the NGOs, the international program for human rights would be a mere shadow of itself."[9]

All these men and women acting either by themselves or in cooperation with others, despite the many differences between them, share a number of characteristics in common. Over a considerable period of time, they have been inspired by some vision of human rights emerging from religious belief, philosophical or political conviction, or their own personal experiences. They have believed that they had a responsibility to go beyond their own self interests and to do something on behalf of those unable to care for themselves or defend their rights. Toward this end, they have been willing to confront powerful vested interests and fierce opposition. They also have been able to overcome the skepticism generated by the imperfections in humankind and society. Moreover, they all have concluded that they need not resign themselves to meekly accepting the world as it was — but envisioning what it might become and believing that their efforts on behalf of international human rights could make a difference.

Some people of vision and action also include individuals serving in official capacities on behalf of governments. This may appear strange, since government leaders themselves historically have been the greatest violators of human rights, and none could survive a test of either consistency or untarnished achievement. As John Humphrey concluded after many years of working in this area for the United Nations, "in matters relating to human rights, individuals and governments are usually on opposite sides of the ring. In such matters, governments usually move when and only when they are forced to do so."[10] They are the ones, as we have seen, who traditionally have used the great power of the state at their disposal to abuse rights, to retain privilege, to keep international norms and institutions weak, and to hide behind the claims of national sovereignty. It is for this very reason that governments draw such wrath from human rights activists and are so frequently described as "the enemy."[11] But it is also true that in the world of international relations, the major actors are leaders of governments, and some of them have taken actions that in their own way, and whether intended or not, contributed to the evolution of international human rights.

One thinks, for example, of the early decisions of people such as Abraham Lincoln emancipating slaves in the United States, Alexander II liberating at least fifty million serfs in Russia, and William Gladstone using pressure to protect those persecuted for their religious beliefs overseas. Others include the policy decisions of Nobuaki Makino representing Japan and Wellington Koo representing China to make efforts to obtain a clause on racial equality in the Covenant of the League of Nations, Peter Fraser representing New Zealand and official delegates from the Latin American countries to secure human rights provisions in the Charter of the United Nations, and the many representatives including Eleanor Roosevelt who negotiated and then adopted on behalf of their governments the Universal Declaration of Human Rights. Further examples can be found in the cases of those leaders willing to create regional bodies on behalf of human rights and all those from Asia and Africa, along with their supporters in the West, who worked so hard to move the United Nations out of a long and debilitating deadlock into a mode of action to adopt binding covenants and conventions on international human rights.

It is important to remember that in this regard none of the many activities taken by the United Nations in the field of human rights can be done without the approval of the leaders of member governments. Indeed, and for better or worse, the organization can take no action, including any in the entire human rights program, without their support. As Kofi Annan acknowledged recently, "The ultimate success of that effort remains, of course, in the hands of Member States."[12] Thus, all the standards that are set, the treaties that are drafted, the implementation mechanisms that are created, the decisions made by the Commission on Human Rights, the special rapporteurs that are sent to investigate abuses, the technical assistance and advisory services that are provided, and tribunals that are created to prosecute those who commit genocide, among the many other activities, all occur because the leaders of governments determine that they will. At the same time, government leaders decide whether their countries will honor their commitments in treaties, whether they will impose sanctions on other governments for violations of human rights, whether they will pay their bills to allow the organization to function, and, like Jimmy Carter as president of the United States, Nelson Mandela as president of South Africa, Mikhail Gorbachev as head of the Soviet Union, or Mary Robinson as president of Ireland, whether they will speak out on behalf of rights in the world — or not.

With such an incredibly wide variety of people ranging from dissidents to government leaders involved in one way or another with international human rights, it is hardly surprising that there would be vastly different visions, personalities, motives, and methods. Some champions of human rights believe that all rights are completely inseparable and indivisible, while others focus exclusively on certain kinds of rights that are self-serving and suit their own ideology or interests. Some advocates move with humble quietness or calm self-assuredness outside of public attention, while others openly seek publicity and often proceed with vocal stridency and arrogant self-righteousness. Some proponents genuinely value the intrinsic worth of human rights for their own sake, while others give their support only if it serves a political purpose such as responding to unwelcomed pressure at home or embarrassing an adversary abroad. In addition, historical experience reveals an enormous capacity for human beings to see the speck in the eyes of others while ignoring the mote in their own.

These features about people help to explain why support for human rights sometimes appears so erratic, selective, inconsistent, confusing, self-serving, and hypocritically fraught with double standards. During the eighteenth century, for example, many of those who spoke so eloquently on behalf of the inalienable and natural rights of all individuals had no intention of including women, black slaves, indigenous peoples, or the unpropertied among those who should receive protection. Not all of those who campaigned in the nineteenth century for the abolition of the slave trade or for the protection of the persecuted supported rights for exploited workers or for those subjected to colonial domination. Woodrow Wilson could advocate the right of self-determination and the right to enjoy religious freedom, but simultaneously and firmly reject the principle of racial equality. During the height of the Cold War, it was not at all difficult to find politicians in the United States eager to publicly criticize the Soviet Union and its clients in Eastern Europe in the name of human rights while at the same time determinedly supporting authoritarian, anti-Communist regimes and opposing the civil rights movement in their own home states. It was not uncommon to hear Communist governments strongly supporting the right of self-determination for peoples in Western colonial empires, but fiercely resisting the extension of that same right for those under their own control. Similarly, it is not unusual to hear some countries today speak loudly on behalf of economic and social rights and the right to development while at the same time restricting civil and political rights and failing to accord equal rights to women. But despite these serious problems and inconsistencies, each in their own way has made some contribution to the evolution of human rights.

Events of Consequence

None of these many individual men and women, however, existed with their visions in a vacuum. They all lived in specific times, places, and cultures around the world influenced by the course of events. During certain periods and in particular areas, of course, change proceeded slowly and traditional patterns of behavior remained much as they had been for centuries before. In these circumstances, contributions on behalf of human rights found themselves largely confined to the realm of theory rather than practice. On other occasions, historical events of great consequence created not only a context but also the conditions for change. They drastically transformed existing structures, vested interests, habits of thought, and cultural values that allowed, encouraged, or actually forced changes that enhanced international human rights.

One of the most interesting — and perhaps tragically ironic — features of this whole evolution is the fact that the major efforts to promote dimensions of human rights have been coupled with enormous human traumas and catastrophes. The early bills and declarations of civil and political rights, for example, emerged only with the upheavals of the English Revolution, the American Revolution, and the French Revolution. The end of the slave trade came only when the horrendous brutality of the Middle Passage and the treatment of several million human beings as mere property became so gruesome that it could no longer be ignored. The abolition of slavery and serfdom resulted only after traumatic civil and foreign wars. The energies expended to advance economic and social rights first resulted from the extent of massive suffering on the part of men, women, and children exploited by the Industrial Revolution. Efforts to create the Red Cross and establish humanitarian law came in the wake of agonized suffering on battlefields. Moreover, the practice of humanitarian intervention emerged only when the level of persecution became so brutal and so extreme as to provoke international outrage.

This pattern proceeded with even greater force in the twentieth century. The innovative Minorities Treaties, extension of humanitarian law, the League of Nations, refugee assistance, and efforts to promote global health all came in the wake of the human tragedies resulting from the catastrophes of World War I, the Bolshevik Revolution, and massive epidemics. Serious discussions about international standards of human rights resulted from the extraordinary abuses perpetrated under totalitarian regimes, especially those of Stalin and Hitler. It was the experience of World War II and its crusade and the unimagined destruction of human life in the genocide of the Holocaust's "Final Solution" that exceeded all previously known bounds, however, that finally tipped the scales. After this, individuals, NGOs, and the governments of the international community refused to remain silent in the face of large-scale violations of human rights by creating the United Nations and adopting the Universal Declaration of Human Rights. With the subsequent destruction of colonial empires in Asia and Africa, the determination for international human rights grew even stronger, resulting in a whole series of efforts to set standards, establish binding covenants and conventions, create implementation mechanisms, and promote and enhance human rights around the world. More recently, the traumas of "ethnic cleansing" in the former Yugoslavia and the genocide in Rwanda have had much the same effect.

One of the reasons why these cause-and-effect relationships occur is that events such as revolutions and wars destroy existing structures of authority, privilege, and vested interests, thus making change possible. Violence and upheaval—whether they occur in Europe, North America, Latin America, Asia, Africa, the Middle East, or islands of the Pacific—result in a transformation of established institutions of control. And, whether they involve political, military, diplomatic, economic, social, or cultural dimensions, the consequence is a tearing away of power from those unwilling to share it voluntarily. Upheaval, of course, always contains the serious danger of leading to merely reshaped forms of abuse and control. But it also can open up new possibilities to make changes only previously imagined in dreams. Due to their duration and extent, the two world wars of the twentieth century certainly created revolutions in their own right, destroying monarchies, authoritarian and totalitarian regimes, social hierarchies, and empires, ultimately emancipating millions of men, women, and children around the world and launching a revolutionary movement on behalf of international human rights.

But events of consequence do much more than this, for they can change habits of thought as well. They often force people, as we have seen constantly throughout this book, out of the limitations of their established ways of thinking and previously accepted values into considering new possibilities of what might be and how people ought to treat each other. Sometimes they provide dramatic reminders that cultural values in any society can themselves be the result of the particular interests of those with power seeking to benefit from the way that culture is defined, and therefore not immutable. In this process, the visions themselves can be transformed. Perhaps this is what Secretary-

General Boutros-Ghali had in mind when he declared before the 1993 World Conference on Human Rights: "It is always when the world is undergoing a metamorphosis, when certainties are collapsing, when the lines are becoming blurred, that there is greatest recourse to fundamental reference points, that the quest for ethics becomes more urgent, that the will to achieve self-understanding becomes imperative."[13]

Upheavals compel those who lived through them to test their assumptions and seriously consider the legitimacy of existing authority, the purposes of government, the degree to which individuals should have certain basic human rights, and evolving visions of what those rights might entail. The revolutions of the seventeenth and eighteenth centuries, for example, raised questions about a first generation of human rights focused on civil and political rights. The socialist and Marxist revolutions of the nineteenth and first half of the twentieth centuries provoked discussions about a second generation of economic and social rights. World War II did much to radically transform the thinking of many women, racial minorities, and indigenous peoples from colonial empires who up to this point had been taught to think that they were somehow inferior. As Reverend Ndabaningi Sithole writes of the experience from Africa:

During the war the African came in contact with practically all the peoples of the earth. He met them on a life-and-death basis. He saw the so-called civilized and peaceful and orderly white people mercilessly butchering one another just as his so-called savage ancestors had done in tribal wars. He saw no difference between the primitive and the civilized man. In short, he saw through the European pretensions that only Africans were savages. This had a revolutionary psychological impact upon the African.[14]

The anticolonialist revolutions immediately following the war continued this evolving process by drawing attention to yet a third generation of human rights, concentrating on collective or "solidarity" rights such as those of self-determination and economic and social development.[15]

Traumas and catastrophes also affect patterns of thinking in still another, perhaps more powerful way. That is, they often dramatically and shockingly reveal just how inhumane people can be to others. Shackled human beings packed like cord wood onboard slave ships, soldiers and civilians writhing in pain, floods of helpless refugees fleeing for their lives from persecution, bodies and minds mutilated by torture, unearthed graves of victims of summary executions, and mounds of corpses piled high as a result of genocide seize attention. Whether witnessed personally with horrifying directness or viewed through pen-and-ink drawings, photographs, the printed word, or visual images now sent instantaneously around the world by modern technology, these staggering scenes force people to confront their thinking and their values. They demonstrate perhaps as nothing else can the consequences of apathy, of ignoring human rights abuses, or of allowing leaders to hide behind a shield of national sovereignty. Just as important, if not more so, they stir the individual and collective conscience to reconsider the meaning of justice, of responsibility to others, and of being truly human. Time and time again, those men and women either eagerly or reluctantly involved with the evolution of international human rights have spoken about this feature of events and its power to move what they variously have called "global moral opinion," "the conscience of the international community," or "the conscience of mankind."[16]

Process, Politics, and Perspective

The evolution of international human rights thus has been — and continues to be — one of considerable complexity, involving interaction among these elements of visions, people, and events in dynamic and often unanticipated ways. Visions possess considerable power, but they differ widely, and are constantly subject to modification, and what is seen clearly by some may remain completely invisible to others. Those women and men and involved with human rights play absolutely critical roles, but they vary greatly in their personalities, methods, and motives. At the same time, although revolutions, wars, and upheavals provide often necessary conditions for change, they remain highly volatile and unpredictable. For all these reasons, the process of evolution most certainly is neither orderly nor precise. It is instead composed of twists and turns, fits and starts, advances and setbacks, and progressive movement and diversions, all heavily influenced by domestic and international politics.

Political factors, as we have explored from the very beginning, help to explain a great deal about the determined and long-standing opposition to human rights. Most of those with vested interests, power, and special privilege at stake fiercely resist sharing what they have with others or acknowledging that all people possess certain basic rights simply by being human beings. At the global level, this tendency also applies to those states adamantly unwilling to surrender the claims of national sovereignty or cultural uniqueness by allowing the international community to pass judgment on their behavior or how they treat people under their control. This can be seen not only in the past, but in the abuses and double standards that persist today against women, racial or religious minorities, the dispossessed and unpropertied, certain ethnic groups, and political prisoners, among others. Some governments confine themselves to symbolic gestures and lip-service, refusing to ratify, and thus be bound by, the international covenants and conventions on human rights. Others have ratified the treaties, but in practice do not comply with their obligations or do so only selectively, claiming special circumstances make them exempt from the established norms.

Given these features, it certainly is not surprising to hear many advocates of human rights despair over the heavy influence of politics. They accuse governments of being interested only in "political motivations" that seek self-serving advantages or narrow interests instead of the intrinsic merits of human rights. They express their "disappointment and consternation" over the constant tendency of members of the United Nations to resort to weakened compromises of politics rather than determined stands of principle, to be seduced by arguments that "cultural relativism" should exempt certain governments from internationally established norms, or to selectively apply standards by criticizing comparatively small countries while allowing the big and powerful to escape serious scrutiny. They deplore the role of official representatives on the Commission on Human Rights as being no more than "stripped-pants dignitaries rather than people of substance," and criticize them for playing "a ping-pong game of diplomacy between nation-states" and creating no more than a "circus of hypocrisy and rhetoric." If only it were not for "politics," they argue, international human rights would be even further advanced than it is today.[17]

Considerable merit resides in some of these arguments, for political forces have often greatly hindered and obstructed the evolution of international human rights. But it is also the case that the advances that have been made in this evolution are the result of politics. Regardless of the motives, none of the many achievements discussed in this book would have taken place without the political forces and political will necessary to make them happen. The human rights provisions in the United Nations Charter, for example, would not be there if it had not been for the influence wielded by the small- to medium-sized states and the NGOs, and the people they represented, gathered together at the San Francisco Conference. The Universal Declaration of Human Rights would have never been negotiated and adopted without the political determination of the vast majority of member states to do so. It took a new majority of the states from Asia and Africa emerging from the decolonization revolution to finally break a protracted deadlock and create the array of international human rights covenants and conventions. Similarly, the treaty mechanisms, special procedures, and tribunals, as well as the several regional human rights bodies, in existence today are all the result of political decision.

Not all developments in this evolution of international human rights, it is important to observe, have been so deliberate or direct. Indeed, sometimes politics plays strange tricks on the unsuspecting and produces unanticipated consequences. Those who issued the Atlantic Charter and then the Declaration of the United Nations during the course of World War II, for example, did so primarily to generate support for the temporary military crusade against their enemies. It was certainly not their intention to permanently upset the international balance of power or to jeopardize their own empires. But the consequence of openly advocating certain human rights, such as that of self-determination, eventually and transformed dramatically the status of colonial possessions throughout the world. As one African nationalist writes,

During the war the Allied Powers taught the subject peoples (and millions of them!) that it was not right for Germany to dominate other nations. They taught the subjugated peoples to fight and die for freedom rather than live and be subjugated by Hitler. Here then is the paradox of history, that the Allied Powers . . . set in motion those powerful forces which are now liquidating, with equal effectiveness, European domination in Africa.[18]

At the same time, in drawing attention to the attitudes of racial superiority in Nazi Germany during the war, they did not intend to have their own words be used against them to overthrow their domestic policies of segregation or discrimination in postwar peace. But this was the result.

Similarly, at the time of the adoption of the Universal Declaration of Human Rights, many governments did everything they possibly could to make sure that the text was not construed by their own people or by others to mean any more than they originally intended. They made speeches in the General Assembly, held news conferences, and issued press releases to inform all who would listen that the proclaimed vision represented "only a declaration" and a "mere recommendation." They insisted that it was "simply" a general statement of principle and contained no legal obligations or binding commitments.[19] It thus came as a great surprise — and sometimes profound shock — to them when the Universal Declaration began almost immediately to take on an authority and normative character of its own, serving as a model for national constitutions, influencing court decisions, inspiring new international legal instruments, and arousing critics at home and abroad to challenge their very claims of national sovereignty and their own records on human rights.

This same pattern continued during the height of the Cold War when the Soviet Union joyously welcomed the surprise announcement that the United States would never sign any of the United Nations-sponsored covenants and conventions on human rights as a glorious gift. Such a decision allowed the Soviets suddenly to present themselves as the only superpower who defended the exploited and championed human rights. In their enthusiasm, they energetically supported the right of self-determination for colonial peoples, cooperated with others in the United Nations in drafting the treaties, and then gave enormous publicity to their efforts in opposing apartheid. They had no intention whatsoever of jeopardizing the nature of their own regime or their own iron-fisted control over their Eastern European satellites. But this followed as the unintended consequence, for by drawing so much ideological and political attention to their support for certain aspects of international human rights, they made these issues well known to their own public. Dissidents quickly invoked the principles of the Universal Declaration of Human Rights and the obligations of the International Covenant on Civil and Political Rights and the International Covenant on Economic, Social, and Cultural Rights against their own authorities. By giving such prominence to human rights for other purposes, therefore, Soviet authorities gave them respectability and thereby sowed seeds that eventually helped lead to the collapse both of the Soviet Union and its empire in Eastern Europe.[20]

Other governments have also found themselves surprised by politics and the consequences of their own rhetoric and actions in the area of human rights. China, to illustrate, eagerly threw itself into the struggle of decolonization and actually competed with the Soviet Union as to who could be the most prominent advocate for the right of self-determination in colonial territories. It enthusiastically endorsed arguments on behalf of the right to racial equality and the right to development, and ratified international conventions on the right to be protected against torture and rights for women and children. In the name of the Universal Declaration of Human Rights, it actively supported strong punitive measures against the "pariah regimes" of the white minority in South Africa for its policy of apartheid and of Israel for its suppression of the rights of the Palestinians in occupied territories. Yet, in taking these actions, the Chinese leaders unintentionally gave ammunition and legitimacy to their own human rights activists such as Fang Lizhi and international critics regarding the repression of the rights of Tibetans, the suppression of political expression at Tiananmen Square, and restraints on the right of citizens to fair trials, among other abuses.[21]

These political influences on the process of the evolution of international human rights should come as no surprise at this stage. As we have seen, they have always been there. The reason for this is that human rights raise some of the most profound of all issues of politics in the world. They challenge the authority of the state over its own people, attempt to impose defined limitations upon the arbitrary exercise of power, endeavor to eliminate special privileges, and seek to hold governments accountable to

certain norms of behavior. Political factors shape any formulation of rights, any obligation incurred, any procedure for implementation, and any practical means of enforcement. Thus, notes one observer with a lifetime of experience in this field, human rights
by definition can never be divorced from politics. Indeed, he writes, "In a sense,
nothing could be more political; and it would have been quite unreal had the great
international debate on human rights not reflected the deep differences which divide
nations and groups."[22]

All those who sought to advance the cause of human rights had to confront this fact of
politics, then decide how to deal with it. Some saw the obstacles and in fear or frustration
largely gave up, declaring the task to be "impractical," "naive," or "impossible," and
confining themselves to the margins of verbal complaint or silence. Others decided to
face the problems head-on with action, regardless of the consequences, and not only
refused to be intimidated but even to compromise in any way with what they regarded as
the "impure," "wickedness," and "evil" of politics. Still others determined that they
would proceed as they could by progressive steps, accepting politics as the art of the
possible in an imperfect world, making accommodation to the realities and constraints
of the time when necessary, and acknowledging that half a loaf might be considerably
better than no bread at all. They believed that desirable measures should not be post-
poned or rejected simply because someday there might be agreement on a perfect and
complete solution.[23] As concluded by one observer of this persuasion, the evolution of
human rights normally proceeds when taken one step at a time beginning with successes
"in *some* matters, to *some* extent, for *some* people, against *some* organ of the State."[24]

Indeed, this very process of progressive steps explains much about the entire evolution of international human rights itself. Challenges to the exercise of power, hierarchical patterns of behavior, prevailing cultural values, and the degree of governmental
authority over the lives of people came only as circumstances permitted. Interpretations over the legitimacy of "national sovereignty," the extent and mechanisms of
"international responsibility," and the intention of what was or was not "essentially
within the domestic jurisdiction of any state" emerged in different measure as time and
place allowed. The same can be said about the very definition of "human rights" which
has expanded through time to accommodate a variety of aspirations among people of
different cultural and philosophical traditions around the world in accordance with the
conditions, range of choice, and possibilities available. To fully appreciate this evolution, it is necessary to bring a sense of historical perspective to bear and to measure
them not against a perfectionist abstraction or simply the last few years, but rather
against the human condition over the last five centuries or more.

For nearly the entirety of human history, almost all of those who lived and died never
knew the meaning nor the enjoyment of human rights. During most times and in most
places of the world, they found themselves facing one kind of abuse or another. They
confronted various forms of discrimination and patterns of dominance based on gender, race, class or caste, religion, ethnicity, or some other form of difference that divided
people from one another. They encountered traditional societies, cultures, and despotic
regimes that emphasized hierarchical relationships, sharp divisions between the few
rulers and the many ruled, stratification between the powerful and the weak, and the

performance of obedience rather than the exercise of rights. Misogyny, racial prejudice, intolerance, segregation, torture, conquest, and human bondage in serfdom or slavery were the norm rather than the exception. Moreover, victims of these practices suffered under governments who confidently knew in advance that how they treated those under their control would be regarded as a matter exclusively within their own domestic jurisdiction and not at all subject to the scrutiny of distant states. Over the course of centuries, the practices, institutions, and laws of international affairs thus remained essentially silent on the subject of rights and precluded victims from ever having recourse to any assistance beyond their own borders. For all practical purposes, and throughout most of history, therefore, international human rights did not even exist.

Today, as a result of the extraordinary evolution discussed in this book, we live in a drastically different setting. Universal norms, or standards, have been set with the participation of all governments around the world representing different systems and cultures, and a sense of responsibility to others beyond one's own borders has grown enormously. A widespread belief exists that serious human rights violations in one country in one way or another do threaten the peace and security of others. For this reason, claims of exclusive national sovereignty, insofar as abuses against people are concerned, most certainly do not carry the conviction or the force they once did. In fact, during a recent international conference of government representatives meeting on the subject of war crimes, one spokesman even went so far as to declare: "There is no longer any such thing as 'domestic affairs' when it comes to human rights."[25] As a result of the technological revolution and a heightened determination among concerned men and women to investigate problems, serious abuses and gross violations of rights can no longer remain hidden for long and often appear in graphic detail on television screens. Moreover, a vast array of organizations, declarations, resolutions, judicial rulings, binding covenants and conventions, treaty-monitoring bodies, special procedures, technical assistance, NGOs, and thousands of experts and civil servants are now devoted to promoting and protecting international human rights. The availability of these collective norms and continuous means provide states, groups, and individuals innumerable opportunities to air complaints and file petitions, express aspirations, and seek practical protection for their rights or those of others. Never before in history have human rights been such a part of the political, legal, and moral landscape, or played such an important role in world affairs. Indeed, Nelson Mandela—who found himself transformed from a prisoner to president, hence dramatically able to see visions become a reality—recently declared that "human rights have become the focal point of international relations."[26]

When one considers all of the differences in the world and the formidable opposition faced all along the way, the magnitude of these remarkable achievements and the prominent role now played by human rights becomes all the more impressive. Phenomenal accomplishments have been realized, especially during the last fifty years, following the vision of the Universal Declaration of Human Rights. While recognizing how far the world has come, of course, it also is important to acknowledge how far it still has to go. Problems tenaciously persist, and not all issues of human rights are resolved and not all difficulties are solved. Abuses still occur, and at times there even appears to be retrogression.[27] There thus remains what has been called "the unfinished ethical agenda of our time" and "the unfinished revolution — the revolution of placing the human person squarely at the center of national and international values."[28] But in the tasks that lay ahead and in the vigilance and courage that will always be required to protect the rights of all men, women, and children wherever they might be, the perspective of history may offer considerable hope not only for the future, but also for the power of visions seen.

The Universal Declaration of Human Rights

Preamble

Whereas recognition of the inherent dignity and of the equal and inalienable rights of all members of the human family is the foundation of freedom, justice, and peace in the world,

Whereas disregard and contempt for human rights have resulted in barbarous acts which have outraged the conscience of mankind, and the advent of a world in which human beings shall enjoy freedom of speech and belief and freedom from fear and want has been proclaimed as the highest aspiration of the common people,

Whereas it is essential, if man is not to be compelled to have recourse, as a last resort, to rebellion against tyranny and oppression, that human rights should be protected by the rule of law,

Whereas it is essential to promote the development of friendly relations between nations,

Whereas the peoples of the United Nations have in the Charter reaffirmed their faith in fundamental human rights, in the dignity and worth of the human person and in the equal rights of men and women and have determined to promote social progress and better standards of life in larger freedom,

Whereas Member States have pledged themselves to achieve, in cooperation with the United Nations, the promotion of universal respect for and observance of human rights and fundamental freedoms,

Whereas a common understanding of these rights and freedoms is of the greatest importance for the full realization of this pledge,

Now, therefore, The General Assembly,

Proclaims this Universal Declaration of Human Rights as a common standard of achievement for all peoples and all nations, to the end that every individual and every organ of society, keeping this Declaration constantly in mind, shall strive by teaching and education to promote respect for these rights and freedoms and by progressive measures, national and international, to secure their universal and effective recognition and observance, both among the peoples of Member States themselves and among the peoples of the territories under their jurisdiction.

Article 1

All human beings are born free and equal in dignity and rights. They are endowed with reason and conscience and should act towards one another in a spirit of brotherhood.

Article 2

1. Everyone is entitled to all the rights and freedoms set forth in this Declaration, without distinction of any kind, such as race, color, sex, language, religion, political or other opinion, national or social origin, property, birth, or status.
2. Furthermore, no distinction shall be made on the basis of the political, jurisdictional, or international status of the country or territory to which a person belongs, whether it be independent, trust, non-self-governing, or under any other limitation of sovereignty.

Article 3

Everyone has the right to life, liberty, and security of person.

Article 4

No one shall be held in slavery or servitude; slavery and the slave trade shall be prohibited in all their forms.

Article 5

No one shall be subjected to torture or to cruel, inhuman, or degrading treatment or punishment.

Article 6

Everyone has the right to recognition everywhere as a person before the law.

Article 7

All are equal before the law and are entitled without any discrimination to equal protection of the law. All are entitled to equal protection against any discrimination in violation of this Declaration and against any incitement to such discrimination.

Article 8

Everyone has the right to an effective remedy by the competent national tribunals for acts violating the fundamental rights granted him by the constitution or by law.

Article 9

No one shall be subjected to arbitrary arrest, detention, or exile.

Article 10

Everyone is entitled in full equality to a fair and public hearing by an independent and impartial tribunal, in the determination of his rights and obligations and of any criminal charge against him.

Article 11

1. Everyone charged with a penal offense has the right to be presumed innocent until proven guilty according to law in a public trial at which he has had all the guarantees necessary for his defense.
2. No one shall be held guilty of any penal offense on account of any act or omission which did not constitute a penal offense, under national or international law, at the time when it was committed. Nor shall a heavier penalty be imposed than the one that was applicable at the time the penal offense was committed.

Article 12

No one shall be subjected to arbitrary interference with his privacy, family, home, or correspondence, nor to attacks upon his honor and reputation. Everyone has the right to the protection of the law against such interference or attacks.

Article 13

1. Everyone has the right to freedom of movement and residence within the borders of each state.
2. Everyone has the right to leave any country, including his own, and to return to his country.

Article 14

1. Everyone has the right to seek and to enjoy in other countries asylum from persecution.
2. This right may not be invoked in the case of prosecutions genuinely arising from non-political crimes or from acts contrary to the purposes and principles of the United Nations.

Article 15

1. Everyone has the right to a nationality.
2. No one shall be arbitrarily deprived of his nationality nor denied the right to change his nationality.

Article 16

1. Men and women of full age, without any limitation due to race, nationality, or religion, have the right to marry and to found a family. They are entitled to equal rights as to marriage, during marriage, and at its dissolution.
2. Marriage shall be entered into only with the free and full consent of the intending spouses.
3. The family is the natural and fundamental group unit of society and is entitled to protection by society and the State.

Article 17

1. Everyone has the right to own property alone as well as in association with others.
2. No one shall be arbitrarily deprived of his property.

Article 18

Everyone has the right to freedom of thought, conscience, and religion; this right includes freedom to change his religion or belief, and freedom, either alone or in community with others and in public or private, to manifest his religion or belief in teaching, practice, worship, and observance.

Article 19

Everyone has the right to freedom of opinion and expression; this right includes freedom to hold opinions without interference and to seek, receive, and impart information and ideas through any media and regardless of frontiers.

Article 20

1. Everyone has the right to freedom of peaceful assembly and association.
2. No one may be compelled to belong to an association.

Article 21

1. Everyone has the right to take part in the government of his country, directly or through freely chosen representatives.
2. Everyone has the right of equal access to public service in his country.
3. The will of the people shall be the basis of the authority of government; this will shall be expressed in periodic and genuine elections which shall be by universal and equal suffrage and shall be held by secret vote or by equivalent voting procedures.

Article 22

Everyone, as a member of society, has the right to social security and is entitled to realization, through national effort and international cooperation and in accordance with the organization and resources of each State, of the economic, social, and cultural rights indispensable for his dignity and the free development of his personality.

Article 23

1. Everyone has the right to work, to free choice of employment, to just and favorable conditions of work and to protection against unemployment.
2. Everyone, without any discrimination, has the right to equal pay for equal work.
3. Everyone who works has the right to just and favorable remuneration ensuring for himself and his family an existence worthy of human dignity, and supplemented, if necessary, by other means of social protection.
4. Everyone has the right to form and to join trade unions for the protection of his interests.

Article 24

Everyone has the right to rest and leisure, including reasonable limitation of working hours and periodic holidays with pay.

Article 25

1. Everyone has the right to a standard of living adequate for the health and well-being of himself and of his family, including food, clothing, housing, and medical care and

necessary social services, and the right to security in the event of unemployment, sickness, disability, widowhood, old age, or other lack of livelihood in circumstances beyond his control.

2. Motherhood and childhood are entitled to special care and assistance. All children, whether born in or out of wedlock, shall enjoy the same social protection.

Article 26

1. Everyone has the right to education. Education shall be free, at least in the elementary and fundamental stages. Elementary education shall be compulsory. Technical and professional education shall be made generally available and higher education shall be equally accessible to all on the basis of merit.

2. Education shall be directed to the full development of the human personality and to the strengthening of respect for human rights and fundamental freedoms. It shall promote understanding, tolerance and friendship among all nations, racial or religious groups, and shall further the activities of the United Nations for the maintenance of peace.

3. Parents have a prior right to choose the kind of education that shall be given to their children.

Article 27

1. Everyone has the right to freely participate in the cultural life of the community, to enjoy the arts, and to share in scientific advancement and its benefits.

2. Everyone has the right to protection of the moral and material interests resulting from any scientific, literary, or artistic production of which he is the author.

Article 28

Everyone is entitled to a social and international order in which the rights and freedoms set forth in this Declaration can be fully realized.

Article 29

1. Everyone has duties to the community in which alone the free and full development of his personality is possible.

2. In the exercise of his rights and freedoms, everyone shall be subject only to such limitations as are determined by law solely for the purpose of securing due recognition and respect for the rights and freedoms of others and of meeting the just requirements of morality, public order, and the general welfare in a democratic society.

3. These rights and freedoms may in no case be exercised contrary to the purposes and principles of the United Nations.

Article 30

Nothing in this Declaration may be interpreted as implying for any State, group, or person any right to engage in any activity or to perform any act aimed at the destruction of any of the rights and freedoms set forth herein.

Notes

Introduction

1. Universal Declaration of Human Rights, preamble.
2. Jan Mårtenson, in Asbjørn Eide (ed.), *The Universal Declaration of Human Rights: A Commentary* (Oslo: Scandinavian University Press, 1992), p. 27.

Chapter 1: My Brother's and Sister's Keeper

1. Veda, as cited in S. S. Subramuniyaswami, *Dancing with Śiva: Hinduism's Contemporary Catechism* (Concord, Calif.: Himalayan Academy, 1993), p. 195. Also see Kana Mitra, "Human Rights in Hinduism," in Arlene Swidler (ed.), *Human Rights in Religious Traditions* (New York: Pilgrim Press, 1982), pp. 77–84.
2. Genesis, 4:9.
3. See Louis Henkin, "Judaism and Human Rights," *Judaism* (Fall 1976): 435–446.
4. Isaiah, 58:6–7.
5. Martin Buber, as cited in N. N. Glatzer (ed.), *The Way of Response: Martin Buber* (New York: Schocken, 1966), p. 86.
6. Buddha, as cited in "Disappearance of Buddhism," *Observer of Business and Politics*, 8 August 1993.
7. Dalai Lama, *Ocean of Wisdom: Guidelines for Living* (Santa Fe: Clear Light, 1989), p. 13. Also see L. P. N. Perera, *Buddhism and Human Rights* (Columbo: Karunaratne, 1991).
8. Confucius, as cited in H. G. Creel, *Confucius: The Man and the Myth* (New York: Day, 1949), p. 150. His chapters entitled "The Philosopher" and "The Reformer" are still regarded as classics. See also Tu Weiming, *Way, Learning, and Politics: Essays on the Confucian Intellectual* (Albany: State Universities of New York Press, 1993); and William McNaughton (ed.), *The Confucian Vision* (Ann Arbor: University of Michigan Press, 1974).
9. *The Analects*, XV, 23.
10. *Great Learning*, as cited in Huston Smith, *The Religions of Man* (New York: Harper & Row, 1958), p. 181.
11. Luke, 10:29–37.
12. Galatians, 3:28.
13. Smith, *The Religions of Man*, p. 249. Also see the thoughtful and detailed book by Ann Elizabeth Mayer, *Islam and Human Rights: Tradition and Politics* (San Francisco and Boulder: Westview/HarperCollins, 1995); Riffat Hassan, "On Human Rights and the Qur'anic Perspective," in Swidler (ed.), *Human Rights in Religious Traditions*, pp. 51–65; and Mahmood Monshipouri, "Islamic Thinking and the Internationalization of Human Rights," *The Muslim World* (July–October 1994): 217–239.

14. This expression is used in Stanley Hoffmann, *Duties Beyond Borders: On the Limits and Possibilities of Ethical International Politics* (Syracuse: Syracuse University Press, 1981).

15. Mahatma Gandhi, as cited in UNESCO, *The Birthright of Man* (Paris: UNESCO, 1969), p. 24.

16. Mo Zi, as cited in H. Maspero, *La Chine antique* (Paris: Presses Universitaires de France, 1927), pp. 253–254. I am grateful to the late Tu Baixiong for insightful conversations on this subject.

17. Mencius, as cited in "Evolution of Human Rights," *Weekly Bulletin of the United Nations*, 12 August 1946.

18. Hsün-tzu, as cited in UNESCO, *Birthright of Man*, p. 303.

19. Hammurabi, as cited in J. M. Roberts, *History of the World* (New York: Knopf, 1976), p. 48.

20. Precepts for Merikare, third millenary B.C., as cited in ibid., p. 301.

21. Cited in P. Modinos, "La Charte de la Liberté de l'Europe," *Revue des Droits de l'Homme*, 8 (1975): 677.

22. Āpastamba-Dharmasūtra II, 450–350 B.C., as cited in UNESCO, *The Birthright of Man*, p. 94.

23. Asvaghosa, as cited in ibid., p. 268.

24. Pampa, as cited in ibid., p. 508.

25. "Spirit of Sacrifice Ennobles Man," *Hindu Times*, 22 January 1977.

26. As cited in Christian Daubie, "Cyrus le Grand: Un Precurseur dans le Domain des Droits de l'Homme," *Revue des Droits de l'Homme*, 5 (1972): 304.

27. See Sultanhussein Tabandeh, *A Muslim Commentary on the Universal Declaration of Human Rights* (London: Goulding, 1970), p. 5. For an earlier period, see Mohammed Arkoun, *L'humanisme Arabe au iv/v siècle* (Paris: Vrin, 1970).

28. See Asmarom Legesse, "Human Rights in African Political Culture," in Kenneth Thompson (ed.), *The Moral Imperatives of Human Rights* (Washington, D.C.: University Press of America, 1980), pp. 123–138.

29. Akan proverb, as cited in UNESCO, *Birthright of Man*, p. 43.

30. Burundi proverb, as cited in ibid., p. 269.

31. Djerma-Songhai proverb, as cited in ibid., p. 189.

32. A. H. Robertson and J. G. Merrills, *Human Rights in the World* (Manchester: Manchester University Press, 1992 ed.), p. 9.

33. Alan Rosenbaum (ed.), *The Philosophy of Human Rights: International Perspectives* (Westport, Conn.: Greenwood, 1980), pp. 9–10.

34. Sophocles, *Antigone*, lines 453–457.

35. Marcus Tullius Cicero, *De Legibus*, Book 1, 5–16, Loeb Classical Library (New York: Putnam, 1928 ed.), pp. 317–345.

36. Marcus Tullius Cicero, *De Re Publica*, Book 3, 22, Loeb Classical Library (New York: Putnam, 1928 ed.), p. 211.

37. See the concise discussion in Burns H. Weston, "Human Rights," in Richard Pierre Claude and Burns H. Weston (eds.), *Human Rights in the World Community* (Philadelphia: University of Pennsylvania Press, 1992 ed.), p. 15.

38. Magna Carta, translated by W. Stubbs, *Select Charters* (Oxford: Clarendon Press, 1921), pp. 294ff.

39. See "Evolution of Human Rights," *United Nations Weekly Bulletin* (12 August 1946), p. 12.

40. Jan Hus, 1415, as cited in H. Gordon Skilling, *Charter 77 and Human Rights in Czechoslovakia* (London: George Allen & Unwin, 1981), epigraph.

41. Erasmus of Rotterdam, as cited in Mark Kishlansky et al., *Civilization in the West* (New York: HarperCollins, 1995 ed.), p. 392.

42. I am grateful to J. Herman Burgers for this citation from the 1581 Dutch Act of Abjuration.

43. See A. S. P. Woodhouse (ed.), *Puritanism and Liberty* (London: Dent & Sons, 1938), p. 444; and G. E. Aylmer, *The Struggle for the Constitution* (London: Blandford, 1975 ed.), pp. 132–136.

44. Bill of Rights, in Walter Laqueur and Barry Rubin (eds.), *The Human Rights Reader* (New

York: Meridian, 1989 ed.), pp. 104–106. Also see Bernard Schwartz, *The Roots of Freedom* (New York: Hill & Wang, 1967).

45. Carl Cohen (ed.), *Communism, Fascism, and Democracy: The Theoretical Foundations* (New York: Random House, 1962), p. 436.

46. John Locke, *Two Treatises of Government* (New York: Hafner Library of Classics, 1947 ed.), pp. 124, 128, 163.

47. Jean-Jacques Rousseau, *Contrat social, ou Principes du droit politique* (Paris: Garnier, 1900 ed.), p. 236.

48. Immanuel Kant, *Grundegung zur Metaphysik der Sitten* (Riga: Hartknoch, 1785).

49. Francis Hutcheson, *System of Moral Philosophy*, as cited in Gary Wills, *Inventing America* (New York: Vintage, 1979), p. 216.

50. As cited in Stanley Chodorow et al., *The Mainstream of Civilization* (Fort Worth: Harcourt Brace, 1994 ed.), p. 547.

51. Denis Diderot and Jean Le Rond d'Alembert (eds.), *L'Encyclopédie*, as cited in Lynn Hunt, *The French Revolution and Human Rights* (Boston: Bedford Books, 1996), p. 37.

52. Maurice Cranston, as cited in Weston, "Human Rights," p. 16.

53. Abigail Adams to John Adams, 31 March 1776, as cited in Diane Ravitch and Abigail Thernstrom (eds.), *The Democracy Reader* (New York: HarperCollins, 1992), p. 104.

54. Thomas Jefferson, *Summary View of the Rights of British America* (1774), as cited in J. P. Foley (ed.) *The Jefferson Cyclopedia*, 2 vols. (New York: Russell and Russell, 1967 ed.), 2: 609.

55. "The Virginia Bill of Rights, 1776," in *The Federal and State Constitutions, Constitutions, Colonial Charters, and Other Organic Laws*, 2 vols., B. Poore (comp.) (reprint, New York: Franklin, 1972), 2:1908–1909.

56. Declaration of Independence, 4 July 1776, in John Garraty, *The American Nation*, 2 vols. (New York: HarperCollins, 1991 ed.), 2:A-1. See also the discussion in Wills, *Inventing America*.

57. See James MacGregor Burns and Stewart Burns, *The Pursuit of Rights in America* (New York: Vintage, 1993), p. 41.

58. Thomas Jefferson to James Madison, 20 December 1787, in P. L. Ford (ed.), *The Writings of Thomas Jefferson*, 10 vols. (New York: Putman, 1892–1899), 4: 477.

59. Duke Mathieu de Montmorency, 1 August 1789, as cited in Hunt, *The French Revolution and Human Rights*, pp. 73–74.

60. Henri Chantavoine, *Les principes de 1789; la Déclaration des droits, la Déclaration des devoirs* (Paris: Société français d'imprimerie et de librairie, 1906). See also M. B. Mirkine-Guetzevitch, "Quelques Problèmes de la mise en Œuvre de la Déclaration Universelle des Droits de l'Homme," *Recueil des Cours de l'Académie de Droit International* (1953): 274–275.

61. Lord Acton, as cited in Robertson and Merrills, *Human Rights in the World*, p. 4.

62. Frede Castberg, "Natural Law and Human Rights," in Asbjørn Eide and August Schou (eds.), *International Protection of Human Rights* (Stockholm: Almquist & Wiksell, 1968), p. 19. See also Dale Van Kley (ed.), *The French Idea of Freedom: The Old Regime and the Declaration of Rights of 1789* (Stanford: Stanford University Press, 1994).

63. On this important point of the "demonstration effect," see Richard P. Claude, "The Classical Model of Human Rights Development," in Richard P. Claude (ed.), *Comparative Human Rights* (Baltimore: Johns Hopkins University Press, 1976), p. 23.

64. Déclaration des Droits de la Femme et de la Citoyenne, 1791, in Olympe de Gouges, *Œuvres* (Paris: Mercure de France, 1986 ed.), pp. 99–112. Olympe de Gouges served as the pen name of Marie Gouze.

65. Condorcet, as cited in Kishlansky et al., *Civilization in the West*, pp. 625–626.

66. See Irving Brant, *The Bill of Rights: Its Origin and Meaning* (New York: New American Library, 1967).

67. Thomas Paine, *The Rights of Man* (New York: Heritage Press, 1961 ed.), p. 18. The original reads "human right" in the singular, but the context is plural.

68. Ibid., p. 39.

308 Notes to pages 20–29

69. Ibid., p. 114.

70. This account is taken from Burns and Burns, *The Pursuit of Rights in America*, p. 71.

71. Edmund Burke, *Reflections on the Revolution in France* (Chicago: Regnery, 1955 ed.), pp. 64, 87, 90, 96, and 201.

72. Burke, *Reflections on the Revolution in France*, pp. 313 and 341; and Edmund Burke, as cited in Weston, "Human Rights," p. 16.

73. Jeremy Bentham, as cited in Weston, "Human Rights," p. 16.

74. Thomas Hobbes, *Leviathan* (1651) (reprint, New York: Washington Square Press, 1964), pp. 84–85.

75. Ibid, pp. 120–128.

76. Sir Robert Filmer, *Patriarcha: Or the Natural Power of Kings* (London: W. Davis, 1680).

77. Jacques Bénigne Bossuet, "Politics Drawn from the Very Words of Scripture," in James Harvey Robinson (ed.), *Readings in European History* (Boston: Ginn, 1906), 2: 275–276.

78. Jacob Sprenger, *Malleus Maleficarum*, as cited in Eva Figes, *Patriarchal Attitudes* (London: Faber & Faber, 1970), pp. 62–63.

79. See Kenneth Lockridge, *On the Sources of Patriarchal Rage* (New York: New York University Press, 1992); Felicity Nussbaum, *The Brink of All We Hate* (Lexington: University Press of Kentucky, 1984); and Carole Pateman, *The Sexual Contract* (Stanford: Stanford University Press, 1988).

80. See Donna Guy, " 'White Slavery,' Citizenship, and Nationality in Argentina," in Andrew Parker et al. (eds.), *Nationalisms and Sexualities* (New York: Routledge, 1992), p. 203.

81. Jean Baptiste Amar, 30 October 1793, in France, *Archives parlementaires*, 78 (Paris: Imprimerie nationale, 1911), p. 50. See also Harriet Applewhite and Darline Levy (eds.), *Women and Politics in the Age of the Democratic Revolution* (Ann Arbor: University of Michigan Press, 1990).

82. For more discussion, see Paul Gordon Lauren, *Power and Prejudice* (Boulder and San Francisco: Westview/HarperCollins, 1996 ed.), chapter 1.

83. André Thevet, *Cosmographie universelle* (Paris: Huilier, 1575), p. 67; and Alexandre Valignamo, as cited in C. R. Boxer, *The Portuguese Seaborne Empire* (New York: Knopf, 1969), p. 252.

84. Johann Friedrich Blumenbach, *On the Natural Varieties of Mankind* (1775) (reprint, New York: Bergman, 1969), pp. 209, 264, and 269.

85. Burke, *Reflections on the Revolution in France*, pp. 115 and 344.

86. See the excellent treatment of the subject in Burns and Burns, *The Pursuit of Rights in America*, pp. 79–92; and Thomas Horne, *Property Rights and Poverty* (Chapel Hill: University of North Carolina Press, 1990).

87. Locke, *Two Treatises of Government*, p. 184.

88. Jean-Jacques Rousseau, *A Discourse on Political Economy*, in *The Social Contract and Discourses* (New York: Dutton, 1950 ed.), p. 311.

89. See the discussion of property rights in Noel Coulson, "The State and the Individual in Islamic Law," *International and Comparative Law Quarterly*, 6 (1957): 49–60.

90. Jean Bodin, *Les Six Livres de la République* (1576), 6 vols. (Paris: Fayard, 1986 ed.), 1: 179–228 and 295–310.

91. See Derek McKay and H. M. Scott, *The Rise of the Great Powers, 1648–1815* (London: Longmans, 1983); and Leo Gross, "The Peace of Westphalia," *American Journal of International Law*, 42 (January 1948): 28–29.

92. Hobbes, *Leviathan*, chapter 18, pp. 120–128.

93. Hans Morgenthau, *Politics Among Nations: The Struggle for Power and Peace* (New York: Knopf, 1978 ed.), p. 315. See also René Brunet, *La Garantie internationale des Droits de l'homme* (Geneva: Grasset, 1947), pp. 29ff.

94. See L. Oppenheim, *International Law: A Treatise* (London: Longmans, 1912 ed.), 1: 362; and Thomas Buergenthal, *International Human Rights in a Nutshell* (St. Paul: West, 1988), pp. 2–3.

95. Confucius, as cited in Kumari Jayawardena, *Feminism and Nationalism in the Third World* (London: Zed Press, 1986), p. 167.

96. Bartholomé de Las Casas, *In Defense of the Indians*, trans. and ed. by S. Poole (DeKalb:

Northern Illinois University Press, 1974), p. 362. See also "Las Casas protecteur des Indiens, défenseur des droits de l'homme," *Revue historique*, 589 (January–March 1994): 51ff.

97. J. H. Parry, *The Spanish Seaborne Empire* (New York: Knopf, 1966), p. 150.

98. See David Brion Davis, *The Problem of Slavery in Western Culture* (Ithaca: Cornell University Press, 1966), pp. 62–128; David Brion Davis, *Slavery and Human Progress* (New York: Oxford University Press, 1984); James Watson (ed.), *Asian and African Systems of Slavery* (Berkeley: University of California Press, 1980); and Orlando Patterson, *Slavery and Social Death* (Cambridge, Mass.: Harvard University Press, 1982).

99. "Board of Trade to the Governors of the English Colonies," 17 April 1708, in E. Donnan (ed.), *Documents Illustrative of the History of the Slave Trade to America*, 4 vols. (Washington, D.C.: Carnegie Institution, 1930–35), 2:45.

100. Davis, *Slavery and Human Progress*, pp. xvii and 51.

101. For more discussion, see Lauren, *Power and Prejudice*, chapter 1; Davis, *The Problem of Slavery*, p. 453; and Winthrop Jordan, *White Over Black* (Chapel Hill: University of North Carolina Press, 1968), p. 80.

102. *Colección de documentos para la formación social de Hispanoamérica, 1493–1810*, as cited in Magnus Morner, *Race Mixture in the History of Latin America* (Boston: Little, Brown, 1967), p. 47.

103. Harley Ross Hammond, "Race, Social Mobility, and Politics in Brazil," *Race*, 4 (1963): 4.

104. "The Fundamental Constitutions of 1669," in Poore, *The Federal and State Constitutions, Constitutions, Colonial Charters, and Other Organic Laws*, 2:1408.

105. Jean-Jacques Rousseau, *Émile* (Paris: Editions Garnier Frères, 1964 ed.), especially livre 5, pp. 445–614.

106. Baron de Montesquieu, *De l'Esprit des lois*, livre 12, chap. 2, in *Œuvres complètes*, 3 vols. (Paris: Hachette, 1908 ed.), 2:15.

107. Voltaire, as cited in William Cohen, *The French Encounter with Africans* (Bloomington: University of Indiana Press, 1980), pp. 88, 133, and 137. Also see Davis, *Slavery and Human Progress*, pp. 107–08.

108. David Hume, "Of National Characters," in *The Philosophical Works*, 4 vols., T. Green and T. Grose (eds.) (London: Longmans, Green, 1882–1886), 3:252n.

109. See the discussion in Jan Lewis, " 'Of Every Age, Sex, and Condition': The Representation of Women in the Constitution," *Journal of the Early American Republic*, 15 (Fall 1995): 368; and Burns and Burns, *The Pursuit of Rights in America*, pp. 60–61.

110. Citations in Ronald Wright, *Stolen Continents* (Boston: Houghton Mifflin, 1992), pp. 116, 126, and 139; Richard Drinnon, *Facing West* (New York: Schocken, 1990 ed.), 98; and David Stannard, *American Holocaust* (New York: Oxford University Press, 1992), p. 120.

111. Marcel Garaud, *La Révolution et l'égalité civile* (Paris: Sirey, 1953).

112. See Richard Schifter, "Human Rights Day, 1989," U.S. Department of State, *Current Policy*, No. 1242 (1989): 2.

113. Abigail Adams to John Adams, 31 March 1776, as cited in Ravitch and Thernstrom (eds.), *The Democracy Reader*, p. 104.

114. Mary Wollstonecraft, *A Vindication of the Rights of Woman* (New York: Norton, 1988 ed.).

115. E. P. Thompson, *The Making of the English Working Class* (New York: Pantheon, 1964), p. 163.

116. Patrick Henry to Robert Pleasants, 18 January 1773, as cited in *OAH Magazine of History* (Spring 1995), p. 40.

117. Petition of New Hampshire Slaves, 12 November 1779, as cited in ibid., p. 39.

118. Anthony Benezet, as cited in George Mellor, *British Imperial Trusteeship, 1783–1850* (London: Faber & Faber, 1951), p. 32.

119. London Revolution Society to the Society of Friends of the Constitution, 2 September 1792, as cited in ibid., p. 22.

120. See Schwartz, *The Roots of Freedom*, pp. 210–211, on the 1772 Somerset decision; and

Arthur Zilversmit, *The First Emancipation: The Abolition of Slavery in the North* (Chicago: University of Chicago Press, 1967).

121. Roger Burns (ed.), *Am I Not a Man and a Brother: The Antislavery Crusade of Revolutionary America, 1688–1788* (New York: Chelsea House, 1983); and Davis, *Slavery and Human Progress*, pp. 107–153, are particularly good in understanding the religious motivation.

122. James Beattie, *Elements of Moral Science*, 2 vols. (Edinburgh: Creech, 1793), 2:164.

123. Madame de Gasparin, as cited in Pierre Boissier, *From Solferino to Tsushima* (Geneva: Henry Dunant Institute, 1985), p. 344.

124. R. H. Tawney, *The Agrarian Problem in the Sixteenth Century* (New York: Longmans Green, 1912), p. 44.

Chapter 2: To Protect Humanity and Defend Justice

1. See W. E. Gladstone, *Bulgarian Horrors and the Question of the East* (London: Murray, 1876), p. 57; and Gustave Moynier and Louis Appia, *La Guerre et la Charité: Traité théorique et pratique de philanthropie appliquée* (Geneva: Cherbuliez, 1867), passim.

2. For much more discussion, see Paul Gordon Lauren, *Power and Prejudice* (Boulder and San Francisco: Westview/HarperCollins, 1996 ed.), pp. 14ff.

3. Thomas Branagan, in 1805, as cited in Dwight Lowell Dumond, *Antislavery* (New York: Norton, 1966), p. 81.

4. Thomas Jefferson, 2 December 1806, in James D. Richardson (ed.), *A Compilation of the Messages and Papers of the Presidents*, 10 vols. (Washington, D.C.: Government Printing Office, 1896–1899), 1: 408.

5. Britain, Parliament, *Substance of the Debates on a Resolution for Abolishing the Slave Trade* (London: Phillips and Fardon, 1806), especially pp. 99–101, 146, 149, 168, and 202–210.

6. Act to Prohibit the Importation of Slaves, 2 March 1807, in United States, Congress, *Annals of Congress*, 9th Congress, 2nd Session (Washington, D.C.: Gales and Seaton, 1852), pp. 1266–1270; and Act for the Prohibition of the Slave Trade, 25 March 1807, in Elizabeth Donnan (ed.), *Documents Illustrative of the History of the Slave Trade*, 4 vols. (Washington, D.C.: Carnegie Institution, 1930–1935), 2: 659–669. Denmark had set the first example by prohibiting its own nationals from participating in the trade in 1802.

7. Samuel Taylor Coleridge, as cited in Ellen Gibson Wilson, *Thomas Clarkson* (New York: St. Martin's, 1990), p. 1.

8. See the discussion in Betty Fladeland, "Abolitionist Pressures on the Concert of Europe, 1814–1822," *Journal of Modern History*, 38 (December 1966): 355–360.

9. Lord Castlereagh, as cited in F. J. Klingberg, *The Anti-Slavery Movement in England* (New Haven: Yale University Press, 1926), p. 144.

10. "Déclaration des 8 cours, relative à l'abolition universelle de la traité des nègres," 8 February 1815, in Great Britain, Foreign Office, *British and Foreign State Papers, 1815–1816*, 3: 971–972.

11. Great Britain, Public Record Office, Foreign Office (hereafter cited as Britain, PRO/FO) 92/30, "Traité défintif entre Grande Bretagne et la France," 20 November 1815.

12. "Treaty of Peace and Amity," 18 February 1815, in United States, Department of State, *Treaties and Other International Agreements of the United States*, C. Bevans (comp.), 12 vols. (Washington, D.C.: Government Printing Office, 1974), 12:47.

13. Fladeland, "Abolitionist Pressures," p. 366.

14. See Betty Fladeland, *Men and Brothers: Anglo-American Antislavery Cooperation* (Urbana: University of Illinois Press, 1972), passim; and the various publications of the British and Foreign Anti-Slavery Society, beginning in 1840.

15. See Suzanne Miers, *Britain and the Ending of the Slave Trade* (New York: Africana, 1975), pp. 3–166; A. H. Robertson and J. G. Merrills, *Human Rights in the World* (Manchester: Manchester University Press, 1992 ed.), p. 14; and, for an economic interpretation, Eric Williams, *Capitalism and Slavery* (New York: Capricorn Books, 1966).

16. William Lloyd Garrison, as cited in Gary Nash et al., *The American People* (New York: Harper-Collins, 1990 ed.), p. 435.

17. James G. Birney, in his acceptance speech for the presidency of the party, as cited in Dwight Lowell Dumond, *Antislavery: The Crusade for Freedom in America* (New York: Norton, 1961), p. 301.

18. See James MacGregor Burns and Stewart Burns, *The Pursuit of Rights in America* (New York: Vintage, 1993), p. 109.

19. Winthrop Jordan et al., *The United States* (Englewood Cliffs, N.J.: Prentice-Hall, 1987 ed.), p. 327.

20. See ibid., p. 328; Nash, *The American People*, p. 485; and Fladeland, *Men and Brothers*, pp. 350–355.

21. Salvador de Madariaga, *The Fall of the Spanish American Empire* (New York: Collier, 1963 ed.), p. 340.

22. Wendell Phillips, as cited in James B. Stewart, *Holy Warriors* (New York: Hill & Wang, 1976), p. 3.

23. General Act of the Conference of Berlin, 26 February 1885, in Edward Hertslet (ed.), *The Map of Africa by Treaty*, 3 vols. (London: Harrison & Sons, 1909), 2: 468ff.

24. General Act of the Brussels Conference, 2 July 1890, in ibid., 2: 488ff.

25. See Miers, *Britain and the Ending of the Slave Trade*, pp. 236–319; and Davis, *Slavery and Human Progress*, pp. 302–07.

26. For more discussion on this point, see Lauren, *Power and Prejudice*, pp. 32ff.

27. George King, as cited in Leon Litwack, *Been in the Storm Too Long* (New York: Knopf, 1979), p. 224.

28. As cited in Burns and Burns, *The Pursuit of Rights in America*, p. 127.

29. For more discussion, see Lauren, *Power and Prejudice*, pp. 41–48.

30. Mark 16:15.

31. For a fascinating survey of the many missionary societies formed during this time and the thousands of missions they established, see Harlan Beach and Burton St. John (eds.), *World Statistics of Christian Missions* (New York: Foreign Missions Conference of North America, 1916).

32. As cited in William T. Hagen, *The Indian Rights Association* (Tucson: University of Arizona Press, 1985), p. 19.

33. The terms of reference for the Aborigines' Committee, as cited in George Mellor, *British Imperial Trusteeship, 1783–1850* (London: Faber & Faber, 1951), p. 249.

34. Decision of the Court in *Ex Parte Milligan*, 1866, in John Wallace (ed.), *Cases Argued and Adjudged in the Supreme Court of the United States* (New York: Banks, 1910), 4: 119.

35. Decision in *United States ex rel. Standing Bear v. Crook*, 1879, Case No. 14,891, in United States, Federal Circuit and District Courts, *Federal Cases: Circuit and District Courts, 1789–1880* (St. Paul: West, 1896), 25:695–701.

36. Chief Joseph, speech of January 1879 delivered in Washington, D.C., as reprinted in *North American Review* (April 1879): 412–433.

37. General Act of the Conference of Berlin, 26 February 1885, in Edward Hertslet (ed.), *The Map of Africa by Treaty*, 2: 468ff. Also see Charles Pelham Groves, "Missionary and Humanitarian Aspects of Imperialism," in L. H. Gann and Peter Duignan (eds.), *Colonialism in Africa*, 5 vols. (Cambridge: Cambridge University Press, 1969), 1:462–96.

38. General Act of the Brussels Conference, 2 July 1890, in ibid., 2:488 ff.

39. See Jan Lewis, " 'Of Every Age, Sex, and Condition': The Representation of Women in the Constitution," *Journal of the Early Republic*, 15 (Fall 1995): 359–387.

40. Abby Kelley Foster, as cited in Jordan et al., *The United States*, p. 267. Also see Blanche Hersh, *The Slavery of Sex: Feminist-Abolitionists in Nineteenth-Century America* (Urbana: University of Illinois Press, 1978).

41. See Dwight Lowell Dumond, *Antislavery: The Crusade for Freedom in America* (New York: Norton, 1966), p. 278.

42. Sarah Grimké, *Letters on the Equality of the Sexes and the Condition of Woman* (Boston: Knapp, 1838).

43. E. P. Hurlbut, *Essays on Human Rights* (New York: Greeley & McElrath, 1845).

44. "Declaration of Sentiments and Resolutions," Seneca Falls Convention of 1948, in Elizabeth Cady Stanton, Susan B. Anthony, and Matilda Joslyn Gage (eds.), *History of Woman Suffrage*, 2 vols. (New York: Mann, 1881), 1:70–71.

45. See John Stuart Mill, *On Liberty* (London: Parker & Son, 1859); John Stuart Mill, *The Subjection of Women* (London: Longmans, 1869); Mehrdad Kia, "Mizra Fath Ali Akhundzade and the Call for Modernization of the Islamic World," *Middle Eastern Studies*, 31 (July 1995): 422–448; Ono Kazuko, *Chinese Women in a Century of Revolution, 1850–1950*, Joshua Fogel (ed.), (Stanford: Stanford University Press, 1989 ed.), pp. 34–37; and Mioko Fujieda, "Japan's First Phase of Feminism," in Kumiko Fujimura-Fanselow and Atsuko Kameda (eds.), *Japanese Women* (New York: Feminist Press, 1995), pp. 324–326.

46. Rosa Guerra, as cited in Anthony Esler, *The Western World* (Upper Saddle River, N.J.: Prentice-Hall, 1997 ed.), p. 540.

47. Eleanor Flexner, *Century of Struggle: The Woman's Rights Movement in the United States* (Cambridge, Mass.: Belknap, 1975 ed.), p. 153.

48. Elizabeth Cady Stanton, as cited in Elisabeth Griffith, *In Her Own Right* (New York: Oxford University Press, 1984), p. 193.

49. See W. E. Mosse, *Alexander II and the Modernization of Russia* (New York: Collier, 1962 ed.), p. 41; and Jerome Blum, *Lord and Peasant in Russia* (New York: Atheneum, 1967), pp. 568 and 616.

50. N. E. Wrangel, *The Memoirs of Baron N. Wrangel* (Philadelphia: Lippincott, 1927), p. 40.

51. Nicholas Riasanovsky, *A History of Russia* (New York: Oxford University Press, 1993), pp. 372–373.

52. Alexander II, Decree of Emancipation, 3 March 1861, as cited in Raymond Stearns (ed.), *Pageant of Europe* (New York: Harcourt, Brace & World, 1961 ed.), p. 664.

53. See W. G. Beasley, *The Modern History of Japan* (Tokyo: Tuttle, 1982 ed.), pp. 120ff.

54. See Mehrdad Kia, "Constitutionalism, Economic Modernization and Islam in the Writings of Mirz Yusef Khan Mostashar od-Dowle," *Middle Eastern Studies*, 30 (October 1994): 751–777.

55. Stanley Chodorow et al., *The Mainstream of Civilization* (Fort Worth: Harcourt, 1994 ed.), p. 628.

56. As cited in Hunt et al., *The Challenge of the West*, p. 754.

57. See the stimulating discussion in Burns and Burns, *The Pursuit of Rights*, pp. 75–76; and George Rudé, *Ideology and Popular Protest* (New York: Pantheon, 1980).

58. William Cobbett, as cited in E. P. Thompson, *The Making of the English Working Class* (New York: Pantheon, 1964), p. 761.

59. John Stuart Mill, *Principles of Political Economy with Some of Their Applications to Social Philosophy* (reprint, New York: Kelley, 1961), p. 366.

60. See especially Moynier and Appia, *La Guerre et la Charité*, pp. vi and 370.

61. See Gwilym Beckerlegge, "Human Rights in the Ramakrishna Math and Mission: 'For Liberation and the Good of the World,'" *Religion* (April 1990): 119–137.

62. Kishlansky et al., *Civilization in the West*, p. 689.

63. Karl Marx, as cited in Louis Henkin, *The Rights of Man Today* (Boulder: Westview, 1978), p. 160 n. 74.

64. Karl Marx and Friedrich Engels, *Manifesto of the Communist Party* (New York: Socialist Labor Party, 1888 ed.), p. 28.

65. "Inaugural Address of the International Working Men's Association," 1864, as cited in Saul Padover (ed.), *Karl Marx Library*, 7 vols. (New York: McGraw-Hill, 1972–1977), 3:5–12.

66. Pope Leo XIII, *Rerum Novarum* (New York: Paulist Press, 1939), passim.

67. Some notable exceptions began to occur with the Treaty and Conventions of Frankfurt in 1743, Louis XV after the Battle of Fontenoy in 1745, and the English General Amherst after the Battle of Montreal in 1762 wherein equal medical treatment was given to all wounded. For more discussion about early practices, see Pierre Boissier, *Histoire du Comité International de la Croix-Rouge*

de Solférino à Tsoushima (Paris: Plon, 1963), Part 2; and Geoffrey Best, *Humanity in Warfare* (London: Weidenfeld & Nicolson, 1980).

68. Sun Tzu, *The Art of War*, S. Griffith (trans.), (London: Oxford University Press, 1963), p. 76.

69. The International Conference of Red Cross Societies, as cited in Cecil Woodham-Smith, *Florence Nightingale, 1820–1910* (London: Constable, 1950), p. 592. Also see her own publications, including *Notes on Matters Affecting the Health, Efficiency, and Hospital Administration of the British Army* (London: Harrison & Sons, 1858).

70. J. Henry Dunant, *Un Souvenir de Solférino*, first published in 1862, in translation as *A Memory of Solferino* (Washington, D.C.: American National Red Cross, 1939 ed.), pp. 20, 33, 35, 36, and 51.

71. Ibid., pp. 47 (my emphasis), 54, and 73.

72. Ibid., p. 93.

73. The official invitation, as cited in Area 4 of the Musée international de la Croix-Rouge et du Croissant-Rouge.

74. C. J. Hambro, 10 December 1963, Nobel Peace Prize Ceremony, as found in Hoover Institution Archives, Red Cross International Committee, Box 3. The original name of the organization was the Comité International de Secours aux Blessés Militaires.

75. John Hutchinson, *Champions of Charity: War and the Rise of the Red Cross* (Boulder and Oxford: Westview, 1996), is particularly insightful in discussing the religious motivations of these founders.

76. See "Amelioration of the Condition of the Wounded on the Field of Battle (Red Cross Convention)," 22 August 1864, Treaty Series 377, in United States, Department of State, *Treaties and Other International Agreements of the United States of America* (Washington, D.C.: Government Printing Office, 1968), 1:7–11.

77. See David Forsythe, *Humanitarian Politics: The International Committee of the Red Cross* (Baltimore: Johns Hopkins University Press, 1977), p. 7.

78. Société ottomane de secours aux blessés et malades militaires, *Annuaire, 1877–1878* (Constantinople: La Turquie, 1878).

79. The words are those of "100 Years of the Red Cross," *Daily Telegraph*, 29 December 1962. For detailed discussions of the early efforts of the Red Cross, see Boissier, *Histoire du Comité International*, passim; and Hutchinson, *Champions of Charity*, passim.

80. See David Forsythe, *The Internationalization of Human Rights* (Lexington: Lexington Books, 1991), p. 146; and Henri Coursier, "L'Evolution du Droit International Humanitaire," *Recueil des Cours de l'Académie de Droit International*, 99 (1960):361–465.

81. "Convention with Respect to the Laws and Customs of War on Land," Hague II, 29 July 1899, which secured twenty-four signatures, in United States, Department of State, *Treaties and Other International Agreements*, 1:247–262. Also see Waldemar Solf, "Protection of Civilians Against the Effects of Hostilities," *American University Journal of International Law and Policy*, 1 (1986): 117–135.

82. "Convention for the Adaption to Maritime Warfare of the Principles of the Geneva Convention," Hague III, 29 July 1899, in ibid., pp. 263–269.

83. The theme of the Red Cross societies being used by states for their own aggressive nationalism and militarism is developed with particular force in Hutchinson, *Champions of Charity*, passim.

84. For more discussion on the convergence of humanitarian and human rights law, see Coursier, "L'Evolution du droit international humanitaire," pp. 369ff.; and David Weissbrodt, "The Role of International Organizations in the Implementation of Human Rights and Humanitarian Law in Situations of Armed Conflict," *Vanderbilt Journal of Transnational Law*, 21 (1988): 313–365.

85. Alberico Gentili, as cited in Theodore Meron, "Common Rights of Mankind in Gentili, Grotius, and Suárez," *American Journal of International Law*, 85 (1991):114.

86. Hugo Grotius, as cited in Jean-Pierre Fonteyne, "The Customary International Law Doctrine of Humanitarian Intervention," *California Western International Law Journal*, 4 (1974): 203–258.

314 Notes to pages 63-66

87. Emerich de Vattel, *Le Droit des Gens, ou Principes de la Loi Naturelle* (reprint, Washington, D.C.: Carnegie, 1916), livre 2, chapitre 4, p. 298; originally published in 1758.

88. The protection of aliens under international law recognized that a nation could demand respect for the rights of its own nationals when living in another country. See Richard Lillich, "The Current Status of the Law of Injury to Aliens," in Richard Lillich (ed.), *International Law of State Responsibility for Injury to Aliens* (Charlottesville: University Press of Virginia, 1983); and Louis Sohn and Thomas Buergenthal, *International Protection of Human Rights* (Indianapolis: Bobbs-Merrill, 1973), pp. 6–7.

89. For more discussion on the nature of coercive diplomacy, see Alexander George and William Simons (eds.), *The Limits of Coercive Diplomacy* (Boulder: Westview Press, 1994 ed.); and Paul Gordon Lauren, "Theories of Bargaining with Threats of Force," in Lauren (ed.), *Diplomacy: New Approaches in History, Theory, and Policy* (New York: Macmillan, 1979), pp. 183–211.

90. For earlier examples, see provisions in the Treaty of Westphalia (1648) that there should be an equality of rights for Roman Catholics and Protestants, or in the Treaty of Utrecht (1713) that French Protestants should be released from imprisonment if held solely on the basis of religious belief.

91. Act of the Acceptance of Sovereignty of the Belgic Provinces, annexed to the Treaty Between Great Britain, Austria, Prussia, Russia, and the Netherlands, 31 May 1815, in Edward Hertslet (ed.), *Map of Europe by Treaty*, 4 vols. (London: Butterworths, 1875–1891), 1:38.

92. The Vienna Congress Treaty, 9 June 1815, in ibid., p. 255.

93. Federative Constitution of Germany, annexed to the Vienna Congress Treaty, 9 June 1815, in ibid., p. 205.

94. See the discussion in H. A. R. Gibb and Harold Bowen, *Islamic Society and the West* (London: Oxford University Press, 1957), pp. 207ff.

95. As early as 1649, for example, Louis XIV unilaterally issued the Proclamation of French Protection of the Maronite Community in Lebanon. By the Treaty of Kutchuk-Kainardji of 1774 the Russians claimed themselves to be the protectors of Christian minorities living under the jurisdiction of the Ottoman Empire.

96. *Hatti-i Sherif*, 3 November 1839, in Robert Landen, *The Emergence of the Modern Middle East* (New York: Van Nostrand Reinhold, 1970), pp. 38–42.

97. *Islahat Fermani*, as cited in Walter Laqueur and Barry Rubin (eds.), *The Human Rights Reader* (New York: Meridian, 1989 ed.), pp. 132–136.

98. Peace of Paris, 30 March 1856, Article IX, in Hertslet, *The Map of Europe by Treaty*, 2:1255. Similar pressure was exerted on the Ottoman Empire from 1866 to 1868 in order to protect the persecuted Christian population of Crete.

99. London Treaty Between Great Britain, France, and Russia for the Pacification of Greece, 6 July 1827, in Hertslet, *The Map of Europe by Treaty*, 1:769–772. This intervention eventually resulted in the independence of Greece in 1830.

100. Earl Cowley to Lord John Russell, British Secretary of State for External Affairs, 5 July 1860, in Great Britain, Parliament, House of Commons, Command Paper No. 2800, *Correspondence Relating to the Affairs of Syria* (London: Her Majesty's Stationery Office, 1861), p. 1.

101. M. Thouvenel to Count de Persigny, Paris, 16 July 1860, in ibid., pp. 3–6.

102. See Manouchehr Ganji, *International Protection of Human Rights* (Geneva: Droz, 1962), p. 25.

103. Lord John Russell to Earl Cowley, Foreign Office, 28 July 1860, in Great Britain, Parliament, Command Paper No. 2800, *Correspondence Relating to the Affairs of Syria*, p. 24.

104. As cited in Lord Kinross, *The Ottoman Centuries* (New York: Morrow, 1977), p. 509.

105. See "The War," in *Illustrated London News*, 19 August 1876.

106. William Ewart Gladstone, *Bulgarian Horrors and the Question of the East* (London: Murray, 1876), pp. 13, 19–20, and 53.

107. Ibid., pp. 17, 20, 43, and passim. Also see "Das Recht der Europaischen Intervention in der Turkei," *Die Gegenwart*, 9 December 1876.

108. William Ewart Gladstone, *Lessons of the Massacre* (London: Murray, 1877), pp. 77–79.

109. Gladstone, *Bulgarian Horrors*, p. 43.

110. Gladstone, *Lessons of the Massacre*, p. 80.

111. Treaty Between Great Britain, Austria-Hungary, France, Germany, Italy, Russia, and Turkey for the Settlement of the Affairs of the East, 13 July 1878, in Hertslet, *The Map of Europe by Treaty*, 4:2759–2769 and 2796.

112. International Convention of Constantinople, 24 May 1881, in Great Britain, Foreign Office, *British and Foreign State Papers, 1880–1881* (London: Ridgway, 1885), 72:382–387.

113. Abdul Hamid, as cited in Kinross, *The Ottoman Centuries*, p. 555.

114. Adam Wandruszka and P. Urbanitsch (eds.), *Die Habsburger-monarchie, 1848–1918* (Vienna: Verlag der Osterreichischen Akademie der Wissenschaft, 1973–1993); Alan Sked, *The Decline and Fall of the Hapsburg Empire, 1815–1914* (London: Longman, 1989), pp. 209ff.; Robert Burns, *Pobedonostsev: His Life and Times* (Bloomington: Indiana University Press, 1968), pp. 109ff.; and Matthew Jacobson, *Special Sorrows* (Cambridge: Harvard University Press, 1995), passim. Other cases involve the humanitarian interventions in Crete during 1866 and 1894.

115. Instructions from Secretary of State Frederick Frelinghuysen, 15 April 1882, as cited in Ellert C. Stowell, *Intervention in International Law* (Washington, D.C.: Byrne, 1921), p. 75.

116. See the various contemporary contributions of Arntz and Rolin-Jaequemyns, in *Revue de Droit International et de Législation Comparée*, 8 (1876); M. Pillet, "Le droit international public," *Revue Générale de Droit International Public*, 1 (1894); Antoine Rougier, "La Théorie de l'intervention d'humanité," *Revue Générale de Droit International Public*, 17 (1910): 468–526; Ganji, *International Protection of Human Rights*, pp. 9–44; Jean-Pierre Fonteyne, "The Customary International Law Doctrine of Humanitarian Intervention," pp. 203–258; Richard B. Lillich, *International Human Rights: Problems of Law, Policy, and Practice* (Boston: Little, Brown, 1991 ed.), pp. 576–582; and W. G. Grewe, *Epochen der Völkerrechtsgeschichte* (Baden-Baden: Nomos, 1988).

117. Russian intervention into the Ottoman Empire was always suspicious, as were claims by the United States from 1895 to 1898 that its interests in Cuba were designed only to defend the laws of humanity and to protect people from persecution from the malevolent Spanish. See M. Le Fur, "Chronique sur la guerre hispano-américaine," *Revue Générale de Droit International Public*, 5 (1898): 665ff.; and Michael Walzer, *Just and Unjust Wars* (New York: Basic Books, 1992 ed.), pp. 101–104, exploring the issue of mixed motives.

118. See the discussion in Peter Malanczuk, *Humanitarian Intervention and the Legitimacy of the Use of Force* (Amsterdam: Het Spinhuis, 1993), pp. 8–11.

119. Marquis of Salisbury (Berlin) to Her Majesty's Principal Secretary of State (London), 13 July 1878, as cited in René Albrecht-Carrié, *The Concert of Europe, 1815–1914* (New York: Harper & Row, 1968), pp. 279–280.

120. C. Musurus to Lord John Russell (London), 30 July 1860, in Great Britain, Parliament, Command Paper No. 2800, *Correspondence Relating to the Affairs of Syria*, p. 36.

121. For more discussion, see Lauren, *Power and Prejudice*, pp. 32–70.

Chapter 3: Entering the Twentieth Century

1. Henry Adams, *The Education of Henry Adams: An Autobiography* (Boston: Houghton Mifflin, 1918), pp. 489–498.

2. See Paul Morand, *1900* (Paris: Éditions de France, 1931), pp. 71–130; and Barbara Tuchman, *The Proud Tower* (New York: Macmillan, 1966), pp. 269–270.

3. See Paul Gordon Lauren, *Diplomats and Bureaucrats* (Stanford: Hoover Institution Press, 1976), pp. 34–68; and Maurice Paléologue, *Un grand tournant de la politique mondiale, 1904–1906* (Paris: Plon, 1934).

4. Lord Vansittart, *The Mist Procession* (London: Hutchinson, 1958), p. 40.

5. France, Archives diplomatiques du Ministère des Affaires étrangères (hereafter cited as

France, MAE), collection of *Annuaire diplomatique et consulaire*, and Comptabilité, Décrets et décisions ministérielles, Carton 50, No. 237, "Note pour le Ministre," 10 May 1906; and Germany, Politisches Archiv des Auswärtiges Amt, Politisches Archiv und Historisches Referat (hereafter cited as Germany, PA/AA), budgets for 1903, 1904, and 1905 "für kartographische Arbeiten."

6. Gabriel Hanotaux, "L'Europe qui naît," *La revue hebdomadaire* 48 (30 November 1907): 561–570.

7. F. S. L. Lyons, *Internationalism in Europe* (Leyden: Sythoff, 1963), p. 14.

8. Henri Sée, *Histoire de la Ligue des Droits de l'Homme, 1898–1926* (Paris: Ligue des Droits de l'Homme, 1927), p. 11. The *Bulletin officiel* was first published in January 1901, although the organization itself formed three years earlier by Ludovic Trarieux in response to the Dreyfus Affair.

9. Ibid., p. 81; and the various issues of *Bulletin officiel* from 1901 to 1914.

10. Mehrdad Kia, "Nationalism, Modernism, and Islam in the Writings of Talibov-i Tabrizi," *Middle Eastern Studies*, 30 (April 1994): 201–223.

11. Larry Burgess, *The Lake Mohonk Conference of Friends of the Indian: Guide to the Annual Reports* (New York: Clearwater, 1975), pp. 6–8.

12. Peter Woo, "A Metaphysical Approach to Human Rights from a Chinese Point of View," in Alan S. Rosenbaum (ed.), *The Philosophy of Human Rights: International Perspectives* (Westport: Greenwood, 1980), pp. 117–118.

13. See the insightful discussion in Ono Kazuko, *Chinese Women in a Century of Revolution* (Stanford: Stanford University Press, 1989), pp. 40–42 and 212.

14. See the general discussion in Peter J. Coleman, *Progressivism and the World of Reform* (Lawrence: University Press of Kansas, 1987).

15. Among many examples, see Great Britain, Parliament, House of Commons, Command Paper 3933, *Papers Relating to the Geneva Convention, 1906* (London: His Majesty's Stationery Office, 1908); and "Convention Respecting the Laws and Customs of War on Land," Hague IV, 18 October 1907, and "Convention for the Adaption to Maritime Warfare of the Principles of the Geneva Convention," Hague X, 18 October 1907, in United States, Department of State, *Treaties and Other International Agreements* (Washington: Government Printing Office, 1968), 1:631–653 and 694–710.

16. As cited in Antoine Rougier, "La Théorie de l'intervention d'humanité," *Revue Générale de Droit International Public*, 17 (1910): 477.

17. Manouchehr Ganji, *International Protection of Human Rights* (Geneva: Droz, 1962), pp. 33–40.

18. Theodore Roosevelt, 6 December 1904, in James D. Richardson (ed.), *A Compilation of the Messages and Papers of the Presidents*, 20 vols. (New York: Bureau of National Literature, 1897–1916), 16:6924. Also see David Weissbrodt, "Human Rights Legislation and United States Foreign Policy," *Georgia Journal of International and Comparative Law*, 7 (1977): 232–233.

19. See Paul Gordon Lauren, *Power and Prejudice* (Boulder and San Francisco: Westview/HarperCollins, 1996 ed.), pp. 50ff.

20. W.E.B. Du Bois, as cited in United Nations, Centre Against Apartheid, *International Tribute to W.E.B. Du Bois* (New York: United Nations, 1982 ed.), p. 48.

21. W.E.B. Du Bois, in P. S. Foner (ed.), *W.E.B. Du Bois Speaks: Speeches and Addresses, 1890–1919* (New York: Pathfinder Press, 1970), pp. 170–171.

22. Arthur Vandenberg, as cited in Louis Fischer, *Gandhi: His Life and Message for the World* (New York: Mentor, 1982), p. 8.

23. J. A. Hobson, as cited in L. H. Gann and Peter Duignan, *Burden of Empire* (New York: Praeger, 1967), p. 40.

24. See E. D. Morel, *The British Case in French Congo: The Story of a Great Injustice* (London: Heinemann, 1903); and Henry Nevinson, *A Modern Slavery* (reprint, New York: Schocken, 1968), originally published in 1906.

25. Alfred Zimmern, *The Third British Empire* (London: Oxford University Press, 1926), p. 82. Also see René Pinon, *La Lutte pour le Pacifique* (Paris: Perrin, 1906), p. 165.

26. Jean Jaurès, 28 June 1912, in France, Assemblée nationale, Chambre des Députés, *Débats parlementaires* (Paris: Imprimerie des Journaux officiels, 1912), p. 923.

27. Frances Balfour, as cited in Tuchman, *The Proud Tower*, p. 354.

28. Winthrop D. Jordan et al., *The United States* (Englewood Cliffs, N.J.: Prentice-Hall, 1987 ed.), p. 563.

29. See Jacqueline Van Voris, *Carrie Chapman Catt: A Public Life* (New York: Feminist Press, 1996). The original name of this NGO when first created in 1902 was the International Alliance of Women for Suffrage and Equal Citizenship.

30. Jiu Jin, as cited in Elizabeth Croll, *Feminism and Socialism in China* (New York: Schocken, 1980), pp. 68–69.

31. Suga Kanno, as cited in Sharon Sievers, *Flowers in Salt: The Beginnings of Feminist Consciousness in Modern Japan* (Stanford: Stanford University Press, 1983), p. 149.

32. See Tarrosa Subido, *The Feminist Movement in the Philippines, 1905–1955* (Manila: National Federation of Women's Clubs, 1955), p. 18.

33. See Kumari Jayawardena, *Feminism and Nationalism in the Third World* (London: Zed, 1986), passim.

34. See Donna Guy, " 'White Slavery,' Citizenship, and Nationality in Argentina," in Andrew Parker et al. (eds.), *Nationalisms and Sexualities* (New York: Routledge, 1992): 206–208.

35. The 25 August 1912 platform of the Guomindang, as cited in Kazuko, *Chinese Women in a Century of Revolution*, p. 88.

36. Franz Conrad von Hötzendorff, *Aus Meiner Dienstzeit, 1906–1918*, 5 vols. (Vienna: Rikola Verlag, 1921–1925), 4:194.

37. Hanson Baldwin, *World War I* (New York: Harper & Row, 1962), p. 159.

38. A. J. P. Taylor, *The History of World War I* (London: Octopus, 1974), p. 279.

39. As cited in André Durand, *From Sarajevo to Hiroshima: History of the International Committee of the Red Cross* (Geneva: Henry Dunant Institute, 1984), p. 32.

40. See ibid.; displays of the Musée international de la Croix-Rouge et du Croissant-Rouge; John Hutchinson, *Champions of Charity* (Boulder: Westview, 1996), pp. 282–283; and David Forsythe, *Humanitarian Politics* (Baltimore: Johns Hopkins University Press, 1977), p. 20.

41. As cited in Gordon Wright, *France in Modern Times* (Chicago: Rand McNally, 1966), pp. 403–404.

42. W.E.B. Du Bois, "Close Ranks," from *Crisis*, July 1918, as cited in W.E.B. Du Bois, *Dusk of Dawn* (New York: Harcourt Brace, 1940), p. 254.

43. As cited in John Hope Franklin, *From Slavery to Freedom* (New York: Knopf, 1974), pp. 343–344.

44. Kelly Miller, *An Appeal to Conscience* (reprint, Miami: Mnemosyne, 1969), first published in 1918; and Kelly Miller, *The World War for Human Rights* (reprint, New York: Negro Universities Press, 1969), first published in 1919.

45. Mohamed Duse, "Today: India and Africa," *African Times and Orient Review*, March 1917, p. 46.

46. This discussion is based upon the insightful comments in Gordon A. Craig, *Europe Since 1815* (New York: Holt, Rinehart & Winston, 1971 ed.), p. 474.

47. Anthony Livesey, *The Historical Atlas of World War I* (New York: Holt, 1994), p. 182.

48. Hoover Institution Archives, Commission for Relief in Belgium, Box 1, cablegram from Herbert Hoover (Washington) to Cravath (London), 3 July 1918.

49. Based upon the archival evidence in Hoover Institution Archives, Commission for Relief in Belgium, Boxes 1–11. Also see Commission for Relief in Belgium, *Annual Report, 1914–1916* (London: Crowther & Goodman, 1916).

50. Herbert Hoover, as cited in Joan Hoff Wilson, *Herbert Hoover, Forgotten Progressive* (Boston: Little, Brown, 1975), p. 7.

51. As cited in Richard Hovannisian, "Etiology and Sequelae of the Armenian Genocide," in George Andreopoulos (ed.), *Genocide: Conceptual and Historical Dimensions* (Philadelphia: University of Pennsylvania Press, 1994), p. 125.

52. United Nations, ECOSOC, Commission on Human Rights, Sub-Commission on Prevention and Discrimination and Protection of Minorities, Doc. E/CN.4/sub.2/1985/SR.36, "Summary Record of the 36th Meeting, of the 38th Session," 29 August 1985. Also see Robert Melson, *Revolution and Genocide* (Chicago: University of Chicago Press, 1992).

53. As cited in Comités arméniens, *Aspirations et agissements révolutionaires des comités arméniens* (Constantinople: Comités arméniens, 1917), pp. 317–318.

54. As cited in Arthur Marwick, *Women at War, 1914–1918* (London: Fontana, 1977), epigraph.

55. Gary Nash et al., *The American People* (New York: HarperCollins, 1990 ed.), p. 772.

56. Marwick, *Women at War*, p. 152.

57. E. S. Montague, as cited in ibid., p. 156.

58. Ziya Gokalp, as cited in Jayawardena, *Feminism and Nationalism in the Third World*, p. 32.

59. Sedition Act of 1918, in United States, *Statutes at Large*, 40, pt. 1 (Washington, D.C.: Government Printing Office, 1919), p. 553–554.

60. See the discussions in Craig, *Europe Since 1815*, pp. 474–480; Sée, *Histoire de la Ligue des Droits de l'Homme*, pp. 143–163; and Burns and Burns, *The Pursuit of Rights in America*, pp. 204–213.

61. Cited in Hunt et al., *The Challenge of the West*, p. 904.

62. Shigenobu Okuma, as cited in United States, Congress, *Congressional Record, 1916*, 53, pt. 1 (Washington, D.C.: Government Printing Office, 1916), pp. 754–755.

63. See Albert Verdoodt, *Naissance et signification de la Déclaration universelle des Droits de l'homme* (Louvain-Paris: Éditions Nauwelaerts, 1964), p. 41.

64. Woodrow Wilson, as cited in Norman Graebner, "Human Rights and Foreign Policy," in Kenneth Thompson (ed.), *The Moral Imperatives of Human Rights* (Lanham, Md.: University Press of America, 1980), p. 40.

65. Woodrow Wilson, 11 February 1918, as cited in Arthur Link (ed.), *The Papers of Woodrow Wilson*, 69 vols. (Princeton: Princeton University Press, 1984), 46:321.

66. V. I. Lenin, *Collected Works* (New York: International Publishers, 1929–1945), 18:367.

67. Arno Mayer, *Wilson vs. Lenin* (New York: World, 1964), p. 299.

68. Declaration of Rights of the Toiling and Exploited People, January 1918, as cited in E. H. Carr, "The Rights of Man," *United Nations Weekly Bulletin*, 21 October 1946.

69. E. J. Dillon, *The Inside Story of the Peace Conference* (New York: Harper & Brothers, 1920), p. 5.

70. Harold Nicolson, *Peacemaking 1919* (New York: Grosset & Dunlop, 1965), pp. 31–32.

71. Guiseppe Mazzini, as cited in Craig, *Europe Since 1815*, pp. 488–489.

72. W.E.B. Du Bois, "Opinion," *Crisis*, 18 (May 1919): 7.

73. Dillon, *The Inside Story*, p. 6.

74. See Library of Congress, Manuscripts Division, Robert Lansing Papers, diary entries for 20 December and 30 December 1918.

75. See, for example, France, Archives diplomatique du Ministère des Affaires étrangères, Nouvelle série, Correspondance politique et commerciale, Congrès de la Paix, Carton 1001, Dossier 2, "Représentation des nationalités."

76. General Sir Henry Wilson, as cited in Arno Mayer, *The Politics and Diplomacy of Peacemaking* (New York: Knopf, 1967), p. 311.

77. See Columbia University, Rare Book and Manuscript Library, Wellington Koo Papers, Box 1, File 3, Memorandum of Meeting with Woodrow Wilson and Wellington Koo, 26 November 1918; and Hoover Institution Archives, Commission for Relief in Belgium, Box 1, Address of Woodrow Wilson, 12 November 1918.

78. These included the Treaty of Versailles with Germany, Treaty of St. Germain-en-Laye with Austria, Treaty of Neuilly with Bulgaria, Treaty of Trianon with Hungary, and the Treaty of Sèvres with Turkey.

79. Woodrow Wilson, as cited in League of Nations, *Protection of Linguistic, Racial, or Religious Minorities*, I.B. Minorities, 1931 I.B.1 (C.8.M.5.1931.I), p. 159.

80. See "Note Sur le Congrès de la Paix," November 1918, in David Hunter Miller, *Diary*, 21 vols. (New York: privately printed, 1924), 2:11–13; and Jacques Duparc, *La Protection des minorités de race, de langue et de religion* (Paris: Dalloz, 1922), pp. 141–171.

81. Document No. 822, "Proposals for Protection of Minorities," 20 April 1919, in Miller, *Diary*, 8:422–423.

82. Texts of these treaties are to be found in Société des Nations/League of Nations, Document C.L.110. 1927. I, Annex, *Protection of Linguistic, Racial, and Religious Minorities* (Geneva: Société des Nations, 1927). See, for example, the Treaty Between the Allied and Associated Powers and Poland Concerning Protection of Minorities, Chapter I, Articles 2 and 12.

83. Herbert Hoover, as cited in Hoover Institution Archives, Commission for Relief in Belgium, Box 11, letter from Woodrow Wilson to Secretary of War Newton Baker, 9 January 1919.

84. See United States, Department of State, *Foreign Relations of the United States* (hereafter cited as *FRUS*): *The Paris Peace Conference, 1919*, 13 vols. (Washington, D.C.: Government Printing Office, 1942–1947), 2:627–725; and 10: passim. The name was subsequently changed to the Food Section on the Supreme Economic Council.

85. See Hoover Institution Archives, Commission for Relief in Belgium, Box 11, joint letter from Woodrow Wilson, David Lloyd George, Georges Clemenceau, and Vittoria Orlando to Fridjof Nansen, 9 April 1919; and Box 12, Memorandum on the Economic Situation of Europe, from Herbert Hoover, 3 July 1919.

86. See, for example, France, Archives Nationales, 94-AP, Fonds Albert Thomas, Cartons 357, 358, and 406.

87. See the comments of Samuel Gompers and James Duncan in United States, Department of State, *FRUS: Paris Peace Conference, 1919*, 11:6 and 71. Also see 1:149, 178, 409–412, 461, and 539–542; and Ernst Haas, *Beyond the Nation State* (Stanford: Stanford University Press, 1964), pp. 140ff.

88. The countries included Belgium, Britain, Cuba, Czechoslovakia, France, Italy, Japan, Poland, and the United States. On the actual deliberations, see James T. Shotwell (ed.), *The Origins of the International Labor Organization*, 2 vols. (New York: Columbia University Press, 1934); and Léon-Eli Troclet, *Législation sociale internationale*, 3 vols. (Brussels: Librairie Encyclopédique, 1952).

89. Treaty of Versailles, Articles 387–427, in United States, Department of State, *FRUS: Paris Peace Conference, 1919*, 13:692–719; the provisions of which are repeated in the other treaties of peace.

90. W.E.B. Du Bois, *Crisis*, 17 (January 1919): 130–131. Also see Lauren, *Power and Prejudice*, pp. 83–85; and Immanuel Geiss, *Panafrikanismus: Zür Geschichte der Dekolonisation* (Frankfurt am Main: Europäische Verlagsanstalt, 1968), pp. 180ff.

91. Jane Addams, *Peace and Bread in Time of War* (New York: Macmillan, 1922), pp. 152–153.

92. Woodrow Wilson, 8 January 1918, in United States, Congress, *Congressional Record*, 1918, pt. 1, p. 681.

93. As cited in Jordan et al., *The United States*, p. 586.

94. Covenant of the League of Nations, Articles 23 and 25, in United States, Department of State, *FRUS: Paris Peace Conference, 1919*, 13:104–105.

95. Document No. 211, Draft Covenant, in Miller, *Diary*, 3:455.

96. See David Hunter Miller, *The Drafting of the Covenant*, 2 vols. (New York: Putnam, 1928), 1:191, 196, 267–269, 462; and 2:273, 282, and 555.

97. For a fuller account, see Lauren, *Power and Prejudice*, pp. 82–107.

98. W.E.B. Du Bois, as cited in United Nations, Centre Against Apartheid, *International Tribute*, p. 48; first stated in 1900 but repeated again in Paris during 1919.

99. Dillon, *The Inside Story*, p. 493; and Steven Bonsal, *Unfinished Business* (Garden City, N.Y.: Doubleday, Doran, 1944), p. 169.

100. *Asahi*, as cited in "Racial Discrimination to End," *Japan Times*, 31 January 1919.

101. See Library of Congress, Manuscripts Division, Woodrow Wilson Papers, Breckinridge Long to Wilson, 4 March 1919, and Memorandum from the Japanese Government, 4 March 1919; and Japan, Delegation to the Paris Peace Conference, Documents Distributed to the Public, located at the Hoover Institution.

102. Arthur Balfour, as cited in Miller, *Diary*, entry of 9 February 1919, 1:116.

103. As cited in L. F. Fitzhardinge, *William Morris Hughes* (Sydney: Angus & Robertson, 1964), pp. 116 and 136; and in "Equality of Races," *Age* (Melbourne), 21 March 1919.

104. *Otago Witness*, "The Week: Racial Equality," 23 April 1919.

105. See Britain, Public Record Office, Foreign Office (hereafter cited as Britain, PRO/FO), 371/3817, Despatch No. 55 from Conyngham Greene (Tokyo) to Lord Curzon (London), 6 February 1919; and "Do to Others," *Japan Times*, 9 February 1919.

106. Conférence de la Paix, 1919–1920, *Recueil des actes de la Conférence*, "Secret," Partie 4, Commission de la Société des Nations (Paris: Imprimerie nationale, 1922), p. 90; and Columbia University, Rare Book and Manuscript Library, Wellington Koo Papers, Box 1, File 3, Memorandum of Interview with Col. House, 2 April 1919.

107. As cited in John Hope Franklin, *From Slavery to Freedom* (New York: Knopf, 1974 ed.), p. 352.

108. Document No. 773, in Miller, *Diary*, 8:279; and Conférence de la Paix, 1919–1920, *Recueil des actes de la Conférence*, "Secret," Partie 4, passim. Those voting in favor of the equality provision included Brazil, China, Czechoslovakia, France (2), Greece, Italy (2), Japan (2), and Yugoslavia.

109. *Sacramento Union*, 13 April 1919.

110. William Tuttle, Jr., "Views of a Negro During 'The Red Summer' of 1919," *Journal of Negro History*, 51 (July 1966): 209–218.

111. *Asahi*, as cited in "The League's Amended Covenant," in *Japan Times*, 18 April 1919; and *Nichinichi*, as cited "Anglo-Saxons Want to Dominate the World," in ibid., 26 April 1919.

112. Shigenobu Okuma, "Illusions of the White Race," in K. K. Kawakami (ed.), *What Japan Thinks* (New York: Macmillan, 1921), p. 170.

113. Woodrow Wilson, in United States, Congress, *Congressional Record, 1918*, 56, pt. 1, pp. 680–681.

114. Columbia University, Rare Book and Manuscript Library, Wellington Koo Papers, Box 1, File 3, Note of 22 January 1919, Strictly Confidential.

115. Cited in Roland Oliver and Anthony Atmore, *Africa Since 1800* (Cambridge: Cambridge University Press, 1981 ed.), p. 161.

116. Nicolson, *Peacemaking 1919*, p. 193.

117. See H. A. L. Fisher, *A History of Europe*, 3 vols. (London: Eyre & Spottiswoode, 1938), 3:1174; and Ronald Segal, *The Race War* (New York: Bantam, 1967), p. 58.

118. The words are those of Neil Sheehan, *A Bright Shining Lie* (New York: Random House, 1989), p. 147.

119. Chen Duxiu, as cited in Lin Yü-sheng, *The Crisis of Chinese Consciousness: Radical Anti-Traditionalism in the May Fourth Era* (Madison: University of Wisconsin Press, 1979), p. 76.

120. Sée, *Histoire de la Ligue*, p. 174.

121. Kikujiro Ishii, *Diplomatic Commentaries*, W. R. Langdon (trans.) (Baltimore: Johns Hopkins University Press, 1936), pp. 270–271.

Chapter 4: Opportunities and Challenges

1. Erich Maria Remarque, *All Quiet on the Western Front* (New York: Fawcett, 1968), pp. 160–161; first published in 1928 as *Im Westen Nichts Neues*.

2. J. Herman Burgers, "The Road to San Francisco: The Revival of the Human Rights Idea in the Twentieth Century," *Human Rights Quarterly*, 14, 4 (November 1992): 447.

3. See Sean Brawley, *The White Peril* (Sydney: University of New South Wales Press, 1995), pp. 8–9.

4. A. Harrison, "A New Order?" *English Review*, 28 (February 1919): 160.

5. Jane Addams, *Peace and Bread* (New York: Macmillan, 1922), pp. 196 and 198.

6. Ibid., p. 224. See also Gertrude Bussey and Margaret Tims, *Women's International League for Peace and Freedom* (London: Allen & Unwin, 1965).

7. Equal Rights Amendment to the U.S. Constitution, 1923, as cited in Eleanor Flexner, *Century of Struggle: The Women's Rights Movement in the United States* (Cambridge: Belknap, 1975 ed.), p. 342.

8. As cited in Sachiko Kaneko, "The Struggle for Legal Rights and Reforms: A Historical View," in Kumiko Fujimura-Fanselow and Atsuko Kameda (eds.), *Japanese Women* (New York: Feminist Press, 1995), p. 7.

9. Kemal Atatürk in 1923, as cited in Kumari Jayawardena, *Feminism and Nationalism in the Third World* (London: Zed, 1986), p. 36.

10. See United Nations, Document 1949.I.15, *Political Rights of Women: 56 Years of Progress* (New York: United Nations, 1949).

11. See UN Document 1948.I.10(1)F, "Pour les Droits de la Femme," p. 2.

12. See Margaret Sanger, *International Aspects of Birth Control* (New York: American Birth Control League, 1925); and Ellen Chesler, *Woman of Valor* (New York: Simon and Schuster, 1992).

13. See discussion below.

14. Based on Henri Sée, *Histoire de la Ligue des Droits de l'Homme* (Paris: Ligue des Droits de l'Homme, 1927), pp. 188ff.; and personal letter to author from Herman Burgers, 14 March 1966, recounting information from Daniel Jacoby, president of the FIDH.

15. Mao Zedong, "Report on an Investigation of the Peasant Movement in Hunan," 1927, in M. J. Coye et al., *China* (New York: Bantam, 1984), pp. 213–214.

16. Rhoades Murphey, *A History of Asia* (New York: HarperCollins, 1996 ed.), pp. 318, 341–342, and 346.

17. See Percy Martin (ed.), *Who's Who in Latin America* (Stanford: Stanford University Press, 1940), pp. 19–20.

18. Mohandas Gandhi, as cited in W. T. de Bary et al. (comp.), *Sources of Indian Tradition* (New York: Columbia University Press, 1958), pp. 811 and 818.

19. This theme is developed at length in Jayawardena, *Feminism and Nationalism in the Third World*.

20. Habib Bourguiba, in Roland Oliver and Anthony Atmore, *Africa Since 1800* (Cambridge: Cambridge University Press, 1981 ed.), p. 177.

21. Britain, PRO/FO, 371/6684, Memorandum entitled "Racial Discrimination and Immigration," Confidential, 10 October 1921; and *Ta Ya*, as cited in Britain, PRO/FO, 371/3823, Despatch No. 553 from Sir J. Jordon (Beijing) to Lord Curzon (London), 10 December 1919.

22. Cited in Britain, PRO/FO, 371/11700, Memorandum A.D. 35/24, "Secret," from J. G. Fearnley to Naval Secretary (Melbourne), 30 December 1925. See also "Mr. F.A. Graham to Leave for Orient," *Victoria Daily Colonist*, 27 January 1926.

23. Walter Nash, as cited in Keith Sinclair, *Walter Nash* (Auckland: Auckland University Press, 1976), p. 82.

24. Second Pan-African Congress, as cited in W. E. B. Du Bois, *The World and Africa* (New York: International Publishers, 1965 ed.), p. 238. See also Immanuel Geiss, *Panafrikanismus: Zür Geschichte der Dekolonisation* (Frankfurt am Main: Europäische Verlagsanstalt, 1968), pp. 189ff.

25. Marcus Garvey, as cited in Edmund David Cronon, *Black Moses: The Story of Marcus Garvey and the Universal Negro Improvement Association* (Madison: University of Wisconsin Press, 1969), p. 39.

26. See Académie Diplomatique Internationale, *Séances et Travaux*, 2 (January–March 1928), pp. 9 and 20.

27. See André N. Mandelstam, "La Protection internationale des droits de l'homme," *Recueil des Cours de l'Académie de Droit International*, 38 (1931): 205–206; Britain, PRO/FO, 372/2553, File T 14526/1761/377; Louis Sohn, "How American International Lawyers Prepared for the San Francisco Bill of Rights," *American Journal of International Law*, 89 (July 1995): 541–546; and Burgers, "The Road to San Francisco," p. 452.

28. See, for example, A. Aulard and Boris Mirkine-Guetzévitch, *Les Déclarations des Droits de l'Homme: Textes constitutionnels concernant les droits de l'homme et les garanties des libertés individuelles dans tous les pays* (Paris: Payot, 1929).

29. André Mandelstam, "La déclaration des droits internationaux de l'homme adoptée par l'Institut de Droit international," *Revue de Droit International* (1930); André Mandelstam, "Der

internationale Schutz der Menschenrechte und die New-Yorker Erklärung des Instituts für Völkerrecht," *Zeitschrift für ausländisches öffentliches Recht und Völkerrecht*, 2 (1931); and André Mandelstam, *Les Droits internationaux de l'Homme* (Paris: Éditions internationales, 1931); among others.

30. For a summary of his life and contributions, see "André Mandelstam (1869–1949)," in Institut de Droit International, *Annuaire de l'Institut de Droit International*, 43 (September 1950): 482–484.

31. Burgers, "The Road to San Francisco," pp. 453–454; and André Mandelstam, "Les dernières phases du mouvement pour la protection internationale des droits de l'homme," *Revue de Droit International*, 1 (1934): 62–69.

32. See André Mandelstam, "La Protection internationale des droits de l'homme," *Les Cahiers des droits de l'homme*, 31 (10 December 1931): 723–733; and André Mandelstam, "Les dernières phases du mouvement pour la protection internationale des droits de l'homme," *Revue de Droit International*, 4 (1933): 486.

33. Georges Gurvitch, *La Déclaration des Droits Sociaux* (Paris: Vrin, 1946); and Burgers, "Road to San Francisco," p. 454. See also Victor Basch, "Projets de complément a la déclaration des droits ou de nouvelle déclaration," in *Les Cahiers des Droits de l'homme* (1935): 342.

34. "Lima Declaration in Favor of Women's Rights" and "Defense of Human Rights," of December 1938, in United States, Department of State, *Conference Series 50: Report of the Delegation of the United States of America to the Eighth International Conference of American States* (Washington, D.C.: Government Printing Office, 1941), pp. 123 and 128–129. For a broader history of previous efforts, see Samuel Guy Inman, *Inter-American Conferences* (Washington, D.C.: University Press of America, 1965), pp. 97, 122–123, 188–189, and 194.

35. René Albrecht-Carrié, *A Diplomatic History of Europe* (New York: Harper & Row, 1973 ed.), p. 379.

36. Guiseppe Molta, in Société des nations, *Actes de la première assemblée, Séances plenières* (Geneva: Renaud, 1920), pp. 25–27.

37. Paul Hymans, in ibid., p. 31.

38. Covenant of the League of Nations, especially Articles 10, 14, 22, 23, and 25, in United States, Department of State, *FRUS: The Paris Peace Conference, 1919*, 13 vols. (Washington, D.C.: Government Printing Office, 1947), 13: 69–106.

39. The details are clearly revealed in France, Archives nationales, Fonds Albert Thomas (94 AP).

40. See Paul Périgord, *The International Labor Organization* (New York: Appleton, 1926), p. 217; Albert Thomas, *International Social Policy* (Geneva: International Labor Office, 1948); and Léon-Eli Troclet, *Législation sociale internationale* (Brussels: Éditions de la Librairie Encyclopédique, 1952).

41. Treaty texts in Société des Nations/League of Nations, Document C.L.110. 1927. I, Annex, *Protection of Linguistic, Racial, and Religious Minorities* (Geneva: Société des Nations, 1927).

42. André N. Mandelstam, "La Protection des minorités," *Recueil des Cours de l'Académie de Droit International*, 1 (1923): 367–519; and André N. Mandelstam, *La Protection internationale des minorités* (Paris: Sirey, 1931).

43. Société des Nations, *Journal officiel*, supplément 9, *Résolutions et Vœux adoptés par l'Assemblée*, 21 September 1922 (Geneva: Société des Nations, 1922), p. 35.

44. Britain, PRO/FO, 371/50843, Memorandum entitled "Minority Protection Under the League of Nations," RRI/101/ii, Restricted, 2 March 1945.

45. Permanent Court of International Justice, Advisory Opinion of 6 April 1935, in *Publications of the Court*, Series A/B, No. 64, Series A/B (Leyden: Sijthoff, 1935).

46. Permanent Court of International Justice, Judgment No. 12, 26 April 1928, in *Publications of the Court*, Series A, No. 15 (Leyden: Sijthoff, 1928), pp. 46–47. See also Manouchehr Ganji, *International Protection of Human Rights* (Geneva: Droz, 1962), pp. 52–69; and A. H. Robertson and J. G. Merrills, *Human Rights in the World* (Manchester: Manchester University Press, 1992 ed.), pp. 19–21.

47. New Zealand, National Archives, External Affairs 2, File 114/3/2, pt. 5, Despatch No. 2315 from Thomas Wilford (London) to Prime Minister (Wellington), 6 November 1933 (hereafter cited as NANZ, EA).

48. See Hannah Arendt, *The Origins of Totalitarianism* (New York: Harcourt, Brace, 1951), pp. 273–274; United Nations Document LIB/96/6, *The League of Nations, 1920–1946*, pp. 49–54; and American Jewish Committee, *Human Rights in the Peace Treaties* (New York: American Jewish Committee, 1946), p. 3.

49. Lord Balfour, as cited in Quincy Wright, "Sovereignty of the Mandates," *American Journal of International Law*, 17 (1923): 692.

50. See League of Nations, Permanent Mandates Commission, *Minutes*, and the often hard-hitting *Reports*. See also F. P. Walters, *A History of the League of Nations*, 2 vols. (London: Oxford University Press, 1952), 1:121–122, 171–173, and 211–213.

51. The texts of these treaties all appear in the *American Journal of International Law*, supplement, 17 (1923): 138–194.

52. Société des Nations, Document A.25.1924.VI, *La Question de l'Esclavage, Memorandum du Secretaire General*, 4 August 1924 (Geneva: Société des Nations, 1924).

53. International Convention for the Abolition of Slavery and the Slave Trade, 25 September 1926, in League of Nations, *Treaty Series*, 60 (Geneva: League of Nations, 1926): 253–270; and United Nations, Economic and Social Council, Document E/AC.33/2, *The Work of the League of Nations for the Suppression of Slavery, Memorandum by the Secretary-General*, 23 January 1950 (New York: United Nations, 1950).

54. "The Slave Trade Rapidly Vanishing," *Evening Post* (Wellington), 29 December 1927.

55. League of Nations, Council Document 23/5359/3554, "Resolution Officially Transmitted to the Secretariat by a Deputation from the International Woman Suffrage Alliance," 12 June 1920.

56. United Nations, Document 1949.I.15, *Political Rights of Women*.

57. International Convention for the Suppression of Traffic in Women and Children, 31 March 1922, in League of Nations, *Treaty Series*, 9 (1922): 415–433; and International Convention for the Suppression of Traffic in Women of Full Age, 11 October 1933, in League of Nations, *Treaty Series*, 150 (1933): 431–443.

58. See League of Nations, *Official Journal*, Special Supplement 169, *Records of the Eighteenth Ordinary Session of the Assembly* (1937), pp, 136–137; "Status of Women," *Weekly Bulletin of the United Nations*, 16 September 1946; and Britain, PRO/FO, 372 (Treaty Series)/2636, File T 1315/11/377, Minute of 6 February 1930.

59. Société des Nations, Document 20/48/160, "Intervention en faveur des enfants des pays éprovés par la guerre," 2 December 1920.

60. For materials on the extensive work of this committee, see League of Nations, Document C.264.M.103.1926.IV, "Child Welfare Committee"; and Document C.337.M.137.1930.IV, "Child Welfare Committee."

61. International Council of Women, as cited in United Nations, Economic and Social Council, Document E/CN.5/44, *Report of the Social Commission, Third Session*, 19 February 1948, p. 45.

62. Declaration of the Rights of the Child, resolution of the League Assembly, in League of Nations, Document A.127.1924.IV, "Protection of Children," 26 September 1924.

63. Y. Sugimura, in League of Nations, *Official Journal*, Special Supplement 33, *Records of the Sixth Assembly* (1925), p. 131.

64. See the informative issues of the *Bulletin of the Health Organization*; and Walters, *A History of the League of Nations*, 1:181–183; and 2:752–753.

65. International Opium Convention, in League of Nations, *Treaty Series*, 81 (1925): 317–358; and Convention for Limiting the Manufacture and Regulating the Distribution of Narcotic Drugs, in League of Nations, *Treaty Series*, 139 (1931): 301–349.

66. "Protocol for the Prohibition of the Use in War of Asphyxiating, Poisonous, and Other

Gases and of Bacteriological Methods of Warfare," 17 June 1925, in League of Nations, *Treaty Series* 94 (1929): 65–74; and Henri Coursier, "L'Evolution du Droit International Humanitaire," in *Recueil des Cours de l'Académie de Droit International,* 99 (1960): 361–465.

67. Convention Relative to the Treatment of Prisoners of War, 27 July 1929, in League of Nations, *Treaty Series,* 118 (1931–1932): 345–397.

68. League of Nations, Document C.484.M.201.1923, Letter from Lieutenant General C. H. Harington, 14 July 1923, describing events beginning in 1920.

69. NANZ, EA 2, File 114/3/2, pt. 5, Despatch 2315 from Thomas Wilford (London) to Prime Minister (Wellington), 6 November 1933; Walters, *A History of the League of Nations,* 1:187–189; UN Document LIB/96/6, *The League of Nations,* pp. 74–80; and Claudena Skran, *Refugees in Inter-War Europe: The Emergence of a Regime* (Oxford: Clarendon Press, 1995).

70. Hoover Institution Archives, Anna Mitchell Papers, Box 2, Letter from A. Mitchell (Constantinople) to F. Nansen (Geneva), undated, but probably June 1925.

71. Ibid., Letter from F. Nansen (Geneva) to A. Mitchell (Constantinople), 11 June 1925.

72. League of Nations, Document A.107.1923.IV, "Work of the High Commission for Refugees," 26 September 1923; Document A.114.1924.II, "Questions Concernant les Réfugiés, 25 September 1924; and Elmer Bendiner, *A Time for Angels* (New York: Knopf, 1975), pp. 187ff. In 1930 the organization was renamed the Nansen International Office for Refugees.

73. See League of Nations, *Official Journal,* 8 (August 1927): 997–1035; and League of Nations, *Treaty Series,* 159 (1935–1936): 199–217.

74. Société des Nations, *Journal officiel,* supplément 9, *Résolutions et Vœux adoptés par l'Assemblée* (October 1922), p. 35.

75. Covenant of the League of Nations, Article 15 (8) and Article 21.

76. Convention of the International Labor Organization, Article 19.

77. Library of Congress, Manuscript Division, Robert Lansing Papers, Confidential Memoranda and Notes, Box 87, "Consideration as to a League of Nations," 27 October 1918.

78. NANZ, EA 2, File 114/3/2, pt. 5, Despatch No. 2315, from Thomas Wilford (London) to Prime Minister (Wellington), 6 November 1933.

79. William Hughes, as cited in Sean Brawley, *The White Peril,* pp. 41–42 and 44.

80. James Reed, as cited in Ralph Stone, *The Irreconcilables* (Lexington: University of Kentucky Press, 1970), p. 88.

81. Henry Cabot Lodge, *The Senate and the League of Nations* (New York: Scribners, 1925), p. 246, speech of 28 February 1919.

82. N. W. Rowell of Canada, as cited in National Industrial Conference Board, *The International Labor Organization of the League of Nations* (New York: Century, 1922), p. 145.

83. Warington Smith of South Africa, as cited in Périgord, *The International Labor Organization,* p. 197.

84. Périgord, *The International Labor Organization,* pp. 192–217; National Industrial Conference Board, *The International Labor Organization of the League of Nations,* pp. 118–159.

85. Maharajah of Nawanagar, in Société des Nations, *Actes de la Troisième Assemblée, Séances Plénières* (1922), 1:176.

86. Tcheo-Wei, in League of Nations, *Records of the Sixth Assembly,* special supplement 39, *Minutes of the Sixth Committee* (1925), p. 19.

87. Robert Cecil, in ibid, p. 18. See also League of Nations, *Records of the Eleventh Assembly,* special supplement 90, *Minutes of the Sixth Committee* (1930), pp. 15ff.

88. United Nations, Document E/CN.4/Sub.2/384/Rev.1, *Study on the Rights of Persons Belonging to Ethnic, Religious, and Linguistic Minorities* (New York: United Nations, 1979), pp. 16–26; and P. de Azcárate, *League of Nations and National Minorities: An Experiment* (Washington, D.C.: Carnegie Endowment, 1945).

89. See Paul Gordon Lauren, *Power and Prejudice* (Boulder and San Francisco: Westview/HarperCollins, 1996 ed.), pp. 108–118.

90. Britain, PRO/FO, 371/6684, Memorandum entitled "Racial Discrimination and Immigration," "Confidential," 10 October 1921, F 4212/223/23.

91. Archives de la Société des Nations (hereafter Archives de la SDN), General 40/151/78, "Petition for an Amendment to the League of Nations," 3 July 1919.

92. Archives de la SDN, General, 40/1827/1827, letter from the Alliance Universelle pour Favoriser le Développement des Relations Amicales entre les Nations, 30 October 1919.

93. Archives de la SDN, Mandates, 1/15865/13940, letter from W. E. B. Du Bois, 15 September 1921.

94. Archives de la SDN, Mandates, 1/37672/21159, letter from Marcus Garvey, 23 May 1923.

95. Archives de la SDN, Mandates, 1/37672/21159, note by A. S., 12 August 1922; and note from E. H. F. Abraham, 15 June 1922.

96. See Archives de la SDN, Mandates, 6A/7158/7158, passim.

97. As cited in Ronald Wright, *Stolen Continents* (Boston: Houghton Mifflin, 1992), pp. 323–324. See also Deskaheh (Levi General), *The Redman's Appeal for Justice* (Brandtford, Ontario: Moore, 1924).

98. Société des Nations, *Journal officiel*, 9 (July 1928), p. 942.

99. J. S. Smit, in League of Nations, *Official Journal*, special supplement 64, *Records of the Assembly* (September 1928), p. 93.

100. Archives de la SDN, Mandates, 1/2444/2444, note by Robert Cecil of Britain.

101. Walters, *A History of the League of Nations*, 1:173 and 211; and Lord Balfour, as cited in Wright, "Sovereignty of the Mandates," p. 697.

102. Winston Churchill, as cited in Fischer, *Gandhi*, pp. 103 and 135.

103. Société des Nations, Document A.25.1924.VI, *La Question de l'Esclavage*, 4 August 1924, p. 3.

104. See Britain, PRO/FO, 370/365, Despatch No. 195 from Tyrrell (Paris) to Arthur Henderson (London), 20 February 1931; Gertrude Bussey and Margaret Tims, *Women's International League for Peace and Freedom* (London: Allen & Unwin, 1965), pp. 73–81; and Walters, *A History of the League of Nations*, 1: 184–188.

105. American Jewish Committee, *Human Rights and the Peace Treaties* (New York: American Jewish Committee, 1946), p. 3.

106. See Mandelstam, "La Protection Internationale des Droits de l'Homme," pp. 146–155.

107. Adolf Hitler, *Mein Kampf*, translated by Ralph Manheim (Boston: Houghton Mifflin, 1962 ed.), pp. 177–178, 338–339, 383, 403, 624, 627, and 657.

108. The original petition is in Archives de la SDN, Minorities, File 4/4150/3643, "Juifs en Haute Silesie allemande," and entitled "Petition des Franz Bernheim, deutscher Reichsangehöriger aus Gleiwitz, Deutsch-Oberschlesien im Sinne des Artikels 147 des deutsch-polnischen Abkommens über Oberschlesien vom 15. Mai 1922," dated 12 May 1933. Eventually reproduced as League of Nations, Document C.314.1933.I.

109. *The Times* (London), "Treatment of Jews in Upper Silesia," 22 May 1933.

110. *Daily Express*, "A Jew May Thwart Hitler," 22 May 1933. See also Burgers, "The Road to San Francisco," pp. 455–459; Manouchehr Ganji, *International Protection of Human Rights* (Geneva: Droz, 1962), pp. 56–70; and Leni Yahil, *The Holocaust*, Ina Friedman and Haya Galai (trans.) (New York: Oxford University Press, 1990).

111. Germany, PA/AA, Referat Völkerbund, Deutschland und der Judentum, Band 1, Telegram from Neurath (Berlin) to German Delegation (Geneva), 24 May 1933.

112. Castillo Najera, 27 May 1933, in League of Nations, *Official Journal* (July 1933), p. 835.

113. The open debates can be found in League of Nations, *Official Journal* (July 1933), *Minutes of the Seventy-Third Session of the Council*, 22 May–6 June 1933. See also Archives de la SDN, Minorities, File 4/4470/3643, "Jews in Upper Silesia," Confidential.

114. See Britain, PRO/FO, 371/17384, File W 4149/120/98, Minute of 17 May 1933.

115. See Britain, PRO/FO, 371/16725 and 371/16726.

116. Marshall Lee, "Failure in Geneva: The German Foreign Ministry and the League of Nations," Ph.D. dissertation, University of Wisconsin, 1974, pp. 215ff., is especially good on this point.

117. August von Keller, 4 October 1933, in League of Nations, *Official Journal*, special supple-

ment 120, *Minutes of the Sixth Committee*, pp. 22–28. The internal German Foreign Office discussion on this matter can be found in Germany, PA/AA, Büro des Reichsministers, Aktenzeichen 18, Völkerbund, Bände 32–35; Politische Abteilung IV/Polen, Aktenzeichen Po.Juden 1. OS, Fall Bernheim, Band 5; and Referat Völkerbund, Aktenzeichen Deutschland und der Judentum, Band 1.

118. "Les Droits de l'homme et du citoyen devant la 14e Assemblée de la S.D.N.," *La Revue Diplomatique* (31 October 1933): 6–7.

119. Antoine Frangulis, 30 September 1933, in League of Nations, *Official Journal*, special supplement 115, *Records of the Fourteenth Ordinary Session of the Assembly, Plenary Meetings*, pp. 50–51.

120. Antoine Frangulis, 4 October 1933, in League of Nations, *Official Journal*, special supplement 120, *Minutes of the Sixth Committee*, pp. 32–33. See also René Brunet, *La Garantie internationale des Droits de l'homme* (Geneva: Grasset, 1947), pp. 47–49 and 90–93.

121. Britain, PRO/FO, 371/17386, File 9391/191/98, Minute by Ashley Clarke, 9 August 1933.

122. See Antoine Frangulis, "Droits de l'Homme," *Dictionnaire Diplomatique* (Paris: Hoche, 1937 ed.).

123. See Britain, PRO/FO, 371/17386, Minute by Ashley Clark, quoting Sir Vansittart, 9 August 1933; and Despatch No. 223, from Douglas Hacking (Geneva) to Sir John Simon, 11 October 1933, Confidential.

124. Ibid. Frangulis brought his proposal before the League again in 1934, but it met the same result.

125. Boris Pasternak, as cited by Roy Medvedev, "New Pages from the Political Biography of Stalin," in Robert C. Tucker (ed.), *Stalinism* (New York: Norton, 1977), p. 212.

126. Robert Conquest, *The Harvest of Sorrow: Soviet Collectivization and the Terror-Famine* (New York: Oxford University Press, 1986), p. 306, uses the figure 14.5 million while acknowledging that the resource base simply does not allow a more precise accounting.

127. As cited in Antonio Banzi, *Razzismo fascista* (Palermo: Agate, 1939), pp. 226–231. See also Renzo de Felice, *Mussolini il duce: Lo Stato totalitario, 1936–1940* (Rome: Einaudi, 1981), pp. 102 ff.

128. Hora Tomio, *Nankin jiken*, as cited in Ono Kazuko, *Chinese Women in a Century of Revolution* (Stanford: Stanford University Press, 1989), p. 162.

129. Judge Hanson, as cited in League of Nations, Document A.11.1937.XII, *Nansen International Office for Refugees, Report of the Liquidation of the Office*, 14 June 1937, pp. 1–2.

130. For more on this neglect, see Burgers, "The Road to San Francisco,'"pp. 459–464.

131. Nansen, as cited in Bendiner, *A Time for Angels*, p. 197.

132. *Neues Volk*, "Wie Rassenfragen entstehen Weiss und Schwarz in Amerika," 4 (1936): 9–15; "700 Jahre Rassenkampf," 5 (1937): 16–21; "Rassenmischmasch," 5 (1937): 22–23; and "Italiens Kolonialreich unter Rassenschuss," 6 (1938): 26–31.

133. Adolf Hitler, 22 August 1939, in United States, Department of State, *Documents on German Foreign Policy, 1918–1945*, Series D (Washington, D.C.: Government Printing Office, 1949–   ), 7:205.

Chapter 5: A "People's War"

1. See, among many others, Angus Calder, *The People's War* (London: Panther, 1969).

2. "The Einsatzgruppen Case," in International Military Tribunal, *Trials of War Criminals*, 15 vols. (Washington, D.C.: Government Printing Office, 1946–1948), 4:412–413.

3. See Hoover Institution, Heinrich Himmler Collection, File 286, containing aprivate correspondence concerning the notorious publication, *Der Untermensch*. Also see *Das Schwarze Korps* 27 (July 1941); and various issues of *Volkischer Beobachter* in the summer of 1941.

4. Franklin Roosevelt Library, Franklin Roosevelt Papers, President's Secretary File, Safe File, Box 6, File "Welles Report, 1940, Part II."

5. Franklin Roosevelt, Address of 6 January 1941, in Samuel Rosenman (ed.), *The Public Papers and Addresses of Franklin D. Roosevelt*, 13 vols. (New York: Random House, 1938–1950), 9:672. For a background, see "Five Freedoms Can Assure Peace, Says Roosevelt," *Daily Herald*, 6 July 1940.

6. For more discussion about this domestic pressure, see the section below entitled "Visions and Proposals."

7. This expression was used frequently in order to maintain secrecy in the face of likely German submarine attacks. See League of Nations Union, *The Atlantic Charter* (London: Hodgson, 1942), p. 1.

8. The details of the trip can be found in the Franklin Roosevelt Library, Franklin Roosevelt Papers, President's Secretary's File, Safe File, Box 1, File "Atlantic Charter (1)," "Log of the President's Cruise, 3–16 August 1941." See also Theodore Wilson, *The First Summit* (Boston: Houghton Mifflin, 1969).

9. Winston Churchill, *The Grand Alliance* (New York: Houghton Mifflin, 1950), p. 432.

10. Churchill's original draft and the final declaration can all be found in Franklin Roosevelt Library, Franklin Roosevelt Papers, President's Secretary's File, Safe File, Box 1, File "Atlantic Charter (1)."

11. See Holly C. Shulman, *The Voice of America* (Madison: University of Wisconsin Press, 1990), p. 72; and Sumner Welles, *The Time for Decision* (New York: Harper & Brothers, 1944), p. 178.

12. "Reaction to the Roosevelt-Churchill Parley," *New York Times*, 15 August 1941.

13. NANZ, EA 1, File 101/1/3 (1), Telegram (10) R, from Peter Fraser (London) to the Cabinet in Wellington, "Most Secret," 12 August 1941; and Circular from Walter Nash, 14 August 1941. During the war Nash served as deputy prime minister, minister of finance, and minister to the United States.

14. Nelson Mandela, *Long Walk to Freedom* (Boston: Little, Brown, 1994 ed.), pp. 83–84. I am grateful to Bert Lockwood for bringing this passage to my attention.

15. See "Japanese Scorn the Eight Points," and "Wilson Revival Seen by Berlin," in *New York Times*, 15 August 1941.

16. Declaration of the United Nations, 1 January 1942, in United States, Department of State, *FRUS, 1942*, 1:25–26. See also Britain, PRO/FO, 371/67605, Minute from Research Department, "Human Rights," 2 June 1947; Wellington Koo Papers, Rare Book and Manuscript Library, Columbia University, Box 54, File 2; and René Brunet, *La Garantie international des Droits de l'homme* (Geneva: Grasset, 1947), pp. 102–105. These words were inserted by Franklin Roosevelt in his own handwriting in the draft of the declaration.

17. Franklin Roosevelt, Annual Message to Congress, 6 January 1942, as cited in Louise Holborn (ed.), *War and Peace Aims of the United Nations* (Boston: World Peace Foundation, 1943), pp. 66–67. Thomas A. Bailey, *A Diplomatic History of the American People* (New York: Appleton-Century-Crofts, 1968 ed.), p. 744, describes the Declaration as "of supreme importance in American diplomatic history."

18. Final Act, Resolution XXXV, "Support and Adherence to the Principles of the 'Atlantic Charter,'" Pan American Union, *Congress and Conference Series*, No. 36 (Washington, D.C.: Pan American Union, 1942). They also referred to the earlier Convention on Rights and Duties of States approved at the International Conference of American States held at Montevideo in 1933.

19. Joseph Goebbels, entry of 27 March 1942, *Diaries, 1942–1943*, translated by Louis Lochner (New York: Doubleday, 1948), p. 147.

20. An eyewitness account, as reproduced in "Dokumentation," *Vierteljahrshefte für Zeitgeschichte*, I (1953): 190–191. The evidence on this subject is vast, as can be seen in International Military Tribunal, *Trial of Major War Criminals*, 42 vols. (Nuremberg: International Military Tribunal, 1947–1949); Germany, PA/AA, Abteilung Inland, Inland I Partei, Aktenzeichen 82–35, "Rassenfrage und Rassenfoerderung," Band 6; Rudolf Hoess, *Kommandant in Auschwitz; Auto-*

biolgraphische Aufzeichnungen (Stuttgart: Deutsche Verlags, 1958); and Primo Levi, *Survival in Auschwitz: The Nazi Assault on Humanity* (New York: Collier, 1993 ed.), among many others.

21. Mark Kishlansky et al., *Civilization in the West* (New York: HarperCollins, 1995 ed.), p. 898. Thomas G. Paterson, *On Every Front* (New York: Norton, 1979), p. 8, uses the figure of twelve million.

22. See John Dower, *War Without Mercy: Race and Power in the Pacific* (New York: Pantheon, 1986); and Lauren, *Power and Prejudice*, pp. 138–140, in Japanese translation as *Kokka to Jinshuhenken* (Tokyo: TBS-Britannica, 1995).

23. Among many others, see Rhoads Murphey, *A History of Asia* (New York: HarperCollins, 1996 ed.), pp. 355–356.

24. See Dower, *War Without Mercy*, p. 175.

25. As cited in W. H. Elsbree, *Japan's Role in Southeast Asian Nationalist Movements, 1940–1945* (Cambridge, Mass.: Harvard University Press, 1953), p. 163.

26. The Goho Report, as cited in Christopher Thorne, "Racial Aspects of the Far Eastern War," *Proceedings of the British Academy*, 66 (1980): 343.

27. Cited in Irwin Gellman, "The *St. Louis* Tragedy," *American Jewish Historical Quarterly*, 61 (December 1971): 156.

28. See David Wyman, *The Abandonment of the Jews* (New York: Pantheon, 1986); Monty Penkower, *The Jews Were Expendable: Free World Diplomacy and the Holocaust* (Urbana: University of Illinois Press, 1983), pp. 94–95 and 120; and Arthur Morse, *While Six Million Died* (New York: Random House, 1967).

29. Sir Frederick Maze, as cited in Thorne, "Racial Aspects of the Far Eastern War," p. 339.

30. See *Sydney Morning Herald*, 27 December 1941 and 2 January 1942; "The Japanese," *Fortune*, 25 (February 1942): 53ff; and Christopher Thorne, *Allies of a Kind* (New York: Oxford University Press, 1979), pp. 1–5.

31. As cited in Dower, *War Without Mercy*, p. 7.

32. Winston Churchill, as cited in Thorne, *Allies of a Kind*, p. 191.

33. As cited in Dower, *War Without Mercy*, p. 7.

34. Winston Churchill, as cited in Thorne, *Allies of a Kind*, p. xxiii.

35. Winston Churchill, 10 November 1942, as cited in Louis Fischer, *Gandhi* (New York: Penguin, 1982), p. 135.

36. Hoover Institution Archives, Joseph Stilwell Diaries, entries of 18 February and 21 February 1942.

37. See United States, Commission on Wartime Relocation and Internment of Civilians, *Personal Justice Denied* (Washington, D.C.: Government Printing Office, 1982); Roger Daniels, *Concentration Camps USA* (New York: Holt, Rinehart & Winston, 1971); Peter Irons, *Justice at War* (New York: Oxford University Press, 1983); and D. R. Hughes and E. Kallen, *The Anatomy of Racism: The Canadian Dimension* (Montreal: Harvest House, 1974).

38. John Rankin, as cited in Virginius Dabney, "Nearer and Nearer the Precipice," *Atlantic Monthly*, 171 (January 1943): 95.

39. See Lauren, *Power and Prejudice*, pp. 140 and 151.

40. See Britain, PRO/FO, 371/27889, File F/1899/17/23.

41. Lord Moyne, 1941, as cited in Laura Tabili, *"We Ask for British Justice"* (Ithaca: Cornell University Press, 1994), p. 161.

42. See Sean Brawley, *The White Peril* (Sydney: University of New South Wales Press, 1995), pp. 174–175.

43. Jan Smuts to M. C. Gillett, 7 June 1942, in J. van der Poel (ed.), *Selections from the Smuts Papers*, 7 vols. (Cambridge: Cambridge University Press, 1973), 6:568.

44. P. S. Gerbrandy, in "Dutch Diamonds," *Bombay Chronicle*, 14 February 1942.

45. Franklin Roosevelt Library, Eleanor Roosevelt Papers, Box 3855, Walter White to Franklin Roosevelt, 4 May 1942.

46. Eleanor Roosevelt, as cited in John Hope Franklin, *From Slavery to Freedom* (New York: Knopf, 1984), p. 456.

47. His study eventually appeared as Gunnar Myrdal, *An American Dilemma: The Negro Problem and Modern Democracy*, 2 vols. (New York: Harper, 1944).

48. "Willkie Says War Liberates Negroes," *New York Times*, 20 July 1942.

49. H. G. Wells, *The Times* (London), "War Aims: The Rights of Man," 25 October 1939. See also the discussion in David C. Smith, *H. G. Wells, Desperately Mortal* (New Haven: Yale University Press, 1986), pp. 428–449; and J. Herman Burgers, "The Road to San Francisco," *Human Rights Quarterly*, 14 (November 1992): 465–468.

50. See Lord Ritchie Calder, *On Human Rights* (London: H. G. Wells Society, 1968), pp. 3–5.

51. H. G. Wells, *The Rights of Man or What Are We Fighting For?* (Harmondsworth: Penguin Books, 1940), p. 127. Other books of the same year that discussed the declaration included H. G. Wells, *The New World Order* (London: National Peace Council, 1940); and H. G. Wells, *The Commonsense of War and Peace* (Harmondsworth: Penguin, 1940).

52. Clarence Streit, *Union Now: A Proposal* (New York: Harper and Brothers, 1939). I am very grateful to Clarence Streit for conversations on this subject prior to his death.

53. Catholic Association for International Peace, *American Peace Aims* (Washington, D.C.: Catholic Association for International Peace, 1941), Report of Several Committees, and Appendix C, "An International Bill of Rights."

54. World Citizens Association, *The World's Destiny and the United States* (Chicago: World Citizens Association, 1941).

55. Franklin Roosevelt Library, Sumner Welles Papers, Box 192, letter from Arnold Toynbee to B. Cohen, 17 May 1941.

56. Eduard Beneš, 10 November 1941, in Holborn (ed.), *War and Peace Aims of the United Nations*, p. 420.

57. National Conference of Christians and Jews, Statement of February 1942, in Holborn (ed.), *War and Peace Aims of the United Nations*, pp. 633–634; and Jacques Maritain, *Les Droits de l'Homme de la Loi Naturelle* (New York: Éditions de la Maison française, 1942).

58. Franklin Roosevelt, message of 14 August 1942, in Roosevelt Library, Franklin Roosevelt Papers, President's Secretary's File, Safe File, Box 1, File: Atlantic Charter (1). A note in this file from M. J. McDermott to Joseph Barnes, 10 August 1942, makes clear that Churchill could not be persuaded to jointly sign this statement.

59. Lauren, *Power and Prejudice*, pp. 155–156; and Immanuel Geiss, *Panafrikanismus: Zur Geschichte der Dekolonisation* (Frankfurt am Main: Europäische Verlagsanstalt, 1968), pp. 300–309.

60. S. Sjahrir, *Out of Exile* (reprint, New York: Greenwood Press, 1969), pp. 248–249.

61. Pearl S. Buck, *American Unity and Asia* (New York: Day, 1942), p. 25.

62. See, among many examples, NANZ, EA 1, File 101/1/3 (1), including the letter from T. T. Wetere to Peter Fraser, 21 September 1942, asking for the text of the Atlantic Charter.

63. Institute of Pacific Relations, December 1942, as cited in Brian Urquhart, *Ralph Bunche* (New York: Norton, 1993), p. 105.

64. As cited in Myrdal, *An American Dilemma*, 2:1006.

65. See Brenda Gayle Plummer, *Rising Wind: Black Americans and U.S. Foreign Affairs, 1935–1960* (Chapel Hill: University of North Carolina Press, 1996), p. 102.

66. Alison Bernstein, *American Indians and World War II* (Norman: University of Oklahoma Press, 1991), pp. 112ff.

67. United Nations, Document 1949.I.15, *Political Rights of Women: 56 Years of Progress* (New York: United Nations, 1949), chapter 1.

68. As cited in Ono Kazuko, *Chinese Women in a Century of Revolution* (Stanford: Stanford University Press, 1989), p. 166.

69. Women's Bureau, as cited in William Chafe, *The Paradox of Change: American Women in the 20th Century* (New York: Oxford University Press, 1991), p. 133. See also Karen Anderson, *Wartime Women* (Westport: Greenwood, 1982); and Sherna Gluck, *Rosie the Riveter Revisited* (New York: New American Library, 1988).

70. See United Nations, Economic and Social Council, Document E/CN.5/44, Social Commission, Third Session, 19 February 1948, pp. 46–47.

71. Franklin D. Roosevelt, State of the Union Address, 11 January 1944, in U.S., Congress, *Congressional Record*, 90, pt. 1, pp. 55–57.

72. As cited in F. L. W. Wood, *The New Zealand People at War* (Wellington: Department of Internal Affairs, 1958), p. 348.

73. See NANZ, Peter Fraser Papers; NANZ, Walter Nash Papers, especially Folio 142; James Thorn, *Peter Fraser, New Zealand's Wartime Prime Minister* (London: Odhams, 1952); 162ff.; Keith Sinclair, *Walter Nash* (Auckland: Auckland University Press, 1976), pp. 237ff.; and ibid., p. 349.

74. See Renu Chakravartty, *Communists in the Indian Women's Movement* (New Delhi: People's Publishing House, 1980).

75. Sir William Beveridge, *Social Insurance and Allied Services* (New York: Macmillan, 1942 U.S. edition), p. 6

76. Citation in Calder, *The People's War*, pp. 607–614.

77. Wood, *The New Zealand People at War*, p. 349. Negotiations to create the UNRRA lasted from 1941 to 1943.

78. See Hoover Institution Archives, Loda Mae Davis Papers, Box 1, memorandum "UNRRA, An Experiment in International Cooperation," spring 1947; and Thomas Paterson and J. Garry Clifford, *America Ascendant* (Lexington, Mass.: Heath, 1995), p. 34.

79. Quincy Wright, "Human Rights and the World Order," *International Conciliation*, 389 (April 1943): 238–262. See also Burgers, "The Road to San Francisco," pp. 472–473.

80. Irving Isaacs, *The International Bill of Rights and Permanent Peace Concordance* (Boston: The International Bill of Rights Committee of the Twentieth Century Association, 1943); and Charles Baylis, "Towards an International Bill of Rights," *The Public Opinion Quarterly*, 8 (Summer 1944): 244–253.

81. Hersch Lauterpacht, *An International Bill of the Rights of Man* (New York: Columbia University Press, 1945).

82. American Law Institute, *Report to the Council of the Institute and Statement of Essential Human Rights* (New York: American Law Institute, 1944), p. 5, a copy of which is on file in U.S. National Archives, RG 59, Alger Hiss Files, Box 2. See also Louis Sohn, "How American International Lawyers Prepared for the San Francisco Bill of Rights," *American Journal of International Law*, 89 (July 1995): 546–553.

83. Walter Nash, in New Zealand, Parliament, *Appendix to the Journals of the House of Representatives, Session 1944* (Wellington: Government Printer, 1945), 1:A-7, pp. 2–24.

84. Brunet, *La Garantie internationale des Droits de l'homme* (Geneva: Grasset, 1947), pp. 93–94. See also Albert Verdoodt, *Naissance et signification de la Déclaration universelle des Droits de l'homme* (Louvain-Paris: Éditions Nauwelaerts, 1964), pp. 40–41.

85. Commission to Study the Organization of Peace, *International Safeguard of Human Rights* (New York: Commission to Study the Organization of Peace, 1944), p. 11. See also U.S. National Archives, RG 59, Alger Hiss Files, Box 2, memorandum written by Alice McDiarmid, "Proposals for an International Bill of Rights," August 1944.

86. For a useful and lengthy compilation of these many public speeches, see Holborn, *War and Peace Aims of the United Nations*, passim.

87. Calder, *On Human Rights*, p. 4.

88. Inter-American Juridical Committee, Preliminary Recommendation on Postwar Problems, 5 September 1942, in Pan American Union, *Preliminary Recommendation on Postwar Problems* (Washington, D.C.: Pan American Union, 1942), pp. 17–22.

89. United Nations Declaration on Jewish Massacres, 17 December 1942, in Great Britain, Parliament, House of Commons, *The Parliamentary Debates*, 5th Series, 385: 2083. See also Penkower, *The Jews Were Expendable*, pp. 87–92.

90. Declaration of Four Nations on General Security, in United States, Department of State, *FRUS, 1943*, 1:756.

91. Winston Churchill, as cited in League of Nations Union, *The Atlantic Charter*, p. 1. See also Lauren, *Power and Prejudice*, pp. 146–147.

92. Britain, FO/PRO, 371/24232, Telegram No. 95, from Lothian (Washington, D.C.) to Foreign Office (London), 8 October 1940.

93. K. Ross Toole Archives at The University of Montana, Clarence Streit Papers, Box 11, File 41, "Your Sovereignty—or Your Nation's?"

94. See Baylis, "Towards and International Bill of Rights," p. 252.

95. The documentation for the work of this Advisory Committee can be found in U.S. National Archives, RG 59, Records of Harley A. Notter; and Franklin Roosevelt Library, Sumner Welles Papers. For a published account, see United States, Department of State, *Postwar Foreign Policy Preparation, 1939–1945* (Washington, D.C.: Government Printing Office, 1949). The precise composition and membership changed from time to time during the course of the war.

96. Some of his many wartime speeches and writings can be found in Franklin Roosevelt Library, Sumner Welles Papers, Box 195; Franklin Roosevelt Library, President's Secretary's File, Safe File, Box 1, File "Atlantic Charter." See also Sumner Welles, *World of the Four Freedoms* (New York: Simon & Schuster, 1943); and Welles, *The Time for Decision*.

97. The membership included at various times G. H. Hackworth, Hamilton Fish Armstrong, Adolf Berle, Benjamin Cohen, Brooks Emeny, and James Shotwell, assisted by Durward Sandifer, John Halderman, Alice McDiarmid, and Lawrence Preuss.

98. The various drafts and language changes can be seen in U.S. National Archives, RG 59, Records of Harley A. Notter, Box 75, Advisory Commission on Postwar Foreign Policy, from "Bill of Rights. Preliminary Draft," L. Document 2, Confidential, 31 July 1942, to the final "Bill of Rights," L. Document 55, Secret, 3 December 1942.

99. Ibid., "Bill of Rights," L. Document 1, Secret, 31 July 1942.

100. Ibid., "Bill of Rights—International Implementation," L. Document 30, Secret, 4 November 1942.

101. Ibid.

102. Franklin Roosevelt Library, Sumner Welles Papers, Box 189, P-IO, Document 3, untitled, 31 July 1942. See also P-IO, Document 5, "Preliminary Memorandum on International Organization," 7 August 1942.

103. U.S. National Archives, RG 59, Records of Harley A. Notter, Box 215, Advisory Commission on Postwar Foreign Policy, "Draft Commentary, First Revision," written by Alice McDiarmid, 3 September 1943.

104. Ibid.

105. See Kingsbury Smith, "Our Foreign Policy Goes Realist," *American Mercury*, December 1943.

106. Franklin Roosevelt Library, Sumner Welles Papers, Box 189, P Minutes 60, 19 June 1943, Secret.

107. Robert Hilderbrand, *Dumbarton Oaks* (Chapel Hill: University of North Carolina Press, 1990), p. 67.

108. The Soviets attended only the first phase and the Chinese attended only the last.

109. Cordell Hull, as cited in United States, Department of State, *Postwar Foreign Policy Preparation*, p. 280.

110. The final results are found in "[The Dumbarton Oaks] Proposals for the Establishment of a General International Organization," 7 October 1944, in ibid., pp. 611–619.

111. Roosevelt, as cited in the extract from the diary of Edward Stettinius, 27 September 1944, in United States, Department of State, *FRUS, 1944*, 1:890.

112. T. V. Soong, in an early speech of 9 June 1942, in Document 26831–11, "Public Statements by Chinese Leaders on International Organization," from the British Foreign Office in NANZ, EA 2, 1945/6b, File 111/8/8(1).

113. Wei Tao Ming to Cordell Hull, 3 June 1944 (transmitting text of the letter from Chiang Kai-shek to Franklin Roosevelt), in United States, Department of State, *FRUS, 1944*, 1:640.

114. "Tentative Chinese Proposals for a General International Organization," 23 August 1944, in ibid., 1:718.

115. Columbia University, Rare Book and Manuscript Library, Wellington Koo Papers, Box 70, File 4, "Ancient China's 'League of Nations,' " 23 August 1944.

116. Ibid., Box 76, File 5, Speech of H. H. Kung before the U.S. Senate, 24 August 1944.

117. See the extracts from the personal diary of Edward Stettinius, 29 August 1944, in United States, Department of State, *FRUS, 1944*, 1:750; United States, Department of State, *Postwar Foreign Policy Preparation*, pp. 301–338; and Ruth Russell, *A History of the United Nations Charter* (Washington, D.C.: Brookings Institution, 1958), p. 329.

118. Ibid., pp. 789, 797, and 825.

119. Britain, PRO/FO, 371/40716, Telegram No. 5318 from Lord Halifax (Washington, D.C.) to Foreign Office, with addition from Alexander Cadogan, 29 September 1944.

120. See U.S. National Archives, RG 59, Alger Hiss Files, Box 2, memorandum entitled "Proposals for an International Bill of Rights," August 1944.

121. See "Welles Warns," in *New York Times*, 25 October 1944.

122. "Additional Paragraph Suggested . . . for Inclusion in Section II, Principles, of the Draft Proposals," in United States, Department of State, *FRUS, 1944*, 1:791.

123. See Britain, PRO/FO, 371/40716, WR.208/126, letter from the Dominion Office to the Foreign Office, "Secret and Immediate," 30 September 1944; and the earlier RR I/50/1, "An International Bill of Rights," in Franklin Roosevelt Library, Sumner Welles Papers, Box 192.

124. Andrei Gromyko, as cited in Memorandum from Edward Stettinius to Cordell Hull, "Progress Report on Dumbarton Oaks Conversations — Eighteenth Day," 9 September 1944, in United States, Department of State, *FRUS, 1944*, 1:789.

125. See United States, Department of State, *Postwar Foreign Policy Preparation*, pp. 246–338; and United States, Department of State, *FRUS, 1944*, 1:838.

126. Columbia University, Rare Book and Manuscript Library, Wellington Koo Papers, Box 77, File 2, Notes of a Conversation Between Wellington Koo and Sir Alexander Cadogan, 29 September 1944.

127. See ibid., Box 76, File 5, especially the memorandum entitled "Notes on the Principle of the Equality of Races."

128. Churchill, as cited in Diane Shaver Clemens, *Yalta* (New York: Oxford University Press, 1970), p. 48.

129. Wellington Koo, in Plenary Record 3, Informal Record, Secret, 3 October 1944, File of Wellington Koo, "Washington, D.C. Conversations on International Organization" (on microfilm at Columbia University School of Law).

130. Ruth Russell, *A History of the United Nations Charter*, p. 420.

131. Hilderbrand, *Dumbarton Oaks*, p. 246.

132. Franklin Roosevelt, as cited in NANZ, EA 2, 1945/6B, File 111/8/8 (1), Memorandum 26831–5, "Private Statements by Members of United States Administration," Most Secret, undated.

133. Leo Pasvolsky, as cited in Joint Formulation Group, Record 3, "Secret," 6 October 1944, File of Wellington Koo, "Washington, D.C. Conversations on International Organization" (on microfilm at Columbia University Law Library).

134. "Welles Warns," *New York Times*, 25 October 1944.

Chapter 6: A "People's Peace"

1. Cordell Hull, as cited in United States, Department of State, *Postwar Foreign Policy Preparation* (Washington, D.C.: Government Printing Office, 1949), p. 304.

2. Carl Berendsen, as cited in F. L. W. Wood, *The New Zealand People at War* (Wellington: Department of Internal Affairs, 1958), pp. 324–325.

3. Peter Fraser, 30 June 1944, in Canada, Parliament, House of Commons, *Debates*, Session 1944 (Ottawa: Edmond Cloutier, 1945), 5:4424.

4. This is clear from NANZ, Peter Fraser Papers, Series 1, File 7; NANZ, Walter Nash Papers; New Zealand, Parliament, *Appendix to the Journals of the House of Representatives, Session 1944* (Wellington: Government Printer, 1945), 1, A-7, "International Labor Conference," p. 2; James Thorn, *Peter Fraser, New Zealand's Wartime Prime Minister* (London: Odhams, 1952), pp. 232ff.; and Keith Sinclair, *Walter Nash* (Auckland: Auckland University Press, 1976), pp. 237ff.

5. NANZ, EA2, 1945/9B, File 111/8/6 (2), Note entitled "Mr. Berendsen's Comments."

6. Joint statement from the 1944 Wellington Conference, as cited in NANZ, EA 2, 1945/9B, File 111/8/6 (2), "Document Prepared by the Australian Minister for External Affairs on International Organization," March 1945. See also in the same file a memorandum entitled "World Organization, Note for File," Secret, concerning a discussion between A. D. McIntosh and H. V. Evatt.

7. Secretary of State for Dominion Affairs to New Zealand Minister of External Affairs, 14 November 1944, as cited in Wood, *The New Zealand People at War*, p. 322.

8. Ibid.

9. "The Position of the Government of Uruguay Respecting the Plans of Postwar International Organization," 28 September 1944, in United Nations Conference on International Organization, *Documents of the United Nations Conference on International Organization* (hereafter cited as UNCIO, *Documents*), 22 vols. (London and New York: United Nations Information Organization, 1946–1955), 3:26–33.

10. "Opinion of the Department of Foreign Relations of Mexico Concerning the Dumbarton Oaks Proposals," 31 October 1944, in ibid., pp. 55ff. See also NANZ, EA2, 1945/6B, File 111/8/8 (1).

11. "Observations of the Government of Venezuela on the Recommendations Adopted at the Dumbarton Oaks Conferences," 31 October 1944, in ibid., pp. 189ff.

12. The words are those of Samuel Guy Inman, *Inter-American Conferences* (Washington, D.C.: University Press of America, 1965), p. 213.

13. The words are those of Harley Notter, in United States, Department of State, *Postwar Foreign Policy Preparation*, p. 401.

14. The U.S. delegation conveyed to the others that in the spirit of good neighborliness they were willing to listen to Latin American opinion, but would not sign any binding agreement. See United States, Department of State, *FRUS, 1945, The American Republics* (Washington, D.C.: Government Printing Office, 1969), 9:1–153.

15. See, for example, Columbia University, Rare Book and Manuscript Library, Wellington Koo Papers, Box 85, File 59, "Comments at Inter-American Conference."

16. See Political Memorandum No. 4, "Conversation Between Licenciado Alfonso García Robles . . . and Messrs. Bohan and Sanders," 6 February 1945, in United States, Department of State, *FRUS, 1945, The American Republics*, 9:90–95.

17. Document No. 24, CI-PR-4, "Proposal of the Delegation of the Republic of Cuba on the Declaration of the International Duties and Rights of the Individual," 27 February 1945, in Inter-American Conference on Problems of War and Peace, Document TC-9986, No. 219, C2-V-17, "An Account of the Essential Comments Made by the Delegations to the Inter-American Conference . . . Concerning the Bases of Dumbarton Oaks . . . Dr. C. Parra-Perez, Minister of Foreign Affairs of Venezuela," a copy of which is on file in Columbia University, Rare Book and Manuscript Library, Wellington Koo Papers, Box 85, File 59.

18. Final Act of the Inter-American Conference on Problems of War and Peace, 8 March 1945, in Inter-American Conference on Problems of War and Peace, Document TC-9986, No. 219, C2-V-17, "An Account of Essential Comments."

19. Pan American Union, *Inter-American Conference on War and Peace*, Congress and Conference Series No. 47 (Washington, D.C.: Pan American Union, 1945), especially the "Declaration of Mexico," "Reaffirmation of the Principles of the Atlantic Charter," "Rights of Women in the Americas," "International Protection of the Essential Rights of Man," and "Racial Discrimina-

tion," pp. 39–40, 61–62, and 69–70. See also "Evolution of Human Rights," *Weekly Bulletin of the United Nations*, 12 August 1946.

20. Inman, *Inter-American Conferences*, pp. 210 and 213.

21. Britain, PRO/FO, 371/50699, "Results of Inter-American Conference (Mexico City, 21 February–8 March 1945) in Regard to World Organization, &c.," Confidential, 8 March 1945.

22. See Edward Stettinius, "Statement by the Secretary of State on the Conclusion of the Conference," 8 March 1945, in United States, Department of State, *Department of State Bulletin*, 12, 298 (11 March 1945): 398–400; and United States, Department of State, *FRUS 1945, The American Republics*, 9:140 and 143.

23. See United States, Department of State, *Department of State Bulletin*, 12, 289–313 (7 January–24 June 1945), passim.

24. United States, Department of State, *Postwar Foreign Policy Preparation*, pp. 378–379; and the observations in NANZ, EA2, 1945/9A, File 111/8/6 (1), Memorandum entitled "United States of America," Confidential, 30 October 1944.

25. Americans United for World Organization, *Statement of Essential Human Rights* (New York: Americans United for World Organization, 1945).

26. Commission to Study the Organization of the Peace, *International Safeguard of Human Rights* (New York: Commission to Study the Organization of the Peace, 1944). See also Louis B. Sohn, "How American International Lawyers Prepared for the San Francisco Bill of Rights," *American Journal of International Law*, 89 (July 1995): 540–553.

27. See Jacob Robinson, *Human Rights and Fundamental Freedoms in the Charter of the United Nations: A Commentary* (New York: Institute of Jewish Affairs, 1946), pp. 32–34; Albert Verdoodt, *Naissance et signfication de la Déclaration universelle des Droits de l'homme* (Louvain-Paris: Éditions Nauwelaerts, 1964), pp. 42–43; and J. Herman Burgers, "The Road to San Francisco," *Human Rights Quarterly*, 14, 4 (November 1992): 476.

28. Commission on a Just and Durable Peace, *Christian Standards and Current International Developments*, as reproduced in *International Conciliation*, 409 (March 1945): 142–149.

29. Her complaints began early and attracted international attention, as seen by NANZ, EA2, 1945/9B, File 111/8/6 (2), Memorandum from Berendsen (Washington, D.C.) to McIntosh (Wellington) 30 August 1944.

30. Statement of Broadus Mitchell, in *International Conciliation*, 409 (March 1945): 166.

31. Ernest Johnson, "A Voice at the Peace Table?" *Crisis* (November 1944): 345.

32. Rayford W. Logan, "Dumbarton Oaks Proposals Ignore Colonial Problem," *Chicago Defender*, 9 December 1944.

33. See Brenda Gayle Plummer, *Rising Wind: Black Americans and U.S. Foreign Affairs, 1935–1960* (Chapel Hill: University of North Carolina Press, 1996), p. 120.

34. Declaration of Philadelphia, as reproduced in United States, Congress, Senate, 81st Congress, 1st Session, Committee on Foreign Relations, Document No. 1223, *A Decade of American Foreign Policy* (Washington, D.C.: Government Printing Office, 1950), pp. 25–26.

35. Commission to Study the Organization of the Peace, *International Safeguard of Human Rights*, as reproduced in *International Conciliation*, 403 (September 1944): 554 and 569.

36. Declaration on Liberated Europe, 11 February 1945, in United States, Department of State, *Department of State Bulletin*, 12, 295 (18 February 1945): 215.

37. The Anti-Slavery and Aborigines Protection Society, *An International Colonial Convention* (London: Anti-Slavery and Aborigines Protection Society, 1943); Immanuel Geiss, *Panafrikanismus: Zur Geschichte der Dekolonisation* (Frankfurt am Main: Europäische Verlagsanstalt, 1968), pp. 440ff.; Columbia University, Rare Book and Manuscript Library, Wellington Koo Papers, Box 76, File 5; Wood, *The New Zealand People at War*, pp. 327–339; and Commission on a Just and Durable Peace, *Christian Standards and Current International Developments*, as reproduced in *International Conciliation*, 409 (March 1945): 142–149.

38. See Chapter 5 above; and Lauren, *Power and Prejudice* (Boulder and San Francisco: Westview/HarperCollins, 1996 ed.), pp. 145–153.

39. U.S. National Archives, RG 59, Records of Harley A. Notter, Box 215, Advisory Commission on Postwar Foreign Policy, "Draft Commentary, First Revision," 3 September 1943; Franklin Roosevelt Library, Sumner Welles Papers, Boxes 189 and 195; Columbia University, Rare Book and Manuscript Library, Wellington Koo Papers, Boxes 70 and 76; New Zealand, Parliament, *Appendix to the Journals of the House of Representatives, Session 1944*, 1:A-7, especially p. 24, among many others.

40. American Jewish Committee, *A World Charter for Human Rights* (New York: American Jewish Committee, 1945).

41. Final Act of the Inter-American Conference on Problems of War and Peace, as cited in Britain, PRO/FO, 371/50699, "Results of Inter-American Conference," Confidential, 8 March 1945.

42. Commission to Study the Organization of the Peace, *International Safeguard of Human Rights*, as reproduced in *International Conciliation*, 403 (September 1944): 554.

43. Document No. 24, CI-PR-4, "Proposal of the Delegation of the Republic of Cuba on the Declaration of the International Duties and Rights of the Individual," 27 February 1945, in Inter-American Conference on Problems of War and Peace, Document TC-9986, No. 219, C2-V-17, "An Account of the Essential Comments Made by the Delegations to the Inter-American Conference," a copy of which is on file in Columbia University, Rare Book and Manuscript Library, Wellington Koo Papers, Box 85, File 59; Declaration of Philadelphia, as reproduced in United States, Congress, Senate, 81st Congress, 1st Session, Committee on Foreign Relations, Document No. 1223, *A Decade of American Foreign Policy*, pp. 25–26; and Commission on a Just and Durable Peace, *Christian Standards and Current International Developments*, as reproduced in *International Conciliation*, 409 (March 1945): 142–149.

44. Franklin D. Roosevelt, as cited in United States, Department of State, *Postwar Foreign Policy Preparation*, p. 411.

45. Jan Smuts, Verbatim Minutes of the Sixth Plenary Session, 1 May 1945, in UNCIO, *Documents*, 1:420–421.

46. Harry Truman, Verbatim Minutes, 25 April 1945, in ibid., 1:113–115.

47. See Jan Smuts, in ibid., 1:425.

48. Ramaswami Mudaliar, Verbatim Minutes, 28 April 1945, in ibid., 1:245.

49. See Franklin D. Roosevelt Library, President's Secretary's File, Safe File, Boxes 5 and 6, File "United Nations Conference (1)."

50. The only major changes from the Dumbarton Oaks proposals made at Yalta were the compromise on voting procedures that allowed the Soviets to have three votes in the General Assembly and the decision that the veto could not be used for procedural questions but could be applied to substantive matters like economic or military sanctions.

51. Winston Churchill, as cited in Robert F. Sherwood (ed.), *The White House Papers of Harry L. Hopkins*, 2 vols. (London: Eyre & Spottiswoode, 1949), 2:854.

52. Alexander Cadogan to Theodosia Cadogan, 15 May 1945, in David Dilks (ed.), *The Diaries of Sir Alexander Cadogan* (New York: Putnam, 1971), p. 742.

53. V. M. Molotov, speech at the First Plenary Session, 26 April 1945, in UNCIO, *Documents*, 1:131–136.

54. Harry Truman, as cited in Memorandum by Charles Bohlen, 23 April 1945, in United States, Department of State, *FRUS, 1945*, 5:253.

55. See Brenda Gayle Plummer, *The Rising Wind*, p. 142; and United States, Department of State, *Postwar Foreign Policy Preparation*, p. 416.

56. Leo Pasvolsky, in Minutes of the Fifth Meeting of the U.S. Delegation, 9 April 1945, in United States, Department of State, *FRUS, 1945*, 1:223.

57. Britain, Foreign Office, U 8657/180/70, "Some Comments on the Dumbarton Oaks Proposals by Dr. C.W. Jenks," Confidential, 12 January 1945, as on file in NANZ, EA2 1945/6B, File 111/8/8 (1).

58. Proposals submitted prior to May 1945: Doc 2, G/7 (c); Doc 2, G/7 (d); Doc 2, G/7 (f);

Doc 2, G/7 (l) Doc 2, G/7 (o); Doc 2, G/7 (q); as contained in UNCIO, *Documents*, 3:54ff., 254–256, 345–347, 383, 446–448, and 474.

59. Proposals submitted during the first four days of May 1945 prior to the joint amendments of the Great Powers: Doc 2, G/7 (n) (l); Doc 2, G/14 (c); Doc 2, G/14 (f); Doc 2, G/14 (g); and Doc 2, G/14 (h); as contained in ibid., 3:365, 472, 486, 495–502, and 527.

60. Doc 2, G/7 (q), "Suggestions of the Egyptian Government," 16 April 1945, in ibid., 3:447.

61. Britain, PRO/FO, 371/50703, "Memorandum for Submission to His Majesty's Government for Their Consideration in View of the San Francisco Conference," 12 April 1945; and handwritten comment on the cover.

62. "A Declaration to the Nations of the World," issued by the Non-European United Committee, Cape Town, South Africa, 1945, as cited in W.E.B. Du Bois, *The World and Africa* (New York: International Publishers, 1965 ed.), pp. 39–41. For more discussion about the NGOs at San Francisco, see René Brunet, *La Garantie internationale des Droits de l'homme* (Geneva: Grasset, 1947), pp. 119–121.

63. See United States, Department of State, "Designation of Consultants to the United States Delegation," *Department of State Bulletin*, 12, 304 (22 April 1945): 724–725.

64. See the excellent discussion in Plummer, *Rising Wind*, pp. 125–140.

65. Walter White, *A Man Called White* (Athens: University of Georgia Press, 1995 ed.), p. 295.

66. Walter Kotschnig, Transcript of Proceedings, Conference on the International Declaration of Human Rights, 31 October 1947, as cited in M. Glen Johnson, "The Contributions of Eleanor and Franklin Roosevelt to the Development of International Protection for Human Rights," *Human Rights Quarterly*, 9, 1 (1987): 25.

67. "Suggestions Presented by the Government of India for the Amendment of the Dumbarton Oaks Proposals," Doc 2, G/14 (h), 4 May 1945, in UNCIO, *Documents*, 3:527.

68. "Proposed Amendments to the Dumbarton Oaks Proposals Submitted by the Philippine Delegation," Doc 2, G/14 (k), 5 May 1945, in ibid., 3:535; and Verbatim Minutes of the Third Meeting of Commission II, Document 1144, II/16, 21 June 1945, in ibid., 8:134.

69. "Amendments to the Dumbarton Oaks Proposals," Doc 2, G/25, 5 May 1945, in ibid., 3:602.

70. See Russell, *A History of the United Nations Charter*, p. 793.

71. "New Urguayan Proposals," Doc 2 G/7 (a) (l), 5 May 1945; and "Additional Amendments Proposed by the Delegation of the Republic of Panama," Doc 2, G/7 (g) (2), 5 May 1945, in ibid., 3:35 and 269.

72. "Amendments Proposed by the French Government," 21 March 1945, in ibid., 3:383.

73. U.S. National Archives, RG 59, Box 2259, 501.BD Human Rights/11–1349, UNCIO CONS, Secret, Meeting 1, 2 May 1945; and United States, Department of State, *FRUS, 1945*, 1:546, statement of Leo Pasvolsky.

74. Francis Michael Forde, 27 April 1945, as cited in NANZ, EA1, File 111/8/7 (1).

75. See UNCIO, *Documents*, 10:434; and NANZ, Peter Fraser Papers, Series 3, Official Administrative Papers, File 2a, "Papers of the UN Conference," handwritten note regarding the amendment on this subject proposed by Wellington Koo.

76. Carlos Romulo, as cited in Verbatim Minutes of the Third Meeting of Commission II, Document 1144, II/16, in UNCIO, *Documents*, 8:138–139.

77. For the long list of proposals and amendments on this single issue, see UNCIO, *Documents*, 1:704–707.

78. Fraser's many speech notes are found in loose pages in NANZ, EA1, File 111/8/7 (1). I am grateful to Colin Aikman for personal interviews sharing his insights on Fraser at this time. See also Alister McIntosh, "Working with Peter Fraser in Wartime," *New Zealand Journal of History*, 10, 1 (April 1976): 3–20.

79. Harold Stassen, in Minutes of the Forty-Fifth Meeting of the U.S. Delegation, 18 May 1945, in United States, Department of State, *FRUS*, 1:791.

80. NANZ, EA1, File 111/8/32 (1), Report of the Prime Minister, *United Nations Conference on*

International Organization, 1945, p. 46. See also Fraser's own papers and notes in NANZ, Peter Fraser Papers, Series 3, Official Administrative Papers, File 2a, "Papers of the UN Conference"; UNCIO, *Documents*, 10; and Russell, *A History of the United Nations Charter*, pp. 808–842.

81. See UNCIO, *Documents*, 3:648–657, especially 652–653.

82. For a listing of the many amendments proposed on this matter, see ibid., 3:690–697.

83. See Minutes of the Twenty-Sixth Meeting of the U.S. Delegation, 2 May 1945; Minutes of the Twenty-Eighth Meeting of the U.S. Delegation, 3 May 1945; and Minutes of Second Four-Power Consultative Meeting, 3 May 1945; in United States, Department of State, *FRUS, 1945*, 1:532, 570, and 581.

84. "Amendments Proposed by the Four Sponsoring Governments," printed on 5 May 1945, as reproduced in UNCIO, *Documents*, 3:640–710. Proposals by the United States were stronger on trusteeship but weaker on non-discrimination, as evidenced in United States, Department of State, *Postwar Foreign Policy Preparation*, pp. 661–663; 679–681, 686–689.

85. See UNCIO, *Documents*, 3:308, 314, and 448; and Wood, *The New Zealand People at War*, p. 384.

86. The British attributed the change of position on human rights by the United States to pressure from these Latin American countries, as seen in Britain, PRO/FO, 371/50712, Telegram No. 374 from UK Delegation San Francisco to Foreign Office, 20 May 1945.

87. See the statements of Arthur Vandenberg in United States, Department of State, *FRUS, 1945*, 1:228; and discussion about the "domestic jurisdiction" subcommittee of the delegation in United States, Department of State, *Postwar Foreign Policy Preparation*, pp. 443–445.

88. See the description of the ceremony in Columbia University, Rare Book and Manuscript Library, Wellington Koo Papers, Box 216, Diaries.

89. The Charter of the United Nations, Preamble and Article 1. This opening phrase was suggested by Virginia Gildersleeve, as described in Russell, *A History of the United Nations Charter*, p. 913.

90. Charter of the United Nations, Articles 10, 13, 24, 34, and 39. See also the discussion in Robinson, *Human Rights and Fundamental Freedoms in the Charter*, pp. 65ff.

91. NANZ, EA1, File 111/8/32 (1), Report of the Prime Minister, *United Nations Conference on International Organization*, 1945, p. 11.

92. Charter of the United Nations, Articles 55, 56, 60, 62, 68, and 71.

93. Charter of the United Nations, Chapter XI, Articles 73 and 74.

94. Charter of the United Nations, Chapter XII, especially Articles 75 and 76; and Chapter XIII, Articles 86–91.

95. Charter of the United Nations, Articles 92, 93, and 94; and Statute of the International Court of Justice, Article 34.

96. See UNCIO, *Documents*, 5:311 and 17:230–231; and Russell, *History of the United Nations Charter*, pp. 806–807.

97. Charter of the United Nations, Articles 77, 82, and 83.

98. UNCIO, *Documents*, 5:311 and 17:230–231; NANZ, EA1, File 111/8/32 (1); and Russell, *History of the United Nations Charter*, pp. 806–807.

99. Charter of the United Nations, Articles 10, 13, 55, 62, 76, and 87.

100. Document 2 6/7 (h) (1), "Comments of the Government of Costa Rica," 4 May 1945, in UNCIO, *Documents*, 3:280.

101. Philip Jessup, as cited in Commission to Study the Organization of Peace, *International Safeguard of Human Rights*, p. 16.

102. Ibid., pp. 23–24.

103. Arthur Vandenberg, Minutes of the Sixth Meeting of the U.S. Delegation, 10 April 1945, in United States, Department of State, *FRUS, 1945*, 1:228.

104. John Foster Dulles, Minutes of the Fifty-First Meeting of the U.S. Delegation, 23 May 1945, in United States, Department of State, *FRUS, 1945*, 1:853–854.

105. See Britain, PRO/FO, 371/46324, "World Organization: Racial Equality and Domestic

Jurisdiction," 8 June 1945; Columbia University, Rare Book and Manuscript Library, Wellington Koo Papers, Box 77, Notes of a Conversation Between Herbert Evatt and Koo, 22 June 1945; Lauren, *Power and Prejudice*, pp. 162–167; and Sean Brawley, *The White Peril* (Sydney: University of New South Wales Press, 1995), pp. 210–221.

106. Herbert Evatt, in Document 696 I/1/39, "Amendment by the Australian Delegation to Proposed Paragraph 8 of Chapter II (Principles)," 14 June 1945, in UNCIO, *Documents*, 6:436–438.

107. Charter of the United Nations, Article 2.

108. Tom Connally, in Minutes of the Fifty-First Meeting of the U.S. Delegation, 23 May 1945, in United States, Department of State, *FRUS, 1945*, 1:854.

109. Among many sources, see NANZ, Personal Papers, Peter Fraser Papers, Series 1, Files 7,8, and 9, and Series 3, File 2a; Columbia University, Rare Book and Manuscript Library, Wellington Koo Papers, Boxes 70–72 and 94–99; United States National Archives, RG 59, Records of Harley Notter; and published materials in UNCIO, *Documents*, passim.

110. Edward Stettinius, in UNCIO, *Documents*, 1:691. See also the speeches by Wellington Koo of China, Joseph Paul-Boncour of France, Jan Masaryk of Czechoslovakia, and Ezequiel Padilla of Mexico, in the same source; NANZ, Peter Fraser Papers, Series 1, File 7, letter of Edward Stettinius to Peter Fraser, 23 June 1945; and Thorn, *Peter Fraser*, p. 236.

111. *Time*, as cited in Robert Divine, *Second Chance: The Triumph of Internationalism in America During World War II* (New York: Atheneum, 1967), p. 297.

112. Rayford Logan, as cited in Plummer, *Rising Wind*, p. 149.

113. W.E.B. Du Bois, 11 July 1945, in United States, Congress, Senate, Committee on Foreign Relations, *The Charter of the United Nations: Hearings Before the Committee on Foreign Relations*, 79th Congress, 1st Session (Washington, D.C.: Government Printing Office, 1945), p. 392. See also W.E.B. Du Bois, *Color and Democracy: Colonies and Peace* (New York: Harcourt Brace, 1945).

114. See Britain, PRO/FO, 371/40843; United States, Senate, Committee on Foreign Affairs, *The Charter of the United Nations: Hearings*, passim; and Brawley, *The White Peril*, pp. 220ff.

115. Lord Halifax, Verbatim Minutes, 26 June 1945, in UNCIO, *Documents*, 1:698.

116. Jan Smuts, in ibid., 1:710. See also Britain, Parliament, House of Commons, Command Paper No. 6666, *A Commentary on the Charter of the United Nations* (London: His Majesty's Stationery Office, 1945).

117. NANZ, EA1, File 111/8/32 (1), Report of the Prime Minister, United Nations Conference on International Organization, pp. 12–14 and 49; and Fraser's own speech notes in EA1, File 111/8/7 (1).

118. Harry Truman, Verbatim Minutes, 26 June 1945, in UNCIO, *Documents*, 1:715–716

Chapter 7: Proclaiming a Vision

1. See Hersch Lauterpacht, *International Law and Human Rights* (New York: Garland, 1973), pp. 3–47 and 145–165.

2. As cited in Kwane Nkrumah, *Towards Colonial Freedom* (London: Panaf, 1973 ed.), pp. 44–45. See also Immanuel Geiss, *Panafrikanismus: Zur Geschichte der Dekolonisation* (Frankfurt am Main: Europäische Verlagsanstalt, 1968), pp. 385ff; and George Padmore, *Pan-Africanism or Communism?* (New York: Roy, 1956).

3. See Philippe Devillers, *Histoire du Viet-Nam de 1940 à 1952* (Paris: Seuil, 1952); and Berhard Dahm, *Sukarnos Kampf um Indonesiens Unabhängigkeit* (Frankfurt am Main: Metzner, 1966).

4. Walter White, *A Rising Wind* (New York: Doubleday, 1945), p. 155.

5. Among many examples, see the wealth of material in United States, National Archives, RG 59, Box 4650; "Shameful Act," *Morning Standard* (Bombay), 16 October 1945; "Treatment of Negroes a Blot on U.S.," *Sunday Standard* (Bombay), 8 July 1945; and *Trud* (Moscow), passim; and American Jewish Committee, *Human Rights in the Peace Treaties* (New York: American Jewish Committee, 1946).

6. Note addressed from Eduardo Rodríquez Larreta to the Chiefs of Mission of the American Republics, 21 November 1945, as reprinted in United States, Department of State, *FRUS, 1945*, 9:190–191.

7. Address of the Argentine Minister for Foreign Affairs, 29 November 1945, in ibid., pp. 198–203.

8. Ernst B. Haas, *Beyond the Nation State: Functionalism and International Organization* (Stanford: Stanford University Press, 1964), pp. 163–165 and 343ff.

9. UNESCO, *Conference for the Establishment of the United Nations Educational, Scientific, and Cultural Organization*, ECO/CONF./29, 16 November 1945, p. 93.

10. Bradley Smith, *Reaching Judgment at Nuremberg* (New York: New American Library, 1977), pp. 14–16, 60, 66–67; and Robert Woetzel, *The Nuremberg Trials in International Law* (London: Stevens, 1962).

11. Robert Jackson, Opening Statement, 21 November 1945, in International Military Tribunal, *Trial of the Major War Criminals*, 42 vols. (Nuremberg: International Military Tribunal, 1947–1949), 2:98–99 and 130.

12. Hermann Goering, as cited in G. M. Gilbert, *Nuremberg Diary* (New York: New American Library, 1961), p. 39.

13. See Johannes Morsink, "World War Two and the Universal Declaration," *Human Rights Quarterly*, 15, 2 (May 1993): 357–405.

14. See Paul Gordon Lauren, *Power and Prejudice* (Boulder and San Francisco: Westview/HarperCollins, 1996 ed.), pp. 170–171.

15. United Nations, Document 1949.I.15, *Political Rights of Women*.

16. Wm. Roger Louis, *The British Empire in the Middle East, 1945–1951* (New York: Clarendon Press, 1984), p. 8.

17. United Nations, Document 1949.I.15, *Political Rights of Women*.

18. Constitution of Japan, Article 24, as cited in Kumiko Fujimura-Fanselow and Atsuko Kameda (eds.), *Japanese Women* (New York: Feminist Press, 1995), p. 354.

19. See U.S. National Archives, RG 59, Box 6, Project No. 126, "The Negotiation of the Human Rights Articles in the Treaties of Peace with Italy, Rumania, Bulgaria, and Hungary," Secret, August 1949.

20. United Nations, General Assembly (hereafter cited as UN/GA), *Official Records, Plenary Meetings of the General Assembly, Verbatim Records, 1946* (Flushing Meadows: United Nations, 1947), pp. 953–973.

21. Vijaya Lakshmi Pandit, 7 December 1946, in ibid., pp. 1016-1019. See also Lauren, *Power and Prejudice*, pp. 179–184; and United States, National Archives, RG 84, U.S. Mission to the United Nations, Box 78, File "Discrimination, Race: South Africa."

22. Ibid., pp. 1009–1058; and UN Resolution A/RES/44 (I), "Treatment of Indians in the Union of South Africa," 8 December 1946.

23. UN Resolution A/RES/96 (I), "The Crime of Genocide," 11 December 1946.

24. See John P. Humphrey, *Human Rights and the United Nations* (Dobbs Ferry: Transnational Publishers, 1984), p. 15. The Tokyo War Crimes Trials occurred between May 1946 and November 1948.

25. New Zealand Minister of External Affairs, as cited in F. L. W. Wood, *The New Zealand People at War* (Wellington: Department of Internal Affairs, 1958), p. 344.

26. Resolution 63 (I), "Approval of Trusteeship Agreements," 13 December 1946; Resolution 64 (I), "Establishment of the Trusteeship Council," 14 December 1946; Resolution 65 (I), "Future of South West Africa," 14 December 1946; Resolution 66 (I), "Transmission of Information," 14 December 1946; and Resolution 67 (I), "Regional Conferences of Representatives of Non-Self-Governing Territories," 14 December 1946, in UN/GA, *Official Records, Resolutions, 1946*, pp. 122–127. The details and the intensity of the debates on this subject is revealed in UN/GA, *Official Records, Summary Records of the Fourth Committee, 1946*.

27. "Status of Women," *United Nations Weekly Bulletin*, 16 September 1946.

28. UN Resolution A/RES/56 (I), "Political Rights of Women," 11 December 1946. See also

"Political Rights of Women," *United Nations Weekly Bulletin*, 25 November 1946; and the discussion in UN/GA, *Official Records, Third Committee, Summary Records, 1946*, pp. 121 ff. See also NANZ, EA 2, File 108/23/1 (1), personal letter from Agnes McIntosh to Peter Fraser, 16 August 1948; and U.S. National Archives, RG 84, Records of the U.S. Delegation to the United Nations, Box 94, File "Women and Women's Rights, 1946–1948."

29. Trygve Lie, as cited in "Human Rights," *United Nations Weekly Bulletin*, 4 November 1946.

30. Aase Lionaes, 14 December 1946, as cited in UN/GA, *Official Records, Verbatim Records of the General Assembly, Plenary Meetings, 1946*, p. 1377.

31. Resolution 59 (I), "Calling of an International Conference on Freedom of Information," 14 December 1946, in UN/GA, *Official Records, Resolutions, 1946*, p. 95.

32. UN Document A/C.3/10, "Statement on the Refugee Question by the Delegate of the Netherlands," 29 January 1946.

33. Constitution of the World Health Organization, 22 July 1946, as reproduced in "World Health Organization," *United Nations Weekly Bulletin*, 3 August 1946. I am grateful to Sandy Lauren for bring this provision to my attention. The debates surrounding the creation of these many specialized agencies can be found in UN/GA, *Official Records, Verbatim Records of the General Assembly, Plenary Records, 1946*; and UN/GA, *Official Records, Third Committee, Summary Records, 1946*.

34. See Chapters 4, 5, and 6 above.

35. Harry Truman, 26 June 1945, Verbatim Minutes of the Closing Plenary Session, in UNCIO, *Documents of the United Nations Conference on International Organization*, 22 vols. (London and New York: UNCIO, 1946–1955), 1:715–716.

36. Resolution 43 (I), "Draft Declaration on Fundamental Human Rights and Freedoms," 11 December 1946, in UN/GA, *Official Records, Resolutions, 1946*, p. 68. See also U.S. National Archives, RG 84, Box 89, File "Rights: Human, 1946–1949," memorandum from James Hendrick, "Panamanian Declaration on Human Rights," 13 November 1946.

37. Edward Stettinius, as cited in United States, Department of State, Publication 2349, *Charter of the United Nations; Report to the President on the Results of the San Francisco Conference* (Washington, D.C.: Government Printing Office, 1945), pp. 118–119. See also Philip C. Jessup, "A Good Start," *Commentary* (January 1946): 56–58; and O. Frederick Nolde, "Possible Functions of the Commission on Human Rights," *Annals of the American Academy of Political and Social Science*, 243 (January 1946): 144–149.

38. Britain, PRO/FO, 371/57317, "Commission on Human Rights," A.C.U. (46), 25 March 1946.

39. The United Nations Preparatory Commission had met in London from August to October 1945 to make recommendations regarding the organization's structure and procedure prior to the first meeting of the General Assembly. See UN Archives/New York, DAG-1/2.3, Office of the Under-Secretary-General for Special Political Affairs [Urquhart Papers], Box 2, "Report of the Preparatory Commission"; and U.S. National Archives, RG 84, Box 103, File "IO: ECOSOC: Human Rights, 1946–1949," letter of William Fowler (Department of State) to H. T. Chu (Human Rights Division, United Nations), 29 October 1946.

40. Humphrey, *Human Rights and the United Nations*, p. 2.

41. See the thoughtful discussion in Blanche Wiesen Cook, "Eleanor Roosevelt and Human Rights," in Edward Crapol (ed.), *Women and American Foreign Policy* (Wilmington: Scholarly Resources, 1992 ed.), pp. 91–117; and M. Glenn Johnson, "The Contributions of Eleanor and Franklin Roosevelt to the Development of International Human Rights," *Human Rights Quarterly*, 11, 1 (1987): 33–47.

42. Eleanor Roosevelt, in UN Document E/HR/10, "Commission on Human Rights, Summary Record of Meetings," 6 May 1946.

43. Ibid.

44. UN Document E/38/Rev.1, "Report of the Commission on Human Rights," 21 May 1946.

45. Britain, PRO/FO, 371/57318, Telegram No. 599 from Ward to Cadogan, 14 June 1946; and Telegram No. 616 from Foreign Office to UN Delegation, 16 June 1946.

46. Resolution 5 (I), 16 February 1946; and Resolution 9 (II) 21 June 1946, in United Nations, Economic and Social Council, *Official Records, 1946–1949*, pp. 163–164 and 400–402.

47. "Extract from the Weekly Political Intelligence Summary," No. 379, 5 February 1947, generated in London, copy on file in NANZ, EA 2, File 108/11/1(1A).

48. There were times when these individuals could not always attend the meetings in person or were replaced by alternates. For a personal account by one of the members, see René Cassin, "La Déclaration universelle et la mise en oeuvre des Droits de l'homme," in *Recueil des Cours de l'Academie de Droit International*, 79 (1951), especially pp. 258ff.

49. For the details of the actual discussion in the Human Rights Commission, see UN Documents E/IIR/1–31 and then E/CN.4/1-and E/CN.4/SR.1–22. See also Albert Verdoodt, *Naissance et signification de la Déclaration universelle des Droits de l'homme* (Louvain-Paris: Éditions Nauwelaerts, 1964), passim; and Humphrey, *Human Rights and the United Nations*, pp. 23ff.

50. Citation from UN Document 1948.I.12, *For Fundamental Human Rights*, p. 17.

51. UN Archives/Geneva, SOA 317/1/01(1), Box 346, Part C, draft memorandum of 12 November 1948 recounting the history.

52. See Alison Dundes Renteln, *International Human Rights: Universalism Versus Relativism* (Newbury Park: Sage, 1990), p. 51.

53. See UN Archives/Geneva, SOA 317/1/01(2), Box 347; and UN Archives/New York, Central Registry, RAG-1, Box 73, File 605-2-1-4-1, "Representatives from Specialized Agencies."

54. UN Archives/Geneva, SOA, Box 341, File 317/03, contains interesting correspondence between the Division of Human Rights and the United Nations War Crimes Commission and the Office of Chief of Counsel for War Crimes. The addition of Dr. Egon Schwelb, who worked on the trials as a permanent staff member of the secretariat, made this connection even stronger.

55. See UN Archives/New York, Central Registry, RAG-1, Box 73, File 605–5-1–1-1, "Human Rights. Bill of Rights. Proposed Drafts by Governments"; Great Britain, Foreign Office, *United Kingdom Draft of an International Bill of Human Rights* (London: His Majesty's Stationery Office, 1947); UN/GA, Document A/148, "Statement of Essential Human Rights Presented by the Delegation from Panama," 24 October 1946; and Leo Baeck Institute, Ernst Hamburger Papers, Box 6, "Final Draft of a Commentary to the Universal Declaration of Human Rights."

56. UNESCO, Document Phil/1/1947, "Memorandum on Human Rights," 27 March 1947.

57. U.S. National Archives, RG 59, Box 2257, 501.BD Human Rights/12–1747, letter from Le Zhongshu (Chung-Shu Lo) to George Marshall, 19 December 1947.

58. The responses of these philosophers to the invitation from UNESCO received widespread attention by being reproduced in *United Nations Weekly Bulletin*, 3 (July-December 1947): 520–522, 586–588, 642–644, 672–674, 692–694, 732–735, 777–781, and 811–813. See also the complete listing of responses in UNESCO, Document Phil./8, "Report of the First Meeting of the Committee of Experts Convened by UNESCO on the Philosophical Principles of the Rights of Man," 31 July 1947.

59. Letter from Mohandas Gandhi to Julian Huxley, as reproduced in "The Rights of Man," ibid., p. 521.

60. UNESCO, Document Phil./10/1947/Rev., "The Grounds of an International Declaration of Human Rights," 31 July 1947. Cassin and Malik both credited this report as having considerable significance on the commission, as in René Cassin, "La Déclaration universelle et la mise en oeuvre des Droits de l'homme," *Recueil des Cours de l'Académie de Droit International*, 79 (1951): 272.

61. Ibid. Fifty copies of this report were sent directly to Laugier, Humphrey, and the Commission on Human Rights by the Director General of UNESCO, Julian Huxley, and they in turn asked for more, as indicated in UN Archives/Geneva, SOA 317/1/01(2), Box 347, File A. Due to some initial concerns about relative roles and jurisdiction, however, the commission did not seek to reproduce this report for distribution. It was eventually published by UNESCO itself in two forms: UNESCO, *The Basis of an International Bill of Rights* (Paris: UNESCO, 1949); and UNESCO, with an introduction by Jacques Maritain, *Human Rights: Comments and Interpretations* (London: Allan Wingate, 1949).

62. See, among many examples, U.S. National Archives, Department of State, RG 84, Records

of the US Delegation to the United Nations, Box 103, File "IO:ECOSOC:Human Rights, 1946–1949," Telegram No. 103 to Eleanor Roosevelt, 25 May 1948, with attached letters of instruction and position papers.

63. Franklin Roosevelt Library, Eleanor Roosevelt Papers, Box 4561, Diary entry of 4 February 1946; and Britain, PRO/FO, 371/59740, memorandum entitled "Human Rights Commission," filed on 11 September 1946.

64. Edward Lawson, who served on the Division of Human Rights during these years, uses the expression, "thousands," in Edward Lawson (ed.), *Encyclopedia of Human Rights* (New York: Taylor & Francis, 1991), p. x; as does United Nations, Department of Public Information, Background Paper No. 25, "Commission on Human Rights," 18 November 1947, p. 10.

65. Among many examples, see UN Archives/Geneva, SOA, Box 350, File 317/1/01(4)(B), letter from J. M. Smoot to Eleanor Roosevelt, 18 February 1948; and U.S. National Archives, RG 59, Boxes 2257 and 2258.

66. UN Archives/Geneva, SOA 317/1/01(3), Box 348, File A, telegram from Wolynec Czubko Iwaniuk to Eleanor Roosevelt, 2 February 1947.

67. UN Archives/New York, Branch Registries, Series: Commission on Human Rights, RAG 2/169, Box 168–7, File 169/5/01.

68. Howard Tolley, Jr., *The U.N. Commission on Human Rights* (Boulder and London: Westview, 1987), p. 16.

69. Franklin D. Roosevelt Library, Eleanor Roosevelt Papers, Box 3766, Walter White to Eleanor Roosevelt, 20 October 1947.

70. Copies of the petition can be found in Library of Congress, Manuscript Division, W.E.B. Du Bois Papers, Reel 86, Petitions, frames 1490-1545; and Franklin D. Roosevelt Library, Eleanor Roosevelt Papers, Box 3766.

71. Library of Congress, Manuscript Division, W.E.B. Du Bois Papers, Reel 60, Correspondence, frame 1079, "Statement of Dr. W.E.B. Du Bois to the Representatives of the Human Rights Commission and Its Parent Bodies," 23 October 1947. See also U.S. National Archives, RG 84, Box 78, File "Discrimination, Race: U.S., 1947"; and Brenda Gayle Plummer, *Rising Wind: Black Americans and U.S. Foreign Affairs* (Chapel Hill: University of North Carolina Press, 1996), pp. 178–184.

72. Library of Congress, Manuscript Division, W.E.B. Du Bois Papers, Reel 60, Correspondence, frames 708–709, Report by H. H. Smythe of the NAACP entitled "Afro-Americans Petitioning the United Nations for Equal Rights."

73. See Library of Congress, Manuscript Division, W.E.B. Du Bois Papers, Reel 60, "Press Reaction to the NAACP United Nations Petition," frames 788ff.; and U.S. National Archives, RG 59, Box 4651.

74. For more discussion, see Paul Gordon Lauren, "The Diplomats and the Diplomacy of the United Nations," in Gordon A. Craig and Francis Lowenheim (eds.), *The Diplomats, 1939–1979* (Princeton: Princeton University Press, 1994), pp. 459 ff.

75. See B. Ponomaryov, A. Gromyko, and V. Khvostov, *History of Soviet Foreign Policy* (Moscow: Progress Publishers, 1974), pp. 158–159.

76. Andre Vyshinsky, as cited in Joseph Lash, *Eleanor: The Years Alone* (New York: New American Library, 1973), p. 99; and G. Petrov, "The Unbecoming Role of Eleanor Roosevelt," *Literary Gazette*, 85 (23 October 1948).

77. For more on the relationship between the Cold War and the issue of racial discrimination, see Lauren, *Power and Prejudice*, pp. 197–208; and U.S. National Archives, RG 59, Boxes 2256, 2257, 4650, and 2651.

78. Hersch Lauterpacht, *International Law and Human Rights* (New York: Garland, 1973), pp. 157–158.

79. United States, President's Committee on Civil Rights, *To Secure These Rights* (Washington, D.C.: Government Printing Office, 1947), pp. 147–148.

80. Among many examples, see Britain, PRO/FO, 371/59741, memorandum from the Work-

ing Party on Human Rights, Confidential, 25 October 1946; PRO/FO, 371/67606, letter from Geoffrey Wilson to Paul Gore-Booth, 18 June 1947; and U.S. National Archives, RG, Box 2257, 501.BD Human Rights/12–2647, Telegram A-118 from Troutman to Secretary of State, Confidential, 26 December 1947.

81. See UN Archives/Geneva, SOA 317/1/01(1), Box 346, File A, Memorandum from Egon Schwelb to Henri Laugier, 15 March 1948.

82. Jan Smuts, as cited in Hugh Tinker, *Race, Conflict, and the International Order* (London: Macmillan, 1977), p. 111.

83. U.S. National Archives, RG 59, Box 2258, 501.BD Human Rights/9–3048, Telegram A-1069 from Caffery (Paris) to Secretary of State, Secret, 30 September 1948.

84. Dean Acheson, *Present at the Creation* (New York: Norton, 1969), pp. 111–112; V. L. Pandit, *The Scope of Happiness: A Personal Memoir* (New York: Crown, 1979), pp. 250–251; and Plummer, *Rising Wind*, p. 131.

85. UN Archives/New York, Central Registry, Box 73, File 605-2-1-6, "Cooperation and Support. Human Rights Program," speech by John Humphrey.

86. See UN Archives/New York, Registry Files, RAG-1, Box 73, File 605–1, "Social Affairs, Human Rights Commission"; UN Archives/Geneva, SOA, Box 348, File 317/1/01(3), and Box 350, File 317/1/02(3); U.S. National Archives, RG 84, Box 89, File "Rights: Human, 1946–1949"; and "Non-Governmental Organizations," *United Nations Weekly Bulletin*, 8 April 1947. Some of these possessed official consultative status, and others did not.

87. Humphrey, *Human Rights and the United Nations*, p. 46.

88. UN Archives/Geneva, SOA 317/1/01(3), Box 348, File A, letter from Louis Sohn to John Humphrey, 24 February 1948. See also "Declaration of Human Rights: Canadian, American Bars Ask for Delay of Action," *American Bar Association Journal*, 34 (October 1948): 881–885.

89. W. R. Hodgson, as cited in ibid., p. 27. See also NANZ, EA 2, File 108/11/13/1(1), "Report of the Australian Representative at the First Meeting of the Human Rights Commission."

90. See the report in UN Archives/Geneva, SOA 317/1/01(1), File C, memorandum from John Humphrey to Edward Lawson, 4 November 1948.

91. Ibid., p. 29.

92. UN, ECOSOC, Document E/CN.4/AC.1/3, "Draft Outline of International Bill of Rights," 4 June 1947; and Document E/CN.4/AC.1/3/Add.1, "Documented Outline," 4 June 1947.

93. Vladimir Koretsky, as cited in Humphrey, *Human Rights and the United Nations*, p. 40. See also U.S. National Archives, RG 59, Box 2256, 501.BD Human Rights/6–2147, Telegram 7594 from W. Austin to Department of State, Restricted, 21 June 1947.

94. Hansa Mehta, as cited in "Economic and Social Council," *United Nations Weekly Bulletin*, 25 March 1947.

95. NANZ, EA 2, File 108/11/1(1A), Memorandum "Human Rights," 13 March 1947.

96. U.S. National Archives, RG 84, Box 103, File "IO: ECOSOC, Human Rights 1946–1949," instructions from Durward Sandifer to Eleanor Roosevelt, 5 February 1947. See also Eleanor Roosevelt, "Statement Regarding Order of Work," copy on file in Britain, PRO/FO, 371/67606.

97. UN, ECOSOC, Document E/CN.4/21, "Report of the Drafting Committee to the Commission on Human Rights," 1 July 1947; E/CN.4.52, "Report Submitted to the Commission on Human Rights," 6 December 1947; and E/CN.4/57, "Report of the Working Group on the Declaration of Human Rights," 10 December 1947.

98. UN, ECOSOC, Document E/600, "Report of the Commission on Human Rights, Second Session," 17 December 1947. It is interesting to note that this three-step strategy was first suggested by André Mandelstam during the 1920s and 1930s.

99. "First Drafts of Human Rights Bill Completed," *United Nations Weekly Bulletin*, 15 January 1948.

100. See France, Assemblée nationale, Chambre des Députés, *Rapport fait au nom de la Commission des Affairs étrangères, 26 février 1948* (Paris: Imprimerie nationale, 1948), located in the collec-

tion at the Ministère des Affaires étrangères; Britain, PRO/FO, 371/72803, Letter No. U2410/62, "The International Political Situation," from R. E. Ormerod to E. B. Boothby, 7 April 1948; and United States National Archives, RG 59, Box 2256, 501.BD Human Rights, among others.

101. Documentation of their work and internal discussions can be found respectively in Britain, PRO/FO, 371/72800–07; U.S. National Archives, RG 59, Boxes 2256, 2257, and 2258, 501.BD Human Rights; and NANZ, EA 2, File 108/11/13/1(1).

102. "American Declaration of the Rights and Duties of Man," as reproduced in UN Document E/CN.4/122, 10 June 1948. See also Samuel Guy Inman, *Inter-American Conferences* (Washington, D.C.: University Press of America, 1965), pp. 233ff.

103. Britain, PRO/FO, 371/72806, Telegram No. 1523 from G. Wilson to Foreign Office, 18 May 1948.

104. UN, ECOSOC, Document E/CN.4/85, *Collation of the Comments of Governments on the Draft International Declaration on Human Rights, Draft International Covenant on Human Rights, and the Question of Implementation*, 1 May 1948.

105. UN Archives/Geneva, SOA 317/1/01(1), Box 346, Part B, letter from the Union of South Africa to the Secretary-General, 23 April 1948.

106. UN Archives/Geneva, SOA 317/1/01(1), Box 346.

107. UN/ECOSOC, Document E/CN.4/95, "Report of the Drafting Committee to the Commission on Human Rights," 21 May 1948; and Document E/800, "Report of the Third Session of the Commission on Human Rights," 28 June 1948.

108. NANZ, EA 2, File 108/11/13/1(2), Memorandum entitled "Report by the New Zealand Observer on the Third Session of the Commission on Human Rights [Colin Aikman]," 1 July 1948. I am grateful to Mr. Aikman for personal interviews on his experience with these early days of the commission.

109. UN Document E/CN.4/102, "China: Amendments to the Draft International Declaration on Human Rights," 27 May 1948.

110. UN/GA, Document A/625, "Report of the Economic and Social Council to the General Assembly, 18–29 August 1948, especially pp. 34 ff.

111. See Morsink, "World War Two and the Universal Declaration," *Human Rights Quarterly*, 15, 2 (May 1993): 357; and Humphrey, *Human Rights and the United Nations*, p. 66.

112. The words are those of Humphrey, in ibid., p. 63.

113. These included Eleanor Roosevelt, Charles Malik, René Cassin, P. C. Chang, Alexei Pavlov of the Soviet Union, and Hernan Santa Cruz of Chile who ultimately worked for many years on behalf of the United Nations human rights program.

114. "Searching Study of Human Rights Declaration," *United Nations Weekly Bulletin*, 5 (1 November 1948): 858–861.

115. Vladimir Koretsky, as cited in Humphrey, *Human Rights and the United Nations*, p. 42.

116. Eleanor Roosevelt, as cited in "Searching Study of Human Rights Declaration," *United Nations Weekly Bulletin*, 5 (1 November 1948): 858.

117. UN/GA, Third Committee, *Summary Records of Meetings, 21 September — 8 December 1948*, passim; UN/GA, Document A/C.3/400, "Report of Sub Committee 4," 4 December 1948; and UN/GA, Document A/777, "Draft International Declaration of Human Rights," 7 December 1948, with Emilio St. Lot of Haiti serving as rapporteur.

118. NANZ, EA2, File 108/11/13/1(1), Memorandum entitled "Human Rights Committee, Questions for Discussion," 12 February 1948.

119. The text under consideration was UN/GA, Document A/777, "Draft International Declaration of Human Rights," 7 December 1948. The final version adopted became Resolution 217 A (III), "Universal Declaration of Human Rights," 10 December 1948, which is reproduced in full following the Conclusion to this book.

120. Universal Declaration of Human Rights, Articles 1 and 2 (my emphasis). Descriptions of each of the articles can be found in Verdoodt, *Naissance et signification de la Déclaration universelle des Droits de l'homme*, pp. 78–274; and discussions about how each article relates to contemporary

developments can be found in Asbjørn Eide et al. (eds.), *The Universal Declaration of Human Rights: A Commentary* (Oslo: Scandinavian University Press, 1992).

121. Universal Declaration of Human Rights, Articles 3–14 and 16–20.

122. Allan Rosas, "Article 21," in Eide, *The Universal Declaration of Human Rights*, p. 299.

123. Universal Declaration of Human Rights, Articles 15 and 21.

124. Universal Declaration of Human Rights, Articles 22–28.

125. Torkel Opsahl, "Articles 29 and 30," in Eide, *The Universal Declaration of Human Rights*, p. 449.

126. Eleanor Roosevelt, *This Troubled World* (New York: Kinsey, 1938), also had expressed her belief that an individual had the duty to give the same respect to the rights of others as they claimed for themselves, and that this principle should apply to relations among nations as well.

127. Universal Declaration of Human Rights, Articles 29 and 30.

128. The debates can be found in UN/GA, *Official Records, Plenary Meetings, 1948*, meetings 180–183, pp. 852–934. See also the discussion in Verdoodt, *Naissance et signification de la Déclaration universelle des Droits de l'homme*, pp. 275–300, for those rights not included in the text.

129. The abstentions came from Byelorussia, Czechoslovakia, Poland, Saudi Arabia, Ukraine, Soviet Union, South Africa, and Yugoslavia.

130. UN Resolution A/RES/217 A (III), "Universal Declaration of Human Rights," 10 December 1948.

131. René Cassin, in UN, GA, *Official Records, Plenary Meetings, 1948*, pp. 864–867; and his subsequent assessments in René Cassin, "La Déclaration universelle et la mise en oeuvre des Droits de l'homme," *Recueil des Cours de l'Académie de Droit International*, 79 (1951): 290–296; and René Cassin, *La Pensée et l'action* (Paris: Lalou, 1972), p. 118.

132. Hernan Santa Cruz and Charles Malik, in UN, GA, *Official Records, Plenary Meetings, 1948*, pp. 857 and 863.

133. P. C. Chang and H. V. Evatt, in ibid., pp. 895 and 934.

134. Belarmino de Athayde and Mohammed Kahn, in ibid., pp. 878 and 890.

135. See UN, GA, *Official Records of the Third Committee, 1948*, p. 35.

136. Eleanor Roosevelt, full text of speech in US National Archives, RG 59, Box 2258, 501.BD Human Rights/12–848.

137. UN Archives/Geneva, SOA 317/1/01(4), Box 350, File B, letter from Erwin Loewenfeld (Cambridge) to John Humphrey (New York), 29 December 1948.

138. See Zdenek Augenthaler of Czechoslovakia and L. I. Kaminsky of Byelorussia, in UN, GA, *Official Records, Plenary Meetings, 1948*, pp. 882 and 896–97.

139. Juliusz Katz-Suchy, in ibid., p. 904.

140. Andrei Vyshinsky, in ibid., pp. 854, 857, and 924–927.

141. H. T. Andrews, in ibid., pp. 910–911.

142. See Frank Holman of the American Bar Association, as cited in *New York Times*, "U.S. Delay Urged on U.N. Human Rights Plan," 1 February 1949.

143. For more discussion on this point, see the Conclusion.

144. Humphrey, *Human Rights and the United Nations*, p. 76; and Asbjørn Eide and Gudmundur Alfredsson, introduction, in Eide (ed.), *The Universal Declaration of Human Rights*, p. 5. See also Verdoodt, *La Naissance et signification de la Déclaration universelle des Droits de l'homme*.

145. See U.S. National Archives, RG 59, Box 89, File "Rights: Human, 1946–1949," Memorandum from James Henrick to Louis Hyde, Jr., 24 September 1947.

Chapter 8: Transforming Visions into Reality

1. Universal Declaration of Human Rights, preamble. This point also is emphasized in René Cassin, "La Declaration universelle et la mise en oeuvre des Droits de l'homme," *Recueil des Cours de l'Académie de Droit International*, 79 (1951): 241–367.

2. UN Archives/Geneva, SOA, Box 346, File 317/1/01(1)(C), memorandum from Edward Lawson to John Humphrey, 16 November 1948.

3. On the efforts for both translations and wider publicity, and various reports about the reaction, see UN Archives/Geneva, SOA, Box 365, Files 373/1/01, /04, and /06.

4. "Treaty of Peace with Japan," 8 September 1951, in United States, Department of State, *United States Treaties and Other International Agreements*, 3, no. 3 (1952): 3171.

5. UN Archives/Geneva, SOA, Box 365, File 373/1/04, letter from King Gordon to Frank Scott, 31 May 1951.

6. UN Resolution, A/RES/260 A (III), "Convention on the Prevention and Punishment of the Crime of Genocide," 9 December 1948. See also Paul Gordon Lauren, *Power and Prejudice* (Boulder and San Francisco: Westview/HarperCollins, 1996 ed.), pp. 194–197.

7. See UN Archives/Geneva, SOA, Box 368, File 417/2/01; and Henri Coursier, "L'Evolution du droit international humanitaire," *Recueil des Cours de l'Académie de Droit International*, 99 (1960): 361–465.

8. "Convention for the Protection of Human Rights and Fundamental Freedoms," 4 November 1950, in Council of Europe, *The European Convention on Human Rights: Collected Texts* (Strasbourg: Council of Europe, 1963), pp. 1–19; and Council of Europe, *Yearbook of the European Convention on Human Rights* series.

9. The texts of these conventions can be found in United Nations, *The United Nations and Human Rights, 1945–1995* (New York: United Nations, 1995), pp. 172–187, 198–201, and 202–204.

10. UN Resolution A/RES/217 E (III), "Preparation of a Draft Covenant on Human Rights and Draft Measures of Implementation," 10 December 1948; and UN Document E/800, "Report of the Third Session on the Commission on Human Rights," 28 June 1948, Annex B, "Draft International Covenant on Human Rights."

11. See Humphrey, *Human Rights and the United Nations*, pp. 63ff.; and Edward Lawson (ed.), *Encyclopedia of Human Rights* (Washington, D.C.: Taylor & Francis, 1996 ed.), p. xii.

12. See UN Archives/Geneva, SOA, Box 350, File 317/1/01(6), memorandum to Alva Myrdal (Acting Assistant Secretary-General for Social Affairs) from John Humphrey, 16 June 1949; Richard Lillich and Frank Newman, *International Human Rights* (Boston: Little, Brown, 1979), pp. 53–121; and Egon Schwelb, "The Influence of the Universal Declaration of Human Rights on International and National Law," *American Society of International Law Proceedings* (1959): 217–229.

13. See Paul Gordon Lauren, "The Diplomats and Diplomacy of the United Nations," in Gordon A. Craig and Francis Lowenheim (eds.), *The Diplomats, 1939–1979* (Princeton: Princeton University Press, 1994), pp. 463 ff.

14. These fascinating and tragic letters can be found in UN Archives/Geneva, SOA, Boxes 366ff.

15. See UN Document 1948.I.12, *For Fundamental Human Rights*, p. 35.

16. See UN Archives/Geneva, SOA, Box 356, File 317/9/01; and Lauren, *Power and Prejudice*, pp. 199–209 and 240–246.

17. John Bricker, as cited in Natalie Hevener Kaufman and David Whiteman, "Opposition to Human Rights Treaties in the United States Senate: The Legacy of the Bricker Amendment," *Human Rights Quarterly*, 10 (1988): 309.

18. John Bricker, "U.N. Blueprint for Tyranny," *The Freeman*, 2 (28 January 1952): 265. I am grateful to David Robertson for bringing this reference to my attention.

19. John Bricker, as cited in U.S., Congress, *Congressional Record 1952*, 98, pt. 1 (Washington, D.C.: Government Printing Office, 1952), p. 912.

20. UN Archives/Geneva, SOA, Box 354, File 317/4/01(C), speech by John Humphrey, 1 January 1952.

21. UN/GA, Resolution 421 E (V), "Draft International Covenant on Human Rights," 4 December 1950.

22. Marc Bossuyt, *Guide to the "Travaux Préparatoires" of the International Covenant on Civil and*

Political Rights (Dordrecht: Nijhoff, 1987); Humphrey, *Human Rights and the United Nations*, p. 64; and Howard Tolley, Jr., *The U.N. Commission on Human Rights* (Boulder and London: Westview, 1987), p. 29.

23. See United States, Department of State, *FRUS, 1952–1954*, 3:1536–1581; John Foster Dulles, "The Making of Treaties and Executive Agreements," in United States, Department of State, *Department of State Bulletin*, 28 (20 April 1953): 591–593.

24. Eleanor Roosevelt, *My Day*, 9 and 10 April 1953, as cited in M. Glen Johnson, "The Contributions of Eleanor and Franklin Roosevelt to the Development of International Protection for Human Rights," *Human Rights Quarterly*, 9, 1 (1987): 46–47. See also Franklin D. Roosevelt Library, Eleanor Roosevelt Papers, Boxes 3855, 4560, 4587, and 1588.

25. Norman Bentwich, "Marking Time for Human Rights," *Contemporary Review*, 192 (August 1957): 80–81. See also Louis Henkin, "Editorial Comments — U.S. Ratification of Human Rights Conventions: The Ghost of the Bricker Amendment," *American Journal of International Law*, 89 (1995): 341–351; and Natalie Hevener Kaufman, *Human Rights Treaties and the Senate: A History of Opposition* (Chapel Hill: University of North Carolina Press, 1990).

26. Universal Declaration of Human Rights, Preface and Article 2, (my emphasis).

27. UN Archives/Geneva, SOA, Box 350, File 317/1/02( ), memorandum "Human Rights in Trusteeship Territories," written by Dr. Lin Mousheng, undated 20 April 1949.

28. Charter of the United Nations, Article 76.

29. UN Archives/Geneva, SOA, Box 350, File 317/1/02( ), memorandum "Human Rights in Trusteeship Territories," 20 April 1949.

30. UN Archives/Geneva, SOA, 317/4/01, Box 353, letter from M. R. Turner to the Commission on Human Rights, 24 July 1949.

31. Enrique Ugon, in UN/GA, *Official Records, Plenary Meetings, 1948*, p. 887.

32. Britain, PRO/FO, 371/78945, Circular Despatch No.25102/2/49, from A. Creech Jones (Colonial Office) to Governors of the Colonies, 28 March 1949, Secret. Similar efforts were made to insert a "colonial clause" into other international accords such as the General Agreement on Tariffs and Trade, the genocide convention, and even the European Convention on Human Rights, to prevent application within overseas possessions.

33. Ibid., letter from Lord Listowel (Colonial Office) to C. P. Mayhew, 8 April 1949.

34. UN, Trusteeship Council, Document T/1/Rev., "Rules of Procedure," 23 April 1947; Document T/44, "Provisional Questionnaire," 25 April 1947, especially questions 136–148; and Brian Urquhart, *Ralph Bunche* (New York: Norton, 1993).

35. UN Resolution A/RES/545 (VI), "Inclusion in the International Covenant or Covenants on Human Rights of an Article Relating to the Right of People to Self-Determination," 5 February 1952; and shortly thereafter, UN Resolution A/RES/637 (VII), "The Right of Peoples and Nations to Self-Determination," 16 December 1952.

36. UN Archives/Geneva, SOA, Box 351, File 317/1/03, memorandum from Victor Hoo to Guillaume Georges-Picot, 12 March 1952. See also UN Document E/CN.4/649, "The Right of Peoples to Self-Determination," 24 March 1952; and UN Documents E/CN.4/SR.252–266, "Summary Records of the Commission on Human Rights," April 1952.

37. UN Archives/Geneva, SOA, Box 351, File 317/1/03, memorandum from Egon Schwelb to Philippe de Seynes, 24 February 1955.

38. Sukarno, as cited in Republic of Indonesia, *The Asian-African Conference, 1955* (New Delhi: Information Service of Indonesia, 1955), pp. 13–18.

39. See Lauren, *Power and Prejudice*, pp. 223–227; and Final Communiqué of the Asian-African Conference, 24 April 1955, in Indonesia, *The Asian-African Conference*, pp. 208–215.

40. The expression comes from Bernard Porter, *The Lion's Share* (London: Longmans, 1975), p. 319.

41. W.E.B. Du Bois, "Address to the All-African Peoples' Conference," in his book *The World and Africa* (New York: International Publishers, 1965 ed.), p. 310. At the last moment, ill health prevented him from delivering his speech in person.

42. Immanuel Geiss, *Panafrikanismus: Zur Geschichte der Dekolonisation* (Frankfurt am Main: Europäische Verlagsanstalt, 1968), pp. 328–330.

43. First published as Frantz Fanon, *Les damnés de la terre* (Paris: Masper, 1961).

44. Interview with Frank Corner, 15 April 1994, in Wellington.

45. See, for example, United Nations, *Yearbook on Human Rights for 1960* (New York: United Nations, 1962), passim.

46. UN Resolution A/RES/1514 (XV), "Declaration on the Granting of Independence to Colonial Countries and Peoples," 14 December 1960.

47. U Thant, *View from the UN* (New York: Doubleday, 1978), p. 441; and UN Archives/New York, DAG-1/5.2.7, Papers of the Secretary-General [Thant Papers], Boxes 2 and 3.

48. This was first known as the Special Committee of Seventeen, but expanded in 1962 and given much more authority as the Special Committee of Twenty-Four.

49. See Lauren, *Power and Prejudice*, pp. 239ff.

50. Hendrik Verwoerd, as cited in UN Archives/New York, DAG-1, 5.1.3, Box 4, Confidential Memorandum of Meeting on 10 January 1961 with Dag Hammarskjöld. See also Columbia University, Rare Book and Manuscript Library, Andrew Cordier Papers, Box 136.

51. Nelson Mandela, 22 October 1962, as cited in Thomas Karis and Gwendolen Carter (eds.), *From Protest to Challenge*, 4 vols. (Stanford: Hoover Institution Press, 1977), 3:725–731.

52. See UN Resolution A/RES/1761 (XVII), "The Politics of Apartheid of the Government of the Republic of South Africa," 6 November 1962; and UN Resolution A/RES/1881 (XVIII), "The Politics of Apartheid . . . ," 11 October 1963.

53. Diallo Telli, 20 November 1963, in UN/GA, *Official Records, Plenary Meetings, 1963*, p. 13.

54. UN Resolution A/RES/2106 A (XX), "International Convention on the Elimination of All Forms of Racial Discrimination," 21 December 1965. See also Gerda Weinberger, *Gegen Rassismus und Rassendiskriminierung; Kampfdekade der UNO* (Berlin: Staatsverlag der DDR, 1976); and Marc Bossuyt, *L'Interdiction de la discrimination dans le droit international des droits de l'homme* (Brussels: Bruylant, 1976).

55. Clara Ponce de León, 16 December 1966, in UN/GA, *Official Records, Plenary Meetings, 1966*, 1495th meeting, p. 7.

56. UN Resolution A/RES/2200 A (XXI), "International Covenant on Civil and Political Rights," and "International Covenant on Economic, Social, and Cultural Rights," 16 December 1966.

57. Comments in UN, GA, *Official Records, Plenary Meetings, 1966*, pp. 6ff.

58. UN Resolution A/RES/2200 A (XXI), "Optional Protocol to the International Covenant on Civil and Political Rights," 16 December 1966; and UN Resolution A/RES/44/128, "Second Optional Protocol . . ." 15 December 1989.

59. Tolley, *The U.N. Commission on Human Rights*, pp. 54–57, is particularly good on this point.

60. Seán MacBride, as cited in Howard Tolley, Jr., *The International Commission of Jurists: Global Advocates for Human Rights* (Philadelphia: University of Pennsylvania Press, 1994), p. 98.

61. UN Resolution A/RES/2391 (XXIII), "Convention on the Non-Applicability of Statutory Limitations to War Crimes and Crimes Against Humanity," 26 November 1968.

62. UN Resolution, A/RES/3068 (XXVIII), "International Convention on the Suppression and Punishment of the Crime of Apartheid," 30 November 1973; followed by UN Resolution A/RES/40/64 G, "International Convention Against Apartheid in Sports," 10 December 1985.

63. UN Resolution A/RES/34/180, "Convention on the Elimination of All Forms of Discrimination Against Women," 18 December 1979. See also the earlier UN Resolution A/RES/1763 A (XVII), "Convention on Consent to Marriage," 7 November 1962; Natalie Kaufman Hevener, *International Law and the Status of Women* (Boulder and London: Westview, 1983); and Rebecca J. Cook (ed.), *Human Rights of Women: National and International Perspectives* (Philadelphia: University of Pennsylvania Press, 1994).

64. UN Resolution, A/RES/39/46, "Convention Against Torture and Other Cruel, Inhuman, or Degrading Treatment or Punishment," 10 December 1984. See J. Herman Burgers and Hans Danelius, *The United Nations Convention Against Torture: A Handbook* (Dordrecht: Nijhoff, 1988).

65. UN Resolution A/RES/44/25, "Convention on the Rights of the Child," 20 November 1989; and UN Resolution A/RES/45/158, "International Convention on the Protection of the Rights of All Migrant Workers and Members of Their Families," 18 December 1990.

66. E. N. Nasinovsky, 16 December 1966, in UN/GA, *Official Records, Plenary Meetings, 1966*, p. 13.

67. A. H. Robertson and J. G. Merrills, *Human Rights in the World* (Manchester: Manchester University Press, 1992 ed.), pp. 89–91; and Karl Partsch, "The Committee on the Elimination of Racial Discrimination," in Philip Alston (ed.), *The United Nations and Human Rights* (Oxford: Clarendon Press, 1992), pp. 339–368.

68. Dana Fischer, "Reporting Under the Covenant on Civil and Political Rights," *American Journal of International Law*, 76 (January 1982): 145.

69. Dominic McGoldrick, *The Human Rights Committee: Its Role in the Development of the International Covenant on Civil and Political Rights* (Oxford: Clarendon, 1991); and Human Rights Committee, *Annual Reports*.

70. UN Document E/CN.4/1994/42, "Report on the Effective Functioning of the Various Mechanisms Established for Supervision, Investigation, and Monitoring of the Implementation of the Treaty Obligations Entered Into by States in Regard to Human Rights . . . ," 14 February 1994, p. 4; and Krzysztof Drzewicki, *Social Rights as Human Rights* (Abo: Institute for Human Rights, 1994).

71. See UN Document E/CN.4/1994/42, "Report on the Effective Functioning of the Various Mechanisms . . . ," 1994; Roberta Jacobson, "The Committee on the Elimination of Discrimination Against Women," and Andrew Byrnes, "The Committee Against Torture," in Alston (ed.), *The United Nations and Human Rights*, pp. 444–472 and 509–547; UN Document A/49/41, "Report of the Committee on the Rights of the Child," 1994.

72. John Humphrey, Preface, in Bossuyt, *Guide to the "Travaux Préparatoires" of the International Covenant on Civil and Political Rights*, p. xv.

73. See Thomas Buergenthal, *International Human Rights in a Nutshell* (St. Paul: West, 1995 ed.), pp. 41, 70, and 76.

74. UN, ECOSOC Resolution 75 (V), "Communications Concerning Human Rights," 5 August 1947; and the discussion in the previous chapter.

75. UN Document E/CN.4/SR.332, "Commission on Human Rights, Eighth Session, Summary Record," June 1952, concerning a period from 3 April 1951 to 7 May 1952; and UN Archives/Geneva, SOA, Boxes 352–365.

76. NANZ, EA 2, File 108/11/13/1(4), memorandum entitled "Covenant of Human Rights," [1949].

77. See UN Archives/New York, Branch Registries, RAG-2/169, Box 168–7, File 169/5/01, "Commission on Human Rights," memorandum from Egon Schwelb to Oscar Schachter, 26 May 1948; UN Archives/Geneva, SOA, Box 342, File 317/06, "Study on the Right of Petition," 4 November 1949; UN Resolution E/RES/728 F (XXVIII), "Communications Concerning Human Rights," 30 July 1959; and Jakob Möller, "Petitioning the United Nations," in *Universal Human Rights*, 1 (October–December 1979): 57–72.

78. ECOSOC Resolution 1235 (XLII), "Question of the Violation of Human Rights," 6 June 1967. The resolution also mentioned South Africa's occupation of South-West Africa and racial discrimination in Southern Rhodesia by name.

79. UN Resolution E/RES/1503 (XLVIII), "Procedure for Dealing with Communications Relating to Violations of Human Rights," 27 May 1970.

80. Sub-Commission on Prevention of Discrimination and Protection of Minorities, Resolution 1 (XXIV), "Question of the Violation of Human Rights . . . in All Countries," 13 August 1971 (my emphasis). See also the discussion in Buergenthal, *International Human Rights in a Nutshell* pp. 89–95.

81. The confidentiality requirement had been a part of the original 1503 resolution, but had never been implemented until this particular meeting. I am extremely grateful to Jakob Möller, who served as the Chief of the Communications Unit of the International Instruments and Procedures Section, for several lengthy conversations on this history and subsequent developments.

82. Interview with Jakob Möller.

83. Among others, see Iain Guest, *Behind the Disappearances: Argentina's Dirty War Against Human Rights and the United Nations* (Philadelphia: University of Pennsylvania Press, 1990).

84. The procedure currently entails a four-stage process involving a Working Group on Communications, the Sub-Commission on Prevention of Discrimination and Protection of Minorities, a Working Group on Situations, and the Commission on Human Rights.

85. For a complete listing see "List of Countries Referred to the Commission on Human Rights Under the 1503 Procedure Since 1974," dated 1997, from the Office of the High Commissioner for Human Rights.

86. This characterization has been provided by individuals particularly knowledgeable about petitions and the 1503 procedure, but who for reasons of confidentiality wish to remain anonymous.

87. This has happened in the cases of Argentina, the Philippines, and Uruguay, when radical changes of regimes have brought new governments into power anxious to cooperate with the Commission on Human Rights.

88. The authority is claimed under UN/ECOSOC Resolution 1235 (XLII), "Question of the Violation of Human Rights," 6 June 1967. For more on Boven's role, see Tolley, *The UN Commission on Human Rights*, pp. 79, 95, 98, 104, 107, 144, and 203.

89. UN Document E/CN.4/1994/42, "Effective Functioning of the Various Mechanisms . . . ," 14 February 1994, p. 17; and Helena Cook, "International Human Rights Mechanisms: The Role of Special Procedure in the Protection of Human Rights," *International Commission of Jurists Review*, 50 (1993): 31–55. I am grateful to Bruna Molina-Abram for sharing her observations from extensive experience with special procedures with me.

90. UN Archives/Geneva, SOA, Box 354, 317/4/01(C), speech of John Humphrey, 1 January 1952. See also UN Archives/Geneva, SOA, Box 356, File 317/9/05.

91. See UN Archives/Geneva, SOA, Box 354, File 317/4/01(C); and UNESCO, *Human Rights: Comments and Interpretations* (London: Wingate, 1949).

92. See UN Archives/Geneva, SOA, Box 353, File 317/4/01; Box 365, Files 373/1/01, /04, and /06; and Tolley, *The UN Commission on Human Rights*, pp. 32–54.

93. UN Documents E/CN.4/Sub.2/181/Rev.1, *Study of Discrimination in Education*, 1957; E/CN.4/Sub.2/213/Rev.1, *Study of Discrimination in the Matter of Political Rights*, 1963; E/CN.4/Sub.2/307/Rev.1, *Study on Racial Discrimination*, 1971; and E/CN.4/1108/Rev.1, *The Realization of Economic, Social, and Cultural Rights*, 1975.

94. UN Publication ST/HR/2, *United Nations Action in the Field of Human Rights*, 1974.

95. The first appeared as UN Publication ST/HR/4, *Human Rights — International Instruments: Signatures, Ratifications, Accessions, Etc.*, 1978.

96. See Lauren, *Power and Prejudice*, pp. 244–248.

97. John XXIII, *Pacem in Terris*, 11 April 1963, in Claudia Carlen Ihm (ed.), *The Papal Encyclicals*, 5 vols. (Raleigh: McGrath, 1981), 5:107–129.

98. UN Resolution A/RES 1961 (XVIII), "International Year for Human Rights," 12 December 1963 and UN Resolution A/RES/2081, "International Year for Human Rights," 20 December 1965. See also United Nations, *The United Nations and Human Rights, 1945–1995*, pp. 215–219.

99. Proclamation of Teheran on Human Rights, 13 May 1968, in UN Document A/CONF.32/41, "Final Act of the International Conference on Human Rights," pp. 2–5; and UN Archives/Geneva, SO, Box 218, File 218(1), "International Conference on Human Rights."

100. Annex to UN Resolution A/RES/3057 (XXVIII), "Decade for Action to Combat Racism and Racial Discrimination," 2 November 1973.

101. The Second Decade to Combat Racism and Racial Discrimination occurred from 1983 to 1992, and the Third Decade runs from 1993 to 2002. For more discussion, see Lauren, *Power and Prejudice*, pp. 251–288; and UN Document A/CONF.92/40, "Report of the World Conference to Combat Racism," 1978.

102. Marcus Gee, "Assessing the Decade," *MacLean's*, 29 July 1985, citing a UN report issued in 1980.

103. UN, *The United Nations and Human Rights, 1945–1995*, p. 86; and UN, *Report of the World Conference to Review and Appraise the Achievements of the United Nations Decade for Women: Equality, Development, and Peace*, 1985 (Sales No. E.85.IV.10).

104. Professor Jan Patočka, 7 January 1977, in H. Gordon Skilling, *Charter 77 and Human Rights in Czechoslovakia* (London: Allen and Unwin, 1981), pp. 209–212.

105. Jimmy Carter, *Keeping Faith: Memoirs of a President* (New York: Bantam, 1982), p. 144. I am also grateful to Jimmy Carter for a personal interview on this subject.

106. A. Glenn Mower, *The United States, the United Nations, and Human Rights* (Westport: Greenwood, 1979).

107. Adopted in 1981 and entered into force in 1986. See Fatsah Ouguergouz, *La Charte africaine des droits de l'homme et des peuples* (Paris: Presses Universitaires de France, 1993).

108. Jan Mårtenson, as cited in *Refugees*, 67 (August 1989): 35.

109. UN Publication DPI/1394/Rev.1/HR, *World Conference on Human Rights: The Vienna Declaration and Programme of Action*, June 1993, 1995, p. 2.

110. Thalif Deen, "Heavy Fire Over Gag Rule," *Terra Viva*, 12 June 1993.

111. UN Document A/CONF/93, "Bangkok Declaration," based heavily on China's original proposal. See Jin Yongjian, "Asia's Major Human Rights Concerns," *Beijing Review*, 19–25 April 1993.

112. Jusuf Wanandi, as cited in Leah Makabenta, "Western Wrongs, Asian Rights," *Terra Viva*, 14 June 1993.

113. Lai Suat Yen, as cited in Thomas Beal, "The 1993 World Conference on Human Rights in Vienna," unpublished 1993 manuscript. See also John Shattuck, "The Global Structure of Human Rights, 1996," at http://www.usis.it/hr_reps/index, 15 September 1997.

114. Aung San Suu Kyi, "Freedom, Development, and Human Worth," *Journal of Democracy*, 6, 2 (April 1995): 12–19.

115. Boutros Boutros-Ghali, "Human Rights: The Common Language of Humanity," 14 June 1993, as cited in UN Document DPI/1394/Rev.1/HR, *World Conference on Human Rights*, p. 5.

116. Vienna Declaration and Programme of Action, in ibid., pp. 25–71. Material on the background of the High Commissioner can be found in UN Archives/Geneva, SO, File 218, Box 218.

117. See UN Archives/Geneva, SOA, Box 356, File 317/9/01, memorandum from John Humphrey to Guillaume Georges-Picot, 12 May 1952; and UN Resolution A/RES/926 (X), "Advisory Services in the Field of Human Rights," 14 December 1955.

118. UN Archives/Geneva, G/SO 216/3; and UN Publication ST/HR/2, *United Nations Action in the Field of Human Rights*, 1974, pp. 87, 192–197.

119. See UN Archives/Geneva, SOA, Boxes 352–365, passim; and Box 398, File 420/123/01, "Advisory Services in the Field of Human Rights."

120. UN Resolution A/48/141, "The Post of the United Nations High Commissioner for Human Rights," 20 December 1993; and UN Archives/Geneva, SO, Box 218, File 218, "United Nations High Commissioner for Human Rights."

121. See UN Archives/Geneva, G/SO, 216/1.

122. UN Resolution A/47/20 B, "Authorizing Participation of the United Nations in Cooperation with the Organization of American States in the International Civilian Mission to Haiti (MICIVIH)," 20 April 1993; and UN Resolution A/RES/48/267, "United Nations Mission for the Verification of Human Rights and of Compliance with the Commitments of the Comprehensive Agreement on Human Rights in Guatemala," 19 September 1994.

123. UN Resolution A/RES/48/91, "Third Decade to Combat Racism and Racial Discrimination," 20 December 1993; UN Resolution A/RES/49/184, "United Nations Decade for Human Rights Education," 23 December 1994; and UN Resolution A/RES/49/214, "International Decade of the World's Indigenous People," 23 December 1994.

124. UN Document E/CN.4/1997/L.91, "Draft Resolution on the Situation of Human Rights in China," 10 April 1997.

125. Wu Jiamin, speech of 15 April 1997 before the Commission on Human Rights, as recorded from personal notes.

126. For current activities, see http://www.un.org/ha/ and http://www.reliefweb.int/dha/.

127. See Kelly Pease and David Forsythe, "Human Rights, Humanitarian Intervention, and World Politics," *Human Rights Quarterly*, 15, 2 (May 1993): 302–308; and Peter Malanczuk, *Humanitarian Intervention and the Legitimacy of the Use of Force* (Amsterdam: Spinhuis, 1993).

128. Interviews with Zdzislaw Kedzia and Fiona Blyth-Kubota, among others.

129. UN Resolution S/RES/693, "The United Nations Observer Mission in El Salvador (ONUSAL)," 20 May 1991; UN Resolution S/RES/808, "Establishing an International Tribunal for . . . the Former Yugoslavia," 22 February 1993; UN Resolution S/RES/955, "Establishing an International Tribunal for . . . Rwanda," 8 November 1994; UN Resolution S/RES/1076, "Violations of Human Rights and Humanitarian Law in Afghanistan," 22 October 1996; UN Resolution S/RES/1077, "Human Rights Protection Office in Abkhazia, Georgia," 22 October 1996; and UN Resolution S/RES/1088, "Stabilization Force Succeeds Implementation Force in Bosnia and Herzegovina," 12 December 1966.

130. UN Publication DPI/167, *The United Nations and Human Rights, 1945–1995*; and UN Publication HR/PUB/HCHR/96/1, *Notes of the UN High Commissioner for Human Rights*, No. 1, "An Introduction: Making Human Rights a Reality," 1996.

131. UN CD-ROM, *Human Rights: Bibliographical Data and International Instruments* (UN Sales No. GV.E.97.0.7), 1997.

132. The address is http://www.unhchr.ch. See also the category of "Human Rights" listed under the more general United Nations website, http://www.un.org.

133. Among many examples, see Laurie Wiseberg, "Introductory Essay," in Lawson (ed.), *Encyclopedia of Human Rights*, pp. xx and xxiv–xxvii.

134. The Human Rights Hot Line is a facsimile line (41-22-917-0092) managed by the Special Procedures Branch of the Centre for Human Rights in Geneva.

135. See the excellent treatment of many of these case studies in George Andreopoulos and Richard Pierre Claude (eds.), *Human Rights Education for the Twenty-First Century* (Philadelphia: University of Pennsylvania Press, 1997).

136. UN Document E/CN.4/1997/98, "Follow-Up to the World Conference on Human Rights: Report of the High Commissioner," 24 February 1997; and Jan Mårtenson, in Asbjørn Eide (ed.), *The Universal Declaration of Human Rights: A Commentary* (Oslo: Scandinavian University Press, 1992), p. 27.

Conclusion

1. Among many examples, see U.S. National Archives, RG 84, Box 89, File "Human Rights, 1946–1949," "Statement to the United Nations on Forced Labor"; William Ewart Gladstone, *Bulgarian Horrors and the Question of the East* (London: Murray, 1876); and Henri Coursier "L'Evolution du droit international humanitaire," *Recueil des Cours de l'Académie de Droit International*, 99 (1960): 361–465.

2. John Humphrey, *Human Rights and the United Nations* (Dobbs Ferry: Transnational, 1984), p. 41.

3. Among many examples, see "Sie halten uns wie Sklaven," *Der Spiegel*, 14 October 1996.

4. See the statements cited in Nehemiah Robinson, *The Universal Declaration of Human Rights: Its Origins, Significance, and Interpretation* (New York: Institute of Jewish Affairs, 1950), p. 15.

5. John Foster Dulles, *War or Peace* (New York: Macmillan, 1950), p. 201.

6. Expressions as reported and as used in NANZ, EA 2, File 108/11/13/1(2), memorandum entitled "Human Rights Committee," 12 February 1948, and memorandum entitled "Report by the New Zealand Observer," 1 July 1948.

7. Eleanor Roosevelt, as cited in Blanche Wiesen Cook, "Eleanor Roosevelt and Human

Rights," in Edward Crapol (ed.), *Women and American Foreign Policy* (Wilmington: Scholarly Resources Books, 1992 ed.), p. 114.

8. Edith Balantyne, 7 April 1997, meeting of the Special Committee of International NGOs on Human Rights, Palais des Nations, personal notes.

9. Kofi Annan, 9 April 1997, as cited in United Nations press release, "Discours du Secretaire General"; and interview with an official who wishes to remain anonymous. See also Thomas Buergental, *International Human Rights in a Nutshell* (St. Paul: West, 1995 ed.), pp. 318–329; and Laurie Wiseberg, "Introductory Essay," in Edward Lawson (ed.), *Encyclopedia of Human Rights* (New York: Taylor & Francis, 1996 ed.) pp. xx and xxiv–xxvii.

10. Humphrey, *Human Rights and the United Nations*, p. 13.

11. This expression is frequently heard among nongovernmental organizations, as evidenced in Special Committee of International NGOs on Human Rights, meeting of 7 April 1997, Palais des Nations, personal notes.

12. Kofi Annan, 9 April 1997, in UN Press Release, "Discours du Secretaire General."

13. Boutros Boutros-Ghali, 14 June 1993, as cited in UN Publication DPI/1394/Rev.1/HR, *World Conference on Human Rights*, p. 6.

14. Ndabaningi Sithole, *African Nationalism* (London: Oxford University Press, 1959), p. 23.

15. For more discussion, see Burns H. Weston, "Human Rights," in Richard Pierre Claude and Burns H. Weston (eds.), *Human Rights in the World Community* (Philadelphia: University of Pennsylvania Press, 1992 ed.), pp. 18–20; and Vasak Karel (ed.), *Dimensions internationales des droits de l'homme*, 2 vols. (Paris: UNESCO, 1982).

16. See, among many examples, William Ewart Gladstone, *Lessons of the Massacre* (London: Murray, 1877), passim; NANZ, EA 2, File 108/11/13/1 (4), memorandum entitled "The Problem of Implementation," 1 December 1949; the Universal Declaration of Human Rights, Preamble; UN/GA, *Official Records, Plenary Meetings, 1966*, Meeting of 16 December 1966, p. 10; and H. Gordon Skilling, *Charter 77 and Human Rights in Czechoslovakia* (London: George Allen & Unwin, 1981), p. 153.

17. Expressions from UN Document E/CN.4/1996/NGO/22, "Organisation des Travaux de la Session," 26 March 1996; and the Special Committee of International NGOs on Human Rights, meeting of 7 April 1997, Palais des Nations, personal notes.

18. Sithole, *African Nationalism*, p. 23.

19. See UN/GA, *Official Records, 1948*, passim; and Robinson, *The Universal Declaration of Human Rights*, p. 15.

20. See Skilling, *Charter 77 and Human Rights in Czechoslovakia*, pp. 152 ff. I also am very grateful to J. Herman Burgers for discussions on this issue.

21. See UN Document E/CN.4/1997/L.91, "Draft Resolution on the Situation of Human Rights in China," 10 April 1997.

22. Humphrey, *Human Rights and the United Nations*, p. 25.

23. See Thomas Jefferson to James Madison, 15 March 1789, in Thomas Jefferson, *The Papers of Thomas Jefferson*, 26 vols. (Princeton: Princeton University Press, 1950–1995), 14:660; letter from Peter Benenson to John Humphrey, Private and Confidential, 13 March 1966, and International League for the Rights of Man, "Statement on the United Nations Commissioner on Human Rights," 30 March 1966, both in UN Archives/Geneva, SO 218, Box 218; and Albert Verdoodt, *Naissance et signification de la Déclaration universelle des Droits de l'homme* (Louvain-Paris: Éditions Nauwelaerts, 1964), pp. 317 and 325.

24. H. Lauterpacht, *International Law and Human Rights* (New York: Garland, 1973), p. 131.

25. Participant at the London Peace Implementation Conference on Bosnia, as cited in the British Broadcasting Corporation's "World News Broadcast," 5 December 1996.

26. Nelson Mandela, as cited at http://www.anc.org.sa, 18 August 1997. See also Robin Cook, "Human Rights Into a New Century," press release from the British Foreign Office, 17 July 1997; and Forsythe, *The Internationalization of Human Rights*, passim. among many others.

27. These can be seen in daily news reports; the discussions during the sessions of the Commis-

sion on Human Rights; the annual reports of Amnesty International; at http://www.usis.it/hr_
reps; and in Philip Alston (ed.), *The United Nations and Human Rights: A Critical Appraisal* (Oxford:
Clarendon Press, 1992), pp. 12–21 and 620–675; among others.

28. Blanche Wiesen Cook, "Eleanor Roosevelt and Human Rights," p. 113; and Jan Mårtenson,
"The Preamble of the Universal Declaration of Human Rights and the UN Human Rights Pro-
gram," in Asbørn Eide et al. (eds.), *The Universal Declaration of Human Rights: A Commentary* (Oslo:
Scandinavian University Press, 1992), p. 17.

Selected Bibliography

Archives

Commission for Relief in Belgium. Hoover Institution, Stanford.
China. Chinese Relief and Rehabilitation Administration, Hoover Institution, Stanford.
France. Archives diplomatiques du Ministère des Affairs étrangères, Paris.
Germany. Politisches Archive des Auswärtiges Amt, Bonn.
Great Britain. Foreign Office Correspondence, Public Record Office, London.
Japan. Delegation to the Peace Conference, Hoover Institution, Stanford.
League of Nations. Archives de la Société des Nations, Geneva.
New Zealand. Department of External Affairs, National Archives, Wellington.
United Nations Archives/Geneva. Registry, Records, and Mailing Section at the Palais des Nations, Geneva.
United Nations Archives/New York. Archives of the United Nations, New York.
United States. Department of State, National Archives and Records Service, Washington, D.C.

Private Papers and Personal Collections

Cordier, Andrew (Columbia University)
Davis, Loda Mae (Hoover Institution)
Du Bois, W.E.B (Library of Congress)
Fraser, Peter (National Archives of New Zealand)
Hammarskjöld, Dag (Papers of the Secretary-General, UN Archives/New York)
Himmler, Heinrich (Hoover Institution)
Koo, Wellington (Columbia University)
Lansing, Robert (Library of Congress)
Lie, Trygvie (Papers of the Secretary-General, UN Archives/New York)
Miller, David Hunter (Hoover Institution)
Mitchell, Anna (Hoover Institution)
Munro, Leslie (Alexander Turnbull Library)
Nash, Walter (National Archives of New Zealand)
Pérez de Cuéllar, Javier (Papers of the Secretary-General, UN Archives/New York)
Roosevelt, Eleanor (Roosevelt Library)
Roosevelt, Franklin D. (Roosevelt Library)
Stilwell, Joseph (Hoover Institution)
Streit, Clarence (University of Montana)
Thomas, Albert (France, Archives Nationales)

Urquhart, Brian (UN Archives/New York)
U Thant (Papers of the Secretary-General, UN Archives/New York)
Waldheim, Kurt (Papers of the Secretary-General, UN Archives/New York)
Webster, Sir Charles (London School of Economics)
Welles, Sumner (Roosevelt Library)

Published Documents

Académie Diplomatique Internationale. *Séances et Travaux.*
Canada. Parliament. House of Commons. *Official Debates.*
Commission for Relief in Belgium. *Annual Report, 1914–1916.* London: Crowther & Goodman, 1916.
Council of Europe. *The European Convention on Human Rights: Collected Texts.* Strasbourg: Council of Europe, 1963.
——. *Yearbook of the European Convention on Human Rights.*
——. Commission européenne des Droits de l'Homme. *Compte rendu annuel.*
France. Assemblée nationale. *Archives parlementaires.*
——. Assemblée nationale, Chambre des Députés. *Débats parlementaires.*
——. Assemblée nationale, Chambre des Députés. *Rapports fait au nom de la Commission des Affaires étrangères.*
——. Conférence de la Paix, 1919–1920. *Recueil des actes de la Conférence.* Paris: Imprimerie nationale, 1922.
Germany. Auswärtiges Amt. *Die Grosse Politik der Europäischen Kabinette, 1871–1914,* 40 vols. Berlin: Deutsche Verlagsgesellschaft für Politik, 1922–1927.
Great Britain. Foreign Office. *British and Foreign State Papers.*
——. Parliament. House of Commons. *A Commentary on the Charter of the United Nations.* London: His Majesty's Stationery Office, 1945.
——. Parliament. House of Commons. *The Parliamentary Debates.*
——. Parliament. House of Commons. *Sessional Papers.*
——. Parliament. House of Commons. *Substance of the Debates on a Resolution for Abolishing the Slave Trade.* London: Phillips and Fardon, 1806.
Indonesia. *The Asian-African Conference, 1955.* New Delhi: Information Service of Indonesia, 1955.
International Labor Organization. *The I.L.O. and Human Rights.* Geneva: International Labor Office, 1968.
——. *Official Bulletin.*
International Military Tribunal. *Trial of the Major War Criminals.* 42 vols. Nuremberg: International Military Tribunal, 1947–1949.
Inter-Parliamentary Union. Reports and Documents No. 27, *Women.* Geneva: Inter-Parliamentary Union, 1997.
League of Nations. *Official Journal.*
——. *Protection of Linguistic, Racial, and Religious Minorities.* Geneva: League of Nations, 1927.
——. *La Question de l'Esclavage.* Geneva: Société des Nations, 1924.
——. *Treaty Series.*
——. Permanent Mandates Commission. *Minutes.*
——. Permanent Mandates Commission. *Reports.*
Netherlands, The. Ministry of Foreign Affairs. *Human Rights and Foreign Policy: Memorandum Presented to the Lower House of the States General.* The Hague: Ministry of Foreign Affairs and Ministry of Development Co-operation, 1979.
New Zealand. Parliament. *Appendix to the Journals of the House of Representatives.*
Organization of African Unity. *Basic Documents and Resolutions.*
Organization of American States. La Comisión Interamericana de Derechos Humanos. *Activi-*

dades de la Comisión Interamericana de Derechos Humanos. Washington, D.C.: Comisión Interamericana de Derechos Humanos, 1976.

Pan American Union. *Congress and Conference Series*.

——. *Inter-American Conference on War and Peace*. Washington, D.C.: Pan American Union, 1945.

——. *Preliminary Recommendation on Postwar Problems*. Washington, D.C.: Pan American Union, 1942.

Permanent Court of International Justice. *Publications of the Court*.

United Nations. *The African Charter on Human and People's Rights*. New York: United Nations, 1990.

——. *Official Records*.

——. *The United Nations and Human Rights, 1945–1995*. New York: United Nations, 1995.

——. *United Nations Weekly Bulletin*.

——. *World Conference on Human Rights: The Vienna Declaration and Programme of Action*. New York: United Nations, 1993.

——. *Yearbook on Human Rights*.

——. Economic and Social Council. Commission on Human Rights. *Official Records*.

——. Economic and Social Council. Commission on Human Rights. Sub-Commission on Prevention and Discrimination and Protection of Minorities. *Official Records*.

——. Economic and Social Council. Human Rights Committee. *Annual Reports*.

——. General Assembly. *Official Records*, *Verbatim Reports*, and *Resolutions*.

——. General Assembly. Committee on the Elimination of Racial Discrimination (CERD). *Official Records*.

——. General Assembly. Special Committee Against Apartheid. *Official Records*.

——. General Assembly. Special Committee on the Situation with Regard to the Implementation of the Declaration on the Granting of Independence to Colonial Countries and Peoples. *Official Records*.

——. General Assembly. Third Committee. *Official Records*.

——. High Commissioner for Human Rights. *The High Commissioner for Human Rights: An Introduction*. Geneva: United Nations, 1996.

——. Security Council. *Official Records*, *Verbatim Reports*, and *Resolutions*.

——. Trusteeship Council. *Official Records*.

United Nations Conference on International Organization. *Documents of the United Nations Conference on International Organization*. 22 vols. London and New York: United Nations Information Organization, 1946–1955.

United Nations Educational, Scientific, and Cultural Organization. *The Basis of an International Bill of Rights*. Paris: UNESCO, 1949.

——. *The Birthright of Man*. Paris: UNESCO, 1969.

——. *Human Rights: Comments and Interpretations*. London: Wingate, 1949.

United States. *Statutes at Large*.

United States. Congress. *Annals of Congress*.

——. Congress. Senate. Committee on Foreign Relations. *The Charter of the United Nations: Hearings*. Washington, D.C.: Government Printing Office, 1945.

——. *Congressional Record*.

United States. Department of State. *Current Policy*.

——. *Department of State Bulletin*.

——. *Documents on German Foreign Policy, 1918–1945*. Series D.

——. *Foreign Relations of the United States*.

——. *Postwar Foreign Policy Preparation, 1939–1945*. Washington, D.C.: Government Printing Office, 1949.

——. *Treaties and Other International Instruments of the United States*.

——. President's Committee on Civil Rights. *To Secure These Rights*. Washington, D.C.: Government Printing Office, 1947.

Books

Addams, Jane. *Peace and Bread*. New York: Macmillan, 1922.

Agi, Marc. *De l'idée d'universalité comme fondatrice du concept des droits de l'homme*. Antibes: Alp'Azur, 1980.

Alston, Philip (ed.). *The United Nations and Human Rights: A Critical Appraisal*. Oxford: Clarendon Press, 1992.

American Jewish Committee. *A World Charter for Human Rights*. New York: American Jewish Committee, 1945.

American Law Institute. *Report to the Council of the Institute and Statement of Essential Human Rights*. New York: American Law Institute, 1944.

Andreopoulos, George (ed.), *Genocide: Conceptual and Historical Dimensions*. Philadelphia: Univeristy of Pennsylvania Press, 1994.

An-Na'im, Abdullahi Ahmed (ed.). *Human Rights in a Cross-Cultural Perspective: A Quest for Consensus*. Philadelphia: University of Pennsylvania Press, 1991.

Anti-Slavery and Aborigines Protection Society. *An International Colonial Convention*. London: Anti-Slavery and Aborigines Protection Society , 1943.

Aulard, A., and Boris Mirkine-Guetzévitch. *Les Déclarations des Droits de l'Homme: Textes constitutionnels concernant les droits de l'homme et les garanties des libertés individuelles dans tous les pays*. Paris: Payot, 1929.

Baxi, Upendra. *Inhuman Wrongs and Human Rights: Unconventional Essays*. New Delhi: Har-Anand, 1994.

Beach, Harlan, and Burton St. John (eds.). *World Statistics of Christian Missions*. New York: Foreign Missions Conference of North America, 1916.

Beveridge, Sir William. *Social Insurance and Allied Services*. New York: Macmillan, 1942.

Blum, Jerome. *Lord and Peasant in Russia*. New York: Atheneum, 1967.

Bodin, Jean. *Les Six livres de la République*. Paris: Fayard, 1986 ed.

Boissier, Pierre. *Histoire du Comité International de la Croix-Rouge de Solférino à Tsoushima*. Paris: Plon, 1963.

Bossuyt, Marc. *Guide to the "Travaux Préparatoires" of the International Covenant on Civil and Political Rights*. Dordrecht: Nijhoff, 1987.

———. *L'Interdiction de la discrimination dans le droit international des droits de l'homme*. Brussels: Bruylant, 1976.

Brandt, Irving. *The Bill of Rights: Its Origin and Meaning*. New York: New American Library, 1967.

Brawley, Sean. *The White Peril*. Sydney: University of New South Wales Press, 1995.

Brownlie, Ian (ed.). *Basic Documents on Human Rights*. Oxford: Clarendon Press, 1992 ed.

Brunet, René. *La Garantie internationale des Droits de l'homme*. Geneva: Grasset, 1947.

Buergenthal, Thomas. *International Human Rights in a Nutshell*. St. Paul: West, 1995 ed.

Burgers, J. Herman. "The Function of Human Rights as Individual and Collective Rights," in Jan Berting et al. (eds.), *Human Rights in a Pluralistic World*. Westport and London: Meckler, 1990.

Burgers, J. Herman, and Hans Danelius. *The United Nations Convention Against Torture: A Handbook*. Dordrecht: Nijhoff, 1988.

Burke, Edmund. *Reflections on the Revolution in France*. Chicago: Regnery, 1955 ed.

Burns, James MacGregor, and Stewart Burns. *The Pursuit of Rights in America*. New York: Vintage, 1993.

Burns, Roger (ed.). *Am I Not a Man and a Brother*. New York: Chelsea House, 1983.

Bussey, Gertrude, and Margaret Tims. *Women's International League for Peace and Freedom*. London: George Allen & Unwin, 1965.

Calder, Angus. *The People's War*. London: Panther, 1969.

Calder, Lord Richie. *On Human Rights*. London: H. G. Wells Society, 1968.

Carter, Jimmy. *Keeping Faith: Memoirs of a President*. New York: Bantam, 1982.

Cassin, René. *La Pensée et l'action*. Paris: Lalou, 1972.

Claude, Richard Pierre (ed.). *Comparative Human Rights*. Baltimore: Johns Hopkins University Press, 1976.

Claude, Richard Pierre, and Burns H. Weston (eds.). *Human Rights in the World Community*. Philadelphia: University of Pennsylvania Press, 1992 ed.

Commission to Study the Organization of the Peace. *International Safeguard of Human Rights*. New York: Commission to Study the Organization of the Peace, 1944.

——. *The United Nations and Human Rights*. Dobbs Ferry: Oceana, 1968.

Cook, Rebecca (ed.). *Human Rights of Women: National and International Perspectives*. Philadelphia: University of Pennsylvania Press, 1994.

Cotler, I., and F. P. Eliadis (eds.). *International Human Rights Law: Theory and Practice*. Montreal: Canadian Human Rights Foundation, 1992.

Craig, Gordon A., and Francis Lowenheim (eds.). *The Diplomats, 1939–1979*. Princeton: Princeton University Press, 1994.

Cranston, Maurice. *What Are Human Rights?* New York: Taplinger, 1973.

Dalai Lama. *Ocean of Wisdom*. Santa Fe: Clear Light, 1989.

Davis, David Brion. *Slavery and Human Progress*. New York: Oxford University Press, 1984.

Donnan, Elizabeth. *Documents Illustrative of the History of the Slave Trade*, 4 vols. Washington, D.C.: Carnegie Institution, 1930–1935.

Donnelly, Jack. *Universal Human Rights in Theory and Practice*. Ithaca: Cornell University Press, 1989.

Dower, John. *War Without Mercy: Race and Power in the Pacific*. New York: Pantheon, 1986.

Drinan, Robert. *The Cry of the Oppressed*. San Francisco: Harper & Row, 1987.

Drzewicki, Krzysztof. *Social Rights as Human Rights*. Abo: Institute for Human Rights, 1994.

Du Bois, W.E.B. *Dusk of Dawn*. New York: Harcourt Brace, 1940.

——. *The World and Africa*. New York: International Publishers, 1965 ed.

Dunant, J. Henry. *A Memory of Solferino*. Washington, D.C.: American Red Cross, 1939 ed.

Duparc, Jacques. *La Protection des minorités de race, de langue et de religion*. Paris: Dalloz, 1922.

Durand, André. *From Sarajevo to Hiroshima: History of the International Committee of the Red Cross*. Geneva: Henry Dunant Institute, 1984.

Dworkin, Ronald. *Taking Rights Seriously*. Cambridge: Harvard University Press, 1977.

Eide, Asbjørn, and August Schou (eds.). *International Protection of Human Rights*. Stockholm: Almquist & Wiksell, 1968.

Eide, Asbjørn, et al. (eds.). *The Universal Declaration of Human Rights: A Commentary*. Oslo: Scandinavian University Press, 1992.

Felice, Renzo de. *Mussolini il duce: Lo Stato totalitario, 1936–1940*. Rome: Einaudi, 1981.

Fischer, Louis. *Gandhi: His Life and Message for the World*. New York: Mentor, 1982.

Fladeland, Betty. *Men and Brothers: Anglo-American Anti-Slavery Cooperation*. Urbana: University of Illinois Press, 1972.

Flexner, Eleanor. *Century of Struggle: The Women's Rights Movement in the United States*. Cambridge, Mass.: Belknap, 1975 ed.

Foner, P. S. (ed.). *W.E.B. Du Bois Speaks: Speeches and Addresses*. New York: Pathfinder Press, 1970.

Forsythe, David. *Humanitarian Politics: The International Committee of the Red Cross*. Baltimore: Johns Hopkins University Press, 1977.

——. *The Internationalization of Human Rights*. Lexington, Mass.: Lexington Books, 1991.

Foster, Catherine. *Women for All Seasons: The Story of the Women's International League for Peace and Freedom*. Athens: University of Georgia Press, 1989.

Franklin, John Hope. *From Slavery to Freedom*. New York: Knopf, 1974 ed.

Fujimura-Fanselow, Kumiko and Kameda, Atsuko (eds.). *Japanese Women*. New York: Feminist Press, 1995.

Ganji, Manouchehr. *International Protection of Human Rights*. Geneva: Droz, 1962.

Geiss, Immanuel. *Panafrikanismus: Zur Geschichte der Dekolonisation*. Frankfurt am Main: Europäische Verlagsanstalt, 1968.

Gibb, H. A. R., and Harold Bowen. *Islamic Society and the West*. London: Oxford University Press, 1957.

Gladstone, William E. *Bulgarian Horrors and the Question of the East*. London: Murray, 1976.

Gouges, Olympe de. *Œuvres*. Paris: Mercure de France, 1986 ed.

Griffith, Elisabeth. *In Her Own Right*. New York: Oxford University Press, 1984.

Grimké, Sarah. *Letters on the Equality of the Sexes and the Condition of Woman*. Boston: Knapp, 1838.

Grewe, W. G. *Epochen der Völkerrechtsgeschichte*. Baden-Baden: Nomos, 1988.

Guest, Iain. *Behind the Disappearances: Argentina's Dirty War Against Human Rights and the United Nations*. Philadelphia: University of Pennsylvania Press, 1990.

Gurvitch, Georges. *La Déclaration des Droits Sociaux*. Paris: Vrin, 1946.

Haas, Ernst. *Beyond the Nation State*. Stanford: Stanford University Press, 1964.

Hagen, William T. *The Indian Rights Association*. Tucson: University of Arizona Press, 1985.

Henkin, Louis. *The Age of Rights*. New York: Columbia University Press, 1990.

——— (ed.). *The International Bill of Human Rights*. New York: Columbia University Press, 1984.

Hertslet, Edward (ed.). *The Map of Africa by Treaty*. 3 vols. London: Harrison & Sons, 1909.

———. *The Map of Europe by Treaty*, 4 vols. London: Butterworths, 1875–1891.

Hilderbrand, Robert. *Dumbarton Oaks*. Chapel Hill: University of North Carolina Press, 1990.

Hilpert, Konrad. *Die Menschenrechte: Geschichte, Theologie, Aktualität*. Düsseldorf: Patmos, 1991.

Hobbes, Thomas. *Leviathan*. New York: Washington Square Press, 1964 ed.

Hoffmann, Stanley. *Duties Beyond Borders: On the Limits and Possibilities of Ethical International Politics*. Syracuse: Syracuse University Press, 1981.

Holborn, Louise (ed.). *War and Peace Aims of the United Nations*. Boston: World Peace Foundation, 1943.

Horne, Thomas. *Property Rights and Poverty*. Chapel Hill: University of North Carolina Press, 1990.

Hsiung, James (ed.). *Human Rights in East Asia*. New York: Paragon, 1986.

Hufton, Olwen (ed.). *Historical Change and Human Rights: The Oxford Amnesty Lectures, 1994*. New York: Basic Books, 1995.

Humphrey, John P. *Human Rights and the United Nations*. Dobbs Ferry: Transnational Publishers, 1984.

Hunt, Lynn (ed.). *The French Revolution and Human Rights*. Boston: Bedford Books, 1996.

Hutchinson, John. *Champions of Charity: War and the Rise of the Red Cross*. Boulder: Westview, 1996.

Ihm, Claudia Carlen (ed.). *The Papal Encyclicals*. 5 vols. Raleigh: McGrath, 1981.

Inman, Samuel Guy. *Inter-American Conferences*. Washington, D.C.: University Press, 1965.

Ishay, Micheline R. *The Human Rights Reader*. New York: Routledge, 1997.

Jacobs, F. G. *The European Convention on Human Rights*. Oxford: Oxford University Press, 1975.

Jayawardena, Kumari. *Feminism and Nationalism in the Third World*. London: Zed Press, 1986.

Kanger, Helle. *Human Rights in the U.N. Declaration*. Uppsala: Acta Universitatis Upsaliensis, 1984.

Kant, Immanuel. *Grundegung zur Metaphysik der Sitten*. Riga: Harknoch, 1785.

Karel, Vasak (ed.). *Dimensions internationales des droits de l'homme*, 2 vols. Paris: UNESCO, 1982.

Karis, Thomas, and G. Carter (eds.). *From Protest to Challenge: A Documentary History of African Politics in South Africa*. 4 vols. Stanford: Hoover Institution Press, 1977.

Kaufman, Natalie Hevener. *Human Rights Treaties and the Senate: A History of Opposition*. Chapel Hill: University of North Carolina Press, 1990.

Kawakami, K. K. (ed.). *What Japan Thinks*. New York: Macmillan, 1921.

Kazuko, Ono. *Chinese Women in a Century of Revolution*. Stanford: Stanford University Press, 1989.

Kinross, Lord. *The Ottoman Centuries*. New York: Morrow, 1977.

Landen, Robert. *The Emergence of the Modern Middle East*. New York: Van Nostrand Reinhold, 1970.

Laqueur, Walter, and Barry Rubin (eds.). *The Human Rights Reader*. New York: Meridian, 1989 ed.

Las Casas, Bartholomé. *In Defense of the Indians*. Trans. and ed. S. Poole. DeKalb: Northern Illinois University Press, 1974.

Lauren, Paul Gordon. *Power and Prejudice: The Politics and Diplomacy of Racial Discrimination*. Boulder and San Francisco: Westview/HarperCollins, 1996 ed.

Lauterpacht, Hersch. *An International Bill of the Rights of Man*. New York: Columbia University Press, 1945.

——. *International Law and Human Rights*. New York: Garland, 1973.

Lawson, Edward (ed.), *Encyclopedia of Human Rights*. New York: Taylor & Francis, 1996 ed.

League of Nations Union. *The Atlantic Charter*. London: Hodgson, 1942.

Lenin, V. I. *Collected Works*. New York: International Publishers, 1929–1945.

Leo XIII. *Rerum Novarum*. New York: Paulist Press, 1939.

Lillich, Richard. *International Human Rights: Problems of Law, Policy, and Practice*. Boston: Little Brown, 1991 ed.

——. *International Law of State Responsibility for Injury to Aliens*. Charlottesville: University Press of Virginia, 1983.

Lillich, Richard, and Frank Newman. *International Human Rights*. Boston: Little, Brown, 1979.

Little, David, et al. (eds.). *Human Rights and the Conflict of Cultures*. Columbia: University of South Carolina Press, 1988.

Livezey, Lowell. *Nongovernmental Organizations and the Ideas of Human Rights*. Princeton: Center of International Studies, 1988.

Locke, John. *Two Treatises of Government*. New York: Hafner, 1947 ed.

Luard, Evan (ed.). *The International Protection of Human Rights*. London: Thames & Hudson, 1967.

Malanczuk, Peter. *Humanitarian Intervention and the Legitimacy of the Use of Force*. Amsterdam: Het Spinhuis, 1993.

Mandela, Nelson. *Long Walk to Freedom*. Boston: Little, Brown, 1994 ed.

Mandelstam, André N. *Les Droits internationaux de l'Homme*. Paris: Les Editions internationales, 1931.

——. *La Protection internationale des minorités*. Paris: Sirey, 1931.

Marwick, Arthur. *Women at War, 1914–1918*. London: Fontana, 1977.

Marx, Karl, and Friedrich Engels. *Manifesto of the Communist Party*. New York: Socialist Labor Party, 1888 ed.

Mayer, Elizabeth. *Islam and Human Rights: Tradition and Politics*. San Francisco and Boulder: Westview/HarperCollins, 1995.

McDougal, Myres S., Harold Lasswell, and Lung-chu Chen. *Human Rights and World Public Order*. New Haven: Yale University Press, 1980.

McGoldrick, Dominic. *The Human Rights Committee: Its Role in the Development of the International Covenant on Civil and Political Rights*. Oxford: Clarendon Press, 1991.

Meron, Theodor. *Human Rights Law-Making in the United Nations*. Oxford: Oxford University Press, 1986.

Miers, Suzanne. *Britain and the Ending of the Slave Trade*. New York: Africana, 1975.

Mill, John Stuart. *On Liberty*. London: Parker & Son, 1859.

——. *The Subjection of Women*. London: Longmans, 1869.

Miller, Kelly. *The World War for Human Rights*. Reprint, New York: Negro Universities Press, 1969.

Mitri, Tarek (ed.). *Religion and Human Rights*. Geneva: World Council of Churches, 1996.

Mower, A. Glenn. *The United States, the United Nations, and Human Rights*. Westport: Greenwood, 1979.

Moynier, Gustave, and Louis Appia. *La Guerre et la Charité: Traité théorique et pratique de philanthropie appliquée*. Geneva: Cherbuliez, 1867.

Murphey, Rhoades. *A History of Asia*. New York: HarperCollins, 1996 ed.

Newman, Frank, and David Weissbrodt (ed.). *International Human Rights: Law, Policy, and Process*. Cincinnati: Anderson, 1990.

Nkrumah, Kwame. *Towards Colonial Freedom*. London: Panaf, 1973 ed.

Nolde, O. Frederick. *Freedom's Charter: The Universal Declaration of Human Rights*. New York: Foreign Policy Association, 1949.

Odinga, Oginga. *Not Yet Uhuru*. New York: Hill & Wang, 1967.

Oliver, Roland, and Anthony Atmore. *Africa Since 1800*. Cambridge: Cambridge University Press, 1981 ed.

Oppenheim, L. *International Law: A Treatise*. London: Longmans, 1912 ed.

Ouguergouz, Fatsah. *La Charte africaine des droits de l'homme et des peuples*. Paris: Presses Universitaires de France, 1993.

Paine, Thomas. *The Rights of Man*. New York: Heritage Press, 1961 ed.

Perera, L. P. N. *Buddhism and Human Rights*. Columbo: Karunaratne, 1991.

Périgord, Paul. *The International Labor Organization*. New York: Appleton, 1926.

Plummer, Brenda Gayle. *Rising Wind: Black Americans and U.S. Foreign Affairs*. Chapel Hill: University of North Carolina Press, 1996.

Ramcharan, B. G. *The Concept and Present Status of the International Protection of Human Rights*. Dordrecht: Kluwer, 1989.

Richardson, James D. (ed.). *A Compilation of the Messages and Papers of the Presidents*. 10 vols. Washington, D.C.: Government Printing Office, 1896–1899.

Robertson, A. H., and J. G. Merrills. *Human Rights in the World*. Manchester: Manchester University Press, 1992 ed.

Robinson, Jacob. *Human Rights and Fundamental Freedoms in the Charter of the United Nations*. New York: Institute of Jewish Affairs, 1946.

Robinson, Nehemiah. *The Universal Declaration of Human Rights: Its Origins, Significance, and Interpretation*. New York: Institute of Jewish Affairs, 1950.

Rosenbaum, Alan (ed.). *The Philosophy of Human Rights: International Perspectives*. Westport: Greenwood, 1980.

Rosenman, Samuel (ed.). *The Public Papers and Addresses of Franklin D. Roosevelt*. 13 vols. New York: Random House, 1938–1950.

Rousseau, Jean-Jacques. *Contrat social, ou Principes du droit politique*. Paris: Garnier, 1900 ed.

Rudé, George. *Ideology and Popular Protest*. New York: Pantheon, 1980.

Russell, Ruth. *A History of the United Nations Charter*. Washington, D.C.: Brookings Institution, 1958.

Said, Edward. *Orientalism*. New York: Vintage, 1979.

Schwelb, Egon. *Human Rights and the International Community*. Chicago: Quadrangle Books, 1964.

Sée, Henri. *Histoire de la Ligue des Droits de l'Homme*. Paris: Ligue des Droits de l'Homme, 1927.

Shotwell, James (ed.). *The Origins of the International Labor Organization*. 2 vols. New York: Columbia University Press, 1934.

Siegel, Richard L. *Employment and Human Rights*. Philadelphia: University of Pennsylvania Press, 1993.

Sinclair, Keith. *Walter Nash*. Auckland: Auckland University Press, 1976.

Sithole, Ndabaningi. *African Nationalism*. London: Oxford University Press, 1959.

Sjahrir, S. *Out of Exile*. Reprint, New York: Greenwood Press, 1969.

Skilling, H. Gordon. *Charter 77 and Human Rights in Czechoslovakia*. London: George Allen & Unwin, 1981.

Smith, Bradley. *Reaching Judgment at Nuremberg*. New York: New American Library, 1977.

Sohn, Louis, and Thomas Buergenthal. *International Protection of Human Rights*. Indianapolis: Bobbs-Merrill, 1973.

Stannard, David. *American Holocaust*. New York: Oxford University Press, 1992.

Stanton, Elizabeth Cady, et al. (eds.). *History of Woman Suffrage*, 2 vols. New York: Charles Mann, 1881.

Steiner, Henry, and Philip Alston. *International Human Rights in Context*. Oxford: Clarendon Press, 1996.

Stewart, James B. *Holy Warriors*. New York: Hill & Wang, 1976.

Swidler, Arlene (ed.). *Human Rights in Religious Traditions*. New York: Pilgrim Press, 1982.

Tabandeh, Sultanhussein. *A Muslim Commentary on the Universal Declaration of Human Rights*. London: Goulding, 1970.

Tesón, Fernando. *Humanitarian Intervention*. Ardsley-on-Hudson, N.Y.: Transnational, 1988.

Thompson, E. P. *The Making of the English Working Class*. New York: Pantheon, 1964.

Thompson, Kenneth (ed.). *The Moral Imperatives of Human Rights*. Washington, D.C.: University Press of America, 1980.

Thorn, James. *Peter Fraser, New Zealand's Wartime Prime Minister*. London: Odhams, 1952.

Tolley, Howard, Jr. *The International Commission of Jurists: Global Advocates for Human Rights*. Philadelphia: University of Pennsylvania Press, 1994.

———. *The U.N. Commission on Human Rights*. Boulder and London: Westview, 1987.

Troclet, Léon-Eli. *Législation sociale internationale*. 3 vols. Brussels: Librairie Encyclopédique, 1952.

Urquhart, Brian. *Ralph Bunche*. New York: Norton, 1993.

Van Dyke, Vernon. *Human Rights, the United States, and the World Community*. New York: Oxford University Press, 1970.

Vattel, Emerich de. *Le Droit des Gens, ou Principes de la Loi Naturelle*. Reprint, Washington, D.C.: Carnegie, 1916.

Verdoodt, Albert. *Naissance et signification de la Déclaration universelle des Droits de l'homme*. Louvain-Paris: Éditions Nauwelaerts, 1964.

Vincent, R. J. *Human Rights and International Relations*. Cambridge: Cambridge University Press, 1986.

Vogelgesang, Sandy. *American Dream, Global Nightmare*. New York: Norton, 1980.

Walters, F. P. *A History of the League of Nations*. 2 vols. London: Oxford University Press, 1952.

Weinberger, Gerda. *Gegen Rassismus und Rassendiskriminierung; Kampfdekade der UNO*. Berlin: Staatsverlag der DDR, 1976.

Welch, Claude, and Virginia Leary (eds.). *Asian Perspectives on Human Rights*. Boulder: Westview, 1990.

Welles, Sumner. *The Time for Decision*. New York: Harper & Brothers, 1944.

———. *World of the Four Freedoms*. New York: Simon & Schuster, 1943.

Wells, H. G. *The Rights of Man or What Are We Fighting For?* Harmondsworth: Penguin Books, 1940.

Westerveen, Gert (comp.). *The International Bill of Rights*. Utrecht: Netherlands Institute of Human Rights, 1986.

Wilson, Ellen Gibson. *Thomas Clarkson*. New York: St. Martin's, 1990.

Wollstonecraft, Mary. *A Vindication of the Rights of Woman*. New York: Norton, 1988 ed.

Wood, F. L. W. *The New Zealand People at War*. Wellington: Department of Internal Affairs, 1958.

Wronka, Joseph. *Human Rights and Social Policy in the 21st Century*. Lantham, Mass.: University Press of America, 1992.

Yü-sheng, Lin. *The Crisis of Chinese Consciousness*. Madison: University of Wisconsin Press, 1979.

Zilversmit, Arthur. *The First Emancipation: The Abolition of Slavery in the North*. Chicago: University of Chicago Press, 1967.

Articles

Beckerlegge, Gwilym. "Human Rights in the Ramakrishna Math and Mission: 'For Liberation and the Good of the World.' " *Religion* (April 1990): 119–137.

Bunch, Charlotte. "Women's Rights as Human Rights: A Re-Vision of Human Rights." *Human Rights Quarterly*, 12, 4 (1990): 486–498.

Burgers, J. Herman. "The Road to San Francisco: The Revival of the Human Rights Idea in the Twentieth Century." *Human Rights Quarterly*, 14, 4 (November 1992): 447–477.

Cassin, René. "La Déclaration universelle et la mise en oeuvre des Droits de l'homme." *Recueil des Cours de l'Académie de Droit International*, 79 (1951): 241–367.

Cook, Helena. "International Human Rights Mechanisms: The Role of Special Procedure in the Protection of Human Rights." *International Commission of Jurists Review*, 50 (1993): 31–55.

Coursier, Henri. "L'Evolution du Droit International Humanitaire." *Recueil des Cours de l'Académie de Droit International*, 99 (1960): 361–465.

——. "Les Droits de l'homme et du citoyen." *La Revue Diplomatique* (31 October 1933): 6–7.

Du Bois, W.E.B. "Opinion." *Crisis*, 18 (May 1919): 7.

Duse, Mohamed. "Today: India and Africa." *African Times and Orient Review* (March 1917): 46.

Fischer, Dana. "Reporting Under the Covenant on Civil and Political Rights." *American Journal of International Law*, 76 (January 1982): 142–153.

Fonteyne, Jean-Pierre. "The Customary International Law Doctrine of Humanitarian Intervention: Its Current Validity Under the UN Charter." *California Western International Law Journal*, 4 (1974): 203–258.

Frangulis, Antoine. "Droits de l'Homme." *Dictionnaire Diplomatique*. Paris: Hoche, 1937 ed. "Human Rights: A Suitable Target for Foreign Policy?" *The Economist* (12–18 April 1997): 15–16 and 21–25.

Johnson, M. Glen. "The Contributions of Eleanor and Franklin Roosevelt to the Development of International Protection for Human Rights." *Human Rights Quarterly*, 9, 1 (1987): 33–47.

Kaufman, Natalie Hevener, and David Whiteman. "Opposition to Human Rights Treaties in the United States Senate: The Legacy of the Bricker Amendment." *Human Rights Quarterly*, 10, 3 (1988): 309–337.

Kia, Mehrdad. "Mizra Fath Ali Akhundzade and the Call for Modernization of the Islamic World." *Middle Eastern Studies*, 31 (July 1995): 422–448.

Lewis, Jan. " 'Of Every Age, Sex, and Condition': The Representation of Women in the Constitution." *Journal of the Early Republic*, 15 (Fall 1995): 359–387.

Li, Xiaorong. " 'Asian Values' and the Universality of Human Rights." *China Rights Forum* (Fall, 1996): 32–35.

Mandelstam, André N. "Les dernières phases du mouvement pour la protection internationale des droits de l'homme." *Revue de Droit International* (1933): 469–510; and (1934): 61–104.

——. "Der internationale Schutz der Menschenrechte und die New-Yorker Erklärung des Instituts für Völkerrecht." *Zeitschrft für ausländisches öffentliches Recht und Völkerrecht*, 2 (1931): 335–377.

——. "La Protection internationale des droits de l'homme." *Les Cahiers des Droits de l'Homme*, 31 (10 December 1931): 724–733.

——. "La Protection internationale des droits de l'homme." *Recueil des Cours de l'Académie de Droit International*, 38 (1931): 129–229.

Mirkine-Guetzevitch, M. B." Quelques Problèmes de la mise en Œuvre de la Déclaration Universelle des Droits de l'Homme." *Recueil des Cours de l'Académie de Droit International*, 82 (1953): 255–376.

Modinos, P. "La Charte de la Liberté de l'Europe." *Revue des Droits de l'Homme*, 8 (1975): 676–686.

Möller, Jakob. "Petitioning the United Nations." *Universal Human Rights*, 1 (1979): 57–72.

Monshipouri, Mahmood. "Islamic Thinking and the Internationalization of Human Rights." *The Muslim World* (July–October 1994): 217–239.

Morsink, Johannes. "World War Two and the Universal Declaration." *Human Rights Quarterly*, 15, 2 (1993): 357–405.

Nolde, O. Frederick. "Possible Functions of the Commission on Human Rights." *Annals of the American Academy of Political and Social Science*, 243 (January 1946): 144–149.

Rougier, Antoine. "La Théorie de l'intervention d'humanité." *Revue Générale de Droit International Public*, 17 (1910): 468–526.

Schreiber, Marc. "L'Année internationale de la lutte contre le racisme et la discrimination raciale." *Revue des Droits de l'Homme*, 4 (1971): 311–340. "700 Jahr Rassenkampf," *Neues Volk*, 5 (1937): 16–21.

Sohn, Louis B. "How American International Lawyers Prepared for the San Francisco Bill of Rights." *American Journal of International Law*, 89 (July 1995): 540–553.

Solf, Waldemar. "Protection of Civilians Against the Effects of Hostilities." *American University Journal of International Law and Policy*, 1 (1986): 117–135.

Suu Kyi, Aung San. "Freedom, Development, and Human Worth." *Democracy*, 6, 2 (April 1995): 12–19.

Weissbrodt, David. "The Role of International Organizations in the Implementation of Human Rights and Humanitarian Law in Situations of Armed Conflict." *Vanderbilt Journal of Transnational Law*, 21 (1988): 313–365.

Wiseberg, Laurie. "Protecting Human Rights Activists and NGOs." *Human Rights Quarterly*, 13, 4 (1991): 525–544.

Wright, Quincy. "Human Rights and the World Order." *International Conciliation*, 389 (April 1943): 238–262.

Yongjian, Jin. "Asia's Major Human Rights Concerns." *Beijing Review*, 36 (19–25 April 1993): 10–11.

Zayas, Alfred de. "The Follow-Up Procedure of the UN Human Rights Committee." *International Commission of Jurists Review*, 47 (1991): 28–35.

Dissertations

Lee, Marshall. "Failure in Geneva: The German Foreign Ministry and the League of Nations." Madison: University of Wisconsin, 1974.

Sun, Ali Nusret. "La Discrimination raciale et l'Organisation des Nations Unies." Paris: Sorbonne, 1954.

Svensson-McCarthy, Anna-Lena. "The International Law of Human Rights and States of Exception." Geneva: University of Geneva, 1996.

Newspapers

Age (Melbourne)
Bombay Chronicle
Chicago Defender
China Daily
Daily Herald
Daily Telegraph
Gegenwart
Hindu Times
Illustrated London News
Japan Times
Journal de Genève
Le Monde
Le Monde diplomatique
Morning Standard (Bombay)
New York Times
News Letter [of the League of Colored Peoples]
Otago Witness
Sacramento Union
The Times (London)
Tribune de Genève
Victoria Daily Colonist
Volkischer Beobachter
Xinhau General Overseas News Service
Die Zeit

CD-ROMs

United Nations. *Human Rights: Bibliographical Data and International Instruments.* UN No. GV.E.97.0.7. Geneva: United Nations, 1997.

Sound Recordings

Radio Suisse Romande. *La Déclaration universelle des droits de l'homme.* CD RSR 6101. Geneva: United Nations, 1994.

Radio Suisse Romande and *Journal de Genève. Une Mémoire internationale: La Société des Nations, 1920–1946.* CD RSR 6104. Geneva: United Nations, 1995.

United Nations and *Tribune de Genève. Les Nations Unies et la Genève internationale.* CD RSR 6103. Geneva: Radio Suisse Romande, 1995.

Websites

American Association for the Advancement of Science. Human Rights Resources on the Internet. http://shr.aaas.org/dhr.htm

Amnesty International. http://www.amnesty.org

United Nations. http://www.un.org

United Nations. Office of the High Commissioner for Human Rights. http://www.hchr.ch

Index

About the Author

PAUL GORDON LAUREN is the Regents Professor at the University of Montana where he also has served as the founding director of the Mansfield Center and as the Mansfield Professor of Ethics and Public Affairs. He earned his Ph.D. from Stanford University. Lauren has published many articles, chapters, and books, including the nationally and internationally acclaimed *Power and Prejudice: The Politics and Diplomacy of Racial Discrimination* (1996), which has been translated into Japanese. He has lectured widely, including before the United Nations, where he has been described as possibly the world's leading authority on the history of human rights.